597.177 MIC
Michael, Scott W.
Reef fishes

Reef Fishes

VOLUME 1

Reef Fishes

VOLUME 1

*A Guide to Their
Identification, Behavior, and Captive Care*

Text & Principal Photography by

SCOTT W. MICHAEL

With a Foreword by Dr. John E. Randall

Additional Photography by
Foster Bam, Fred Bavendam, Janine Cairns-Michael, John P. Hoover, Paul Humann, Keisuke Imai,
Rudie H. Kuiter, Dr. John E. Randall, Roger Steene, Larry Tackett, and Denise Nielsen Tackett

MICROCOSM

SHELBURNE, VERMONT 05482

Copyright © 1998 by Scott W. Michael
Illustrations copyright © 1998 by Joshua Highter

All rights reserved. No part of this book may be reproduced or transmitted in any form or by any electronic or mechanical means, including information storage and retrieval systems, without permission in writing from the Publisher, except for the inclusion of brief quotations in a review.

Published by
Microcosm Ltd.
Shelburne, VT 05482

Library of Congress Cataloging-in-Publication Data
Michael, Scott W.
    Reef fishes: a guide to their identification, behavior, and captive care/by Scott W. Michael; foreword by John E. Randall.
    p. cm.
    Includes bibliographical references and index.
    ISBN 1-890087-21-1 (hardcover)
    1. Coral reef fishes. I. Title.
    QL620.M47   1998
    597.177'89—dc21   98-34408

Printed and bound in U.S.A. by
World Color Book Services

Color separations by Digital Media Inc. U.S.A., Grants Pass, OR.

Designed by Eugenie Seidenberg Delaney

Front Cover (background photograph by Fred Bavendam; inset photographs by Scott W. Michael)
Background: *Pseudanthias huchtii* and *Pavona clavus* coral in Milne Bay, Papua New Guinea
Left: Shortfin Lionfish (*Dendrochirus brachypterus*)
Center: Hawaiian Longfin Anthias (*Pseudanthias hawaiiensis*)
Right: Goldentail Moray (*Gymnothorax miliaris*)

Back Cover (photographs by Scott W. Michael)
Top: Ornate Ghost Pipefish (*Solenostomus paradoxus*)
Center: Threadfin Anthias (*Nemanthias carberryi*)
Bottom: Golden Moray (*Gymnothorax melatremus*), variant

*This series of books is dedicated to my lifelong dive buddy,
my soulmate, and my reason for living,
Janine Cairns-Michael.
Without her constant guidance, patience,
encouragement, and companionship, this book
would still be a dream, not a reality.*

Contents

Foreword, by Dr. John E. Randall 8

Preface 11

Acknowledgments 12

CORAL REEF FISHES—AN INTRODUCTION 15

CHAPTER 1: THE HISTORY & ANATOMY OF REEF FISHES 33

CHAPTER 2: TAXONOMY 63

CHAPTER 3: CORAL REEF HABITATS 159

CHAPTER 4: THE FISHES 235

    Family Muraenidae / Moray Eels 245

    Family Heterocongridae / Conger and Garden Eels 287

    Family Ophichthidae / Snake Eels 295

    Family Plotosidae / Eel Catfishes 308

    Family Synodontidae / Lizardfishes 311

    Family Bythitidae / Livebearing Brotulas 318

    Family Batrachoididae / Toadfishes 321

    Family Antennariidae / Frogfishes 329

    Family Ogcocephalidae / Walking Batfishes 358

    Family Anomalopidae / Flashlight Fishes 363

    Family Monocentridae / Pineapple Fishes 367

Subfamily Holocentrinae / Squirrelfishes 370
Subfamily Myripristinae / Soldierfishes 384
Family Aulostomidae / Trumpetfishes 393
Family Pegasidae / Sea Moths 398
Family Solenostomidae / Ghost Pipefishes 401
Family Syngnathidae / Seahorses and Pipefishes 409
Family Centriscidae / Shrimpfishes 440
Family Caracanthidae / Coral Crouchers 443
Family Tetrarogidae / Waspfishes 445
Family Scorpaenidae / Scorpionfishes, Devilfishes, and Stonefishes 453
Subfamily Pteroinae / Lionfishes 491
Family Platycephalidae / Flatheads 509
Family Dactylopteridae / Helmut Gurnards 515
Subfamily Serraninae / Dwarf Seabasses and Hamlets 519
Subfamily Anthiinae / Anthias 543

REFERENCES

Glossary 590
Bibliography 594
Photography Credits 600
Index 601
About the Author 624

Foreword

"You are standing on a metal ladder in water up to your neck. Something round and heavy is slipped gently over your head, and a metal helmet rests upon your shoulders. Thus were the knights of old helmed by their squires for the grim business of war. Instead of a slotted visor, however, you find two large frames of glass before your eyes. . . .

"You wave good-by and slowly descend . . . for a brief space of time the palms and the beach show intermittently through waves which are now breaking over your very face. Then the world changes. There is no more harsh sunlight, but delicate blue-greens with a fluttering of shadows everywhere. Huge pink and orange growths rise on all sides—you know they are living corals . . . a quartet of swimming rainbows—four gorgeously tinted fish who rush up and peer at you. You reach out for them, and they vanish."

—William Beebe
Beneath Tropic Seas (1928)

One day in 1947, I went to an Army-Navy surplus store in Los Angeles to buy anchor line for a small sloop I was rebuilding. There I saw a steel cylinder wrapped in wire and painted green with zinc chromate; there was a rubber hose coming off one end to what was the regulator, and another hose to a mouthpiece. I asked the salesman what it was, and he said you could put compressed air in the tank and go underwater and breathe. The price was twenty-five dollars. Instead of the anchor line, I bought the tank. I made a simple backpack and mounted the regulator on the shoulder strap. Then I decided I would be very clever and put oxygen in the tank instead of air. Why waste four-fifths of the volume on worthless nitrogen? Besides, it was easy to get oxygen from a welding shop. Fortunately, I confined my diving with this gear to the shallows, or I would not be relating this tale.

As a teenager, I had avidly read the books by William Beebe on his explorations of the marine realm—especially *Beneath Tropic Seas*, about diving with helmet and hose on Haitian coral reefs. It was a major inspiration for my becoming a marine biologist and spending my adult life studying reef fishes.

The first functional hard-hat diving helmet, such as that worn by Beebe, was invented in 1820. Its early use was mainly for various commercial operations such as salvaging wrecks, not for viewing marine life. Before that, man's knowledge of the wealth of life below the surface of the sea was limited to what he could catch by hook and line, trap, seine, trawl, or dredge. The early European naturalists who explored the tropical world in their wooden sailing ships brought back preserved specimens of reef fishes and other forms of marine life to museums where they were described, often without documentation of their life color. They could never have appreciated the lovely colors and beauty of tropical reefs as Beebe and his successors have.

After World War II, skindiving became a popular sport with the use of rubber swim fins and face mask. My own first mask was a far cry from today's equipment, perfectly round and made of narrow, hard, black rubber that had to be carved and sanded to fit one's face. I was skindiving then in southern California before the advent of the wet suit, and I always emerged from the sea shivering with cold. This led to my making a wet suit of sorts. I dipped the long-john underwear from my military service into a washtub of latex rubber and hung it up to dry. However, I did not have sense enough to add a closing collar, and the icy water kept coming in the large opening at my neck. Still, it helped.

The year after purchasing my rudimentary scuba apparatus, I took the first course in ichthyology offered at UCLA, where Professor Boyd Walker had an Aqua-Lung for fish collecting. From these crude and somewhat risky beginnings half a century ago, the modern era of marine biology was born. With this gear, scientists were finally able to move freely in the realm of the coral reef, to make observations and selectively collect new species of fishes to depths of about 200 feet. And now with the current use of mixed-gas rebreathing devices, divers are beginning to explore the next 200 feet or more. The development of underwater cameras with strobes and of video cameras has also been very important to our documentation of marine life and its behavior. Not only have we been able to discover, describe, and illustrate a multitude of new species of fishes, but we have been able to learn much more of the ecology and habits of fishes by diving in their environment.

How long might it have taken for us to determine, for example, the sexual dichromatism of so many wrasses and parrotfishes, without scuba? Early naturalists, even great ones like Pieter Bleeker, described the very differently colored males and females of these fishes as separate species. So would any of us today, were we not able to see them in courtship or spawning. I remember being bewildered when I was studying the aggregate spawning of the Redfin Parrotfish (*Sparisoma rubripinne*) off St. John, Virgin Islands. On one occasion, I observed what was then regarded as another species, the green *Sparisoma axillare*, wildly chasing various drab individuals of the spawning aggregation. Why, I wondered, would one species of fish try to disrupt the spawning of another? Later I saw a parrotfish intermediate in coloration to the drab form and the green, and I realized I had been observing only one species. Ultimately my wife, Helen, and I wrote our 1963 paper in *Zoologica* on the two different spawning patterns of this and other parrotfishes and of the wrasse *Thalassoma bifasciatum*: group spawning by like-colored fish and pair spawning by a drab female fish with a more colorful terminal male who maintains a sexual territory and fights with other males at the periphery. We might envy the experiences of such fish, who first get to experience life as females and end up as males with a harem of female partners.

IN RECENT DECADES THERE HAS BEEN AN INCREASING awareness of the sea and its life—and not just as a source of food. There is today more understanding and more enjoyment of the beauty and fascinating biology of the living animals, in particular the coral reef fishes. Ever-increasing numbers of divers and snorkelers are now traveling to and exploring distant reefs. Many are avid fish watchers comparable to their terrestrial counterparts, the birders.

So too has the marine aquarium hobby enjoyed increasing popularity, partly due to the greater success saltwater aquarists are having, not only in maintaining fishes, but also in keeping invertebrates, including corals and gorgonians, and algae. Now a landlocked aquarist thousands of miles from the Tropics can be exposed to and learn to appreciate the living beauty and complexity of the coral reef.

One very bold and well-informed young man, Scott W. Michael, has realized that the time has come for a series of volumes on coral reef fishes of the world to serve not only the marine biological community, but the many divers, snorkelers, fishermen, and aquarists anxious to know more about the fishes they have encountered, collected, or maintained.

I first met Scott in 1989 at the annual meeting of the American Society of Ichthyologists and Herpetologists in San Francisco. He was an undergraduate student in biology at the time and was presenting a paper on the reproductive behavior of the round stingray. Scott cornered me on several occasions at the conference and besieged me with questions concerning the taxonomy of a variety of different reef fish groups. Since our first meeting, we have corresponded on a regular basis on matters ichthyological.

Scott is a keen aquarist, dedicated diver, skilled underwater photographer, and as I can see from this text, a gifted writer. His familiarity with the scientific literature on reef fishes and his personal experience as a diver and aquarist have provided the qualifications to embark on the writing and photographing of these volumes, which will cover 68 fish families from the moray eels (Muraenidae) to the curious species of porcupinefishes of the Family Diodontidae. The *Reef Fishes* series is unique in that it has extensive information on the natural history, husbandry, dietary requirements, and compatibility for myriad fishes. One of the important consequences of Scott Michael's work will be a much greater appreciation and understanding of the biology of reef fishes. He has made it clear which species are appropriate for captive systems and which should be left on the reef. Examples of the latter are the many species of butterflyfishes that feed exclusively on coral polyps. If one observes such fishes in the sea, one soon realizes that they never take more than a small bite or two from any one coral head at one time. They are natural conservationists. Because their coral-grazing activity is spread over their large territories, the corals are able to regenerate. It would not be possible to maintain an aquarium in the home large enough to keep sufficient live coral for even a single adult coral-feeding butterflyfish.

Although our general knowledge of the coral reef ecosystem has progressed substantially in the past decades, there is still much to be learned. Scott's three volumes will summarize much of our knowledge of reef fishes, but they will also serve to reveal the need for more research on reef fish biology and of aquariology.

With a greater appreciation of the fishes of the coral reefs, there is also growing concern over the degradation of so many reefs around the world. Pollutants are still pouring into the sea in frightening quantities. Cutting down rainforests has resulted in the destruction of coral reefs from siltation (witness the loss of the reefs of the east coast of Madagascar). The use of dynamite and cyanide is still going on in many regions, especially the islands of Southeast Asia, where it is estimated that 3,000 species of reef and shore fishes are found. Overfishing continues unabated, and many major fisheries' stocks are seriously depleted. Overfishing on coral reefs results in the removal of the larger fishes, many of which are predators that keep the community in balance. Scientific studies have shown that the best way to conserve the biota of coral reefs is to set aside a minimum of 30% as complete preserves where no fishing or collecting of any kind is allowed. Fishes in these preserves can grow to full reproductive maturity, and their eggs and larvae will provide the recruits to the other 70% of local reef areas where fishing is allowed. In some places, such as the small resort island of Balicasag in the Philippines, the residents have learned that creating a reserve for the island and stopping all fishing is far more lucrative than fishing itself. It attracts divers and snorkelers who only want to observe and photograph the fishes.

All of us who want to maintain the coral reefs and their fishes for future generations should do all we can to promote the development of marine reserves. It is my hope that well-researched books such as this will enhance the awareness of aquarists, divers, snorkelers, and amateur naturalists to the biology and diversity of coral reef fishes. Wider and better-informed appreciation of these species can only serve to improve the chances that they and their habitats will be preserved for posterity.

—*John E. Randall, Ph.D.*
Kaneohe, Hawaii

Dr. John E. Randall is Senior Ichthyologist Emeritus of the Bishop Museum in Honolulu, member of the Graduate Faculty in Zoology of the University of Hawaii, and Distinguished Fellow of the American Society of Ichthyologists and Herpetologists. He is the author of more than 500 publications, principally on the biology and classification of coral reef fishes.

Preface

THIS SERIES OF VOLUMES IS MEANT as a reference tool for marine aquarists, as well as divers, snorkelers, and underwater naturalists with an interest in fish species that are associated with the coral reefs of the world. Because of the scope and volume of this work, the family groupings have been divided into three equal volumes, as follows. A fourth volume will provide a full photographic index to all species covered in the set.

VOLUME 1		**VOLUME 2**		**VOLUME 3**	
Families / Groups		**Families / Groups**		**Families / Groups**	
Muraenidae	Moray Eels	Serranidae	Groupers, Soapfishes, Reef Basslets	Labridae	Wrasses
Heterocongridae	Conger & Garden Eels			Scaridae	Parrotfishes
Ophichthidae	Snake Eels	Pseudochromidae	Dottybacks	Pholidichthyidae	Convict Blenny
Plotosidae	Eel Catfishes	Grammatidae	Grammas	Trichonotidae	Sand Divers
Synodontidae	Lizardfishes	Plesiopidae	Longfins	Pinguipedidae	Sand Perches
Bythitidae	Livebearing Brotulas	Opistognathidae	Jawfishes	Tripterygiidae	Triplefins
Batrachoididae	Toadfishes	Priacanthidae	Bigeyes	Labrisomidae	Weed Blennies
Antennariidae	Frogfishes	Cirrhitidae	Hawkfishes	Chaenopsidae	Tube & Pike Blennies
Ogcocephalidae	Walking Batfishes	Cheilodactylidae	Morwongs	Blenniidae	Blennies
Anomalopidae	Flashlight Fishes	Apogonidae	Cardinalfishes	Gobiesocidae	Clingfishes
Monocentridae	Pineapple Fishes	Malacanthidae	Tilefishes	Callionymidae	Dragonets
Holocentridae	Squirrelfishes & Soldierfishes	Echeneidae	Remoras	Gobiidae	Gobies
		Carangidae	Jacks	Microdesmidae	Dartfishes & Wormfishes
Aulostomidae	Trumpetfishes	Lutjanidae	Snappers & Fusiliers	Ephippidae	Spadefishes & Batfishes
Pegasidae	Sea Moths	Haemulidae	Grunts	Siganidae	Rabbitfishes
Solenostomidae	Ghost Pipefishes	Nemipteridae	Spinecheeks	Zanclidae	Moorish Idol
Syngnathidae	Seahorses & Pipefishes	Sciaenidae	Drums & Croakers	Acanthuridae	Surgeonfishes
Centriscidae	Shrimpfishes	Mullidae	Goatfishes	Bothidae	Lefteye Flounders
Caracanthidae	Coral Crouchers	Pempheridae	Sweepers	Soleidae	Soles
Tetrarogidae	Waspfishes	Monodactylidae	Monos	Balistidae	Triggerfishes
Scorpaenidae	Scorpionfishes, Lionfishes	Chaetodontidae	Butterflyfishes	Monacanthidae	Filefishes
		Pomacanthidae	Angelfishes	Ostraciidae	Trunkfishes
Platycephalidae	Flatheads	Pomacentridae	Damselfishes	Tetraodontidae	Pufferfishes & Tobies
Dactylopteridae	Helmut Gurnards			Diodontidae	Porcupinefishes & Burrfishes
Serranidae	Dwarf Seabasses, Hamlets, Anthias				

Acknowledgments

It is impossible to imagine creating this series of books without the help, expertise, contributions, advice and unfailing encouragement of a great many generous people in many disciplines and many countries. Over the 10 years I have been gathering material for this book and its companion volumes, I have been aided by countless folks from the worlds of marine biology, ichthyology, diving, aquarium keeping, and underwater photography. The following acknowledgments are painfully incomplete, and I apologize to any of you who have contributed and whose assistance is not noted here.

I must begin by expressing my gratitude to an international group of scientists and reef fish experts who have unselfishly aided my efforts to identify fishes, gather photographs and ecological information, and provide behavioral observations on many species. These contributors include Dr. Gerald R. Allen, Eugene Böhlke, Keisuke Imai, Rudie H. Kuiter, Dr. John E. McCosker, Robert F. Myers, Richard Pyle, Dr. John E. Randall, and Roger Steene.

My colleagues in marine fishkeeping circles have also provided a constant source of new information and insights on the species of interest to aquarists. My sincere thanks to Gary Barth, Chip Boyle, Dr. Bruce Carlson (Waikiki Aquarium), J. Charles Delbeek, Greg Godwin, William Gordy, Richard Harker, Larry Jackson, Ron Mascarin, Martin A. Moe, Jr., Bronson Nagreda, Tony Nahacky, Alf Jacob Nilsen, Michael S. Paletta, Vince Rado, Mike Schied, Matt Schuler, Julian Sprung (Two Little Fishies), Dr. Hiroyuki Tanaka, Tony Wagner, Joyce Wilkerson, and Bill Zarnick.

I am especially appreciative of years of support from many fine friends and acquaintances in the aquarium trade, including Bill and Arlene Addison (C-Quest), Wayne Sugiyama (Wayne's Underwater World), Millie, Ted, and Edwin Chua (All Seas Marine), Steven Freed (Seashell Pet Shop), Kyle and Mark Haeffner (Fish Store Inc.), Roy and Teresa Herndon (Sea Critters), Edwin Mowka (Aquarium Systems), David and Kathy Smith (Reef Encrustaceans), Robert Stern (Sea Dwelling Creatures), George Teodora and Philip Shane (Quality Marine), Jeffrey Turner (Oceans, Reefs & Aquariums), Jeff Voet (Tropical Fish World), Matt Walker (Animal Talk Pet Center), Randy Walker (Marine Center), Jim Walters (Old Town Aquarium), and Forrest Young and Angus Barnhart (Dynasty Marine). My friend and expert fishfinder Dennis Reynolds of Aqua Marines in Hermosa Beach, California, deserves special recognition for all the unusual fishes and reliable information he has provided over the years.

Many individuals, companies, and resorts have also assisted me in traveling to exotic locations to photograph the fishes contained within these volumes. They include Debbie Baratta (Adventure Express), Bart, Eric, Murphyn, and Martin (Buddy Beach and Dive Resort, Bonaire), Margo Chornlesky (Caribbean Adventures), Mike and Mimi Degruy, Mark Ecenbarger (Kungkungan Bay Resort, Sulawesi), Carol Evans (Mike Ball Expeditions), Exmouth Fishing and Dive Center (Exmouth, Australia), Garuda Indonesia, Avi Klapfer (Undersea Hunter, Coco Island), Mary Kukral (Boulder Scuba Tours), Carol Palmer (Ambon Dive Centre, Ambon), Larry Smith, Martin and Lori Sutton (Fisheye, Grand Cayman), and Rob Vanderloss (Chertan, Papua New Guinea).

I would never have been able to assemble a comprehensive collection of species photographs without the help of some of the best fish photographers in the world. I thank Dr. Gerald R. Allen, Helmut Debelius (IKAN), John P. Hoover, Paul Humann, Keisuke Imai, Rudie H. Kuiter, Robert F. Myers, Dr. John E. Randall, Roger Steene, and Larry Tackett, who helped to fill the gaps with their own magnificent photographs. Special thanks to Fred Bavendam, Denise Nielsen Tackett and Dave and Theresa Schrichte and others for providing some of the most outstanding reef habitat photographs I have ever seen.

A number of other accomplished photographers were gracious enough to let us use their photographs of hard-to-get species. Among them are: Mike Bacon, Foster Bam, Steven Frink, Joe Froelich, John Greenamyer, Tsuyoshi Kawamoto, Ken Marks, Hiroshi Nagano, Aaron Norman, Doug Perrine, Ross Robertson, Graeme Teague, Masae and Satoshi Ueda, Norbert Wu, and last, but far from least, my wife, Janine Cairns-Michael. Also thanks to my photographic advisor, Alan Broder of AB Sea Photo, for taking care of all of my underwater camera needs (sometimes in emergency situations) and my good friends at Images II, who have provided unequaled film developing services for more than a decade.

I can never fully thank all who have encouraged my writing and publishing efforts over the years. Very special thanks are owed to the editors of *Aquarium Fish Magazine*, Kathleen Wood and Edward Bauman, for keeping me on task and encouraging me to expand upon my monthly contributions to their magazine and put them in book form. I also appreciate the ongoing support of Thomas A. Frakes (*SeaScope*).

I can't fail to recognize my diving companions over the years, for they have put up with my frequent fossiking in reef crevices, my lying motionless for long periods of time on sand plains and mud flats, and my constant tendency to lag behind. This list of dive buddies includes, Mary Findlay, Joe and Melissa Hancock, Terry Majewski, Terry Parsons, Phyllis Randall, Roy Smathers, Cameron Snow, and Roger Steene.

I am extremely appreciative of the work of my publishing team at Microcosm, especially Alesia Depot, Alice Lawrence, Eugenie Seidenberg Delaney, Tanya Stone, Kerry Lawrence, and Editor James Lawrence for the many months they have invested in editing, designing, and organizing these volumes and their dedication to book-publishing excellence.

On a more personal level, I want to express sincere thanks to my family, especially Duane and Donna Michael, my parents, for encouraging my interest in the ocean's inhabitants and saltwater aquarium keeping. Thanks also to my New Zealand mum, Margaret, and to the late, great William Cairns for providing a friendly waystation during our South Pacific expeditions, and for letting me use their compost pile as a postdissection repository for Carpet Shark remains. I also wish to express thanks to our Creator for the marvelous planet on which we dwell, and for the extraordinary creatures and natural wonders we marvel at and which demand our responsible stewardship.

Finally, along with ichthyophiles everywhere, I am forever indebted to Jack Randall for dedicating his life to the study of coral reef fishes. Through his astonishing volume of scientific papers and books, and our regular communications, he was a constant influence for me over the many years that I was writing this text. Without his enormous contribution to the science of ichthyology, our knowledge about the taxonomy and ecology of this wonderful guild of fishes would be sorely lacking.

—*Scott W. Michael*
Lincoln, Nebraska

INTRODUCTION

Coral Reef Fishes

"The earth has spun with its real stars under a beautiful blue robe ever since the beginning of time."
—Romesh Gunesekera, *Reef*, 1994

As the skipper throttled back the engines and our boat glided quietly up to the day's first dive site, I was overcome with that rare sense of elation triggered by a new adventure in a strange location. Backpacking around the South Pacific on a low budget, my wife, Janine, and I were about to have our first underwater experience in the Fiji Islands. The deckhand launched an anchor from the bow, and the boat settled to a stop. Immediately, I began to scan the dark blue water beneath the boat. I could make out the top of a large coral pinnacle, with small, freely moving shapes hanging above it.

I have found that there is a strong correlation between being the first in the water and being the one to encounter shy, large fish species like the Napoleon Wrasse (*Cheilinus undulatus*) and various reef sharks that might be spooked by a group of divers. Whenever possible, I like to be submerged ahead of the pack, with camera at the ready. On this particular dive, I had no more than slipped into the water when I found myself surrounded by a huge, gaudy school of plankton-feeding fishes.

The coral reef is a shallow oasis of color and diversity in the world's deep blue oceans. Female *Pseudanthias squamipinnis*, Lyretail Anthias, hover near soft and stony corals (Indo-Pacific).

The primary species in this fluorescent cloud was the Lyretail Anthias (*Pseudanthias squamipinnis*)—mainly bright orange females with an occasional purple male darting among them. Bicolor Chromis (*Chromis dimidiatus*), Klein's Butterflyfish (*Chaetodon kleini*), Twotone Wrasses (*Thalassoma amblycephalum*), and Pinktail Triggerfish (*Melichthys vidua*) comprised the rest of the aggregation that hung above the multicolored lagoon pinnacle. Larger Coral and V-tailed Hinds or Groupers (*Cephalopholis miniata* and *Cephalopholis urodeta*) darted from one crevice to another on the reef top, their full bellies seemingly packed with the smaller planktivores from the swarm above them. I looked over the edge of the pinnacle in time to see an adult Clown Triggerfish (*Balistoides conspicillum*) moving past. Its pace suddenly quickened when a much smaller, but equally aggressive, damselfish raced out and chased it from its territory. Suddenly, a large Freckled Hawkfish (*Paracirrhites forsteri*) dashed from its coralline perch to snatch a passing Blue Green Chromis (*Chromis viridis*). The hawkfish returned to its ambush site—a promontory adorned with cherry red soft corals, mustard-colored fire coral, and purple clumps of the branching stony coral *Pocillopora*—with its victim's head protruding from its capacious jaw. As I looked around, my senses were swamped with stimuli.

Biological Keys

Returning home to Nebraska (more than 800 miles from the nearest ocean), I was determined to recreate at least part of the vista we had seen on that lagoon pinnacle. I acquired a used 55-gallon tank and gathered various items from both local aquarium stores and generous friends. Within several months, the Fijian reef scene—excluding the corals and big predators—was beginning to take shape in my landlocked living room. My desire to try to duplicate a small niche of coral reef was motivated by several things: an unshakable attraction to the behaviors and beauty of reef fishes, the unforgettable habitat we had visited, and a growing belief that captive ma-

Paracirrhites forsteri, Freckled Hawkfish: "To appreciate these fishes fully in any aquarium setting, providing a semblance of the natural reef habitats where they are found is a vital first step."

Deep reef in Kimbe Bay, Papua New Guinea: *Lutjanus biguttatus,* Twospotted Snappers, with red *Ctenocella* sp. gorgonians and hard coral plates.

rine species will acclimate and thrive best in an environment that mimics their natural home as closely as possible. To appreciate these fishes fully in an aquarium setting, providing a semblance of the natural reef habitats where they are found is a vital first step.

For most of the early history of saltwater aquarium keeping, aquascaping had more in common with a Japanese Zen garden than a coral reef: a flat expanse of sand with a scattering of dead, bleached coral skeletons. Some fishes will settle into such surroundings, but the survival rate of marine specimens in these stark tanks was notoriously low. As a marine aquarium keeper from the age of 12, I had created a succession of such conventional systems myself, but continuing exposure to reef fishes in their native habitats and years of observing their relative adaptability to captivity finally convinced me that we

Red Sea patch reef scene: *Pseudochromis fridmani*, Orchid Dottyback, with gorgonians, red *Dendronephthya* sp. soft corals, and a commensal mollusk.

needed to bring more of the biology and complexity of the coral reef into our aquariums.

Today there is no longer any reason to pluck fishes from a vibrant reef environment and place them in stark, artificial surroundings. The aquarist now has access to a profusion of reef-collected and propagated live rock and live reef sand from many regions, beautiful macroalgae, and invertebrates that range from cultures of mysid shrimp and tiny zooplankters to aquarium-hardy soft and stony corals. These, perhaps even more than improved aquatic technologies, are important keys to keeping and watching healthy, thriving reef fishes in captive systems.

In years past, marine aquarists were often content merely to be able to identify their specimens and know what foods they would accept. Today, we are beginning to be able to do much more. In order to replicate the habitat and conditions of a particular fish, for example, it is important to learn about the geographical distribution of the species and the types of habitat in which it naturally occurs. In order to set up and successfully maintain it in a captive reef fish community, we also need to know about the fish's feeding behavior in the wild, how it avoids predators, and its place in a social organization of other fishes.

A growing number of marine aquarists are now taking their hobby to a new level, breeding and raising piscine gems that were once thought impossible to propagate. Obviously, to do this demands research and careful observation of the fishes' sexual characteristics, reproductive behavior, and the feeding habits of their larvae and fry. Having insight into the natural history of a fish not only enables you to be a better fishkeeper, it also increases your appreciation of these amazing creatures and the complex communities in which they live.

Coral Reef Ecosystems

Coral reefs are the largest biologically produced structures on Earth. Some reef systems stretch for thousands of miles and extend to great depths. These impressive calcareous labyrinths are the creation of minuscule coral polyps and other simple plants and invertebrates, but they have wrecked countless ships and aroused deep fear, awe, and curiosity in humans for millennia. True coral reefs are limited in their distribution to areas where the minimal surface temperature is 18°C (64.4°F) or higher. Coral communities are, however, also found in cooler environs. But most reefs that are full of life usually occur in warm, clear, nutrient-impoverished water, arising oasislike from a watery desert.

Reefs can be divided into various zones and habitats, which are often characterized by different abiotic and biotic characteristics. Parameters such as light intensity, water movement, nutrient levels, and substrate type can vary dramatically from one zone to the next within the same reef. To varying degrees, the flora and fauna of the various reef habitats and zones are also unique.

Coral reefs rival the species-dense rainforests for their diversity of life. Although the undersea environment lacks the insects that give tropical forests their astronomical species counts, it is characterized by an astonishing diversity of sponges, anemones, stony corals, soft corals, polychaete worms, crustaceans, tunicates, and others. Many of these groups have more representatives in the coral reef ecosystem than in any other aquatic biome.

> *"Having insight into the natural history of a fish not only enables you to be a better fishkeeper, it also increases your appreciation of these amazing creatures and the complex communities in which they live."*

Diversity's Apex

Marine fishes also reach their apex of diversity on and around coral reefs. Although coral reef areas account for less than 1% (latest estimate is 255,000 km^2 or 0.07%) of the total area of the world's oceans, about half of all known species of marine fishes are found associated with coral reefs. The total number of reef fish species has been estimated at about 7,000, with vast areas of the Tropics waiting to be explored, and many new fishes remaining to be cataloged. (The total of all saltwater species is approximately 14,600, while all freshwater fish species number about 10,000.) Square meter for square meter, coral reefs support the richest concentration of fish diversity on Earth.

The diversity of species in some locations is astonishing. For example, the Philippines are known to have about 2,500 fish species, Papua New Guinea has more than 2,000, and the Great Barrier Reef in Australia has more than 1,500. Approximately 460 inshore species have been reported from the Hawaiian Island chain, 510 from the Bahamas, more than 600 from Alligator Reef off the Florida Keys, and 827 species from the Marshall Island reefs.

Every square centimeter of reef is utilized by one or more species, with a single patch reef providing a home for hundreds of different fishes. Because this community is packed with so many forms, many of which have overlapping resource requirements, the life of a coral reef fish can be very complex. Not only must it compete with its neighbors (both members of its own and different species) for food and shelter, it must constantly avoid being eaten. If it is successful in these endeavors, it will attempt to reproduce.

Coral reef fish communities vary from one reef habitat to the next, between reefs in a specific region, and from one geographical location to another. Many regions have unique, or endemic, components. The reefs surrounding the Hawaiian chain have a large endemic component—24% of the 460 species found there occur nowhere else. While the Hawaiian Islands are a special case, all major reef

Below: *Centropyge hotumatua,* Hotumatua's Angelfish, is an unusual Easter Island endemic much sought after by aquarists.

Facing page: coral grotto in Milne Bay, Papua New Guinea, with a large gorgonian sea fan, (*Melithaea* sp.), a Barrel Sponge (*Xestospongia testudinaria*), and a surrounding shoal of anthias.

areas of the world have species found only there, and/or a unique collection of species. On Easter Island, for example, 26% of the species are endemic to the reefs surrounding the island, and some of these fishes are highly sought after by aquarists. One species found there, as well as around the neighboring Pitcairn Group, Rapa, and Austral Island, is the exquisite Hotumatua's Angelfish (*Centropyge hotumatua*). This royal angel, which is the coveted Holy Grail for many pomacanthid aficionados, was named after one of the original Polynesian chiefs who inhabited Easter Island.

The serious aquarist may want to try to duplicate a particular habitat, zone, or region in his or her tank, perhaps a Coral Sea fore reef, a reef flat from Mombasa, or an Indonesian coastal patch reef. With some information on zoogeography, as well as the proper equipment and knowledge of fish husbandry, we can now recreate reef fish communities from around the world.

Strategic Adaptations

Because of the intense competition that exists in reef fish communities, many species have special anatomical features, behaviors, or distribution patterns to aid them in survival. A good example of how specialized some reef species have become is found in the Hawaiian surgeonfish community. Over 23 species of surgeonfishes live on the reefs off the Kona coast. But because some occupy different reef habitats or have dissimilar diets, they are not all in competition with each other. The Orange-shoulder Surgeonfish (*Acanthurus olivaceous*) occupies the sand areas adjacent to reefs and feeds on the layer of diatoms (brown microalgae) and detritus (decaying organic matter and bacteria) on the sand surface. The Achilles Surgeonfish (*Acanthurus achilles*) occupies a territory on the turbulent reef crest and feeds primarily on the microalgae "turf" that grows on hard substrates. And the Orange-spine Unicornfish (*Naso lituratus*) is found in less turbulent areas of the reef and browses on leafy brown macroalgae. The Yellow Tang (*Zebrasoma flavescens*) also lives in quieter areas on the reef, but it picks mainly on filamentous microalgae, which it can better extract from interstices with its elongate snout. Finally, the Sleek Unicornfish (*Naso hexacanthus*) forms schools in the water column above the reef and ingests passing plankton. As demonstrated in this surgeonfish community, all tangs are not the same, closely related species may have very different approaches to living on or near the reef. They may occupy different habitats, display different social behaviors, feed on different food items, and utilize different foraging strategies—all to help reduce competition among sympatric species.

> "The serious aquarist may want to try to duplicate a particular habitat, zone, or region in his or her tank, perhaps a Coral Sea fore reef, a reef flat from Mombasa, or an Indonesian coastal patch reef."

Surgeonfishes grazing in the boulder zone: *Acanthurus achilles* (Achilles Surgeonfish), *Acanthurus guttatus* (Whitespotted Surgeonfish), and *Zebrasoma flavescens* (Yellow Tang).

Cirrhilabrus lineatus, Lined Fairy Wrasse (male): the "poster-paint" colors and dazzling patterns of coral reef fishes have long puzzled biologists and produced many explanations and theories.

Riotous Colors

"Wow, there is so much color!" This is virtually always the first thing any neophyte diver or snorkeler says when coming up from seeing his or her first coral reef. Pastel-colored stony corals, brightly hued soft corals, iridescent clam mantles, ostentatious crinoids, and richly colored macroalgae make a spectacular backdrop for the more vagile (wandering) characters in the aqueous drama—the fishes.

Although not all the bony fishes of the reef are "chromatically blessed," many do possess dazzling colors and patterns. For many years, ethologists have speculated on the function of these bright hues. Konrad Lorenz, the father of ethology, suggested that the colors help to advertise the presence of territorial species in order to decrease aggressive encounters. He coined the term "poster coloration" to refer to these color patterns. But not all brightly colored reef fishes are territorial, and some drably colored forms display intense levels of site-attached aggression. Many species that shoal—such as the anthias—are brilliantly colored, while many of the highly territorial damsels of the genus *Stegastes* have dull colors. As will be discussed in Chapter 1, reef fish coloration defies easy explanations.

One thing we must remember is that we view the reef fish's world differently than it does. Water affects light, filtering out shorter wavelengths at relatively shallow depths. Thus, a lionfish that looks red and white under a bank of fluorescent lights would appear black and light blue on a deep forereef slope. The retinal pigments of coral reef fishes and their optical sensitivity also differ from ours, and vary between species. Most diurnal fishes (those that hunt during the day) have relatively small eyes with numerous cones (responsible for color vision) and few rods (responsible for vision in low-light conditions). This makes them sensitive to the distinction of colors and movement when light is bright. At dawn and dusk, predatory reef piscivores, as well as nocturnal and deep-water species, which have larger eyes with a high concentration of rods, function successfully in the subdued lighting. These predators are less adept during the day. The number of visual pigments in the rods and cones also determines the visual acuity and color perception of a fish's eye.

A predator pauses: a large *Pterois volitans* (Volitans Lionfish) allows itself to be cleaned by a juvenile *Labroides dimidiatus* (Bluestreak Cleaner Wrasse), in the Red Sea.

Predator-Prey Tactics

Although the reef appears to teem with potential prey, many of these organisms are equipped with defenses that make them unavailable as food for the generalized piscivorous carnivore. Even creatures as inoffensive looking as the lovely soft corals are equipped with spines, spicules, and chemicals to put off all but the most specialized predators. An "arms race" is occurring on the reef between predators and prey. Predators have

Scorpaenopsis oxycephala, Tasseled Scorpionfish: an ambush predator, armed with complex camouflage and venomous spines to ward off attackers, it patiently awaits a prey item to pass within striking distance (Banda Sea).

developed anatomical features and behaviors to deal with the defenses of prey species. In response, new defenses are selected to thwart the effectiveness of these predators. These defensive adaptations may be morphological or behavioral in nature. Some prey species have sharp spines, hard shells, toxins, or cryptic chromatic attire to reduce the chances that they will be eaten. Behavioral adaptations include speed, schooling, and refuging. Some edible species even mimic the appearance and behavior of unpalatable forms, fooling the predator into looking elsewhere for a tastier morsel.

Some of the most fascinating features of reef fish communities are the hunting strategies of its carnivorous members. Some species remain quiet on the seafloor, mimicking the appearance and "behavior" of either harmless organisms or the seafloor itself, and inhale any fish or crustacean that moves too close. Other species hide behind nonthreatening fishes, using them as a mobile blind from which to sneak up on their prey. There are some species that fool their prey by resembling a fish that does not eat them. This is called aggressive mimicry. Some carnivores are adapted to take advantage of the small, free-floating eggs, larvae, and minute adult organisms that constitute the broth that surrounds the reef. Some of these hunters feed during the day, while others leave their reef lairs at night to enter the water column and catch zooplankton. Because these fishes are themselves more vulnerable to predators, and because they are often far from shelter, they may take advantage of the protection afforded by living in aggregations and shoals. Many of these fascinating food-collecting behaviors and feeding relationships can be observed in our aquariums.

Algae are the most abundant plants on any reef. Although they look harmless, some algae have developed noxious chemicals and physical structures to dissuade hungry herbivores. But there are still many forms that are utilized by reef vegetarians. These fishes take different approaches when it comes to their feeding behavior. Some herbivores move over the reef in roving shoals, which drop out of the water column to pillage the substrate. Others, such as the gregory damsels, are farmers—they defend and tend a lush algal turf. The turf within the territories of these plant-eaters is many times more productive than in those areas not tended by these fishes.

Mating Games

Not only do reef fishes display a number of disparate feeding strategies, they also employ a diversity of reproductive modes. Although the majority of bony fishes fertilize their eggs outside of the body, there is a wide spectrum of reef fish sexuality and mating systems. In some species, females change to males. In others, females result from male sex changes. Some adult individuals of certain species have functional ovaries and testes simultaneously. Recently, it was discovered that several site-attached goby genera engage in "both way" sex changing—they are able to change back and forth from one sex to the other, depending on the social circumstances.

Many female reef fishes are selective about whom they mate with, choosing various physical or behavioral attributes. In turn, mates compete with each other to attract and spawn with one or more females. Many male reef fishes engage in elaborate behaviors to entice potential mates and to drive away male competitors.

In most reef fishes, the fertilized eggs are sent adrift as they are expelled during the spawning act. The currents then disperse the eggs from one area of the reef to the next, from one reef to another, or even between islands or land masses. But there are species that incubate their eggs in either specialized pouches or their mouths. Some tend nests, fanning and defending the developing eggs from predators. Even in these species, the newly hatched fry enter the plankton where they spend weeks to months before settling into an appropriate and vacant reef habitat.

Chaetodon semilarvatus, Golden Butterflyfish: in typical butterflyfish fashion, a mated pair works its way in tandem over Jackson Reef in the Red Sea.

Social Behavior

Social behaviors function to reduce competition within and between reef fish species. Some fishes aggressively evict members of their own species—as well as other competing fishes—from a specific area referred to as a territory. This effectively spreads the food competitors out over the reef, so that there are enough resources for more individuals in a specific area. The selective pressure of predation is strong enough to force some species to form shoals or schools in order to reduce the chances that they will become a meal. By forming groups, some species are able to overpower the defenses of those herbivores that stake out a feeding territory.

Although fascinating to observe in the wild, some of these behaviors can make life difficult for the aquarist. Territorial fishes, of which there are many on the reef, can mangle their tankmates and cause the blood pressure of even the calmest caretaker to rise. However, being informed about the ways of a fish and what stimuli catalyze certain undesirable behaviors can make the fishkeeper's life much more serene.

Aquarium Ethics

With recent advances in filtration, nutrition, and disease prevention and control, and with the opening of collecting stations in far-flung locations, there is no better time to be a marine fishkeeper. It is now possible for even landlocked reef lovers to enjoy marine fishes from reefs around the world, rather than only being able to observe them in public aquariums or on those infrequent dive trips.

For the saltwater aquarist, however, this brings with it the ethical responsibility of being a caretaker to some of nature's most beautiful subjects. An aquarist's obligation should not be taken lightly. Among the reef fish species commonly kept by aquarists, none is considered endangered at this writing—a consequence of their widespread distributions, the localized activities of most ornamental fish collectors, and the prolific reproduction capabilities of most reef species. Nevertheless, this is a resource that must be harvested and used with care and respect.

Most assessments of reef fish collection for the aquarium trade have shown minimal environmental impact when traditional hand-fishing methods are used, primarily nets. The use of sodium or potassium cyanide to stun reef fishes, both for sales to gourmet markets in the Orient and to the pet-fish trade, are having tragic consequences on reefs in the Philippines and Indonesia. Cyanide application can kill or weaken coral heads, and areas heavily

fished with these chemicals typically lose their natural habitat and their population of fishes and invertebrates. In addition to the long-term or permanent environmental damage, fishes harvested with cyanide may never recover fully, and informed aquarists are actively involved in trying to put a stop to this and other nonsustainable collection practices.

Most of the species in the marine trade are collected from the wild, and the aquarist who ensures that his or her specimens survive well in captivity is helping to prevent needless pressure on natural stocks. (A marine fish can live from 5 to 25 years if properly cared for in the aquarium.) Captive-bred marine fishes are also becoming more commonly available, an exciting development that is providing the aquarist with specimens that are beautiful, well-adapted to aquarium conditions, and that also have a propensity to reproduce in captive conditions. While many species will likely continue to come primarily

Amphiprion clarkii, Clark's Anemonefish: a young pair nestles in the stinging tentacles of its host anemone in North Sulawesi. Captive propagation efforts are taking collection pressures off this and other anemonefish species.

Pygoplites diacanthus, Regal Angelfish: although an alluring and coveted species, this sponge-eater often adapts poorly to captivity and is avoided by many knowledgeable aquarists, while experts try to understand its husbandry requirements (Red Sea).

from Third World collectors, it is important that all who buy and sell marine fishes (wholesalers, retailers, and hobbyists) support those suppliers that are propagating marine species in captivity or in aquaculture settings. Many species are spawning and being raised in facilities in Puerto Rico, Florida, and other areas. Marine invertebrates, including giant clams, soft corals, and reef-building stony corals are all being farmed in various locations close to their native reefs, including Belau, the Solomon Islands and Guam. The pioneers in these efforts will only succeed if hobbyists demand and buy captive-raised stock—or if reefs are closed to collection because of overharvesting.

There are some species that should be avoided by most aquarists, because they present special feeding challenges. For example, unless you are willing to provide the natural diet of those butterflyfishes that eat only stony coral polyps, they should be left on the reef to thrive and procreate. There are also certain fish species that refuse to live in captivity for other reasons. The Pinnate Batfish (*Platax pinnatus*) does not have a specialized diet, as indicated by food habit studies, but it still rarely accepts aquarium fare and fails to thrive in captivity. Until their husbandry requirements are discovered, it is important that we refuse to buy those fishes that are nearly impossible to keep. If there is not a demand for them, collectors will stop removing them from the wild.

Some of the species offered in the trade also get far too large for the vast majority of home aquariums. The juvenile Giant Grouper (*Epinephelus lanceolatus*) is attractively marked, "personable," and occasionally shows up in the aquarium trade. But what is the ill-informed hobbyist going to do when junior grows into a ravenous behemoth? This fish can reach a maximum length of 300 cm (9.8 ft.) and weigh over 400 kg (882 lbs.). Other unsuitable "gargantuans" that enter the aquarium trade in small numbers include some shark and ray species, several morays, most of the jacks (they not only get large, they are also very active and need plenty of swimming room), and the Napoleon Wrasse (*Cheilinus undulatus*). There are many other species that reach considerable proportions and need more room than the hobbyist can readily provide. If these fishes are forced to live in crowded confines, they usually perish prematurely. Many aquarists are under the false impression that they can dump an overgrown fish at a local public aquarium. But these institutions often don't have the space for these animals—don't rely on them to rescue you from your indiscretions.

Reef Connections

In this book, I have attempted to give the aquarist, diver, biologist, and reef naturalist a detailed look into the lives of some of the most fascinating creatures and communities on this planet. I especially hope that these insights will aid aquarists in succeeding with the long-term husbandry of these animals and facilitate the duplication of reef environments and reef fish communities from around the world in our home aquariums. Despite the unsuitability of certain families and species, a huge selection of reef fishes make excellent aquarium specimens, able to lead long, healthy lives in captivity, giving us great satisfaction and providing countless others with an educational face-to-face look at live coral reef creatures.

My ultimate goal is to encourage a greater appreciation of reef fishes and the ecosystem that they inhabit. In turn, I trust that this will lead to an increase in the well-being of the animals we keep in our home aquariums, better awareness of coral reef ecosystems, and an active interest in their future. Anyone with a marine aquarium has a living link to the coral reefs of the world, however distant and unreal they may seem.

Only within the past half century, with the development of scuba apparatus, have we become fully aware of the natural beauty and complexity of living reefs. Given the rapidity of development and resource harvesting in the Tropics, many reef areas are predicted to be decimated or greatly diminished within the next half century. (By some estimates, coral reefs are now the most threatened ecosystems on earth, with the possibility of massive coral habitat losses in the coming decades.) Perhaps the allure of reef fishes can bring together aquarists, divers, naturalists, scientists, and others who share a concern for the reefs and their myriad species. If so, it will be an extraordinary demonstration of the powerful attractions—the fantastic colors, shapes and behavioral patterns—of these endlessly fascinating fishes.

> *"... a huge selection of reef fishes make excellent aquarium specimens, able to lead long, healthy lives in captivity, giving us great satisfaction and providing countless others with an educational face-to-face look at live coral reef creatures."*

CHAPTER

1

The History & Anatomy of Reef Fishes

A Primer on Some of Nature's Most Successful and Fantastic Works

"Why such an explosion of fishes, so brilliantly adorned in pattern, so famously varied in contour? No one knows."
—Carlos Safina, *Song for a Blue Ocean*, 1997

In the foothills of the Alps in northern Italy, there is a fossilized coral reef where scientists have found the remains of more than 80 families of saltwater fishes, including members of the Acanthuridae, Chaetodontidae, Labridae, Pomacentridae, and Zanclidae—all strikingly similar to the modern-day forms of marine angelfishes, butterflyfishes, wrasses, damselfishes, and even the Moorish Idol. The victims of a mass die-off, perhaps caused by an algal bloom, these exceptional fossils represent the first-known record of a complete community of coral reef fishes. Known as Monte Bolca, the reef and its fossil fishes is an estimated 50 million years old.

Reef fishes are ancient life forms, with many of them traced back to the Eocene Epoch, which followed shortly after the extinctions of the dinosaurs of the late Cretaceous Period. It was a time of great change in marine environ-

Mene rhombeus, a fossilized acanthomorph—related to present-day surgeonfishes—about 57 million years old from Monte Bolca, Italy: fossil records reveal that reef fishes are ancient life forms.

ments, with the appearance, diversification, and spread of the reef-building stony corals (which had come close to obliteration at the time of the mass extinction of the dinosaurs), and the creation of new, shallow-water habitats. Over a 20-million-year period, most of the modern reef fish families appear in the fossil record, and from that time until today, a period of over 50 million years, they have remained relatively unchanged.

The precursors to the reef fishes are much older and among the first vertebrates known on Earth. The first fishes in the fossil record date back roughly 500 million years. Fossil evidence of the first-known hominids, by way of comparison, dates back a mere 5 million years. Of the 48,170 recognized living vertebrates found on Earth, more than half—or about 24,600—of these are fishes. Birds and mammals together account for less than 14,000 species.

Clearly, living in water can have long-term advantages. The fishes are an evolutionary success story, with anatomies and survival modes that have carried them through some of the worst geological and meteorological conditions and disasters Earth has known. Long before the appearance of mammals and birds in the fossil record, the fishes survived the tremendous mass extinction of 225 million years ago that killed 95% of all marine invertebrate species. Then, whatever wiped out the dinosaurs 65 million years ago was dodged by a great array of fishes—enough to give us greater species diversity today than at any time in Earth's history.

Almost 60% of the world's known fish species live only in saltwater. Not surprisingly, the coral reefs of the world are home to an amazing variety of bony fishes. Almost every niche on the reef, as well as nearby ecosystems (mangrove areas, seagrass beds, etc.), is occupied by one or more fish species.

In general terms, reef fishes are smaller, more colorful, and more diverse than the oceanic fishes. They are also relatively long-lived and more sedentary, often spending their entire lives on the same reef, with the exception of a larval period in which many species spend days or weeks drifting in the plankton before settling out.

Specialized Anatomies

Fishes live in a medium that is very different from our own. Water is 800 times denser than air and holds just 3.3% of the oxygen that our atmosphere contains. Water also reduces the amount of light that permeates its depths (by refraction). The quality of those light rays that do penetrate is altered. Sound is also affected by the density of this noncompressible medium, traveling over four times faster underwater than it does in air.

> *"Clearly, living in water can have long-term advantages. The fishes are an evolutionary success story, with anatomies and survival modes that have carried them through some of the worst geological and meteorological conditions and disasters Earth has known."*

Istiblennius chrysospilos, Redspotted Blenny: as with all reef fishes, marvelously adapted to its particular niche in a highly complex environment (North Sulawesi).

Fishes possess numerous anatomical adaptations to meet the unique challenges presented by the environment in which they live. Because water is denser than air, a fish must be stronger than a similarly sized terrestrial animal. Fishes display a wide array of body shapes and forms of locomotion in order to move with greater efficiency in their aqueous environment. Many species have organs that allow them to achieve neutral buoyancy. This buoyancy increases their ability to maneuver in tight places and allows them to expend less energy when swimming or maintaining their position in the water column. Fishes also possess respiratory organs, called gills. The fishes are able to extract oxygen efficiently from the water by either pumping or pushing water (ram-jet ventilation) over the gills. Specialized body coverings protect them from their enemies as well as the external environment, while modified sensory organs enable them to sample their surroundings quickly.

Body Form and Function

Reef fishes are found in a dazzling array of shapes and sizes. They range from minute, elongate fishes that sit on hard substrate to giant, beaked leviathans that roam over the reef like the herds of ungulates that range over the African savanna. The body form of a reef fish provides useful information about its lifestyle. Not surprisingly, most can be classified into a particular group based on the characteristics of their form. The following is a list of the most common fish-body plans, with the common locomotory habits employed by representatives of each group:

Anguilliform Body Plan

A number of reef fishes have very elongate, snakelike bodies. In many

Gymnothorax meleagris, Whitemouth Moray: exhibits the anguilliform body plan.

cases, the posterior portion of the body in these species is flattened, which aids in propulsion. These fishes swim by flexing the whole body in the lateral plane, creating sinusoidal waves down the fish's length. This type of locomotion is known as anguilliform swimming. Some of the best examples of this body plan are the moray eels. These fishes may or may not have spineless dorsal and anal fins, they have no paired fins, and they may or may not have a tail fin—which, when present, consists of a lobe joined to the other median fins. They are not strong swimmers and spend most of their time slithering over the substrate. This elongate body plan is ideal for entering tight crevices and holes in the reef either to seek refuge or to ferret out crustaceans and fishes.

Compressiform Body Plan

One of the most common body shapes of reef fishes is a laterally compressed, or compressiform, plan, with the degree of compression varying considerably from one group to the next. For example, butterflyfishes are highly compressed with a saucer-shaped body, while groupers are slightly to moderately compressed and somewhat elongate. The laterally compressed body of the butterflyfish is excellent for slipping between coral branches when seeking shelter or food, and its exaggerated depth, along with its stout dorsal and anal spines, presents an unappetizing target for most predators. Those species that are highly compressed (like angelfishes and butterflyfishes) swim by employing short lateral strokes of the posterior portion of the body and tail and are not strong swimmers. There are other deep-bodied fishes (like triggerfishes) that move by undulating the dorsal and anal fins, a swimming mode referred to as balistiform locomotion.

Those fishes with bodies that are less compressed and more elongate (like groupers) are capable of bursts of speed, but most cannot sustain a rapid rate of movement. Many of these fishes are ambush predators, while others stalk macroinvertebrates. The most common mode of locomotion practiced by these fishes is subcarangiform swimming (sometimes classified as a form of anguilliform swimming). In this type of locomotion, the body is undulated in the lateral plane, but not to the same degree as in anguilliform swimming.

Taeniform Body Plan

Relatively few coral reef fishes display this architecture, which is extremely laterally compressed and ribbonlike. Some of the best examples of this body plan are the ribbon gobies (*Oxymetopon* spp.), which are found on mud or sand slopes adjacent to coral reefs. The Hair-tail Blenny (*Xiphasia setifer*) also exhibits the taeniform plan and, like the ribbon gobies, is a resident of soft bottoms. These species swim much like the eels, employing typical anguilliform locomotion.

Left: *Oxymetopon cyanoctenosum*, Bluebarred Ribbon Goby: exemplifies the taeniform body plan.
Right: *Pomacanthus imperator*, the Emperor Angelfish: displays the compressiform body plan.

Cirrhilabrus rhomboidalis, Rhomboid Fairy Wrasse (male): illustrative of the sagittiform body plan.

Sagittiform Body Plan

Some reef fishes are only slightly compressed with more elongate bodies that are round to slightly oval in cross section. These include fishes such as the barracudas and many of the wrasses. Some of these species feed on motile invertebrates and rely on sudden bursts of speed to capture their wary prey, while others feed on zooplankton. For example, the lizardfishes hurl themselves off the bottom to capture passing prey species, while the fairy wrasses swim above the reef and snap up small, free-floating crustaceans. Some fishes with a sagittiform body plan spend most of their time hovering in the water column (like fairy wrasses), while others perch on the substrate (like lizardfishes, sand perches, and gobies).

While many of the reef fishes that display this body plan employ subcarangiform swimming, there are some (the wrasses) that also—or instead—engage in labriform locomotion. This mode of swimming consists of using the pectoral fins like oars to propel the fish through the water. There are also some fishes (including some wrasses, parrotfishes, and surgeonfishes) that do not have a sagittiform body plan but that do employ labriform locomotion.

Depressiform Body Plan

Many bottom-dwelling fish species have flattened or dorsally compressed bodies that enable them to better blend with the substrate. Some of these species also bury themselves just under the sand or mud surface. The flatfishes exemplify this body type. These fishes swim by undulating the edges of the dorsal and anal fins, or by swinging the tail and posterior portion of the body up and down. This latter swimming style can best be described as sub-carangiform.

Fusiform Body Plan

Fishes that rely on sustained speed to survive possess a fusiform body plan. This streamlined package is ideal for rapid movement through the water. Although not usually considered to be associated with reefs, the tunas are the best example of this form. These fishes are stiff-bodied; when they swim, they flex only the posterior portion of the body and the rigid tail, with the latter providing almost all of the propulsive thrust. The caudal peduncle is round in cross section, narrow, and often has lateral keels that reduce turbulence as the tail beats rapidly from side to side. This type of swimming pattern is known as carangiform locomotion.

Left: *Bothus lunatus*, Peacock Flounder: showing the depressiform body plan.
Right: a school of *Caranx sexfasciatus*, Bigeye Trevally: classic fusiform body plan.

Globiform Body Plan

Some fishes have lumpish or globe-shaped bodies. These include the frogfishes, the puffers, and some of the porcupinefishes. In cross section, they are round and often have poorly developed fins or fins that are modified for moving over the substrate. Most of these fishes are weak swimmers, relying on other strategies to capture prey or to avoid predators. For example, the puffers feed on sessile invertebrates and are toxic, while the frogfishes lure their prey and are extremely well camouflaged. Representatives of both of these families can inflate with water when threatened. Some of these fishes (like puffers) swim by beating their undersized dorsal and anal fins from side to side, while the caudal fin is used for steering. This mode of propulsion is known as tetraodontiform locomotion. Puffers and porcupinefishes can also engage in a diodontiform mode of swimming, in which the pectoral fins are rhythmically undulated. The frogfishes actually "walk" on the substrate by employing modified paired fins or propel themselves by expelling streams of water out of small gill apertures (jet propulsion). The puffers and frogfishes are also capable of ingesting air to disperse from one reef to another by floating with the current on the water's surface.

Box-Shaped Body Plan

A smaller number of fishes have box-shaped bodies. The trunkfishes and boxfishes are almost square in cross section. Members of this group use their single dorsal and anal fins to propel themselves forward, curling their tails to one side or the other. The tail is used as a rudder to change course or as a paddle to increase propulsion. This mode of locomotion is referred to as os-

Left: a juvenile *Arothron mappa*, Map Puffer: typical globiform body plan.
Right: *Ostracion solorensis*, Reticulate Boxfish (male): an obvious box-shaped body plan.

traciform swimming. These fishes are relatively poor swimmers that rely on toxic slime and body armor to deter potential predators.

Other Body Plans

A number of unusual reef fish body types cannot be placed in any of the categories described above. Consider the members of the genus *Hippocampus*, the seahorses. These fishes display one of the most unusual reef fish anatomical structures, with ringlike segments that encircle the laterally compressed body, and long, prehensile caudal peduncles. They swim with their bodies in an upright position by rapidly beating their pectoral fins and the single dorsal fin. When they want to remain stationary, they wrap their tails around seagrasses, sponges, or soft corals or use their tails as anchors on soft bottoms.

Solenostomus paradoxus, Ornate Ghost Pipefish: related to the seahorses (genus *Hippocampus*), with a dermal skeleton made up of stellate plates that form a unique body plan (North Sulawesi).

Fins

Fish fins have several different functions. These include locomotion, stabilization, defense, and prey capture. Fins may also have other functions. In some fishes, the fins can help both conspecifics (and aquarists) in differentiating between the sexes. For example, many male fairy wrasses (*Cirrhilabrus* spp.) have elongate pelvic fins. One disadvantage of having fins is that they create turbulence, which increases the amount of drag experienced by the body as it moves through the water. The best way to reduce fin-induced drag is to reduce the surface area of these structures.

The fins can be classified as either median or paired. The median fins occur along the midline of the body and include the dorsal fin or fins, anal fin, caudal fin, and adipose fin, which is present in only a few reef-dwelling forms. In most cases, the median fins are larger in fish species that have deeper bodies in order to prevent the body from rolling as it moves through the water. The paired fins include the pectoral fins and the pelvic or ventral fins. In many fishes, there is an interesting correlation between the position

Left: *Zanclus cornutus*, Moorish Idol: displays an elogated dorsal fin filament that serves to reduce drag and make for more efficient swimming.
Right: *Antennarius striatus*, Striated Frogfish: note the cleverly adapted lurelike structure called the esca, which is attached to the first dorsal spine, or illicium. This feature is used by frogfishes to attract prey to within striking range. (The esca will regenerate if actually bitten off.)

of the paired fins and a change in their function. As pectoral fin placement moves higher up on the body, the pelvic fins move farther forward. In this way, the pelvic fins provide for increased stabilization.

A fin is typically comprised of a membrane that extends between spines or rays. Both of these structures are modified scales, but spines are derivations of rays. All fishes have rays, but some of the more "primitive" forms lack spines. Spines are stouter (adding more support), are often sharp, and may even be equipped with venom glands (as in the scorpionfishes). Spines are limited to the dorsal, pelvic, and anal fins, while all fins have rays. The number of spines and rays in the fins can provide important clues when differentiating certain species. For example, one of the best ways to distinguish the Percula Anemonefish (*Amphiprion percula*) from the Ocellaris Anemonefish (*Amphiprion ocellaris*) is by counting the number of dorsal spines (*A. percula* usually has 10 spines, while *A. ocellaris* typically has 11). The membrane between the rays (and sometimes the rays themselves) is often damaged during aggressive or predatory interactions. If the fish is in a "healthy" environment, however, the membrane is quick to heal and regenerate. Rays will also grow back, but spines rarely do.

Dorsal Fin

Dorsal fins are located along the midline of the back. In fishes that cruise or are midwater hunters, the dorsal fin acts as a stabilizer to prevent them from yawing, or rolling to one side or the other. Certain teleosts can also curl the posterior portion of the dorsal fin to one side and use it for braking, while in other body forms it is an important component in propulsion. In the triggerfishes and filefishes, for example, the dorsal and anal fins are undulated and act to propel the body forward or backward. The dorsal fin is also used for swimming in seahorses and pipefishes.

The dorsal fin, however, is not just an important component in locomotion. In certain species (especially benthic forms), dorsal fins are used for display during courtship or aggressive interactions. In many male dragonets, for example, the fin is exaggerated in length and adorned with striking colors. The fin is inconspicuous when lying along the back, but very obvious when it is raised up and extended forward during agonistic or courtship displays.

Reef fishes can have zero, one, or two dorsal fins. If you have difficulty differentiating a goby from a blenny, you can use the dorsal fin(s) to tell them apart. The vast majority of gobies have two dorsal fins, while blennies always have one long continuous fin. In the more "advanced" bony fishes, the dorsal fin is divided into the spinous dorsal fin—the most anterior portion of the fin—and the soft dorsal, which is supported only by rays. The dorsal spines of some fish species (like scorpionfishes) are equipped with venom glands that help protect them from predators. Others species have one or more long filaments that extend from the posterior edge of this fin (like the bannerfishes and the Moorish Idol) and guide turbulence away from it. This reduces drag and increases swimming efficiency.

In some species, a modified dorsal spine is employed as a lure to attract prey. For example, in the frogfishes, the first dorsal spine—called an illicium—is moved in a variety of ways to entice smaller fishes into striking range. In most species, there is also a tuft of filaments and/or a flat piece of skin to serve as "bait." This is known as the esca. Some fishes (like the Decoy Scorpionfish, *Iracundus signifier*) seem to use the entire dorsal fin to attract prey. In another group, the sharksuckers, the dorsal fin is modified to form a sucking disc. These fishes often adhere to sharks, rays, whales, and large bony fishes.

Pectoral Fins

A fish's pectoral fins can function as oars, brakes, pivots, paddles, balancing tools, and hydroplanes. It is the pectoral fins that have given "advanced" bony fishes the ability to make minor adjustments in position, allowing them to exploit a larger number of reef niches. The pectoral fins can be used for forward and backward propulsion, making sudden stops or sharp turns, and maintaining a fish's position in the water column. For example, juvenile Panther Groupers (*Cromileptes altivelis*), Percula Anemonefish (*Amphiprion percula*), and the Graceful Shrimp Goby (*Lotilia graciliosa*) can maintain their

Fin rays of *Pterois antennata*, Spotfin Lionfish: these exaggerated pectorals are used to threaten would-be aggressors and even to prevent the escape of prey fishes being hunted.

Scorpaenopsis papuensis, Papuan Scopionfish: the reef-tone colors, along with skin flaps and tassles, enable it to disappear against the variegated background of the reef (North Sulawesi).

positions in the water column by sculling with their oversized pectoral fins. In some species, the pectoral fins are a primary means of forward propulsion. Wrasses and parrotfishes, for example, "flap" their pectoral fins like wings during "normal" swimming (when they need a burst of speed, they use their caudal fins). In sharks, which are usually negatively buoyant, the stiff pectoral fins are important for both lift and braking. Some eels lack these fins, while others have pectorals, but they are very small in relation to body length. Eels either slither along the substrate or use their tails for forward thrust.

Some species have pectoral fins that are analogous to legs. In some of these fishes, the pectoral fin rays actually function like toes. The frogfishes and walking batfishes have such appendages and use them to "walk" along the seafloor. In fact, when a frogfish wants to move quickly over the substrate, it employs a tetrapodlike gait, "galloping" along on its pectoral and pelvic fins. Other species, like devilfishes, stingfishes, and flying gurnards, have several modified pectoral rays that are used either to move over the bottom or to displace substrate as they look for benthic invertebrates. The insides of the pectoral fins of some species are ornately marked with bright colors and striking patterns that are displayed during aggressive interactions or when the fish is threatened. Some of these species are venomous and the colors send this warning to predators. The lionfishes have greatly enlarged pectoral fins that they use to corner their prey against the reef.

Pelvic Fins
The pelvic fins act as stabilizers to prevent active fishes from tumbling forward as they swim. They are also used for braking, as a base on which a fish can rest on the substrate (as in certain roundheads and gobies), or for locomo-

tion in benthic species (like sea robins). The first three pelvic fin rays in sea robins are enlarged and not bound together by a membrane. These rays are used to crawl over the seafloor. In other species, the pelvic fins are either enlarged or filamentous and may be important when an individual engages in displays during aggressive or reproductive interactions. In still other species, the pelvic fins are reduced or absent. For example, the triggerfishes and filefishes have a prominent spine instead of "true" pelvic fins; in eels, puffers, and boxfishes, the pelvic fins are completely absent. In the clingfishes, the pelvic fins are modified to form a thoracic sucker disc, which they use to adhere to rocks, macroalgae, or benthic invertebrates (like crinoids and gorgonians).

Anal Fin

The anal fin is located along the midline of the ventrum, just posterior to the anal opening. It can bear spines at its anterior end and, like the dorsal fin, acts as a stabilizer. It is often extended when a fish displays, which increases the individual's apparent size. Some species (like triggerfishes and filefishes) swim by undulating the anal and dorsal fins. The males of certain blenny species have fleshy tissue on top of the anal spines that is believed to secrete pheromones that attract mates. The only coral reef fishes that lack this fin are the pipefishes.

Above: *Gobiesox punctulatus*, Stippled Clingfish: modified pelvic fins form a suction device. Below: *Paracheilinus mccoskeri*, McCosker's Flasher Wrasse: displaying a bright red anal fin.

Caudal Fin

Most fishes use the caudal fin, or tail, as their major source of propulsion. When a fish needs to beat a hasty retreat or move over a short distance to capture prey, it will often lay all its fins flat against its body (which diminishes the amount of surface area subjected to turbulence), and propel itself forward with the caudal fin. When a fish is maneuvering, it will keep its median fins erect to provide stabilization. The caudal fin is expanded when some fishes display, is used to beat rivals during aggressive encounters (tail-beating), and in at

Caudal or tail fin of *Sparisoma viride*, Stoplight Parrotfish (terminal male): lunate or crescent-moon shape allows strong propulsion with turbulence diverted to the elongated tips.

least one group of fishes (the shrimp gobies) it is used to communicate with a symbiont. The surgeonfishes have modified scales in front of the tail, on the narrow portion known as the caudal peduncle. These scales consist of either a sharp spine that can lie along the peduncle, or a rigid thornlike structure that is perennially erect. They wield these spines when attempting to dissuade competing rivals and potential predators. Some reef "speedsters" also have scutes and/or a keel along the caudal peduncle that may aid in channeling turbulence or enabling the peduncle to be moved through the water with greater efficiency. This is true for many of the jacks.

Caudal fins come in a number of different shapes and sizes and, in many species, can be divided into an upper and lower lobe. The form of the tail often gives clues about the swimming abilities of a fish. For example, swift-moving predators often have a lunate, or moon-shaped tail that enables it to swim at a greater speed. In these species, the shape of the tail acts to divert turbulence to the tips so that the tail experiences less drag. This also applies to forked tails. Species with truncate tails can be strong swimmers, but cannot move at the speeds exhibited by those with lunate tails. And fishes with rounded or paddlelike caudal fins are capable of short bursts of speed, but are not able to maintain a fast pace. Species that have caudal fins contiguous with the dorsal and anal fins are poor swimmers, and most spend their time crawling over the substrate.

In those fishes that do not use the caudal fin as the primary means of propulsion, there are often fewer caudal rays, and the tail is not as well developed. The caudal fin can also have long filaments (often called streamers) that act to reduce drag on the fin. For example, large Orangespine Unicornfish (*Naso lituratus*) have long trailing filaments on the edge of the upper and lower caudal lobes.

Swim Bladder

Many teleost fishes have an air-filled bladder in the body cavity referred to as a swim, or air, bladder. The main function of this organ is as a buoyancy-compensation device to enable the fish to achieve neutral buoyancy. By being weightless, the fish expends less energy when moving or maintaining its position in the water column. The swim bladder, which occupies about 7% of a "typical" marine fish's body volume, allows precise adjustments in buoyancy and is an important factor contributing to the success of these more "advanced" fish groups. If a fish did not have a swim bladder (or was not weightless), it would not be able to make abrupt changes in direction. For this reason, sharks, which lack swim bladders, require relatively large spaces in which to swim and maneuver, whereas most bony fishes can live in much smaller areas.

There are two types of swim bladders, physostomous and physoclistous. The physostomous (or "open") swim bladder has a connection between the bladder and the gut that allows gas to enter or exit. Fishes with physostomous swim bladders gulp air at the water's surface in order to inflate it; they usually occupy shallow-water habitats. The only reef-associated fishes with this type of swim bladder are the moray, snake eel, conger eel, and eel catfish families. The most prevalent type of swim bladder among coral reef fishes is the physoclistous (or "closed") swim bladder. In these species, the organ has no connection with the gut, and the fishes rely on diffusion for the bladder's deflation and inflation. When the swim bladder is deflated, excess gas moves from the bladder into the bloodstream and then diffuses out of the body through the gills.

Some fishes have "lost" the swim bladder as a result of their benthic lifestyles. For example, the hawkfishes have no need for a swim bladder because they spend their time sitting on the seafloor. When these fishes hang in the water column, they have to beat furiously with their pectoral and caudal fins in order to maintain their position. Some species that lack swim bladders are unable to "hover" in the water column because of their heavy body armament. The scorpionfishes, for example, which have a large, heavy cranium with profuse spination, rarely enter the water column, except possibly when they swim from one position to another.

In a few reef fishes, the swim bladder not only serves to achieve weightlessness, it is also used in sound production, acting as a resonation device to amplify the sounds produced by other organs or making the sound itself. For example, grunts have denticles (modified toothlike scales) in their phar-

> *"If a fish did not have a swim bladder (or was not weightless), it would not be able to make abrupt changes in direction. For this reason, sharks, which lack swim bladders, require relatively large spaces in which to swim and maneuver, whereas most bony fishes can live in much smaller areas."*

ynx that they rub together when alarmed or defending a territory (this type of sound production is known as stridulation). The swim bladder acts as a resonator—the character of the sound varies depending upon whether it is deflated or inflated. The triggerfishes also use the swim bladder as a resonator, rubbing or beating the pectoral fins against the thin skin adjacent to the bladder. In squirrelfishes and bigeyes, two muscles that extend from the skull are attached to the swim bladder. These muscles—often referred to as sonic muscles—contract rapidly to manipulate the swim bladder, creating audible noises. Toadfishes, well known for their ability to produce a wide range of sounds, have two broad muscles along the lateral surface of the swim bladder that are responsible for sound production. In sea robins, the sound-producing mechanism is similar to that of the toadfishes.

The swim bladder not only provides buoyancy control and serves to produce sound, it may also facilitate hearing by acting as a transducer, reflecting sonic energy to the ear bones. If this is true, fishes with swim bladders should hear better than those without this organ. Studies to prove or disprove this hypothesis have been inconclusive.

During collection, the swim bladder can be damaged. A physics principle called Boyle's Law says that as pressure decreases, volume increases. If a fish ascends too quickly (moving into water of decreased pressure), the gas in its air bladder will expand, damaging it and the surrounding organs. A fish brought to the surface too fast may have its stomach protruding from its mouth. This is caused by the air bladder overfilling the abdomen, forcing the stomach out of the mouth. To avoid this problem, most fishes have to be brought to the surface slowly so that some of the gas can be liberated through the bloodstream, or the swim bladder must be vented as the fish is lifted to the surface in stages. The latter is done by sticking a hypodermic needle through the fish's side into the swim

Paracirrhites forsteri, Freckled Hawkfish, "Typee" form: a diurnal predator without a swim bladder that must hunt by darting from a perching position (Maldives).

bladder. Although this technique could result in irreparable damage to a fish if done incorrectly, experienced fish collectors rarely cause serious injuries when "needling" a fish. Fishes that have been improperly decompressed are usually easy to recognize. They will have a difficult time maintaining a stationary position in the water column, will often wedge themselves among rockwork to keep from floating to the surface, and when they swim, the tail will rise higher than the level of the head.

Lateral Line Organ

The lateral line is made up of sense organs located on the head (head-canal system) and along the trunk (trunk-canal system). Some fishes (like gobies) lack lateral line organs, but most are well equipped with sensory pores and papillae on their heads. The lateral line organ consists of neuromasts located on the body surface (free neuromasts) or in shallow pits, grooves, or canals (most reef bony fishes have the latter arrangement). The neuromast is made up of a cupula, a long, jelly-filled projection that ensheathes sensory hairs. These hairs are embedded in a sensory cell under the epidermis and are stimulated when the cupula is bent. Although the neuromasts continuously send nerve impulses to the brain, the frequency of impulses increases when the cupula is flexed in one direction and decreases when it is bent the opposite way.

This organ provides a sense of "distant touch." Because water is a noncompressible medium, molecules move when it is displaced or disturbed. The lateral line organ detects these movements, allowing a fish to gauge approximately how fast an object is approaching and how far away it is.

This system explains why it is difficult or impossible to sneak up on a fish. When you move a net toward a fish, the net displaces water molecules and the fish can "feel" the movement with its lateral line organ. The lateral line not only aids a fish in avoiding nets, it also facilitates navigation, orienting to the current, and the detection of a predator or a prey item. When a fish swims in the dark or in turbid water, the lateral line can detect the presence of an object to help avoid collision. One interesting adaptation many fishes have is the configuration of the lateral line in relation to the pectoral fin. As a fish swims, the beating of the pectoral fin can push water over the lateral line canal, creating "noise." To avoid this, the lateral line of many fishes is deflected upward, well above the beating pectoral fins. The next time you are at the aquarium store or in front of your own tank, examine the lateral lines of several fishes for examples of this adaptation.

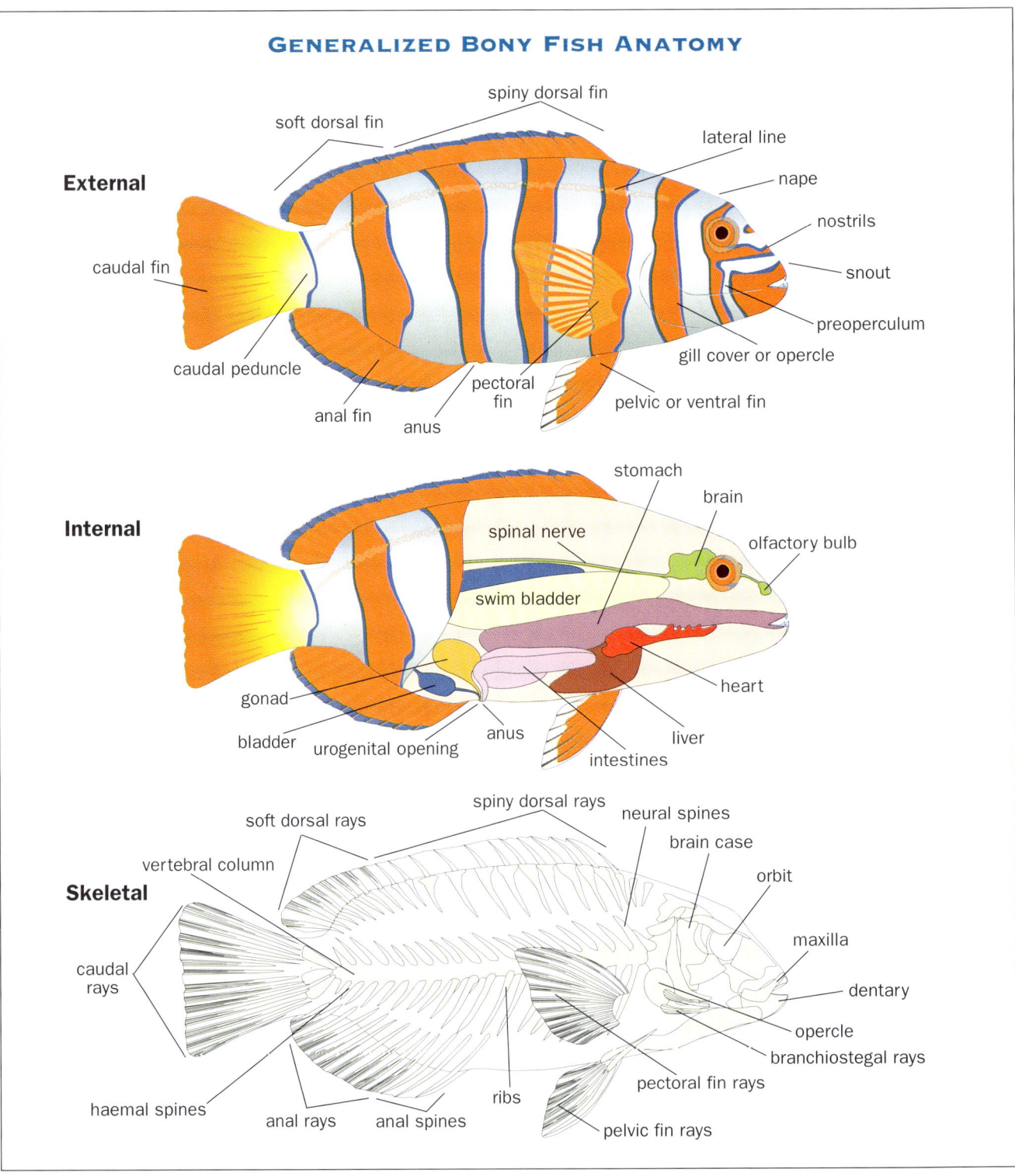

Gills

Even in highly oxygenated water, the concentration of oxygen available to an organism is only 1/30 of that found in air. Therefore, fishes must have a well-developed set of gills, with a large surface area. Most reef fishes also have an efficient pumping system to push oxygenated water over these organs.

A bony plate known as the opercle bone, or operculum, protects the gills of most bony fishes. The operculum sports spiny ornamentation in some groups. For example, scorpionfishes often have numerous small spines on the gill cover and head, while angelfishes have a single large spine on the operculum. In some angelfishes (like the *Centropyge* spp.), there is a ridge on the gill cover with a serrated edge. The Spinecheek Anemonefish (*Premnas biaculeatus*) has two spines on the operculum. These species must be handled with care as their spines can easily pierce the skin of an aquarist or get caught in mesh netting. In fact, fishes with head or operculum spines should always be captured with a specimen container, not a net.

In some species, there is a relatively small aperture through which the water that passes over the gills is expelled. This is the case for the moray, snake, conger, and garden eels, as well as the frogfishes. Triggerfishes also lack the bony operculum; instead, they simply have a short gill slit.

The gill itself consists of a gill arch—which supports gill filaments on the dorsal surface—and, at least in some species, gill rakers on the opposing side. Oxygen is extracted from the water as it flows past the gill filaments, while the gill rakers prevent food from passing out of the gill opening. In some species, the gill rakers are long, fine, and closely spaced to enable the fish to strain plankton from the water as it passes over the gill arch.

Gill morphology differs depending on a fish's lifestyle. In active, fast-swimming species like the Yellowtail Jack (*Seriola quinqueradiata*), the

Pomacanthus semicirculatus, Koran Angelfish: vital oxygenating organs are well-armored by the opercle covering the gills. Note the stout opercular spine, in this case blue, typical of many angelfishes.

water comes in closer contact with the blood than it does in a sluggish group like frogfishes. In addition, the epithelium of the Yellowtail's gill filaments is convoluted, increasing the surface area and the ability of the filaments to extract oxygen from the water that flows past. These differences make the Yellowtail's gills about 2.5 times more efficient at extracting oxygen than those of a frogfish.

Aquarium fishes are sometimes subjected to high levels of toxins (like ammonia) when they are shipped. This can affect the structure of the gill filaments and cause subsequent respiration problems. For this reason, it is a good idea to watch a fish's breathing rate before you purchase it. If breathing is labored, it is possible that the gills have been damaged or are infected by parasites. These specimens should be avoided. But remember that not all fishes breathe at the same rate. A hyperactive fish like a wrasse will breathe much more heavily than a less active scorpionfish. In addition, fish may breathe faster and harder if food is present, if they have been newly introduced to the aquarium, or if they are being harried by their tankmates.

Enchelycore pardalis, Dragon Morays: razor-sharp and needlelike teeth allow efficient catching, holding, and swallowing of fishes that are its primary prey.

Mouth and Dentition

Reef fishes display considerable diversity of mouth size and tooth morphology. These characteristics can provide valuable information about the food habits of a species. For example, many piscivores have large, upturned mouths with small, sharp teeth lining the edge of the jaw, as well as the roof of the mouth. Some species have protruding jaws with comblike teeth for scraping polyps from stony coral calyxes. And in other reef fishes, the jaw or snout is elongate, allowing them to consume prey items that are not available to their short-snouted relatives.

Teeth can be classified as incisiform, villiform, molariform, spatulate, canine, or conical. They can be tiny and almost nonfunctional—as in

some zooplankton feeders—or they can be large and essential in prey capture and handling, as in the Ornate Butterflyfish (*Chaetodon ornatissimus*). In some species, like parrotfishes and puffers, the teeth are fused and form a beaklike structure that is effective at scraping algae and/or encrusting invertebrates off the substrate.

The teeth-bearing bones of the teleost fishes include the premaxilla, vomer, maxilla, palatine, parasphenoid, and pterygoid in the upper jaw and the dentary, glossohyal (tongue), and basibranchial in the lower jaw. Not all reef fishes have teeth on all of these bones, and many also have teeth on the bones of the pharynx. These pharyngeal teeth can be conical, pebblelike, or platelike and can occur on either the ventral or dorsal bones, or on both. The form of

Scorpaena plumieri, Spotted Scorpionfish: a huge mouth allows this sedentary predator to take very large prey items when they happen to stray into its target zone.

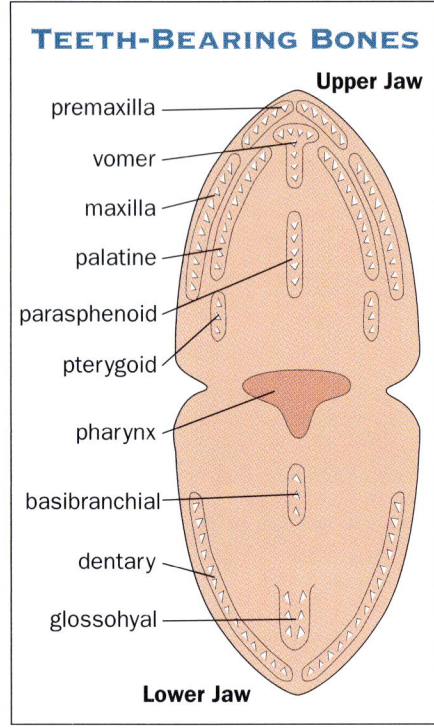

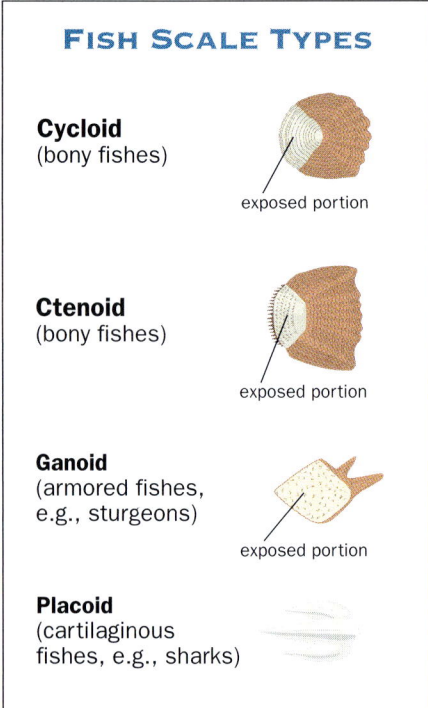

these teeth may change as a fish grows and its diet changes. In many fishes, the pharyngeal teeth are used to grind up hard-shelled prey items. At least one group (the parrotfishes), has a "pharyngeal mill" that it uses to pulverize calcareous substrate in order to exploit boring algae as a food source.

Barbels

Several reef fish families have sensory barbels on the chin. These structures have taste receptors that enable the fish to locate concealed prey. One family with well-developed barbels is the goatfishes. These fishes use their barbels to dig in the sand, probe reef crevices, and flip over small pieces of coral debris when hunting. Certain gobies also have barbels, as do the eel catfishes, some cusk eels, and armorheads. In these species, the barbels also have a sensory function.

Scales and Skin

Most reef fishes have scales. These thin bony plates act as both armor to protect the fishes from predators and parasites and as a barrier to prevent freshwater from being lost to the surrounding seawater. The two most common scale types in bony fishes are cycloid and ctenoid—both are lightweight and do not encumber active movement. Cycloid scales are typically round and thin and are found on cusk eels, some scorpionfishes, soapfishes, some dottybacks, longfins, hawkfishes, some cardinalfishes, jacks, some drums, certain sweepers, wrasses, jawfishes, some gobies, dartfishes, barracudas, rabbitfishes, and puffers.

The majority of reef fishes have ctenoid scales, which are similar to cycloid scales except that they have toothlike projections (ctenii) on the posterior edge. Some reef fishes, such as the Clearfin Lionfish (*Pterois radiata*), Deep-water Lionfish (*Pterois mombasae*), sand tilefishes, certain flatfishes, and batfishes, have both cycloid and ctenoid scales. The Moorish Idol (*Zanclus cornutus*) has slightly modified ctenoid scales, with ctenii that are recurved and stick straight up. These give the skin a rough, sandpaperlike texture.

A handful of reef fishes have dermal spinules, which are modified scales with elongate spines. The frogfishes, for example, have numerous spinules on the head, body, and fins. In most frogfishes, there are two spines that vary in length and extend from a common base. In the genus *Echinophryne* (the prickly frogfishes), the spinules are so long that they give the fish a furry appearance. Puffers of the Subfamily Tetraodontinae also have smaller spinules on the head and body, while the porcupinefishes have elongate spines that

Left: *Pseudupeneus maculatus*, Spotted Goatfish: large barbels are both sensory organs and tools for digging in the substrate to find buried targets. Right: *Cirrhilabrus solorensis*, Redheaded Fairy Wrasse: scales in marine fishes go far beyond ornamentation, offering protection from predators, parasites, and the loss of freshwater from body tissues into the surrounding saltwater.

are actually modified scales. In some species, the spines are permanently erect. In others, they can be laid flat against the body until the fish inflates its abdomen. The triggerfishes have tubercles over most of the body, and many also have enlarged spines (with points that curve toward the fish's tail) on the posterior part of the body and on the caudal peduncle. These spines may serve to inhibit piscivores from ingesting them and are effective offensive weapons when tail-beating intruders or rivals.

Some fishes, like the moray, snake, and conger eels, are scaleless, as are most toadfishes, the eel catfishes, some adult cornetfishes, certain scorpionfishes (stingfishes [*Choridactylus* spp.], devilfishes [*Inimicus* spp.], stonefishes [*Synanceia* spp.]), some stargazers, blennies, certain gobies, clingfishes, and dragonets. Certain fishkeepers have advised that treating "scaleless" fishes with copper-based medications should be avoided. Although there is some truth to this suggestion, I don't believe that all scaleless fishes are harmed by typical treatment levels of copper. Many of these fishes are also reported to be sensitive to other medications, like organophosphates.

Other species, although they may appear scaleless, have small, deeply embedded scales. These include the cusk eels, waspfishes, and jawfishes.

Some fishes have bony plates rather than small, lightweight scales. In general, they are not rapid swimmers and rely on this bony "exoskeleton" to provide protection from predators. Some reef fishes that fall into this group include the pincapple fishes, sea moths, seahorses, pipefishes, shrimpfishes, and boxfishes. Pineapple fishes, for example, have platelike scales that are equipped with a large spine directed toward the tail, while the shrimpfishes are encased in thin, transparent bony plates. Seahorses and pipefishes have bony

Pteroidichthys amboinensis, Ambon Scorpionfish: numerous dermal appendages represent an extreme in skin modification, with a profusion of flaps that mimic lush filimental algae growth (North Sulawesi).

rings that encircle the body and tail.

Most fishes produce significant amounts of mucus, or slime, secreted by unicellular mucus glands in the epidermis. This coating protects the body from parasites, makes the fish more difficult for a piscivore to grasp, and helps prevent chloride from migrating into the body. Some fishes, such as the Yellowmouth Moray (*Gymnothorax nudivomer*), soapfishes, Green Mandarinfish (*Synchiropus splendidus*), Shadow Goby (*Yongeichthys nebulosus*), moses soles (*Pardachirus* spp.), and boxfishes, produce toxic body slime to deter potential predators. Soapfishes and boxfishes can cause problems in the closed-system aquarium because the toxins in the body slime can be released in the tank (especially when these fishes are stressed) and kill the fish's tankmates. The parrotfishes, as well as certain wrasses, produce a mucus envelope when they sleep that may serve to make them less conspicuous to nocturnal predators like moray eels. Fish mucus may also function to bind certain irritants, such as heavy metal salts, which are then sloughed off with the slime. When you add copper to a tank, it causes the fish to produce excessive amounts of slime. The slime, possibly containing the parasites, is then sloughed off. Some scorpionfishes shed their outer cuticle (a skin by-product) on occasion to rid their bodies of fouling organisms like algae and sessile invertebrates.

Some fishes are slimier than others. Many of the scaleless fishes, like eels and dragonets, produce copious amounts of slime to compensate for not having scales. Some scaleless forms also have thicker skin: the epidermis of most morays is four to six times as thick as that of many scaled fish species. They also have a very thick dermis (the layer of cells below the epidermis) made up of compact collagen fibers. The thicker skin of these eels is an adaptation to their benthic, crevice-dwelling lifestyles, protecting them from coral cuts and other abrasions that can be inflicted by the substrate.

A number of bottom-dwelling reef fishes have dermal appendages, or skin flaps, on the body. This ornamentation helps to break up the outline of the fish so that it blends in better with its natural surroundings. The presence or development of dermal appendages can vary within a species and is usually a function of the environment in which the individual is found. For example, Striated Frogfish (*Antennarius striatus*) that live in macroalgae or filamentous algal beds usually develop long filaments on the skin to enhance their camouflage. There are also species of toadfishes and scorpionfishes that possess skin flaps. A few species that spend more of their time in the water column are covered with dermal appendages: the Tasseled Filefish (*Chaetoderma penicilligera*) sports branching, fleshy filaments on the head and body. This species lives in seagrasses and macroalgae beds and is camouflaged by its skin ornamentation. Some ghost pipefishes, which live near the substrate, have a hairy appearance caused by long filaments on the head, body, and fins.

Coloration

Reef fishes are celebrated for their diverse coloration. Although not all are brilliantly colored, many do sport striking hues that have delighted and fascinated humans for centuries.

In a fish-eat-fish world, bright pigments would seem to be an open invitation to predators, and outside reef areas other fishes and many animals do tend to blend into their surroundings. A typical color scheme for open-water marine fishes, for example, is darker on the dorsal or back surface and lighter on the ventral or belly area. Thus a predator approaching from above might miss the fish as it blends with deep water or the bottom far below, while a hunter coming up from beneath would be less likely to spot the white belly against a bright sky above.

Several theories have emerged over the years to explain why many reef fishes exhibit chromatic attire so far outside of this logical defensive-

Cirrhilabrus scottorum, Scott's Fairy Wrasse: elegant and complex, the color schemes of this and other reef fishes are far from fully understood.

Sphaeramia nematoptera, Pajama Cardinalfish: a popular aquarium species displays a comically unusual color pattern that defies simple biological explanation (North Sulawesi).

color scheme. Some have proposed that the bright colors are in place to remind predators of toxins or other distasteful or lethal defenses—a mechanism used by certain insects (butterflies, for example), snakes and spiders. This idea may have some merit, as many reef fishes have sharp spines and barbs and some may have chemical defenses that make them distasteful. This explanation comes up short, however, when we consider that many colorful reef fishes are readily eaten in large numbers by their predators.

Nobel Prize-winning ethologist Konrad Lorenz proposed what seemed to many a sensible answer—that the "poster" colors are there to signal possession of a patch of reef territory. His theory at first attracted great interest, but critics soon pointed out that many species with vivid, contrasting color patterns are not the least bit territorial. On the other hand, certain rather drab reef fishes are exceptionally aggressive in defending their territories. There seems to be no obvious correlation between color pattern and territoriality in many species.

Another school of thought suggests that many reef fishes do not require defensive coloration or camouflage. For diurnal or daytime feeders, the hours of bright sunlight when they are out and foraging on the reef is a time when many of the bigger fish-eating predators like jacks, barracudas, and certain groupers are relatively inactive. In addition, a great many reef fishes are extremely quick and agile, well able to duck into the protection of corals, rocks or rubble to evade large pursuers.

The hours of vulnerability come at dawn and dusk, when many fish-eating predators are most active. While these hunters have extremely good eyesight for twilight conditions, they have poor color vision and are believed to hunt by perceiving shapes and movement rather than detailed color patterns. The electrifying colors of many reef fishes would not make them obvious targets in these circumstances of heightened predation.

One theory about reef fish coloration that is difficult to refute is its importance during reproduction. In the dense populations of the reef, distinctive color patterns may very well assist males and females of the same species in finding each other at the appropriate times. Fishes that attempt to mate with members of the wrong species are wasting their gametes and reproductive energies. Clearly, there is a strong survival advantage to species that spawn consistently and efficiently.

While many questions remain about the development of distinctive, electrifying, and sometimes bizarre colors, more is known about the actual anatomy of these hues. Pigments present in chromatophores—irregularly shaped cells in both the dermis and epidermis—are responsible for most of these colors. Three classes of chromatophores include pigments for various colors: melanophores for shades of brown or black; xanthophores for shades of yellow; erythrophores for shades of red. In addition, iridophores contain

Colorful Confusions

We often use color when describing or identifying a fish species. It is not hard to see why. A fish's color is a conspicuous external feature—especially in many reef fishes. Not only do humans use color to tell one fish species from another, some fish rely on chromatic characteristics to recognize potential mates, competitors, or possible aggressors. While a fish's chromatic attire is often useful in distinguishing it from its close relatives, it is not always a salient characteristic when it comes to distinguishing one species from another.

There are a number of reef fishes whose coloration can be quite variable within the same species. Some of these fishes change their color to better match the substrate they are living on, while in other species, the function of chromatic plasticity is not known.

For example, the color of the Bloody Frogfish (*Antennarius sanguineus*) can vary greatly and is somewhat dependent on the color of its sponge or rock ambush site (as seen in the photographs below).

In contrast, the Redheaded Fairy Wrasse (*Cirrhilabrus solorensis*) exhibits a variety of color forms, within and between populations, which apparently serve no obvious function. This chromatic infidelity among members of the same species has led to great consternation in both the ichthyological and aquarist communities.

It should be kept in mind that although the coloration of some fishes can give important clues to their identity, in other species the appearance of another color form—even one that seems dramatically different—may prove useless for precise species identification.

Antennarius sanguineus: white coloration.

Antennarius sanguineus: orange coloration.

Antennarius sanguineus: red-pink coloration.

mirrorlike guanine crystals, which can produce white and sparkling silver, as well as modifying the appearance of other colors. Areas of blue are created by layering iridophores over darker melanin; the melanin absorbs the longer wavelengths of light passing through the iridophores while the shorter blue wavelengths are reflected.

Most chromatophores consist of a central body with branchlike extensions. When a fish undergoes rapid color change, the color pigments may migrate from the core out into the branches (making the color darker), or from the irregular cell extensions back into the main cell body (making the color lighter or paler). Hues or shades are altered when one chromatophore is covered by, or combined with, another of a different color. They are also altered by changes that occur within cells that have more than one type of pigment granule. These changes are under both nervous and hormonal control and, in part, are catalyzed by visual stimuli. Therefore, when a Tasseled Scorpionfish (*Scorpaenopsis oxycephala*) moves from a pink sponge to a variegated, hard reef substrate, it will change hues to more closely resemble the substrate on which it rests. In some cases, more dramatic color changes take days or weeks. For example, frogfishes can change from black to orange over the course of several weeks. The pigments found in reef fishes include carotenoids (yellow, orange, bright red, and green—created when yellow overlies a blue structure) and melanins (dark red, brown, and black). Purines are crystalline, reflective substances responsible for the iridescent colors of many reef fishes, as well as the silvery sheen of pelagic fishes like jacks.

A fish species may display a number of different color forms and color phases. A color form, or color morph, refers to the permanent chromatic characteristics of an individual, while a color phase is used to refer to a color pattern that can, and often does, change. Many wrasses, for example, show different color phases based on the age and gender of the fish. The color phase can change as the fish grows and may be altered when an individual changes sex. Color forms (morphs) are more permanent differences that are often seen between, rather than within, populations. Around the Fijian and Tongan Islands, for example, Herald's Angelfish (*Centropyge heraldi*) has a black saddle on the soft portion of the dorsal fin. In other geographic areas where this angelfish occurs, the black saddle is lacking. The Lyretail Anthias (*Pseudanthias squamipinnis*) displays a number of different color forms over its wide geographical range. Often, these differences in color between populations are the result of genetics. Some ichthyologists (those referred to as "splitters") refer to these isolated populations as different species or subspecies.

> *"One theory about reef fish coloration that is difficult to refute is its importance during reproduction. In the dense populations of the reef, distinctive color patterns may very well assist males and females of the same species in finding each other at the appropriate times."*

Left: *Arothron meleagris*, Guinea Fowl Puffer: showing the xanthic or yellow color form. Right: *Amphiprion clarkii*, Clark's Anemonefish: like a number of reef fishes, the color of this species is somewhat variable. The black color form from the Maldives is shown here.

Other ichthyologists ("lumpers") suggest that more than a disparity in coloration is necessary to classify members of two different populations as distinct species.

Two color phases observed in a relatively small number of reef fishes are xanthism and melanism. Xanthism describes the exhibition of yellow or gold. An occasional Blackspotted Puffer (*Arothron nigropunctatus*) or Guinea Fowl Puffer (*Arothron meleagris*) will turn yellow or yellowish orange. Xanthism is also observed in trumpetfishes, groupers, and possibly in assessors, butterflyfishes, and morays. There may be advantages to those individuals that have been recipients of the "Midas touch." In one study of a freshwater cichlid, xanthic males enjoyed greater mating success. For some reason, females often selected xanthic individuals over those with a more "normal" color pattern.

Melanistic fishes are not as spectacular as their xanthic counterparts. A melanistic individual has an abundance of melanin that results in it being black over much, or all, of its body. A melanistic form of the Blackspotted Puffer has been showing up in the aquarium trade from the Solomon Islands—it is completely black.

Explanations for the color patterns of reef fishes are far from complete, with much research to be done on the role of coloration in survival and reproductive strategies. There is not likely ever to be a simple, general answer as to why reef fishes are so colorful, but the success of the designs can be found in the millions of years these species have survived and thrived in the competitive, complex world of the reef.

CHAPTER

2

Taxonomy

CLASSIFYING THE FISHES
AND A SURVEY OF CORAL REEF FAMILIES

"Systematics is mostly science but also a bit of art."
—EDWARD O. WILSON, *The Diversity of Life*, 1992

IMAGINE BEING CONFRONTED WITH A LIVING DISPLAY OF EVERY species of fish found on Earth. Imagine that your sample for each species includes males, females, juveniles, and all possible variants—supermales, color morphs, and all other known forms. Imagine also that you have before you fossil specimens for every species of fish or fishlike animal ever found. As mind-boggling as this seems, there is one way to deal with the overwhelming chaos: start sorting.

Such is the challenge—and the response—for taxonomists who deal with some 24,600 valid species of living fishes and thousands of extinct species known only from their fossil records. Making sense of the phenomenal diversity of living and fossil fishes is no easy matter. Even trying to define the term "fish" can trigger debate among some scientists. Some taxonomists prefer to separate out the jawless groups (such as the lampreys) and even the elasmobranchs (sharks, rays, and chimeras), leaving only the bony fishes with jaws as legitimate "true" fishes.

Joseph S. Nelson, a preeminent fish taxonomist, acknowledges that "fish"

Epinephelus striatus, Nassau Grouper:
clearly a magnificent fish, but the very term "fish" is debated by taxonomists.

is an artificial label with no clear taxonomic rank. In his classic reference work, *Fishes of the World*, he wryly resorts to this as one possible definition: "... fish are those vertebrates studied by ichthyologists and covered in ichthyological courses." This is the equivalent of saying that a group of animals must be described by the people who study it, rather than by the characteristics of the group itself.

While academic controversies rage about how to classify the living fishes and their prehistoric ancestors, taxonomy is still the tool that brings us a sense of order out of the awesome profusion of fishes in the world's waters.

Grouping fishes by their anatomies and genetic connections allows us to see them within the grander scheme of genera and families, rather than treating each and every species as an isolated case. The practical returns for the amateur fish observer or aquarium keeper are considerable—once you are acquainted with a member of the genus *Zebrasoma*, perhaps from firsthand experience with the common Yellow Tang (*Zebrasoma flavescens*), you have many clues about how its related species may behave, feed, and adapt to captivity. When, and if, a much rarer Gem Tang (*Zebrasoma gemmatum*) ever crosses your path, you will quickly have a frame of reference for its possible behavior and its requirements in captivity.

Centropyge flavissima x *C. vroliki*, Lemonpeel x Halfblack Angelfish hybrid: taxonomy and scientific names bring order to biological chaos, erase language barriers, and allow us to communicate accurately with others.

Taxonomy also gives us the ability to communicate accurately with others. Common names for fishes vary wildly from language to language, country to country, region to region—even from one aquarium shop to the next. A scientific name, however, applies to only one species and is good throughout the world. The naming convention we all use is called the Linnean or binomial system of nomenclature, introduced by the Swedish naturalist Carolus Linnaeus in the 1750s.

Although using Latin, Greek or fabricated words, the essentials of scientific names are simple: both genus and species are printed in italic type; the genus comes first and is always

TABLE 1
Classification of the Yellow Tang

Kingdom: Animalia
Phylum: Vertebrata
Superclass: Gnathostomata
Class: Actinopterygii
Order: Perciformes
Suborder: Acanthuroidei
Family: Acanthuridae
Subfamily: Acanthurinae
Tribe: Zebrasomini
Genus: *Zebrasoma*
Species: *flavescens*

capitalized when written—as in *Zebrasoma*; the species name comes next, and is never capitalized—as in *flavescens* for the Yellow Tang. A complete classification of this fish is shown in the above table. The value of a unique scientific name for each species becomes apparent even for this ubiquitous aquarium fish; there are several other species sold under the common name of "yellow tang," including the juvenile form of the Atlantic Blue Tang, *Acanthurus coeruleus*.

In older reference works, you may find a third name, also lowercase, that designates a subspecies (as in *Scorpaenodes guamensis scabra*) but the use of formal subspecies names has largely been abandoned. Hybrids are designated in this manner: *Centropyge flavissima* x *C. vroliki*, indicating a cross between *Centropyge flavissima* and *Centropyge vroliki*.

The "author" (the person or persons who first described and named the species) is sometimes included with a full reference to the name. For example the Tinsnip Moray is properly known as *Gymnothorax breedeni* McCosker & Randall, 1977, having been described by well-known ichthyologists John E. McCosker and John E. Randall in 1977. When a species has subsequently been placed in a genus other than that used by the original author, the author's name is indicated in parentheses. For example, the Latticetail Moray is known to science as *Gymnothorax buroensis* (Bleeker, 1857). It was first described by Bleeker in 1857, although not under the currently accepted genus name.

Among those who take these things seriously, there is also a subtle but important distinction between the terms "fishes" and "fish." "Fishes" is a plural noun, used when two or more species are being discussed. "Fish" can be either singular or plural, but is only used to describe one specimen or a group of specimens of the same species. Thus, a shoal of Blue Green Chromis (*Chromis viridis*), for example, is a group of *fish*, while the community of species in which they live is a group of *fishes*.

Classification Basics

Although taxonomists still wrangle over what the word "fish" really means, for most, Nelson's own working definition makes good sense: "aquatic vertebrates that have gills throughout life and limbs, if any, in the shape of fins."

For our purposes, we will view the fishes as falling into four distinct classes:
Myxini (hagfishes)
Cephalaspidomorphi (lampreys)
Chondrichthyes (sharks, rays, and others)
Actinopterygii (bony fishes)

Coral reef fishes are made up of the latter two groups, with the bony fishes constituting the overwhelming majority of species and individuals in shallow-water tropical environments.

A **species** is a natural population of organisms that can interbreed and produce viable offspring and that are reproductively isolated from other populations of organisms. The count of valid, living species of fishes grows each year, with most observers expecting thousands more to be found and identified. (This is actually the definition for a "biological species." Evolutionary biologists have a more complex definition, in which a species is identified by its ancestors, genetic lineage, and evolutionary history.) According to Nelson (1994), there are more than 24,600 recognized species of fishes, with the number expected to grow annually for years to come.

A **genus** (plural **genera**) is a grouping of species with similar characteristics. There are 4,258 recognized genera of extant fishes, both freshwater and marine.

A **family** is a grouping of related genera with common characteristics. There are 482 recognized families of living fishes. The average number of species per family is 51, with the median being just 10.9 species per family.

An **order** is a grouping of related families with common characteristics. There are 57 orders of living fishes.

A **class** is a major division of a phylum, including one or more orders. The fishes, if viewed as a group, can be divided into two superclasses:

> *"The count of valid, living species of fishes grows each year, with most observers expecting thousands more to be found and identified."*

Superclass Agnatha: (jawless fishes: hagfishes and lampreys)

Superclass Gnathostomata: (jawed fishes: sharks, rays, and bony fishes)

The jawed fishes can then be split into two major groups of interest to observers of reef fishes:

Class Chondrichthyes: (cartilaginous fishes: sharks, rays, skates, chimaeras)

Class Actinopterygii (formerly Osteichthyes): (spiny-rayed or bony fishes)

Among the fishes associated with coral reefs and adjacent habitats, there are 15 orders, over 90 families, and approximately 7,000 species at this writing. Many of these are available to marine fish hobbyists, and it is this incredible access to biological diversity that attracts many people to the keeping of saltwater aquariums.

What follows is an overview of the fish families that typically occur on and around coral reefs. (Rocky shallow-water areas are also popularly called reefs, but are not of biological origin and not included here.) Members of some of the following groups of fishes are never or only rarely collected for the ornamental marine fish trade or are inappropriate for home aquariums. These are described briefly in this chapter, while those families of special interest to aquarists are covered in greater detail in the family, genus, and species accounts that begin on page 245.

This survey follows classical taxonomic organization, beginning with the most "primitive" groups and working its way up to the most "advanced" families. The term "advanced" is applied to those fishes whose morphology and anatomy are the most highly modified, or "derived." (It has nothing to do with them being better adapted or more successful.) For example, the Anguilliformes (eels) are found near the beginning of the list because of their simple anatomical plan, while the Tetraodontiformes (including the triggerfishes, filefishes, and puffers) are considered to be one of the most advanced groups because of their sophisticated anatomical structures that display a reduction of skeletal elements.

Dr. John E. Randall, the preeminent reef fish authority, examines *Pseudanthias* specimens in a makeshift laboratory aboard a dive vessel off the coast of NW Australia in 1987. (Subsequently he and Dr. Gerald R. Allen described it as *Pseudanthias sheni*, Shen's Anthias.)

TABLE 2
Classification of Bony Fishes (Class Actinopterygii) Associated with Coral Reefs

Order Elopiformes
    Family Megalopidae (tarpons)
Order Albuliformes
    Family Albulidae (bonefishes)
Order Anguilliformes
    Suborder Muraenoidei
        Family Muraenidae (moray eels)
    Suborder Congroidei
        Family Heterocongridae (conger eels and garden eels)
        Family Ophichthidae (snake eels and worm eels)
Order Siluriformes
    Family Plotosidae (eel catfishes)
Order Aulopiformes
    Suborder Alepisauroidei
        Family Synodontidae (lizardfishes)
Order Ophidiiformes
    Suborder Bythitoidei
        Family Bythitidae (livebearing brotulas)
    Suborder Ophidioidei
        Family Carapidae (pearlfishes)
        Family Ophidiidae (cusk eels)
Order Batrachoidiformes
    Family Batrachoididae (toadfishes)
Order Lophiiformes
    Suborder Antennarioidei
        Family Antennariidae (frogfishes)
    Suborder Ogcocephalioidei
        Family Ogcocephalidae (walking batfishes)
Order Beloniformes
    Suborder Belonoidei
        Family Belonidae (needlefishes)
        Family Hemiramphidae (halfbeaks)

Order Beryciformes
    Suborder Trachichthyoidei
        Family Anomalopidae (flashlight fishes)
        Family Monocentridae (pineapple or pinecone fishes)
    Suborder Holocentroldei
        Family Holocentridae (squirrelfishes and soldierfishes)
Order Gasterosteiformes
    Suborder Syngnathoidei
        Family Aulostomidae (trumpetfishes)
        Family Fistulariidae (cornetfishes)
        Family Pegasidae (sea moths)
        Family Solenostomidae (ghost pipefishes)
        Family Syngnathidae (seahorses and pipefishes)
        Family Centriscidae (shrimpfishes)
Order Scorpaeniformes
    Suborder Scorpaenoidei
        Family Caracanthidae (coral crouchers)
        Family Tetrarogidae (waspfishes)
        Family Scorpaenidae (scorpionfishes)
        Family Aploactinidae (velvetfishes)
        Family Triglidae (sea robins)
    Suborder Platycephaloidei
        Family Platycephalidae (flatheads)
    Suborder Dactylopteroidei
        Family Dactylopteridae (helmut gurnards)
Order Perciformes
    Suborder Percoidei
        Family Serranidae (groupers and anthias)
        Family Pseudochromidae (dottybacks)
        Family Grammatidae (grammas)
        Family Plesiopidae (roundheads or longfins)
        Family Opistognathidae (jawfishes)
        Family Priacanthidae (bigeyes)

TABLE 2 (CONTINUED)

Family Cirrhitidae (hawkfishes)
Family Cheilodactylidae (morwongs)
Family Apogonidae (cardinalfishes)
Family Malacanthidae (tilefishes)
Family Echeneidae (sharksuckers or remoras)
Family Carangidae (jacks)
Family Lutjanidae (snappers)
Family Gerreidae (mojarras)
Family Haemulidae (grunts and sweetlips)
Family Lethrinidae (emperor snappers and large-eye breams)
Family Nemipteridae (spinecheeks)
Family Sciaenidae (drums and croakers)
Family Mugilidae (mullets)
Family Mullidae (goatfishes)
Family Pempheridae (sweepers)
Family Monodactylidae (monos)
Family Chaetodontidae (butterflyfishes)
Family Pomacanthidae (angelfishes)
Family Pentacerotidae (armorheads or boarfishes)
Family Kyphosidae (sea chubs)
Family Teraponidae (grunters and tigerfishes)
Family Kuhliidae (flagtails)
Family Microcanthidae (stripies)
Family Cepolidae (bandfishes)
Suborder Labroidei
    Family Pomacentridae (damselfishes)
    Family Labridae (wrasses)
    Family Scaridae (parrotfishes)
Suborder Trachinoidei
    Family Pholidichthyidae (Convict Blenny)
    Family Trichonotidae (sand divers)
    Family Pinguipedidae (sand perches)
    Family Uranoscopidae (stargazers)
Suborder Blennioidei
    Family Tripterygiidae (triplefins)
    Family Dactyloscopidae (sand stargazers)
    Family Labrisomidae (weed blennies)
    Family Clinidae (clinid blennies)
    Family Chaenopsidae (tube blennies and pike blennies)
    Family Blenniidae (blennies or combtooth blennies)
Suborder Gobiesocoidei
    Family Gobiesocidae (clingfishes)
Suborder Callionymoidei
    Family Callionymidae (dragonets)
Suborder Gobioidei
    Family Gobiidae (gobies)
    Family Microdesmidae (dartfishes and wormfishes)
Suborder Acanthuroidei
    Family Ephippidae (spadefishes and batfishes)
    Family Scatophagidae (scats)
    Family Siganidae (rabbitfishes)
    Family Zanclidae (Moorish Idol)
    Family Acanthuridae (surgeonfishes)
Suborder Scombroidei
    Family Sphyraenidae (barracudas)

Order Pleuronectiformes
Suborder Pleuronectoidei
    Family Bothidae (lefteye flounders)
    Family Samaridae (samarid flounders)
    Family Soleidae (soles)

Order Tetraodontiformes
Suborder Tetraodontoidei
    Family Balistidae (triggerfishes)
    Family Monacanthidae (filefishes)
    Family Ostraciidae (trunkfishes)
    Family Tetraodontidae (puffers and tobies)
    Family Diodontidae (porcupinefishes and burrfishes)

References: Hughes & Umezawa (1983), Myers (1989), Nelson (1994), Randall (1995), Randall (1997).

Survey of Reef Fish Families

Family Megalopidae (tarpons)

Genera: 1

Species: 2

The megalopids belong to the Order Elopiformes. Members of this order are large, herringlike fishes that produce leptocephalus larvae (this trait has linked them to the Orders Albuliformes and Anguilliformes). They possess many "primitive" characteristics, such as cycloid scales, a gular plate, and pectoral fins located low on the body. It is an enigmatic group whose position in the grand scheme of fish systematics is still nebulous. They have elongate, laterally compressed bodies with the following characteristics: a terminal or superior mouth, a swim bladder that lies up against the skull, a single dorsal fin with an elongate ray extending from the posterior margin, pelvic fins positioned well behind the pectoral fins (which are located low on the body), a broad-based anal fin, and lateral line tubes radiating over the surface of the lateral line scales. The largest tarpon reaches a maximum length of 2.4 m (7.8 ft.). Both species inhabit marine ecosystems in tropical and subtropical seas—although one will enter freshwater on occasion. The Eastern Atlantic species is sometimes found refuging on reef faces or fore-reef slopes. Megalopids are active fishes that have been observed attacking smaller schooling fishes at night.

Captive Care: The tarpons are too large and free-ranging to keep in the home aquarium, although they are displayed in public oceanariums.

Family Albulidae (bonefishes)

Subfamilies: 2

Genera: 2

Species: 4

The bonefishes are currently placed in the Order Albuliformes, with a group of deep-water fishes known as the spiny eels (notacanthoids) by most fish experts. However, this small group of fishes is very similar to the Elopiformes and was once included in this order. These fishes have compressed, elongate bodies, with a single, short-based dorsal fin, pelvic fins that are located well behind the pectoral fins (which are positioned low on the body), no teeth on the maxilla, and basihyal and crushing teeth on the parasphenoid. They have leptocephalus larvae. The largest species attains a maximum length of 105

Facing page: Tarpons (*Megalops atlanticus*): a congregation moves through Tarpon Alley (Grand Cayman, British West Indies).

cm (41 in.). These are tropical species, most of which live in marine environments, although they can be found in freshwater as well. Members of the genus *Albula* are often found on sand flats adjacent to coral reefs and are also observed over sandy lagoon bottoms.

Captive Care: The bonefishes get too large for the home aquarium, but are kept in public aquariums.

Family Muraenidae (moray eels)

Subfamilies: 2

Genera: about 15

Species: 200+

The Order Anguilliformes contains most of the marine fishes recognized as eels, including the moray, snake eels, and congers. The morays are characterized by elongate bodies, a lack of scales (if scales are present, they are deeply embedded cycloid scales), no pelvic fins or pelvic girdle, caudal fins that (when present) are confluent with the dorsal and anal fins, swim bladders with a duct, and leptocephalus larvae. Among the Muraenidae or morays, most are marine fishes, although several occur in brackish conditions or will enter freshwater. The largest moray attains a maximum length of 3.9 m (12.7 ft.). Many of these fishes have long, needlelike teeth, while some have round, molariform dentition. The morays have posterior nostrils that are usually located above the eyes. Morays are particularly adept at slipping through tight openings and small holes in the reef, where they refuge and capture prey.

Gymnomuraena zebra, Zebra Moray.

Captive Care: Most of the morays readily acclimate to captivity, although some get too large and aggressive for the average home aquarium. Be sure to know the maximum length attained by any species being considered for purchase, and use care when handling or working in a tank with a species that is a known biter. The morays are renowned for jumping or slithering out of the tank. Be sure that the aquarium is of adequate size and that it is securely covered. Provide suitable hiding places, such as stable rocky caves.

Feeding: Offer a varied diet that includes fresh fish and crustacean meat. Avoid the use of feeder fish, which may cause some species to become more of a threat to fish tankmates. Note that morays may fast when first acquired and are able to go without feeding for weeks at a time without apparent ill effect.

Other Advice: Morays may eat any crustacean or fish tankmate that can be swallowed whole (some will bite chunks from larger prey species). Exercise care in selecting a moray species or placing one in a community aquarium.

Family Heterocongridae (conger eels and garden eels)

Subfamilies: 4
Genera: 42
Species: 110

The conger and garden eels have a complete lateral line, and pectoral fins are usually absent. All of the congrids occur in marine habitats—in tropical and temperate seas—and have leptocephalus larvae. The two subfamilies encountered by aquarists are very different in form and behavior. Members of the Subfamily Heterocongrinae (garden eels) are elongate with narrow bodies, the dorsal and anal fins have rays that are not segmented, the pectoral fins are minute, they have a short mouth with a lower jaw that projects beyond the tip of the snout, and they often live in large colonies. The garden eels dig burrows in the sand (which they rarely leave) and feed on zooplankters that drift past in the current. There are 2 genera and about 25 species in this subfamily. Members of the Subfamily Congrinae (conger eels) have elongate bodies, but are not nearly as slender as the garden eels. They have dorsal and anal rays that are segmented, well-developed pectoral fins, and posterior nostrils located above the middle of the eye. There are about 25 genera in this subfamily. The congers live in rocky or coral crevices and most are nocturnal, foraging for fishes and crustaceans at night.

Captive Care: Conger eels are best observed in an aquarium equipped with a red light to illuminate their nightly feeding activities. Provide a tank with a secure cover and suitable hiding places. Garden eels require a tank that is at least 51 cm (20 in.) in height, with a thick layer of sand (15 to 20 cm [6 to 8 in.] deep) in which to burrow. A gentle current should be directed along the bottom of the aquarium, and other decor should be kept to a minimum.

Feeding: Garden eels require a diet that consists primarily of very small crustaceans, including frozen mysid shrimp and small shavings of table shrimp.
Other Advice: Congers will eat any crustacean or fish tankmate that can be swallowed whole. Garden eels are extremely shy and should be placed in a tank in a low-traffic area or one with a piece of one-way glass covering the front panel.

Family Ophichthidae (snake eels and worm eels)

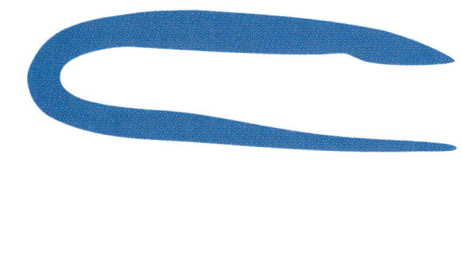

Subfamilies: 2
Genera: 55
Species: 250+

Snake eels (Subfamily Ophichthinae) have elongate bodies, upper lips pierced by the rear nostril, tongues attached to the floor of the lower jaw, and numerous branchiostegal rays that overlap to form a basketlike structure in the bottom of the throat (the jugostegalia). Pectoral fins are either present or absent. The tail can have a fleshy tip, or it can be rigid with a sharp tip, enabling the eel to burrow backward into the sand. The anal and dorsal fins are both absent. Members of this subfamily often have spots and/or stripes. Most snake eels live in saltwater, although some will enter freshwater. They spend much of their time under the sand and feed on crustaceans and fishes. Worm eels (Subfamily Myrophinae) have a flexible tail tip, are uniform in color, and are small and inconspicuous—living in sand and mud bottoms near coral reefs.

Captive Care: Snake eels should be provided with ample swimming room and a thick layer of sand (minimum 10 cm [4 in.]) in which to bury. The aquarium should also be tightly covered to prevent them from jumping out.
Feeding: In captivity, some snake eels may be finicky eaters. Try offering these specimens live shrimp or crabs after the tank lights have been turned off, although some are more likely to accept feeder fish.
Other Advice: Snake eels should not be housed with overly aggressive tankmates or efficient food competitors.

Family Plotosidae (eel catfishes)

Genera: 9
Species: 32

This is the only family in this huge group of fishes—Order Siluriformes—that is represented on coral reefs. Most members of this immense order occur in freshwater in neotropical regions. The plotosids occur in estuarine conditions, although one is found on coral reefs in the Indo-Pacific. These fishes have an eel-like body with contiguous dorsal, caudal, and anal fins; a pointed or rounded tail; typically four pairs of barbels; and no adipose fin (as found in many catfishes). They also have venomous fin spines that can inflict a painful sting. The one reef-dwelling species forms compact schools as juveniles and subadults, while adults are solitary and secretive.

Captive Care: A school of juvenile eel catfish makes an interesting aquarium display, but individuals can outgrow smaller tanks and adults may feed on desirable fishes and crustaceans. Provide an expanse of sandy bottom to allow active foraging.

Feeding: In captivity, they are hardy and are skilled at scavenging food particles from the bottom. Provide a varied diet.

Other Advice: Use caution to keep from being stung by venomous spines. (Not recommended for tanks to which children have access.) Do not treat with nonchelated copper medications or organophosphates.

Family Synodontidae (lizardfishes)

Subfamilies: 3
Genera: 5
Species: about 55

This is the only family in the Order Aulopiformes that occurs on coral reefs. Most other members of this order are deep-water fishes that are either benthic, pelagic, or bathypelagic. One of the largest families in this order is Myctophidae, the lanternfishes. This is a group of light-emitting fishes that roams the ocean depths. All of the Aulopiformes have specialized gill arches, a feature that is unique to the order. The Synodontidae are the only group in this order that occurs in coral reef environs. Synodontids lack enlarged scales along the lateral line and usually have an adipose fin. The largest reaches 60 cm (23.6 in.) in length. Most lizardfishes live in marine habitats, although a few can be found in brackish environments. Representatives of the Subfamily Synodontinae are found on or near coral reefs. These fishes are ambush hunters that conceal themselves on the ocean floor, either by remaining still or burying just under the substrate. They dart up to capture unsuspecting fishes that move too close.

Captive Care: Lizardfishes do well in the aquarium, but are highly predaceous. Tankmates have to be carefully selected. Provide a system with a secure cover, ample surface area, and open bottom space for those species that bury or live on soft substrates.

Synodus intermedius, Sand Diver (Bonaire).

Feeding: Provide a varied diet including marine fish and crustacean meat.

Other Advice: Lizardfishes are predatory, cannibalistic, and can be territorial. Do not keep with small fishes or crustaceans, except possibly cleaner shrimp, which should be introduced before the lizardfish.

Family Bythitidae (livebearing brotulas)

Subfamilies: 2

Genera: 31

Species: 90+

The livebearing, or viviparous, brotulas have elongate bodies that are slightly compressed. Scales are usually present, as well as swim bladders. Most have pronounced preopercular spines, rounded pectoral fins, small eyes, and pelvic

fins that are elongate filaments. They swim by undulating the edges of their dorsal and anal fins. Some of these fishes can attain over 70 cm (27.5 in.) in length. Most occur in marine habitats, although five species have been found in brackish and/or freshwater. Some occur in coral reef habitats, others around rocky reefs, and one genus—with blind and poor-sighted species—occurs in limestone caves and sinkholes.

Captive Care: Livebearing brotulas are rare in the aquarium trade, and those that do show up are quite secretive. In a large aquarium with numerous hiding places, the aquarist may never spot the brotula after introducing it. An appropriate system is small, with one or two easily observed hiding places.

Feeding: Brotulas in the wild thrive on a diet of crustaceans and will eat ornamental shrimps if they are present in an aquarium system. Feed live or frozen brine shrimp, mysid shrimp, or shreds of table shrimp, being sure the food gets to the brotula. Feeding in a darkened aquarium may be necessary.

Other Advice: It may be necessary to mount a red light over the aquarium or to use a flashlight that emits a red beam to view the brotula at night.

Family Carapidae (pearlfishes)

Subfamilies: 2

Genera: 7

Species: 32

Carapidae and the next two families belong to the Order Ophidiiformes. Members of this unusual group have elongate bodies, pointed fins, no (or filamentlike) pelvic fins, and cycloid scales (if scales are present at all). They occur in shallow and deep water; some deep-water forms have photophores (light-producing organs) and very small eyes. Many of the ophidiiforms that live in shallow water are very cryptic. The pearlfish family has to be one of the oddest groups in the order. They have an anus and anal fin that are far forward on the body (they can be under the pectoral fin), and a few species lack pectoral fins. They have no scales, their gill openings are wide and extend far forward, and there are no spines on the operculum. All family members occur in marine waters, and the Subfamily Carapinae includes a number of species that live on or near coral reefs. Many of these are parasitic, entering the anus of sea cucumbers and feeding on their internal organs. Others are commensal, living with clams, sea stars, sea cucumbers, and tunicates. There are also some pearlfishes that are free-living. These pearlfishes pass through two larval stages. The first stage is pelagic, while the second is demersal (the second stage can be absent in free-living forms). Parasitic and commensal forms begin associating with their host during the second larval stage. The largest pearlfish attains a maximum length of 30 cm (11.8 in.). The most species encountered around coral reefs are members of the genus *Carapus*.

Captive Care: Pearlfishes are not intentionally collected for the aquarium trade, although they may be incidentally brought in with their hosts (e.g., sea cucumbers).

Family Ophidiidae (cusk eels)

Subfamilies: 4

Genera: 46

Species: 209

Cusk eels have dorsal and anal fins with numerous rays, most of which are equal in height or are longer in the dorsal fin. In addition, the dorsal and anal fins are contiguous with the caudal fin, the anus and anal fin originate behind the tip of the pectoral fin, scales are present, some species have a spine or spines on the operculum, and pelvic fins are usually present and consist of long filaments. The largest cusk eel reaches a maximum length of 2 m (6.5 ft.). They are relatively uncommon on coral reefs, although the family is well represented in temperate waters on either rocky reefs or open bottoms at depths of over 8,000 m (26,000 ft.). The genus *Brotula*, of the Subfamily Brotulinae, is sometimes seen in the aquarium trade. These fishes have barbels on the chin and snout. They are nocturnal and very secretive, hiding deep in reef crevices during the day.

Captive Care: The cryptic habits of the cusk eels make them less than desirable aquarium fishes and they are seldom kept in home systems.

Family Batrachoididae (toadfishes)

Subfamilies: 3

Genera: 24

Species: 71

The toadfishes form the only family in the Order Batrachoidiformes, with most occurring in marine environments, although a few enter brackish waters and several are limited to freshwater. The Subfamily Batrachoidinae (15 genera, 43 species) is well represented on coral reefs. They have stout opercular and dorsal spines (some have associated venom glands), as well as subopercular spines. Scales are either present or lacking; in those species with scales, they are cycloid in form. They have no photophores, no canine teeth, and one or three lateral lines. Most live on soft substrate (sand or mud), although some (e.g., *Sanopus*) also occur in coral reef habitats. Some of these toadfishes defend their eggs and young and feed on crustaceans, sea urchins, and small fishes. Several species from the Subfamily Thalassophryninae also occur on coral reefs in the Caribbean. These species have two hollow dorsal and opercular spines that inject venom produced by an associated gland. These fishes have no subopercular spines, scales, or photophores. They have either a single lateral line or no lateral line. There are 2 genera and 11 species in this subfamily, and at least 2 of them inhabit freshwater (e.g., *Thalassophryne amazonica* occurs only in the Amazon River). The members of the final subfamily, the Porichthyinae, are deep-water and/or soft-bottom forms, many of which have photophores.

Captive Care: Only one toadfish species commonly shows up in aquarium stores. It is a voracious predator that will eat small fishes and crustaceans, and will spend much of its time hiding under rocks. Provide a small- to large-sized aquarium with a bed of sand at least 5 cm (2 in.) deep and numerous hiding places that cannot be toppled by the digging toadfish.

Feeding: Offer a varied diet that includes plenty of crustacean meat such as shrimp and large krill.

Other Advice: Keep no more than one toadfish per tank, unless they are a mated pair. Do not house with desirable motile invertebrates (snails, crabs, urchins, sea stars) that may fall prey to the toadfish. Use a red light for after-dark viewing of hunting habits. Note that some Caribbean toadfishes have venomous opercular and dorsal spines.

Family Antennariidae (frogfishes)

Genera: 12

Species: about 43

The frogfishes and walking batfishes (the family that follows) are the only members of the Order Lophiiformes that occur on coral reefs. However, there are others that occur on temperate water rocky reefs, such as the goosefishes (Family Lophiidae), the handfishes (Family Brachionichthyidae), and the coffinfishes (Family Chaunacidae). They also share this order with the deep-sea anglers, well known for their light-emitting lures and for the unusual life history of the males, which attach to and are nourished by the much larger females. The frogfishes are equally unusual. They are globular in form, with modified pectoral fins that look and function like legs, a first dorsal spine that functions to lure prey items, no swim bladder, and no stout spines. They have small, round opercular openings usually located under the "armpit" of

Antennarius multiocellatus, Longlure Frogfish (Bonaire).

the pectoral fin. They also lack scales, but have dermal spinules instead. The largest member of the family reaches a maximum length of 34 cm (13.4 in.). All but one of the frogfish species live in marine habitats (one species occurs in brackish and freshwater conditions) and occur in tropical to temperate seas. Some species display parental care of the eggs, while others produce a pelagic egg raft.

Captive Care: The frogfishes make unique aquarium inhabitants, although great care should be exercised when selecting tankmates for these fishes. Their voracious feeding habits (sometimes attempting to swallow prey much larger than themselves) make them best suited to housing in a species aquarium. The tank does not have be large to accommodate the many smaller species, but it should be provided with suitable rocky hiding places.

Feeding: Provide frogfishes with a varied diet of meaty marine foods. Freshwater feeder fish should be offered sparingly or not at all. Never feed oversize prey and be sure that all fish tankmates are at least twice the length of the frogfish—for the protection of both predator and prey.

Other Advice: Never lift a live frogfish from the water; always use a specimen container rather than a net to keep it immersed.

Family Ogcocephalidae (walking batfishes)

Genera: 9

Species: 62

The walking batfishes occupy marine habitats and occur in tropical and subtropical seas. They have a depressiform body, a short illicium, an illicial cavity that houses the esca when the illicium is retracted, a horizontal mouth, and a gill opening located above or on the pectoral fin base. They also have modified scales known as tubercles or bucklers (i.e., multispine tubercles), and there are modified scales associated with the lateral line organs. The largest species attains 40 cm (15.7 in.) in length. Aquarists often apply the vernacular name "batfish" to members of the Family Ephippidae (the spadefishes) and "walking batfish" to the ogcocephalids (the latter have long been known to ichthyologists and naturalists as batfishes). Most of these fishes occur in marine habitats, but several species have been reported from brackish and freshwater conditions. They typically occur on sand, mud, or rubble bottoms, with some species inhabiting seagrass beds. They walk along the bottom on modified pectoral and pelvic fins and are poor swimmers.

Captive Care: Walking batfishes are occasionally available to aquarists but require special attention in order to survive in captivity. They may damage themselves by swimming against the glass and aquarium decor, and the aquarium housing them should be placed in a low-traffic area or be equipped with a one-way-glass viewing panel. Place a 15 cm (5.9 in.) wide strip of black plastic along the outside bottom of the tank to prevent the batfish from rubbing up against the aquarium glass.

Feeding: Live food (adult brine shrimp, grass shrimp, black worms) may be needed to induce an initial feeding response. Continue to offer a varied diet of live and high-protein fresh and frozen foods.

Other Advice: Walking batfishes are often parasitized by intestinal worms, and should be dewormed immediately after being purchased. Do not house them with large herbivores or sessile invertebrate feeders that may pick at the batfish.

Family Belonidae (needlefishes)

Genera: 10

Species: 32

The needlefishes and halfbeaks are members of the Order Beloniformes. This order also contains the flyingfishes, which are well known for their aerial acrobatics. Belonids are elongate with pelvic fins located far behind the pectoral fin base. They have small scales, a large mouth opening with long jaws and needlelike teeth, and occur in marine and freshwater in both tropical and temperate seas. Few needlefishes live around coral reefs, and those that do most often inhabit shallow lagoon waters. They swim near the surface and are capable of catapulting themselves out of the water. The largest species attains a maximum length of about 1 m (3.3 ft.). When they first hatch, the jaws of the fry are short and equal in length. As they grow, the lower jaw grows faster (so they look like halfbeaks) and then the upper jaw begins to catch up. The needlefishes feed on small fishes and will leap out of the water when startled (people have actually been impaled and killed by airborne needlefish). They produce large pelagic eggs with filaments that adhere to floating debris.

Captive Care: The needlefishes are not available to aquarists; most get too large and are too active to be kept in the home aquarium.

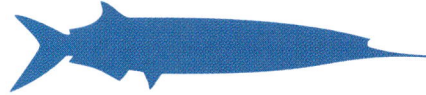

Family Hemiramphidae (halfbeaks)

Genera: 12

Species: 85

The halfbeaks display an upper jaw that is much shorter than the lower jaw, which is elongate in both juveniles and adults. The pectoral and pelvic fins are short. The largest species reaches a maximum length of 45 cm (17.7 in.). These fishes occur in both marine and freshwater habitats. They tend to inhabit coastal waters and are often found swimming near the surface in schools. Representatives of the genus *Hemiramphus*, which is the largest genus, are most frequently encountered near coral reefs. The halfbeaks feed on zooplankton, small fishes, and floating plant material. When threatened, they leap from the water and often skip along the surface—some species also glide using their pectoral fins for lift. Some species produce large eggs with adhesive threads that stick to floating debris or seagrass, while other species are ovoviviparous, giving birth to live young.

Captive Care: Although marine species are not seen in the aquarium trade, there is a species of freshwater halfbeak that is available to aquarists.

Family Anomalopidae (flashlight fishes)

Genera: 5

Species: 6

This family and the two that follow belong to the Order Beryciformes. This order is comprised of a hodgepodge of spiny-rayed fishes that share several "primitive" osteological characteristics. The most remarkable feature of these fishes is the kidney-shaped photophore under each eye. This organ harbors bioluminescent bacteria that continually produce a greenish glow. The fish "turns off" the light by covering it with a black membrane or by rotating it downward (depending on the genus in question), and employs it to communicate with conspecifics, to find and possibly attract zooplankton, and to confuse predators. The flashlight fishes have one continuous dorsal fin or a dorsal fin with a notch. The largest member of the family attains a maximum length of 27 cm (10.6 in.). They occur near the surface to depths of 365 m (1,186 ft.). Those species that live at greater depths often make nocturnal migrations toward the surface, while shallow-water forms leave the shelter of the reef on moonless nights.

Captive Care: The flashlight fishes can be successfully kept in aquariums if special requirements are met. They should be provided with a dimly lit (or totally dark) tank in a dark room without a high volume of human traffic. Provide them with an aquascape of caves and overhangs.

Feeding: Offer live, enriched brine shrimp and gradually begin to vary the diet.

Other Advice: View flashlight fishes after dark with a flashlight that emits a red beam or a with red light mounted over the tank.

Family Monocentridae (pineapple or pinecone fishes)

Genera: 2

Species: 3

Like the flashlight fishes, the pineapple or pinecone fishes possess light organs. The photophores of the pineapple fishes are located on the lower jaw. These fishes are covered with heavy scales, they have a stout pelvic spine with two to four soft rays, two dorsal fins, an anal fin with no spines and 10 to 12 soft rays, and a large eye. The largest species attains 21 cm (8.2 in.). The pineapple fishes occur in tropical and warm temperate seas, and are typically found at depths of 30 to 300 m (98 to 975 ft.). However, two species are found at shallower depths on rocky reefs in certain locations.

Captive Care: Pineapple fishes are occasionally offered to marine hobbyists and can be successfully kept if provided with caves and overhangs as hiding places

and housed either with peaceful species or on their own. Keep the tank dimly lit or totally dark and in a quiet room without bright lights or sunlight.
Feeding: Offer live, enriched brine shrimp and gradually begin to vary the diet.
Other Advice: View these fishes after dark with a flashlight that emits a red beam or a with red light mounted over the tank. Use a specimen container to capture and move a pineapple fish, as its spines may get entangled in a net.

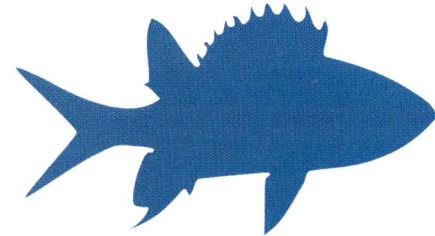

Family Holocentridae (squirrelfishes and soldierfishes)
Subfamilies: 2
Genera: 8
Species: 65

The squirrelfishes and soldierfishes are a ubiquitous group of reef dwellers that are found in tropical marine waters and are able to produce a variety of sounds (including clicks and growls) that they use to communicate with each another. Members of the Subfamily Holocentrinae, commonly called the squirrelfishes, have a stout spine on the preopercle (which is venomous in some), with the longest anal spine exceeding the length of the longest dorsal spine, and a tubular swim bladder that extends the entire length of the body cavity. The 3 genera and 32 species in this subfamily are nocturnal fishes, many of which refuge in reef caves and under ledges during the day. They feed on crustaceans, polychaete worms, and small fishes. The Subfamily Myripristinae, known as the soldierfishes, lack the large, preopercular spine (except for one Atlantic species). The longest anal spine is usually shorter than the longest dorsal spine, and the swim bladder is divided into two chambers. There are 5 genera and 33 species in this subfamily. The members of the largest soldierfish genus (*Myripristis*) are nocturnal zooplanktivores that feed on larger plankters like crab larvae. Members of the three smaller genera prey more heavily on benthic invertebrates and small fishes. Little is known about their reproductive behavior, but the pelagic larvae settle out at a large size (3 cm [1.2 in.] in some species).
Captive Care: All of the holocentrids are excellent aquarium inhabitants, and a group of soldierfishes in a large tank makes an attractive and interesting display. Many species can be kept in social groupings with no territoriality problems. Provide subdued lighting or caves and overhangs in which these fishes can find shelter.
Feeding: Offer a varied diet that includes planktonic crustaceans.
Other Advice: Squirrelfishes and soldierfishes can be added to a large reef aquar-

ium, although some species will eat smaller fishes and ornamental shrimps. Do not attempt to keep them with overly aggressive, crevice-dwelling species. Use a red light to observe their after-dark activities.

Myripristis vittata, Whitetip Soldierfish (Maldives).

Family Aulostomidae (trumpetfishes)

Genera: 1

Species: 3

This family, as well as the five that follow, are members of the Order Gasterosteiformes. The trumpetfishes have a very elongate body that is slightly depressed, a long and tubelike snout, very expandable jaws, a row of short dorsal spines before the small dorsal fin, and a barbel on the chin. When moving at a leisurely pace, they employ undulations of the dorsal and anal fins.

Aulostomus maculatus, Atlantic Trumpetfish.

When they beat a hasty retreat or make a lunge at a prey item, however, they beat their caudal fins. All the trumpetfishes attain a maximum length of about 80 cm (31.5 in.). The trumpetfishes are tropical marine species that often associate with rocky or coral reefs. The juveniles generally reside in seagrass beds or among soft corals. Aulostomids are usually found singly and feed mainly on small fishes and crustaceans. They are master hunters, utilizing a considerable repertoire of tactics to capture unwary prey species. For example, they will position themselves in the middle of a shoal of feeding herbivores or lie along the back of a larger fish in order to sneak up on their unsuspecting quarry. They are capable of rapid color change and a xanthic, or golden, morph has been reported in one species. These fishes spawn in pairs, with males having been observed competing for females. They produce pelagic eggs.

Captive Care: Although the trumpetfishes grow too large for the majority of home aquariums, they are engaging display animals that thrive in aquarium confines. The juveniles are occasionally offered in the trade, and may be started in a medium-sized tank but will eventually require a system of 200 gallons or more. The tank should have ample swimming room, as well as appropriate vertical structures where the fish can find shelter. A full cover and well-protected filter intakes and siphon tubes are required.

Feeding: Offer feeder fish and live crustaceans initially, gradually converting the fish to a varied diet of fresh and frozen meaty marine foods.

Other Advice: Trumpetfishes are a threat to any smaller fish or crustacean that fits within their expandable jaws, but they, in turn, can be harassed by aggressive tankmates.

Family Fistulariidae (cornetfishes)

Genera: 1

Species: 4

The cornetfishes are very similar to Family Aulostomidae, having a very slender, elongate body that is slightly depressed, and a long snout. However, they lack the dorsal spines that precede the single dorsal fin and they have a forked caudal fin with a filament that extends from the middle. The fistularids often swim by undulating the body in an anguilliform (eel-like) fashion. All the cornetfishes live in tropical and warm-temperature marine environments, inhabiting coral reefs, deep sand slopes, and estuaries. Also like the trumpetfishes, these fishes are stealthy predators, stalking small fishes and crustaceans. They are even known to engage in "hunting by riding," a common hunting tactic employed by the aulostomids. Cornetfishes occur singly or in small shoals and typically do not stray far from the seafloor.

Captive Care: Cornetfishes are rarely, if ever, offered in the marine aquarium trade, and are too large and active for most home aquariums. Their care requirements are similar to those of the trumpetfishes.

Family Pegasidae (sea moths)

Genera: 2

Species: 5

The unusual sea moths have bodies that are depressed and encased in bony plates, winglike pectoral fins, and modified pelvic rays that function as legs with which they drag themselves over the substrate. A sea moth has one dorsal fin, a tail that is encircled in bony rings, an inferior mouth that folds up

Solenostomus cyanopterus, Robust Ghost Pipefish (North Sulawesi).

into a cavity beneath the snout, and an elongate, flattened rostrum. They lack both fin spines and a swim bladder. They live in marine environments (although one species is known to enter brackish water estuaries) on soft substrates—often adjacent to coral reefs—and feed on small, benthic invertebrates. The mouth is highly protractile. When the jaws are extended and the buccal cavity expands, enough suction is created to draw prey into the mouth.

Captive Care: Although rare in the marine fish trade, sea moths can make interesting aquarium inhabitants if special care is taken to ensure that they get enough to eat. Provide an aquarium that is wide and shallow, rather than tall, with a large expanse of open sandy bottom and little other decor.

Feeding: Sea moths will eat only food that is sitting on or near the substrate. Small, live crustaceans are often necessary to induce feeding. Offer a varied diet of enriched adult brine shrimp, mysid shrimp, and amphipods.

Other Advice: Sea moths are best kept in a species tank or with peaceful fishes that are not food competitors.

Family Solenostomidae (ghost pipefishes)

Genera: 1

Species: 6 (3 undescribed)

Ghost pipefishes have long bodies that are encased in bony plates. They have a long snout with a small mouth on the end and two dorsal fins with no fin spines. The pelvic fins of the females are connected along the margins to form an incubation pouch for the eggs. Ghost pipefishes live in marine habitats, typically in or around coral reef ecosystems. They feed on small, swarming crustaceans like mysid shrimp, and often occur in male-female pairs. The ghost pipefishes often masquerade as calcareous algae, such as *Halimeda*, or parts of sessile invertebrates, such as sponges, crinoids, or soft corals.

Captive Care: Ghost pipefishes are rarely collected for the aquarium trade, and often do poorly in captivity unless given both a quiet tank and expert care. They should be kept in a system with gentle water movement and adequate shelter, possibly including some of the plants or invertebrates they mimic. Be sure to place strainers or covers on filter intakes and siphon tubes.
Feeding: Live food, such as vitamin-enriched adult brine shrimp, mysid shrimp, and *Grammarus*, must be offered.
Other Advice: Connecting a ghost pipefish aquarium to a refugium with a healthy population of copepods, amphipods, and mysid shrimp will help provide a constant supply of live foods.

Family Syngnathidae (seahorses and pipefishes)

Subfamilies: 2
Genera: 52
Species: 200+

The seahorses and pipefishes all have elongate bodies encased in bony rings, a small anal fin, and no pelvic fins. Most have pectoral fins and a single dorsal fin. When present, the caudal fin is small. Gill openings are also small, and they have a tubelike snout with a small mouth at the end. Members of the Subfamily Hippocampinae, the seahorses, swim with their bodies upright and have a prehensile tail. Members of the Subfamily Syngnathinae, the pipefishes, either crawl over the substrate or hover just above it, with their bodies in a horizontal orientation. The Pipehorse (*Acentronura tentaculata*) is an anomalous member of the pipefish subfamily—it has a head like a pipefish, but a prehensile tail like a seahorse. The extravagant sea dragons, residents of warm temperate rocky reefs, are also members of the Subfamily Syngnathinae. Permits are required to collect sea dragons, and they must be housed in a cool-water system and fed live mysid shrimp if they are to thrive in captivity. The males of all the syngnathid species carry the eggs on the ventral surface of the abdomen or in a brood pouch, where they are incubated until they hatch. Almost all seahorses are found in marine environments (one species lives in freshwater rivers in Vietnam); some pipefishes only occur in freshwater. All members of the family feed on small crustaceans, both benthic forms and those that swarm near the substrate.
Captive Care: Seahorses and pipefishes will readily acclimate to captive living if healthy individuals are acquired and they are provided with proper food and peaceful tankmates. They are best kept in quiet, small- to medium-sized species systems or with a limited population of peaceful tankmates that are not

Hippocampus reidi, Longsnout Seahorse (Bonaire).

food competitors. Seahorses require an abundance of structures that can be safely grasped with their prehensile tails. A gentle water current should be provided, but do not use airstones or filters that produce fine bubbles that may be mistaken for food items. Do not attempt to house seahorses with piscivorous anemones or with corals that have a potent sting. Be sure to examine potential seahorse acquisitions for diseases and parasites and always quarantine new specimens. Place strainers or covers on filter intakes or siphon tubes.

Feeding: Offer live foods, such as enriched adult brine shrimp or frozen mysid shrimp. Feed at least four times per day or provide a constant supply of live foods. Starvation is a major cause of death of these fishes—be sure to have an adequate supply of foods they will accept.

Other Advice: Seahorses are being overcollected—largely for use in Asian folk medicine—and aquarists are being asked to assist in preservation efforts. Do not purchase seahorses if you aren't prepared to offer the foods and care they require. Purchase larger specimens, leaving younger stock in the wild to reproduce. Look for captive-bred seahorses or consider becoming a home propagator. (Some species will breed readily in the home aquarium.)

Family Centriscidae (shrimpfishes)

Genera: 2

Species: 4

Shrimpfishes have greatly compressed bodies with a sharp ventral edge (hence their other common name, the razorfishes). Specimens have thin, bony plates—expansions of the vertebral column that encase the body—a long, tubelike snout, a small mouth that lacks teeth, a single dorsal fin placed where the caudal fin usually exists (the latter has been displaced in a more ventral location), a rigid or jointed dorsal spine, and no lateral line. They typically adopt a vertical orientation (with their heads down) when at rest, or as they move over the bottom beating the median fins. All the shrimpfishes occur in marine environments, and all four species can be found on coral reefs or in adjacent habitats such as seagrass beds. They most often live in schools, commonly associating with invertebrates like ramose stony corals, gorgonians, and sea urchins. These fishes ingest small swarming and benthic crustaceans.

Captive Care: If given the appropriate attention and aquarium venue, the shrimpfishes make unique and interesting "pets." They are best housed in a system with live rock, live sand, macroalgae growths, and natural foraging opportunities. A gentle current is required.

Feeding: They almost always require live food, such as enriched adult brine shrimp. A well-established reef aquarium, especially one with a refugium, can provide a constant source of healthy mysid shrimp, copepods, and other live prey.

Other Advice: An especially appropriate setting for shrimpfishes would include long-spined sea urchins (*Diadema* spp.) or branching stony corals.

Family Caracanthidae (coral crouchers)

Genera: 1

Species: 4

The coral crouchers, along with the next six families, are members of the Order Scorpaeniformes. They are extremely compressed and oval in shape, with a stout preopercular spine, five to six spines on the "cheek" margin, a

body covered with papillae (which gives them a rough texture), one notched dorsal fin, and small pelvic fins. All of these fishes live on coral reefs; in fact, they are all obligatory stony coral inhabitants, wedging themselves deep among the branches of ramose species (e.g., *Pocillopora*). They rarely leave their calcareous shelters but feed on small crustaceans and small fishes that cohabit these coral heads.

Captive Care: Coral crouchers are seldom available to aquarists, and when they do turn up in the aquarium trade, they are usually mislabeled as "gobies." The coral crouchers are secretive and difficult to maintain and are best suited to a small species exhibit or with other fishes that inhabit ramose stony corals. They must be provided with a live, branching coral head, or at least a coral skeleton, in which to hide.

Feeding: Offer live foods, such as grass shrimp and enriched adult brine shrimp.

Other Advice: The coral crouchers are venomous and must be handled with care. Use a specimen container to capture this fish, as its spines may become entangled in a net.

Family Tetrarogidae (waspfishes)

Genera: 11+

Species: 35

Waspfishes are laterally compressed, often with a single, high dorsal fin that originates on the head (often over or in front of the eyes) and that may be contiguous with the caudal fin. They have venomous fin spines that can deliver a very potent and potentially dangerous "sting." Most of the waspfishes occur in marine habitats, although at least one species is known from freshwater and others have been reported from brackish, estuarine environments. They are often more abundant on nutrient-rich coastal reefs, as opposed to oceanic habitats. Most waspfishes are nocturnal, often spending the daylight hours amid macroalgae. Some enhance their camouflage by swaying from side to side like a piece of plant debris. They feed on worms, crustaceans, and small fishes.

Captive Care: Waspfishes can be kept in aquariums and are often available to the hobbyist, but they can be finicky eaters and demand special care. Provide a 5-cm (2-in.) deep layer of sand,(especially for those species that bury themselves), rubble, and/or macroalgae substrate.

Feeding: They will typically refuse to eat anything but live food, such as grass shrimp or baby livebearers. Live grass shrimp can often initiate a feeding re-

sponse and can be followed by a varied diet that includes nonliving foods.
Other Advice: The waspfishes are one of the most venomous groups of fishes and are capable of causing human fatalities. Great care should be taken when handling or maintaining a tank that houses one of these menacing "stingers," and they should never be kept in a tank that is accessible to children. Use a specimen container, rather than a net, for safe handling and moving. Do not house them with sessile invertebrate feeders or large herbivores, and view nocturnal activities with a red light.

Family Scorpaenidae (scorpionfishes)

Subfamilies: 11

Genera: 45

Species: 388+

The scorpionfishes have compressed bodies often attired with fleshy, dermal flaps. They have large, heavily ridged and spined heads, one to two opercular spines, and three to five preopercular spines. The single dorsal fin is often notched, and they have 11 to 17 dorsal spines, 8 to 17 soft rays, one to three anal spines, one pelvic spine, and large pectoral fins. Scorpionfishes either have cycloid and/or ctenoid scales, or no scales at all. They are best known for their venom glands, which are associated with the fin spines. The 3 subfamilies that are best represented on coral reefs are the Scorpaeninae (over 150 species), the Pteroinae (with 16 species), and the Synanceinae (with 10 species). The latter subfamily includes the most venomous fishes in the sea—the stonefishes. Most of the scorpionfishes are benthic, sluggish, and masters of disguise and deception. They typically exhibit chromatic characteristics that enable them to disappear against the substrate. Many of the boldly colored species, such as the lionfishes and some members of the genus *Rhinopias*, appear to be exceptions to this rule of thumb. Even these animals, however, may masquerade as benthic invertebrates, often selecting ambush sites among the crinoids that they resemble. Most of the scorpionfishes exercise a sit-and-wait hunting strategy, although some species either passively or actively lure their prey. For example, algae grow on the heads and body surfaces of many scorpionfishes and may attract potential prey. At least one species has a dorsal fin that looks like a swimming fish as sinusoidal waves move down the fin. Their food habits vary somewhat between species, but worms, cephalopods, crustaceans, and fishes are their primary prey. Some of the scorpionfishes lay gelatinous egg masses that float about the ocean until they hatch, at which time the larvae enter the plankton.

Scorpaenopsis papuensis, Papuan Scorpionfish (Ambon).

Captive Care: The scorpionfishes are durable aquarium fishes, but they do carry an inherent risk of seriously stinging their keepers. These are not appropriate for young aquarists or in tanks that are accessible to children. Provide hiding places and a 5 cm (2 in.) deep layer of substrate for those species that bury.

Feeding: Although live food may be required to induce an initial feeding response, with a little effort and ingenuity, most individuals can be coaxed into accepting chunks or strips of seafood. Do not feed oversized prey items.

Other Advice: Great care should be taken when handling or working in a tank that contains one of these fishes. Do not house with sessile invertebrate feeders or large herbivores, and view nocturnal activities with a red light. Use a specimen container, rather than a net, for safe handling and moving.

Family Aploactinidae (velvetfishes)

Genera: 17

Species: 25

The velvetfishes are elongate and compressed, often with a steep head profile, bony knobs rather than spines on the head, and thick fins. They have long dorsal fins that originate over or in front of the eyes; zero, one, or two notches; rounded caudal fins; and rather loose, often wrinkly looking skin with microscopic bristles instead of scales. All velvetfishes are marine species, although some do enter estuaries, with the majority inhabiting the warm, temperate waters of Australia. A few species occur on sand or rubble bottoms near coastal reefs where they feed most heavily on small shrimps.

Captive Care: The velvetfishes are rarely encountered in the aquarium trade.

Family Triglidae (sea robins)

Genera: 13

Species: 120

Sea robins have long, slightly compressed bodies, with large, armored heads adorned with ridges and spines. They also have pointed snouts (some species have bilobed snouts consisting of two forward projecting spines), large eyes, no barbels on the chin, slightly inferior mouths, a spinous and a soft dorsal fin, and large winglike pectoral fins that often have brightly colored inner surfaces, with the three lowest rays enlarged and free from the rest of the fin. These free pectoral rays are used to crawl across the seafloor and dig for buried prey. All sea robins live in marine environments, but few occur on or near coral reefs. Instead, most inhabit deep sand or mud plains. The sea robins are always found on or near the seafloor and sometimes bury under the substrate. When threatened, they will open the expansive pectoral fins and exhibit their bright colors, or (in some juveniles) false eyespots. These displays are probably used to startle potential predators. The sea robins feed on benthic invertebrates (mollusks and crustaceans) and small fishes. They can produce sounds by using the swim bladder and have acquired their common name because of their habit of "chirping" when removed from the water. Members of this family are rarely encountered in aquarium stores. Those species that do show up come from the tropical Western Atlantic.

Captive Care: Sea robins can be successfully maintained in captivity if provided with a large tank, limited decor, and a sandy bottom with a minimum of 5 cm (2 in.) of substrate. Locate the tank in a low-traffic area and keep these fishes with peaceful tankmates that will not nip at their large pectoral fins.

Feeding: Offer a steady diet of live, vitamin-enriched brine shrimp, black worms, and grass shrimp.

Other Advice: To move these fishes, use a specimen container rather than a net, which could result in damaging entanglements. View after dark with a flashlight that emits a red beam or a red light mounted over the tank.

Family Platycephalidae (flatheads)

Genera: 19

Species: 60+

The flatheads have long, slightly depressed bodies and moderately to strongly flattened heads with bony ridges that bear spines and serrations. They have two dorsal fins—the first is spinous with 7 to 10 spines, and the second has 10 to 15 soft rays. The pelvic fins originate behind the pectoral fin base. Flatheads lack a swim bladder, and their eyes are equipped with an iris lappet, a branching structure that hangs over the eye and can expand or contract to let in either more or less light. All of these fishes live in saltwater, although some enter brackish estuaries and inhabit tropical and temperate seas. Relatively few flatheads are found on sand and mud bottoms adjacent to reefs, while even fewer species live on coral reef substrate. They occur at depths of less than 1 to 300 m (3.3 to 975 ft.). Most flatheads bury under the substrate during the day and emerge to forage after dark. Even those that do not bury are extremely cryptic and are easily overlooked by both potential prey and predators. The dorsal surface of the body is usually attired with shades of brown, gray, and black—although individuals of some species can sport red, pink, or green hues.

Captive Care: Often called "crocodilefishes," a few flathead species occasionally enter the aquarium trade. They are easy to keep if provided with live food and some open, sandy bottom on which to rest.

Cymbacephalus beauforti, Beaufort's Crocodilefish (North Sulawesi).

Feeding: Offer grass shrimp or feeder fish to initiate a feeding response. The aquarist will probably be able to train most individuals to take nonliving foods, such as strips of fish, squid, and crustacean meat, from a feeding stick.

Other Advice: True to their predatory appearance, the flatheads will eat small fishes and ornamental crustaceans that can be swallowed whole. Their nocturnal activities can best be viewed with a red light.

Family Dactylopteridae (helmut gurnards)

Genera: 2

Species: 7

As with most of the members of this suborder (Dactylopteroidei), helmut gurnards are bottom-dwellers. They have large pectoral fins, large armored heads, and an orbital stay (a bony ridge that runs across the operculum). The bulbous head has a rounded snout, and the body tapers toward the tail and is covered with scutelike scales. There are no venomous fin spines, two dorsal fins, one or two independent spines before the first dorsal fin, immense, winglike pectoral fins, and a shoulder girdle that extends backward and ends in a sharp spine. The helmut gurnards possess a relatively small mouth with small, granular teeth. All of these fishes live in marine environments; two are often found in the vicinity of coral reefs on either soft substrates or coral rubble. The helmut gurnards typically crawl over the bottom, employing four modified pelvic rays to pull themselves along. When they are threatened, they flare open their large pectoral fins—seeming to increase in size—and rapidly beat their tail fins. They are not fast swimmers and usually swim in circles in an attempt to outmaneuver pursing predators. The helmut gurnards feed on benthic crustaceans, mollusks, and small fishes and produce sounds by stridulation of the hyomandibular bone.

Captive Care: The young of the two reef-dwelling forms are occasionally offered in the ornamental marine fish trade and make an unusual addition to a large tank with an open expanse of sandy substrate and little decor. They demand a quiet setting in a low-traffic area with nonaggressive tankmates.

Feeding: Live foods are essential in maintaining most individuals in captivity. Offer a steady diet of adult vitamin-enriched brine shrimp, black worms, and other small crustaceans.

Other Advice: The large pectoral fins of the helmut gurnards make them vulnerable to tankmates that nip. Always house them with peaceable species that do not actively compete for their live food items.

Family Serranidae (groupers and anthias)
Subfamilies: 3
Genera: 62
Species: 449+

The serranids belong to the largest order of vertebrates, the Perciformes. This order contains about 7,000 species. All members have spines in the fins, pectoral fins on the side of the body, pectoral fin bases with a vertical orientation, fewer than 17 principal caudal rays, and pelvic fins (when present) that are in a jugular position. All of the families from groupers to barracudas are members of this order. The Family Serranidae is a large, diverse family ranging in size from 5-cm (2-in.) dwarfs to 2.5-m (8.1-ft.), 400-kg (660-lb.) giants. The vast majority live in marine habitats, although some occur in brackish water, and a few live in freshwater. The opercle bears three spines; the lateral line is complete and continuous in all but one species but does not run onto the caudal fin; the dorsal fin is continuous (although in many it is notched); the caudal fin is rounded, truncate, or lunate; and the lower jaw extends beyond the end of the snout. They are either simultaneous or synchronous hermaphrodites that produce pelagic eggs (a small number of species may lay demersal eggs). The Subfamily Serraninae contains about 13 genera with 75 species, many of which are smaller predators on fishes and motile invertebrates. The Subfamily Anthiinae consists of about 20 genera and 170 species, a large number of which are zooplankton feeders that form shoals over the reef. The Subfamily Epinephelinae is a diverse group that consists of five tribes. It includes the Niphonini—which contains a single species; the Epinephelini—which includes 14 genera with about 164 species, including the more well-known groupers; the Diploprionini, which contains three genera; the Liopropomini, which consists of 3 genera (including the reef basslets, genus *Liopropoma*); and the Grammistini, which contains 8 genera and about 21 species. The soapfishes (Tribes Diploprionini and Grammistini) exude a toxic slime to dissuade predators; this mucus can kill aquarium tankmates. Some authors raise the status of the soapfish tribes to the family level.

Captive Care: Most of the groupers are durable, easily kept aquarium inhabitants. Many will outgrow the moderate-sized aquarium, and most will feed on small fishes or ornamental crustaceans. Groupers are heavy feeders that should be provided with a large tank with ample circulation and filtration capacity. Aquascaping should include adequate caves and crevices. The anthias are popular for reef aquariums, although many of these fishes demand frequent feedings and some do poorly in captivity. Provide a full aquarium cover to prevent

Cephalopholis miniata, Coral Hind (Maldives).

jumping, along with strong circulation and excellent water quality. Some deep-water species require dimly lit tanks.

Feeding: Groupers are greedy eaters that should be offered a varied diet of fresh and frozen meaty marine foods. (Freshwater feeder fish should be used sparingly, if at all.) Do not overfeed. The anthias are planktivores that require a varied diet of live and high-quality prepared foods offered several times a day. Hard-to-keep anthias species will do better in a reef-type aquarium connected to a well-established refugium with breeding populations of mysid shrimp, amphipods, and copepods.

Other Advice: Many of the groupers and anthias can be territorial and should often be kept singly, except in larger aquariums. The aquarist is urged to know the growth and social habits of any species being considered for purchase. Some groupers grow very large, and the anthias vary widely in their hardiness and aggressiveness. Severely stressed soapfishes will exude a toxic slime that can be lethal to their tankmates. Groupers are a threat to smaller fishes and ornamental shrimps, while the anthias are generally well-behaved members of a reef-tank community.

Family Pseudochromidae (dottybacks)

Subfamilies: 4
Genera: 16
Species: 100+

The dottybacks are most similar to small serranids, all occurring in tropical marine habitats. Each dorsal and anal fin of these fishes has one to three dorsal spines. They have pelvic fins located below the pectoral fin base, a variable lateral line, a ligament between the lower jaw and the hyoid arch, and eggs with threads. The largest member of the family attains 40 cm (15.7 in.), but most are much smaller (less than 11 cm [4.3 in.]). The most popular subfamily with aquarists is the Pseudochrominae, the dottybacks. The members of this group have an interrupted lateral line, scales on the head, pelvic fins with one spine and five branched soft rays, and teeth on the palatine. They live on coral or rocky reefs and spend most of their time peeking from interstices or hovering just above a shelter site. The dottybacks feed mostly on small crustaceans (often planktonic) and worms, and many are both colorful and territorial. The Subfamily Pseudoplesiopinae contains two genera and eight species, many of which are very secretive. They have pelvic fins with a single spine with three or four unbranched soft rays. The Subfamily Anisochrominae is made up of one genus with two species. These have pelvic fins with one spine and one unbranched and three branched pelvic rays. The Subfamily Congrogadinae is a very divergent group. They have an eel-like body with cycloid scales, one spine before the dorsal fin, no anal spines, some without pelvic fins, and a caudal fin that is continuous with the long dorsal and anal fins. The largest congrogadin attains a maximum length of 40 cm (15.7 in.), and they inhabit coral reefs, gravel, and mud bottoms at depths of less than 1 to 140 m (3.3 to 455 ft.). There are 8 genera and 19 species in this subfamily.

Captive Care: Members of the Subfamily Pseudochrominae are durable and popular aquarium fishes, although most will wreak havoc in a peaceful community tank. Some will do well in small aquariums, while the more aggressive, territorial species should be provided a larger tank with plenty of hiding places. (Only one member of the Subfamily Congrogadinae regularly shows up in the aquarium trade, where it is sold as the "wolf eel.")

Feeding: Most dottybacks will eagerly accept both prepared and live foods. Offer a varied diet that includes some items with color-enhancing pigments.

Other Advice: With few exceptions, a rule of one dottyback per tank should be followed. Larger species are a threat to small fishes and ornamental crustaceans, but some will also help rid a reef tank of noxious bristleworms and mantis shrimp.

Family Grammatidae (grammas)

Genera: 2

Species: 11

The grammas are a Western Atlantic family in which the lateral line is interrupted or absent, and the pelvic fins have one spine and five soft rays, with 11 to 13 spines in the dorsal fin. The largest member of the family attains 10 cm (3.9 in.). All of these fishes occur on coral reefs or rubble slopes, and many live at great depths (deeper than 75 m [244 ft.]). Most of these fishes hover just above the substrate or hang upside down under ledges or in caves, feeding on passing zooplankters. The eggs of at least some members of the family have a filament that anchors them to the substrate; the eggs are often deposited in a hole that the male lines with algae.

Captive Care: One species in this family, the Royal Gramma (*Gramma loreto*), is one of the most popular aquarium fishes. Members of the genus *Gramma* are hardy and relatively docile, while species of the genus *Lipogramma* that enter the trade are diminutive, often secretive, and require special care. Provide plenty of hiding places, vertical rock faces, overhangs, and rubble substrates (for deep-water species). *Lipogramma* species may do better in dimly lit systems.

Feeding: Offer a varied diet that includes some enriched and color-enhancing prepared foods.

Other Advice: Use caution if adding more than one member of a species to a tank. Watch for and avoid individuals suffering from maladies related to improper decompression.

Gramma loreto, Royal Gramma (Bonaire).

Calloplesiops altivelis, Comet or "Marine Betta" (North Sulawesi).

Family Plesiopidae (roundheads or longfins)

Subfamilies: 2
Genera: 11
Species: 38

The roundheads or longfins all have an incomplete or disjunct lateral line, no scales on the head or gill cover, pelvic fins with one spine, and two or four soft rays. The largest species in this group reaches a length of 20 cm (7.9 in.). The most specious subfamily, the Plesiopinae (roundheads or longfins) contains the well-known Comet (*Calloplesiops altivelis*) and the assessors (*Assessor* spp.)—the latter group containing three species that typically shoal in caves or under overhangs. The assessors also incubate their eggs orally while other plesiopins lay demersal eggs that are tended by the male. Most members of the subfamily are more drably attired than the Comet and assessors, and many of these occur in shallow, intertidal areas. The Subfamily Acanthoclininae, the spiny basslets, contains 4 genera with about 12 species, most of which occur on rocky reefs in the South Pacific.

Captive Care: The Comet is a deservedly popular species, and the roundheads or longfins are generally resistant to disease and are durable aquarium inhabitants, although most are quite secretive. Provide them with suitable hiding places, such as live rock, which also creates an ongoing source of the invertebrate fauna that form their natural diet.

Feeding: Offer a variety of meaty marine foods, and be sure that they receive several meals per week if productive live rock is not present in their system.

Other Advice: Roundheads are best kept one per tank. Some will consume small fish tankmates and all will eat ornamental crustaceans. Their nocturnal hunting activities can be viewed with a red light.

Family Opistognathidae (jawfishes)

Genera: 3

Species: 100+ (about 40 undescribed)

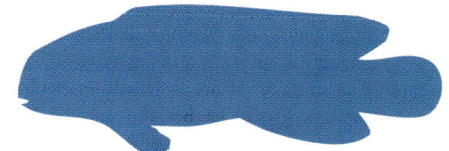

The jawfishes have a large mouth, cycloid scales on the body, pelvic fins that have one spine, and five soft rays situated in front of the pectoral base, a long dorsal fin, and a lateral line high on the body. They range in size from 3 to 40 cm (1.2 to 15.7 in.). Jawfishes live in burrows that they dig in soft substrates. The males incubate the eggs orally, and in some species have larger mouths than the females. The eggs have filaments that hold them together in a mass. Some jawfishes form colonies, while others occur singly. Certain species feed primarily on zooplankton, while others consume crustaceans and small fishes.

Captive Care: Their comical appearance and fascinating behavior have long made jawfishes popular with many aquarists. Most are easy to keep, provided the aquarium has a deep substrate and a tight-fitting top to keep them from jumping out. Create an open bed of sand, shell fragments, and bits of rubble that is at least 10 cm (3.9 in.) in depth.

Feeding: Offer a varied, meaty diet that includes small crustaceans, such as small frozen krill, mysid shrimp, and shavings of table shrimp.

Other Advice: Some jawfishes may be kept in colonies, while others should be housed singly. Larger jawfishes will eat small fish tankmates and ornamental shrimps.

Family Priacanthidae (bigeyes)

Genera: 4

Species: 18

The bigeyes are aptly named, with very large eyes—and a capacious mouth to match. The dorsal fin is continuous, a membrane connects the posterior pelvic rays to the body, the scales are modified cycloid with strong spines, and most are red in overall color. The largest bigeye reaches a maximum length of around 52 cm (20.4 in.). They can undergo rapid color change, transforming from a solid red to a blotchy or silvery pattern. They have a unique tapetum lucidum, a reflective layer that increases their visual sensitivity under low-light conditions and is responsible for the "eyeshine" observed in these fishes. Bigeyes occur in marine environments, in tropical and subtropical seas. They feed on motile invertebrates, small fishes, and larger zooplankters, and some form large schools. Bigeyes are nocturnal fishes, many of which refuge under overhangs and in caves during the day.

Captive Care: Bigeyes make interesting inhabitants for a large aquarium where they are provided with suitable caves, overhangs, or other shelter sites. They prefer dimly lit conditions, at least initially, and low-traffic areas.

Feeding: Offer a varied diet that includes fish and crustacean meats.

Other Advice: These fishes will eat small fishes and crustaceans, but may themselves be bullied by overly aggressive tankmates. In a darkened tank, their activities can be viewed with a red light.

Family Cirrhitidae (hawkfishes)

Genera: 9

Species: 35

Mostly occurring in the Indo-Pacific (only 4 are known from the Atlantic), the hawkfishes have 14 rays in the pectoral fins (the lower 5 to 7 are larger and unbranched), with a single, notched dorsal fin, and one or more cirri present on the tips of the dorsal spines and around the rear edge of the nostril. They have two flat spines on the opercle and no swim bladder. The largest hawkfish attains a maximum length of about 55 cm (21.7 in.). These are benthic fishes, most of which are diurnally active and feed on crustaceans and small fishes. These species usually rest on the substrate and dart out to capture passing prey items. There are also some hawkfishes that hunt crustaceans after dark, while one species feeds on zooplankton. Most cirrhitids are haremic, although a few form long-term pair bonds—at least when limited resources keep male individuals from attracting more females. All produce pelagic eggs.

Cirrhitichthys oxycephalus, Coral Hawkfish (Maldives).

Captive Care: Many of the hawkfishes are available in fish stores and all are durable aquarium inhabitants. Provide a covered tank with plenty of hiding places and substrate where these fishes can "perch."
Feeding: Offer a varied diet that includes some prepared foods with color-enhancing pigments.
Other Advice: Keep only one individual of a species per tank, unless a mated pair has been acquired. Some hawkfishes are very aggressive toward smaller tankmates and will eat any fish or motile invertebrate they can fit into their mouths. Note that some species (e.g., *Paracirrhites* spp.) will not tolerate the presence of fellow family members in the same aquarium.

Family Cheilodactylidae (morwongs)

Genera: 5

Species: 18

The morwongs have a long, continuous dorsal fin, and the lower-most pectoral rays are thickened, elongate, and separated from the rest of the fin. They have small mouths, thick lips, and forked tails. The largest morwong attains a maximum length of 1 m (3.3 ft.). All of these are marine fishes, with many of them inhabiting rocky reefs in subtropical and warm temperate seas (none occur in tropical seas). Most of these fishes feed on small invertebrates.

Captive Care: Morwongs rarely show up in aquarium stores. Provide a very large aquarium with open swimming areas as well as a spacious cave or overhang where they can find shelter.
Feeding: Offer a varied diet based on crustacean fare, including brine shrimp, krill, and mysid shrimp.
Other Advice: Morwongs exhibit an antitropical distibution and do best at lower water temperatures (23°C [74°F]).

Family Apogonidae (cardinalfishes)

Subfamilies: 2

Genera: 22

Species: 207

All of the cardinalfishes have two dorsal fins—the first with six to eight spines and the second with one spine. The second dorsal fin has 8 to 14 soft rays, and most of these fishes have ctenoid scales, although some have cycloid or lack scales altogether. These fishes incubate their eggs orally, with the male most frequently engaging in the care of the eggs. The male of at least one species also

Cheilodipterus quinquelineatus, Fivelined Cardinalfish (juvenile) (North Sulawesi).

holds the newly hatched young in its mouth. Many of the cardinalfishes live on coral reefs, while others occur in brackish and even freshwater habitats. Most are thought to be active at night, but some do feed during the day. They occur singly, in shoals, or in schools.

Captive Care: The cardinalfishes are excellent additions to the peaceful community aquarium, however some species will consume small fishes and ornamental crustaceans. They will ignore corals and other sessile invertebrates and are a popular choice for reef tanks. Provide hiding places, such as caves, or, for species such as *Pterapogon kauderni*, seagrass and long-spined sea urchins (*Diadema* spp). Many cardinalfishes are small and slow-moving and are prime targets for many piscivores, such as groupers and lionfishes.

Feeding: Offer a varied diet, including live adult brine shrimp to encourage reproduction.

Other Advice: Keep more than one individual of those species that form shoals or schools. Others may be kept singly or in mated pairs to avoid fighting. Some species will readily spawn, providing a display of marine mouthbrooding behavior. Nighttime behaviors can be observed with a red-beamed flashlight or red overhead lighting.

Family Malacanthidae (tilefishes)

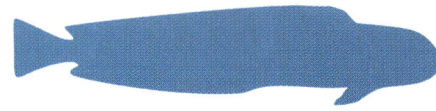

Subfamilies: 2
Genera: 5
Species: 39

The tilefishes all have a long, continuous dorsal fin, a relatively long anal fin, and a spine on the operculum. The larvae have numerous spines on the head and scales. The Subfamily Malacanthinae, the sand tilefishes, contains the species encountered in the aquarium trade. This group consists of 2 genera with 12 species. The largest member of the group attains a maximum length of 60 cm (23.6 in.). Most live on sand flats—often adjacent to coral reefs—and some species form large mounds out of shell fragments and coral rubble. These mounds provide shelter and food for many small fish species, as well as a refuge for the tilefishes. Some feed on zooplankton, while others eat crustaceans, worms, and small fishes. Many species occur in pairs.

Captive Care: The sand tilefishes vary in their suitability to aquarium life. Some rarely acclimate to captive conditions, while others thrive in larger tanks if provided with frequent feedings and suitable habitat. All are prone to leaping out of open aquariums. Place the aquarium in a low-traffic area and avoid sudden movements when working in or around the tank. Provide a coral head, a flat rock forming a cave in the sand, or a a mound of coral rubble where the tilefish can hide.

Feeding: Getting some of these species to feed can be a challenge, and keeping them with dither fishes, such as torpedo gobies, may help. Offer live foods, such as adult brine shrimp, to induce feeding, with high-quality frozen foods such as mysid shrimp as part of a varied long-term diet. Feed *Hoplolatilus* species several times daily.

Other Advice: Check for and avoid specimens suffering from improper decompression. Members of the genus *Malacanthus* are more durable than most of the *Hoplolatilus* species. The latter require peaceful tankmates and some do best in conspecific or heterospecific pairs.

Family Echeneidae (sharksuckers or remoras)
Genera: 4
Species: 8

These unique, wide-ranging fishes attach themselves to sharks—as well as sea turtles, marine mammals, and other fishes. The sharksuckers or remoras have a modified spinous dorsal fin that forms a sucking disc, an elongate body, a lower jaw that projects beyond the upper jaw, no spines in the dorsal and anal fins, and no swim bladder. They range from 17 cm to 1 m (6.7 in. to 3.3 ft.) in length. Some species feed on parasites that infect their hosts or on scraps resulting from predation events. Larger individuals rely on small fishes for food. The sharksuckers will enter the spiracles, gills, and cloaca of large sharks. They are opportunistic predators that also eat crustaceans.

Captive Care: The sharksuckers will do well in the aquarium, but some species grow much too large for most home systems. Be sure to know the maximum

Hoplolatilus chlupatyi, Flashing Tilefish.

length attained by the species of interest before making a purchase. They are agile swimmers and will jump—making an aquarium cover a necessity.

Feeding: These are greedy eaters that should be given a varied diet of meaty marine foods.

Other Advice: Remoras do not need their pelagic companions (like sharks and rays) to thrive in captivity. They have ample jaws and will eat fishes and crustaceans that they can swallow.

Family Carangidae (jacks)

Subfamilies: 4

Genera: 32

Species: 140

The jacks are quite variable in shape, ranging from deep-bodied forms to more elongate and fusiform species. Most have small cycloid scales, while a few have ctenoid scales. Some have small scutes, and finlets may be present behind the dorsal and anal fins. Larger juveniles and adults have two dorsal fins. The caudal peduncle is slender, and the caudal fin is usually lunate or highly forked. Most jacks live in marine environments, but juveniles of some species may enter brackish estuaries. They are active predators that feed on motile invertebrates and fishes. Some species may associate with large predators like sharks.

Caranx ruber, Bar Jacks.

Captive Care: Most jacks are too large (exceeding 60 cm [24 in.]) and active for the majority of home aquariums, but will do well in captivity if provided with enough space. Identify the species before making a purchase. Be ready to provide an extra-large tank, preferably with a circular perimeter, with plenty of swimming room, filtration capacity, and a secure cover. Smaller fishes and crustaceans put into the same tank will be eaten.

Feeding: Offer a varied diet, including marine fish, squid, large krill, and shrimp flesh.

Other Advice: Jacks are strong, fast swimmers, and care should be taken when working in or around the aquarium not to startle them, which may cause them to ram into the glass or leap out.

Family Lutjanidae (snappers)

Subfamilies: 5
Genera: 21
Species: 125+

The snappers have a continuous dorsal fin (in some species a shallow notch is present), pelvic fins that originate just behind the pectoral fin base, a moderate to large mouth that is in a terminal position, large canine teeth on the jaws and palatines (and often on the vomer), and a caudal fin that is either truncated or forked. They attain a maximum length of 1 m (3.3 ft.). Most snappers live in marine environments, although some occur in brackish water and freshwater. Many live in coastal habitats on coral reefs or in adjacent habitats (sand flats and seagrass meadows), but some species can be found at depths of 550 m (1,788 ft.). The members of the Subfamily Caesioninae (which some authors give family status) are schooling fishes that feed on zooplankton—usually near coral reefs. Most of the other snappers feed on benthic invertebrates.

Lutjanus apodus, Schoolmaster (Bonaire).

Captive Care: Many snappers grow too large for the average home aquarium, but some of the smaller species will do well if given enough room and proper filtration and water conditions. Be sure to identify the species and know its maximum length before purchasing. Provide plenty of swimming room, rocky hiding places, and tankmates that fend for themselves.

Feeding: Offer a varied diet, including marine fish, squid, and crustacean flesh.

Other Advice: Snappers are successful reef predators that target smaller fishes, ornamental clams, snails, echinoderms, and crustaceans.

Family Gerreidae (mojarras)

Genera: 8

Species: 40

The mojarras have highly protrusible jaws that extend downward, tiny brush-like teeth, a scaly head and sheath along the base of the anal and dorsal fins, and a deeply forked tail. Most live in marine environments, although some occasionally enter brackish water or freshwater. Those that occur near coral reefs usually occupy sand flats, where they feed heavily on infaunal invertebrates. They plunge their jaws into the substrate, take a mouthful, and eject inedible material through the gill openings. The largest mojarra reaches a maximum length of 35 cm (13.7 in.).

Captive Care: The mojarras are rarely, if ever, seen in the aquarium trade, although they would be ideal for helping to agitate bottom substrates.

Family Haemulidae (grunts and sweetlips)

Subfamilies: 2

Genera: 17

Species: 150

All members of the Haemulidae have a continuous dorsal fin, small mouths, cardiform teeth on the jaws, no teeth present on the vomer, and pores present on the chin. Most members of the Subfamily Haemulinae occur in the tropical Atlantic and Eastern Pacific. These fishes have a short dorsal fin (13 to 16 soft rays) and include the porkfishes and grunts. The Subfamily Plectorhynchinae, commonly known as sweetlips, are distributed in the Indo-Pacific and Eastern Atlantic. They have a long dorsal fin (17 to 26 soft rays) and often have large, fleshy lips. Some of the grunts are nocturnal and form large aggregations during the day. Most feed on benthic invertebrates and infaunal prey.

Captive Care: The Subfamily Plectorhynchinae includes the sweetlips, which are the most popular of the haemulids in the aquarium trade because of their bright colors and interesting chromatic patterns. Most sweetlips are more delicate and difficult to keep than their family mates, the grunts. They vary in their aquarium suitability, with some rarely acclimating to captivity, and others thriving in these conditions. Many attain larger proportions and will require an extremely large tank. Be sure to make a proper identification before buying any of these fishes. Provide an extra-large aquarium with plenty of swimming room and suitable sheltering places.

Feeding: Some are reluctant feeders that will require live foods, such as vitamin-enriched brine shrimp, grass shrimp, and live marine worms. Once eating, they should be fed a varied diet of marine fish, squid or octopus, and crustacean flesh.

Other Advice: Juveniles of most species should be housed with peaceful tankmates to ensure that they adapt to captivity and are able to compete for food.

Plectorhinchus polytaenia, Yellow-ribbon Sweetlips (North Sulawesi).

Family Lethrinidae (emperor snappers and large-eye breams)
Subfamilies: 2
Genera: 5
Species: 39

The emperor snappers and large-eye breams have a long, continuous dorsal fin (with 10 spines and 9 or 10 soft rays) and an anal fin with 3 spines and

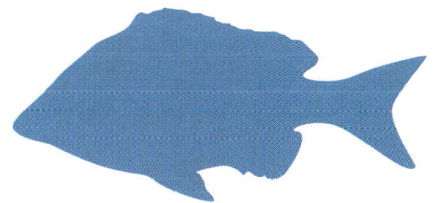

8 to 10 soft rays. These are marine fishes, most of which occur in the Indo-Pacific (only one is found in the Atlantic). Most are drably colored and often change colors when they rest on or near the bottom. The Subfamily Lethrininae, commonly called emperor snappers, have scaleless cheeks and nine soft dorsal fin rays. Some of these fishes occur on coral reefs, in seagrass meadows, or over rubble or rocky substrates. Some species have molarlike teeth that they use to crush clams and other hard-shelled invertebrates, while others feed on small fishes. Certain emperor snappers have long jaws that they plunge into the sand. They take a mouthful of substrate and sort invertebrates from the inedible materials, which are then expelled through the gill openings. The Subfamily Monotaxinae are known as the large-eye breams. They have some scales on the cheeks and ten soft dorsal fin rays. These fishes are often found over sand or rubble bottoms near reefs and feed on invertebrates.

Captive Care: The lethrinids are rarely, if ever, offered in the aquarium trade.

Family Nemipteridae (spinecheeks)

Genera: 5

Species: 64

Many of the spinecheeks, or threadfin breams, are found on or near coral reefs. They have a continuous dorsal fin (with ten spines and nine soft rays), an anal fin with three spines and seven to eight soft rays, and a caudal fin that is either emarginate or deeply forked. In some species, there may be filaments extending from the upper and lower lobe of the tail. There is a flat spine on the opercle. Spinecheeks have a small- to moderate-sized terminal mouth with small conical teeth in the jaws and no teeth on the vomer or palatines. These fishes often feed on sand-dwelling invertebrates. Several species are Batesian mimics of blennies that have venomous fangs.

Captive Care: The genus *Scolopsis* is most often encountered in the aquarium trade and will do well in captivity if housed in a large tank where much of the bottom is dedicated to sandy substrate at least 5 cm [2 in.] deep. Do not house them with overly aggressive tankmates, and keep only one specimen per tank unless the system is very large.

Feeding: Offer a varied diet of marine fish flesh, pieces of cephalopod, and crustacean meat. Live foods, such as grass shrimp and adult brine shrimp, will help initiate captive feeding.

Other Advice: Spinecheeks will eat ornamental crustaceans, but some will also hunt noxious bristleworms.

Family Sciaenidae (drums and croakers)

Subfamilies: 10
Genera: 70
Species: 270

Equetus lanceolatus, Spotted Drum (juvenile) (Bonaire).

Most of the drums and croakers occur in marine habitats, but some do live in brackish water and/or freshwater. The sciaenids have a moderately compressed and elongate body, a deeply notched dorsal fin, and lateral line scales that extend onto the caudal fin. The caudal fin is slightly emarginate or rounded, and there are large pores on the front of the snout and chin. The drums and croakers are most common in coastal, continental waters; few occur around islands. They get their common name from their ability to create a drumming sound that is resonated by the swim bladder. Some species have a barbel or patch of barbels on the chin, which facilitate food location. The species of interest to aquarists are collected from the tropical Western Atlantic and are coral reef inhabitants. These species are nocturnal and hide in reef crevices and caves during the day. However, most drums and croakers occur on open soft bottoms. The majority of species feed on invertebrates, although some include small fishes in their diet.

Captive Care: Relatively few of the drums and croakers are collected for the aquarium trade. They are susceptible to being bullied by aggressive tankmates, and need a large aquarium with plenty of caves and crevices to hide in during the daylight hours.

Feeding: These fishes may require live foods—such as vitamin-enriched adult brine shrimp, grass shrimp, or black worms—to induce an initial feeding response. Once settled, they may be switched to a varied diet of crustacean and mollusk flesh.

Other Advice: These fishes will eat many motile invertebrates kept by aquarists: ornamental shrimp, hermit crabs, porcelain crabs, and snails. Some will also help control troublesome bristleworms. Use a flashlight with a red beam or a red light mounted over the tank to view their nocturnal behaviors.

Family Mugilidae (mullets)

Subfamilies: 2

Genera: 14

Species: 64

The mullets have a slightly compressed and elongate body, a considerable distance between the eyes, two dorsal fins, pelvic fins that are placed well behind the pectoral fin base, large cycloid scales (in some cases, ctenoid), a small terminal mouth with no teeth or minute teeth, a gizzardlike stomach, and a very long intestine. The majority of mullets are silvery in color, being slightly darker dorsally. These fishes are found in marine, brackish, and freshwater environments and usually occur in shallow water. The mullets form schools and descend to the substrate to feed on algae and detritus, which they suck up and filter through elongate gill rakers. Some also eat zooplankton and small invertebrates.

Captive Care: The muted colors and unspectacular form and behavior of the mullets have little appeal to most aquarists. As a result, they are not collected for the aquarium trade.

Family Mullidae (goatfishes)

Genera: 6

Species: 55

The goatfishes have elongate bodies, two separate dorsal fins, a forked caudal fin, and ctenoid scales. The most distinguishable goatfish attribute is the long barbels present on the chin that are employed to locate food. They also use them to flip over rubble, probe soft sediments, and flush prey from reef crevices. Most live and feed on sand or mud bottoms—often adjacent to coral reefs—while some rest and feed on hard substrates. Other goatfishes prefer seagrass habitats. These fishes feed mostly on invertebrates, although at least two species are also piscivorous. Opportunistic predators often follow the mullids to capture prey exposed by their activities.

Captive Care: A number of goatfishes are available in the marine fish trade. They are active fishes that need plenty of swimming room and an open expanse of sand substrate (5 cm [2 in.] deep) in which to grub. They will help stir and aerate the sand on the bottom of an aquarium and are good scavengers, even taking noxious bristleworms and mantis shrimp.

Feeding: Ever-hungry juveniles should be fed at least three times per day with meaty fresh or frozen foods. An established bed of sand with a healthy population of small crustaceans and infaunal worms will help provide captive

goatfishes with a constant source of live foods.
Other Advice: Some individuals suffer from intestinal worms and will become skinny and die, even though they continue to feed. Be prepared to deworm these fishes if they feed well but still grow thin.

Parapriacanthus ransonneti, Slender Sweepers (foreground) (Andaman Sea, Thailand).

Family Pempheridae (sweepers)
Genera: 2
Species: 25
The sweepers primarily occur in the Indo-Pacific (only two are known from the tropical Western Atlantic). Sweepers have deep, compressed bodies, large

eyes, a single short dorsal fin, no adipose fin, and a lateral line that extends onto the caudal fin. They have bands of small, recurved teeth in the jaws and a V-shaped patch of teeth on the vomer. The sweepers also have long gill rakers and, usually, a forked caudal fin. Some species have bioluminescent organs associated with the digestive tract. Most sweepers form aggregations or schools, either in caves or under overhangs during the day. At night, they disperse to capture zooplankton.

Captive Care: Sweepers are rarely available to aquarists, but can be kept in a large aquarium with one or more spacious caves or overhanging ledges. The system should be dimly lit and located in a low-traffic area. Exclude any aggressive tankmates.

Feeding: Offer live or frozen foods, such as adult brine shrimp, that mimic zooplankters.

Other Advice: When keeping schooling sweeper species, add a small group rather than a single individual. Their nocturnal actions can be viewed with a red light over the tank or a flashlight with a red beam.

Family Monodactylidae (monos)

Genera: 2

Species: 5

The monos have a short snout, a single dorsal fin with a long base, and anal and dorsal fins mostly covered with scales. Most of these fishes are silver overall in color. The pelvic fins are found in juveniles but are lost or vestigial in adult *Monodactylus* species. These fishes occur near coral and rocky reefs, in estuaries, and in mangrove swamps. They can tolerate saltwater, brackish water, and freshwater, and usually occur in schools. They feed on zooplankton and plant material.

Captive Care: Monos are very popular with aquarists who maintain brackish-water tanks. They are active, flashy fishes that do well in saltwater systems, especially when given plenty of swimming room in an aquarium that has ample length and height.

Feeding: Offer a varied diet, including vegetable matter, to these unfinicky eaters.

Other Advice: Monos are best kept in small schools, although some intraspecific aggression may be seen in the more sensitive *Monodactylus sebae*. Some monos may cause damage to ornamental feather duster worms or large-polyped stony corals.

Family Chaetodontidae (butterflyfishes)

Genera: 11

Species: 120

The butterflyfishes have a laterally compressed body, no spine on the preopercle, stout dorsal and anal fin spines, a continuous or slightly notched dorsal fin, scales extending onto the dorsal and anal fins, a small mouth at the end of a snout (which can vary in length), and brushlike teeth. Butterflyfish larvae (known as the tholichthys stage) are both different from their parents and distinct from other reef fishes. They have bony head armor that often sports serrated spines. The largest member of the butterflyfish family attains a maximum length of 30 cm (11.8 in.). Most butterflyfishes are brightly colored, often sporting false eyespots and obliterative eye lines to deflect the attacks of predators. These fishes all occur in marine habitats and reach their apex of diversity on coral reefs. The majority of species are most abundant at depths of less than 20 m (65 ft.), although there are some deep-water forms that range to depths of at least 200 m (650 ft.). Many are specialized feeders that consume coral polyps and/or other sessile invertebrates; others are also omnivores, while a smaller number are zooplankton feeders. Long-term pair bonding appears to be common in this family, with pair members defending a large territory from conspecifics and food competitors.

Heniochus diphreutes, Schooling Bannerfish (Maldives).

Captive Care: The butterflyfishes vary greatly in their suitability to aquarium life. In many cases, this is a function of their diet. Some species (the obligate coral feeders) rarely, if ever, survive in captivity, while others are durable aquarium inhabitants. These fishes are best kept by the more experienced aquarist. Provide a large aquarium with plenty of swimming room and a number of "bolt holes"—hiding places into which they can dash if threatened. Do not keep with overly aggressive tankmates, or add the butterflies first to let them become established before introducing any potentially belligerent species.

Feeding: The butterfly species that typically do well in captivity will eat many different live, fresh, and prepared foods. Offer a varied diet and feed frequently—at least twice per day.

Other Advice: With the butterflyfishes, it is essential to select the species to be kept very carefully. While some butterflyfishes adapt well to captive conditions, many other species offered for sale have very narrow feeding requirements that are difficult—if not impossible—to meet in an aquarium.

Family Pomacanthidae (angelfishes)

Genera: 9

Species: 74

The marine angelfishes are closely related to the butterflyfishes, but are easily separated by the prominent spine present on the preopercle. They also have a long, continuous dorsal fin. Both the anal and dorsal fin often have long filaments extending from the trailing edge. The caudal fin can be truncate or lunate (as in the zooplankton-feeding *Genicanthus* spp.). The largest pomacanthid reaches a maximum length of 46 cm (18.1 in.). Many are chromatically blessed, exhibiting striking colors and remarkable patterns. In some species, the juveniles are much different in color from the adults. Some are facultative cleaners, removing parasites and necrotic tissue from other fishes. There are also some species (including all the *Genicanthus* spp.) that display striking sexual dichromatism and sexual dimorphism (males are usually larger than females). Many of these fishes are haremic, and most feed on sessile invertebrates and algae.

Captive Care: Some of the angelfishes are well suited to aquarium life, while others ignore most foods in captivity and gradually perish. (Some species have a difficult time switching from their natural diets, which may include sponges and tunicates, and are not good aquarium candidates.) Provide a suitably sized aquarium with both ample swimming room and rocky hiding places. Keep only one specimen of each species per aquarium (unless you aquire a mated pair), and limit yourself to just one member of the family per tank, unless you have a large tank and are an experienced aquarist.

Feeding: Offer a varied diet that includes plant material (especially for juveniles and pygmy angelfishes) and special frozen angelfish rations that include marine sponges. Feed at least twice a day. Many angelfishes do best if placed in a tank with a lush turf of filamentous algae and/or well-established live rock that offers constant foraging opportunities.

Other Advice: Always know the traits and captive care requirements of an an-

Facing page: *Pomacanthus imperator*, Emperor Angelfish (Fiji).

gelfish species before making a purchase. Always quarantine angelfishes in an adequately sized hospital tank before introduction to the display aquarium. Some angelfish species (e.g., *Centropyge* spp.) can be housed in reef aquariums, although many will nip at large-polyped stony corals, gorgonians, and/or tridacnid clam mantles.

Family Pentacerotidae (armorheads or boarfishes)
Subfamilies: 3

Genera: 7

Species: 11

The armorheads or boarfishes are compressed, deep-bodied fishes with a steep or gently sloping head profile, an armored head, an elongate snout with a small mouth at the end, and bands of fine, conical teeth in the front of the jaws (some species have molariform teeth in the back of the jaws). Some have short, whiskerlike barbels on the chin, rough bones, a long continuous dorsal fin with 4 to 15 stout spines, a high, sail-like dorsal fin, and large pelvic fins with a strong spine. Many of the shallow-water forms sport thick, dark bands on the body. The armorheads are found in marine habitats in warm temperate and tropical seas. They occur at depths of 15 to 650 m (49 to 2,113 ft.) and are found singly, in pairs, and even in large groups. The long snout of the armorheads enables them to pluck crustaceans, worms, and echinoderms from reef cracks and crevices. At least one of these species, the Whiskered Armorhead (*Evistias acutirostris*), apparently feeds heavily on brittle stars.

Captive Care: These fishes are rarely encountered in the aquarium trade. The Whiskered Armorhead can be kept in the aquarium, although it may need to be given brittle stars to incite a feeding response.

Family Kyphosidae (sea chubs)
Subfamilies: 5

Genera: 15

Species: 42

The sea chubs are moderately deep-bodied, with a small head, a small mouth, incisiform teeth, a long continuous dorsal fin, and a forked caudal fin. All of the sea chubs are marine species. Most occur inshore and feed on algae, which they crop off of hard substrates. A few (especially juvenile individuals) are found associating with rafts of *Sargassum*. Some of the sea chubs are solitary, while others form schools. Although they are usually drab in color, a few of these fishes do produce an occasional xanthic, or golden, individual.

Captive Care: Because of their normal lack of dramatic color, sea chubs are rarely sought by aquarists but may be acquired by amateur collectors. Provide a medium- to large-sized aquarium with plenty of swimming room.

Feeding: Offer a diet heavy in vegetable matter.

Other Advice: An appropriate sea chub system would include lush algae growth, which is discouraged in more typical aquarium settings.

Family Teraponidae (grunters and tigerfishes)

Genera: 16

Species: 45

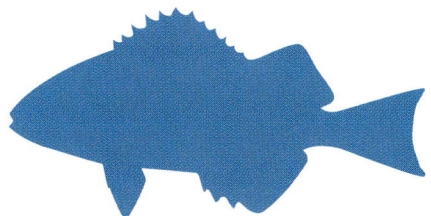

Many of the grunters and tigerfishes occur in freshwater, while others live in brackish and marine habitats, and a few occur near coral reefs. One genus (*Terapon*) is found in adjacent habitats like mangrove swamps. Teraponids are oblong and slightly compressed. They have two spines on the opercle, a notched dorsal fin (the spinous portion of which can be depressed into a groove formed by a sheath of scales), a pelvic fin base behind the pectoral fin base, and a lateral line that is continuous and extends onto the caudal fin. In most species, there are no teeth on the vomer and palatines. These fishes produce sound with their transversely divided swim bladders. The largest member of the family reaches 80 cm (31.5 in.) in length.

Captive Care: The grunters and tigerfishes are virtually never seen in the marine aquarium trade, but at least one species is occasionally sold for brackish-water tanks.

Family Kuhliidae (flagtails)

Genera: 1

Species: 8

The flagtails have moderately deep, slightly compressed bodies, with a notched dorsal fin, which, along with the anal fin, has a scaly sheath along the base. They have relatively large eyes and two spines on the opercle. Most species are silver overall. The flagtails occur in marine and brackish environments, and at least one species lives in freshwater. One species lives along rocky coastlines, often forming schools in the surge zone. These fishes are nocturnal and feed on zooplankton.

Captive Care: Flagtails are not a favorite with marine aquarists and are only occasionally found in aquarium stores.

Family Microcanthidae (stripies)

Genera: 3

Species: 5

In the past, the stripies have been regarded as a subgroup within the butterflyfish (Chaetodontidae) and chub (Kyphosidae) families. (Some still consider them a subfamily of the latter group.) They have compressed, deep bodies, with a small mouth that has numerous rows of slender teeth in the jaws. They have large eyes, a single continuous dorsal fin, and bold color patterns. Most of these fishes occur in warm temperate seas and are restricted in distribution to the Pacific (most are found around Australia and New Zealand). The Stripey (*Microcanthus strigatus*) has been reported from coral reefs, where it occurs in harbors, lagoons, and coastal bays. It usually occurs in small to large shoals and feeds on plant material and small invertebrates. This species attains 16 cm (6.3 in.), and individuals can be pale to a brilliant yellow.

Captive Care: The Stripey is occasionally available to aquarists and is a hardy aquarium fish suitable for the beginning hobbyist. Provide a large tank with ample swimming space.

Feeding: Easy to feed, the Stripey should be offered a varied diet including both meaty marine items and vegetable matter.

Other Advice: Stripies can be kept in schools and make an attractive and unusual display.

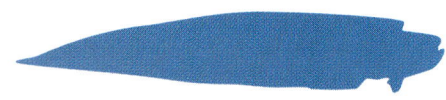

Family Cepolidae (bandfishes)

Subfamilies: 2

Genera: 4

Species: 19

The bandfishes are an odd family that has an elongate body that becomes tapered toward the tail, a long dorsal fin that has zero to four spines, dorsal and anal fins that are contiguous with the pointed caudal fin, and a lateral line along the base of the dorsal fin. Most bandfishes are red or pink in color. The largest species attains a maximum length of 70 cm (27.5 in.). At least one species occurs in sand or mud slopes near coastal reefs; this fish occurs in small to large colonies, in burrows it digs in the substrate. It feeds on zooplankton.

Captive Care: On rare occasions, one species of bandfish does show up in the aquarium trade, but it is very difficult to keep.

Family Pomacentridae (damselfishes)

Subfamilies: 4
Genera: 28
Species: 320+

Pomacentrids belong to the Suborder Labroidei, which includes the popular freshwater fish family known as cichlids (Cichlidae), the surfperches (Family Embiotocidae), the wrasses (Labridae), and the parrotfishes (Scaridae). The damselfishes have a deep, compressed body with a small mouth, an incomplete or interrupted lateral line, a toothless palate, and a single continuous dorsal fin. The largest pomacentrid reaches 35 cm (13.8 in.). The Subfamily Amphiprioninae (anemonefishes) includes some of the most popular aquarium fishes. They are well known for the symbiotic relationship they form with sea anemones. These anemonefishes have a serrated opercle, and most have 10

Amphiprion nigripes, Maldives Anemonefish, with its host, *Heteractis magnifica*, Magnificent Sea Anemone (Maldives).

dorsal spines (9 or 11 observed in some species). There are 2 genera and 26 species (some include *Amphiprion leucokranos* as a distinct species, although data indicates this is a hybrid). Most of these are colorful and many have white bands on the head or body. The Subfamily Chrominae contains 4 genera and 87 species, many of which are obligatory stony coral dwellers that feed on passing plankton. Some of these have deep bodies with a truncate tail (e.g., *Dascyllus*), while others are more elongate with a forked caudal fin. The Subfamily Lepidozyginae includes one planktivorous species that forms shoals. This fish, known as the Fusilier Damselfish (*Lepidozygus tapeinosoma*), is also a social mimic, adopting the color patterns of other shoaling zooplanktivores (especially anthias, *Pseudanthias* spp.). The Subfamily Pomacentrinae is the most specious group, consisting of 21 genera with about 199 species. Most of these fishes are territorial, defending a feeding territory from conspecifics and other food competitors. These fishes actively "farm" their territories, which greatly increases the productivity of their algal lawn. Many of these damselfishes lay demersal eggs, which the male tends and protects.

Captive Care: The damselfishes are durable and often-colorful aquarium inhabitants. The only drawback with these fishes is that some can be very aggressive, terrorizing other fishes and making it difficult to achieve a social balance in the confines of a tank. Damselfishes are accustomed to darting for cover to avoid predation, and they should be provided with a habitat that contains numerous hiding places.

Feeding: Offer a varied diet that includes plenty of plant material.

Other Advice: Know the difference between damselfish species to avoid buying bullies or fishes that are beautiful as juveniles but that become drably colored and aggressive as adults. Do not try to keep members of the genus *Stegastes* or *Eupomacentrus* in a peaceful community aquarium or with small-polyped stony corals (they may nip off the polyps to farm filamentous algae). Keep members of the genus *Chromis* in shoals and do not house them with overly aggressive tankmates.

Family Labridae (wrasses)
Genera: 60

Species: 500+

One of the largest reef fish families, wrasses are very diverse in shape, but all species have a protractile mouth, teeth that are separated and that project outward, a dorsal fin with 8 to 21 spines and 6 to 21 rays, an anal fin with 4

Paracheilinus angulatus, Lyretail Flasher Wrasse.

to 6 spines and 7 to 18 soft rays, cycloid scales, and a continuous or interrupted lateral line. Most wrasses have pelvic fins—the only species that does not have pelvic fins or a pelvic girdle is *Conniella apterygia*. Wrasses range in size from 5 cm (2.0 in.) to over 2 m (6.5 ft.) and all are found in marine habitats, occurring in tropical to temperate seas. The color of the wrasses is incredibly diverse. The food habits and feeding behavior of the wrasses is also quite variable, although most are carnivorous and feed on benthic invertebrates. Some are also fish-eaters, while others feed on zooplankton. Many of the zooplankton feeders form shoals, while many wrasses exhibit a haremic social structure. Some labrids pick parasites, dead tissue, and slime off other fishes.

Captive Care: Most wrasses do well in aquarium confines, although there are some that reject aquarium fare and/or that ship poorly. Many species are well suited to the reef aquarium, and some of these can perform a beneficial function in this setting (e.g., eating problem flatworms or parasitic snails). In this very diverse group are bold members that can be kept with aggressive tankmates and others that are easily intimidated and do best if housed in a peaceful community setting. Wrasses are accomplished jumpers and should always be kept in a securely covered tank.

Feeding: Feed a varied diet that includes plenty of crustacean meat (enriched brine shrimp, mysid shrimp, and appropriate-sized krill are good staple foods). Several groups must be housed with live rock or in an aquarium with a productive refugium if they are going to thrive. Zooplankton-feeding species, like the fairy wrasses (*Cirrhilabrus* spp.) and flasher wrasses (*Paracheilinus* spp.), are best suited for the reef aquarium.

Other Advice: Research a prospective wrasse purchase very carefully. Some species grow too large for the home aquarium and others are simply unsuited to reef-tank conditions (some will avidly feed on desirable invertebrates, others will flip over hard corals when searching for food).

Family Scaridae (parrotfishes)

Subfamilies: 2

Genera: 9

Species: 83

Found in the Suborder Labroidei with the wrasses, parrotfishes are distinguished by a mouth that is not protractile, teeth that are fused to form a beak, and large cycloid scales. The dorsal spine has 9 spines and 10 soft rays, the anal fin has 3 spines and 9 soft rays. All of the parrotfishes occur in marine habitats, and many occur on coral reefs. They use their beaklike teeth to scrape boring algae out of carbonate substrates, while a few bite off chunks of living corals or browse on macroalgae. Some form schools or shoals, while others are solitary creatures. Most parrotfishes are sexually dichromatic and protogynous hermaphrodites. The feeding behavior of these fishes is responsible for the production of much of the sand that occurs around coral reefs.

Captive Care: Although several species do appear in the aquarium trade, most of the parrotfishes are too active and too large for the confines of a home-scale system. Provide an extra-large aquarium (at least 240 gallons for most species) with plenty of swimming space.

Feeding: Feed them a varied diet composed primarily of plant material. Offer plaster-matrix feeding blocks impregnated with plant matter, flake food, and/or shrimp; pieces of coral rubble with boring algae are needed to help wear down their beaks. Some species will eat live stony corals.

Other Advice: Many aquarists believe that the parrotfishes are best left on the reef or in the hands of professional aquarists with huge systems.

Family Pholidichthyidae (Convict Blenny)

Genera: 1

Species: 1

The single species in this family, *Pholidichthys leucotaenia*, is an elongate, eel-like fish that has no scales, one nostril on each side of the head, pelvic fins that are located just below the pectoral fin base, and a round caudal fin that

Sparisoma viride, Stoplight Parrotfish (terminal male) (Bonaire).

is contiguous with the dorsal and anal fins. The color of this fish changes as it grows. The juveniles school—apparently mimicking groups of the venomous Striped Eel Catfish (*Plotosus lineatus*). They lay demersal eggs, which the parents tend.

Captive Care: The Convict Blenny is an industrious digger that will excavate holes and extensive tunnels under aquarium decor. This behavior can be advantageous, as it helps put detritus into suspension where it can be removed by external filters. It can also be problematic, as it can undermine aquarium decorations placed atop sand substrates and cause them to collapse. Provide a medium- to large-sized aquarium with plenty of hiding places. Prepare the tank for the introduction of the Convict Blenny by arranging a foundation of rockwork directly on the bare aquarium floor, then add 5 cm (2 in.) of live sand around the rock.

Feeding: Feed a varied diet that includes small crustaceans (mysid shrimp is an excellent staple food).

Other Advice: Larger adults will eat ornamental shrimps and tiny fishes.

Family Trichonotidae (sand divers)

Genera: 1

Species: 6

Sand divers are very elongate fishes, with the anterior rays of the dorsal fin being elongate in the males of some species, and the lower jaw extending past the upper jaw. The scales along the lateral line have a deep V-shaped notch. Epineural and pleural ribs are present. These species are all marine, and most occur on sand flats adjacent to coral reefs. The sand divers typically occur in shoals consisting of fewer males than females; they escape predators by diving under the sand.

Captive Care: Sand divers are rare in the aquarium trade but do show up occasionally. They are sensitive fishes and difficult to sustain in most captive settings, although they can be kept if provided with an extra-large tank that has plenty of open bottom space with a thick layer of sand substrate—at least 10 cm (3.9 in.) in depth. Be sure the system is equipped with a top that covers the entire tank. Keep the aquarium in a low-traffic area (or use one-way glass for the front panel) and move very slowly when working around or inside the aquarium. Decor should be excluded or kept to a minimum.

Feeding: Offer live foods, including vitamin-enriched brine shrimp.

Other Advice: Do not attempt to keep sand divers with aggressive tankmates.

Family Pinguipedidae (sand perches)

Genera: 4

Species: 50

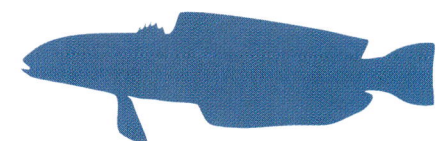

Sand perches have elongate, cylindrical bodies, with pelvic fins placed slightly in front of the pectorals, a continuous dorsal fin with 4 to 7 short spines and 19 to 27 rays, and a continuous lateral line. The sand perches are all found in marine habitats in tropical to temperate seas. Many occur on or near coral reefs, where they spend their time sitting on or scooting over sand or rubble bottoms. Most feed on benthic invertebrates and small fishes, although one species is a zooplanktivore. At least some species are haremic, with males defending a large territory that contains several females. Males differ in color from females in some species.

Captive Care: Sand perches are durable aquarium residents, although not recommended for communities with smaller fishes, tubeworms, or ornamental shrimps. Provide a medium- to large-sized aquarium with a full cover and sand or coral rubble substrate on the bottom.

Feeding: Provide a varied diet, including crustaceans.

Other Advice: Sand perches can be aggressive toward fish tankmates that live on the substrate, while large adults will eat small fishes. Some species will eat undesirable bristleworms.

Family Uranoscopidae (stargazers)

Genera: 8

Species: 50

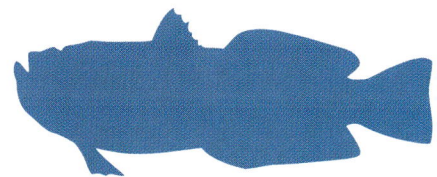

Most stargazers are found on open sand or mud bottoms—not on or near reefs. They have a large head and elongate body that tapers toward the tail; a large, oblique mouth; small, smooth scales, or no scales; fringed lips that prevent sand from entering the mouth; eyes on top of the head; a lateral line that is on the upper part of the side; and pelvic fins far forward on the body (under the throat). They have a long dorsal and anal fin, with the spinous portion of the dorsal being absent in many species. Other species have a wormlike appendage that is attached to the bottom of the mouth. This structure extends from the mouth and apparently functions to attract small fishes. Members of at least one genus (*Astroscopus*) possess electric organs. The stargazers often bury in the substrate—with only the top of the head exposed—and ambush passing fishes and crustaceans. They are marine fishes that sometimes enter brackish-water estuaries.

Captive Care: These fishes are rarely offered in the marine aquarium trade.

Provide them with a medium- to large-sized aquarium that has a deep (10 cm [3.9 in.]) layer of sand in which they can bury. As in nature, they will eat small fishes and ornamental shrimps.

Feeding: Live foods, such as feeder fish and grass shrimp, may be needed to induce an initial feeding response, after which these fishes should gradually be switched to a more varied diet of nonliving foods.

Other Advice: View after dark with a flashlight that emits a red beam or with a red light mounted over the tank.

Family Tripterygiidae (triplefins)

Genera: 20

Species: 115

The triplefins are elongate fishes with the dorsal fin divided into three parts (hence the name)—the first two parts have spines, while the third has only soft rays. There are no cirri on the nape, and the pectoral fins are large. These are small fishes, the largest attaining a maximum length of 5 cm (2.0 in.). Many live on coral reefs, and all but one are limited to marine environments. They occur in tropical and temperate seas, with New Zealand possibly boasting the greatest number of species. Many are colorful, but are easily overlooked because of their small size. They feed on small benthic invertebrates.

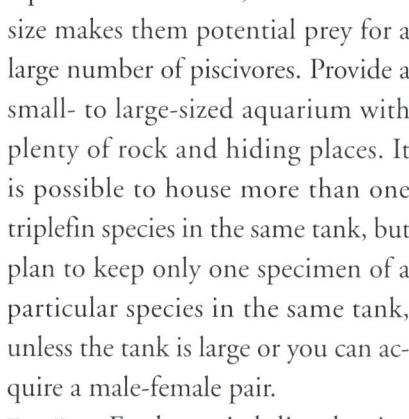

Helcogramma striata, Striped Triplefin (North Sulawesi).

Captive Care: The triplefins are desirable aquarium inhabitants, but their small size makes them potential prey for a large number of piscivores. Provide a small- to large-sized aquarium with plenty of rock and hiding places. It is possible to house more than one triplefin species in the same tank, but plan to keep only one specimen of a particular species in the same tank, unless the tank is large or you can acquire a male-female pair.

Feeding: Feed a varied diet that includes plenty of small crustaceans, such as brine shrimp.

Other Advice: Triplefins are an excellent choice for the reef aquarium, where they can forage on and among the live rock.

Family Dactyloscopidae (sand stargazers)

Genera: 9

Species: 41

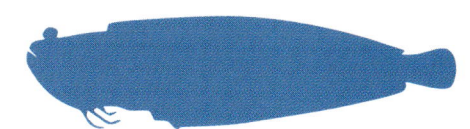

The sand stargazers have an elongate body, a big head, and an oblique mouth with fringed lips. The eyes are on top of the head and, in some species, rest on a stalk. Most of the sand stargazers also have fingerlike projections on the edge of the gill membrane, which may prevent sediment from plugging the branchial chamber. The largest sand stargazer attains a maximum length of 15 cm (5.9 in.). These fishes are all marine (a few will enter estuaries) and live on soft substrates, under which they bury. They respire by branchiostegal pumping, rather than by opercular pumping.

Captive Care: Sand stargazers are rare in the aquarium trade, although one species is occasionally collected and sold from Florida. Provide a small- to medium-sized aquarium with a 5 cm (2 in.) bottom layer of sand.

Feeding: Because they are so reclusive, these fishes can be very difficult to feed. Offer very small crustaceans, including brine shrimp, small krill, and mysid shrimp.

Other Advice: Don't expect to see much of these fishes. Most sand stargazers are very secretive, burrowing under the sand during the day.

Family Labrisomidae (weed blennies)

Genera: 16

Species: 100

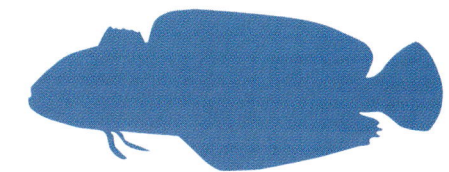

The weed blennies have an elongate body with cirri present on the nape, near the nostril, and above the eye. The long dorsal fin has more spines than soft rays. The largest species in this family reaches a maximum length of 23 cm (9.1 in.). Some of these fishes are ovoviviparous (give birth to live young), while members of one genus (*Starksia*) have an intromittent organ that is used to transfer sperm. These are marine species, most of which occur in the tropical Western Atlantic, with some species living among the tentacles of sea anemones.

Captive Care: Weed blennies do make their way into the aquarium trade and are suitable for both fish-only tanks and reef aquariums. Provide a small to large aquarium with plenty of hiding places. It is possible to house more than one weed blenny species in the same tank, but keep only one specimen of each particular species, unless the tank is extra large or you can acquire a male-female pair.

Feeding: Offer a varied diet with primary emphasis on small crustaceans.

Other Advice: Large individuals may prove too predatory for reef systems, eating chitons, limpets, snails, serpent stars, and small fishes.

Family Clinidae (clinid blennies)

Genera: 20

Species: 73

The clinid blennies are elongate fishes, with a long continuous dorsal fin that has more spines than soft rays and no cirri on the nape (although they can be present in other locations). The largest member of the family reaches a maximum length of 60 cm (23.6 in.), but most are much smaller. These are marine fishes, the majority of which occur in temperate regions. A few are coral reef dwellers. Some are ovoviviparous (eggs hatch within the parent), with the male possessing an intromittent organ.

Captive Care: Clinid blennies rarely enter the aquarium trade. They can be kept by providing a small to large aquarium with rocky aquascaping and plenty of hiding places. It is possible to house more than one clinid blenny species in the same tank, but don't try to keep more than one specimen of a particular species together, unless you have a large system or a male-female pair.

Feeding: Offer a varied diet that includes regular feedings of small crustaceans.

Other Advice: Large individuals will eat chitons, limpets, snails, serpent stars, and small fishes.

Family Chaenopsidae (tube blennies and pike blennies)

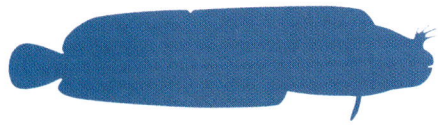

Genera: 9

Species: 60

The tube blennies are elongate and compressed, with a long, continuous dorsal fin that can be sail-like in some species. They have no lateral line, no scales, no cirri on the nape, and they may or may not have cirri over the eyes and nostrils. The head is often spiny or rough. All of the tube blennies occur in marine habitats and all associate with coral or rocky reefs. The tropical Western Atlantic and Eastern Pacific support the most diverse tube blenny communities. Most of these fishes live in empty, calcareous tubes constructed by serpulid worms. They back into the opening of the tube and dart out to capture passing plankton. The pike blennies (*Chaenopsis* spp.), which are eel-like in form, are often observed in repose on sand and hard substrates and are more voracious, feeding on small fishes and crustaceans. The pike blennies are also the largest members of the family, with the giant of the genus measuring 16 cm (6.3 in.) in length. Most of the tube blennies attain less than 6 cm (2.4 in.) in length.

Captive Care: Although the tube and pike blennies are only occasionally offered in aquarium stores, they make interesting and durable aquarium inhabitants—especially in a smaller tank. Provide a rocky aquascape, if possible, including rocks with small holes, such as empty calcareous tubeworm tubes, where they can hide. With the exception of the pike blennies (*Chaenopsis* spp.), it is possible to house more than one of these blennies, of the same or different species, in the same tank.

Feeding: Feed a varied diet based on small crustaceans, such as brine shrimp, frozen ocean plankton, and mysid shrimp.

Other Advice: Large pike blennies will eat ornamental crustaceans and small fishes, while the tube blennies are harmless.

Family Blenniidae (blennies or combtooth blennies)

Genera: 53

Species: 345

The blennies are a diverse group of elongate, laterally compressed fishes, with no scales, a blunt head, pelvic fins that are positioned in front of the pectoral fin base (members of the genus *Plagiotremus* lack pelvic fins), comb-like teeth, a long, continuous dorsal fin that has fewer spines than soft rays (in the majority of species). The adults of most species lack a swim bladder (the members of the genera *Aspidontus, Meiacanthus, Petroscirtes*, and *Plagiotremus* have a very small swim bladder). Almost all the blennies inhabit marine habitats, although at least one (*Meiacanthus anema*) enters freshwater. Others may occur in brackish estuaries. Most of the blennies scrape diatoms and filamentous algae off hard substrates. Some blennies have venomous fangs and will bite the inside of a piscivore's mouth if they are ingested. Harmless blennies, cardinalfishes, and sea breams mimic some of these venomous species. There are also predatory blennies that prey on small invertebrates, while others meet their nutritional needs by biting scales and slime from the bodies of unsuspecting fishes.

Captive Care: A relatively small number of blennies are available to aquarists. For example, only two species in the genus *Ecsenius*, which is comprised of 46 small species—most of them attractively marked—are regularly seen in the aquarium trade. Many do well in captivity, especially if the tank contains a healthy growth of microalgae. Provide a small to large aquarium aquascaped

Parablennius marmoreus, Seaweed Blenny.

with an ample quantity of rock for hiding and grazing. Except when keeping a mated pair, a single specimen of a particular species per aquarium is the rule. However, it is possible to keep blennies of different species in the same aquarium, although closely related forms may fight.

Feeding: Feed a varied diet that includes regular offerings of plant material. (Some species require an established system with a rich growth of microalgae to thrive.)

Other Advice: Some of the blennies feed on the scales of larger fishes, while others have poison fangs they can use if attacked by a piscivore. Some blennies eat live stony corals, while others will nip tridacnid clam mantles.

Family Gobiesocidae (clingfishes)

Genera: 36

Species: 120

Clingfishes are often tadpole-shaped, with a large head and a body that tapers toward the tail. They have modified pelvic fins that form a suction disc, which enables them to cling to hard bottoms in areas with a lot of surge. These fishes are characterized by urogenital papillae behind the anus, no swim bladder, no scales, and no fin spines. They also produce copious amounts of slime (in at least one species, the slime is toxic). All of these fishes are marine, and most occur in shallow, inshore waters. In fact, many inhabit the intertidal zone, living in small tidepools in crevices and under rocks. Several species associate with crinoids or live among the spines of sea urchins. Most feed on small benthic invertebrates (including barnacles, limpets, and small crustaceans). Some of the larger forms will ambush small fishes that swim past. At least one rocky reef species is known to move over the bodies of larger fishes and remove parasites. Clingfishes are resilient to desiccation, having been known to live out of water (if kept moist) for several days, and many can withstand a wide range of temperatures. Males (or sometimes both parents) of some species guard a nest of adhesive eggs, which they cover with secreted slime when the tide recedes.

Captive Care: Although few of these unusual fishes enter the aquarium trade, those that do are very durable—although often secretive—aquarium inhabitants. Provide a small aquarium with suitable hiding places.

Feeding: Larger individuals will eat a wide array of foods, including small feeder fishes. Some species are microhabitat specialists, with specialized diets.

Other Advice: Clingfishes generally will not bother other fishes, but may fight with conspecifics if housed in a smaller aquarium.

Family Callionymidae (dragonets)

Genera: 11

Species: 155

The dragonets are elongate fishes and most are slightly depressed in shape. They have a small, protrusible mouth, small gill openings, and a stout spine on the preopercle. Most of the dragonets occur in marine environments, although at least two are known to enter rivers. Some of the species are very colorful. Many dragonets are sexually dichromatic or sexually dimorphic (the male typically has longer spines in the spinous dorsal fin and is usually larger than the female). The largest dragonet attains a maximum length of

25 cm (9.8 in.). They pick small invertebrates off the substrate and produce pelagic eggs. Certain dragonets also exude copious amounts of slime, which may be toxic or at least distasteful.

Captive Care: Two dragonets, *Synchiropus picturatus* and *Synchiropus splendidus*, commonly called mandarinfishes, are extremely popular with aquarists, although most are difficult to maintain unless they are housed in an aquarium full of live rock or live sand. Provide a small- to large-sized aquarium with a layer of live sand on the aquarium bottom for those species that live on soft substrates. Create an aquascape of live rock with numerous hiding places for those species that live on hard reef substrates. Hard-substrate dwellers are great choices for reef aquariums.

Feeding: Dragonets should only be placed in well-established systems that have populations of small crustaceans, such as copepods and amphipods, breeding in the live rock and/or live sand. Growths of filamentous algae are a good sign in a dragonet system. Reinoculate the aquarium with potential prey cultures by replacing some of the live rock and live sand on occasion and/or connect the display tank to a productive refugium. Supplement the dragonet diet with live brine shrimp and other small crustaceans and worms.

Other Advice: Do not place mandarin fishes in the same aquarium with other active hunters of small invertebrate prey, such as wrasses in the genera *Halichoeres* and *Pseudocheilinus*, which will prove too competitive. Some dragonets will help control populations of noxious flatworms.

Family Gobiidae (gobies)

Subfamilies: 5

Genera: 212+

Species: 2,000+

The gobies represent the largest family of marine fishes, with new genera and species still being discovered and identified. Most of the gobies are elongate and slightly compressed, with large, united pelvic fins that serve as an adhesive disc in some species. Most species have two dorsal fins (the spinous dorsal is absent in some species). Cycloid or ctenoid scales are usually present (scales are absent in a few species). The majority of gobies are relatively small (the shortest fish in the world is a goby), but the largest species can reach 50 cm (20 in.). Most live in marine environments, but some occur in brackish water or freshwater. A large number of gobies associate with other marine organisms. For example, a number of gobies live in burrows with snapping shrimps, others are found only on black corals or sea whips, and

Amblygobius rainfordi, Rainford's Goby (North Sulawesi).

some live in sponge lumens or among the branches of stony corals. Most of these fishes feed on small motile invertebrates, while some also pick parasites from the mouth, gills, and body surfaces of larger fishes—including piscivorous species. Most gobies produce demersal eggs. In some species, the male guards and fans the eggs.

Captive Care: Gobies are popular aquarium fishes, but come from a very large family whose members vary greatly in their life histories and aquarium hardiness. Research group members carefully before purchasing. Provide a small to large aquarium, depending on the species. Be sure the tank is equipped with a full top and has ample decor and suitable hiding places for species that live on hard substrates. For those found on soft substrates, provide a layer of live sand (minimum 5 cm [2 in.]) with a large, open expanse of bottom space.

Feeding: Feed a varied diet that includes small, vitamin-enriched crustaceans. Some species should be fed several times a day, while others require infrequent food introduction. Some (*Amblygobius* spp.) do best if housed in a tank with lush filamentous algae growth.

Other Advice: Many gobies are well-suited for the reef aquarium. Some species will consume noxious bristleworms and are effective for bioturbation of the upper layers of the substrate.

Family Microdesmidae (dartfishes and wormfishes)

Subfamilies: 2

Genera: 10

Species: 73

The dartfishes and wormfishes have very elongate, slightly compressed bodies, with small, deeply embedded cycloid scales, and no lateral line. The members of the Subfamily Microdesminae, commonly known as the wormfishes, have a large lower jaw that protrudes beyond the snout tip and a long continuous dorsal fin. The wormfishes employ an anguilliform locomotory mode and bury under the substrate both when threatened and at night. There are 5 genera with 30 species in this subfamily. The Subfamily Ptereleotrinae, which are known as dartfishes and fire gobies, have a vertical mouth, without the protruding lower jaw. Most have two separate dorsal fins (except *Ptereleotris monoptera*, which has connected fins). The dartfishes swim above the substrate and feed on zooplankton. Some live in pairs, while others form shoals; most dash into burrows when threatened. This subfamily is composed of 5 genera with 43 species.

Nemateleotris helfrichi, Helfrich's Firefish.

Captive Care: A number of dartfishes are available to aquarists, and all are highly desirable additions to a quiet fish-only system or a reef aquarium without aggressive tankmates. A small to large aquarium with a top that covers the entire tank should be provided with a layer of coral sand (a minimum of 5 cm [2 in.]) and/or rubble with some small live rock caves and plenty of open bottom space.

Feeding: Feed a varied diet that includes small, vitamin-enriched crustaceans. Most will only require a single feeding per day.

Other Advice: These fishes are well-suited for the reef aquarium.

Family Ephippidae (spadefishes and batfishes)

Genera: 7

Species: 20

Ephippids are highly compressed and deep-bodied, with a small mouth and bands of small teeth. The spinous portion of the dorsal fin is distinct from the soft portion in some (*Chaetodipterus* spp.) and hard to differentiate in others (*Platax* spp.). The rear nostril is elongate, and many have a steep head profile. In members of the genus *Platax* (commonly called batfishes, not to be confused with walking batfishes, Family Ogcocephalidae), the juveniles have long dorsal and anal fins with a deeper body, but the fins become shorter and the body longer as they grow larger. Most of the spadefishes are marine, although some do enter brackish habitats. A number of species live on or near coral reefs; the juveniles of some of these species inhabit mangrove areas where they float near the water's surface, mimicking fallen leaves. The juveniles of one species appear to mimic a noxious flatworm, while the young of other *Platax* have been observed floating out at sea with algae and other drifting objects. The spadefishes feed on a wide variety of invertebrates, especially jellyfishes and sessile forms like anemones, hydroids, and polychaete worms.

Captive Care: Although most will outgrow the standard home aquarium, many ephippids are hardy captives. However, one of the most beautiful specimens, the Pinnate or Red-finned Batfish (*Platax pinnatus*), is notorious for refusing captive fare. Provide an extra-large, high aquarium, with plenty of swimming room and minimal decor. Conspecifics and heterospecifics can be kept

Chaetodipterus faber, Atlantic Spadefish.

in the same tank together, but do not attempt to keep these fishes with overly aggressive species or with potential fin-nippers.

Feeding: Offer a varied diet that includes some vegetable matter. Feed several times a day.

Other Advice: The spadefishes and batfishes are not good candidates for a reef tank and will eat a wide variety of invertebrates, including cnidarians (e.g., corals, anemones). They are also prone to contracting skin parasites, especially marine ich (*Cryptocaryon irritans*).

Family Scatophagidae (scats)

Genera: 1

Species: 4

All of the scats are highly compressed with a steep head profile. They have a small mouth with brushlike teeth, and the dorsal fin is deeply notched with stout spines in the anterior portion (which may be venomous). These fishes occur in marine, brackish, and freshwater habitats, such as mangrove areas and estuaries. The scats, or "dung eaters" (this is the literal translation of the family name), feed on algae, small invertebrates, and offal.

Captive Care: Juvenile scats, which are often more colorful than the adults, are regularly sold in aquarium stores for freshwater and brackish-water tanks, but can also be kept in full-strength seawater. Provide a medium to large aquarium with plenty of swimming room. Scats can be kept in small groups in larger aquariums.

Feeding: Offer a varied diet, including regular feedings of vegetable matter.

Other Advice: Scats are prone to contracting skin parasites and fungal infections. In reef tanks, they will consume decorative macroalgae and may pick at some sessile invertebrates.

Family Siganidae (rabbitfishes)

Genera: 1

Species: 27

The rabbitfishes have a highly compressed, elliptical-shaped body, with stout, venomous dorsal and anal spines, protruding incisiform teeth (hence the common name), and small, deeply embedded cycloid scales. These fishes occur in saltwater and brackish water, with about half of the species being more common in inshore seagrass beds and estuaries. The other half are abundant on coral reefs. The reef-dwelling forms are often brightly colored and may form pairs or small shoals. Most rabbitfishes are herbivores that browse on macroalgae, although at least one species is also coprophagous—it consumes the feces of other fishes.

Captive Care: Unfortunately, relatively few of the rabbitfishes show up in the aquarium trade. Those that do, however, are durable fishes that will help control some forms of undesirable algae. Provide a large aquarium with ample swimming space. Most species can be kept in pairs or with other members of the family.

Feeding: Offer a varied diet, including regular portions of vegetable matter. Feed several times a day, unless the tank has lots of algae, or secure pieces of dried macroalgae (i.e., nori) to the side of the tank with a lettuce clip.

Other Advice: Rabbitfishes have venomous fin spines and should be handled with care. They will consume decorative algae and may pick at some sessile invertebrates, like large-polyped stony corals. Some species will even graze on encrusting coralline algae.

Family Zanclidae (Moorish Idol)

Genera: 1

Species: 1

A lone species in its own genus, the Moorish Idol (*Zanclus cornutus*), is one of the most recognizable reef fishes in the world and commonly seen throughout its wide Indo-Pacific range. It is deeply compressed, with a long snout, brushlike teeth, no modified spines on the caudal peduncle, protuberances over the eyes in adults, and a long filament on the dorsal fin. Postlarval Moorish Idols settle out of the plankton at a very large size (about 8 cm [3.1 in.]). Its long snout is used to graze on coralline algae and sponges that inhabit reef crevices. The Moorish Idol often occurs singly, but will also form pairs or large shoals.

Captive Care: Although its graceful form and striking color pattern have attracted the attention of many marine aquarists, the Moorish Idol is typically difficult to acclimate and maintain for any length of time in the home aquarium. Experienced hobbyists who attempt to keep it should provide a well-established, extra-large aquarium with plenty of swimming room. Offer suitable hiding places in a formation of live rock, including a "bolt hole" (a hiding place it can dash into if threatened). Keep with peaceful, noncompetitive tankmates.

Feeding: Attempt to feed live, vitamin-enriched brine shrimp, frozen mysid shrimp, and vegetable matter. Provide with natural food sources, such as coralline algae and sponge-encrusted live rock.

Other Advice: This species has a very poor survival record, even among professional aquarists. Younger specimens may adapt more successfully than older, larger fishes.

Family Acanthuridae (surgeonfishes)

Subfamilies: 3
Genera: 6
Species: 72

Also known as the tangs or doctorfishes, the surgeonfishes are laterally compressed and have a continuous dorsal fin, a small, terminal mouth with spatulate, acute, or brushlike teeth, and a modified spine or spines on the side of the caudal peduncle. All the surgeonfishes have long intestines, and some have a gizzardlike stomach that facilitates mastication of food materials. There are three subfamilies, whose members are easily distinguished by the number and morphology of the caudal peduncle spines. The Subfamily Nasinae, the unicornfishes, has one or two fixed spines. The Subfamily Prionurinae has three to ten bony plates on the side of the caudal peduncle. The Subfamily Acanthurinae has a single spine that folds into a groove on the side of the caudal peduncle. The majority of the members of all three subfamilies occur on or adjacent to coral reef habitats. Some live in warm temperate seas, and these species normally inhabit rocky reefs. Most of the surgeonfishes are detritivores and/or herbivores, but the types of plant material consumed and the feeding behavior of each species varies within the family. For example, some suck detritus and diatoms off the sand, some browse on macroalgae, and others graze on unicellular algae growing on hard substrates. Surgeonfishes may defend a feeding territory, pairs may roam over a large home range, or roving shoals may form that swamp the defenses of territorial species.

Captive Care: Surgeonfishes constitute one of the most popular groups of marine aquarium species. They vary somewhat in their husbandry requirements and hardiness, but most need large quantities of plant material every day, a large-sized aquarium, and lots of swimming room. Be sure to know the maximum length attained by any species being considered for purchase (some surgeonfishes get too large for the average home aquarium). Provide suitable hiding places, including a "bolt hole" (a hiding place they can dash into if threatened). Provide brisk current and well-oxygenated water. Many surgeonfishes behave aggressively toward other fishes, especially other herbivores introduced after the surgeonfishes are established in the aquarium. It is

Acanthurus pyroferus, Chocolate Surgeonfish (juvenile) (North Sulawesi).

risky to keep members of the same species together in the same tank. Unless you have a large tank and are an experienced aquarist, keep no more than one member of the family per tank.

Feeding: Offer a diet that consists primarily of vegetable matter, including dried and frozen marine algae and leafy green lettuce. Feed several times a day, or secure pieces of dried macroalgae (i.e., nori) to the side of the tank with a lettuce clip.

Other Advice: Surgeonfishes, mostly from the genus *Zebrasoma*, are often employed to control undesirable algal growth in reef aquariums. Most reef aquarists have success with this arrangement, but acanthurids will also consume decorative macroalgae, and some species are prone to picking at sessile invertebrates like large-polyped stony corals. The surgeonfishes are susceptible to skin parasites. Because these fishes have sharp spines on the caudal peduncle, use care in handling them; large specimen containers are advised for capturing any surgeonfish to avoid having them become entangled in the mesh of an aquarium net.

Family Sphyraenidae (barracudas)

Genera: 1
Species: 20

The barracudas are elongate fishes with a large mouth, a lower jaw that juts far forward on the tip of the snout, long, sharp teeth, two dorsal fins, and a well-developed lateral line. The largest species reaches a total length of 1.8 m (5.9 ft.). These highly predatory fishes feed primarily on piscine prey. All are marine fishes, although some will enter estuaries, and some occur on or near coral reefs. Some species, such as the Great Barracuda (*Sphyraena barracuda*), usually lead a solitary life. Others, such as the Chevron Barracuda (*Sphyraena putnamiae*), often occur in schools.

Captive Care: The barracudas are too large for the typical home aquarium, but they are sometimes exhibited in public oceanariums.

Family Bothidae (lefteye flounders)

Genera: 20
Species: 115

The lefteye flounders, as well as the two families that follow, are members of the Order Pleuronectiformes. These fishes are a highly derived group, whose members are not bilaterally symmetrical. Instead, both eyes are on one side of the body, while the other side is unpigmented and lies flat on the substrate. The larvae are similar to those of other fishes—with one eye on each side of the head—but as they develop, one eye migrates to the other side of the head. As the common name implies, both eyes in this family end up on the left side. They have no fin spines, the dorsal fin originates before or just above the eye, and the dorsal and anal fins are long and not contiguous with the caudal fin. The pelvic fin base on the blind side is short, while the pelvic fin on the ocular side has a long base. Males of some lefteye flounder species have a spine or spines on the snout. In some species, the eyes are more widely separated. All occur in marine habitats and a number occur either on, or adjacent to, coral reefs. They live on the substrate—usually sand or mud—and are masters at matching the hue of the bottom on which they lie. The lefteye flounders are ambush predators and are primarily piscivo-

Sphyraena barracuda, Great Barracuda.

rous (they also eat crustaceans). When threatened, or to better conceal themselves from potential prey, they bury just under the substrate surface.

Captive Care: The flounders are occasionally available to aquarists. To keep a lefteye flounder, provide a layer of coral sand (a minimum of 5 cm [2 in.]) on the bottom of a spacious aquarium with limited decor. These are highly piscivorous, large-mouthed species, so choose tankmates accordingly.

Feeding: Offer a diet consisting of live crustaceans, frozen mysid shrimp, frozen krill, and live feeder fish. (These fishes will only take food that is moving just above or on the substrate.)

Other Advice: Do not house with ornamental shrimps or fishes small enough to become prey for the flounder.

Family Samaridae (samarid flounders)

Genera: 3

Species: 20

This taxon was separated from the Family Pleuronectidae, which has no current aquarium representatives. All samarid flounders have depressiform bodies, with eyes located on the right side of the head. There are no fin spines, the dorsal fin originates behind the eye, and the long dorsal and anal fins are not contiguous with the caudal fin. Most occur in deep water in marine habitats. Only one species, the Threespot Flounder (*Samariscus triocellatus*), is regularly encountered on or near coral reefs. This fish inhabits silty bottoms, feeding on small invertebrates and benthic fishes.

Captive Care: The Threespot Flounder does turn up in aquarium stores on occasion. A captive specimen should be provided with sand substrate in a large aquarium with plenty of open bottom on which to move and rest.

Feeding: Offer a diet consisting of live crustaceans, frozen mysid shrimp, and live feeder fish. (These fishes will only take food that is moving just above or on the substrate.)

Other Advice: The Threespot Flounder will eat ornamental shrimps and fish tankmates that can be swallowed whole.

Family Soleidae (soles)

Genera: 20+

Species: 89

The soles are depressiform in shape, with eyes located on the right side of the head, and the preopercle margin not distinct (it is covered with scales and skin). There are no fin spines, and the dorsal and anal fins may or may not be united with the caudal fin. Most of these fishes live in marine environments in tropical and temperate seas, but relatively few are found on or near coral reefs. A few of these fishes inhabit brackish water and freshwater. Most soles exhibit substrate-tone coloration that helps them blend in with the seafloor, although a few sport more striking attire. For example, the Peacock Sole (*Pardachirus pavoninus*) has small yellow spots and dark-edged white spots all over the body. There are also a few smaller, colorful species that may mimic distasteful flatworms. Some of the soles exude a toxic slime that deters potential predators. All the soles will bury under the substrate to avoid detection. The anterior nostril (on the eyed side of the body) is elongate and tubular and remains above the sand surface when the fish is buried. The soles feed on small benthic fishes and motile invertebrates.

Pardachirus pavoninus, Peacock Sole (Ambon).

Captive Care: Occasionally, a few species of sole do show up in aquarium stores. They will acclimate to captivity if they are not housed with voracious competitors and are given an expanse of sandy substrate in which to bury. Some of the more colorful smaller species would make ideal aquarium inhabitants, but they are rarely collected.

Feeding: Offer a diet of live foods, such as adult brine shrimp (initially), gradually adding frozen mysid shrimp and other crustacean fare. The soles will only eat food that is moving just above or on the substrate.

Other Advice: They will swallow ornamental shrimps and should not be trusted with small fishes.

Pseudobalistes fuscus, Blueline Triggerfish (juvenile) (North Sulawesi).

Family Balistidae (triggerfishes)
Genera: 12
Species: 37

The final five families of fishes associated with coral reefs are all members of the Order Tetraodontiformes. This group is considered to be highly "advanced" because of its sophisticated anatomical plan: fewer teeth, massive fusion of the jaw bones, no lower ribs, no pelvic fins, no pelvic girdle (in some), and a reduction in the number of bones in the skull. Some other families in this order that are not described here include the Triacanthidae (spikefishes), which are deep-water bottom dwellers; the Triodontidae (triplespines), which have long dorsal and pelvic spines and are considered to be the most primitive members of this order; and the Molidae (molas), which are huge, highly compressed, seagoing fishes that either lack or have a highly modified caudal fin. The triggerfishes are laterally compressed and deep-bodied, with eyes set high on the head. They have two dorsal fins, with the first dorsal having three spines that can be depressed into a groove along the back. All the soft fin rays are branched, they have no pelvic fins, and the teeth are well suited for crushing hard-shelled prey. They have stout pharyngeal teeth, with eight teeth protruding in the front of the jaw and six set right behind them. The skin is tough, with large, nonoverlapping scales. Some of the balistids have forward-curved spines on the posterior portion of the body and caudal peduncle. These spines may be employed during intraspecific aggressive interactions. The first dorsal spine can be locked into an erect position by the smaller second dorsal, or "trigger," spine. The triggerfishes are all marine species, many of which occur in tropical and coral reef environments. They swim by undulating the anal and dorsal fins and often blow jets of water out their mouths to excavate buried prey. Most triggers feed on a wide range of prey items, especially benthic invertebrates. A few species specialize in zooplankton or floating algae. Those triggerfishes studied to date lay demersal eggs—often in a depression in the sand—which the males aggressively defend. Some nest-tending males have been known to attack and inflict harm to human divers. At least some of the triggerfishes are sexually dichromatic.

Captive Care: A number of triggerfishes are highly sought after by aquarists, and for good reason: they are durable, often very colorful, and exhibit an interesting array of behaviors. Many of these fishes are aggressive and predatory, and their tankmates should be chosen very carefully. Zooplankton-feeding triggerfishes are best suited for a community setting, and several species can even be housed in reef aquariums. However, most triggerfishes feed on a wide array of sessile and motile invertebrates and will eat small fishes. Provide a medium to extra-large aquarium with suitable hiding places.

Feeding: Offer a varied diet that includes crustacean meat and some hard-shelled invertebrates (like mollusks), or occasionally place a piece of coralline algae-encrusted coral rubble in the tank to help them wear down their ever-growing teeth. Try to feed them several times a day. Triggers tend to become more aggressive if given a diet that includes live feeder fish.

Other Advice: Be careful when handling or working in a tank that contains a large specimen—it can deliver a painful (and potentially serious) bite. Never try to extract a triggerfish that has locked itself into a hiding place. Use a specimen container when capturing one of these fishes as the fin spine and bristles on the caudal peduncle may get tangled in the mesh of an aquarium

> *Zooplankton-feeding triggerfishes are best suited for a community setting, and several species can even be housed in reef aquariums.*

net. It is possible to place different triggerfish species together in a large aquarium, but keep only one member of a species in the same tank, unless you can acquire a male-female pair.

Family Monacanthidae (filefishes)

Genera: 31

Species: 95

Once incorporated into the Family Balistidae, the filefishes have deep, laterally compressed bodies. They have two dorsal fins, with the first fin usually having two spines—the first spine is long and narrow, and the second spine is much smaller and may be absent in some species. They have unbranched (simple) soft rays in the fins, and small scales with tough skin. (They are sometimes called "leatherjackets" because of their skin texture.) The jaws have six outer teeth and four inner teeth. These teeth are smaller than those of the triggerfishes and are better suited for nibbling the algae and/or sessile invertebrates on which filefishes feed. The males of some species have hooklike scales in front of the caudal peduncle that may be employed during intrasexual combat. The filefishes lay demersal eggs, which are often deposited on toxic algae. In at least one species, the eggs are deposited into the lumen of a sponge. The female of one filefish species takes her parental duties very seriously—she will push the egg mass into the algal mat with her snout and circulate water over it with her mouth and fins. A solitary parent (the female, in most cases) may drive off egg predators until the eggs hatch, while others simply ignore the spawn. At least one filefish species is known to form long-term monogamous pairs, while others practice a promiscuous mating system.

Oxymonacanthus longirostris, Longnosed Filefish.

Captive Care: Although less popular than the closely related triggerfishes, filefishes regularly appear in the aquarium trade and some make colorful and interesting captive specimens. Most have polyphagous diets, making them simple to keep, but some (e.g., the Longnosed Filefish [*Oxymonacanthus longirostris*]) are very specialized coral predators. These species almost never adapt to an aquarium diet and should be avoided. Provide a medium to large aquarium with suitable rocky hiding places. Most filefishes are unsuitable for reef tanks and pose a threat to various ornamental invertebrates, including sponges, corals, crustaceans, and echinoderms.

Feeding: Feed a varied diet that includes crustacean meat and some hard-shelled invertebrates (such as table clams or mussels), or occasionally place a piece of coralline algae-encrusted coral rubble in the tank to help the filefishes wear down their ever-growing teeth. Provide food several times a day.

Other Advice: Be careful when handling or working in a tank that contains a large specimen as it may inflict a painful (and potentially serious) bite. Use a specimen container when capturing one of these fishes—the fin spine and teeth may get tangled in the mesh of an aquarium net. Generally plan to place only one member of a species in the same tank, unless you can acquire a male and female. In a large aquarium, it is possible to keep different filefish species together, but note that some species will nip the fins of their tankmates.

Family Ostraciidae (trunkfishes)

Subfamilies: 2
Genera: 14
Species: 33

The trunkfishes all have a bony carapace that encases the body, no pelvic skeleton or pelvic fins, no spinous dorsal fin, and a small soft dorsal and anal fin. When stressed, they can also exude a potent toxin, called ostracitoxin, to dissuade potential predators. (If released in an aquarium, this toxin can kill all of the tank's inhabitants.) Members of the Subfamily Aracaninae have an opening behind the dorsal and anal fins and are most common in warm-temperate Australian waters. The Subfamily Ostraciinae, whose members have no opening behind the anal fin, are found in tropical seas and often inhabit coral reefs or adjacent habitats. Their small mouths are used to rasp sessile invertebrates (e.g., sponges) and tunicates off hard substrate or to pluck more motile prey from the sand. Those species that inhabit sand flats and seagrass beds often expose buried prey by blowing a jet of water at the substrate (a behavior known as hydraulic jetting). All of the trunkfishes studied to date are haremic, with the male defending an area in which his females live. They produce pelagic eggs, and at least one species is known to "hum" during the spawning act. In some trunkfishes, the sexes are dichromatic.

Captive Care: Except for the possibility that some species can decimate a fish collection by exuding their highly toxic body slime when stressed, the trunkfishes are often highly desirable aquarium inhabitants. Provide a small to large aquarium with plenty of hiding places. Do not keep with cleaner wrasses or aggressive species that may cause them to produce excessive amounts of toxic slime. Trunkfishes are not good reef tank candidates because they will nip at sessile animals (clams and corals) and small, slow-moving invertebrates.

Feeding: Offer a varied diet that includes crustacean meat with an occasional piece of coralline algae-encrusted coral rubble. Do not offer floating flake foods unless you saturate them with water before adding to the tank. Feed several times a day unless the system is very large and produces a sufficient supply of natural foods (e.g., algae, encrusting invertebrates, small crustaceans).

Other Advice: Trunkfishes are prone to skin parasites, viral infections, and funguses. Promptly remove severely ill or dying individuals from the display aquarium and place them in a hospital tank. It is generally advisable to place only one member of a species in the same display tank, unless you can acquire a male and female. However, different trunkfish species (especially females) can be kept together in a large aquarium.

Family Tetraodontidae (puffers and tobies)

Subfamilies: 2
Genera: 19
Species: 121

The puffers have the ability to inflate the abdomen by filling the stomach with water or air. They have one small dorsal fin, a small anal fin, fused teeth that form a beaklike structure, stout pharyngeal teeth, no scales (just short prickles), and no ribs. The puffers also assimilate a highly toxic alkaloid in the skin and organs known as tetraodotoxin, which can be fatal if consumed by predators, including humans. The members of the Subfamily Tetraodontinae have a round body and a short snout, and all but one genus lack a ridge along the middle of the back and belly. Although some of the 95 species in this subfamily occur on or near coral reefs, many live in cooler, warm-temperate seas. Others are restricted to freshwater. Those puffers that inhabit coral reefs feed on a wide range of benthic invertebrates, including sponges, stony corals, tubeworms, bivalves, sea urchins, and sea stars. At least one species is even known to consume the dreaded reef-wrecking Crown-of-Thorns Sea Star (*Acanthaster planci*). Some of these fishes scatter their eggs over the substrate,

Canthigaster solandri, Ocellated Toby.

while others deposit them in an algal nest. The Subfamily Canthigastrinae contains 26 species characterized by a body that is slightly compressed, a long snout, and ridges of skin along the midline that are erected during either combat or courtship. Almost all members of this subfamily are coral reef dwellers. At least one, and probably all, of the *Canthigaster* species have toxic eggs that are avoided by egg predators.

Captive Care: The puffers and tobies make delightful aquarium inhabitants, although some species are notorious fin-nippers. All of them are a threat to many types of reef aquarium life, including sponges, corals, snails, crustaceans, echinoderms, and desirable coralline algae. Be sure to know the maximum size of any species being considered for purchase as some species get much too large for the home aquarium. Tobies make excellent choices for smaller fish-only systems that won't accommodate a full-sized puffer. Provide plenty of swimming room, but also include crevices or a cave for them to hide in.

Feeding: Offer a varied diet that includes crustacean meat and some hard-shelled invertebrates (including mollusks from the seafood counter), which will help wear down the ever-growing teeth. (It may be necessary to have the teeth ground down.) Try to provide food at least twice a day.

Other Advice: Never encourage puffers to inflate, as this can lead to irreversible health problems. Some may suffer from intestinal parasites and may need to be given a deworming medication. Immediately remove dead individuals from the aquarium as some of their organs are highly toxic. Puffers are vulnerable to skin parasites, which should be treated in a hospital tank. It is possible to place different *Arothron* species, and even members of the same species, together in larger aquariums, but some species are more quarrelsome than others. Be careful when handling or working in a tank that contains a large specimen—it can inflict a deep bite wound.

Family Diodontidae (porcupinefishes and burrfishes)
Genera: 6

Species: 19

All porcupinefishes and burrfishes can inflate their bellies with water or air, they have spines on the body, and fused teeth. The spines of some (e.g., *Diodon*) lie flat against the body when the fish is deflated and are erected when the body swells. In other species, the spines are always erect. The skin and organs of these fishes may contain tetraodotoxin. All of the porcupine and burrfishes live in marine biomes, and many inhabit coral reef habitats or areas adjacent to them. At least one species (*Diodon eydouxii*) lives a pelagic lifestyle. The burrfishes of the genus *Chilomycterus* are often found in seagrass meadows in protected bays or lagoons. The fused, beaklike teeth of the diodontids are used to crush sea urchins, sea stars, hermit crabs, crabs, and snails. Many of these fishes hunt primarily at night, resting in reef crevices during the day. Males, sometimes more than one, may bite and hold onto a female during courtship and spawning. The expelled eggs are pelagic.

Captive Care: The "personable" porcupinefishes make entertaining pets, readily acclimating to the rigors of captive life, although they are a threat to many types of invertebrates and some are notorious fin-nippers. Know the potential size of large species you are interested in before purchasing (at least one species gets too large for most home aquariums). Provide plenty of swimming room, but also include a crevice or cave where the fish can hide. These

Diodon holacanthus, Spiny Puffer (Bonaire).

fishes are not reef-tank safe and will eat snails, crustaceans, and echinoderms.
Feeding: Offer a varied diet that includes crustacean meat and some hard-shelled invertebrates (clams, mussels, table crabs, and the like), which will help wear down their ever-growing teeth. Try to feed at least twice a day.
Other Advice: Never encourage a porcupinefish to inflate. Be careful when handling or working in a tank that contains a large specimen—it can bite. Immediately remove a dead individual from the aquarium to prevent having the system poisoned by the breakdown of the fish's highly toxic organs. These fishes often contract skin parasites and can even carry ich (*Cryptocaryon irritans*) in their internal organs. More than one specimen can be housed in the same aquarium.

CHAPTER

3

Coral Reef Habitats

WEBS OF COMPLEXITY: AN INTRODUCTION
TO THE REALMS OF CORAL AND THEIR FISHES

"The ocean is a wilderness reaching round the globe..."
—HENRY DAVID THOREAU, *The Sea and the Desert*, 1855

IT WAS A CLEAR, SUNNY DAY ON THE SOUTHERN GREAT BARRIER Reef as I eased myself into the shallow water on the Heron Island reef flat. The tide was out, so my observation efforts were limited to the large tidepools that remained. I was surprised at the large number of fish species that resided, or were stranded, in these shallow pools. These temporary ponds were as warm as bath water, enabling me to spend hours closely observing and photographing the inhabitants.

Suddenly, a chill went up my spine. I noticed the shimmering appearance—like heat devils dancing above hot pavement or desert sand—that the water near the seaward edge of the pool had developed. This happens when water masses at different temperatures collide. The tidal flat was beginning to flood with the cooler oceanic water that had been standing off the reef face.

As the tide came in, the temperature of the sun-warmed water in the tidal pool began to plummet. Fishes that had left the reef flat as the tide was going out were migrating back onto the reef flat. I observed butterflyfishes,

---

Complex cover for myriad reef fishes, a garden of hard corals just beneath the water's surface at Bunaken Island Manado Tua Marine National Park (North Sulawesi).

159

Great Barrier Reef, Australia: the largest structure ever built by animals on the face of the Earth and a mecca for reef fish observers.

wrasses, and parrotfishes either swimming through the mixing masses of water or traveling from warm to cold (or cold to warm) without hesitation. As an aquarist, I was surprised because I had always been told these fishes (especially butterflyfishes) could not stand dramatic changes in temperature. (Indeed, I had always taken great care to avoid stressing my fishes with abrupt changes in water temperature.) It was the beginning of an important lesson for me: reef conditions are not as simple and stable as most of us have been led to believe.

Complexity

Informed by the popular literature and nature documentaries in the electronic media, many of us have come to think of the environment on a coral reef as being very stable and relatively homogeneous. While this is more true of deeper areas, anyone who has actually spent time in the shallows—where most marine aquarium specimens are collected—knows that sometimes shocking variations can and do occur. While the coral reef ecosystem, as a whole, may be more stable than many other aquatic or terrestrial biomes, parameters such as light level, temperature, salinity, water movement, water quality, and substrate type can vary in time and space—from tide to tide and from one niche or habitat to the next—on the very same reef as well as from one reef to another.

Here is coral biologist Dietrich Kühlmann's assessment of the highly variable reefscape: "The coral reef in its three-dimensional expanse, with horizontal, diagonal, vertical to overhanging substrates, level stretches, gorges, terraces, caves and hollows, pedestals and clefts, with sunshine, shade and darkness, with windward and leeward aspects, with the progressive decline in light and water movement from the surface downward, offers the marine organisms a uniquely varied supply of habitats."

Because these environmental differences exist, it is important to know where the fishes we keep originate, as well what their natural or "preferred" habitats are. Many species have evolved over millions of years to function best under specific environmental conditions. Certain gobies, such as the common Citron Goby (*Gobiodon citrinus*), are virtually always found perching in thickets of branching stony coral, while others, such as the Yellowhead Sleeper Goby (*Valenciennea strigata*) prowl down in the rubble zone or over sandy bottoms. Placed in an aquarium without a reasonable approximation of these natural habitats, such fishes will not thrive. Forced through a window of unnatural habitat parameters, many of these reef species may either be difficult to maintain or will live abbreviated lives. A fish in a substandard situation is more prone to disease, weight loss, color infidelity, and listlessness or hyperactivity. These conditions are all the result of stress, which can be reduced if we provide our aquarium residents with a captive environment as similar to their natural homes as possible.

Knowing the differences in "preferred" environmental conditions for the species we keep can greatly aid us in keeping them successfully. For example, diurnally active (daytime-feeding) species from the reef flat or shallow fore reef are less sensitive to high light levels than those from the deep fore-reef slope. The Lyretail Anthias (*Pseudanthias squamipinnis*), which is most abundant in shallow, clear water, will feel at home in a reef tank that is lit with intense metal halide lamps. But the Longfin Anthias (*Pseudanthias ventralis*), which is most abundant in water deeper than 45 m (146 ft.), will

Pseudanthias ventralis, Longfin Anthias: typically found on the deep fore reef, in which it has adapted to a habitat with dim light, stable water conditions, and a profusion of places where it can instantly seek refuge.

have a difficult time adjusting to such bright conditions.

Another reason to know the geographical distribution and habitat preferences of a particular species is to be able to create a model of a specific fish community. By recreating a particular habitat of a specific region, we are more likely to see natural interactions and associations that have evolved between sympatric species. For example, by keeping fishes that occur together in a sand and rubble habitat, it is possible to observe their feeding interactions. Perpetually grubbing in the soft substrate, the whiskered Dash-and-Dot Goatfish (*Parupeneus barberinus*) may be followed by an opportunistic species, such as the Threespot Wrasse (*Halichoeres trimaculatus*), eager to pick off any prey items stirred up by the hard-working but less nimble goatfish.

The following sections examine the different types of reefs found around the world and the various zones, habitats, and microhabitats that comprise these magnificent formations, along with some of the environmental parameters that can vary from one area of the reef to the next.

Reef Types

Coral reefs are carbonate structures formed by stony corals, calcareous or coralline algae, hydrocorals (e.g. fire coral), organ-pipe coral, blue coral, mollusks, coral sponges, and tube-building polychaete worms. The stony corals and calcareous algae are the primary frame builders of these bioherms. Coral reefs typically occur in warm, clear, nutrient-impoverished water. This is not always the case, however. There are some reefs present in turbid, nutrient-rich coastal waters.

One environmental condition that limits the development of coral reefs is water temperature. Coral reefs are found in areas where the minimal surface temperature is 64°F (18°C) or higher. Cold currents and cold water upwellings limit the growth of coral reefs. For example, coral reefs are absent or poorly developed along the coasts of western Africa and the west coast of North and South America because of these two factors.

The availability of suitable growing substrate, the presence of river-borne sediments, and freshwater runoff can also determine if coral reefs will develop. Sediment can smother corals. It also reduces water transparency, which cuts down light levels. Even in clear water, the penetration of sunlight limits the vertical distribution of stony corals and coral reef growth. Other factors that affect coral reef formation are turbulence, water circulation, nutrient supplies, and salinity.

There are five basic types of reef: the **fringing reef**, the **platform reef**, the

Species of the lagoon and fringing reefs:
Top: *Apogon sealei*, Seale's Cardinalfish (North Sulawesi).
Bottom: *Cynarina lacrymalis*, a large-polyped stony coral.

bank reef, the **barrier reef**, and the **atoll**.

Fringing reefs are the most common type of reef formation. They develop along the coasts of continents and high islands. In most cases there is only a narrow, shallow lagoon between the inner edge of the reef and the coastline. The fringing reef itself can be narrow or wide, depending on the width of the platform it is growing on, and is either bordered on its seaward side by a lagoon or by the open ocean. The zones of the fringing reef include a poorly developed back reef or reef flat on its shoreward edge and a reef face and fore-reef slope on the seaward side.

Fringing reef: the most common type of coral reef formation, fringing reefs skirt tropical mainland areas and islands, often creating a narrow, shallow lagoon between the reef itself and the land mass (Red Sea).

The fringing reefs that form in more nutrient-rich coastal waters are frequently colonized by different flora and fauna than those represented on "clean" oceanic reefs. For example, these coastal reefs often support a prolific algae community, a greater diversity of sponges, and more large-polyped stony corals than are found on barrier reefs or atolls. The coastal fringing reefs of northeastern Sulawesi exemplify these differences. There, one can find large sections of reef comprised almost entirely of the large-polyped stony coral known as *Euphyllia ancora*, or Hammer Coral. On more oceanic reefs, hammer coral usually occurs in isolated heads or small colonies.

Other large-polyped stony corals are abundant on these fringing reefs, including Elegance Coral (*Catalaphyllia jardinei*), Bubble Coral (*Plerogyra sinuosa*), Open Brain Coral (*Trachyphyllia geoffroyi*), and Meat Polyp Coral (*Cynarina lacrymalis*). Certain soft corals, including leather corals (*Sarcophyton* spp.), flower leather corals (*Lobophytum* spp.), star polyps (*Pachyclavularia* spp.), pulse corals (*Xenia* spp.), branching xenia (*Cespitularia* spp.), clove polyps (*Clavularia* spp.), and finger leather corals (*Alcyonium* spp.), as well as heavy growths of macroalgae (e.g., *Caulerpa*, *Padina*, *Sargassum* spp.) are also more common biotic elements of nutrient-rich coastal reefs. These plants may compete with, and even overgrow and kill, stony corals in some areas. It is

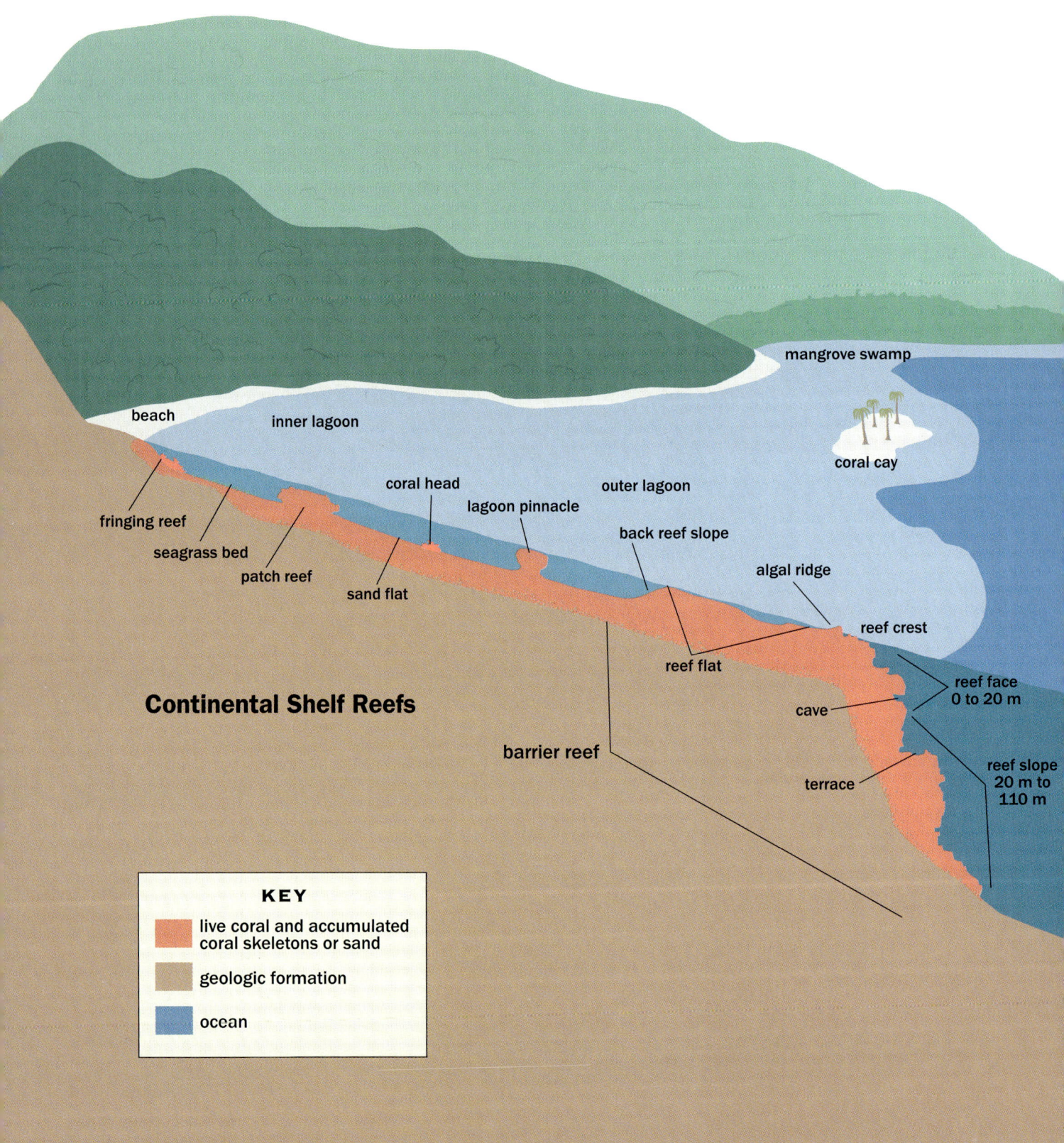

Coral Reef Types and Zones

Generalized cross-section of various coral reef types, including those that develop as Continental Shelf Reefs, *left*, and Oceanic Reefs, *right*. Also indicated are reef zones and habitats that support populations of coral reef fishes. (For an aerial view of some common reef zones, see illustration on page 203.)

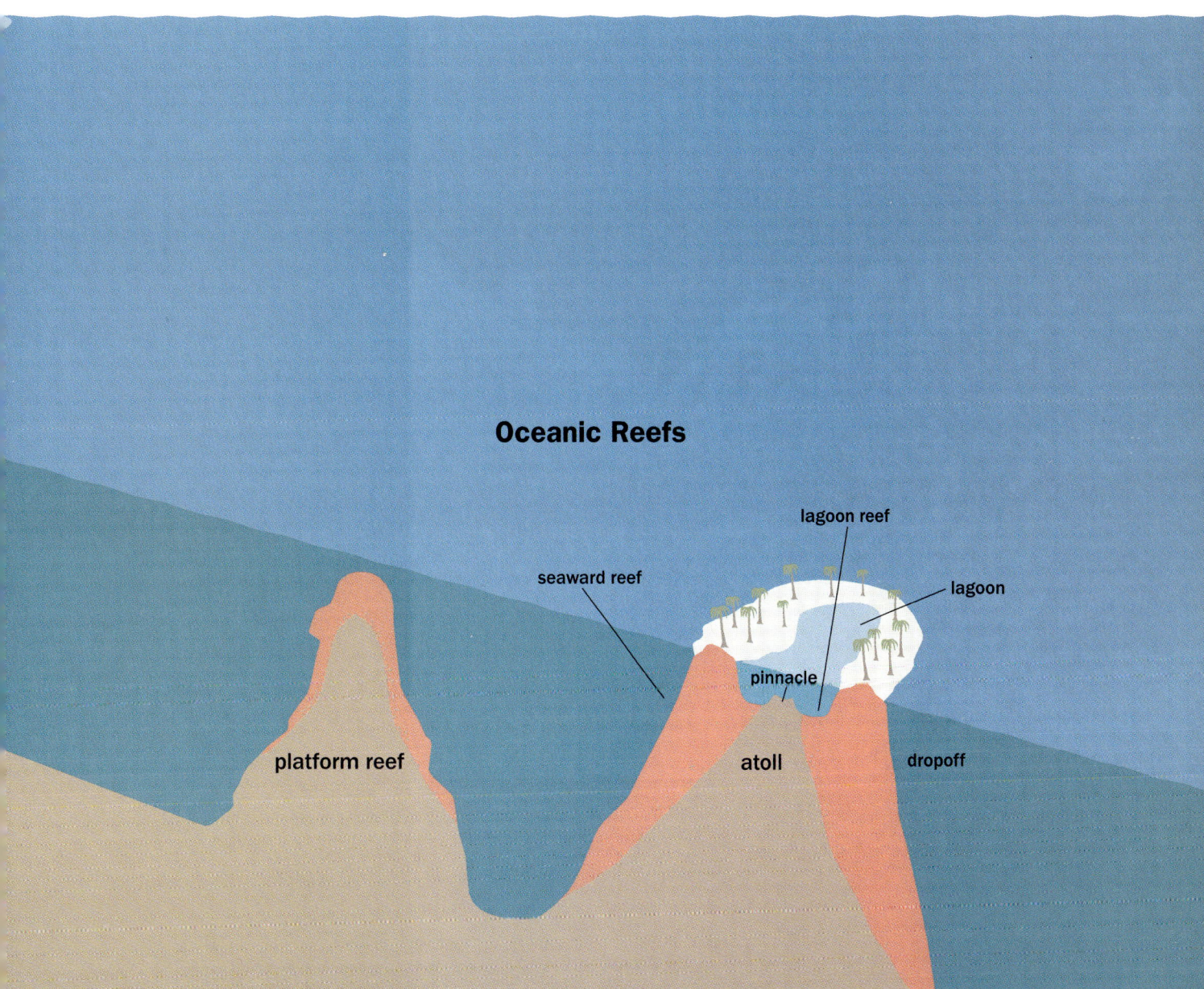

Patch reef: engulfed by *Parapriacanthus ransonneti*, Slender Sweepers, and *Rhabdamia gracilis*, Slender Cardinalfish (North Sulawesi).

not uncommon for water clarity to be reduced around coastal fringing reefs. As a result, they rarely extend into deep water. Reefs in nutrient-rich waters often support a very rich fish fauna as well, including species that are less common on reefs in "cleaner" conditions (see Table 3.).

Fringing reefs are found throughout the tropical world and are the most easily accessed by snorkelers and divers entering from the shoreline or small boats, while also providing aquarists with a preponderance of their shallow-water fishes and corals.

Platform reefs grow on solid bottom substrates or rocky irregularities—such as carbonate platforms, stone outcroppings, or sea mounts—on the continental shelf. These coral reefs grow upward and, in most cases, portions of the reef actually break the water's surface. Sand may accumulate on these exposed areas and form coral quays. Platform reefs vary widely in their shape and size. They can be up to 20 km (12.4 mi.) wide and contain a shallow, central lagoon. They often have well-developed reef flats, portions of which are exposed at low tide.

Platform reefs are found in large lagoons—such as the one formed off the Queensland coast by the Great Barrier Reef—or in open ocean environs. Two of the most famous platform reefs are Elizabeth and Middleton Reefs off the northern coast of New South Wales, Australia. These two oceanic reefs are surrounded by very deep water and support rich fish communities

TABLE 3

Some Fishes from Indonesian Nutrient-Rich Coastal or Fringing Reefs

Fimbriated Moray	(*Gymnothorax fimbriatus*)	Blackbanded Cardinalfish	(*Apogon cooki*)
Barredfin Moray	(*Gymnothorax zonipectus*)	Hartzfeld's Cardinalfish	(*Apogon hartzfeldii*)
White-eye Moray	(*Siderea thyrsoidea*)	Northern Orangestriped Cardinalfish	(*Apogon properupta*)
Ribbon Eel	(*Rhinomuraena quaesita*)	Semilined Cardinalfish	(*Apogon semilineatus*)
Giant Frogfish	(*Antennarius commerson*)	Twobelt Cardinalfish	(*Apogon taeniatus*)
Hispid Frogfish	(*Antennarius hispidus*)	Whitelined Goatfish	(*Parupeneus ciliatus*)
Wartskin Frogfish	(*Antennarius maculatus*)	Manybar Goatfish	(*Parupeneus multifasciatus*)
Painted Frogfish	(*Antennarius pictus*)	Blackstriped Goatfish	(*Upeneus tragula*)
Striated Frogfish	(*Antennarius striatus*)	Eightbanded Butterflyfish	(*Chaetodon octofasciatus*)
Spiny Waspfish	(*Ablabys macracanthus*)	Latticed Butterflyfish	(*Chaetodon rafflesi*)
Cockatoo Waspfish	(*Ablabys taenianotus*)	Twoeye Coralfish	(*Coradion melanopus*)
Longspine Waspfish	(*Paracentropogon longispinus*)	Keyhole Angelfish	(*Centropyge tibicen*)
Shortfin Lionfish	(*Dendrochirus brachypterus*)	Halfblack Angelfish	(*Centropyge vroliki*)
Zebra Lionfish	(*Dendrochirus zebra*)	Vermiculated Angelfish	(*Chaetodontoplus mesoleucus*)
Spotfin Lionfish	(*Pterois antennata*)	Pink Skunk Anemonefish	(*Amphiprion perideraion*)
Tasseled Scorpionfish	(*Scorpaenopsis oxycephala*)	Red and Black Anemonefish	(*Amphiprion melanopus*)
Papuan Scorpionfish	(*Scorpaenopsis papuensis*)	Maroon Anemonefish	(*Premnas biaculeatus*)
Raggy Scorpionfish	(*Scorpaenopsis venosa*)	Redheaded Fairy Wrasse	(*Cirrhilabrus solorensis*)
Spiny Devilfish	(*Inimicus didactylus*)	Cigar Wrasse	(*Cheilio inermis*)
Thorny Seahorse	(*Hippocampus histrix*)	Batu Coris	(*Coris batuensis*)
Robust Ghost Pipefish	(*Solenostomus cyanopterus*)	Wandering Cleaner Wrasse	(*Diproctacanthus xanthurus*)
Ornate Ghost Pipefish	(*Solenostomus paradoxus*)	Purplestriped Wrasse	(*Halichoeres leucurus*)
Bluespotted Hind	(*Cephalopholis cyanostigma*)	Chainlink Wrasse	(*Halichoeres richmondi*)
Blueline Hind	(*Cephalopholis formosa*)	Twotone Wrasse	(*Halichoeres prosopeion*)
Freckled Hind	(*Cephalopholis microprion*)	Zigzag Wrasse	(*Halichoeres scapularis*)
Redcheek Anthias	(*Pseudanthias huchtii*)	Oneline Tubelip Wrasse	(*Labropsis unilineatus*)
Stocky Anthias	(*Pseudanthias hypselosoma*)	Filamented Flasher Wrasse	(*Paracheilinus filamentosus*)
Longfin Dottyback	(*Pseudochromis polynemus*)	Pink Flasher Wrasse	(*Paracheilinus* sp.)
Splendid Dottyback	(*Pseudochromis splendens*)	Fingered Dragonet	(*Dactylopus dactylopus*)
Comet	(*Calloplesiops altivelis*)	Green Mandarinfish	(*Synchiropus splendidus*)
Ringeye Jawfish	(*Opistognathus* sp.)	Neon Pygmy Goby	(*Eviota pellucida*)
Golden Cardinalfish	(*Apogon aureus*)		
Manyline Cardinalfish	(*Apogon chrysotaenia*)		
Ochre-striped Cardinalfish	(*Apogon compressus*)		

Barrier reef: reef-building scleractinian corals populate the shallows of a back barrier reef in Bora Bora, French Polynesia.

that include numerous pelagic species such as sharks, tunas, and mackerels.

Bank reefs begin on a similar substrate as platform reefs, but unlike most platform reefs, bank reefs develop in deeper water well away from any landmass and never extend to the surface. The top of the bank reef may be as deep as 40 m (130 ft.) under the ocean's surface, with the richest growths of stony corals occurring on the shallowest portions of the reef (e.g., the reef top) where light levels are highest. At depths greater than 50 m (163 ft.), bank reefs do not support prolific stony-coral communities, but instead serve as a growing substrate for other invertebrates.

For example, in the Gulf of Mexico, large stands of black corals (antipatharian zone) or rich growths of crustose coralline algae and sponges (algae/sponge zone) grow on the deeper portions of bank reefs. Some of the best known bank reefs include the Flower Garden Reefs in the northern Gulf of Mexico, the Great Bahama Bank, Ten Mile Banks off Grand Cayman Island, and Osprey Reef in the Coral Sea. The outer-reef formations that parallel the Florida Keys are generally classified as bank reefs, although some regard the whole assemblage as a bank/barrier reef.

Barrier reefs are linear in form, and are separated from a landmass by an elongated lagoon, which is usually quite expansive. Barrier reefs run parallel to continental coastlines and can either develop along the edge of the continental shelf—with the seaward edge of the reef plummeting into the abyssal depths of the open ocean—or at a considerable distance away from the shelf edge. The distance from the shore to the barrier reef also varies, and in some cases the barrier reef may actually come so close to the coastline that it takes on the form of a fringing reef.

The lagoon and seaward sides of a barrier reef are quite different in their structure, prevailing conditions, and associated flora and fauna. The lagoon side, or back reef, usually has an irregular outline, is more protected, and tends

Barrier reef: fairy basslets and damselfishes swim above a section of hard coral reef festooned with feather star crinoids.

to be colonized by large stands of more delicate stony corals. The seaward margin of the barrier reef, in contrast, is more regular in form. The stony corals that grow there are more robust and massive in form in order to withstand the pounding of the incoming swell.

The best example of this type of reef is the Great Barrier Reef, known widely as the GBR, off the northeast Australian coast. It is actually an aggregation of individual reefs, numbering more than 2,900, that stretch over a distance of 1,900 km (1,178 mi.) and cover an area of 350,000 km^2 (220,000 mi.^{2}). The Swain Reefs, forming the southern tip of the GBR's densely-packed formation, lie some 200 km (125 mi.) off the coast of Australia. The shoreward side is a channel extending from south-central Queensland northward to Papua New Guinea.

The Great Barrier Reef is often described as the largest structure built by animals, mankind included, on the face of the Earth, but there are other impressive barrier reefs in other parts of the world, such as off the coasts of New Caledonia (644 km [400 mi.] long), the main Fijian Island of Viti Levu (265 km [165 mi.] long), and the Sudan (330 km [205 mi.] long). A significant barrier reef (257 km [160 mi.] long) is found off the coast of Belize, formerly British Honduras, in the Western Caribbean Sea. The Andros Barrier Reef in the Bahamas runs some 110 km (70 mi.), but is regarded by some as a fringing reef.

An **atoll** is a ring or oval-shaped reef that encloses a central lagoon. The lagoon can vary in size and depth. The largest atoll is Kwajelin in the Marshall Islands, which is 100 km (34 mi.) in length and reaches a maximum depth of 55 m (179 ft.). In contrast, Astore Atoll, in the Indian Ocean, is only 3 km (1.9 mi.) long, and the maximum depth of the lagoon is only about 1 m (3.3 ft.). The number of passes that connect the atoll lagoon with the open ocean also varies, but is much less on average than the number found bisecting barrier reefs.

For example, Rangiroa, the second-largest atoll in the world, has only 2 major passes; a neighboring atoll, Kaukura, has none; and Kwajelin is reported to have 28. While most atolls are found rising from deep water in oceanic environments, some smaller atolls have formed on the continental shelf. Atolls are often found in chains, developing on what were once mountain ranges. Although common in the Pacific, where they have developed on submerged volcanos, atolls are rare in the Western Atlantic. The relatively few Atlantic atolls, such as Hogsty in the Bahamas and Chinchirro off the Yucatan Peninsula, do not have volcanic bases.

Barrier reef, Moorea Island, French Polynesia (left).
Atoll lagoon: Rangiroa , French Polynesia, the second largest atoll in the world (right).

Reef Zones and Habitats

Coral reefs are comprised of a number of different zones and habitats, each of which has unique abiotic and biotic elements. Reef zones can be geological (abiotic) or ecological (biotic) in nature. For example, the zone referred to as the reef flat is defined by its geological features—the upper reef platform falls within the intertidal and upper subtidal portion of the reef. The *Acropora palmata* zone, on the other hand, is an ecological zone that gets its name from the dominant coral species in that area. Two of the primary factors that affect ecological zonation on coral reefs are current direction and intensity. For example, massive stony corals occur in areas with higher wave energy, while fragile, branched corals usually predominate in areas where wave energy is reduced.

Acropora palmata zone: an ecological zone in the Caribbean and Florida Keys where Elkhorn Coral is the dominant species.

An ecological zone can be subdivided into habitats. The term habitat is used to define the characteristics —both abiotic and biotic—that exist within an area where an animal lives. A microhabitat is a subdivision of a habitat. To illustrate: the lagoon is a reef zone, a patch reef is a habitat within this reef zone, and a large sea anemone on the patch reef is a microhabitat (for anemonefishes) within this habitat.

Not all reefs possess all the zones and habitats listed. Most Caribbean reefs lack the outer-reef flat characteristic known as the **algal ridge**. Instead, reefs in this region often have extensive growths of fire coral (*Millepora* spp.). The calcareous green algae, *Halimeda*, which could be regarded as providing a distinct microhabitat, are also more prolific on reef flats in the Caribbean than on the majority of reefs in the Indo-Pacific.

What follows is a brief description of the zones and habitats characteristic of coral reefs, with a list of their representative fish faunas. Although some fish are more abundant in a certain zone or habitat, there are species that are not

MAJOR CORAL REEFS OF THE WORLD

CORAL REEF HABITATS 173

Coral head: the bane of sailors but an essential habitat for countless small reef species, such as this population of Blue Green Chromis (*Chromis viridis*) in the Maldives.

restricted to just one area of the reef. Habitat preferences may also vary from one geographical area to the next.

Lagoon

A lagoon is an area enclosed by the inner edge of an atoll, barrier reef, or (in rare cases) a fringing reef. It can range from less than 1 m (3.3 ft.) to over 90 m (292 ft.) deep. Lagoons tend to be deeper and more extensive in the Indo-Pacific than in the tropical Western Atlantic. A lagoon bottom is composed of sand (comprised of *Halimeda* plates, foraminifer shells, and pulverized coral) or mud. Coral rubble is often present near the seaward edge of the fringing reef, the backside of the barrier reef and atoll, or around pinnacles or patch reefs. The clarity of a lagoon is dependent on water circulation, bottom composition, and the presence of river runoff. Tidal and wind-driven currents affect water exchange between a lagoon and the open ocean. Water exchange is also a function of the size of a lagoon and the number of channels that connect a lagoon with the surrounding ocean. For example, the exchange rate of the lagoonal water mass with open ocean water in the Caribbean can range from an entire turnover in 1 or 2 days to over 2 months, depending upon the lagoon.

The **inner lagoon** is often calmer and less turbulent than other reef habitats. Its inner edge may harbor seagrass meadows, which are utilized for shelter and as food by a number of reef fishes and invertebrates. Calcareous green macroalgae, like *Udotea* and *Halimeda*, may sprout from the sand, and *Caulerpa* species may also be present. In some lagoons, these algae contribute

TABLE 4
Some Fishes That Associate with Lagoon Coral Heads and Patch Reefs

Fimbriated Moray	(*Gymnothorax fimbriatus*)	Manybar Goatfish	(*Parupeneus multifasciatus*)
Whitemouth Moray	(*Gymnothorax meleagris*)	Goldenstriped Butterflyfish	(*Chaetodon aureofasciatus*)
Monochrome Moray	(*Gymnothorax monochrous*)	Speckled Butterflyfish	(*Chaetodon citrinellus*)
Yellowhead Moray	(*Gymnothorax rueppelliae*)	Raccoon Butterflyfish	(*Chaetodon lunula*)
Painted Frogfish	(*Antennarius pictus*)	Pacific Redfin Butterflyfish	(*Chaetodon lunulatus*)
Longspine Squirrelfish	(*Holocentrus rufus*)	Rainford's Butterflyfish	(*Chaetodon rainfordi*)
Red Soldierfish	(*Myripristis murdjan*)	Teardrop Butterflyfish	(*Chaetodon unimaculatus*)
Scarlet Soldierfish	(*Myripristis pralina*)	Vagabond Butterflyfish	(*Chaetodon vagabundus*)
Violet Soldierfish	(*Myripristis violacea*)	Saddleback Anemonefish	(*Amphiprion polymnus*)
Roughscale Soldierfish	(*Plectrypops lima*)	Blue Green Chromis	(*Chromis viridis*)
Network Pipefish	(*Corythoichthys flavofasciatus*)	Humbug Dascyllus	(*Dascyllus aruanus*)
Messmate Pipefish	(*Corythoichthys intestinalis*)	Blacktail Dascyllus	(*Dascyllus melanurus*)
Sixline Soapfish	(*Grammistes sexlineatus*)	White Damselfish	(*Dischistodus perspicillatus*)
Goldbelly Cardinalfish	(*Apogon apogonides*)	Biglip Damselfish	(*Cheiloprion labiatus*)
Ochre-striped Cardinalfish	(*Apogon compressus*)	Bird Wrasse	(*Gomphosus varius*)
Orangestriped Cardinalfish	(*Apogon cyanosoma*)	Hardwick's Wrasse	(*Thalassoma hardwicke*)
Threadfin Cardinalfish	(*Apogon leptacanthus*)	Hector's Goby	(*Amblygobius hectori*)
Orangestriped Cardinalfish	(*Archamia fucata*)	Stellate Dragonet	(*Synchiropus stellatus*)
Pajama Cardinalfish	(*Sphaeramia nematoptera*)	Striped Bristletooth	(*Ctenochaetus striatus*)
Fivelined Cardinalfish	(*Cheilodipterus quinquelineatus*)	Picasso Triggerfish	(*Rhinecanthus aculeatus*)

a significant amount of oxygen during the day as they photosynthesize.

As you move out into a lagoon, you will find **coral heads** and **patch reefs** (also known to yachties and divers as bommies). Coral heads are comprised of a single colony or a group of colonies representing a single species. Patch reefs are composed of a variety of different stony-coral species and tend to be larger than coral heads. Both of these structures are like an oasis in the middle of the desert, providing sanctuary for small reef-dwelling fishes and sessile invertebrates, such as delicate, branching staghorn corals (*Acropora* spp.) and fire corals (*Millepora* spp.). Although fish diversity in most parts of a lagoon is relatively low compared to the outer-reef slope, it dramatically increases around coral heads and patch reefs. At Canton Atoll, for example, areas along the lagoon shoreline may support from 8 to 23 different species of fishes, while as many as 43 species have been reported on patch reefs in the

Coral head: *Dascyllus aruanus*, Humbug Dascyllus, hover over a pink-tipped coral (*Acropora* sp.), ready to dart for cover at the first sign of a predator.

middle of the lagoon, especially those exposed to greater water flow. In the Caribbean, lagoon substrate is an important growing surface for gorgonians; in some areas, they grow profusely. Like coral heads and patch reefs, these gorgonian forests provide food and shelter for a number of reef fish species.

The Florida Reef Tract includes more than 6,000 patch reefs, most of them seaward of Hawk Channel, which runs for more than 100 miles parallel to the Florida Keys. Many of these reefs are circular patches 10 m to 700 m [33 to 2,300 ft.] in diameter and consist of stony corals (*Diploria*, *Acropora*, *Montastraea*, and *Porites* spp.) and fire corals (*Millepora* spp.).

In deep Indo-Pacific lagoons, large, steep-sided **pinnacles** (knolls) may rise from the bottom. Hundreds of these structures may be present. If they are located in an area exposed to strong currents, their tops are often covered with stony corals, zooxanthellae-bearing soft corals, fire corals, and anemones. The sides provide a growing surface for soft corals such as *Dendronephthya* and *Scleronephthya*, large sea fans, whip corals, wire corals, and thorny oysters. These pinnacles are also permeated with caves, tunnels, and arches that are utilized by a number of different fish species, including lionfishes, squirrelfishes, soldierfishes, sweetlips, Humphead Bannerfish (*Heniochus varius*), and Regal Angelfish (*Pygoplites diacanthus*). Some of these caves and overhangs contain profuse growths of colorful soft corals.

Moving away from the fringing reef, the open lagoon bottom is often featureless and provides no cover for fish other than those that burrow in the sand. However, it is the preferred habitat for a variety of sand-dwelling mollusks, which are an attractive food source for some larger, more free-ranging fish species such as stingrays and emperor snappers.

Bottom substrate of deep lagoons may consist of mud or fine sediment,

TABLE 5

Some Fishes That Associate with Sand and/or Rubble Bottoms Adjacent to the Fringing Reef or Back-Reef Slope

Yellow Stingray	(*Urolophus jamaicensis*)	Pastel Green Coris	(*Coris chloropterus*)
Pacific Spotted Snake Eel	(*Myrichthys maculosus*)	Slippery Dick	(*Halichoeres bivittatus*)
Crocodile Snake Eel	(*Brachysomophis crocodilinus*)	Threespot Wrasse	(*Halichoeres trimaculatus*)
Striped Eel Catfish	(*Plotosus lineatus*)	Ocean Surgeonfish	(*Acanthurus bahianus*)
Blackblotch Lizardfish	(*Synodus jaculum*)	Doctorfish	(*Acanthurus chirurgus*)
Graceful Lizardfish	(*Saurida gracilis*)	Peacock Flounder	(*Bothus lunatus*)
Snakefish	(*Trachinocephalus myops*)	Scrawled Filefish	(*Aluterus scriptus*)
Reef Scorpionfish	(*Scorpaenodes caribbaeus*)	Fringed Filefish	(*Monacanthus ciliatus*)
Starry Conchfish	(*Astrapogon stellatus*)	Scrawled Cowfish	(*Acanthostracion quadricornis*)
Dusky Cardinalfish	(*Phaeoptyx conklini*)	Sharpnose Puffer	(*Canthigaster rostrata*)
Whitelined Goatfish	(*Parupeneus ciliatus*)	Greeley's Puffer	(*Sphoeroides greeleyi*)
Spotted Goatfish	(*Pseudupeneus maculatus*)	Southern Puffer	(*Sphoeroides nephelus*)
Manybar Goatfish	(*Parupeneus multifasciatus*)	Bandtail Puffer	(*Sphoeroides spengleri*)
Blackstriped Goatfish	(*Upeneus tragula*)	Spiny Puffer	(*Diodon holacanthus*)
Batu Coris	(*Coris batuensis*)		

which is often home to large-polyped stony corals. In the Indo-Pacific, these may include flowerpot corals (*Goniopora* spp.), Open Brain Coral (*Trachyphyllia geoffroyi*), and Meat Polyp Coral (*Cynarina lacrymalis*). It is also home to small-polyped scleractinians that are able to shed sediment, including

Coral head: *Dascyllus albisella*, Hawaiian Dascyllus, hang in the water column above antler coral growing in a deep lagoon (left).

Cave: a dark cavity festooned with soft corals (right).

Mangrove swamp: a nutrient-rich habitat that serves as a vital nursery ground for many juvenile marine fishes (Grand Cayman).

Leptoseris, Pachyseris, and *Montipora.* In the tropical Atlantic and Caribbean, lagoon and patch-reef species include Corky Sea Fingers (*Briareum asbestinum*), Encrusting Gorgonians (*Erythropodium caribaeorum*), sea rods (*Plexaura* spp.), sea fans (*Gorgonia* spp.), Lettuce Coral (*Agaricia agaricites*) Rose Coral (*Manicina areolata*), and others. Plants and motile invertebrates found on the lagoon floor include cohesive mats of blue-green algae, Turtle Grass (*Thalassia testudinum*), calcareous macroalgae, sea cucumbers, mollusks, sea stars, and sea urchins.

Mangrove Habitat

Mangrove swamps are typically found in tranquil water, on the shoreward edge of a lagoon or fringing reef. In some regions, mangroves grow in brackish water estuaries. In others, they develop in "full strength" seawater. The salinity may drop slightly (e.g., from 35 to 27 parts per thousand)—especially in the surface layer—during the rainy seasons of the year. Mangroves rarely grow in water that exceeds 2 m (7 ft.) in depth. Because of the prevalence of silty bottom material and freshwater runoff, water clarity is often reduced when compared to adjacent reef habitats (less than 1 m [3.3 ft.]) of horizontal visibility is not uncommon, while a visibility of 5 m [16 ft.] would be exceptional). The water in mangrove swamps is usually tealike in color as a result of dissolved organics leaching from the mangrove roots and the decomposing leaves that have fallen off the trees. Decaying leaves, macroalgae, and occasionally seagrasses (e.g., Turtle Grass) are present on either the mud or fine sand bottom. This fine substrate provides a home for burrowing bivalves, worms, crustaceans, and upside-down jellyfishes. The prop root system created by many mangrove species serves as a shelter for fishes and as a living substrate for sessile invertebrates (sponges), bivalves, and some corals. As many as 45 prop roots can occur in an area of 1 m^2 (10.8 ft.^{2}). Mangrove swamps also serve as important nursery areas for many juvenile fishes, including a number of reef-associated species. The latter is especially true in areas where a mangrove swamp is located near an extensive coral reef system. In one study of the barrier reef complex

The Mangrove Aquarium

Mangrove propagules (or seedpods) have become readily available in the aquarium trade in the past few years. The species most often sold is the Red Mangrove (*Rhizophora mangle*), which can be grown in both freshwater and saltwater. In most cases, mangroves need to be kept in a tank without a cover or canopy so that they can grow upward. Even without a top on the aquarium, it is necessary to prune the tree to prevent it from growing too tall. You will need to give your mangroves a sufficient amount of light and humidity. A bank of fluorescent lights, a metal halide pendant light, or natural light may be used to provide adequate illumination. The closer the light source is to the tree's leaves, without causing heat damage, the better. In dry environs, you must also mist your mangrove's leaves at least once a week. When a mangrove is doing poorly, place it in freshwater under strong illumination.

The best tank for mangroves is one with plenty of surface area—height is not important. For example, a shallow aquarium on a low stand with overhanging pendant lights can make an interesting display tank for mangroves. You can place the propagules in a hole in a piece of live rock, or you can crowd several of the seedpods into a plastic container filled with freshwater until they form an actual prop root system. After the roots of the trees become entangled, just lift them out of the container and set them on their root base. It may be necessary to place a piece of rock or rubble on the roots to prevent the trees from being upended. Sprung (1995) recommends securing the mangrove roots to the live rock with plastic toothpicks. One final note; it is illegal to remove mangrove trees from their natural environment in the U.S., although collecting and selling the seedpods is permitted. See Table 6, below, for ideas on what types of fishes are found in this habitat.

TABLE 6
Some Reef Fishes Found in Mangrove Habitats

Blacktipped Shark (juv.)	(*Carcharhinus limbatus*)	Spiny Devilfish	(*Inimicus didactylus*)
Lemon Shark (juv.)	(*Negaprion brevirostris*)	Mangrove Waspfish	(*Tetraroge barbata*)
Undulated Moray	(*Gymnothorax undulatus*)	Leopard Sea Robin	(*Prionotus scitulus*)
Longtail Moray	(*Strophidon sathete*)	Bighead Sea Robin	(*Prionotus tribulus*)
Saddled Snake Eel	(*Leiuranus semicinctus*)	Speckled Grouper	(*Epinephelus cyanopodus*)
Blacksaddled Snake Eel	(*Ophichthus cephalozona*)	Highfin Grouper	(*Epinephelus maculatus*)
Striped Eel Catfish	(*Plotosus lineatus*)	Butter Hamlet	(*Hypoplectrus unicolor*)
New Guinean Frogfish	(*Antennarius dorehensis*)	Bronze Cardinalfish	(*Apogon altus*)
Wartskin Frogfish	(*Antennarius maculatus*)	Bridled Cardinalfish (juv)	(*Apogon aurolineatus*)
Lined Seahorse	(*Hippocampus erectus*)	Gilbert's Cardinalfish	(*Apogon gilberti*)
Thorny Seahorse	(*Hippocampus histrix*)	Threadfin Cardinalfish	(*Apogon leptacanthus*)
Brownbanded Pipefish	(*Corythoichthys amplexus*)	Bay Cardinalfish	(*Foa brachygramma*)
Horrid Stonefish	(*Synanceia horrida*)		(continued on next page)

TABLE 6 (CONTINUED)

Variegated Cardinalfish	(*Fowleria variegata*)	Striped Fang Blenny	(*Meiacanthus grammistes*)
Crocodile Cardinalfish	(*Pseudamia amblyuroptera*)	Mangrove Dragonet	(*Callionymus enneactis*)
Orbiculate Cardinalfish	(*Sphaeramia orbicularis*)	Hover gobies	(*Parioglossus* spp.)
Golden Jack	(*Gnathanodon speciosus*)	White Goby	(*Amblygobius bynoensis*)
Mojarras	(*Gerres* spp.)	Link's Goby	(*Amblygobius linki*)
Twostriped Sweetlips	(*Plectorhinchus albovittatus*)	Nocturn Goby	(*Amblygobius nocturnus*)
Brown Sweetlips	(*Plectorhlnchus gibbosus*)	Danded Goby	(*Amblygobius phalaena*)
Lined Sweetlips	(*Plectorhinchus lineatus*)	Bluespotted Goby	(*Asterropteryx semipunctatus*)
Porkfish	(*Anisotremus virginicus*)	Puntang Goby	(*Exyrias puntang*)
French Grunt (juv.)	(*Haemulon flavolineatum*)	Crested Goby	(*Lophogobius cyprinoides*)
Bluelined Grunt (juv.)	(*Haemulon sciurus*)	Decorated Goby	(*Istigobius decoratus*)
Twolined Spinecheek	(*Scolopsis bilineatus*)	Ornate Goby	(*Istigobius ornatus*)
Indian Goatfish	(*Parupeneus indicus*)	Spinecheek Goby	(*Oplopomus oplopomus*)
Blackspot Goatfish	(*Parupeneus spilurus*)	Flagfin Prawn Goby	(*Mahidolia mystacina*)
Blackstriped Goatfish	(*Upeneus tragula*)	Teardrop Sleeper Goby	(*Valenciennea longipinnis*)
Yellowbanded Goatfish	(*Upeneus vittatus*)	Ocean Surgeonfish	(*Acanthurus bahianus*)
Orbiculate Batfish	(*Platax orbicularis*)	Ringtail Surgeonfish	(*Acanthurus blochii*)
Mono	(*Monodactylus argenteus*)	Doctorfish	(*Acanthurus chirurgus*)
Spotted Scat	(*Scatophagus argus*)	Elongate Surgeonfish	(*Acanthurus mata*)
Threadfin Butterflyfish	(*Chaetodon auriga*)	Yellowfin Surgeonfish	(*Acanthurus xanthopterus*)
Foureye Butterflyfish	(*Chaetodon capistratus*)	Golden Rabbitfish	(*Siganus guttatus*)
Banded Butterflyfish	(*Chaetodon striatus*)	Lined Rabbitfish	(*Siganus lineatus*)
Gray Angelfish	(*Pomacanthus arcuatus*)	Vermiculate Rabbitfish	(*Siganus vermiculatus*)
Beaugregory	(*Stegastes leucostictus*)	Starry Triggerfish	(*Abalistes stellatus*)
Sergeant Major	(*Abudefduf saxatilis*)	Fringed Filefish (juv.)	(*Monacanthus ciliatus*)
Twospot Wrasse	(*Halichoeres biocellatus*)	Slender Filefish	(*Monacanthus tuckeri*)
Saowisata Wrasse	(*Halichoeres binotopsis*)	Whitespotted Puffer	(*Arothron hispidus*)
Slippery Dick	(*Halichoeres bivittatus*)	Immaculate Puffer	(*Arothron immaculatus*)
Threespot Wrasse	(*Halichoeres trimaculatus*)	Manila Puffer	(*Arothron manilensis*)
Blackedge Thicklip Wrasse	(*Hemigymnus melapterus*)	Reticulate Puffer	(*Arothron reticularis*)
Hogfish	(*Lachnolaimus maximus*)	Sharpnose Puffer	(*Canthigaster rostrata*)
Cylindrical Sand Perch	(*Parapercis cylindrica*)	Laticeps Puffer	(*Chelonodon laticeps*)
Rippled Rockskipper	(*Istiblennius edentulus*)	Bandtail Puffer	(*Sphoeroides spengleri*)

off the coast of Belize, it was demonstrated that mangrove creeks have a higher relative abundance of fish species than two other lagoon habitats (seagrass beds and sand/rubble zones).

Seagrass Habitat

Seagrass beds are usually most extensive in the protected waters of a lagoon, but they also grow on the shoreward side of the fringing reef and barrier reef flat. The major botanical components of this habitat vary from one geographical location to the next. In the Caribbean, seagrass beds are dominated by Turtle Grass and Manatee Grass (*Syringodium filiforme*), but other plants are also common in this community, including green calcareous algae like leaf algae (*Halimeda* spp.), Shaving Brush (*Penicillus capitatus*), and Mermaid's Fan (*Udotea flabellum*). In the Indian Ocean, seagrass of the genera *Cymodacea, Thalassodendron, Diplanthera, Syringodium, Halophila, Thalassia,* and *Enhalus* are all represented in seagrass communities. In some locations, corals are also found in seagrass beds. Around some Indian Ocean islands, heads of *Favia, Favites, Goniastrea, Pavona, Platygyra, Pocillopora, Porites, Psammocora,* and *Turbinaria* grow in seagrass meadows (although most species will not survive in areas where grass growth is too dense). The exception is *Turbinaria ornata*, which will grow up through openings in the turf. In these same seagrass beds, carpet anemones (*Stichodactyla* spp.), sea cucumbers, urchins (including *Culcita, Diadema,* and *Tripneustes*), and sea stars (including *Acanthaster, Linckia,* and *Oreaster*) are also common. And in the tropical Eastern Atlantic and Caribbean, fire corals (*Millepora* spp.), Rose Coral (*Manicina areolata*), Ivory Bush Coral (*Oculina diffusa*), and Starlet Coral (*Siderastrea radians*) are found in Turtle Grass beds.

Seagrass bed: growing in the flat, sandy waters shoreward of fringing reefs and barrier reefs, seagrass beds host a diverse population of fishes and invertebrates (Papua New Guinea).

> ### The Seagrass Bed Aquarium
>
> It is actually possible to create a captive seagrass meadow in an aquarium. Unfortunately, live seagrasses are rarely available in the aquarium trade. In most cases, you will have to collect the seagrass yourself. You may also be able to special-order it from Floridian fish collectors, and a few livestock importers can also provide Indo-Pacific seagrasses. When selecting a tank to use for a seagrass-bed display, choose an aquarium with a greater surface area. Placing a mirror on the back of the tank will help increase the illusion of tank width, which will make the seagrass bed look more extensive.
>
> Live seagrass should be rooted in 10 to 13 cm (4 to 5 in.) of live sand and provided with bright lighting. Although seagrasses will grow under a bank of fluorescent lights, greater success with these plants is often had by using metal halide lamps. (These species are adapted to very intense sunlight in their natural environment.) Urchins, parrotfishes, surgeonfishes, puffers, and tobies should not be kept with seagrass as they are likely to graze it down rapidly. Sand-sifting and burrowing worms, crustaceans, echinoderms, and fishes will help keep the substrate agitated.
>
> Some aquarists without access to live seagrasses have used plastic plants to achieve the look of a seagrass bed. The artificial plants that most closely resemble these marine angiosperms are replicas of those in the freshwater genus *Vallisneria*. Although not truly realistic, plastic plants do allow one to keep a greater selection of fishes, including herbivores, and there is no need to worry about providing intense illumination.
>
> For variation, you can also include some of the green macroalgae that naturally live among seagrasses, such as *Arrainurellea*, *Caulerpa*, *Halimeda*, *Penicillus*, and *Udotea*. Some invertebrates that occur in this habitat include the Pinktipped Anemone (*Condylactis gigantea*), Corkscrew Sea Anemone (*Macrodactyla doreensis*), Giant Sea Anemone (*Stichodactyla gigantea*), Haddon's Sea Anemone (*Stichodactyla haddoni*), Sun Anemone (*Stoichactis helicanthus*), Elegance Coral (*Catalaphyllia jardinei*), zoanthids (*Zoanthus* and *Parazoanthus* spp.), sea hares (*Aplysia* spp.), Lettuce Sea Slug (*Tridachia crispata*), cone snails (*Conus* spp.), conchs (*Strombus* spp.), burrowing polychaete worms, snapping shrimps (*Alpheus* spp.), hermit crabs, swimming crabs, sea cucumbers, Many-spined Sea Star (*Pentaceraster multispinus*), African Sea Star (*Protoreaster lincki*), Chocolate Chip Sea Star (*Protoreaster nodosus*), Green Serpent Star (*Ophioarachna incrassata*), and other serpent stars (*Ophiolepisi* spp.).

Like mangrove swamps, seagrass beds provide a sanctuary for the juveniles of many reef species. There are fewer piscivores in this habitat than on the reef itself, and the increased turbidity in these habitats, as well as the seagrass itself, provides protection from predators that hunt by sight. Other advantages gained by juveniles that settle and grow up in seagrass beds are diminished competition from adults and greater prevalence of food.

Several factors can influence the abundance and composition of fish communities in seagrass meadows. For example, seagrass beds that are more sheltered from incoming waves are usually inhabited by a greater number of fish species. Salinity, which can vary greatly from one grass bed to the next and from one season to another, can influence the ichthyfauna to some degree, but its effects are minimal. Although the bottom salinity of one seagrass bed off the coast of eastern Panama ranged from 21.25 to 33.45 parts per thousand, many species that also occur on coral reefs were present.

The composition of the seagrass fish community is also affected by its proximity to a coral reef. If the seagrass meadow is adjacent to a reef, there will be a large number of juvenile reef fishes occupying the grass bed. In most cases, a handful of species comprise the bulk of the ichthyfauna. For example, although 106 species of fish have been reported from seagrass beds along the eastern coast of Panama, only 14 to 17 species made up 90% of the total number of individuals. The ichthyfauna of the seagrass beds may also differ from daytime to nighttime. In the Caribbean, morays, cardinalfishes, drums, grunts, and jacks are more abundant at night than during the day.

TABLE 7
Some Reef Fishes Found in Seagrass Beds

Yellow Stingray	(*Urolophus jamaicensis*)	Threespot Wrasse	(*Halichoeres trimaculatus*)
Purplemouth Moray	(*Gymnothorax vicinus*)	Seagrass Wrasse	(*Novaculichthys macrolepidotus*)
Inshore Lizardfish	(*Synodus foetens*)	Threeribbon Wrasse	(*Stethojulis strigiventer*)
Striated Frogfish	(*Antennarius striatus*)	Bullethead Parrotfish	(*Scarus sordidus*)
Polkadot Batfish	(*Ogcocephalus cubifrons*)	Bucktooth Parrotfish	(*Sparisoma radians*)
Gulf Toadfish	(*Opsanus beta*)	Sphinx Goby	(*Amblygobius sphynx*)
Plumed Scorpionfish	(*Scorpaena grandicornis*)	Bluespotted Goby	(*Asterropteryx semipunctatus*)
Spotted Scorpionfish (juv.)	(*Scorpaena plumieri*)	Ornate Shrimp Goby	(*Vanderhorstia ornatissima*)
Lined Seahorse	(*Hippocampus erectus*)	Blacklined Wormfish	(*Gunnelichthys pleurotaenia*)
Longsnout Seahorse	(*Hippocampus reidi*)	Forktail Rabbitfish	(*Siganus argenteus*)
Dwarf Seahorse	(*Hippocampus zosterae*)	Seagrass Rabbitfish	(*Siganus canaliculatus*)
Messmate Pipefish	(*Corythoichthys intestinalis*)	Scribbled Rabbitfish	(*Siganus spinus*)
Anderson's Shortnose Pipefish	(*Micrognathus andersonii*)	Yellowfin Surgeonfish	(*Acanthurus xanthopterus*)
Florida Pipefish	(*Syngnathus floridae*)	Blackbelly Triggerfish	(*Rhinecanthus verrucosa*)
Bluespotted Cornetfish	(*Fistularia tabacaria*)	Seagrass Filefish	(*Acreichthys tomentosus*)
Red Grouper (juv.)	(*Epinephelus morio*)	Fringed Filefish	(*Monacanthus ciliatus*)
Nassau Grouper (juv.)	(*Epinephelus striatus*)	Pygmy Filefish	(*Monacanthus setifer*)
Lantern Bass	(*Serranus baldwini*)	Slender Filefish	(*Monacanthus tuckeri*)
Twospot Bass	(*Serranus flaviventris*)	Scrawled Cowfish	(*Acanthostracion quadricornis*)
Harlequin Bass	(*Serranus tigrinus*)	Longhorn Cowfish	(*Lactoria cornuta*)
Fivelined Cardinalfish	(*Cheilodipterus quinquelineatus*)	Buffalo Trunkfish	(*Lactophrys trigonus*)
Banggai Cardinalfish	(*Pterapogon kauderni*)	Humpback Turretfish	(*Tetrasomus gibbosus*)
Orbiculate Cardinalfish	(*Sphaeramia orbicularis*)	Fingerprint Toby	(*Canthigaster compressa*)
Dash-and-Dot Goatfish	(*Parupeneus barberinus*)	Sharpnose Puffer	(*Canthigaster rostrata*)
Manybar Goatfish	(*Parupeneus multifasciatus*)	Southern Puffer	(*Sphoeroides nephelus*)
Whitesaddle Goatfish	(*Parupeneus porphyreus*)	Bandtail Puffer	(*Sphoeroides spengleri*)
Spotted Goatfish	(*Pseudupeneus maculatus*)	Whitespotted Puffer	(*Arothron hispidus*)
Bluelined Grunt	(*Haemulon sciurus*)	Immaculate Puffer	(*Arothron immaculatus*)
Yellowtail Snapper (juv.)	(*Ocyurus chrysurus*)	Bridled Burrfish	(*Chilomycterus antennatus*)
Foureye Butterflyfish (juv.)	(*Chaetodon capistratus*)	Web Burrfish	(*Chilomycterus antillarum*)
Cigar Wrasse	(*Cheilio inermis*)	Striped Burrfish	(*Chilomycterus schoepfi*)
Dwarf Wrasse	(*Doratonotus megalepis*)	Spiny Puffer	(*Diodon holacanthus*)
Schwartz's Wrasse	(*Halichoeres schwartzi*)		

Pass: a channel cutting through an Indian Ocean reef displays walls laden with soft and stony corals. Several Giant Squirrelfish (*Sargocentron spiniferum*) can be seen in the foreground (Maldives).

Passes

The passes, or channels, that cut through barrier reefs and atolls provide a connection between the fore reef and the lagoon. The walls of these passages are often laden with stony and soft corals. In some passes, tidal currents move through so vigorously and at such accelerated rates (the narrow channels act like funnels or nozzles to boost the speed of incoming swells) that the walls and seafloor are devoid of encrusting invertebrates. Passes are often a favorite haunt of schooling zooplanktivores because of the large quantities of planktonic organisms brought through by the tidal currents. In turn, the planktivores attract larger predatory fishes, including groupers, jacks, and reef sharks. The fish diversity within some reef passes equals that found on the fore-reef face.

Back-Reef Slope

The lagoon side of a barrier reef or atoll is called the back reef. This zone is often protected from strong water movement. As a result, much of the substrate may be covered by fine sediment. In large atolls, portions of the back reef are often exposed to strong winds and are buffeted by a strong, constant surge. In these areas, the back reef will display characteristics similar to that of the windward reef face (i.e., a distinct spur-and-groove formation will be present). Light intensity is high if the lagoon is shallow.

On narrow barrier reefs, the back-reef slopes are often exposed to sudden changes in temperature resulting from tidal influx. Coral heads and rubble typically characterize the area. In lagoons not choked with sediment, there is often an area of prolific coral growth, including a variety of faviid species, *Galaxea astreata*, *Leptoria* species, *Montipora,* and *Porites* species In some back-reef areas, large stands of *Acropora* are present. Coral growth is especially profuse on back reefs that have a gradual, rather than a steep, slope. In some regions, large anemones are also common.

TABLE 8

Some Fishes from Reef Channels

Snowflake Moray	(*Echidna nebulosa*)	Blackback Butterflyfish	(*Chaetodon melannotus*)
Variegated Lizardfish	(*Synodus variegatus*)	Merten's Butterflyfish	(*Chaetodon mertensii*)
Bloodspot Squirrelfish	(*Neoniphon sammara*)	Pacific Redfin Butterflyfish	(*Chaetodon lunulatus*)
Giant Squirrelfish	(*Sargocentron spiniferum*)	Doublesaddle Butterflyfish	(*Chaetodon ulietensis*)
Brick Soldierfish	(*Myripristis amaena*)	Schooling Bannerfish	(*Heniochus diphreutes*)
Red Soldierfish	(*Myripristis murdjan*)	Masked Bannerfish	(*Heniochus monoceros*)
Pacific Trumpetfish	(*Aulostomus chinensis*)	Emperor Angelfish	(*Pomacanthus imperator*)
Saddleback Coral Grouper	(*Plectropomus laevis*)	Weber's Chromis	(*Chromis weberi*)
Lyretail Anthias	(*Pseudanthias squamipinnis*)	Blue Green Chromis	(*Chromis viridis*)
Manybar Goatfish	(*Parupeneus multifasciatus*)	Powderblue Surgeonfish	(*Acanthurus leucosternon*)
Sidespot Goatfish	(*Parupeneus pleurostigma*)	Striped Bristletooth	(*Ctenochaetus striatus*)
Fusiliers	(*Caesio* spp.)	Vlamingi's Unicornfish	(*Naso vlamingii*)
Bluestriped Snapper	(*Lutjanus kasmira*)	Moorish Idol	(*Zanclus cornutus*)
Saddled Butterflyfish	(*Chaetodon ephippium*)	Clown Triggerfish	(*Balistoides conspicillum*)
Klein's Butterflyfish	(*Chaetodon kleini*)	Saddled Filefish	(*Paraluteres prionurus*)
Raccoon Butterflyfish	(*Chaetodon lunula*)	Yellow Boxfish	(*Ostracion cubicus*)

TABLE 9

Some Fishes of the Back Reef

Pacific Trumpetfish	(*Aulostomus chinensis*)	Yellowtail Coris	(*Coris gaimard*)
Smooth Cornetfish	(*Fistularia commersonii*)	Bird Wrasse	(*Gomphosus varius*)
Giant Squirrelfish	(*Sargocentron spiniferum*)	Checkered Wrasse	(*Halichoeres centriquadrus*)
Arc-eye Hawkfish	(*Paracirrhites arcatus*)	Chocolate Surgeonfish	(*Acanthurus pyroferus*)
Whitespot Hawkfish	(*Paracirrhites hemistictus*)	Convict Surgeonfish	(*Acanthurus triostegus*)
Lemonpeel Angelfish	(*Centropyge flavissima*)	Striped Bristletooth	(*Ctenochaetus striatus*)
Threadfin Butterflyfish	(*Chaetodon auriga*)	Brown Tang	(*Zebrasoma scopas*)
Speckled Butterflyfish	(*Chaetodon citrinellus*)	Pinktail Triggerfish	(*Melichthys vidua*)
Chevron Butterflyfish	(*Chaetodon trifascialis*)	Yellow Boxfish	(*Ostracion cubicus*)
Doublesaddle Butterflyfish	(*Chaetodon ulietensis*)	Ocellated Toby	(*Canthigaster solandri*)
Blue Green Chromis	(*Chromis viridis*)	Guinea Fowl Puffer	(*Arothron meleagris*)
Reticulated Dascyllus	(*Dascyllus reticulatus*)	Porcupinefish	(*Diodon hystrix*)
Twinspot Coris	(*Coris aygula*)		

Back reef: out of reach of waves crashing on the reef crest, the back reef (left) often serves as a site for dense growths of stony corals that support many families of reef fishes (Great Barrier Reef).

Reef flat: a broad expanse of shallow water between the outer reef crest and the inner or back reef, the reef flat (right) is subject to extreme conditions brought on by tides, heavy seas and tropical storms (Heron Island, Australia).

Reef Flat

The reef flat is the upper reef platform that falls within the intertidal to the upper subtidal zone. It can be devoid of structure or it can be replete with channels, tidepools, sand patches, crevices, microatolls, and rubble tracts. The reef flat can range from several meters (7 ft.) to over 100 m (325 ft.) in width. The inner-reef flat may support seagrass meadows, fields of *Halimeda,* thickets of staghorn coral (*Acropora* spp.), faviids, and massive heads of *Porites* coral. Other scleractinian genera represented on the reef flat include *Echinopora, Goniastrea, Leptoria, Montipora, Pavona, Pocillopora, Stylophora,* and *Turbinaria.* In some locations, fire corals (*Millepora* spp.) are ubiquitous.

Large tidepools are important homes for many fishes on the reef flat. Some smaller fishes—such as damselfishes, gobies, and blennies—occupy them permanently, while others use them for temporary sanctuary during low tide (e.g., butterflyfishes, wrasses, and surgeonfishes). Invertebrates such as sponges, stony corals, soft corals, bryozoans, tridacnid clams, and tunicates also occur in tidepools and are especially abundant if there is frequent influx of fresh oceanic water. On the outer-reef flat, tunnels create a network of passages. The tunnels consist of grooves in the reef that have had stony corals grow over them, forming a roof. Some of these tunnels connect to pools on the reef flat, surge openings, or blow holes. The cavities are home to numerous invertebrates, including ahermatypic stony corals like *Balanophyllia, Culicia, Tubipora, Tubastraea,* and the hydrozoan *Distichopora*. These cavities are also used as a sanctuary by secretive and nocturnal fish species. Coralline boulders and rubble accumulate on the outer edge of some windward reef flats.

During extreme low tides, some of the reef platform may be exposed. There is reduced water circulation, especially in the shoreward section of this

Scleractinian corals: many species of reef-building corals compete for sunlight and space in the brilliant shallows adjacent to a reef flat (left). Planktivorous fishes: clouds of anthias and other fishes hang in the water column of the outer-reef flat, capturing passing zooplankton (right).

TABLE 10
Some Fishes from the Reef Flat

Snowflake Moray	(*Echidna nebulosa*)	Pacific Redfin Butterflyfish	(*Chaetodon lunulatus*)
Banded Moray	(*Echidna polyzona*)	Blackback Butterflyfish	(*Chaetodon melannotus*)
Longfang Moray	(*Enchelynassa canina*)	Teardrop Butterflyfish	(*Chaetodon unimaculatus*)
Blotchnecked Moray	(*Gymnothorax margaritophorous*)	Vagabond Butterflyfish	(*Chaetodon vagabundus*)
Tiger Moray	(*Gymnothorax enigmaticus*)	Yellowhead Butterflyfish	(*Chaetodon xanthocephalus*)
Undulated Moray	(*Gymnothorax undulatus*)	Coral Beauty	(*Centropyge bispinosa*)
White Ribbon Eel	(*Pseudechidna brummeri*)	Banded Sergeant	(*Abudefduf septemfasciatus*)
Peppered Moray	(*Siderea picta*)	Blackspot Sergeant	(*Abudefduf sordidus*)
White-eye Moray	(*Siderea thyrsoidea*)	Blue Green Chromis	(*Chromis viridis*)
Pacific Spotted Snake Eel	(*Myrichthys maculosus*)	Humbug Dascyllus	(*Dascyllus aruanus*)
Variegated Lizardfish	(*Synodus variegatus*)	Brighteye Damselfish	(*Plectroglyphidodon imparipennis*)
Graceful Lizardfish	(*Saurida gracilis*)	Whiteband Damselfish	(*Plectroglyphidodon leucozonus*)
Scarlet Frogfish	(*Antennarius coccineus*)	Phoenix Damselfish	(*Plectroglyphidodon phoenixensis*)
Guam Scorpionfish	(*Scorpaenodes guamensis*)	Speckled Damselfish	(*Pomacentrus bankanensis*)
Bigscale Soldierfish	(*Myripristis berndti*)	Maroon Anemonefish	(*Premnas biaculeatus*)
Bloodspot Squirrelfish	(*Neoniphon sammara*)	Bird Wrasse	(*Gomphosus varius*)
Crown Squirrelfish	(*Sargocentron diadema*)	Peacock Wrasse	(*Halichoeres argus*)
Network Pipefish	(*Corythoichthys flavofasciatus*)	Checkered Wrasse	(*Halichoeres centriquadrus*)
Serrate Cornetfish	(*Fistularia petimba*)	Zigzag Wrasse	(*Halichoeres scapularis*)
Striped Eel Catfish	(*Plotosus lineatus*)	Cutribbon Wrasse	(*Stethojulis interrupta*)
Peacock Hind	(*Cephalopholis argus*)	Hardwick's Wrasse	(*Thalassoma hardwicke*)
Honeycomb Grouper	(*Epinephelus merra*)	Goldbar Wrasse	(*Thalassoma hebraicum*)
Redfinned Longfin	(*Plesiops caeruleolineatus*)	Klunzinger's Wrasse	(*Thalassoma klunzingeri*)
Bluegill Longfin	(*Plesiops corallicola*)	Cylindrical Sand Perch	(*Parapercis cylindrica*)
Secretive Soapfish	(*Pseudogramma polyacantha*)	Jeweled Rockskipper	(*Salarias fasciatus*)
Broadstriped Cardinalfish	(*Apogon angustatus*)	Citron Goby	(*Gobiodon citrinus*)
Aurita Cardinalfish	(*Fowleria aurita*)	Rivulate Goby	(*Gobiodon rivulatus*)
Mojarras	(*Gerres* spp.)	Yellowhead Sleeper Goby	(*Valenciennea strigata*)
Threelined Spinecheek	(*Scolopsis trilineatus*)	Sohal Surgeonfish	(*Acanthurus sohal*)
Dash-and-Dot Goatfish	(*Parupeneus barberinus*)	Striped Bristletooth	(*Ctenochaetus striatus*)
Copper Sweepers	(*Pempheris oualensis*)	Indian Ocean Sailfin Tang	(*Zebrasoma desjardinii*)
Threadfin Butterflyfish	(*Chaetodon auriga*)	Honeycomb Toby	(*Canthigaster janthinoptera*)
Speckled Butterflyfish	(*Chaetodon citrinellus*)	Saddled Toby	(*Canthigaster valentini*)
Raccoon Butterflyfish	(*Chaetodon lunula*)	Immaculate Puffer	(*Arothron immaculatus*)

reef zone, and conditions are most variable there—especially in small, isolated tidepools. During low tide, the nitrogen levels, temperature, and salinity may rise appreciably, while oxygen levels will drop. For example, the temperature on the Heron Island reef flat may increase by 6°C (11°F) during low tide. At low tide, the salinity in tidepools may decrease if there is substantial precipitation. Temperature changes are often sudden, when the cooler water from the fore reef irrigates the reef flat at high tide. As a result of these environmental fluctuations, the fishes that occupy these microhabitats must be very resilient. Light is extremely intense and wave action can be strong, depending on the fish's location on the reef flat, the stage of the tidal cycle, and how exposed the reef is to the wind.

Reef Crest (Algal Ridge)

The reef crest is the most seaward portion of the reef flat. On windward reefs, it is pounded by incoming waves, and its top portion is usually pavementlike, with little or no coral growth due to the strong wave action. On Indo-Pacific reefs, there is usually a well-defined algal ridge—formed by calcareous, encrusting algae (mainly coralline algae)—that is honeycombed with small holes and tunnels. This ridge can extend for more than 1 m (3.3 ft.) above the water level at low tide. On most reefs in the tropical Western Atlantic, the algal ridge is either poorly developed or nonexistent. There are also surge channels, depressions, and grooves present on the reef crest, and subsurface cavities that provide sanctuary for zoanthids, small cowries, shrimps, crabs, and other invertebrates. Some of the depressions in the algal ridge are created by the boring activities of urchins. In some locations, small colonies of stony corals (including *Goniastrea*, *Hydnophora*, *Montipora*, and *Porites*) are found in this zone. On sheltered leeward reefs, where wave action has less of an impact on the zonation of plants and animals, you will find more delicate

Surge zone: *Kuhlia sandvicensis*, Hawaiian Flagtails, feed in the turbulence of the seaward edge of a reef where only strong-swimming species can thrive.

TABLE 11

Some Fishes from the Reef Crest

Latticetail Moray	(*Gymnothorax buroensis*)	Neon Damselfish	(*Pomacentrus coelestis*)
Bluelined Dottyback	(*Pseudochromis cyanotaenia*)	Philippine Damselfish	(*Pomacentrus philippinus*)
Fourspot Butterflyfish	(*Chaetodon quadrimaculatus*)	Ward's Damselfish	(*Pomacentrus wardi*)
Orange Skunk Anemonefish	(*Amphiprion sandaracinos*)	Bluntsnout Gregory	(*Stegastes lividus*)
Sergeant Major	(*Abudefduf saxatilis*)	Bluespotted Wrasse	(*Anampses caeruleopunctatus*)
Whitley's Sergeant	(*Abudefduf whitleyi*)	Cuvier's Wrasse	(*Anampses cuvier*)
Midget Chromis	(*Chromis acares*)	Surge Wrasse	(*Thalassoma purpureum*)
Lined Chromis	(*Chromis lineata*)	Redspeckled Blenny	(*Cirripectes variolosus*)
Vanderbilt's Chromis	(*Chromis vanderbilti*)	Achilles Surgeonfish	(*Acanthurus achilles*)
King Demoiselle	(*Chrysiptera rex*)	Whitespotted Surgeonfish	(*Acanthurus guttatus*)
Yellowtail Demoiselle	(*Neopomacentrus azysron*)	Lined Surgeonfish	(*Acanthurus lineatus*)
Banded Scaleyfin	(*Parma polylepis*)		

TABLE 12

Some Fishes from the Reef Face

Tinsnip Moray	(*Gymnothorax breedeni*)	Pink Skunk Anemonefish	(*Amphiprion perideraion*)
Coral Hind	(*Cephalopholis miniata*)	Maldives Anemonefish	(*Amphiprion nigripes*)
V-tailed Hind	(*Cephalopholis urodeta*)	Twisti Wrasse	(*Anampses twistii*)
Whitemargined Grouper	(*Gracila albomarginata*)	Harlequin Tuskfish	(*Choerodon fasciatus*)
Lyretail Grouper	(*Variola louti*)	Napoleon Wrasse	(*Cheilinus undulatus*)
Dispar Anthias	(*Pseudanthias dispar*)	Slingjaw Wrasse	(*Epibulus insidiator*)
Lyretail Anthias	(*Pseudanthias squamipinnis*)	Ring Wrasse	(*Hologymnosus annulatus*)
Twospotted Hawkfish	(*Amblycirrhitus bimacula*)	Foxface Rabbitfish	(*Siganus vulpinus*)
Whitespot Hawkfish	(*Paracirrhites hemistictus*)	Whitecheek Surgeonfish	(*Acanthurus nigricans*)
Flame Hawkfish	(*Neocirrhites armatus*)	Orangespine Unicornfish	(*Naso lituratus*)
Twobar Goatfish	(*Parupeneus bifasciatus*)	Yellow Tang	(*Zebrasoma flavescens*)
Bennett's Butterflyfish	(*Chaetodon bennetti*)	Sailfin Tang	(*Zebrasoma veliferum*)
Saddled Butterflyfish	(*Chaetodon ephippium*)	Orangelined Triggerfish	(*Balistapus undulatus*)
Speculum Butterflyfish	(*Chaetodon speculum*)	Black Durgon	(*Melichthys niger*)
Doublesaddle Butterflyfish	(*Chaetodon ulietensis*)	Blue Boxfish	(*Ostracion meleagris*)
Yellow Longnose Butterflyfish	(*Forcipiger flavissimus*)	Blackspotted Puffer	(*Arothron nigropunctatus*)
Masked Bannerfish	(*Heniochus monoceros*)	Guinea Fowl Puffer	(*Arothron meleagris*)

corals and a larger assemblage of fishes. The windward reef crest is usually dominated by microalgae. As a result, it is a popular place for many herbivorous fishes.

Reef Face (Reef Front, Shallow Fore Reef)

The reef face, which is usually limited to depths of 0 to 20 m (0 to 65 ft.), is found on fringing and barrier reefs. Some biologists define this zone as the area that begins at the seaward edge of the reef crest and ends at the limit of abundant coral growth. One prominent characteristic of this zone is the spur-and-groove formation, which is made up of fingerlike projections of coral with alternating sand and/or rubble-floored channels. The lower portions of spur are scoured by the sand that is transported by the energy of incoming waves. As you progress down the slope, coral cover is very high. The coral community can be comprised of a potpourri of small-polyped scleractinians, or there can be monotypic thickets of branching corals such as staghorn corals (*Acropora* spp.), with an occasional boulder or mound-type coral colony amid the staghorn forest. Sand channels often bisect these areas of heavy coral growth. The percentage of soft coral cover on the reef face typically increases as you progress into deeper water. For example, on the outer reefs of the Great Barrier Reef, soft coral cover equals that of stony corals at about 10 m (33 ft.), and exceeds it below 15 m (49 ft.). Some soft coral species found in this zone include *Lobophytum, Sarcophyton, Sinularia,* and *Xenia.* Conditions

Reef face: the shallow fore reef, an area of great biological interest, is generally defined as the zone from the reef crest down to about 20 meters or 65 feet (Sipadan, East Malaysia).

here are relatively homogeneous, with little change in temperature, salinity, or other water parameters. This zone has the richest fish fauna, both in total fish numbers and in the number of species present. Some reef faces have well-developed terraces that can either be covered with a veneer of stony coral or can serve as an accumulation site for coral rubble—with scattered coral heads. This terrace is usually contiguous with the reef slope on its seaward side.

Reef Slope (Outer Slope, Fore-Reef Slope, Deep Fore Reef)

The reef slope is the portion of the reef that begins at the bottom of the reef face and extends into the depths. It is a zone found on both fringing and barrier reefs, although it tends to extend into much deeper water on a barrier reef. The water bathing the reef slopes of barrier reefs also tends to be clearer and "cleaner" (i.e., nutrient-poor) than that found near fringing reefs.

The reef slope usually occurs at a depth below 20 m (65 ft.) and is typically steeper than 30 degrees. Both sand and coral rubble are common bottom constituents. Small to massive coral heads protrude from the slope and provide a focal point for much fish activity. At shallower depths, coral diversity can be high. Soft coral cover increases as one moves down the slope. In certain locations, large fields of whip corals may be present at depths below 25 m (81 ft.). On the reef slope, branching stony corals disappear at about 60 m (195 ft.) and are replaced by platelike forms that can occur at a maximum depth of about 110 m (358 ft.). Stony coral cover is sparse (as low as 1% of bottom coverage) below 90 m (293 ft.), with gorgonians, black corals, and sponges being the most dominant sessile invertebrates at these depths. Clumps of the calcareous algae *Halimeda* occur at depths of at least 100 m (325 ft.), while some algal film and small macroalgae may be found as deep as 140 m (455 ft.). The light intensity falls greatly as you descend the slope, and the predominant wavelength of light becomes blue. All environmental parameters tend to be constant in the deeper parts of the reef slope, except in locations where there are occasional upwellings (e.g., Oman, Bali). In these areas, cooler water from the deep is pushed into warmer shallow waters. On the deeper reef slope, water movement consists of a constant current of varying velocity, not pulses of wave energy characteristic of the shallower zones.

Some outer-reef slopes are nearly vertical or even undercut. These are known as walls, or dropoffs. They tend to occur on leeward reefs that are sheltered from heavy wave action. This is a great habitat in which to find deepwater fishes at shallower depths. The Burgess' Butterflyfish (*Chaetodon*

Reef slope: a soft-coral-covered reef slope near Flores, Indonesia (above).

Deep fore-reef slope: *Hemitaurichthys polylepis*, Pyramid Butterflyfish, swarm near a deep fore-reef slope in Kimbe Bay, Papua New Guinea (facing page).

TABLE 13

Some Fishes of the Reef Slope

Finspot Soldierfish	(*Myripristis botche*)	Deep-reef Chromis	(*Chromis delta*)
Twinspot Anthias	(*Pseudanthias bimaculatus*)	Flame Wrasse	(*Cirrhilabrus jordani*)
Purple Queen Anthias	(*Pseudanthias pascalus*)	Rhomboid Fairy Wrasse	(*Cirrhilabrus rhomboidalis*)
Princess Anthias	(*Pseudanthias smithvanizi*)	Carpenter's Flasher Wrasse	(*Paracheilinus carpenteri*)
Orangeback Bass	(*Serranus annularis*)	Filamented Flasher Wrasse	(*Paracheilinus filamentosus*)
Steene's Dottyback	(*Pseudochromis steenei*)	Burgess' Butterflyfish	(*Chaetodon burgessi*)
Blackcap Basslet	(*Gramma melacara*)	Caribbean Longnose Butterflyfish	(*Prognathodes aculeatus*)
Ridgeback Bass	(*Liopropoma mowbrayi*)	Debelius Angelfish	(*Centropyge debelius*)
Longnose Hawkfish	(*Oxycirrhites typus*)	Ornate Angelfish	(*Genicanthus bellus*)
Flashing Tilefish	(*Hoplolatilus chlupatyi*)	Blackspot Angelfish	(*Genicanthus melanospilos*)
Skunk Tilefish	(*Hoplolatilus marcosi*)	Bandit Angelfish	(*Desmoholacanthus arcatus*)
Yellow Chromis	(*Chromis analis*)	Whiskered Armorhead	(*Evistias acutirostris*)
Blueaxil Chromis	(*Chromis caudalis*)	Bluethroat Triggerfish	(*Xanthichthys auromarginatus*)

burgessi), Yellowcrowned Butterflyfish (*Chaetodon flavocoronatus*), and the Multicolor Angelfish (*Centropyge multicolor*) can all be observed at much shallower depths along walls than on a more gradual outer slope.

Cave, Overhang, and Archway Habitats

Cave habitats, which are prevalent on some walls, provide protection from major currents, intense light, and active, visually oriented predators. Overhangs and archways are also reef structures utilized by cryptic fishes and nocturnal species that refuge during the daylight hours, like squirrelfishes, soldierfishes, and cardinalfishes.

The ceilings and walls of caves are usually covered by encrusting invertebrates that do not require light to survive (these organisms are referred to as scyaphilic). These include sponges; hydroids; certain soft corals including *Dendronephthya* species, *Scleronephthya* species, *Siphonogorgia* species, Spiral Coral (*Cirripathes spiralis*); gorgonians (*Acabaria* spp., *Muricella* spp.); black corals (*Antipathes* spp.); cup corals (*Dendrophyllia* spp., *Tubastraea* spp., and *Tubipora* spp.); and lace coral (*Stylaster* spp. and *Distichopora* spp.). Coral rubble is often present on the bottoms of caves and under overhangs, which provides hiding places for smaller fishes. The occasional soft coral (*Dendronephthya* spp.) or stands of whip corals (*Junceella* spp.) may also "sprout" from the bottom.

Archway or overhang: soft corals and sponges blanket a densely packed arch in North Sulawesi (above). Cave: a sheltering hole for *Cephalopholis sexmaculata*, Sixspot Hind, and other fishes (facing page).

TABLE 14
Some Species That Inhabit Caves, Overhangs, or Archways

Giant Moray	(*Gymnothorax javanicus*)	Venustus Angelfish	(*Paracentropyge venusta*)
Barredfin Moray	(*Gymnothorax zonipectus*)	Regal Angelfish	(*Pygoplites diacanthus*)
Soldierfishes	(*Myripristis* spp.)	Whitebarred Pygmy Wrasse	(*Wetmorella albofasciata*)
Roughscale Soldierfish	(*Plectrypops lima*)	Blackspot Pygmy Wrasse	(*Wetmorella nigropinnata*)
Squirrelfishes	(Holocentrinae)	Randall's Shrimp Goby	(*Amblyeleotris randalli*)
Flashlight Fishes	(Anomalopidae)	Bluestriped Cave Goby	(*Trimma tevegae*)
Harlequin Hind	(*Cephalopholis polleni*)	Candycane Goby	(*Trimma* sp.)
Reef basslets	(*Liopropoma* spp.)	Girdled Goby	(*Priolepis cincta*)
Assessors	(*Assessor* spp.)	Rusty Goby	(*Priolepis hipoliti*)
Bigeyes	(Priacanthidae)	Leopard Toby	(*Canthigaster leoparda*)
Drums	(*Equetus* spp.)	Easter Island Toby	(*Canthigaster cyanetron*)
Indian Butterflyfish	(*Chaetodon mitratus*)	Tyler's Toby	(*Canthigaster tyleri*)
Colin's Angelfish	(*Centropyge colini*)	Porcupinefish	(*Diodon hystrix*)

Rocky Reefs

The coral reef is not the only habitat used by reef fishes. A number of other natural and man-made structures attract them. Among these are rocky reefs, artificial reefs, shipwrecks, pier pilings, oil rigs, sponge/macroalgae beds, and specific coral or algae zones.

Rocky reefs can take many different forms. They can consist of boulders strewn over the seafloor or spilling from the beach into the water, a rocky cliff face of a high island, a continental coastline that plummets into the sea, or a sea mount or rocky escarpment protruding from the seafloor. Rocky reefs are most commonly found in areas where coral growth is limited by water temperature, water depth, turbidity, or an extreme tidal range—or around relatively "young" islands (e.g., Hawaii). Stony corals may be present on rocky reefs, but the suboptimal conditions that usually exist do not allow for extensive coral reef development.

Another difference between coral reefs and subtropical rocky reefs is that the latter structure tends to support large stands of macroalgae. For example, in the middle Gulf of California, the rocky reefs support extensive growths of *Sargassum*, which can provide shelter and food for the fishes in this area.

Rocky reef fish communities can be as complex as those found on coral reefs. Depending on where they are located, however, rocky reefs are typically

Rocky reef: an assemblage of *Holacanthus clarionensis*, Clarion Angelfish, moves across a boulder-strewn area near the Revillagigedo Islands in the Eastern Pacific.

home to fewer species. One thing that will influence the number of fish species present on a rocky reef is the number of habitats present. Holes, crevices, caves, and ledges all provide shelter for fishes and motile invertebrates.

In deep water (between 40 and 110 m [130 and 358 ft.]), there is not enough light penetration for reef-building corals to thrive. At these depths, reefs are often comprised of limestone or carbonate rock and can be covered with sponges, hydroids, certain stony corals, whip corals, gorgonians, black corals, and crinoids. In deep water off North Carolina, one can find flat rocks, less than 1 m^2 (10.8 ft.^{2}), strewn over the sand slope near the rocky reef's edge. These rock "islands" often have sponges, gorgonians of the genus *Lophogorgia*, Wire Coral (*Cirripathes leutkeni*), Brilliant Sea Fingers (*Tianideum frauenfeldii*), and crinoids on their upper surface. A handful of fish

Shipwreck: *Lutjanus monostigma*, Onespot Snappers, cruise through a sunken ship in the Red Sea. Whether the result of misfortune or intential sinking, such wrecks are often rich in fish and invertebrate life.

species live in burrows they have dug under these rock islands, including Squirrelfish (*Holocentrus ascensionis*), Red Barbier (*Hemanthias vivanus*), Sand Perch (*Diplectrum formosum*), Tattler Bass (*Serranus phoebe*), Wrasse Bass (*Liopropoma eukrines*), Short Bigeye (*Pristigenys alta*), and the Caribbean Chromis (*Chromis enchrysura*).

Artificial Reefs

In the last decade, more artificial reefs have been created to support reef fish communities. These man-made structures can be in the form of wrecked cars, concrete blocks, old tires, or cement modules specifically designed to encourage algae and sessile invertebrates to settle on them and provide sanctuary for motile organisms. Another type of artificial reef that has become more prevalent in the last few years is piles of carbonate rock that have been laid down off the west coast of Florida by people propagating live rock for the aquarium hobby. These piles of rock deposited on sand bottoms are utilized by a variety of local reef fishes.

Artificial reefs attract and retain fish communities soon after they are put in place. Some of these fish species use these structures as a place to hide and feed on associated plants or invertebrates. Others take refuge in the artificial reef and feed on organisms living on or in the surrounding sand or mud substrates. Reef fishes that colonize artificial reefs are often the same species that utilize patch reefs. Morays, toadfishes, squirrelfishes, groupers, soapfishes, dottybacks, spadefishes, grunts, croakers, cardinalfishes, damselfishes, butterflyfishes, wrasses, filefishes, triggerfishes, puffers, and boxfishes have all been reported to reside on artificial reefs.

Shipwrecks

One of the most interesting man-made "reefs" is the shipwreck. These provide a structure for invertebrates to grow on and plenty of hiding places for both invertebrates and fishes. The type of animals that grow on or frequent a shipwreck is a function of the environmental conditions that the wreck is exposed to (e.g., amount of light, water movement). For example, if all or part of the wreck is located in an area where there is a strong current, the superstructure will often be festooned with beautiful soft corals and gorgonians. Small and large-polyped stony corals may also grow on the areas of the structure exposed to direct sunlight, while certain large-polyped species (e.g., Bubble Coral, *Plerogyra sinuosa*), cup corals (*Tubastraea* spp.), and soft corals that lack zooxanthellae often grow in more shaded parts of the wreck. The environmental parameters also affect the fish assemblages found around wrecks. If there is considerable water movement, it is not uncommon to see one or more anthias (*Pseudanthias*) species swimming over the superstructure, feeding on zooplankton. A number of fish species seem to prefer wreck habitat. The Volitans Lionfish (*Pterois volitans*), for example, is often found on shipwrecks, sometimes in very large numbers. The Map Puffer (*Arothron mappa*) is also frequently encountered there. The hull of a ship provides an artificial cave for nocturnal species like flashlight fishes, soldierfishes, and squirrelfishes to hide during the day.

One of the most popular shipwrecks in the world for scuba diving is the *Liberty*, which is located off the northeastern coast of Bali, Indonesia. This is a great place to observe and photograph fishes, with over 600 species of fishes

> "A number of fish species seem to prefer wreck habitat. The Volitans Lionfish, for example, is often found on shipwrecks, sometimes in very large numbers. The Map Puffer is also frequently encountered there."

Pier pilings: *Callyspongia vaginalis*, Branching Vase Sponge, growing on pier pilings, which often become encrusted with invertebrates, in turn attracting an astonishing array of fishes.

having been reported from the wreck and the surrounding sand. Chuk Lagoon (formerly Truk) is another well-known diving destination, where most of a Japanese naval fleet was sunk during World War II. The once-barren lagoon bottom is now covered with structures where corals can grow and fish can hide.

Pier Pilings

Pier pilings are often encrusted with invertebrates like sponges, corals, and tunicates that provide shelter and food for a variety of motile invertebrates and reef fishes. If a pier is constructed in an area where there is little other available structure, it will attract a wide variety of reef fish species. Typically trash and debris (e.g., tires, bottles, pipes, logs, palm fronds) litter the bottom around piers. Although unsightly, this material provides suitable hiding places for smaller reef fishes. The shade, created by the pier platform, encourages the organisms that prefer, or are not deleteriously affected by, low light conditions, such as cup corals (*Tubastraea* spp.) and tube sponges. These grow on the pier pilings under the platform and on the insides of the outer pilings. Piers also provide a diurnal shelter site for fishes that are more active at night, like moray eels (*Gymnothorax* spp.) and soldierfishes (*Myripristis* spp.). Pier pilings are some of the best places to find frogfishes (*Antennarius* spp.), seahorses (*Hippocampus* spp.), certain scorpionfishes, including the Shortfin Lionfish (*Dendrochirus brachypterus*), pufferfishes (*Arothron* spp.), and a host of juvenile reef fishes.

One of the most incredible dive sites I have ever explored was a pier on the island of St. Croix, known as the Fredricksted Pier. In one week of investigating the sponge-laden pilings of this pier, I found seven Longlure Frogfish (*Antennarius multiocellatus*), several Longsnout Seahorses (*Hippocampus reidi*), and a hoard of other fishes. These included Spotted Morays (*Gymnothorax moringa*), scorpionfishes, Atlantic Trumpetfish (*Aulostomus maculatus*), juvenile angelfishes, Spotfin Butterflyfish (*Chaetodon ocellatus*), wrasses, triplefin blennies, filefishes, and trunkfishes. Unfortunately, this structure has been replaced because of hurricane damage. But in time, the new structure will become as invertebrate-encrusted and fish-infested as its predecessor.

Oil Platforms

Oil platforms are composed of a drilling platform on steel legs that have been driven deep into the seafloor. These structures are very common in certain areas; approximately 3,000 oil platforms occur off the Louisiana coast. One of the most interesting characteristics of oil platforms is that they provide an artificial habitat that stretches from the seafloor to the ocean's surface. In the Gulf of Mexico, these structures range from shallow, inshore waters to depths of 130 m (423 ft.). While fish diversity around oil platforms is not as great as that found on natural reefs in the Gulf of Mexico, these structures often attract a large number of individuals. In one study, 49 species of fish were reported from oil platforms, and although most of these species were also observed on natural reefs, 12 were seen only around these man-made structures. Some species that were common around platforms in this region include the Warsaw Grouper (*Epinephelus nigritus*), Whitespotted Soapfish (*Rypticus maculatus*), Blue Runner (*Caranx crysos*), Yellowtail Snapper (*Ocyurus chrysurus*), Atlantic Spadefish (*Chaetodipterus faber*), Blue Angelfish (*Holacanthus bermudensis*), French Angelfish (*Pomacanthus paru*), Gray Triggerfish (*Balistes capriscus*), and

Pier pilings: *Aplysina fistularis*, Yellow Tube Sponge, and other sponge species cover a pier piling in the Caribbean.

Planehead Filefish (*Monacanthus hispidus*). Other species common in the aquarium trade that occasionally utilize this habitat include the Flamefish (*Apogon maculatus*), Queen Angelfish (*Holacanthus ciliaris*), Spotfin Butterflyfish (*Chaetodon ocellatus*), the Atlantic Blue Tang (*Acanthurus coeruleus*), and the Sharpnose Puffer (*Canthigaster rostrata*).

Macroalgae/Sponge Beds

In certain coastal areas of the Western Pacific (e.g., northeast coast of Sulawesi, Milne Bay, and Papua New Guinea), one can find low-profile structures composed primarily of brown macroalgae. The few sponges that are found among the macroalgae are usually small globular or fingerlike forms. Occasionally, a large barrel sponge may also be present. These beds are found in areas protected from surge, in more turbid, nutrient-rich water, and can extend from the shallows (2 m [7 ft.]) to depths of at least 30 m (98 ft.). Macroalgae/sponge beds usually develop on soft mud or sand bottoms and trap debris, including trash (e.g., plastic bags, cans, and bottles) and terrestrial plant material (e.g., leaves and palm fronds). Large polyped-stony corals, including the Elegance Coral (*Catalaphyllia jardinei*) and Open Brain Coral (*Trachyphyllia geoffroyi*), some soft corals, and anemones such as *Stichodactyla* species and *Actinodendron* species grow near the edges of this living carpet or in open patches within the bed. The intricate network of holes and tunnels created by this cluster of plant, animal, and man-made material provides sanctuary for numerous invertebrates and fishes. Some of the fishes that frequently associate with these beds include the Wartskin Frogfish (*Antennarius maculatus*), Painted Frogfish (*Antennarius pictus*), Raggy Scorpionfish (*Scorpaenopsis venosa*), Spiny Devilfish (*Inimicus didactylus*), waspfishes (*Paracentropogon* spp.), Stocky Anthias (*Pseudanthias hypselosoma*), Twospot Maori Wrasse (*Cheilinus bimaculatus*), Whipfin Fairy Wrasse (*Cirrhilabrus filamentosus*),

Macroalgae/sponge bed: female *Cirrhilabrus filamentosus*, Whipfin Fairy Wrasse shelters among the densely packed sessile invertebrates of a Western Pacific microhabitat created by a mass of brown macroalgae and sponges.

Redheaded Fairy Wrasse (*Cirrhilabrus solorensis*), Filamented Flasher Wrasse (*Paracheilinus filamentosus*), and the Fingered Dragonet (*Dactylopus dactylopus*).

Coralline Algae/Sponge Zone

On bank reefs in the northwestern Gulf of Mexico there is a zone composed of coralline algae (which usually grows in nodular form), colonial sponges, and massive demosponges. This low-relief habitat, known as the coralline algae/sponge zone, occurs at depths of 45 to 98 m (146 to 319 ft.) and supports slightly fewer species than the coral reef communities in shallower water in these same areas.

Species common in this area include Roughtongue Bass (*Holanthias martinicensis*), Orangeback Bass (*Serranus annularis*), Wrasse Bass (*Liopropoma eukrines*), Bigeye (*Priacanthus arenatus*), Cherub Angelfish (*Centropyge argi*), Reef Butterflyfish (*Chaetodon sedentarius*), Caribbean Chromis (*Chromis enchrysura*), and the Spotfin Hogfish (*Bodianus pulchellus*).

Although not common, the Flamefish (*Apogon maculatus*), the Bank Butterflyfish (*Prognathodes aya*), the Blue Angelfish (*Holacanthus bermudensis*), Queen Angelfish (*Holacanthus ciliaris*), Rock Beauty Angelfish (*Holacanthus tricolor*), and French Angelfish (*Pomacanthus paru*) are also found in the coralline algae/sponge zone.

Gorgonian Zone

Gorgonians are members of the Order Gorgonacea and are found on coral reefs of the tropical Atlantic and Indo-Pacific. However, these animals are particularly abundant in the Caribbean and around southern Florida, where one can actually find a habitat known as the gorgonian zone. This zone is located on the shoreward side of the reef face and is characterized by a carbonate platform with a diverse growth of gorgonian species. Fifteen species were found to be significant contributors to the gorgonian zone off Puerto Rico. These belonged to the genera *Eunicea* (4 species), *Plexaura* (3), *Pseudopterogorgia* (2), *Gorgonia* (1), *Iciligorgia* (1), *Muricea* (1), *Muriceopsis* (1), *Plexau-

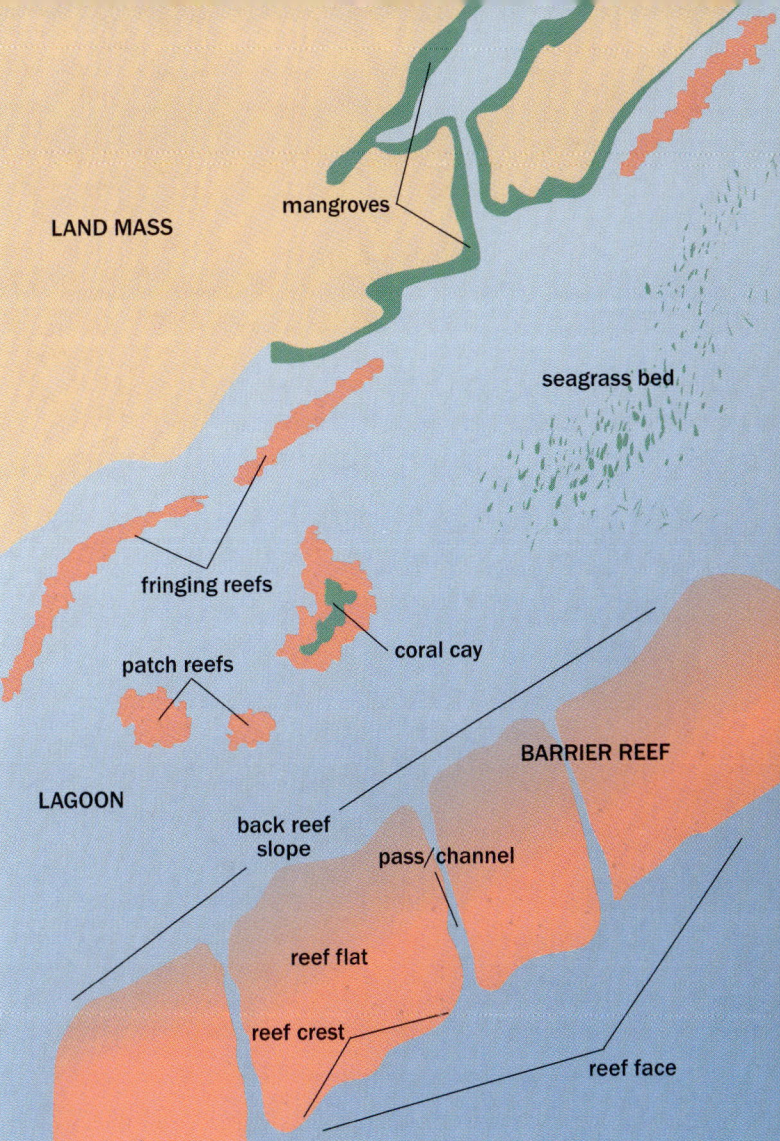

Aerial view of a number of reef zones, including several habitats typically associated with coral reefs and populated by reef fish species.

Gorgonian zone: a pair of Gray Angelfish (*Pomacanthus arcuatus*) hunt through the rubble of a Caribbean gorgonian zone off the Cayman Islands.

rella (1), and *Pterogorgia* (1). Sediment and finer coral rubble cover the bottom in shallow water, but as you move toward the seaward edge of this zone, stony coral colonies become more common until one reaches the reef face. A number of shallow-water reef species can be found in this octocoral forest, including small, shallow-water basses (*Serranus* spp.), butterflyfishes, angelfishes, wrasses, parrotfishes, and surgeonfishes.

Black Coral (Antipatharian) Zone

Another biological zone that has been described on bank reefs off the Gulf of Mexico is the Antipatharian zone. This zone occurs at a depth from 60 to 130 m (195 to 423 ft.), and the horny corals of the genus *Antipathes* (commonly called black corals) are the dominant sessile invertebrates. The substrate consists of algal reefs, encrusted with sponges and soft coral. The fishes most common in this zone are the Roughtongue Bass (*Holanthias martinicensis*),

Tattler Bass (*Serranus phoebe*), Bigeye (*Priacanthus arenatus*), Spotted Drum (*Equetus lanceolatus*), Cubbuyu (*Equetus umbrosus*), Bank Butterflyfish (*Prognathodes aya*), Caribbean Chromis (*Chromis enchrysura*), Spotfin Hogfish (*Bodianus pulchellus*), and the Sharpnose Puffer (*Canthigaster rostrata*).

Sponge "Gardens"

In certain locations, expansive stands of sponges have been discovered on otherwise featureless ocean bottoms adjacent to coral reefs. A spectacular dive site I once visited is located in 28 m (91 ft.) of water off the coast of Exmouth, northwestern Australia. The flat bottom is covered with sponges of every shape and size (I counted at least 12 different species of larger sponge), as well as a number of soft corals, including whip corals, *Dendronephthya* species, sea fans, and Harp Coral (*Ctenocella pectinata*). It looks more like the scenery one would expect to find on a distant planet than any that could be encountered on Earth. This amazing sponge garden is subjected to incredible currents. We were moving over the terrain at such a high speed it was impossible to stop and compose a photograph. It is also home to a number of colorful fish species that are typically associated with coral reefs, including the Spotted Dottyback (*Pseudochromis quinquedentatus*), Double Whiptail (*Pentapodus emeryii*), Western Butterflyfish (*Chaetodon assarius*), Margined Butterflyfish (*Chelmon marginalis*), Yellowtail Angelfish (*Chaetodontoplus personifer*), Scribbled Angelfish (*Chaetodontoplus duboulayi*), and Blue Tuskfish (*Choerodon cyanodus*). Although little information is available on how common this unique habitat is around the world, it is likely that these sponge gardens are found in other parts of the Indo-Pacific as well.

Marine Lakes

Some of the rock islands in Belau, Micronesia, and the island of Kakaban off eastern Borneo have marine lakes. The water in these lakes can range from full-strength seawater to brackish water. In Kakaban, there are no openings to the sea and all the water in the lakes results from seawater seeping up through the ground and from rainwater. In Belau, many of the marine lakes have channels connecting them to the ocean, but in the rainy season the salinity of the lakes is still likely to decrease. Some marine lakes are quite large. The lake at Kakaban occupies almost all of the island interior, covering an area of 5 km^2 (3.1 mi.^{2}) and reaching a maximum depth of 11 m (36 ft.). Mangrove forests often fringe these lakes, and macroalgae (like *Caulerpa* spp.) are abundant. The invertebrates found in these lakes includes unusual

Black coral zone: although seriously depleted in many areas by collectors supplying jewelrymakers, branchy thickets of black corals of the genus *Antipathes* have long served as habitats for a number of fish species.

anemones, sponges, bivalves, tubeworms, crustaceans, and sea cucumbers. But the most numerous invertebrates are the jellyfishes, which include members of the upside-down jellyfish genus *Cassiopea*. Kakaban is the most species-rich of the marine lakes, and its ichthyfauna includes one species of cardinalfish and six species of gobies. The Puntang Goby (*Exyrias puntang*), which is available in the aquarium trade, and the Inshore Cardinalfish (*Apogon lateralis*) are the two most abundant species.

Sargassum Rafts

A floating ecosystem, created by massive rafts of *Sargassum* algae, is found in all tropical seas. *Sargassum* species are brown macroalgae with air-filled bladders that keep them afloat on the ocean's surface. Most of the *Sargassum* that comprise these botanical rafts are concentrated in the upper 1 m (3.3 ft.) of the water's surface and usually occur far offshore. Because this ecosystem is like a floating oasis in the open ocean desert, it attracts numerous invertebrates, which include nudibranchs, worms, barnacles, amphipods, copepods, crabs, shrimps, and fishes. Approximately 170 species of fishes have been reported to associate with *Sargassum* rafts, although most of these species do so infrequently. For example, of 40 species found among *Sargassum* rafts in the Gulf of Mexico, 1 species, the Planehead Filefish (*Monacanthus hispidus*), represented 84.5% of all the fishes collected, and only 13 species were represented by more than 5 individuals. Some fishes, like jacks, shelter under *Sargassum* rafts and feed on its inhabitants, but are not dependent on the raft for survival. Like the jacks, a handful of coral reef fishes are facultative *Sargassum* dwellers. The Lined Seahorse (*Hippocampus erectus*), Spotted Goatfish (*Pseudupeneus maculatus*), Pinnate Batfish (*Platax pinnatus*), Orange Filefish (*Aluterus schoepfi*), Scrawled Filefish (*Aluterus scriptus*), Rough Triggerfish (*Canthidermis maculatus*), Ocean Triggerfish

Sargassum raft: more than 170 fish species have been found in the floating habitat of *Sargassum* algae rafts, including *Syngnathus pelagicus*, the Sargassum Pipefish.

(*Canthidermis sufflamen*), Gray Triggerfish (*Balistes capriscus*), Sargassum Triggerfish (*Xanthichthys ringens*), Porcupinefish (*Diodon hystrix*), and Spiny Puffer (*Diodon holacanthus*) have been reported to associate with *Sargassum* rafts. Some of these species are more frequently found among *Sargassum* as juveniles. There are a few fishes, such as the Sargassum Frogfish (*Histrio histrio*) and Sargassum Pipefish (*Syngnathus pelagicus*), that are obligatory *Sargassum* dwellers —they are always found living among these rafts of brown algae.

This is a difficult habitat to recreate in the aquarium because *Sargassum* algae are rarely available to the home aquarist. A few *Sargassum* dwellers do make it into the aquarium trade and these will usually thrive without the algae. The most popular of these is *Histrio histrio*, the Sargassum Frogfish. The best way to recreate a *Sargassum* raft in your aquarium is to place large amounts of the readily available green macroalgae of the genus *Caulerpa* in your tank. You could also purchase plastic plants that are made for the freshwater aquarium, remove the plastic base, and let them float around the tank. Replicas of a species like Red Ludwigia (*Ludwigia repens*) make an acceptable substitute.

Rubble zone: typically created when storms and waves smash colonies of living stony corals, coral rubble is quickly colonized by invertebrate and fish species, such as this *Pseudocheilinops ataenia*, Pink-streaked Wrasse. This zone also supplies live-rock collectors with a renewable supply of aquascaping materials for marine aquarists.

The Rubble Zone

Along the edge of fringing reefs, and on the terraces and slopes of the fore reef, there are coral graveyards. Pieces of stony corals—broken off by large ocean swells produced by storms and the feeding activities of destructive fishes and urchins—amass in these areas and die. Although the tissue that was once a part of the coral animal perishes, the calcareous skeleton that remains provides a substrate on which other sessile organisms can adhere. In fact, coral rubble is the most common hard substrate on many barrier and atoll reefs.

Like the fallen leaves on the rainforest floor, the accumulated rubble provides sanctuary for myriad plants and animals. Those animals that live among

Rubble zone: *Nemateleotris magnifica*, Fire Goby, hovers close to its hiding place in a mass of dead coral rubble.

the coral rubble are known as cavity dwellers, or coelobites. The cavity dwellers fill an important ecological role. They provide a food source for organisms that live above the rubble, they help to consolidate the reef framework with the sediment they produce, and they recycle nutrients. In surveys conducted in the Caribbean, from 80 to 370 species of cavity dwellers were found. Their abundance is dependent on the geographical location, the water depth, the amount of exposure to current and waves, and the size of the rubble. Flushing by waves and currents provides food to many of these filter-feeding, sessile invertebrates, affecting their distribution among the rubble. Larger pieces of rubble (between 180 and 250 cm^2 [27.9 and 38.7 in.^{2}] in area), which are less likely to be disturbed by turbulence, yield a greater number of plant and animal species than smaller pieces.

Of the encrusting and attached organisms that occur in coral rubble nooks and crannies, encrusting coralline algae and sponges are usually most abundant. Branching red, green, and brown algae, mollusks, bryozoans, tunicates, and foraminiferans are also common. Of the motile invertebrates, crustaceans, peanut worms, and annelid worms (e.g., terebellid worms, bristleworms, and feather dusters) occur among coral debris. The surface of the rubble provides a growing surface for mushroom anemones, soft corals like *Sinularia* species, and stony corals (including *Acropora* spp.). Although not attached to the substrate, solitary corals, like the fungiid corals (known commonly as plate or mushroom corals), are also common on rubble bottoms in the Indo-Pacific. A number of smaller fish species also utilize the rubble interstices as a place to refuge, while for some medium- and larger-sized fishes, rubble tracts are prime hunting grounds.

The aquarist can easily duplicate the rubble zone of a lagoon, barrier

TABLE 15
Some Reef Fishes from the Rubble Zone

Common Name	Scientific Name	Common Name	Scientific Name
Sharptail Snake Eel	(*Myrichthys breviceps*)	Blackdotted Sand Perch	(*Parapercis millepunctata*)
Spotted Snake Eel	(*Ophichthus ophis*)	Nebulosus Sand Perch	(*Parapercis nebulosus*)
Walking batfishes	(*Ogcocephalus* spp.)	Blackflag Sand Perch	(*Parapercis signata*)
Reef toadfishes	(*Sanopus* spp.)	Purple Fire Goby	(*Nemateleotris decora*)
Devil Scorpionfish	(*Scorpaenopsis diabola*)	Bluehead Fairy Wrasse	(*Cirrhilabrus cyanopleura*)
Flasher Scorpionfish	(*Scorpaenopsis macrochir*)	Whipfin Fairy Wrasse	(*Cirrhilabrus filamentosus*)
Devilfishes	(*Inimicus* spp.)	Flame Wrasse	(*Cirrhilabrus jordani*)
Orangeback Bass	(*Serranus annularis*)	Redfin Fairy Wrasse	(*Cirrhilabrus rubripinnis*)
Tobacco Fish	(*Serranus tabacarius*)	Longfin Fairy Wrasse	(*Cirrhilabrus rubriventralis*)
Harlequin Bass	(*Serranus tigrinus*)	Bluestreak Fairy Wrasse	(*Cirrhilabrus temminckii*)
Chalk Bass	(*Serranus tortugarum*)	African Coris	(*Coris africana*)
Sand tilefishes	(*Hoplolatilus* spp.)	Formosan Coris	(*Coris frerei*)
Blanquillo tilefishes	(*Malacanthus* spp.)	Yellowtail Coris	(*Coris gaimard*)
Whitelined Goatfish	(*Parupeneus ciliatus*)	Filamented Flasher Wrasse	(*Paracheilinus filamentosus*)
Spotted Goatfish	(*Pseudupeneus maculatus*)	Dot-and-Dash Flasher Wrasse	(*Paracheilinus lineopunctatus*)
Manybar Goatfish	(*Parupeneus multifasciatus*)	McCosker's Flasher Wrasse	(*Paracheilinus mccoskeri*)
African Flameback Angelfish	(*Centropyge acanthops*)	Secretive Wrasse	(*Pseudocheilinus evanidus*)
Cherub Angelfish	(*Centropyge argi*)	Yamashiro's Wrasse	(*Pseudocoris yamashiro*)
Bicolor Angelfish	(*Centropyge bicolor*)	Spottail Dartfish	(*Ptereleotris heteroptera*)
Cocos Pygmy Angelfish	(*Centropyge joculator*)	Shrimp gobies	(*Amblyeleotris* spp.)
Multicolor Angelfish	(*Centropyge multicolor*)	Dash Goby	(*Gobionellus saepepallens*)
Nahacky's Angelfish	(*Centropyge nahackyi*)	Goldspot Goby	(*Gnatholepis thompsoni*)
Potter's Angelfish	(*Centropyge potteri*)	Pike blennies	(*Chaenopsis* spp.)
Keyhole Angelfish	(*Centropyge tibicen*)	Sailfin blennies	(*Emblemaria* spp.)
Cylindrical Sand Perch	(*Parapercis cylindrica*)	Clinid blennies	(*Malacoctenus* spp.)
Speckled Sand Perch	(*Parapercis hexophthalma*)	Dragonets	(*Synchiropus* spp.)

reef, or fore-reef slope. Since the vertical relief of the decor will be somewhat limited, select a tank with greater surface area. Cover the bottom with a 3 cm (1 in.) layer of live sand and place a variety of sizes of coral rubble on top of the sand. Rubble is currently available from Tonga, Fiji, and the Marshall Islands. If you want more topographic relief in your tank, construct a small coral head of live rock in the middle of the aquarium or pile live rock up at one end of the tank to duplicate the base of the reef face.

Sand flats and slopes: areas of dead substrate, usually crushed coral and tiny mollusk shells, often border coral reefs. Although sometimes appearing desertlike, they are home to many species, such as *Heteroconger taylori*, the Leopard Garden Eel.

The Oceanic Desert

Coral reefs are often fringed by large expanses of sand. This habitat, like its terrestrial counterpart, may appear to be a stark and lifeless underwater desert at first glance. But closer examination will reveal it is anything but lifeless. Although sand slopes and flats are often devoid of living and nonliving structure to provide sanctuary for smaller invertebrates and fishes, some animals possess both physical and behavioral adaptations that allow them to use the sand as a place to shelter. For example, many crustaceans dig their own burrows to hide in, while bivalves bury under the sand for most of their lives. There are also fish, like the razor wrasses (genus *Xyrichtys*), that dive headfirst into the sand when threatened and "swim" underneath the substrate (this behavior is known as sand diving). The snake eels (Family Ophichthidae) also hide under the sand when alarmed. In many of these fishes the tip of the tail is sharp and rigid so that they can enter the substrate tailfirst. The garden eels (Subfamily Heterocongrinae) create burrows in the sand, which they never leave. These eels live in large colonies, deriving some protection by living in groups. Other sand-dwelling fishes rely on toxins, armor, camouflage, or mimicry to avoid predators. The Moses Sole (*Pardachirus marmoratus*) uses toxic slime, the Dragon Sea Moth (*Eurypegasus draconis*) has body armor, many of the lefteye flounders (Family Bothidae) are cryptically colored and disappear against the substrate, and the Black Razorfish (*Xyrichtys niger*) floats over and lies on the substrate, looking like a piece of debris.

A sand slope is easy and inexpensive to recreate in your aquarium. Simply add a 5 to 10 cm (2 to 4 in.) layer of smaller-grade sand, preferably of the live variety, to your tank, some water pumps to provide adequate circulation, and an external filter for supplemental biological filtration. Although you can use a smaller aquarium to recreate this habitat, a larger tank (100 gallons or larger) makes a much more impressive sand-habitat display. Because there is little or no vertical topography, the height of the tank is also unimportant. Instead, select a tank with as much surface area as possible. Many of the species that live in this habitat are active swimmers so more surface area will provide more swimming space. You can make the sand slope look more expansive by placing a mirror on the back of the tank and/or by sloping the sand upward toward the back of the aquarium.

Some of the most interesting additions for the sand-slope aquarium include snake eels, garden eels, Ambon Scorpionfish (*Pteroidichthys amboinensis*), flatheads (Family Platycephalidae), helmut gurnards (Family Dactylopteridae), Tobacco Fish (*Serranus tabacarius*), Chalk Bass (*Serranus tortugarum*), jawfishes (Family Opistognathidae), goatfishes (Family Mullidae), sand divers (*Trichonotus* spp.), razor wrasses (*Cymolutes* spp., *Xyrichtys* spp.), sand perches (Family Pinguipedidae), shrimp gobies (including *Amblyeleotris* spp., *Cryptocentrus* spp., *Stonogobiops* spp., and *Vanderhorstia* spp.), dartfishes (*Ptereleotris* spp.), flatfishes (Order Pleuronectiformes), Bennett's Toby (*Canthigaster bennetti*), the Fingerprint Toby (*Canthigaster compressa*), and Crowned Toby (*Canthigaster coronata*).

Microhabitats

Habitats can be subdivided further into microhabitats. Because space is at a premium on the species-packed coral reefs, a large number of reef fishes utilize specific microhabitats. Many of these "specialists" live in association with other living organisms. Some of the neon gobies (*Gobiosoma* spp.) live only in the lumens of large vase sponges. The anemonefishes (*Amphiprion* spp. and *Premnas biaculeatus*) are obligatory anemone dwellers, while young Urchin Clingfish (*Diademichthys lineatus*) use their host, *Diadema* urchins, as a place to refuge and as a

Deep-water species: *Bodianus bimaculatus*, Twinspot Hogfish (juvenile) on a deep-reef slope.

TABLE 16
Some Deep-Water Fishes*

Hawaiian Deep-water Anthias	(*Holanthias fuscipinnis*)	Scythe Butterflyfish	(*Prognathodes falcifer*)
Roughtongue Bass	(*Holanthias martinicensis*)	Colin's Angelfish	(*Centropyge colini*)
Hawaiian Longfin Anthias	(*Pseudanthias hawaiiensis*)	Debelius Angelfish	(*Centropyge debelius*)
Squarespot Anthias	(*Pseudanthias pleurotaenia*)	Multicolor Angelfish	(*Centropyge multicolor*)
Randall's Anthias	(*Pseudanthias randalli*)	Manybar Angelfish	(*Centropyge multifasciata*)
Longfin Anthias	(*Pseudanthias ventralis*)	Nahacky's Angelfish	(*Centropyge nahackyi*)
Magenta Dottyback	(*Pseudochromis porphyreus*)	Narcosis Angelfish	(*Centropyge narcosis*)
Blackcap Basslet	(*Gramma melacara*)	Ornate Angelfish	(*Genicanthus bellus*)
Dusky Gramma	(*Gramma linki*)	Watanabe's Angelfish	(*Genicanthus watanabei*)
Heliotrope Basslet	(*Lipogramma klayi*)	Blackspot Angelfish	(*Genicanthus melanospilos*)
Wrasse Bass	(*Liopropoma eukrines*)	Boyle's Angelfish	(*Paracentropyge boylei*)
Candy Bass	(*Liopropoma carmabi*)	Longnose Hawkfish	(*Oxycirrhites typus*)
Flashing Tilefish	(*Hoplolatilus chlupatyi*)	Spotfin Hogfish	(*Bodianus pulchellus*)
Green Tilefish	(*Hoplolatilus cuniculus*)	Flame Wrasse	(*Cirrhilabrus jordani*)
Skunk Tilefish	(*Hoplolatilus marcosi*)	Pyle's Fairy Wrasse	(*Cirrhilabrus pylei*)
Bluehead Tilefish	(*Hoplolatilus starcki*)	Helfrich's Firefish	(*Nemateleotris helfrichi*)
Burgess' Butterflyfish	(*Chaetodon burgessi*)		
Tinker's Butterflyfish	(*Chaetodon tinkeri*)		
Indian Butterflyfish	(*Chaetodon mitratus*)		
Caribbean Longnose Butterflyfish	(*Prognathodes aculeatus*)		
Bank Butterflyfish	(*Prognathodes aya*)		

* In certain geographical regions and habitats, some of these species are found in shallower water.

The Deep-Water Aquarium

Some fishes available in the marine aquarium trade are inhabitants of deep fore-reef slopes, terraces, and walls. To ensure that you have success keeping these fish, it is best to recreate their natural habitat. Because light levels in deep water are greatly reduced and temperatures can be slightly cooler, I would suggest lighting the deep-water aquarium with blue fluorescent tubes and keeping the temperature at approximately 22 to 24°C (72 to 76°F). Use only blue bulbs if you have one or two fixtures. If you have three fixtures, try two blue fluorescent bulbs and one dimmer color-enhancing bulb (a color temperature of 10,000°K). If fishes that normally spend time in the water column are reluctant to move away from their hiding places, add illumination over the tank. Under dim light conditions, some species are naturally more wary of the potential of being eaten.

source of food. And over certain parts of its range, the juvenile Whitebelly Damselfish (*Amblyglyphidodon leucogaster*) is found hiding among the branches of the soft coral *Litophyton viridis*. When a piscivore contacts the soft coral's branches, the invertebrate releases a toxic chemical that deters the predator. The damselfish has built up more resistance to this ichthyotoxin than most other fishes, so the fish can use the coral as a chemical

Anemone dwellers: *Amphiprion ocellaris*, Ocellaris Anemonefish pair, with *Heteractis magnifica*, Magnificent Sea Anemone, the stinging-celled invertebrate that serves as their microhabitat (North Sulawesi).

barrier against predators. For a list of microhabitat specialists that associate with other living organisms see Table 17, page 214.

Some fishes that associate with other organisms will adapt to aquarium life without their symbiotic associates, while others will be difficult to acclimate unless provided with an adequate host. For example, the Flame Hawkfish (*Neocirrhites armatus*) and Longnose Hawkfish (*Oxycirrhites typus*) will do fine without their natural invertebrate associates. The coral crouchers (*Caracanthus* spp.), however, do poorly unless provided with a large piece of live or dead branching coral that they can refuge in. These fishes are occasionally seen in fish stores and are often mistakenly sold as "clown gobies" or as "fuzzy nut gobies."

TABLE 17

Some Reef Fishes That Associate with Other Organisms

Fish Species	Microhabitat
Pearlfishes (Family Carapidae)	Some live in sea cucumbers, bivalves, sea stars, and tunicates.
Speckled Scorpionfish (*Sebastapistes coniorta*)	Live among branches of *Pocillopora* coral.
Coral crouchers (*Caracanthus* spp.)	Live among branches of live stony corals (*Pocillopora* spp., *Acropora* spp. and *Stylophora* spp.).
White Pipefish (*Siokunichthys nigrolineatus*)	Live among tentacles of Long-tentacle Mushroom or Plate Coral (*Heliofungia actiniformis*).
Soft Coral Pipefish (*Siokunichthys breviceps*)	Live among branches of soft corals.
Sawcheek (*Apogon quadrisquamatus*) and Bridled Cardinalfishes (*Apogon aurolineatus*)	Live among tentacles of Curleycue anemone (*Bartholomea annulata*).
Starry Conchfish (*Astrapogon stellatus*)	Live inside mantle cavity of live Giant Conch (*Strombus gigas*).
Crown-of-Thorns Cardinalfish (*Siphamia fuscolineata*)	Live among spines of Crown-of-Thorns Sea Star (*Acanthaster planci*).
Sea Urchin Cardinalfish (*Siphamia versicolor*)	Live among spines of long-spined sea urchins (*Diadema* spp.).
Flame Hawkfish (*Neocirrhites armatus*)	Live among branches of live stony corals of the genus *Pocillopora*.
Longnose Hawkfish (*Oxycirrhites typus*)	Live among branches of gorgonians and black corals.
Dascyllus damselfishes (*Dascyllus* spp.)	Live among branches of live stony corals of the genus *Acropora* and *Pocillopora*.
Anemonefishes (*Amphiprion* spp. and *Premnas biaculeatus*)	Live among the tentacles of 10 anemones of the genera *Cryptodendrum*, *Entacmaea*, *Heteractis*, *Macrodactyla*, and *Stichodactyla*.
Tube blennies (*Acanthemblemaria* spp.)	Often live in empty tubes of serpulid worms.
Diamond Blenny (*Malacoctenus boehlkei*)	Live near base of Caribbean Pinktipped Anemone (*Condylactis gigantea*).
Clown gobies (*Gobiodon* spp.)	Live among branches of live staghorn coral (*Acropora* spp.).
Fuzzy gobies (*Paragobiodon* spp.)	Live among branches of live stony corals (*Stylophora* spp. and *Seriatopora* spp.).
Redeye Goby (*Bryaninops natans*)	Live among branches of live staghorn coral (*Acropora* spp.).
Whip Goby (*Bryaninops yongei*)	Live on sea whips (*Cirripathes* spp.).
Black Coral Goby (*Bryaninops tigris*)	Live among branches of black corals.
Shrimp gobies (*Amblyeleotris* spp., *Cryptocentrus* spp., *Ctenogobiops* spp., and *Stonogobiops* spp.)	Live in burrow with pistol shrimp (*Alpheus* spp.).

The Sponge Dwellers

The Caribbean Sea is well known for its incredible populations of tubular, globular, and vaselike sponges—many of which belong to the genera *Callyspongia, Ircinia, Spongia, Aplysina,* and *Xestospongia.* These sponges come in an assortment of different colors and sizes. The chimney of the tubular varieties commonly measures 50 cm (20 in.) in length, while the lumen (the hollow interior) of some of the large barrel sponges is large enough to conceal a medium-sized human. It is not surprising then, that in an ecosystem where space is at a premium, a wide variety of invertebrates live within these sessile organisms. Species of polychaete worms, annelid worms, cleaner shrimps, pistol shrimps, and small crabs can be found residing in sponges. There are also fish species that associate with sponges to varying degrees. These sponge-dwelling fishes can be broken down into three groups—morphologically specialized obligate sponge dwellers, morphologically unspecialized obligate sponge dwellers, and facultative sponge-dwellers.

Sponge dweller: *Antennarius multiocellatus*, Longlure Frogfish, has tucked itself tightly into the barrel of a spawning tube sponge (Bonaire).

The first group—the obligate sponge dwellers—contains relatively few fishes. In the Caribbean, this includes gobies in the genera *Evermannichthys, Pariah,* and *Risor.* These are small, short-lived gobies (*Risor ruber* is sexually mature at 1 cm [0.3 in.] and probably lives for no more than 1 year) that have large, recurved teeth used to widen holes in the sponge's walls and get to hidden invertebrates. They also have scales toward the tail with enlarged ctenii (comblike structures on the back edge of the scale), that help them to cling to the walls of the sponge. These tiny gobies are always found in association with sponges and apparently never leave their invertebrate host. They feed on zooplankton carried in by the sponge's filtering activities and small invertebrates that live in the lumen. As many as 21 of these obligate sponge dwellers have been taken from one 50 cm (20 in.) Loggerhead Sponge (*Speciospongia vesparium*). These secretive fishes are never observed unless their host sponge is dissected, so they are rarely collected for the aquarium trade. It is possible that an aquarist could accidentally acquire one inside a sponge.

Members of the second group—the nonspecialized obligate sponge dwellers—do show up in aquarium stores from time to time. These species are almost always found associating with sponges but do not possess any special anatomical features to facilitate this lifestyle. This group includes the Shortstripe Goby (*Gobiosoma chancei*), the Yellow Prow Goby (*Gobiosoma xanthiprora*), and the Sponge Cardinalfish (*Phaeoptyx xenus*). The gobies are usually observed sitting at the lumen opening or just outside of it, while the Sponge Cardinalfish lives inside the sponge during the day, leaving its host at night to feed on zooplankton.

The third group—the facultative sponge dwellers—includes the largest number of fish species, many of which enter the aquarium trade. These species are not always found in association with sponges, often using the sponge only as a temporary refuge. A number of different gobies, several labrisomid blennies, Mushroom Scorpionfish (*Scorpaena inermis*), Longlure Frogfish (*Antennarius multiocellatus*), several clingfishes, the Sawcheek Cardinalfish (*Apogon quadrisquamatus*), Bluehead Wrasse (*Thalassoma bifasciatum*), and several juvenile damselfishes fall into this category.

There are also a number of fish species that live on or in sponges in the Indo-Pacific. Many gobies in the genus *Trimma* live between the outer ridges or in the lumen of the large Barrel Sponge (*Xestospongia testudinaria*), while the slender Sponge Goby (*Pleurosicya elongata*) lives under the floppy blade-like thallus of the Fan Sponge (*Ianthella basta*). Unfortunately, these species are rarely collected for the home aquarium. If you examine these sponges carefully on your next dive trip, however, you might observe some of these unique sponge dwellers. Other facultative sponge dwellers found in the Indo-Pacific include the Giant Frogfish (*Antennarius commerson*), Striated Frogfish (*Antennarius striatus*), Tasseled Scorpionfish (*Scorpaenopsis oxycephala*), Zebra Lionfish (*Dendrochirus zebra*), Longfin Dottyback (*Pseudochromis polynemus*), Splendid Dottyback (*Pseudochromis splendens*), Spotted Hawkfish (*Cirrhitichthys aprinus*), and the Blackspotted Puffer (*Arothron nigropunctatus*).

Habitat Distribution of Reef Fishes

We have already discussed how reefs can be divided into a number of zones and habitats that differ in both physical and biological characteristics. Studies have demonstrated that many reef fishes are limited in distribution to specific habitats or reef zones. For example, on a reef in Polynesia, 45% of the species observed occurred in only one of four possible reef zones (i.e., fringing reef, lagoon, reef crest, outer slope). The Fourline Wrasse (*Pseudocheilinus tetrataenia*) and the Crosshatch Goby (*Amblygobius decussatus*) were only found on the fringing reef, while the Yellow Boxfish (*Ostracion cubicus*) and the Saddled Toby (*Canthigaster valentini*) were limited in their distribution to the lagoon. Only 5% of the species in this study oc-

Deep reef: many marine species have limited distributions in certain reef zones and habitats. This patch of reef at 45 meters (211 feet) shows a *Choriaster granulatus*, Sea Star, and various sponges, including barrel sponges, crinoids, and small reef fishes (Bali, Indonesia).

curred in all four habitats. These ubiquitous species include the Manybar Goatfish (*Parupeneus multifasciatus*), Vagabond Butterflyfish (*Chaetodon vagabundus*), Black Damselfish (*Stegastes nigricans*), and the Convict Surgeonfish (*Acanthurus triostegus*). In Guam, the Striped Bristletooth (*Ctenochaetus striatus*), Lavender Surgeonfish (*Acanthurus nigrofuscus*), Speckled Butterflyfish (*Chaetodon citrinellus*), Redbreasted Maori Wrasse (*Cheilinus fasciatus*), and the Ocellated Toby (*Canthigaster solandri*) are all found in four or more different reef zones. In a study conducted on Red Sea species, 11 of 38 species were found to be ubiquitous, occurring from the reef flat to a depth of 20 m (65 ft.) on the fore-reef slope. These included the Peacock Hind (*Cephalopholis argus*), Red Sea Goatfish (*Parupeneus forsskali*), Indian Ocean Bird Wrasse (*Gomphosus caeruleus*), the Orangespine Unicornfish (*Naso*

lituratus), the Indian Ocean Sailfin Tang (*Zebrasoma desjardinii*), and the Orangelined Triggerfish (*Balistapus undulatus*).

It should be pointed out that species-specific habitat preferences might also change from one geographical location to another. As far as their husbandry is concerned, it would seem logical that "generalists" would be more likely to adapt to aquarium confines due to their plasticity in habitat selection than habitat specialists would.

Some species may also have different habitat preferences during different phases of their life cycle. Convict Surgeonfish (*Acanthurus triostegus*) live in shallow water as juveniles and move to deeper water as they mature; young Humbug Dascyllus (*Dascyllus aruanus*) usually live among the branches of different coral species than adults do. Likewise, some damselfishes in the Caribbean live among fire corals (*Millepora* spp.) as juveniles, but not as adults. A study conducted near Lizard Island on the Great Barrier Reef showed that young Bluestreak Cleaner Wrasses (*Labroides dimidiatus*) were more abundant in the deeper habitats (the reef slopes and reef base), while larger individuals were more common on the reef flat and reef crest. In Moon Wrasse (*Thalassoma lunare*) populations in the same area, new recruits were encountered more on the reef slope, while adults were more ubiquitous on the deeper reef base and sand slope. The different age classes of 62 other wrasse species studied at Lizard Island showed no differences in habitat distribution.

So what factors influence the distribution of fishes on a coral reef? One of the most important is the type and configuration of the substrate. A number of studies have shown that the greatest number of reef fishes occur in habitats where the substrate varies in vertical relief and has greater rugosity, and where there is prolific stony coral growth. More complex reef habitats attract a larger variety of reef fishes because of the diversity of hiding places and abundance of prey organisms. Areas of low relief devoid of live stony coral do not attract the same variety. Substrate with more vertical relief also has more surface area. And habitats with substantial live-coral coverage are exposed to more water movement and better overall water quality. Wave action, temperature variation, water depth, and bottom slope can all determine the structure of a fish community on a coral reef.

Environmental conditions are not the only factors that influence the fish distribution on a reef. Interspecific competition can also be a factor. For example, the Maroon Anemonefish (*Premnas biaculeatus*) keeps smaller, less aggressive anemonefishes from entering its preferred host, the Bulb Tentacle Sea Anemone (*Entacmaea quadricolor*).

Facing page: volcanic boulders have been colonized by orange soft corals. A shoal of *Pseudanthias* sp. swims above (Mimpang Island, Bali, Indonesia).

Hovering in the current, *Pseudanthias squamipinnis*, Lyretail Anthias, use water motion to bring them live zooplankters that form the basis of their diet (Red Sea).

Water Movement

Water movement can be vital as it pertains to maintaining the health of sessile invertebrates, but it is less important in promoting the well-being of marine fishes (at least in our aquariums). Of course, turbulence at the water's surface is important in facilitating the exchange of gases (e.g., oxygen and carbon dioxide), and in deeper tanks it facilitates water mixing so that conditions do not vary greatly from the surface to the bottom of the aquarium.

There are cases in which water flow affects the behavior of certain fishes. Species that live near the turbulent reef crest, like the Achilles Surgeonfish (*Acanthurus achilles*), will adjust to captivity more readily if provided with similar conditions in the aquarium. Wavemakers, or a series of water pumps that turn off and on to mimic surge action, can enable aquarists to recreate these conditions. In an aquarium without good water flow, for example, the Achilles Surgeonfish has a tendency to pace back and forth at the front of the aquarium. Other active species that inhabit the outer-reef flat, reef crest, or reef face will also appreciate artificially induced surge. Studies have shown that current strength will affect the shoaling behavior of some planktivores, such as the Lyretail Anthias (*Pseudanthias squamipinnis*). This species will form tighter shoals when water flow is increased.

Some species prefer the still waters of protected lagoon areas and are less likely to adapt if they are constantly buffeted by water blasting out of a battery of water pumps, a practice often employed by coral keepers. Juvenile batfishes and spadefishes often reside in shallow, calm mangrove areas or in grass beds on the inner reef flat. The frogfishes, seahorses, pipefishes, dragonets, boxfishes, and pufferfishes often prefer less turbulent conditions.

Temperature

Hobbyists typically think of the coral reef as a relatively stable environment that is subjected to little, if any, temperature fluctuation. This assertion is true for many areas of the reef, but it does not apply to all reef zones. There are typically two different water masses that influence reef habitats. One is a shallow surface water mass that affects the shallow lagoons, reef flats, and reef crests. The other is an oceanic water mass that primarily affects the fore reef, but does infiltrate the reef crest and reef flat at high tide. The oceanic water mass is fairly constant in temperature, while the temperature of the shallow surface water mass can vary greatly. At Arno Atoll, for example, the oceanic water mass is about 28°C (82°F) throughout the year, but water temperatures on the inner reef flat can vary from 27 to 37°C (80 to 98°F). On the reef flat of Heron Island, temperatures commonly fluctuate 2.8 to 5°C (5 to 9°F) during the day, while tidepools on a reef flat in Guam can range in temperature from 27 to 34°C (80 to 93°F). The temperature of a deeper lagoon, such as those found at many atolls, will be more similar to the fore reef than to the reef flat.

When the tide comes in over the

Studies of *Forcipiger longirostris,* Big Longnose Butterflyfish, found it usually occurring in waters that measured between 22 and 27°C (72 and 80°F). The author has found a temperature of 23°C (74°F) is ideal for many captive marine fishes (Sulawesi).

reef flat, the cool oceanic water penetrates the warm surface mass and the temperature of the reef flat drops rather suddenly. Fishes that live in this reef zone experience dramatic changes. If you are snorkeling in this area at flood tide, you can see the obvious mixing of the different water masses. In contrast, fishes that are restricted in distribution to the reef face and fore reef, and especially to the deeper part of this zone, are not exposed to such drastic changes in temperature and other water parameters. Although the annual water temperature on the fore reef may vary in some regions (the fore reef of Heron Island, southern Great Barrier Reef, ranges from 24 to 27°C (76 to 80°F)), daily fluctuations are slight. It is not surprising, then, that fish from intertidal areas, such as the reef flat, are more durable and able to withstand some extreme environmental changes, while those from the fore reef are not as adept at acclimating to rapid changes in their environment. Of course, this does not mean that you should treat more durable fishes with any less care. To avoid undue stress to any fish, it is important that changes in temperature (and other parameters) be made slowly.

Although there may be subtle differences in temperature preferences between species, with the favored measure often being determined by the fish's depth and geographical distribution, the majority of reef fishes will thrive at a moderate range of temperatures. For example, the Yellow Longnose Butterflyfish (*Forcipiger flavissimus*) is usually found in water that is from 22 to 27°C (72 to 80°F) and it will live at temperatures as low as 21°C (70°F). Studies conducted on several species of reef fishes have shown that they will behaviorally thermoregulate. That is, if given a choice of water temperatures they will move to the area that they find most desirable. In these studies, tropical reef fishes "preferred" temperatures between 20 and 30°C (68 and 86°F), depending on the species.

Some species need to be kept at cooler water temperatures in order to thrive. Rocky reef fishes from warm temperate regions are best kept at temperatures lower than those maintained in most tropical marine aquariums. The Catalina Goby (*Lythrypnus dalli*), for example, is best kept at a temperature of 15 to 22°C (59 to 72°F). See Table 18, page 225, for surface temperatures from various geographical regions.

Some deeper-dwelling species also fare better if kept at lower water temperatures. However, depth is less of a determining factor regarding temperature than geographical distribution as temperatures do not usually vary greatly within the depth range from which most reef fishes are collected for the aquarium trade. Off Enewetak Atoll, in the Central Pacific, surface temperatures are

Lythrypnus dalli, Catalina Goby: this cold water fish occurs on rocky reefs along the California coast and is not suitable for the tropical marine aquarium.

typically 29°C (84°F) and drop very little—even at depths of 45 m (146 ft.). At about 90 m (295 ft.) the water temperature is 26°C (78°F), and at 136 m (442 ft.) it drops to 22°C (72°F). There is a similar trend in the Caribbean. Off Belize, the water temperature stays at approximately 28°C (82°F) down to 50 m (163 ft.). The temperature gradually drops below this depth, decreasing to 18°C (64°F) at a depth of 200 m (650 ft.).

Although the majority of species we keep are taken from water no deeper than 30 m (98 ft.), some aquarium species are more abundant in deeper water where temperatures are cooler. The Longfin Anthias (*Pseudanthias ventralis*) is most common near Enewetak at depths between 87 and 116 m (283 and 377 ft.). Although it is not collected for the aquarium trade at this depth, it tends to do better in captivity if kept at water temperatures around 22°C

(72°F). Many of its shallow-water relatives will live at higher water temperatures of up to 28°C (82°F). However, due to their high metabolism, it is best to keep them at lower temperatures.

Most marine fish guides suggest keeping the aquarium at a temperature of 24 to 28°C (76 to 82°F), with the optimal temperature being 26°C (78°F). However, I prefer keeping my aquariums at a lower temperature of about 23°C (74°F). Cooler water slows down the fish's metabolism, so they do not have to be fed as frequently. In addition, hyperactive species are less likely to lose body weight at 23°C. The herbivorous Jewel Damselfish (*Plectroglyphidodon lacrymatus*) is a good example of how much water temperature affects the rate of food ingestion. In a study conducted on its feeding behavior, it was shown that this fish has a mean hourly bite rate of 225 bites at the substrate at 25°C (77°F), while the mean hourly bite rate is approximately 425 at 28°C (82°F). That is a 52% increase in food consumption at a temperature that is only 3°C (5.4°F) higher.

Another advantage to keeping the temperature in the aquarium cooler is that parasites do not reproduce as quickly at lower water temperatures. This gives you more time to deal with a problem if it should arise. Temperature can also have an effect on a fish's disposition. Studies have shown that at least some fish species are more aggressive at higher water temperatures. Although not a concern for every aquarist, fish also grow more slowly at lower water temperatures. I have yet to recognize any deleterious affects resulting from keeping my fish at lower water temperatures.

If you live in a part of the country that is subjected to hot weather, you probably have to fight to keep the aquarium temperatures down in the summer. Although some fish will survive at temperatures as high as 32°C (90°F), it can be lethal if they are maintained at this temperature for extended periods of time. An aquarium at a higher temperature may also "crash" if it is heavily loaded with livestock. If heat suppression is a constant problem, move the aquarium to a cooler part of your home (like the basement) or buy a chiller. For those of you who have yet to set up your aquariums, consider this potential problem carefully. One simple way to prevent your aquarium from heating up is to avoid placing it in direct sunlight. If you are going to mount intense, heat-producing lights in a canopy, make sure you install fans and vents to help evacuate the warm air. Remember, at higher temperatures water has a lower oxygen-carrying capacity (there is less oxygen available for your fish no matter how much you aerate it) and your fishes will need more food to maintain their basal metabolic rates.

> *"Remember, at higher temperatures water has a lower oxygen-carrying capacity (there is less oxygen available for your fish no matter how much you aerate it) and your fishes will need more food to maintain their basal metabolic rates."*

TABLE 18

Geographical Variation in Sea Surface Temperature

LOCATION	TEMPERATURE °C (°F)	LOCATION	TEMPERATURE °C (°F)
Eastern Atlantic		West Pacific	
Canaries	18–22 (64–72)	Singapore	27–31 (80–87)
Western Atlantic		Northern Marianas	25–29 (77–84)
Florida	13–33 (56–91)	Southern Great Barrier Reef	16–35 (60–95)
Caribbean	23–28 (74–82)	Papua New Guinea	26–30 (78–86)
Belize	27–28 (80–82)*	Indian Ocean	
East Coast of Panama		Gulf of Mannar	
(seagrass bed)	27–31 (80–88)	(Southeastern coast of India)	25–30 (77–86)
Gulf of California		Sri Lanka	25–28 (77–83)
Upper Gulf	12–33 (54–91)	Maldives (Addu Atoll)	28–29 (82–84)
Central Gulf	16–33 (60–91)	Mauritius	22–27 (72–80)**
Southern part	20–30 (68–86)	Reunion	21–27 (70–80)**
South and Central Pacific		Madagascar	22–29 (72–84)**
Hawaiian Islands (Kona Coast)	22–29 (72–84)	Aldabra	23–28 (74–82)**
Pitcairn Islands	22–26 (72–78)	Red Sea	
Easter Island	18–24 (64–75)	Northern Red Sea	
Marquesas	26–27 (78–80)**	(e.g., Aqaba, Eilat)	21–28 (70–82)
Tahiti	26–27 (78–80)**	Central Red Sea	
Gambier	21–26 (70–78)**	(e.g., Port Sudan, Jeddah)	27–30 (80–86)
Rapa	20–23 (68–74)**	Southern Red Sea and Gulf of Aden	
		(e.g., Djibouti)	25–32 (77–90)

* Range between October and May.

**Mean surface temperatures from summer and winter months.

Light Levels

As mentioned earlier, light levels can play an important part in assuring that certain fish species will acclimate. In many species, light levels are important in determining what depth you will find them on the reef, what habitat they occupy, their activity patterns, and their reproductive behavior. Water depth and turbidity (i.e., clarity) affect light levels. The intensity and quality of light changes dramatically from the shallow reef areas (less than 10 m [33 ft.] in depth) to the deeper terraces and walls of the reef slope. Water is 1,000 times less transparent than air and selectively absorbs various wavelengths of

Many species from deeper water or those with nocturnal habits, such as these *Apogon sealei*, Seale's Cardinalfish, will do better in an aquarium with subdued lighting (Sulawesi).

light as it penetrates to the depths. For example, 90% of the longer wavelengths of light (red and orange) are filtered out within the first 10 m (33 ft.), yellow is almost gone by 18 m (59 ft.), green has nearly disappeared at around 27 m (88 ft.), and by 41 m (133 ft.) everything looks blue or violet. If you have ever been diving in deep water, you are familiar with this phenomenon.

I remember one of my first deep dives in the Cook Islands during which I spotted what I thought was a new species of anthias at 33 m (107 ft.). It looked like the Purple Queen Anthias (*Pseudanthias pascalus*), but it was blue rather than the characteristic magenta color. After returning home and having some pictures of this unusual fish developed, I realized it was the common Purple Queen—magenta just looks blue at that depth. (Fortunately, the light produced by my strobe had illuminated its true colors.)

Although 30 m (98 ft.) under the ocean's surface sounds like a considerable depth, it is not as drastic if you think of it in terrestrial terms. It is roughly equivalent to the height of three school buses stacked end on end. But light levels drop quickly as we move from the ocean surface to the depths of the fore reef. Measurements taken at noon on a sunny day near Enewetak Atoll showed that the surface irradiance (measured to be about 100,000 lux) drops by 73% (to 27,000 lux) just under the water's surface. At 14 m (46 feet), surface irradiance has dropped 85% (to 15,000 lux); at 30 m (98 ft.) it has decreased 93% (to 7000 lux), and at 45 m (146 ft.) it has dropped 97% (to 3000 lux). These levels can also decrease as much as 50% when the sky is cloudy or as the sun moves across the sky. An example in the beginning of this chapter suggests that certain deep-water anthias are less likely to adapt to an aquarium that is aglow with artificial sunlight. Consider an average-sized reef aquarium illuminated with large metal halide lamps. It may have a reading as high as 15,000 lux at the aquarium bottom. A distribution study of the Longfin Anthias (*Pseudanthias ventralis*) shows that they are most abundant in Enewetak at depths greater than 45 m (146 ft.). The intensity of light in such a reef tank, therefore, would be too high. For those species that inhabit the deep fore reef, the aquarist is wise to mimic the light levels that occur there.

Other cryptic or nocturnal species are also more likely to come out of hiding if kept in a less brightly illuminated tank. Bamboo sharks, catsharks, certain eels, soldierfishes, squirrelfishes, bigeyes, flashlight fishes, pineapple fishes, some cardinalfishes, scorpionfishes, basslets, roundheads, drums, soapfishes, and livebearing brotulas may adapt more readily and be more conspicuous tank residents if exposed to less intense lighting—especially during the acclimation period.

Although less important in determining optimal conditions for most aquarium fishes, turbidity also affects light penetration. The more sediment present in the water, the more difficult it is for light to penetrate. Near-shore reefs subjected to lots of freshwater runoff and silt are not as brightly illuminated as reefs in clear water. Species common to estuarine conditions often occur in more silty conditions and thus are used to lower light levels than those species from the shallow reef face.

The salinity of most of the world's oceans is 34 to 35 ppt, a reasonable target for most aquarium systems. Red Sea fishes, such as this *Plectropomus pessuliferus*, Roving Coral Grouper, come from waters with a salinity of 37 to 42 ppt but will usually adapt well to less saline conditions.

Salinity

Salinity does not require exact duplication in order for a coral reef fish to thrive in captivity, although salinity levels can vary between reef zones and habitats, or from one geographical area to another. The Red Sea is the most hypersaline area that reef fishes are collected from for the aquarium trade, having a salinity 37 to 42 parts per thousand (ppt), depending on the time of year and location. But fish species from this region will readily acclimate to a salinity between 29 and 37 ppt, the salinity level most aquarists maintain in their tanks. (The salinity of most of the world's tropical oceans is between 34 and 35 ppt.)

CORAL REEF HABITATS 227

TABLE 19

Estimating Salinity with a Hydrometer

The most practical tool for measuring the salt content of marine aquarium water is a hydrometer designed to indicate specific gravity at a temperature of 24°C (75°F). The popular "dip-and-read" box hydrometers, along with some glass aquarium hydrometers, are built to give specific gravity (or density) readings at this temperature. On the other hand, many glass hydrometers sold to aquarists are actually meant for laboratory use and are standardized for use with fluid samples at 15°C (59°F). Such a laboratory hydrometer may be used, but its readings need to be corrected to compensate for the actual temperature of the water sample. To do so, first measure the temperature of the water sample and take a hydrometer reading. Next, use the chart below to convert this reading to density. For example, if the temperature of the tank is 24°C (75°F) and the hydrometer reading is 1.0240, the conversion factor would be 0.0021. Add this to the hydrometer reading to get 1.0261.

Now, refer to Table 20, page 229, **Conversion of Density to Salinity**. The density value of 1.026 corresponds to a salinity of 35 ppt (parts per thousand), which is the average value for natural seawater worldwide and a good target for most marine aquarium systems.

Conversion of Observed Hydrometer Readings to Density
TEMPERATURE (°C/°F)

HYDROMETER READING	20°C/68°F	21°C/70°F	22°C/72°F	23°C/74°F	24°C/75°F	25°C/77°F	26°C/78°F
1.0170	.0010	.0012	.0015	.0017	.0020	.0022	.0025
1.0180	.0010	.0012	.0015	.0017	.0020	.0023	.0025
1.0190	.0010	.0012	.0015	.0018	.0020	.0023	.0026
1.0200	.0010	.0013	.0015	.0018	.0020	.0023	.0026
1.0210	.0010	.0013	.0015	.0018	.0021	.0023	.0026
1.0220	.0011	.0013	.0015	.0018	.0021	.0023	.0026
1.0230	.0011	.0013	.0016	.0018	.0021	.0024	.0026
1.0240	.0011	.0013	.0016	.0018	.0021	.0024	.0027
1.0250	.0011	.0013	.0016	.0018	.0021	.0024	.0027
1.0260	.0011	.0013	.0016	.0019	.0022	.0024	.0027
1.0270	.0011	.0014	.0016	.0019	.0022	.0024	.0027
1.0280	.0011	.0014	.0016	.0019	.0022	.0025	.0028
1.0290	.0011	.0014	.0016	.0019	.0022		

At a lower salinity, fish have to expend less metabolic energy to conserve the water in their body tissues. In fact, many coral reef fishes can withstand salinity levels approaching that of freshwater for short periods of time (e.g., 1 week). Emperor Angelfish (*Pomacanthus imperator*) have been kept at a salinity of 7 ppt for one month with no apparent ill effects. These fish were not "stressed," as indicated by the lack of change in their serum cortisol and glucose levels. The angelfish also continued to feed and did not behave abnormally. The lethal limit for the Emperor Angelfish was found to be a salinity of 5 ppt; at this salinity all individuals died within 3 days. Therefore, while fishes from coral reef environments have long been thought of as being stenohaline (only tolerating a narrow salinity range), most species studied to date are actually physiologically euryhaline (tolerating a range of salinities). This can be used to the aquarist's advantage. One effective treatment for certain parasites, like *Cryptocaryon*, is to lower the salinity of your quarantine tank to less than 15 ppt for 1 week. This will kill the parasite, but will not harm the fish. Lowering salinity levels does not decimate all parasites. For example, *Amyloodinium ocellatum* is a euryhaline species that often parasitizes estuarine fishes. Lower salinity may not kill it completely, but may impede its development. A hypersaline condition, or high salinity, is another matter. If you were to raise your salinity much above that found in the area where the fish was collected, the fish would become dehydrated as a result of the loss of water by diffusion to its surrounding environment. This can cause stress, leading to physiological disturbances, disease, and possibly death.

Although salinity on the reef is typically stable over the short term, there are habitats where it can show some daily fluctuation. The salinity of tidepools isolated at low tide can increase as a result of evaporation, or decrease as a result of heavy rain. The specific gravity of tidepools on Guam reefs varied from about 1.014 (about 20 ppt salinity) to over 1.030 (about 40 ppt). As with temperature, it is best to expose your fishes to gradual, rather than sudden, changes in salinity.

Substrate Type

Substrate is defined as the base on which an organism lives or over which it moves. As far as coral reef fish are concerned, there are two broad categories of substrate—living and nonliving. Although the neophyte aquarist may not think the substrate we choose for our aquariums is as important to the fish as the water chemistry, it can have a direct impact on the survival of some specialized fishes.

TABLE 20
Conversion of Density to Salinity

DENSITY	SALINITY (in parts per thousand)	DENSITY	SALINITY (in parts per thousand)
1.0180	25	1.0240	32
1.0185	25	1.0245	33
1.0190	26	1.0250	34
1.0195	27	1.0255	34
1.0200	27	1.0260	35
1.0205	28	1.0265	36
1.0210	29	1.0270	36
1.0215	29	1.0275	37
1.0220	30	1.0280	38
1.0225	30	1.0285	38
1.0230	31	1.0290	39
1.0235	32	1.0295	40
		1.0300	40

Many species are dependent on the proper substrate. Coarse sediment with scattered rubble seems to suit these adult *Valenciennea strigata*, Yellowhead Sleeper Gobies, while juvenile and smaller sleeper gobies tend to prefer small-grained reef sand (Papua New Guinea).

Nonliving substrate includes boulders, rubbles, dead corals, cobbles, pebbles, and sand. The size of the sand grains and pieces of rubble we choose to use in our aquariums can affect the health of those species that bury, construct burrows, or have specialized feeding behaviors. For example, some wrasses bury under the sand at night or when threatened. If they are placed in a tank with coarse carbonate substrate, they often succumb to bacterial and viral infections resulting from damage caused when they attempt to bury under these abrasive materials. On the other hand, jawfishes are better able to construct burrows if the substrate is of varying grain size (this should include small chunks of coral rubble and a coarser grade of crushed coral). Other species, such as the sleeper gobies, sift the substrate through their gills to collect infaunal worms and crustaceans. Studies conducted on the Teardrop Sleeper Goby (*Valenciennea longipinnis*) demonstrated that their distribution on the reef was correlated to the presence of coarse sediment (the substrate that attracted an important prey source, harpacticoid copepods) and a lack of large rubble. However, aquarium observations suggest that smaller sleeper gobies have difficulty sifting coarser bottom materials, such as large grades of crushed coral, and show greater survivorship if small-grained reef sand is used.

Some of the sand around coral reefs is the result of the feeding activity of parrotfishes. These fishes rasp the coral surface with their hard beaks to get at boring algae and then crush the calcareous material into fine particles with a specialized pharynx. The parrotfishes excrete this indigestible debris in large clouds and the resultant material ends up on the seafloor.

Although still classified as a nonliving substrate, "live" sand is a great substrate for sand-sifting gobies and fishes that bury. This substrate can also help improve the environmental parameters of the tank. Live sand varies in its composition, depending on where it was collected, but it typically consists of coral sand (pulverized and eroded pieces of coral), pieces of the calcareous algae *Halimeda,* and the remains of minute, shelled protozoa known as foraminiferans (Order Foraminifera). The live component of the sand includes aerobic and anaerobic bacteria, forams, annelid worms, crustaceans (primarily isopods, copepods, and amphipods), tiny brittle stars, and even lancelets. The grain size varies from very fine to chunky. It is best to go with a medium grade, where the grains are about the same size or slightly larger than a pinhead. Very fine grades may remain suspended, which can result in clogged external filters and destroyed impellers. On the other hand, large grades are more difficult for fishes and invertebrates to stir up.

The advantages of including live sand in the reef aquarium are many. First of all, it looks better than a bare glass bottom or plastic eggcrate material. It also provides refuge for those fishes that bury in the substrate and invertebrates that hide and reproduce in the sand. In turn, these invertebrates can provide an important food source for fishes that feed on infaunal animals. The light color of the sand reflects light off the aquarium bottom and makes the tank look brighter. This reflected light also benefits those zooxanthellae-bearing invertebrates that live near the bottom of the aquarium. Most importantly, the bacteria-laden sand will help reduce ammonia to nitrite, nitrite to nitrate, and the anaerobic forms will break nitrate down into nitrous oxide, which will diffuse from the aquarium. This natural denitrifying process helps control the accumulation of waste products. I have seen nitrate levels drop by half in as a little as 2 days after live sand was added. Adding live sand is also a great way to inoculate a new aquarium with nitrifying bacteria. Live sand will also help maintain your pH and alkalinity levels.

The abundance of caves, overhangs, and catacombs provided by both live and dead substrates affects the density and distribution of fish species on the reef. Shelter sites are of particular importance to the reef's piscine residents and some fish spend

Caves, overhangs and deep crevices provided by live rock and other aquascaping materials seem to be essential for the well being of many naturally cryptic species, such as *Centropyge aurantia*, Golden Angelfish.

"It is not possible to describe a coral reef; to be fully appreciated, it has to be seen," wrote Ernst Haeckel more than 100 years ago. This reef scene includes *Oxycomanthus bennetti*, feather star crinoids, clinging to *Montipora* sp. plate corals while *Pseudanthias* sp. fishes feed in the currents (Milne Bay, Papua New Guinea).

most of their lives hiding in reef recesses. These include the Longjaw Moray (*Channomuraena vittata*), Zebra Moray (*Gymnomuraena zebra*), Ridgeback Bass (*Liopropoma mowbrayi*), Candy Bass (*Liopropoma carmabi*), Golden Angelfish (*Centropyge aurantia*), Blackspot Pygmy Angelfish (*Centropyge nigriocella*), Leopard Toby (*Canthigaster leoparda*), and the Pygmy Toby (*Canthigaster pygmaea*). These species are rarely encountered by divers, except possibly when artificial lights are used to illuminate their hideaways. When keeping cryptic species, you must provide many usable hiding places to ensure acclimation. Many of these cryptic species do better in a reef aquarium because these tanks tend to have a greater number of shelter sites. The number of hiding places can also determine how much your fish quarrel. If shelter sites are limited, fish are likely to fight for those few hiding places.

Live substrates include stony coral, soft coral, sponge, and algae (including macroalgae, turf algae, coralline algae, and *Halimeda*) that can vary greatly in their structural complexity and form. Stony corals can be branching, massive, encrusting, columnar, foliaceous, laminar, or turbinate. One important difference between these growth forms is the amount of shelter each provides for reef fishes. A head of branching staghorn coral has more hiding places than a similar-sized massive *Porites* coral. Likewise, a bed of green macroalgae, such as a *Caulerpa* species, will provide greater refuging opportunities than a veneer of encrusting coralline algae.

Many reef fishes show distinct preferences for a particular type of substrate. A study conducted on the Great Barrier Reef showed that the Dash-and-Dot Goatfish (*Parupeneus barberinus*) and Yellowlined Goatfish (*Mulloides flavolineatus*) associate with sand; the Manybar Goatfish (*Parupeneus multifascia-*

tus), the Yellowsaddle Goatfish (*Parupeneus cyclostomus*), Whitelined Goatfish (*Parupeneus ciliatus*), and Twobar Goatfish (*Parupeneus bifasciatus*) are found over carbonate or coral reef substrate; and the Redspot Goatfish (*Parupeneus heptacanthus*), Indian Goatfish (*Parupeneus indicus*), and the Blackstriped Goatfish (*Upeneus tragula*) are most often found on mixed seagrass and sand substrates. A species predilection to associate with a particular substrate is often a reflection of the substrate preferences of their prey. Whenever possible, an aquarist should try to provide the preferred substrate for the species kept in his or her aquarium. (See the species accounts in the latter half of this volume, starting on page 245, for substrate preferences.)

To understand the complexity of a coral reef, it helps greatly to experience it in person. As Ernst Haeckel noted in his travel diary of more than a century ago, "It is not really possible to describe a coral reef; to be fully appreciated, it has to be seen." Haeckel, of course, was writing before the time of color film and underwater photography, and it is hardly necessary for the aquarist to take up snorkeling or diving before attempting to replicate a realistic reef environment in the aquarium. Not surprisingly, I know many divers who have been attracted to the aquarium hobby and many more aquarists who have taken up mask and fins to get out and study the natural habitats of the fishes they keep.

Fortunately, the armchair naturalist today can view reefscapes and study their fauna and flora in books, videos, and other media, and there is no longer any reason for marine aquariums to be unrealistically barren, artificial, and inhospitable to the fishes we keep. Any effort to duplicate the natural habitats of your specimens will be repaid many times over in the health, vigor, and behaviors they exhibit.

> *". . . there is no longer any reason for marine aquariums to be unrealistically barren, artificial, and inhospitable to the fishes we keep. Any effort to duplicate the natural habitats of your specimens will be repaid many times over in the health, vigor, and behaviors they exhibit."*

References

Bortone et al. (1977), Colin et al. (1986), Dennis & Bight (1988), Edwards & Roswell (1981), Galzin (1987), Gischler & Ginsburg (1996), Green (1996), Grovhoug & Henderson (1976), Hillis-Colinvaux (1986), Jones & Chase (1975), Key (1973), Larson (1983), McCormick (1995), Meesters et al. (1991), Müller (1995), Parker & Ross (1986), Polunin & Klumpp (1989), Polunin & Brothers (1989), Popper & Fishelson (1973), Potts & Swart (1984), Preston & Preston (1975), Reynolds & Casterlin (1980a, 1980b), Sedberry & Carter (1993), Sonnier et al. (1976), Sprung (1995), St. John et al. (1989), Thayer et al. (1987), Tursch (1982), Tyler & Böhlke (1972), Weinstein & Heck (1979), Wells (1952), Woo & Chung (1995).

CHAPTER

4

The Fishes

The Morays (Muraenidae) to the Anthias (Anthiinae): A Guide to the Families, Genera, and Species

"In all things of nature, there is something of the marvelous."
—Aristotle, *Parts of Animals*

A CORAL REEF OR A MARINE AQUARIUM WITHOUT FISHES HAS BEEN likened to a garden without birds or butterflies—beautiful but lacking the flashing colors, the dynamics of movement, and the captivating behaviors that truly complete the scene.

While the gardener must rely on nature to provide the desirable avian and insect life, an aquarist has almost divine control over the fish species that populate his or her created piece of ocean. Given the astonishing diversity of choices available, with fishes from the far reaches of the tropical world, the aquarium keeper today can assemble groupings of marine species that provide endless hours of pleasure—or unhappy scenes of strife, territoriality, and unwanted predation.

Matching species in a marine aquarium is both science and art. Doing it well may take years of experimentation and reading, and it is far from uncommon for inexperienced or bewildered aquarists to select fishes that are inappropriate for one reason or another. The accounts that follow are intended to provide the aquarium keeper with a tool to better understand the families

Sweepers (*Parapriacanthus* sp.) and *Pseudanthias* sp. feeding in the currents above a coral plate festooned with crinoids. (Milne Bay, Papua New Guinea)

Pseudanthias ignitus, Flame Anthias: this displaying male is irresistably appealing to marine aquarists, but it comes with a set of biological requirements that must be known and considered before the specimen is acquired (Maldives).

and species available, to choose intelligently among them and, once the choices have been made, to keep the fishes alive and well.

In these pages and the companion volumes to this work, the aquarist will find information about, and photographs of, the majority of coral reef fishes that can be encountered in the trade by aquarists and by divers exploring reefs around the world. This is not to say that all of these fishes are readily or constantly available. Some of the species covered rarely enter the ornamental marine fish trade, but are included because they would make desirable aquarium specimens—or are of general interest to fishkeepers.

Others, as will be clear from the descriptions, are not suitable for home aquariums, even though they may frequently be offered for sale to marine hobbyists. While even experienced fishkeepers sometimes fall prey to the "must have" or "love at first sight" syndrome when encountering a new species that turns up in the local aquarium shop, uninformed purchases very often have unhappy endings.

The simple rule of thumb is to examine the care requirements of each species very carefully before seeking out or purchasing a particular fish. I have made every attempt to discourage aquarists from purchasing those species that do not fare well in captivity. Although things are improving, it is still possible to see innocent hobbyists heading home with fishes that have, for decades, defied the best efforts of experts—even professional public aquarists—to keep them alive. If you observe such species in your local aquarium store, please point them out to the management. If the store doesn't discontinue the selling of unkeepable species, please shop elsewhere. It is critical that we police our own hobby.

An overview of the systematics, biology, behavioral ecology, and captive care of the group—whether it is a family, subfamily, or genus—is provided in each section. The reader is urged to examine these overviews before moving into the species accounts, as there is often important general information covering a family group that is not repeated for each and every species.

In order to make information more readily available to the hobbyist or diver, the species accounts are broken down into the following divisions and subdivisions.

Scientific Name

This is the most current Latin name applied to the fish by the scientific community. The name is in the form of a binomial. The first name indicates the genus to which the fish belongs, while the second name is the species name. At first mention of a scientific name, the "author" is listed after it. This is the ichthyologist or naturalist who formally described the fish. If the name is in parentheses, it indicates that the species was originally placed in a different genus. For example, the Hispid Frogfish (*Antennarius hispidus*) (Bloch & Schneider, 1801) was originally placed in the genus *Lophius* by its describers, but has since been moved to the genus *Antennarius*.

Common Name

One or more common names are listed for each species. The first name provided is the name most frequently used in the authoritative checklists and field guides written by ichthyologists. It is the name we will use in this series. In many cases, the names used in the aquarium trade are not given as the preferred name. This is often because the trade name(s) are confusing and lend little insight into the systematics or relatedness of various species. For example, in the aquarium trade, the name "scooter

Anampses chrysocephalus, Redtail Tamarin Wrasse: members of this genus are notoriously problematic, even for professional aquarists. Knowing the general characteristics and husbandry requirements of different genera is an essential tool for the informed marine aquarium enthusiast when selecting fishes.

Variola louti, Lyretail Grouper: a gorgeous species whose maximum length of 80 cm (32 in.) demands that it ultimately be housed in a very large aquarium (Red Sea).

blenny" is applied to members of the Family Pinguipedidae and the Family Callionymidae. Members of these two families are referred to as sand perches and dragonets by ichthyologists, while blennies belong to the Family Blenniidae. In assigning the preferred common name to each species, I have attempted to steer away from such misnomers and toward names that will minimize confusion and bring science and hobby closer together.

For example, the names used in ichthyological circles often incorporate the scientific name into the common name. For instance, *Dendrochirus biocellatus* is called the Twinspot Lionfish—*biocellatus* means "two ocelli" or "two spots"—hence the name Twinspot. I believe that by using a common name that is derived from the scientific name, amateur aquarists, divers, and marine scientists can all better communicate with one another. However, to make the book more user-friendly, I have tried to include most of the common names used in the aquarium hobby in the list of common names and in the index.

Maximum Length

This refers to the greatest length that an individual of that particular species can attain—or the longest ever reported—measuring from the end of the snout to the tip of the tail. In most cases, the length of a specimen will fall short of this measure, but the aquarist should always infer that his or her fish will reach a maximum length near to that presented. In some cases, the standard length (SL)—which is measured from the tip of the snout to the base of the caudal (tail) fin—may be given.

Range

The distribution of a fish is presented from its eastern, western, northern, and southern geographical limits. This information is of great value to those aquarists that want to set up a tank that represents a fish community from a specific geographical location. It may also provide clues to the environmental conditions to which a species is subjected (e.g., fishes from Easter Island will tolerate cooler water temperatures than species limited to coral reefs around the Philippines).

Biology

In this section, information is provided on the natural history of the fish. This includes details on the habitats and reef zones occupied by the fish, its depth range, food habits, feeding behavior, reproductive behavior, social organization, and any interspecific relationships. The information was compiled from scientific papers, fish guides, and personal observations.

A koi-like angelfish specimen from an isolated population of *Holacanthus ciliaris*, Queen Angelfish, at St. Paul's Rocks in the Central Atlantic, where inbreeding has apparently caused extreme color aberrations.

Aquarium suitability varies significantly among reef fishes, even among species within the same genus. This series of books suggests a numerical Aquarium Suitability Index, with ratings ranging from a low of 1 (for species that are almost impossible to keep) up to a high of 5 (for fishes that are known to be very hardy and able to adapt easily to captive conditions). This rugged species, *Histrio histrio*, Sargassum Frogfish, has an Aquarium Suitablility Index of 4.

Captive Care

This section includes specific husbandry requirements, food preferences, color fastness, how aggressive a species is toward conspecifics and heterospecifics, unusual habits, suitability of the species for the invertebrate aquarium, and captive breeding information, if available.

Aquarium Size

This is the minimum suitable aquarium size for an adult individual of the species. Of course, juveniles and adolescents can be housed in smaller tanks. Activity levels and behavior patterns of a particular species have been accounted for whenever possible. As this is the minimum suitable size, please note that providing as much room as possible will allow any fish to acclimate better and display less aggression toward its tankmates.

Temperature

This is the temperature range most suitable for the species. The data is based on captive observation and/or examination of the geographical distribution of the species. For example, a species that is found around Pitcairn Island can withstand lower water temperatures than a fish that is limited in its distribution to Micronesia. In many cases, the fish would survive at higher and lower water temperatures than recommended.

Aquarium Suitability Index

I have provided a number from 1 to 5 to give the reader some indication of the durability, hardiness, and/or adaptability of each species. Factors such as readiness to feed, dietary breadth, competitiveness, tolerance of sudden changes, and deteriorating conditions were taken into account when applying a captive suitability rating. A species typically loses one rating point on my scale if live food is usually required. The origin of an individual also influences its likelihood of survival in captivity. In some regions, the fishes being collected are handled with less care or are captured using chemicals. This makes them stressed and less likely to acclimate. Although fishes from the Philippines and Indonesia are most often considered "handicapped" because of the stress they are exposed to before being shipped, I have seen collectors/wholesalers in Florida who housed and handled fish with little regard for their long-term health. The following is a breakdown of the rating system:

1 = These species are almost impossible to keep and should be left on the reef. These fishes may rarely feed, may be prone to disease, may be incurably shy, and, for one or more of these reasons, will almost always waste away and die in the home aquarium.

2 = Most individuals of these species do not acclimate to the home aquarium, often refusing to feed and wasting away in captivity. However, the occasional individual may adapt if kept in optimal water conditions and housed on its own or with noncompetitive tankmates. These species are best left in the wild or ordered only by the experienced aquarist with the aptitude and willingness to devote the time and energy to maintaining them.

One of those species that advanced aquarists are still working to understand, *Macropharyngodon bipartitus*, the Vermiculate Leopard Wrasse, has had a poor survival record in captivity. Aquarium Suitability Index: 2.

3 = These species are moderately hardy, with most individuals acclimating to the home aquarium if special care is provided. This may include offering live food to induce a feeding response, keeping them with less competitive (and less aggressive) tankmates, and providing aquarium conditions that resemble those of their natural habitats. For some of these species, a lush growth of filamentous algae may also provide a natural source of food and increase the chances of their successful maintenance.

4 = These species are durable, with most individuals acclimating to the home aquarium. Even so, they should not be exposed to dramatic changes in environment or to poor water conditions. They will accept a wide range of commercially available

THE FISHES 241

An extremely hardy species, but one with an aggressive disposition, is *Pseudochromis splendens*, the Splendid Dottyback, a sponge dweller.

foods. In the case of some fish or crustacean feeders, live food may either be required to induce feeding or may be the only type of food accepted. These fishes could be kept by aquarists with limited experience (e.g., 6 months).

5 = These species are very hardy with almost all individuals readily acclimating to aquarium confines. They are undemanding and are more likely to withstand some neglect and deteriorating conditions. They will accept a wide range of commercially available fish foods and will not require live food to survive. These fish are great for the beginning hobbyist.

While these rankings are arbitrary, they are based on the collected experiences of hundreds of amateur and professional aquarists, marine biologists, aquarium trade importers, distributors, retailers, and others. (Readers with additional information—or contrary opinions—are invited to contact the author or publisher at the addresses listed on the last page of this book.)

Remarks

If sexual dimorphism and sexual dichromatism exists for the species, details are provided in this section. In addition, information on salient identifying characteristics and color variation is included. In some cases, morphological and chromatic differences between similar species and incorrect or obsolete scientific names often used in the aquarium literature are given—as well as interesting anecdotes about the species.

Wherever possible, at least one photograph is provided for each of the species accounts. In some cases, two or more photographs of the same fish are provided to show color differences between males and females or between adults and juveniles. Multiple photos may also be used to demonstrate the chromatic variability within a species. A complete listing of salient distinguishing characteristics and detailed descriptions of the color pattern is not included, but can be found in more technical reference works listed in the bibliography. Instead, photographs are provided to enable the hobbyist to make a correct identification.

One additional note: while the organization of these volumes follows standard taxonomic order, the reef-dwelling cartilaginous fishes, or elasmobranchs, will be covered separately in *Aquarium Sharks & Rays* (Microcosm, 1999).

Finally, I hope that these volumes will help the aquarist target the species that he or she finds most appealing and that are appropriate for his or her intended aquarium and tankmates. Just using one's buying power to bring home a fish without foresight and planning is something the thoughtful aquarist will want to avoid.

In the words of John Berry, "The bird of paradise alights only upon the hand that does not grasp." Simply acquiring fishes without studying their natural histories and biological requirements too often leads to problems for the animals and expensive and unhappy experiences for their owners—there are better ways of approaching and enjoying these wonderful works of nature.

New and rare species continually appear in the ichthyological literature and aquarium trade, and future volumes of this series will attempt to cover all fishes of interest to marine aquarists and reef naturalists. This fish is a prized *Paracentropyge venusta*, Venustus Angelfish.

Family Muraenidae
Moray Eels

Aquarists and divers are instinctively drawn to moray eels, perhaps because of their menacing, snakelike appearance and their reputation for viciousness and biting. However, as anyone who has ever kept these eels in an aquarium or interacted with them in the wild well knows, most moray species are shy, retiring creatures. They are fishes, not snakes, and most human bites occur accidentally or when the eel is intentionally provoked.

For example, if a diver thrusts his or her hand into a hole containing a moray, the eel may perceive this as a threat and bite. Some attacks may also be the result of mistaken identity. If an aquarist or diver places a hand near a moray's lair, or attempts to hand-feed the eel, the animal may easily mistake the fingers for a natural prey item—and grab one instinctively.

Many years ago, a moray lured me into the marine aquarium hobby. In fact, not only was this eel responsible for my baptism into the saltwater fish hobby, it also landed me in the boy's choir—a fate that seemed worse than death. I was 12 at the time, and I wanted to set up a saltwater tank with a Spotted Moray (*Gymnothorax moringa*). My mother said that I could have the eel if I agreed to join the choir. For most aquarists, the price of owning a moray is considerably lower, and many of the smaller species make excellent, hardy specimens for the home aquarium.

Classification and Biology

Moray eels belong to the Family Muraenidae, which is comprised of 15 genera and approximately 200 species. They range in size from 20 cm (8 in.) to 3.9 m (13 ft.) and are characterized by a lack of pectoral and pelvic fins, gill openings that consist of small holes with no bony cover, dorsal and anal fins that are continuous around the tail (in some species the median fins are absent), and large, tooth-ridden mouths. Morays lack scales. To protect themselves from parasites and abrasions, they exude large amounts of body slime. Morays may appear menacing because their mouths are frequently agape, displaying their formidable dental equipment. But although they look threatening, this is simply how morays respire. The mouth remains open as they pump water over the gills with the muscles in the gill cavity. Some morays have hooked jaws and such large teeth that they are not able to close their jaws completely.

Juveniles differ from adults in their body proportions and, in some species, in their coloration. The body generally becomes thicker with age, and the color pattern may also change dramatically. For example, the juvenile Giant Moray (*Gymnothorax javanicus*) is pale with large, widely scattered dark brown spots. With age, it becomes much darker overall and the spots break up, becoming smaller and more numerous. Although a moray's color pattern can often be used to differentiate species, it can vary somewhat between individuals—even between those in the same size class.

The vast majority of morays occur on coral reefs, but there are also species that live on rocky reefs in temperate waters. One species, *Gymnothorax polyuranodon*, even lives in freshwater in Indonesia, and possibly Fiji and Australia as well. One temperate-water member of the family is the California Moray (*Gymnothorax mordax*), which is a resident of rocky reefs in cooler waters off the west coast of North America. On coral reefs, morays are an important part of the predatory fish community. For example, in the Hawaiian Islands, the moray family is the second-most specious group, with more than 40 species. Because of their secretive natures, however, they are often overlooked by divers watching the more obvious fishes.

Food Habits, Feeding Behavior, and Interspecific Associations

The activity patterns of morays vary from one species to the next. Some hide during the day and come out at night to fossick (prospect) in reef interstices for concealed or nocturnally active prey. Others spend a good portion of the day in the open, moving over the reef and probing coral rubble and reef crevices with their snouts to locate food. Some extremely cryptic species rarely emerge from the reef at all. Although moray species may display a proclivity for either diurnal or nocturnal hunting, most will feed any time the opportunity presents itself. A moray can often be observed with its head protruding from a hole or crevice during the day, and it may ambush unsuspecting prey items that swim past.

The moray's sense of smell and its head and body structure make it a formidable enemy of animals that shelter in the reef. These eels can detect injured or stressed fishes that have hidden

Gymnothorax insigteena, Blackspotted Moray Eel (Bali, Indonesia): similar to the Honeycomb Moray (*G. favagineus*) and a large but easily kept species.

Echidna polyzona, Banded Moray (adult): exhibiting the blunt, molar-form teeth typical of many moray species that feed heavily on crustaceans.

cephalopods. These species have larger eyes, capacious jaws, long teeth, and fewer sensory cells on the nasal lamellae. In most of these species, the teeth have smooth edges to grasp the prey. In a few species, the teeth are serrated, which facilitates cutting chunks from larger prey items. In some species (e.g., *Gymnothorax* spp.), the teeth in the middle of the upper jaw are depressible—they can be folded back against the roof of the mouth. These species use keen vision, as well as olfaction, to help find and capture their prey.

Morays have a relatively wide jaw gape and a flexible buccal region that enable them to swallow prey items that might appear too large to ingest. In most cases, a moray will manipulate a fish in its mouth so that it goes down its gullet headfirst. This facilitates swallowing, since the sharp spines of the prey fish's median fins will be pressed back toward the victim's tail and down against the body. When a captured prey item cannot be swallowed whole, many morays employ a behavior known as knotting. The eel forms two loops around its body with its tail and then rapidly pulls its head through the tightened knot. This

in crevices. With their solid, wedge-shaped heads and muscular, serpentine bodies, morays can squeeze into tight reef fissures to extract them. The eels' keen sense of smell also helps them when hunting after dark or in the deep recesses of the reef. Morays feed infrequently, consuming large prey. One study showed that the Spotted Moray (*G. moringa*) and the Purplemouth Moray (*Gymnothorax vicinus*) only leave their hiding places to forage every three or four days. However, they may also capture prey items taken at their hiding places.

Regarding dietary preferences, morays can be divided into two groups. The first group feeds mainly on crustaceans and other hard-shelled invertebrates. The second group primarily eats fishes, but will occasionally eat crustaceans and cephalopods. The first group includes members of the genera *Echidna*, *Gymnomuraena*, and *Siderea*. They usually have blunt, conical, or molarlike teeth that are good for crushing the exoskeletons of their invertebrate prey. They also tend to have small eyes, short mouths, and olfactory systems rich with sensory cells. Not surprisingly, these morays rely more on smell than sight to locate their prey. When these species approach their prey, they often move their heads from side to side and may actually touch their prey with their noses before making a strike. Taste and touch receptors on the noses, lips, and mouths of morays help them to assess prey items before trying to eat them.

Most morays fall into the second group—feeding more heavily on fishes and occasionally consuming crustaceans and

Gymnothorax fimbriatus, Fimbriated Moray: a reclusive species whose formidable needlelike teeth allow it to capture and consume a diet of fishes.

enables the moray to either rip a mouthful of flesh from an oversized victim or flatten the body of the prey item so that it can be swallowed whole. In some cases, a moray may hold a prey item in a knot for an extended period of time as if constricting it. Two other behaviors many morays employ when feeding are to shake their heads vigorously or to rotate on their longitudinal axes. These actions facilitate swallowing prey whole or tearing pieces off larger food items.

At least one moray species has been reported to engage in prey storing. In this case, a Panamic Green Moray (*Gymnothorax castaneus*) was observed leaving its cave and killing a Blue and Gold Snapper (*Lutjanus viridis*). It returned to its hiding place, which already contained the bodies of two snappers dispatched earlier. The moray stored the fish it had just killed, then swallowed one of the moribund individuals. Whether morays regularly employ this behavior is not known.

As they forage or move over the bottom, morays are often followed by a number of predatory reef fishes. The moray's activities flush small fishes and crustaceans out from hiding, making them vulnerable to the eel's attendants. Lionfishes, groupers, soapfishes, and goatfishes will follow morays. Some of these species will even chafe their bodies against a stationary eel to encourage it to move.

Moray eels are occasionally mobbed by potential prey fishes such as damselfishes. Species of damselfishes that form territorial mosaics will abandon their territories and cooperate to drive smaller eels from the area. Not only has this been observed in nature, I have seen Yellowtail Blue Damselfish (*Chrysiptera parasema*) mob a moray that was eating a conspecific (a member of the same damselfish species), and I also observed Humbug Dascyllus Damsels (*Dascyllus aruanus*) nip and tail-beat smaller morays.

Siderea thyrsoidea, White-eye Moray: accepting grooming services from the Common Cleaner Shrimp (*Lysmata amboinensis*).

Morays are frequently serviced by cleaner wrasses (*Labroides* spp.), Bluestripe Pipefish (*Doryrhamphus excisus*), and cleaner shrimps in the genera *Stenopus, Periclimenes, Leander,* and *Lysmata*. Eels are the favored clients of some cleaners, not only because they harbor crustacean and trematode parasites, but also because of the copious amounts of nutrient-rich slime they produce. Cleaner wrasses and cleaner shrimps will also clean food scraps and parasites from the teeth of moray eels, which open their mouths wide to enable the cleaners to do a thorough job.

Social Organization

There is only limited information available on the social behavior of muraenids. Most morays are solitary animals that roam over a relatively large home range, although they may spend much of their time in one or more preferred coral heads or reef crevices. Some morays have been observed in the same coral head for more than a year. Morays may forage in surrounding areas at night, but frequently return to their "home" cave before dawn. Some morays regularly occur in pairs or small groups. For example, as many as five Gray Morays (*Siderea grisea*) may shelter in the same hole. More than one moray species may also occupy the same cave or crevice. Both the Spotted Moray (*G. moringa*) and the Purplemouth Moray (*G. vicinus*), for example, sometimes occupy the same coral head.

Morays are rarely aggressive toward each other in the wild. I have, however, seen them engaging in agonistic interactions, and there are a few accounts of moray melees in the literature. In one episode that I observed, two Giant Morays (*G. javanicus*)

In knotting behavior, an eel pulls a prey item through the tight loops of its body, ripping a mouthful from the prey or flattening it for easier swallowing.

locked jaws and began twisting and rolling over the bottom until the loser finally released its grip and retreated into a nearby crevice. I swam over to examine and photograph this specimen, and saw that it had shreds of flesh hanging from its lower jaw and bleeding incisions. I have also seen Giant Morays doing battle near the Maldive Islands. In this case, the eels were facing one another with their jaws agape. Every time one individual would strike, the other eel would parry to avoid locking jaws. The two maintained this orientation—even as they moved into the water column—until one abruptly darted away. This jaw-locking behavior, which results in bite marks on the jaws of the combatants, apparently occurs in other species as well. I once encountered a large Honeycomb Moray (*Gymnothorax favagineus*) in the Maldives that had lacerations indicative of this type of fighting. There are also reports that the Speckled Moray (*Gymnothorax obesus*), which is found in subtropical waters off New Zealand, locks jaws in combat. Yellow Morays (*Gymnothorax prasinus*), another subtropical form, will also bite each other, often resulting in serious lacerations.

Morays employ at least two threat displays—head shaking and exaggerated jaw gaping. When approached by another moray, many species perform either or both of these behaviors. It is also not uncommon for an individual to place its open mouth around the body of an intruding eel. In most cases, however, they do not bite down or cause any bodily harm.

Gymnothorax javanicus, Giant Moray: large, aggressive eels often display wounds resulting from fighting members of their own species. Reaching 10 feet in length and 150 pounds, the Giant Moray is for huge aquariums only.

Sexuality, Sexual Dimorphism, and Reproduction

Reef fishes can be classified into several categories based on their sexuality. There are the gonochorists (born either male or female, they do not change sex), simultaneous hermaphrodites (they are both sexes simultaneously), and sequential hermaphrodites (they start life as one sex and then change to the other). This latter group can be broken down into the protogynous hermaphrodites (species that change from female to male) and the protandrous hermaphrodites (species that change from male to female). Although all members of a family typically display the same pattern of sexuality, all three sexual modes have been reported in the morays.

For example, the Ribbon Eel (*Rhinomuraena quaesita*) is a sequential (protandrous) hermaphrodite. The juveniles (which are black) become males (which are blue). The adult males then become females (which are either yellow or yellowish green). Members of the genus *Siderea*—which includes the Gray Moray (*Siderea grisea*) from the Red Sea and Indian Ocean—are simultaneous hermaphrodites, while the White Ribbon Eel (*Pseudechidna brummeri*) is a gonochorist.

With the exception of the Ribbon Eel, sexual dichromatism has not been documented in the Family Muraenidae. However, some species are sexually dimorphic. The dentition of several moray species differs between the sexes. Female Richardson's Morays (*Gymnothorax richardsonii*) have more teeth than males, while male Snowflake Morays (*Echidna nebulosa*) have no medial teeth near the front of the upper jaw (always present in females), and sharper, serrated teeth on the periphery of this same area. The function of these differences is not known, but it is possible that differences in dentition indicate dietary separations between the sexes, thus reducing competition for food. These differences may also be related to mating behavior. Males may have sharper teeth in order to bite females during mating and maintain their grip. (Biting of females by males during courtship has been confirmed in one species and probably occurs in others.) There are also size differences between the sexes: in some species (e.g., the protogynous hermaphrodites), males are larger than females; In others (e.g. protandrous hermaphrodites), females attain greater lengths than males.

Little information exists on the courtship and mating behavior of moray eels. In at least some species, the male and female approach each other with their heads raised above the bottom and their mouths agape. They then wrap around each other, press their abdomens together, and release their gametes as they abruptly separate. At least one species employs group spawning. In this moray (tentatively identified as *Gymnothorax herrei*), up to seven males were observed to entwine around and bite a larger

Gymnothorax albimarginatus, Whitemargin Moray

Dangerous Morays

Most morays rarely bite people—unless they are prodded, grabbed, or mistake a human finger for food while being fed. In some parts of the world, dive-boat operators hand-feed morays to delight and thrill their guests. This is a foolish practice that teaches morays to associate divers with food. Morays exposed to hand-feeding sometimes transform from timid and reclusive to aggressive and confrontational. In July 1996, a woman was scuba diving at Cod Hole on the Great Barrier Reef—an area where divers frequently feed large eels such as the Giant and Yellowmargin Morays (*Gymnothorax javanicus* and *Gymnothorax flavimarginatus*). An eel emerged from the reef and bit her just above the elbow. The young woman almost died from blood loss and ended up having her arm amputated. Several years earlier at this same dive site, a large moray bit a diver on the throat.

Several moray species are aggressive and prone to bite even when food is not present. One of these is the Tinsnip Moray (*Gymnothorax breedeni*). I have had this eel emerge from its hiding place and bite my hand, which I'd placed on the substrate nearby. The Undulated Moray (*Gymnothorax undulatus*) is also aggressive and has been reported to attack divers, while the Yellowhead Moray (*Gymnothorax rueppelliae*) has been described as a "nervous and belligerent species." If you keep any of these morays, observe them closely when your hands are in the aquarium. Although you can hand-feed your moray, it is highly likely that sooner or later you will be bitten. Three species of moray are known to have a mildly venomous bite. One of these is the Whitemargin Moray (*Gymnothorax albimarginatus*), a rare species unlikely to be encountered in the trade.

The greatest danger morays pose to humans is the poison that some assimilate in their bodies. This substance, known as ciguatera, can cause severe illness and even death in anyone who eats the eel's flesh.

female. The whole group of eels then quickly ascended toward the surface and released their gametes. The peak of reproductive activity for most morays takes place during the spring and summer. Some species spawn once a year, while others may do so several times during the reproductive period. Moray eel eggs are fairly large, ranging in size from 1.8 to 4 mm. The larvae are unique in shape, with small heads, large eyes, and elongate, flattened bodies. These are known as leptocephalus larvae and are characteristic of four orders—the true eels (Anguilliformes), the tarpons (Elopiformes), and their relatives the bonefishes (Albuliformes) and the deep sea eels (Notacanthiformes).

Captive Care

When aquascaping an aquarium that will house a moray, you should provide shelter sites that are large enough to hide the eel's entire body. This is especially true for eels like the Zebra Moray (*Gymnomuraena zebra*), which are almost always found deep in reef crevices. You can construct a coral head cave out of live rock or artificial corals, but be sure that your reef structure is stable. It may be necessary to use cable ties to attach rocks together so that they are less likely to be displaced by the moray. These eels often dig under decorations and can topple pieces of live rock or coral that are not fixed into position. This may result in injury to the eel. To create a hideout for a smaller eel, you can also use PVC pipe, a large conch shell, a fish bowl with crushed coral siliconed to the outside and placed on its side on the aquarium bottom, or a large ceramic flowerpot.

Morays can be kept in reef aquariums, although most species will eat smaller fishes and ornamental crustaceans. In addition, the larger species may knock loose corals off your reef structure, causing damage to the invertebrates. This is particularly true for morays that become rambunctious at feeding time. One advantage in placing an eel in your reef tank is that when it moves behind and between your live rocks, it will stir up some of the detritus that collects in these hidden areas.

Morays are the escape artists of the marine fish world. Not only will they emerge, Houdini-like, from an open aquarium, they can and will exit through any hole in the cover through which they can slither or force a passage. I have even had them knock off glass tops—which had been weighted to prevent their escape—and jump out. (Eels are much more acrobatic than many people assume.) Drying up on the living room carpet is probably the leading cause of death in many of the captive moray species. Therefore, it is critical to have a tight-fitting top to prevent such suicidal activities. In the case of larger eels, it may even be necessary to place something heavy on the top to prevent them from knocking it off. One caution, however: if you have a tight top on your tank and are using an undergravel filter with powerheads, it is a good idea to add an alternate oxygen source (such as an airstone connected to an air pump) to oxygenate the air trapped between the aquarium top and the water's surface. Otherwise, carbon dioxide can build up in this air space and cause the pH of the water to drop. If you do find your moray dried up on the floor, return it to the aquarium immediately; you may be surprised to find that it recovers. An eel that has been lying on the floor will shed its outer slime layer, along with any foreign matter stuck to it (dust, dirt, rubber bands), once it is returned to the aquarium. This process can take several hours.

Morays can become particularly frisky when being fed and are most likely to jump out of the tank when feeding stimuli are present. They are also more likely to evacuate their aquarium home after the rockwork in the tank has been rearranged.

Smaller morays may swim down undergravel uplift tubes where airstones are used and get beneath undergravel filter plates. I once had a small Snowflake Moray (*Echidna nebulosa*) swim down an uplift tube where an airstone was being used and come up the other uplift tube, which had a powerhead on it. The moray's head was sucked up against the plastic screen on the intake of the powerhead, resulting in hemorrhaging on the eel's face.

Feeding

In captivity, it is important to offer your moray a varied diet. Although it is interesting to watch morays chase and capture live feeder fish, you also need to include frozen or fresh squid, marine fish flesh, and crustaceans. If you give your eel frozen food, make sure the material is completely thawed before offering it. Most morays can be enticed to eat nonliving food by impaling it on the end of a feeding stick and moving it in front of their head. I use a piece of rigid air line tubing with a sharpened end. It is also important not to feed your moray too frequently. Overfeeding can lead to fatty infiltration of the liver, which impairs its functioning. It is not uncommon to see eels in public aquariums that have excessive fat deposits on the head and body, probably as a result of being overfed. Field studies suggest that morays eat infrequently. Therefore, in order to prevent this overfed condition, I recommend feeding your eel to satiation twice a week. In addition, an overfed moray may regurgitate its partially digested meal, making a mess of your tank. As previously mentioned, morays usually ingest one large meal every three or four days.

Occasionally, a moray will refuse to eat. This may occur if the eel is overfed, the water quality in the tank has deteriorated, or the water temperature drops significantly. It may sometimes occur for no observable reason. This problem can usually be rectified by performing a partial water change, offering your eel different types of food, and being patient. It may take several weeks for the animal to regain its appetite.

Compatibility

More than one moray can be kept in the same tank. A rocky cave or even PVC pipes with numerous moray heads protruding from them is an awesome sight. Occasionally, a new specimen added to a tank that already contains a well-established individual will be chased and bitten by the resident moray—especially if they are members of the same species. But in most cases, a moray will attempt to defend a preferred hiding place simply by pushing the intruder away with the side of its head or placing its open mouth on the body of the other eel.

Morays can however be cannibalistic. I once had a small Snowflake Moray (*E. nebulosa*) that regurgitated a slightly smaller conspecific, and a Honeycomb Moray (*Gymnothorax favagineus*) that ate two eels about half its length. Small eels will often stay out of the way of larger specimens, but in smaller aquariums, they will have a difficult time avoiding a hungry relative. If you are keeping more than one moray in the same tank, it is best to introduce them simultaneously—especially if they are of the same species. Keeping specimens of similar size together is also prudent. Dispersing individuals, by providing numerous hiding

Gymnothorax rueppelliae, Yellowhead Moray, gulping a live goldfish: this captive specimen should be fed a varied diet of fresh and frozen marine fare.

Gymnothorax moringa, Spotted Moray: an aged wild specimen showing cloudy eyes, scarred jaws, and missing teeth. Morays can be long-lived in captivity.

from the body of a large fish by employing knotting behavior. I have had eels capture fish, swallow them tailfirst, and successfully separate the body from the head (as it was too large to ingest). I have also seen a group of smaller morays, including Richardson's Moray (*Gymnothorax richardsonii*) and an undescribed species, attack a newly introduced fish that was too large for a solitary eel to ingest. Even if your moray does not eat your fishes, it may nip at them when feeding stimuli are present. Crustacean-feeders, such as the Snowflake Moray (*E. nebulosa*), will dart about the tank and bite at anything that gets in its way when food is introduced. If morays are regularly fed live feeder fish, there is an increased chance that they will nip at the fish in your tank.

Although morays are often kept in tanks containing other large predators such as sharks or groupers, these animals will occasionally injure or kill an eel. Sharks have been known to bite or maul moray tankmates, while larger groupers and snappers may eat them. For example, a Whitemargin Lyretail Grouper (*Variola albimarginata*) about 35 cm (14 in.) in length had a 15-cm (6-in.) moray in its stomach, while a Dog Snapper (*Lutjanus jocu*) of about 60 cm (24 in.) had eaten a 45-cm (18-in.) Spotted Moray (*Gymnothorax moringa*). Other fishes that are known to feed on morays include the Mutton Hamlet (*Alphestes afer*), Peacock Hind (*Cephalopholis argus*), Red Grouper (*Epinephelus morio*), Nassau Grouper (*Epinephelus striatus*), Lyretail

places, will also help diffuse the potential for those rare aggressive interactions.

Occasionally, one moray will bite another, causing a deep gash or laceration. In some cases, these wounds will even expose the vertebral column. The bleeding usually stops within minutes, and within 1½ days, a thin epithelial covering will develop over the wound. In a few days to 3 weeks, depending on the severity of the injury, the wound is usually totally healed, often with no visible scar. This power of regeneration may also be helpful when morays cut themselves while pushing between sharp coral branches or tight reef fissures. Morays have an extremely thick dermis and epidermis, another apparent adaptation to their benthic, crevice-dwelling lifestyle. This thick covering also substitutes for the protection afforded by scales.

You can house morays with larger fishes, but there are inherent risks—especially if the muraenid you are keeping is a fish-eating species. Morays have a surprisingly large mouth gape, so if you keep fishes with a piscivorous eel, make sure that their bodies are several times deeper than the girth of the moray, and introduce them to the tank before the moray is added. Although not common, it is possible that a moray will tear chunks of flesh

Gymnothorax fimbriatus, Fimbriated Moray: small copepod parasites infest this eel's jaw, but captive morays rarely exhibit serious health problems.

MORAY EELS

Grouper (*Variola louti*), and a Schoolmaster (*Lutjanus apodus*).

Although eels are often groomed by cleaner wrasses in the wild, these fishes are often eaten by captive morays. As far as invertebrates are concerned, morays will not feed on sessile invertebrates such as sponges or corals, but they can do mechanical damage to unattached coral colonies if they accidentally knock them over. Many morays can also be housed with hermit crabs, cleaner shrimps, sea stars, and sea cucumbers, although some of the crustacean-feeders may eat hermit crabs and cleaner shrimps.

Troubleshooting

Most morays are extremely durable. In fact, many would be considered among the hardiest fishes available in the marine hobby. I have yet to have a specimen succumb to disease or parasites. At least one species (the Yellowmouth Moray, *Gymnothorax nudivomer*) produces a toxic body slime that may ward off skin parasites, as well as making itself less palatable to larger predators. On rare occasions, I have had individual morays show signs of external parasite infestations. In these cases, the individual would flick its dorsal fin up and down frequently, engage in repeated head-shaking, or rub its head against hard substrate. Morays are occasionally parasitized by nematode worms, which appear as squiggly, raised bumps under the eel's skin. It has been suggested that moray eels are sensitive to copper compounds and organophosphates, so be careful when treating them with these substances.

Morays kept in tanks with fiberglass decorations (like artificial coral) may develop skin lesions from contact with the fiberglass. This problem can be resolved by removing the decorations. Rarely, a moray may suffer from skin tumors, and older specimens may develop cloudy eyes—a condition I have seen in the wild as well as in captivity.

Morays will often continue to thrive when water conditions deteriorate, and they can go for long periods without eating. Eliciting a feeding response can be difficult in some species. The Ribbon Eel (*Rhinomuraena quaesita*) is often reluctant to feed in captivity and is best left to the more experienced aquarist. The Zebra Moray (*Gymnomuraena zebra*) can also be difficult to feed, but will usually start eating if kept in a tank with deep crevices for hiding and offered live crabs.

I have not found any reports in the literature concerning moray eels spawning in captivity, but it is a possibility in a very large aquarium. My first eel, a large female Spotted Moray (*Gymnothorax moringa*), would routinely expel eggs. A ball-like swelling would appear in her urogenital region several days before she expelled thousands of eggs into the aquarium. This happened several times over a 6-month period.

MORAY SPECIES

Genus *Channomuraena*

This genus contains two unique moray species, the most wide-ranging of which is the **Longjaw or Broadbanded Moray (*Channomuraena vittata*) Richardson, 1844**. This eel is found all around the world, having been reported from Christmas Island in the Indian Ocean, the Hawaiian Islands in the Pacific, Bermuda, the Bahamas, throughout the Caribbean in the Western Atlantic, and in the Eastern Atlantic. The other species, ***Channomuraena bauchotae*, Saldanha & Quero, 1994**, was recently described from Réunion Island in the Indian Ocean. Both species have huge jaws—so large that when the eels yawn, they look more like filter-feeding Basking Sharks (*Cetorhinus maximus*) than eels. Their incredible jaws allow them to swallow fishes that are twice their own girth. The Longjaw Moray has a heavy body, a small cranium, minute eyes positioned near the tip of its snout, and saggy, wrinkled skin. All of these characteristics give this species an unusual appearance. It is tan to gray overall, with reddish brown, brown, or cream bands. In smaller Longjaws, the bands are more pronounced. This species attains a maximum length of at least 1.2 m (3.9 ft.).

The Longjaw Moray is found on reef faces and fore-reef slopes, in water 4.5 to 24 m (15 to 78 ft.) deep. It is a secretive species that spends its days hiding in holes and crevices, although an occasional individual may be observed lying in the open. At night, it moves about the reef in search of sleeping fishes. There are reports that this eel will feign death, lying on its side when extended from a hole. The function of this behavior is unclear.

This moray is rarely seen on the reef or in the aquarium trade.

Channomuraena vittata, Longjaw Moray: a rarity with an awesome gape.

Echidna catenata, Chainlink Moray: handsome and modestly sized.

Echidna delicatula, Finespeckled Moray: secretive but fine for smaller tanks.

Most individuals encountered in public aquariums were taken in fish traps set in deep water. If a Longjaw Moray does show up in an aquarium store, it is likely to be from the Bahamas or the Caribbean. It should be housed in a tank with numerous hiding places and can be kept with other eels. However, it may dine on smaller individuals if it becomes too hungry. If other bony fishes are to be kept with this species, special care must be taken when selecting tankmates. As it can ingest incredibly large prey items, any fish housed with it should exceed the girth of the eel by at least 3 times.

Genus *Echidna* (Pebbletooth Morays)

The genus *Echidna* contains a number of attractive morays, four of which are commonly seen in the aquarium trade. In juveniles, *Echidna* teeth are conical in shape, while those of adults are molarlike. This tooth shape is well suited for masticating the exoskeletons of their primary prey—crustaceans. In the *Echidna* species, the front nostrils are tubelike, while those located over the eyes are simple openings.

Echidna catenata (Bloch, 1795)
Common Names: Chainlink Moray, Chain Moray.
Maximum Length: 71 cm (28.0 in.).
Distribution: South Florida to Bermuda to southern Brazil, east to St. Paul's Rocks and Ascension Island.
Biology: The Chainlink Moray inhabits coral and rocky reefs, being most abundant at depths of less than 1.5 m (5 ft.), but occurring as deep as 12 m (39 ft.). It is most common in near-shore areas of reef rock with sparse, small coral heads and on the reef face among stony corals. It resides under rocks during the day and comes out at night to hunt. Its diet consists primarily of crabs, which it will sometimes pursue out of the water onto the shore. Occasionally, these eels eat shrimps.
Captive Care: I have found that the Chainlink readily adjusts to the home aquarium if it is provided with plenty of hiding places and live crustaceans for food, such as small fiddler crabs and grass shrimp. However, at least one reliable author (Thresher, 1980) reports that this eel is difficult to maintain for long periods of time. I have found that the occasional specimen will accept pieces of fresh shrimp impaled on a feeding stick, but live foods are usually needed to catalyze food intake. Some individuals will snap at other fishes in the tank when food is present. The Chainlink Moray is a secretive fish that will spend most of the day hiding under or between the aquarium decorations.
Aquarium Size: 30 gal. **Temperature:** 22 to 27°C (72 to 80°F).
Aquarium Suitability Index: 4.
Remarks: There is considerable variation in the color pattern of individual Chainlink Morays. The base coloration of *E. catenata* is white to yellow, with brown, gray, or black mottling. Juveniles typically have fewer markings than adults.

Echidna delicatula (Kaup, 1856)
Common Name: Finespeckled Moray.
Maximum Length: 65 cm (26.0 in.).
Distribution: Sri Lanka to Samoa, north to southern Japan.
Biology: The Finespeckled Moray hides among stony corals and occurs in shallow water. It is a gonochoric species.
Captive Care: This is a reclusive eel, which spends most of its time in and under aquarium decor. It will eat small feeder fish and grass shrimp. The Finespeckled Moray can be kept with other eels, as well as any fish that is not small enough to fit into its mouth. Because of its small size, it can be housed with a wide

Echidna nebulosa, Snowflake Moray: an ideal moray for the home aquarium.

Echidna nebulosa, Snowflake Moray: emerging to hunt the reef shallows.

range of tankmates. This species may attempt to eat ornamental shrimps, especially smaller, more delicate forms (e.g., *Periclimenes* spp.).
Aquarium Size: 30 gal. **Temperature:** 23 to 27°C (74 to 80°F).
Aquarium Suitability Index: 5.
Remarks: The color pattern of this moray varies with age. The coloration consists of fine yellow speckles on a dark brown background, which may form fine lines in juveniles.

Echidna nebulosa (Ahl, 1789)
Common Names: Snowflake Moray, Clouded Moray, Starry Moray.
Maximum Length: 75 cm (29.5 in.).
Distribution: East African coast and Red Sea east to Panama, north to the Ryukyus, and south to Lord Howe Island.
Biology: Snowflake Morays occur in lagoons, on reef flats, on reef faces, and on the fore-reef slope at depths of less than 1 to more than 10 m (3.3 to 33 ft.). This eel is common in the intertidal zone and has been observed slithering out of the water at ebb tide to move from one tidepool to another. It occasionally hunts on rubble bottoms at the edge of the lagoon during the day, but generally moves about in the open at night. The Snowflake Moray feeds mainly on crabs, including grapsid, majid, and xanthid crabs. However, mantis shrimps (including *Odontodactylus* spp.) and bony fish remains have also been found in Snowflake Moray stomachs. Larger specimens may also eat cephalopods. This species is a protogynous hermaphrodite.
Captive Care: The Snowflake Moray is a great aquarium fish. It adapts quickly to a captive life, readily accepts most foods, stays relatively small, and is less of a threat to its fish tankmates than members of the genus *Gymnothorax*. However, even the normally mild-mannered Snowflake Moray can become pugnacious when food is present. A hungry eel will often dash about the tank looking for the source of the olfactory stimulus and may snap at anything in the odor corridor. Occasionally, larger specimens may latch onto a fellow tankmate and attempt to rip off a chunk of flesh. You can curtail this undesirable behavior by feeding your moray with a feeding stick. These morays can be kept with other eels, but a resident specimen may chase and bite a conspecific introduced to the aquarium later, and they will occasionally engage in cannibalism.

Like most morays, this eel will spend much of its time with its head protruding from under a rock or from a crevice during the day. In time, it will become more brazen and move about in the open when the aquarium is illuminated. The Snowflake Moray does not tend to be as shy as the Banded Moray (*Echidna polyzona*) or the Zebra Moray (*Gymnomuraena zebra*).
Aquarium Size: 30 gal. **Temperature:** 22 to 28°C (72 to 82°F).
Aquarium Suitability Index: 5.
Remarks: You can determine the sex of a Snowflake Moray by the shape of its teeth. In adult males, the teeth at the front of the upper jaw (the area known as the premaxillary plate) are sharper, with serrated posterior edges. In females, those teeth are conical and smooth. The females also have teeth in the middle of the premaxillary plate, while the males do not. This species also has an ontogenetic transformation in tooth shape (changes that occur as the eel ages). Males over 45 cm (17.7 in.) in total length have serrations on some of their teeth, suggesting that there may be a change in diet as this fish grows.

Although not verified by field studies, large adults may feed more on fishes and cephalopods than their smaller counterparts will.

Echidna polyzona (Richardson, 1844)

Common Names: Banded Moray, Ringed Moray, Barred Moray.
Maximum Length: 60 cm (23.6 in.).
Distribution: Red Sea to the Marquesas, north to the Ryukyus and Hawaiian Islands, south to the Great Barrier Reef and the Tuamotu Islands.
Biology: The Banded Moray occurs at depths of less than 1 to 15 m (3.3 to 49 ft.) on reef flats, coastal reefs, and in clear shallow water lagoons. This secretive species feeds mainly on crabs (including majid, xanthid, and protunid crabs), but it occasionally eats shrimps (including *Saron* spp.). When it feeds, it probes its prey with its snout and open mouth before striking at it. It hides and hunts in reef crevices during the day and moves out onto the reef to search for prey at night.
Captive Care: The Banded Moray is readily available to marine hobbyists. It is suitable for the home aquarium if the aquarist is willing to provide it with live crustaceans, especially small fiddler crabs. With time and persistence, it is possible to switch some specimens over to fresh crustacean and fish flesh. Provide this moray with numerous holes and crevices to refuge in to ensure that it acclimates and does not jump out of the aquarium. It is a nonaggressive species that can be kept with other morays, as well as with fishes (it rarely will consume fish tankmates). It will eat ornamental crustaceans.
Aquarium Size: 30 gal. **Temperature:** 22 to 28°C (72 to 82°F).
Aquarium Suitability Index: 3.
Remarks: The juveniles of this species are superficially similar to young Yellowhead Morays (*Gymnothorax rueppelliae*) and Tiger Morays (*Gymnothorax enigmaticus*) as they share a color pattern of alternating pale and black or dark brown bands. But juvenile Banded Morays have teeth that are conical and rounded, while the teeth are long and sharp in the *Gymnothorax* species. Juvenile Banded Morays also have 25 to 30 bars, some of which do not entirely encircle the body anterior to the anus, and a dark patch at the corner of the mouth.

Young Yellowhead Morays have 16 to 21 bars on the body, some of which do not entirely encircle the body on the throat and head, while the Tiger Morays have 17 to 21 bars that completely encircle the body along the entire length. The Tiger Moray also has light-colored anterior nostrils and lacks a dark spot at the corner of the jaws, which is present in *G. rueppelliae*. As the Banded Moray grows, the bands become more obscure, and the teeth become more flattened and pebblelike. In Banded Moray adult males, the teeth on the premaxillary plate are sharper than in females and there are fewer of them (there are no teeth present on the middle of this plate in males, but they are present in females).

Echidna polyzona, Banded Moray: bold coloration of a juvenile specimen.

Echidna polyzona, Banded Moray: small adult coloration.

Echidna polyzona, Banded Moray: older adult with fading color pattern.

Genera *Enchelycore* and *Enchelynassa* (Dragon and Longfang Morays)

These two genera contain some of the most ominous-looking species in the moray family. This is because they have slender, curved jaws that are jam-packed with long, sharp teeth and cannot be closed entirely. They are secretive morays, rarely seen during the day. Members of both genera are apparently nocturnal, hunting slumbering fishes and octopuses under the cover of darkness.

Enchelycore bayeri (Schultz, 1953)
Common Name: Bayer's Moray.
Maximum Length: 70 cm (27.6 in.).
Distribution: Chagos Island to the Line and Society Islands, north to the Marianas, and south to the Great Barrier Reef.
Biology: Bayer's Moray occurs on coastal reefs, reef flats, reef faces, and fore-reef slopes, to depths of at least 20 m (65 ft.). It is a cryptic, nocturnal species that is rarely observed by divers.
Captive Care: This species is rare in the aquarium trade. Its husbandry requirements are similar to its more commonly encountered relative from the Atlantic—the Viper Moray (*Enchelycore nigricans*). It is a secretive species that needs plenty of deep crevices and caves in which to shelter.
Aquarium Size: 55 gal. **Temperature:** 23 to 28°C (74 to 82°F).
Aquarium Suitability Index: 4.
Remarks: The **Bikini Atoll Moray** (*Enchelycore bikiniensis*) (**Schultz, 1953**) is a similar species known from Micronesia to Samoa and the Marquesas. It differs from Bayer's Moray in that it has short jaws, is mottled in color, the fins have white edges, and the posterior nostrils are very large and surrounded by a fimbriated rim. It attains 60 cm (23.6 in.) in length.

Enchelycore carychoa Böhlke & Böhlke, 1976
Common Name: Chestnut Moray.
Maximum Length: 34 cm (13.4 in.).
Distribution: Bermuda and the east coast of North America, the Gulf of Mexico, throughout the Caribbean, south to Brazil, and east to the Gulf of Guinea.
Biology: This is also a secretive species that lives on patch reefs, fringing reefs, reef faces, fore-reef slopes, and shallow rocky areas. However, it prefers coral to rocky substrate. It occurs at depths of 1.5 to 64 m (5 to 208 ft.), but is most common at depths of less than 15 m (49 ft.). Divers rarely encounter this species during the day. Nothing is known about its food habits, but its dentition suggests that it eats fishes.
Captive Care: The Chestnut Moray will do well in the home aquarium if provided with plenty of hiding places and live food. Although secretive, in the aquarium it will spend a lot of time with its head protruding from its hiding place. Live foods are usually a must to encourage newcomers to feed, but they can be weaned off them later and fed fresh fish flesh, fresh shrimp, and strips of squid. It will eat any fish tankmates that are small enough to swallow, but because of its small maximum size, there is a wider range of fishes that can be kept with it. It does not tend to be aggressive toward heterospecifics. Because it is a solitary fish in the wild, I suggest you keep only one Chestnut Moray per aquarium. You can, however, keep them with other small moray species. Its smaller size also makes it more vulnerable to being preyed upon by larger eels.
Aquarium Size: 20 gal. **Temperature:** 22 to 28°C (72 to 82°F).
Aquarium Suitability Index: 4.
Remarks: Although they are not as colorful as the Dragon Moray (*Enchelycore pardalis*), they are much less expensive and look just

Enchelycore bayeri, Bayer's Moray: a rarity with cryptic, noctural habits.

Enchelycore carychoa, Chestnut Moray: fierce looking but small in size.

as fierce. The Chestnut Moray is reddish brown throughout its life and can be easily separated from the Viper Moray (*E. nigricans*) by the presence of white spots around each pore on the lower and upper jaws, as well as black grooves in the gill area.

Enchelycore nigricans (Bonnaterre, 1788)
Common Name: Viper Moray.
Maximum Length: 87 cm (34.4 in.).
Distribution: Bermuda and Florida south to South America and east to the tropical Eastern Atlantic.
Biology: The Viper Moray is most abundant among coral rock in shallow water, although it is also found in crevices of lagoon patch reefs and on the fore reef. It occurs at depths of less than 1 to over 30 m (3.3 to 98 ft.), but is most common in water less than 6 m (20 ft.) deep. Although common over much of its range, this species is rarely encountered because of its secretive nature. It does move into exposed areas at night.
Captive Care: The Viper Moray should be provided with plenty of hiding places that are large enough for total concealment. Live fishes are often necessary to induce feeding, but with time it will eat strips of fresh fish flesh. It can be kept with other morays, although two Viper Morays housed in the same tank may fight. It will also consume any fish tankmate that can be swallowed whole.
Aquarium Size: 55 gal. **Temperature:** 22 to 28°C (72 to 82°F).
Aquarium Suitability Index: 4.
Remarks: The young of this species are light brown with darker reticulations, while the adults are uniformly chestnut brown to maroon.

Enchelycore nigricans, Viper Moray: reclusive and an agile fish stalker.

Enchelycore pardalis, Dragon Moray (juvenile): prized by the world's aquarists.

Enchelycore pardalis (Temminck & Schlegel, 1846)
Common Names: Dragon Moray, Hawaiian Dragon Moray.
Maximum Length: 80 cm (31.5 in.).
Distribution: Réunion Islands and Comoros in the Indian Ocean east to the Hawaiian, Line, and Society Islands, north to southern Japan and Korea, and south to New Caledonia.
Biology: The only place where the Dragon Moray is commonly observed is on rocky reefs off southern Japan and the northern Philippines—where it is reported at a depth range of 15 to 50 m (49 to 163 ft.)—and in certain habitats off the Hawaiian Islands. In the latter location, it is most often seen among the fingerlike branches of *Porites compressus*. This secretive moray is usually solitary, but occasionally a pair of Dragon Morays will occupy the same crevice. They feed mainly on bony fishes and octopuses.
Captive Care: This moray's contrasting combination of a menacing appearance and colorful attire makes it a great display animal for the larger home aquarium. Unfortunately, the Dragon Moray is rarely encountered in the aquarium trade—and when it is available, it is extremely expensive. It is a fish-eater that will ingest anything that can fit into its expandable jaws. Although an uncommon event, larger specimens have also been known to bite and mutilate fish that are too large to swallow whole. The Dragon Moray is very cryptic, especially smaller specimens, and must be provided with suitable shelter sites to facilitate acclimation. With time, it will become less of a recluse, spending more of the daylight hours with at least its head protruding from a hole or crevice. Some specimens will even begin to lie out in full view and become quite tame. The Dragon Moray will eat live feeder fish in captivity, although it may take several weeks, or even months, before some larger specimens commence feeding. With time, most

Enchelycore pardalis, Dragon Moray (adult form): may attack other eels.

Enchelycore pardalis, Dragon Moray: color variant from Japan.

Dragon Morays can (and should) be switched to long strips of fish flesh (e.g., smelt, orange roughy, haddock) and squid presented on a feeding stick. Because their large teeth can inflict serious injury to conspecifics and fighting is likely to result, I would not risk placing two specimens in the same tank unless they are a mated pair and you have an aquarium that is at least 135 gallons. You can keep juveniles of this species with other morays, but adults may attack other eels housed with them, especially if the other morays are introduced after the Dragon Moray. If you are going to keep other eels with an adult Dragon Moray, they should all be placed in a very large tank with numerous hiding places. In addition, the Dragon Moray should be introduced to the tank last, and all the eels should be of similar size (the Dragon Moray could be slightly smaller).

The threat display of the Dragon Moray is spectacular. It will open its jaws as wide as possible, laterally flatten the gill region, cock its head to one side, and erect its dorsal fin. I have seen other morays that were nearly as long as the Dragon and were well established in a tank before the Dragon Moray was added flee to the upper corner of the tank when threatened by this menacing-looking beast.

Aquarium Size: 55 gal. **Temperature:** 22 to 26°C (72 to 78°F).
Aquarium Suitability Index: 4.
Remarks: This species is one of the most extraordinary members of the entire moray clan. It has an ornate color pattern, consisting of a brownish orange body with dark brown and white spots, and white and orange bars on the head and snout. It has elongate rear nostrils above its eyes that look like horns, and a curved, snaggle-toothed jaw. All the members of the genus *Enchelycore* share the latter characteristic, but no other species is as colorful as *E. pardalis*. Adults differ slightly from the juveniles in their coloration, and as is the case in most morays, youngsters are more slender in build than their elders. The amount of orange on the head and jaws and the spotting pattern on the body can vary between individuals. It has been suggested that males display more of the orange coloration on the head and throat than females and more of a stippled pattern on the body, but this has never been confirmed by internal examination.

Enchelynassa canina (Quoy & Gaimard, 1824)
Common Name: Longfang Moray.
Maximum Length: 1.5 m (4.9 ft.).
Distribution: Chagos to Panama, north to Marcus and the Hawaiian Islands, and south to the Great Barrier Reef, Tonga, and Mangreva.
Biology: This species occurs on outer-reef flats, reef crests, and the upper-reef face, often in areas of heavy surge. It is reported at depths of at least 10 m (33 ft.). It spends its days deep in reef and coral head crevices and moves out in the open to feed at night on octopuses and bony fishes. The Longfang Moray is reported to be very aggressive, sometimes leaving its lair to attack divers without provocation.
Captive Care: The Longfang Moray makes for a frightening display. It needs plenty of room and some deep crevices in which to hide, otherwise it may refuse to take food. Finicky individuals should be fed live fish at night. Great care must be taken when working in the tank of this ominous-looking beast, as it will bite if it gets the opportunity. Although Hawaiian collectors encounter this species, it is rarely taken because of its nasty disposition.
Aquarium Size: 180 gal. **Temperature:** 21 to 27°C (70 to 80°F).
Aquarium Suitability Index: 4.

Remarks: This species has a wrinkled head, white spots on its lower jaw, and a flap on the anterior nostril that has two lobes.

Genus *Gymnomuraena* (Zebra Moray)

The genus *Gymnomuraena* contains only one distinct species, the Zebra Moray (*G. zebra*). It is easily recognized by its bluntly rounded snout and its many narrow white bands on a chocolate brown body.

Gymnomuraena zebra (Shaw, 1797)

Common Name: Zebra Moray.
Maximum Length: 1.5 m (4.9 ft.), although specimens over 1 m (3.3 ft.) are rare.
Distribution: East coast of Africa and the Red Sea east to Panama and the Gulf of California, north to the Ryukyus, and south to the Society Islands.
Biology: The Zebra Moray occurs on rocky and coral reefs. In the latter habitat, it is found on fringing coastal reefs, the reef face, and fore-reef slopes, at depths from the surge zone to at least 39 m (127 ft.). The specialized dentition and strong jaws of this species enable it to feed on larger, more heavily armored crabs than similarly sized *Gymnothorax* species. Although crabs (including majid, xanthid, and grapsid crabs) make up the bulk of its diet, this moray occasionally feeds on snails (including cowries), pencil urchins, and spiny urchins. When hunting, the Zebra Moray will probe its prey with its snout before it strikes. It will also employ different handling techniques when feeding on prey items of varying sizes. For example, when feeding on small crustaceans, the Zebra Moray will usually ingest the entire animal, while it will only bite off and consume the claws and walking legs of larger crabs. Unlike many other moray species, this eel does not employ knotting behavior to disarticulate larger prey (see illustration, page 247). It will, however, rotate on its longitudinal axis with the prey item in its mouth.

The Zebra Moray does much of its hunting in reef crevices and rarely ventures out into the open—except possibly at night. I once encountered a smaller specimen during the day that was moving from one hiding place to another on a reef flat. Some specimens show strong site attachment and remain in the same hiding place for days, or even weeks, at a time. Sometimes more than one Zebra Moray will occupy the same refuge or it will share its hiding place with another eel species such as the Banded Moray (*Echidna polyzona*). I have seen them being cleaned in reef crevices by cleaner shrimps of the genus *Periclimenes*. The Zebra Moray is a protogynous hermaphrodite.

Captive Care: This is an extremely docile species that poses no threat to its fish tankmates or the aquarist, making it an ideal moray for the community fish tank. However, it is imperative that you provide this reclusive eel with crevices that are large enough for it to conceal its entire body. The many nooks and crannies afforded by a tank full of live rock make the reef aquarium an excellent captive habitat for one of these morays. Although they are secretive when acclimating to their new home, if provided with proper shelter and given time, a Zebra Moray's boldness can increase to the point where it will move about the tank searching for food when the lights are still on. Live crabs may be required to encourage adults of this species to feed. Fiddler crabs, available at most aquarium stores for freshwater tanks, will fit the bill nicely. They will also take fresh blue crabs that have had their carapaces cracked. Juveniles accept food more readily and will usually take a wider variety of prey, including fish flesh, clam meat, scallop, and squid—all off the end of a feeding

Enchelynassa canina, Longfang Moray (night photo): nasty disposition.

Gymnomuraena zebra, Zebra Moray: docile crustacean eater.

stick. When using a feeding stick, gently nudge the eel's snout with the food.

Unfortunately, specimens of less than 45 cm (17.7 in.) are rarely seen in the aquarium trade, which would suggest that juveniles are even more secretive than adults. This moray can be kept with other fishes, including individuals that are small enough to be swallowed whole. However, it will eat ornamental crustaceans.

Aquarium Size: 55 gal. **Temperature:** 22 to 28°C (72 to 82°F).
Aquarium Suitability Index: 3.
Remarks: This moray is chocolate to orangish brown overall, with white to pale yellow bands. The thickness of the bands can vary. In most specimens, the light bands are much thinner than the dark interspaces, but occasionally this condition is reversed. This species was once placed in the genus *Echidna*.

Genus *Gymnothorax* (Sharp-toothed Morays)

This is the most specious of all the moray genera and is represented on every coral reef in the world. Its members are characterized by having a tail that is not more than 1.5 times the length of the body, at least some canine teeth (some species may possess molarlike teeth as well), one or more depressible fangs in the middle of the upper jaw, and usually a single row of teeth on the vomer. Other than these subtle similarities, this genus is comprised of a diverse assemblage of morays that vary greatly in color, body depth, and dentition.

Gymnothorax breedeni, Tinsnip Moray: note anthias refuging in its crevice.

Gymnothorax breedeni McCosker & Randall, 1977
Common Names: Tinsnip Moray, Masked Moray.
Maximum Length: 75 cm (29.5 in.).
Distribution: East Africa, Comoros, Seychelles, Maldives, Line, and the Marquesas Islands.
Biology: The Tinsnip Moray is found on the reef flat, reef face, and fore-reef slope at depths of 4 to 25 m (13 to 81 ft.). It is usually a solitary species, but on rare occasions two individuals will hide in the same hole. In the Maldives, groups of Lyretail Anthias (*Pseudanthias squamipinnis*) and Flame Anthias (*Pseudanthias ignitus*) are often found refuging in the same crevice with the Tinsnip Moray. This is the most common moray encountered in the Maldives. It is extremely aggressive, often lunging at any human appendage placed near its lair. (I was bitten on the arm in the Maldives while concentrating on taking a photograph of a scorpionfish.) Although no information is available on the Tinsnip's food habits, the shape of its teeth indicates that it is piscivorous.
Captive Care: This species rarely enters the aquarium trade. It will consume fish that can be swallowed whole and will not hesitate to bite the hand that feeds it.
Aquarium Size: 55 gal. **Temperature:** 23 to 28°C (74 to 82°F).
Aquarium Suitability Index: 4.

Gymnothorax brunneus (Herre, 1923)
Common Name: Brown Moray.
Maximum Length: 25 cm (9.8 in.).
Distribution: Sulawesi, Indonesia, the Philippines, Taiwan, and Okinawa.
Biology: I have encountered this small moray on coastal patch reefs at depths of about 7 m (23 ft.). It spends its time in crevices

Gymnothorax brunneus, Brown Moray: a small eel suited to reef aquariums.

or with its head protruding from reef interstices. More than one of these eels, as well as several other morays (including the Barredfin Moray, *Gymnothorax zonipectus*, and the White-eye Moray, *Siderea thyrsoidea*), were observed in the same area of the patch reef. It probably feeds on the small fishes and crustaceans that are prevalent in this habitat.

Captive Care: This is a smaller species that is well suited for the home aquarium. The Brown Moray will eat a large selection of living and nonliving foods. It can be kept with a variety of fish tankmates, although it is likely to become a meal for one of its larger relatives, and it may eat ornamental shrimps (in the wild it can be found in crevices filled with Dancing Shrimp, *Rhynchocinetes durbanensis* and Humpbacked Cleaner Shrimp, *Lysmata amboinensis*). If you want to keep the Brown Moray with shrimps, add the crustaceans to the aquarium first. It is also a good candidate for the reef aquarium—its smaller size means it is less likely to topple coral pieces.

Aquarium Size: 20 gal. **Temperature:** 22 to 28°C (72 to 82°F).
Aquarium Suitability Index: 5.

Remarks: This is one of several monochromatic morays. It is brown to light brown overall, and in most cases the snout and lower jaw are somewhat paler than the body. The dentition of the Brown Moray is reported to be similar to that of the White-eye Moray (*Siderea thyrsoidea*), which suggests it may actually belong to the same genus.

Gymnothorax buroensis (Bleeker, 1857)
Common Name: Latticetail Moray.
Maximum Length: 33 cm (13.0 in.).
Distribution: East Africa to Panama, north to the Ryukyus and Hawaiian Islands, and south to the Tuamotu Islands.

Biology: The Latticetail Moray is found in shallow lagoons, on coastal reefs, reef faces, and fore-reef slopes. It is most common on reef flats in the surge zone, hiding in among the branches of hard coral colonies, in holes, crevices, and among algae. This species occurs at depths of 2 to 24 m (7 to 78 ft.). I have seen the Latticetail Moray on patch reefs that were also occupied by Barredfin (*Gymnothorax zonipectus*) and White-eye (*Siderea thyrsoidea*) Morays. The Latticetail Moray feeds mainly on crabs (including xanthid crabs like *Trapezia* spp.), but also eats mantis shrimps, shrimps, and small bony fishes. Both males and females mature at a maximum length of 23 cm (9.0 in.).

Captive Care: Although this species is very common in many parts of the Indo-Pacific, it rarely enters the aquarium trade. When it does, it is usually sold as an "assorted moray." Like most morays of the genus, it will consume fish that can be swallowed whole. It can be kept with other morays of similar size and is a great species for the smaller aquarium.

Aquarium Size: 20 gal. **Temperature:** 22 to 28°C (72 to 82°F).
Aquarium Suitability Index: 4.

Gymnothorax chilospilus Bleeker, 1865
Common Names: Whitelip Moray, Lipspot Moray.
Maximum Length: 50 cm (19.7 in.).
Distribution: Gulf of Oman east to Indonesia and Australia.

Biology: This species occurs at a depth range of less than 1 to at least 45 m (3.3 to 146 ft.), but is most common in water less than 5 m (16 ft.) deep. At Heron Island, which is on the southern part of the Great Barrier Reef, this species is relatively common on fore-reef slopes.

Captive Care: Its size makes the Whitelip Moray a good choice for a smaller aquarium. Provide it with numerous hiding places

Gymnothorax buroensis, Latticetail Moray: maximum size a mere 13 inches.

Gymnothorax chilospilus, Whitelip Moray (juvenile): good for a small aquarium.

Gymnothorax chilospilus, Whitelip Moray (variant): note spots on jaw.

Gymnothorax chilospilus, Whitelip Moray (variant): adult lacking jaw spots.

Gymnothorax cribroris, Australian Moray: common on the Great Barrier Reef.

and do not house it with larger morays that are known to consume smaller eels (e.g., *Gymnothorax favagineus*). It will eat both live and nonliving foods and should be fed a varied diet.
Aquarium Size: 30 gal. **Temperature:** 23 to 28°C (74 to 82°F).
Aquarium Suitability Index: 5.
Remarks: This is a readily available species, most often sold in fish stores as an "assorted moray." Some individuals are easily recognized by the white spot on the edge of the lower jaw and the white borders that surround the pores on the jaws (although some individuals may lack the spot on the jaw). This species is usually light brown overall, with dark brown mottling and lighter dendritic blotches. Some may have a green hue.

Gymnothorax cribroris Whitley, 1932
Common Names: Australian Moray, Sievepatterned Moray.
Maximum Length: 45 cm (17.7 in.)—although it has been reported by some to reach 75 cm (29.5 in.).
Distribution: Great Barrier Reef and Western Australia.
Biology: This species is common on the Great Barrier Reef, occurring on the reef flat (where it often resides in tidepools), on the reef face and on fore-reef slopes at depths of 1 to 15 m (3.3 to 49 ft.). It is also found in harbors and estuaries, on rocky reefs, and among man-made debris. The Australian Moray is a secretive species that apparently does most of its hunting after dark.
Captive Care: This diminutive species will do well in smaller aquariums. The Australian Moray should not be housed with larger, more aggressive morays, as it is likely to be preyed upon. It is not common in the aquarium trade because of its limited distribution.
Aquarium Size: 30 gal. **Temperature:** 23 to 28°C (74 to 82°F).
Aquarium Suitability Index: 5.
Remarks: This species is recognized by the spotting behind the eyes.

Gymnothorax enigmaticus McCosker & Randall, 1982
Common Names: Tiger Moray, Enigmatic Moray.
Maximum Length: 58 cm (22.8 in.).
Distribution: Gulf of Aden to the Tuamotu Islands, north to southern Japan, and south to Samoa.
Biology: The Tiger Moray is found in coral heads, among rubble, on fore-reef slopes, and in tidepools in clear, intertidal areas. It occurs at depths of less than 1 to at least 6 m (3.3 to 20 ft.). It is a nocturnal species that leaves its daytime hiding places to forage. I have seen it moving over large areas of the reef at night. No data is available on its feeding habits, but it probably feeds on crustaceans and small bony fishes. It is interesting to note that there are several other morays known to be nocturnal,

Gymnothorax enigmaticus, Tiger Moray (juvenile): hunting at night.

Gymnothorax enigmaticus, Tiger Moray (subadult): note mottling with bands.

Gymnothorax enigmaticus, Tiger Moray (adult): compare with juvenile, above.

such as the Yellowhead Moray (*Gymnothorax rueppelliae*) and the Banded Moray (*Echidna polyzona*), that have a similar color pattern.

Captive Care: The Tiger Moray rarely shows up in the retail aquarium trade. Its small maximum length makes it an ideal species for smaller aquariums. It can be housed with a wide range of fish tankmates.

Aquarium Size: 30 gal. **Temperature:** 23 to 28°C (74 to 82°F).
Aquarium Suitability Index: 5.

Remarks: This handsomely marked species is easily confused with other banded species, such as *Echidna polyzona* and *Gymnothorax rueppelliae*. (For more details on separating these three species, see the remarks section for *Echidna polyzona*, page 255.) In juveniles, the brown bands are more distinct than on the adults, and there is little mottling on the lighter interspaces present in larger specimens.

Gymnothorax eurostus (Abbott, 1861)

Common Names: Stout Moray, Salt and Pepper Moray.
Maximum Length: 65 cm (25.6 in.).
Distribution: Southeast Africa to Cocos Island in the Eastern Pacific, north to southern Japan and the Hawaiian Islands, and south to Lord Howe and Easter Island. It displays an antitropical distribution and is the most common moray in the Hawaiian Islands.

Biology: This moray occurs among live hard coral, coral rubble, and in man-made debris such as metal pipes. At Heron Island on the Great Barrier Reef, it is reported to be most abundant at depths of 1 to 15 m (3.3 to 49 ft.) on the reef flat and the fore-reef slope, but has been reported as deep as 25 m (81 ft.) off Japan. The Stout Moray preys heavily on benthic prey, includ-

Gymnothorax eurostus, Stout Moray: darker color variant (see next page).

Gymnothorax eurostus, Stout Moray: white variant (compare to page 263).

Gymnothorax favagineus, Honeycomb Moray: juvenile specimen.

ing bony fishes and crustaceans. Around southern Japan, crabs are the dominant prey in the diets of specimens measuring 9 to 65 cm (3.5 to 25.6 in.). One study showed that only 19% of 97 specimens examined had empty stomachs, suggesting that this species feeds more frequently than many other moray species.

Captive Care: This is a hardy moray that does not show up often in aquarium stores. It will eat tankmates that can be swallowed whole, and is a predator on ornamental crustaceans. This species should not be kept with morays that are appreciably smaller, as the Stout Moray is likely to prey on smaller eels. Although live food may be necessary to induce a feeding response, this moray can be trained to take marine fish and crustacean flesh off a feeding stick.

Aquarium Size: 30 gal. **Temperature:** 21 to 28°C (70 to 82°F).
Aquarium Suitability Index: 5.
Remarks: The Stout Moray displays two different color forms. One is white overall with dark markings, while the other is brown with lighter mottling.

Gymnothorax favagineus Bloch & Schneider, 1801
Common Names: Honeycomb Moray, Tessellated Moray.
Maximum Length: Attains at least 1.8 m (5.9 ft.) and may become 3 m (9.8 ft.) long.
Distribution: Red Sea and East Coast of Africa, east to Papua New Guinea, north to the Philippines, and south to the Great Barrier Reef.
Biology: This moray occurs at depths of 1 to at least 50 m (3.3 to 163 ft.), inhabiting reef flats, lagoon patch reefs, reef faces, and fore-reef slopes. It is usually a solitary species, but it will occasionally cohabit coral heads with the Giant Moray (*Gymnothorax javanicus*). The Honeycomb Moray feeds, both at night and dur-

Gymnothorax favagineus, Honeycomb Moray: young adult.

Gymnothorax favagineus, Honeycomb Moray: large adult.

Gymnothorax fimbriatus, Fimbriated Moray (juvenile): uncommon species.

Gymnothorax fimbriatus, Fimbriated Moray (adult): highly reclusive.

ing the day, on fishes and octopuses. In the daytime, its head and a large portion of its body often protrude from the reef. It may even lie out in the open.

Captive Care: The Honeycomb Moray readily adapts to aquarium life. However, if you are keeping one in a community tank, be aware that it will eat any fish it can swallow. Furthermore, because it can attain a large size, it is a potential threat to a wide range of fish tankmates. There have been many cases in which one of these morays has lived peacefully in a tank and then suddenly eaten one of its tankmates. This often occurs at night, when most of the other fishes are sleeping. It can consume surprisingly large prey, and a specimen that is not well fed may even bite and attempt to tear a mouthful of flesh out of a fish that is too large to ingest whole. The Honeycomb Moray can be aggressive toward similarly sized morays, and will eat smaller individuals whole or bite them in half. I once observed an unusual association between a large Honeycomb Moray and a porcupinefish housed in a large home aquarium, in which the porcupinefish (*Diodon holacanthus*) would regularly rest on the eel's head. This relationship did not appear to benefit either fish, but the eel would tolerate the porcupinefish's unusual antics. As a result of its pleasing color pattern and its relative scarcity in the hobby, the Honeycomb Moray often costs more than most other eels in the trade.

Aquarium Size: 180 gal. **Temperature:** 23 to 28°C (74 to 82°F).
Aquarium Suitability Index: 5.
Remarks: The color pattern of this species is variable. The black markings can vary in size and shape and there may be some yellow and white between the blotches. The Honeycomb Moray is synonymous with the Blackblotched Moray, *Gymnothorax permistus*. However, there is another species that may be sold under the common name "Tessellated Moray" that is similar—but it is a distinct species. The **Blackspotted Moray,** *Gymnothorax insigteena* (**Richardson, 1845**) (see photograph, page 244) has spots that are equal to or smaller than the eye and are more widely dispersed than those of the Honeycomb Moray. The Blackspotted Moray is distributed from the Maldives to the southern Great Barrier Reef, north to southern Japan. It attains a maximum length of 1.8 m (5.9 ft.). Small specimens are known to feed on shrimps. *Gymnothorax insigteena* is synonymous with *Gymnothorax melanospilos*.

Gymnothorax fimbriatus (Bennett, 1831)

Common Name: Fimbriated Moray.
Maximum Length: 80 cm (31.5 in.).
Distribution: Mauritius to the Society Islands, north to southern Japan, and south to northeast Australia.
Biology: This species is uncommon over most of its range, except around certain islands in the Indonesian Archipelago, where adults are commonly found on patch reefs or in large sponges on steep sand slopes. Juveniles are more secretive and rarely observed. It often inhabits coral heads where the shrimps *Lysmata amboinensis* and *Stenopus hispidus* maintain cleaning stations. This species occurs at depths of 7 to at least 50 m (23 to 163 ft.). I have seen adult Fimbriated Morays sharing small coral heads with White-eye Morays (*Siderea thyrsoidea*). The Fimbriated Moray is a solitary species that feeds mainly on fishes (including parrotfishes), but also consumes crabs and shrimps. It apparently does much of its hunting at night. This species is a protogynous hermaphrodite.
Captive Care: As in its natural habitat, this species is secretive in the aquarium and should be provided with a number of crevices

Gymnothorax flavimarginatus, Yellowmargin Moray: large juvenile specimen.

Gymnothorax flavimarginatus, Yellowmargin Morays: mature adult pair.

and caves in which to hide. Although all specimens are usually shy, especially when first introduced to the tank, smaller individuals are more reclusive during the day. At night, this moray will move about the tank in search of food. Live food, such as grass shrimp and feeder fish, may be necessary to induce food intake. This species can be kept with other morays and fishes that are not small enough to swallow whole. Be aware that it can ingest fishes that measure up to 20% of its total length. Cleaner shrimps can be added to the tank to simulate its naturally preferred habitat, but add them to the tank before placing the eel in order to reduce the likelihood that your moray will eat the cleaners. Because of its reclusive nature, the Fimbriated Moray is not an ideal choice for most reef aquariums.

Aquarium Size: 55 gal. **Temperature:** 23 to 28°C (74 to 82°F).
Aquarium Suitability Index: 5.
Remarks: This species occasionally makes it into the aquarium trade, where it is usually sold under the common name "Yellowhead Moray" or as an "assorted moray." It is gray with scattered black spots of varying shapes and sizes on the body and head. Some individuals, especially younger specimens, may have a yellowish head, hence the misapplied Yellowhead name.

Gymnothorax flavimarginatus (Rüppell, 1828)
Common Name: Yellowmargin Moray.
Maximum Length: 1.2 m (3.9 ft.).
Distribution: Red Sea east to Panama, north to southern Japan and the Hawaiian Islands, and south to New Caledonia, the Tuamotus, and the Austral Islands.
Biology: The Yellowmargin Moray occurs in less than 1 m (3.3 ft.) of water to depths of 150 m (488 ft.). It lives in a variety of different habitats, including lagoon patch reefs, the reef flat, the reef face, and the reef slope. It tends to be a secretive species, spending most of its time with only its head protruding from the reef or entirely hidden in reef crevices. The Yellowmargin Moray feeds on fishes (including goatfishes, gobies, blennies, and damselfishes) and crabs. Juveniles of this species feed mainly on crabs (including swimming crabs), shrimps (including the Dancing Shrimp, *Rhynchocinetes durbanensis*), and small fishes, such as gobies of the genus *Eviota*. This species is thought to be a protogynous hermaphrodite.
Captive Care: This is a hardy aquarium species that should be housed in a larger tank (at least 100 gallons). It will readily accept nonliving foods, such as pieces of fresh fish, squid, and crustacean meat and will consume any fish tankmate whose girth does not greatly exceed the width of the eel's mouth. I had one specimen that swallowed a small scorpionfish tailfirst until it reached the head, which was too large to swallow. The eel proceeded to rasp the scorpionfish's head against the substrate until it broke free from the body! This eel can be housed with other morays, although it may eat individuals that are appreciably smaller than itself.

Aquarium Size: 135 gal. **Temperature:** 22 to 28°C (72 to 82°F).
Aquarium Suitability Index: 5.
Remarks: Although commonly observed by divers, the Yellowmargin Moray is relatively rare in the aquarium trade. It is yellowish brown overall, with dark brown mottling on the body and either a gray or dark brown head. In young specimens, the dorsal fin margin is often bright green, while in adults it is yellow. Other salient chromatic characteristics include the orange eyes and the dark blotch that surrounds the gill opening.

Gymnothorax funebris Ranzani, 1840

Common Name: Green Moray.
Maximum Length: 2.3 m (7.5 ft.).
Distribution: New Jersey and Bermuda south to Brazil.
Biology: The Green Moray occurs at depths ranging from 3 m (10 ft.) to over 30 m (98 ft.) in a variety of different habitats, including seagrass meadows, pier pilings, reef flats, reef faces, forereef slopes, and steep dropoffs. It is often strongly site-attached, with individuals having been reported to occupy the same section of a patch reef for up to 7 years. This massive moray apparently feeds during both the day and night and eats fishes and crabs. It also eats other morays—in one case, a 1.5-m (4.9-ft.) Green Moray regurgitated a 90-cm (35-in.) Spotted Moray (*Gymnothorax moringa*).
Captive Care: Because it can attain such large proportions, only an aquarist with an aquarium of 240 gallons or larger should consider purchasing a Green Moray. Juveniles and adolescents tend to acclimate more readily to aquarium life than larger specimens. I have had large adults refuse to eat for months after being introduced to the aquarium. One of these individuals, which regurgitated a semidigested fish in its shipping bag, refused fish fillets and small feeder fish, but was finally induced to feed by presenting it with live koi. This species (as well as some other morays) may host parasitic nematode worms, which appear as raised, squiggly lines just under the skin. This species can be more aggressive than other morays, biting and locking jaws with heterospecifics. It will eat any fish small enough to ingest and will even eat other morays.
Aquarium Size: 240 gal. **Temperature:** 22 to 27°C (72 to 80°F).
Aquarium Suitability Index: 4.
Remarks: Adult and adolescent individuals are green to greenish brown overall, while small juveniles are dark brown to black, with a white chin. The **Panamic Green Moray** (*Gymnothorax castaneus*) (Jordan & Gilbert, 1882) and the **Finespotted Moray** (*Gymnothorax dovii*) (Günther, 1870) are two closely related forms from the tropical Eastern Pacific. The Panamic Green Moray and *G. funebris* are very similar in appearance, while the Finespotted Moray, as the name implies, is covered with small white spots.

Gymnothorax gracilicaudus Jenkins, 1903

Common Name: Slendertail Moray.
Maximum Length: 32 cm (12.6 in.).
Distribution: Western Australia east to the Tuamotus, Line, and Hawaiian Islands; also the Carolines and Marianas and the Great Barrier Reef.
Biology: This small, secretive species spends much of its time

Gymnothorax funebris, Green Moray (juvenile): destined to become massive.

Adult *Gymnothorax funebris*, Green Moray: too aggressive for most aquarists.

Gymnothorax gracilicaudus, Slendertail Moray: little eel for quiet tanks.

among corals and rocks during the day. It occurs on lagoon reefs, reef faces, and fore-reef slopes. No data is available on its food habits, but the Slendertail Moray probably feeds on fishes and small crustaceans.
Captive Care: This is a great aquarium species because of its small size and the ease with which it settles into captivity. Do not keep it with larger morays, as it is likely to be preyed upon. It can be housed with a wide array of fish tankmates because of its relatively diminutive dimensions.
Aquarium Size: 20 gal. **Temperature:** 22 to 28°C (72 to 82°F).
Aquarium Suitability Index: 5.
Remarks: The Slendertail Moray is whitish overall with brown bars on the body and dorsal fin and brown dendritic blotches on the posterior half of the body.

Gymnothorax herrei Beebe & Tee-Van, 1933
Common Name: Herre's Moray.
Maximum Length: 30 cm (11.8 in.); most under 20 cm (7.9 in.).
Distribution: Red Sea and the Maldives east to New Britain and Indonesia, north to the Philippines, and south to Queensland.
Biology: Herre's Moray is often found on coastal reefs and has been taken from very shallow tidepools to depths of at least 7 m (23 ft.). It is found on sand, cobble, rubble, and stony coral substrate. It feeds on small crustaceans and benthic fishes. It has been observed spawning in groups. Male and female specimens gather in shallow water in the afternoon and begin spawning at about sundown. Females are larger and more swollen in appearance during this time than the more abundant males. Males search for females and upon finding a potential mate they attempt to bite her abdomen, with as many as seven males clamping onto the same female. The rising mass of morays will then rush a short distance above the substrate and release their gametes. This species is sexually mature at 11.5 cm (4.5 in.).
Captive Care: Herre's Moray is ideally suited for the smaller home aquarium. It will feed on grass shrimp and livebearers. Its small size makes it vulnerable to being preyed upon by piscivores, including groupers, snappers, large wrasses, and also other morays. Because of its small size, Herre's Moray is less likely to topple corals in the reef aquarium, but it is also more difficult to relocate after it is placed in a tank full of live rock.
Aquarium Size: 20 gal. **Temperature:** 22 to 28°C (72 to 82°F).
Aquarium Suitability Index: 5.
Remarks: This is one of several small brown moray species. Although the body is brown, the tail tends to be lighter in color. The teeth on the vomer of *G. herrei* are low, nodular, and in a single series—it lacks well-developed canine teeth and may later be reclassified in the genus *Siderea*.

Gymnothorax javanicus (Bleeker, 1828)
Common Names: Giant Moray, Javanese Moray.
Maximum Length: 3 m (9.7 ft.) and a weight of 70 kg (154 lbs.). Although this is one of the largest members of the family, it is not the longest moray. This distinction goes to the giant Longtail Moray (*Strophidon sathete*), which can reach 3.9 m (12.7 ft.) in total length.
Distribution: This moray is distributed from the Red Sea east to the Marquesas and Pitcairn Islands, north to southern Japan, and south to New Caledonia and the southern Great Barrier Reef.
Biology: This immense moray hides in reef interstices, under ledges, in caves on reef walls, or in crevices among live coral on more gradually sloping fore-reef areas. It occurs at depths of 0.3 to 46 m (12 in. to 150 ft.). Typically, only its head is visible

Gymnothorax herrei, Herre's Moray: nice species for the smaller aquarium.

Gymnothorax javanicus, Giant Moray: huge size can make it a true menace.

sticking out of the reef, but occasionally it will spend time with its head and much of its body extending up into the water column. It is usually a solitary species, but occasionally two individuals may be seen sharing the same crevice or cave. I have also seen these eels engaged in combat, which consisted of biting and jaw-locking. The Giant Moray is often hand-fed by experienced divers. It has bitten divers under these conditions and some of these incidents have resulted in very serious injuries. Its natural prey is mainly fishes, but it also eats crabs, shrimps, and octopuses. This species will also eat other eels—the stomach of a 70-cm (28-in.) specimen was reported to contain a 28-cm (11-in.) Largehead Snake Moray (*Uropterygius macrocephalus*). The Giant Moray is often followed by groupers—such as the Peacock Hind (*Cephalopholis argus*)—as it pokes its head in reef crevices and coral heads searching for food.

Captive Care: The Giant Moray should be housed in a very large aquarium. It is potentially dangerous to a wide range of tankmates because it attains such gargantuan proportions. This species is also likely to eat any other eels kept with it, especially if they are crowded into a smaller tank. The Giant Moray is not frequently encountered in the aquarium trade.

Aquarium Size: 180 gal. **Temperature:** 22 to 28°C (72 to 82°F).
Aquarium Suitability Index: 5.
Remarks: The Giant Moray is easily recognized by its large size and its dark spots (which are leopardlike and located behind the head) and the black area around the gill openings. The juveniles, which are rarely seen by divers or aquarists, are paler than the adults overall and have fewer large, dark brown spots.

Gymnothorax kidako (Temminck & Schlegel, 1842)
Common Name: Kidako Moray.
Maximum Length: 1 m (39.4 in.).
Distribution: Japan, Korea, and the Philippines. One record from the southern Great Barrier Reef is probably erroneous.
Biology: The Kidako Moray lives on rocky reefs, hiding under overhangs, in crevices, and among man-made debris (metal pipes). It can be found at water depths of 3 to 60 m (10 to 195 ft.). It has been observed spawning: on one occasion a male and female lifted the anterior one-third of their bodies off the substrate while they faced each other. They suddenly pushed their abdomens together and then abruptly separated, releasing their gametes at this time.
Captive Care: This species shows up in aquarium stores on rare occasions and commands a high price. Its care requirements are similar to most other medium-sized morays.
Aquarium Size: 75 gal. **Temperature:** 19 to 26°C (66 to 78°F).
Aquarium Suitability Index: 5.

Gymnothorax kidako, Kidako Moray: a coveted aquarium rarity.

Gymnothorax melatremus, Golden Moray: excellent reef tank eel.

Gymnothorax melatremus, Golden Moray: uncommonly bright variant.

Gymnothorax meleagris, Whitemouth Moray: large juvenile specimen.

Gymnothorax meleagris, Whitemouth Moray: handsome adult eel.

Gymnothorax meleagris, Whitemouth Moray: "Reverse Comet Moray" variant.

Gymnothorax melatremus Schultz, 1953
Common Names: Golden Moray, Dirty Yellow Moray, Pencil Moray.
Maximum Length: 18 cm (7.1 in.).
Distribution: East Africa to Hawaiian Islands, Marquesas, and Mangareva Islands, south to the Austral Islands.
Biology: This diminutive, secretive moray usually hides in reef holes, in crevices, in sponges, and among coral rubble, from the surge zone to at least 26 m (85 ft.). It is usually a solitary species, but occasionally occurs in pairs. The teeth of the Golden Moray are conical and blunt; it feeds on crustaceans. This species is a protogynous hermaphrodite.
Captive Care: The Golden Moray is ideal for a smaller aquarium. It should be housed in a tank with plenty of suitable hiding places. Although it will hide most of the time during the day, it often does so with its head exposed and can be trained to come out to accept food when the lights are on. This species can be kept in a shallow-water or deep-water reef aquarium. However, because it is quite cryptic, it may not be observed too often in a larger tank replete with live rock. The Golden Moray will eat ornamental crustaceans, but its small maximum size makes it less of a threat to most fishes.
Aquarium Size: 20 gal. **Temperature:** 22 to 27°C (72 to 80°F).
Aquarium Suitability Index: 5.
Remarks: The overall coloration of this species can vary from tan to yellowish orange, with some specimens sporting brown reticulations. All specimens have a dusky spot surrounding the gill openings and a black rim around each eye. It should not be mistaken for the *Gymnothorax miliaris* (yellow form) from Brazil.

Gymnothorax meleagris (Shaw & Nodder, 1795)
Common Names: Whitemouth Moray, Comet Moray, Guineafowl Moray.
Maximum Length: 1.2 m (3.9 ft.).
Distribution: East Africa and the Red Sea to the Galapagos Islands, north to southern Japan and the Hawaiian Islands, south to Lord Howe Island. Most specimens encountered by aquarists originate from reefs around the Hawaiian Islands, where it is one of the most common eels.
Biology: This solitary moray most often occurs in coral-rich areas in lagoons and on the reef face and fore-reef slope, at depths of less than 1 m (3.3 ft.) to at least 36 m (117 ft.). The Whitemouth Moray feeds on bony fishes and crabs during the day and night. This eel is thought to be mimicked by the Comet (*Calloplesiops altivelis*), a small grouperlike fish.
Captive Care: The Whitemouth Moray is an attractive aquarium animal that readily accepts both living and nonliving foods. It can

be kept with other morays and with fishes that are too large for it to ingest. It is not unusual for this species to fast when it is first introduced to the aquarium, but after it has been kept for several weeks, it usually begins eating. This moray may consume ornamental crustaceans, especially if they are introduced to the tank after the eel.

Aquarium Size: 135 gal. **Temperature:** 22 to 28°C (72 to 82°F).
Aquarium Suitability Index: 5.
Remarks: This gorgeous eel regularly enters the aquarium trade. It is easily separated from other Pacific Morays by the inside of its mouth, which is a brilliant white. There are several color forms, or morphs, of this eel. The two most common have snow white spots, but one has a golden brown base color, and the other is chocolate brown overall, with smaller spots (this may represent an age-related color change as large individuals most often display the latter color pattern). There is also a rare morph that is white overall with brown reticulations—this eel is sometimes referred to as the "Reverse Comet Moray" in the trade.

Gymnothorax miliaris (Kaup, 1856)
Common Names: Goldentail Moray, Golden Moray.
Maximum Length: 60 cm (23.6 in.).
Distribution: Southern Florida and Bermuda, south to Brazil, and east across the Atlantic to St. Paul's Rocks, Ascension, St. Helena, and the Cape Verde Islands.
Biology: The Goldentail Moray is a resident of lagoons and coastal coral and rocky reefs. It typically occurs at depths of less than 15 m (49 ft.), living in medium-sized coral colonies on sandy substrate, among smaller corals on reef rock, or among larger pieces of coral rubble. It is usually found singly, but occasionally a pair of these eels may occupy the same coral head. It is strongly site-attached, often staying in the same coral head for up to 2 months before moving to a new coral colony. This species has been observed attacking crabs in the wild. It sometimes forages during the day and may be followed by hunting groupers.
Captive Care: This moray is readily available from dealers specializing in fishes from the tropical Atlantic and Caribbean. The Goldentail Moray is a hardy aquarium inhabitant and is less aggressive than many other morays. It is a threat to smaller fishes and to crustacean tankmates, although it can be kept with cleaner shrimps if they are introduced to the aquarium first. An occasional *G. miliaris* will have a jaw deformity where the lower jaw is crooked. I have seen these individuals in the aquarium trade; the deformity does not interfere with their feeding behavior.
Aquarium Size: 30 gal. **Temperature:** 22 to 27°C (72 to 80°F).
Aquarium Suitability Index: 5.
Remarks: The body and head of most individuals are brown with

Gymnothorax miliaris, Goldentail Moray: hardy, mild-mannered species.

Gymnothorax miliaris, Goldentail Moray: dark-colored variant.

Gymnothorax miliaris, Goldentail Moray: attractive, light-colored variant.

Gymnothorax miliaris, Goldentail Moray: "Golden Brazilian Moray" variant.

Gymnothorax moringa, Spotted Moray: excitable and aggressive species.

Gymnothorax moringa, Spotted Moray (variant): common Caribbean eel.

numerous small yellow spots, while the tail is tipped with yellow or gold. An occasional specimen may be yellow overall, with irregular black markings or brown spots; others may be brown overall with minute gold spots (see photographs of both of these color variants on page 271). The rarer yellow color variety was once thought to be a distinct species known as *Gymnothorax flavopicta* and is often sold in the aquarium trade as the "Golden Brazilian Moray." Like *Gymnothorax meleagris,* it has a white mouth.

Gymnothorax moringa (Cuvier, 1829)
Common Name: Spotted Moray.
Maximum Length: In the western part of its range, the Spotted Moray attains a maximum length of 1.2 m (3.9 ft.), but is reported to reach nearly 3 m (9.8 ft.) at Ascension Island.
Distribution: South Carolina and Bermuda south to Brazil and east to Ascension and St. Helena Islands.
Biology: The Spotted Moray lives in a variety of different habitats, including seagrass meadows, among sponges on pier pilings, in coral heads (usually those that have an area greater than 0.5 m^3 [5 ft.^{3}], on sandy lagoon bottoms, reef faces, and fore-reef slopes. It occurs at depths of less than 1 m to at least 190 m (3.3 to at least 618 ft.). In lagoon habitats, most Spotted Morays stay at the same coral head for less than 5 days and then move on. However, some may be found at the same site for up to 24 days.

Although this species is sometimes found sharing a refuge site with the Purplemouth Moray (*Gymnothorax vicinus*) or Sharptail Snake Eel (*Myrichthys breviceps*), they are rarely, if ever, observed with conspecifics.

I have encountered large individuals that had torn flesh around their jaws, missing teeth, and bite marks on their snouts, indicating that conspecifics may fight on occasion.
The Spotted Moray feeds mainly on bony fishes (including trumpetfishes, grunts, snappers, and the Slippery Dick Wrasse, *Halichoeres bivittatus*) and crabs, but also eats octopuses and spiny lobsters. It will also eat members of its own species on occasion; for example, a 60-cm (24-in.) specimen contained a 32-cm (13-in.) conspecific. It commonly consumes relatively large prey—a 1-m (3.3-ft.) specimen contained a 20-cm (8-in.) snapper. Individuals tracked with telemetry tags were observed to forage nocturnally on 62% of the nights they were tracked. Feeding bouts in this species can range from less than 1 hour to 15 hours.

Spotted Morays that have been hand-fed can become quite aggressive toward divers, with both intentional and accidental bites having been reported.
Captive Care: This species can be aggressive toward other morays and may prey on any eel that it can swallow whole. I once had a

41-cm (16-in.) specimen ingest a White Ribbon Eel (*Pseudechidna brummeri*) and a Ribbon Eel (*Rhinomuraena quaesita*), both of which were considerably longer than it was. It later regurgitated the partially digested *R. quaesita*. In another incident, a *G. moringa* bit the tail off a smaller Green Moray (*G. funebris*). I have also seen this species bite and kill a scorpionfish. The Spotted Moray is a very excitable species and will not hesitate to bite the aquarist, especially when stimulated by the presence of food. It is an extremely hardy aquarium fish that can be kept in a medium- to large-sized tank. I would recommend that adult specimens be housed in larger tanks with at least one sizable coral head in which to shelter.

Aquarium Size: 100 gal. **Temperature:** 22 to 27°C (72 to 80°F).
Aquarium Suitability Index: 5.
Remarks: The Spotted Moray is the most ubiquitous moray in the Caribbean. Not surprisingly, it is also a common moray in aquarium stores. It is an attractively patterned species that is white or yellowish cream overall with brown flecks all over its head and body. The dorsal and anal fin margins are trimmed in black. The amount of flecking on the body can vary greatly. In some cases, individuals may be almost entirely white.

Gymnothorax nudivomer (Playfair, 1867)

Common Names: Yellowmouth Moray, Dinosaur Moray.
Maximum Length: 1 m (39.4 in.).
Distribution: Red Sea to Hawaiian and Marquesas Island, north to the Ryukyus, and south to New Caledonia.
Biology: This species is found on coastal reefs, lagoons, reef faces, and fore-reef slopes. In the northern Red Sea, it is common at depths of less than 15 m (49 ft.). Outside of this area, it is usually found at depths greater than 30 m (98 ft.) and has been reported as deep as 165 m (536 ft.). The Yellowmouth Moray has toxic body slime that may repel predators and parasites. When threatened, it will open its mouth wide, exposing the bright yellow inner lining. This may serve an aposematic function, warning any potential predator that it is unpalatable.
Captive Care: This eel must be provided with plenty of good hiding places and an aquarium with a tight-fitting top. With large specimens, the top should be weighted. Almost all the individuals available in aquarium stores are large, with the vast majority of specimens measuring over 51 cm (20 in.) in total length. Once it is added to its new aquarium home, the Yellowmouth Moray will usually refuse to eat for at least 1 month and may go as long as 8 months before it starts to feed. However, these morays rarely starve to death. Try feeding fasting individuals rinsed table shrimp or squid on a feeding stick. They also pose little threat to fish tankmates (an occasional specimen may eat fish that it can

Gymnothorax nudivomer, Yellowmouth Moray: toxic body slime.

swallow whole) and Yellowmouths can be kept in pairs, with few or no aggression problems.

Aquarium Size: 75 gal. **Temperature:** 22 to 27°C (72 to 80°F).
Aquarium Suitability Index: 4.
Remarks: Juveniles of this species have numerous small spots all over the body. As this eel grows, the spots on the anterior part of the body become smaller. Toward the head, some of the spots disappear, while others increase in size. In the Red Sea, adults of this species have fewer, smaller spots on the posterior part of the body than individuals from other areas.

Gymnothorax richardsonii (Bleeker, 1852)

Common Name: Richardson's Moray.
Maximum Length: 32 cm (12.6 in.).
Distribution: Red Sea to the Society Islands, north to the Ryukyus, and south to the Cook Islands.
Biology: This species occurs on shallow coastal reefs and reef flats, and in lagoons. It is a secretive moray that is found under coral rubble, rocks, and in reef crevices, and it has been reported from areas with rich growths of macroalgae. Richardson's Moray is more active at night than during the day.
Captive Care: This small species is commonly sold in the aquarium trade as an "assorted moray." It does well in the home aquarium and has a voracious appetite. Richardson's Moray will not only eat live foods, but also fresh and frozen fish, and crustacean and scallop flesh. I have seen several of these morays simultaneously attack and tear chunks of flesh from a cardinalfish that was too large for them to swallow whole.

Aquarium Size: 20 gal. **Temperature:** 22 to 27°C (72 to 80°F).
Aquarium Suitability Index: 5.
Remarks: Richardson's Moray has white around the head pores,

Gymnothorax richardsonii, Richardson's Moray: small eel with large appetite.

Gymnothorax rueppelliae, Yellowhead Moray (juvenile): known biter.

dark reticulations on a light background, and a dorsal fin that originates far back over the gill openings. It is sexually dimorphic, with females having significantly more teeth in both the upper and lower jaws than males.

Gymnothorax rueppelliae (McClelland, 1845)
Common Name: Yellowhead Moray.
Maximum Length: 80 cm (31.5 in.).
Distribution: Red Sea east to the Hawaiian Islands, north to the Ryukyus, and south to the Great Barrier Reef.
Biology: This moray is found on coral and rocky substrates. It occurs on reef flats, in clear-water lagoons, on reef faces, and on fore-reef slopes at depths of less than 1 to at least 30 m (3.3 to 98 ft.). It is found deep in reef crevices during the day and moves out of the reef to hunt at night. It has been observed feeding on fishes and chasing crabs over sand patches under the cover of darkness. The Yellowhead Moray has been described as nervous and aggressive—aquarists beware.
Captive Care: This is a durable aquarium species. Juveniles will readily adapt to aquarium life, feeding on grass shrimp and small feeder fish. Adults will also thrive in the large home aquarium if provided with plenty of crevices and caves to hide in when the lights are on. All age classes will eat any fish small enough to swallow whole. The Yellowhead can be housed with other morays, as long as they are equal in size. This is an aggressive moray that will not hesitate to bite.
Aquarium Size: 75 gal. **Temperature:** 22 to 27°C (72 to 80°F).
Aquarium Suitability Index: 4.
Remarks: This is a secretive species that shows up in the aquarium trade on rare occasions. It is characterized by having dark brown bands that completely encircle the body, except near the head.

Gymnothorax rueppelliae, Yellowhead Moray: adult specimen.

Gymnothorax rueppelliae, Yellowhead Moray: large adult color variant.

Gymnothorax saxicola, Ocellated Moray: eastern North American species.

Gymnothorax steindachneri, Steindachner's Moray: durable Hawaiian endemic.

In adults, the head is often yellow, hence the common name (for more information on separating this species from similar forms see the Remarks section in the *Echidna polyzona* species account, page 255). Juveniles are often sold in the trade as "banded morays."

Gymnothorax saxicola (Jordan & Davis, 1891)
Common Name: Ocellated Moray.
Maximum Length: 60 cm (23.6 in.).
Distribution: New Jersey and Bermuda south to southern Florida and the eastern Gulf of Mexico.
Biology: This species does not inhabit coral reefs. It lives in seagrass beds and offshore banks and occurs in water ranging from 9 to 121 m (29 to 393 ft.) deep. These eels are commonly collected in shrimp nets, and those in the aquarium trade are incidentally captured in crab traps.
Captive Care: The Ocellated Moray is the most common of three closely related *Gymnothorax* species in the aquarium trade (see Remarks, below). The maximum length of the Ocellated Moray makes it a good choice for the aquarist with a tank up to 30 gallons. It is a very durable species that can become quite aggressive once it has fully acclimated. When live food is introduced to the tank, the moray will often race about and bite at anything that gets in its way. I once saw a Smoothhound Shark (*Mustelus californica*) that had its gill region ripped out by a large Ocellated Moray. Although no data on its food habits are available, I received one specimen that had regurgitated an octopus during the shipping process. It can be kept with other morays, but will eat smaller fish tankmates and nip at fishes that it cannot swallow whole. Larger individuals may occasionally refuse to eat for long periods of time.

Aquarium Size: 30 gal. **Temperature:** 22 to 27°C (72 to 80°F).
Aquarium Suitability Index: 5.
Remarks: The Ocellated Moray belongs to a species group along with two other closely related forms that may just be color variants. The other two species are the **Blackmargin Moray** (*Gymnothorax nigromarginatus*) Girard, 1859, and the **Blacktail Moray** (*Gymnothorax kolpos*) Böhlke & Böhlke, 1980. These three morays are separated only by their color patterns and the maximum lengths they attain. The Ocellated Moray's maximum size is 60 cm (23.6 in.), the Blackmargin Moray reaches 53 cm (20.9 in.) in length, and the Blacktail Moray reaches 78 cm (30.7 in.) in length. The black markings on the dorsal margin of the Ocellated Moray are broken up into individual semicircular spots, while in the Blackmargin Moray, the black margin is a continuous black edge—this is especially true toward the posterior end of the body. Both of these species have numerous white spots on the head, body, and fins. The Blacktail Moray, in contrast, has more black on the tail and fewer, larger white spots on the body. The bodies of all three species may have a greenish cast as they get larger.

Although there is some overlap, the distribution patterns of these three morays are also different. The Blackmargin Moray is distributed from the Gulf of Mexico to the Yucatan peninsula, while the Blacktail Moray is only known from Florida and the Gulf of Mexico.

Gymnothorax steindachneri Jordan & Evermann, 1903
Common Name: Steindachner's Moray.
Maximum Length: 87 cm (34.3 in.).
Distribution: Hawaiian Islands.
Biology: This species is common in shallow water around the

Northwestern Hawaiian Islands, but is found at greater depths (30 m [98 ft.] or more) around the main islands.
Captive Care: This medium-sized moray is a durable aquarium species that will eat a variety of living and nonliving foods. It may eat ornamental crustaceans but can be kept with other eels. It is usually not a great threat to fish tankmates that are too large to swallow whole. Steindachner's Moray will find its way out of a tank if it is not securely covered.
Aquarium Size: 55 gal. **Temperature:** 21 to 27°C (70 to 80°F).
Aquarium Suitability Index: 5.
Remarks: This species is dirty white to light brown overall, with small, irregular-shaped markings all over the head and body and a black blotch surrounding the gill opening. Although *G. steindachneri* has only been reported from the Hawaiian Islands, a specimen acquired from a fish wholesaler was reportedly collected in Samoa. It occasionally shows up in the aquarium trade but is not common.

Gymnothorax undulatus (Lacépède, 1803)
Common Name: Undulated Moray.
Maximum Length: 1.5 m (4.9 ft.).
Distribution: Red Sea to Panama, north to southern Japan and the Hawaiian Islands, and south to the Great Barrier Reef.
Biology: This moray occurs on reef flats, reef faces, and fore-reef slopes and in lagoon patch reefs. It is found at depths of 5 to 50 m (16 to 163 ft.). This eel is active at night and feeds on fishes, octopuses, and crustaceans. One specimen was observed snatching a cardinalfish from a sponge.
Captive Care: This voracious species will accept fresh or frozen seafood or live feeder fish. A 76-cm (30-in.) specimen can eat up to 25 medium-sized feeder goldfish during a single feeding bout. Although this species can be kept with other morays, it is an aggressive fish that is prone to bite other eels. It can also be aggressive toward the aquarist—beware when you have your hands in the tank.
Aquarium Size: 100 gal. **Temperature:** 22 to 27°C (72 to 80°F).
Aquarium Suitability Index: 4.
Remarks: Large adults often have a greenish yellow head and are sometimes called "Yellowhead Morays" in the aquarium trade.

Gymnothorax vicinus (Castelnau, 1855)
Common Name: Purplemouth Moray.
Maximum Length: 1.2 m (3.9 ft.).
Distribution: Bermuda, south Florida and the Bahamas to Brazil, east to Ascension, Cape Verde, and Canary Islands, and West Africa.
Biology: The Purplemouth Moray spends its days in patch reef caves and crevices. Juveniles of less than 40 cm (16 in.) are extremely cryptic and rarely observed in the open, while adults move about the reef and surrounding sand, rubble, and seagrass areas at night. This species will occasionally share a hiding place with conspecifics, Spotted Morays (*Gymnothorax moringa*), and/or Sharptail Snake Eels (*Myrichthys breviceps*).

The Purplemouth Moray feeds mainly on bony fishes, including squirrelfishes, the Slippery Dick Wrasse (*Halichoeres bivittatus*), and parrotfishes, but on occasion it will eat crabs and octopuses. It also engages in cannibalism. A Purplemouth Moray that was 66 cm (26 in.) in length was reported to have a conspecific 27 cm (11 in.) long in its stomach. This species feeds less frequently than the sympatric Spotted Moray. One study

Gymnothorax undulatus, Undulated Moray (juvenile): active nighttime hunter.

Gymnothorax undulatus, Undulated Moray (adult): prone to bite.

demonstrated that it only foraged on 36% of the nights that its activity was monitored, while the Spotted Moray fed on 62% of the nights it was tracked. A Purplemouth Moray's hunting bout can last from less than 1 hour to as long as 9 hours.

Captive Care: The Purplemouth Moray does well in the home aquarium. Although it might eat fish that are small enough to swallow, it is not as great a threat to its tankmates as some of its close relatives. I did have a Purplemouth Moray, however, that consumed a freshly dead triggerfish whose body depth was much greater than the girth of the eel. This species might also eat other morays, including smaller conspecifics.

The Purplemouth is a nocturnal moray that should be provided with plenty of places in which to hide when the lights are on. It will readily accept squid, fish, and crustacean flesh from a feeding stick. It is not a threat to cleaner shrimps, as long as they are introduced to the tank before the moray.

Aquarium Size: 100 gal. **Temperature:** 22 to 27°C (72 to 80°F).
Aquarium Suitability Index: 5.
Remarks: This sleek, attractive moray is usually yellow or brown overall with darker mottling. In adult specimens, the fins usually have pale edges with dark submargins. The snout and lower jaw are light lavender, while the inside of the mouth is dusky to purplish in color. The iris is yellow.

Gymnothorax zonipectus Seale, 1906
Common Name: Barredfin Moray.
Maximum Length: 47 cm (18.5 in.).
Distribution: East Africa and the Red Sea to the Hawaiian and Marquesas, north to the Ryukyus, south to New Caledonia.
Biology: In certain parts of its range, the Barredfin Moray has been reported to be most abundant in caves in water deeper than 20 m (65 ft.). In Indonesia, however, I found this species to be quite common on coastal reef coral heads and on pier pilings at depths of 4 to 8 m (13 to 26 ft.). During the day, it is found among coral rubble, hard corals, and sponges; under overhangs; and in reef holes and crevices—usually with only its head exposed. At night, it moves over the reef and surrounding rubble zone looking for food. I have seen this species sharing a patch reef with Brown Morays (*Gymnothorax brunneus*), Latticetail Morays (*G. buroensis*), and White-eye Morays (*Siderea thyrsoidea*).
Captive Care: *Gymnothorax zonipectus* is great for the home aquarium. Its small size makes it ideally suited to smaller tanks. Provide this species with plenty of hiding places and feed it a varied diet, including fresh marine fish flesh and crustacean meat. It does well with other morays.
Aquarium Size: 30 gal. **Temperature:** 22 to 28°C (72 to 82°F).
Aquarium Suitability Index: 5.

Gymnothorax vicinus, Purplemouth Moray: piscivorous, nocturnal species.

Gymnothorax zonipectus, Barredfin Moray: great aquarium eel.

Gymnothorax zonipectus, Barredfin Moray: note pale nocturnal coloration.

Echidna sp. or *Siderea* sp., Wrinkled Moray

Gymnothorax sp. 1, Little Brown Moray

Gymnothorax sp. 2, unnamed moray

Undescribed Morays in the Aquarium Trade

Occasionally, a fish that is unknown to science or has yet to be described and given a scientific name shows up in the aquarium trade. Such is the case in the taxonomically chaotic world of the moray eels. In the last two years, I have found three moray species that are new to science. I was able to preserve two of these eels and send them to the world's leading authority on the Family Muraenidae, Eugene Böhlke. After careful examination and x-ray of the specimens, she confirmed that both were new species. One of them (top left) she had previously encountered but had yet to decide whether it belonged to the genus *Echidna* or *Siderea*. Mrs. Böhlke tells me that this species, which I call the Wrinkled Moray, has been reported from Queensland, Australia; Flores, Indonesia; and the Philippines (mine came from the Philippines). The second moray (top center), which I refer to as the Little Brown Moray, is in the genus *Gymnothorax*, and my specimen was supposedly collected in the Philippines. The third specimen (top right) is definitely a *Gymnothorax* but the species is undetermined. The next time you purchase an "assorted moray," you may be buying an animal that has yet to be described by ichthyologists.

Genus *Muraena* (Horned Morays)

The morays of this genus are characterized by having tubular rear nostrils in comparison to those of the *Gymnothorax* species, which consist of a simple opening or a raised rim. Otherwise, the *Muraena* species are very similar to members of the genus *Gymnothorax*.

Muraena clepsydra Gilbert, 1898

Common Name: Hourglass Moray.
Maximum Length: 1.2 m (3.9 ft.).
Distribution: Baja California to Peru, including the Galapagos Islands.
Biology: This species is found among rocks and boulders or on rocky reef walls, where it hides in holes, crevices, and caves. It occurs at a depth of 4.5 to 24 m (15 to 78 ft.).
Captive Care: The Hourglass Moray is a hardy aquarium fish that should be provided with plenty of hiding places. It can be housed with other morays, although larger individuals may prey on smaller eels. It is an aggressive feeder and will eat any fish small enough to swallow whole.
Aquarium Size: 100 gal. **Temperature:** 19 to 26°C (66 to 78°F).
Aquarium Suitability Index: 5.

Remarks: Two other members of this genus occur in the Eastern Pacific. One of these species, the Jewel Moray (*Muraena lentiginosa*), is commonly encountered in the aquarium trade. The other is the **Argus Moray** (*Muraena argus*) (**Steindachner, 1870**), which is very similar in color to *M. clepsydra*, possessing the large dark spot over the gill opening. However, *M. argus*

Muraena clepsydra, Hourglass Moray: hardy Eastern Pacific species.

Strophidon sathete, Longtail Moray: grows to lengths of more than 12 feet.

Uropterygius fasciolatus, Barred Snake Moray: rarely seen crevice dweller.

Genus *Strophidon*

Strophidon sathete (Hamilton, 1822)
Common Names: Longtail Moray, Estuarine Moray.
Maximum Length: 3.75 m (12.2 ft.).
Distribution: Red Sea and Eastern Africa east to Indonesia, south to Queensland.
Biology: The Longtail Moray is found in coastal bays and estuaries. It will even swim up rivers in brackish water. It is sometimes found in very shallow water of less than 1 m (3.3 ft.) but is also found at depths up to 10 m (33 ft.). I have observed it foraging in sandy bays at night at a depth of 6 to 10 m (20 to 33 ft.). During the day, *Strophidon sathete,* may bury itself in the substrate.
Captive Care: This extremely elongate moray is occasionally observed in the aquarium trade and is sold as a "White Ribbon Eel" (a name we reserve in this book for *Pseudechidna brummeri*). It should be kept in an aquarium with a minimal amount of decor and a layer of sand (at least 5 cm [2 in.] deep) on the bottom. Because of its potential size, *Strophidon sathete* will require a very large tank as it grows. Large adult Longtail Morays should be treated with great respect—they are capable of inflicting serious injury to the aquarist.
Aquarium Size: 240 gal. **Temperature:** 22 to 28°C (72 to 82°F).
Aquarium Suitability Index: 3.
Remarks: This species is tan on the dorsum and sides, and is lighter ventrally with a white stripe along the dorsal fin margin. As these morays grow, they become darker in overall color (sometimes chocolate brown) with no distinct markings. *Thyrsoidea macrura* is a junior synonym of this species.

Genus *Uropterygius* (Snake Morays)

The snake morays are rarely encountered by aquarists or divers because of their secretive natures. They spend most of their lives deep in reef crevices and are usually only seen by ichthyologists using toxins to sample cryptic fish populations. These eels live in shallow water on reef flats, coastal reefs, reef faces, and fore-reef slopes. At least one species, the Unicolor Snake Moray (*Uropterygius concolor*), inhabits mangrove swamps and river mouths. They are characterized by having poorly developed fins, a single posterior nostril, and numerous small, needlelike teeth. If you are lucky enough to acquire a snake moray for your aquarium, provide it with plenty of hiding places and be prepared to feed it live feeder fish or grass shrimp until you can coax it to eat fresh seafood from a feeding stick. At least two members of this genus are protogynous hermaphrodites.

Uropterygius fasciolatus (Regan, 1909)
Common Names: Barred Snake Moray, Horned Snake Moray.
Maximum Length: 53 cm (20.9 in.).
Distribution: New Guinea to the Solomons, north to Belau and the Moluccas.
Biology: The Barred Snake Moray is found on coastal reefs and in lagoons. It is a cryptic species that hides in patch reef holes and crevices and among the branches of ramose stony corals. It occurs at depths of less than 1 up to at least 7 m (3.3 to 23 ft.).
Captive Care: The Barred Snake Moray will do well in the home aquarium. It is a secretive eel that should be provided with adequate shelter sites. It may require live foods, like grass shrimp, when first introduced to the aquarium. It is quite aggressive and is likely to bite if the aquarist's hand gets too close.

lacks the white spot that is seen on *M. clepsydra* toward the back of the lower jaw. Like *M. clepsydra*, *M. argus* ranges from Baja to Peru, including the Galapagos Islands.

Muraena lentiginosa Jenyns, 1842
Common Names: Jewel Moray, Mexican Moray.
Maximum Length: 60 cm (23.6 in.).
Distribution: Tropical Eastern Pacific from the Gulf of California to Peru and the Galapagos Islands.
Biology: This eel is a resident of rocky and coral reefs and occurs at a depth range of 1.8 to 24 m (6 to 78 ft.). I have encountered it in rocky reef crevices as well as among stands of large macroalgae in the Gulf of California. It is reported to be nocturnal, but I have also seen it moving about in the open during the daytime. It feeds on fishes and crustaceans.
Captive Care: This is the most common member of the genus *Muraena* in the aquarium trade. It is a great aquarium fish that can be kept in a medium-sized aquarium (30 gallons or larger), but it is also a voracious predator that will eat smaller fishes, including other eels if they differ appreciably in body size. Jewel Morays will fight each other if placed in smaller aquariums, but can be housed together if introduced simultaneously to a larger tank.
Aquarium Size: 30 gal. **Temperature:** 20 to 28°C (68 to 82°F).
Aquarium Suitability Index: 5.
Remarks: *Muraena lentiginosa* has a highly variable color pattern, but most specimens entering the aquarium trade are brown with dark-edged yellow spots. The other common color form in the wild is light brown to white overall, with dark brown mottling instead of spots.

Muraena melanotis (Kaup, 1856)
Common Name: Blackear Moray.
Maximum Length: 1 m (39.4 in.).
Distribution: Tropical Eastern Atlantic, including Ascension and Cape Verde Islands, south to Angola.
Biology: This species occurs on rocky reefs to depths of 1 to 20 m (3.3 to 65 ft.). Although it is most active at night, it is occasionally seen in the open during the day.
Captive Care: I have had only one of these beautiful morays, which was sold to me as a "West African Dragon Moray." This specimen, which was about 30 cm (12 in.) in length, quickly acclimated to captivity and voraciously fed on live feeder fish and fresh fish flesh presented on a feeding stick. It was housed with several other morays and displayed no aggression toward them, even though some were smaller than it was. It can be kept in a medium-sized aquarium (55 gallons). The only drawback

Juvenile *Muraena lentiginosa*, Jewel Moray: commendable aquarium fish.

Adult *Muraena lentiginosa*, Jewel Moray: voracious fish-eater.

Muraena melanotis, Blackear Moray: rarely seen Eastern Atlantic species.

to this species is the very high price it commands (over $250 retail).
Aquarium Size: 55 gal. **Temperature:** 20 to 28°C (68 to 82°F).
Aquarium Suitability Index: 5.
Remarks: The **Reticulate Moray** (*Muraena retifera*) **Goode & Bean, 1812**, is also brown overall with white spots on the body, fins, and head and a black spot surrounding the gill openings. *Muraena retifera* is restricted in distribution to the Western Atlantic, where it has been reported at depths of 15 to 76 m (49 to 247 ft.). It is most common on the outer continental shelf. As a result of its predilection for deeper water, it is rarely encountered by aquarists.

Genus *Pseudechidna*

Pseudechidna brummeri (Bleeker, 1859)
Common Name: White Ribbon Eel.
Maximum Length: 103 cm (40.6 in.).
Distribution: East Africa east to the Cook Islands, north to Taiwan and the Yaeyamas, and south to Fiji.
Biology: The White Ribbon Eel, as the common name suggests, is a very thin species with wide fins. It is a resident of shallow lagoons and reef flats, and is reported to hide in the sand and among coral rubble. However, it will come out to hunt at night. It has been observed (rarely) moving over the reef during the day. I once happened across a specimen on a rocky reef flat one morning—although it rapidly disappeared into a small hole as I approached. It moves in a very exaggerated serpentine fashion. Although food habit data is lacking on this species, it presumably feeds on crustaceans and small fishes. This eel is gonochoric.
Captive Care: In captivity, this eel is very cryptic, spending most of its time hiding among the aquarium decor. Therefore, plenty of rock or coral should be placed in the tank to serve as shelter. A layer of sand can also be placed on the aquarium bottom. In captivity, they require live food such as grass shrimp. My efforts to feed them with a feeding stick have been unsuccessful. In most cases, the White Ribbon Eel will flee when the feeding stick is moved toward its head. I have kept this species with relatively small fish without incident, but I have had larger morays eat them.
Aquarium Size: 55 gal. **Temperature:** 22 to 28°C (72 to 82°F).
Aquarium Suitability Index: 3.

Genus *Rhinomuraena*

Rhinomuraena quaesita Garman, 1888
Common Names: Ribbon Eel, Black Ribbon Eel, Blue Ribbon Eel, Yellow Ribbon Eel.
Maximum Length: 1.2 m (3.9 ft.).
Distribution: From East Africa to the Tuamotus, north to southern Japan, and south to New Caledonia and the Austral Islands.
Biology: This genus contains one extremely elegant and unique species. The Ribbon Eel occurs at a depth range of 1 to 57 m (3.3 to 185 ft.) and is most abundant on coastal reef slopes and in protected lagoons. Although it is sometimes observed living in holes in hard reef substrate, it is most commonly seen in sand or mud or among coral rubble.

In most cases, its head—and possibly a portion of the anterior part of its body—protrudes from a hole. The Ribbon Eel has numerous pouchlike (sacciform), mucus-producing cells in the epidermis of the belly that generate copious amounts of slime. The slime helps cement the substrate grains of the burrow wall together and prevent injury to the eel as it moves over abrasive surfaces. Although you rarely see Ribbon Eels moving over the bottom or swimming in the water column, on occasion they can be seen moving from one hole to another, rapidly undulating their elongate bodies.

Rhinomuraena quaesita tends to be very site-attached, sometimes staying in the same hole for months or even years. Juvenile individuals are found singly, but it is not uncommon to find more than one male in the same area. In some cases, males will even share the same hole. The Ribbon Eel apparently feeds during the day on small fishes that pass too near its burrow entrance.
Captive Care: Ribbon Eels make striking display animals for the home aquarium. In some captive venues, however, they may refuse to feed. There are several things you can do to help initiate feeding in a Ribbon Eel. Provide adequate hiding places by

Pseudechidna brummeri, White Ribbon Eel: cryptic and hard to feed.

placing about 8 to 13 cm (3 to 5 in.) of live sand and 2.5 cm (1 in.) of coral rubble on the aquarium bottom and a mound of live rock on one side of the tank or against the back glass. By setting up your tank in this manner, you will be providing places for the eel to refuge. I have also seen Ribbon Eels adopt artificial caves as hiding places. You can create a cave by gluing crushed coral and chunks of rubble to a fish bowl, which can then be laid on its side on the aquarium bottom. A long piece of PVC pipe, no more than twice the diameter of the eel, may also serve as a sanctuary. Place a 45-degree elbow on one end of the pipe and cap the other end before burying it in the substrate.

Live feeder fish are also necessary to entice a Ribbon Eel to feed. Introduce a dozen or more mollies or guppies to your tank. To increase the concentration of potential prey in the vicinity of the eel, it is best to house it in a smaller tank (30 to 55 gallons) or partition off the eel's preferred hiding place in a larger aquarium. It is also easier to feed a Ribbon Eel if it is not housed with voracious carnivores that will snap up the feeder fish before the eel has a chance to feed. In fact, I would recommend that you keep your Ribbon Eel in a tank on its own or with a conspecific. Some Ribbon Eels can be trained to take small pieces of fish impaled on the sharpened end of a piece of rigid air line tubing, or to take food off the aquarium bottom. When using a feeding stick, it is important to present the food in a nonthreatening manner. Move the food around the tank as if it were natural prey.

Be aware that Ribbon Eels are especially proficient at finding small cracks and holes in the aquarium back stripping through which they can escape. They will also swim up siphon tubes that lack strainer caps.

Some specimens of *R. quaesita* from the Philippines and Indonesia may be collected by using cyanide. This probably has deleterious effects on the long-term health of the animals.

Aquarium Size: 55 gal. **Temperature:** 22 to 28°C (72 to 82°F).
Aquarium Suitability Index: 2.
Remarks: The Ribbon Eel has several characteristics that have led some to suggest that it should be placed in its own family, the Rhinomuraenidae. These include an extremely long, thin body with broad dorsal and anal fins that give it a ribbonlike appearance; delicate jaws; fan-shaped nasal extensions; one barbel-like filament on the upper jaw and several on the lower jaw; and its kidneys and most of its reproductive organs situated posterior to the anus. This last unique condition has not been reported in any other vertebrate.

The Ribbon Eel is a protandrous hermaphrodite—all females are derived from males that have changed sex. As this sexual transformation occurs, the eel also undergoes a chromatic

Rhinomuraena quaesita, Ribbon Eel: jet black and yellow juvenile form.

Rhinomuraena quaesita, Ribbon Eel: typical blue adult male form.

Rhinomuraena quaesita, Ribbon Eel: large adult female.

metamorphosis. As a juvenile, it is jet black with a yellow dorsal fin. Between 65 and 80 cm (23 and 32 in.) it begins to transform into a male, at which time its coloration begins to change from black to blue. The snout and lower jaw also turn bright yellow. This color phase was once thought to be a different species, having been referred to scientifically as *Rhinomuraena amboinensis*. When an individual reaches about 85 cm (33 in.), it begins to develop female sex organs and changes colors until it is either yellowish blue or entirely yellow. In the wild, the blue color phase is most commonly encountered, the black color phase is occasionally observed, and yellow individuals are rarely seen.

Genus *Scuticaria* (Shortfinned Morays)

The genus *Scuticaria* contains two species. Its members have very small dorsal and anal fins that are restricted to the tail tip, the tail is very short, the body is long and is almost cylindrical in cross section, and it gets quite large. (One species may reach 1.4 m [4.5 ft.].) This genus has long been considered a subgenus within the genus *Uropterygius*.

Scuticaria okinawae (Jordan & Snyder, 1901)

Common Name: Okinawan Snake Moray.
Maximum Length: 93 cm (36.6 in.).
Distribution: Mauritius to the Hawaiian Islands, north to Japan, and south to Indonesia.
Biology: Little is known about the biology of this species. It is apparently nocturnal, having rarely been encountered during the day, when it apparently hides deep in coral crevices. It is probably a fish-eater.
Captive Care: The captive care of this species should be similar to the closely related (and more commonly encountered), Tiger Snake Moray (*Scuticaria tigrina*), below. Make sure you provide this species with plenty of crevices and caves to hide in.
Aquarium Size: 75 gal. **Temperature:** 22 to 28°C (72 to 82°F).
Aquarium Suitability Index: 4.

Scuticaria tigrina (Lesson, 1828)

Common Name: Tiger Snake Moray.
Maximum Length: 1.22 m (3.9 ft.).
Distribution: East Africa east to islands of the tropical Eastern Pacific (e.g., Clipperton, Clarion, and the Revillagigedos) and Panama, north to the Philippines and the Hawaiian Islands, and south to the Society Islands.
Biology: This secretive fish is found in lagoons, on the reef face, and on the reef slope. Little is known about its biology.
Captive Care: This moray is usually reluctant to eat for weeks or even months after being first introduced to an aquarium. Entice a fasting Tiger Snake Moray with squid and pieces of table shrimp. After it begins to eat, you can offer other seafoods. This moray will eat fish tankmates but is not as voracious as some other morays; it will rarely bother other morays, including members of its own species. It is usually quite secretive, hiding under reef decor during the day and moving about the tank in search of food at night. These eels will attempt to jump out of the tank if suitable hiding places are lacking (and even in some cases when plenty of sites are available).
Aquarium Size: 100 gal. **Temperature:** 22 to 28°C (72 to 82°F).
Aquarium Suitability Index: 4.
Remarks: This species is very similar to the **Manyspotted Snake Moray** (*Uropterygius polyspilus*) (**Regan, 1909**), which has an anus located about halfway to the end of the tail (it is about two-

Scuticaria okinawae, Okinawan Snake Moray: reclusive and uncommon.

Scuticaria tigrina, Tiger Snake Moray: widespread, secretive eel.

thirds of the way back in *S. tigrina*). The Manyspotted Snake Moray also has a shorter snout and jaw, conical, fanglike upper jaw teeth, a lappetlike posterior nostril tooth, and, in many cases, spots of equal size (the spots vary in size in the Tiger Snake Moray).

Genus *Siderea* (Bluntnosed Morays)

Eels in the genus *Siderea* have no depressible teeth in the middle of the upper jaw and have two rows of short, conical teeth on the vomer. All of the *Siderea* species studied are thought to be simultaneous hermaphrodites—sexually mature individuals that possess both male and female sex organs. Unpublished studies suggest that this genus may be synonymous with *Gymnothorax*.

Siderea grisea (Lacépède, 1803)
Common Names: Gray Moray, Geometric Moray.
Maximum Length: 65 cm (25.6 in.).
Distribution: This species is most abundant in the Red Sea, but also ranges to South Africa and the island of Mauritius.
Biology: The Gray Moray is a diurnal species that hunts small fishes and crustaceans. It will stick its head between pieces of coral rubble and into reef fissures to find its prey. It will even invade the burrows of snapping shrimps and their partners, the shrimp gobies. Crustaceans and small fishes that hide in ramose hard corals, such as *Stylophora*, are not safe from smaller Gray Morays (25 cm [10 in.] in length), which will poke their heads between the coral branches when searching for food. As the Gray Moray moves over the substrate, it is often accompanied by scorpionfishes, groupers, soapfishes, and goatfishes, which all pounce on prey items flushed out of hiding by the eel's hunting activities. On one occasion in the Red Sea, I observed a band of Yellowsaddle Goatfish (*Parupeneus cyclostomus*) and a Lyretail Grouper (*Variola louti*) following a Gray Moray as it moved from one coral head to the next searching for food. Juveniles of this species often occur in aggregations numbering up to ten individuals. Adult Gray Morays are often solitary. Just before spawning, the area from just behind the head to the anus becomes greatly swollen with eggs. A Gray Moray will release from 8,000 to 12,000 planktonic eggs per spawning.
Captive Care: The Gray Moray has become more common in the aquarium trade because of increased collecting in the Red Sea. It is a smaller, less aggressive moray that can be housed with medium-sized fishes as well as with other eels. This moray should be provided with plenty of good hiding places and will usually accept fresh or frozen table shrimp or scallop from a feeding stick. I have even seen smaller specimens eat brine shrimp floating in the aquarium. I enjoy keeping morays and groupers together. If the tank is large enough and you feed them their natural prey (crabs, shrimps, small fishes), you can observe some of the behavioral interactions described in the Biology section, page 245.
Aquarium Size: 55 gal. **Temperature:** 22 to 28°C (72 to 82°F).
Aquarium Suitability Index: 4.
Remarks: The Gray Moray is light yellow to cream overall, with light brown mottling, a grayish brown head, and black spots surrounding the pores on its face.

Siderea picta (Ahl, 1789)
Common Names: Peppered Moray, Painted Moray, Leopard Moray.
Maximum Length: 1.2 m (3.9 ft.).
Distribution: East Africa, east to the islands of the Eastern Pacific, north to the Ryukyus, and south to southern Queensland.

Siderea grisea, Gray Moray: very attractive Red Sea and East African species.

Siderea picta, Peppered Moray: will leave water to catch crabs.

Biology: This moray is usually found near rocky shorelines and on reef flats, in water as shallow as several inches. At low tide, as many as five of these eels may be found living under rocks or ledges in the same tidepool. As the tide rises, the Peppered Morays move out onto the reef flat to hunt crabs (including sally lightfoots, *Grapsus* spp.) and the occasional spiny lobster or small bony fish. Its hunting forays often take it close to the shoreline, where it has been observed to slither out of the water and onto the beach in pursuit of grapsid crabs. It will also jump out of the water to strike at crabs sitting on rocks near the shore.

Captive Care: The Peppered Moray is a durable aquarium animal that will accept nonliving food (fresh table shrimp or pieces of marine fish flesh) as well as live fiddler crabs, small freshwater crayfish, grass shrimp, and feeder fish. This eel is less of a threat to other morays, but it may nip at larger fishes and it will eat any fish that it can swallow whole.

Aquarium Size: 100 gal. **Temperature:** 22 to 29°C (72 to 84°F).
Aquarium Suitability Index: 5.
Remarks: Juveniles have larger spots, which develop pale centers and finally break up into numerous black flecks as the eel matures.

Siderea thyrsoidea (Richardson, 1845)

Common Names: White-eye Moray, Grayface Moray.
Distribution: West Thailand to the Tuamotus, north to the Ryukyu Islands, and south to Tonga.
Maximum Length: 65 cm (25.6 in.), but most individuals do not exceed 40 cm (15.7 in.).
Biology: The White-eye Moray is not regularly seen in the aquarium trade. In certain areas, however, it is common in tidepools on the reef flat, in coral heads in silty lagoons, or under coral outcrops on sand or mud slopes. It is often found in pairs or with other species, such as the Fimbriated Moray (*Gymnothorax fimbriatus*) or the Zebra Moray (*Gymnomuraena zebra*). They often share crevices with Banded Coral Shrimp (*Stenopus hispidus*), cleaner shrimps (*Lysmata* spp.), and Dancing Shrimp (*Rhynchocinetes durbanensis*). Like other members of the genus, it feeds mainly on crustaceans, especially protunid or swimming crabs—but it will also eat octopuses and fishes.

Captive Care: This species does well in the home aquarium if provided with plenty of hiding places. The small size of the White-eye Moray makes it ideally suited for smaller home aquariums. It will eat live feeder fish, fiddler crabs, and grass shrimp. Like many morays, it is usually not a threat to cleaner shrimps and boxer shrimps. However, there is a possibility that the moray will eat the shrimps if they are molting, injured, or distressed. For example, a *Stenopus hispidus* that I had been keeping with a White-eye Moray for several weeks was eaten by the eel as I tried to capture the shrimp. Another way to reduce the chances that shrimps will be eaten by your moray is to introduce them to the aquarium before the eel. The White-eye Moray is not a threat to other eels, but will eat any small fishes housed with it.

Aquarium Size: 30 gal. **Temperature:** 22 to 28°C (72 to 82°F).
Aquarium Suitability Index: 5.
Remarks: The White-eye Moray is a handsome species easily identified by its white irises. There is some controversy as to how many "White-eye Morays" there actually are. Some ichthyologists believe there is only one species, others suggest that there may be three distinct species. This species is synonymous with *Siderea prosopeion*.

Siderea thyrsoidea, White-eye Moray: modest size for smaller aquariums.

Siderea thyrsoidea, White-eye Moray: whitish color variant.

Uropterygius macrocephalus, Largehead Snake Moray: good species for captive systems, but not often encountered because of its highly secretive nature.

Aquarium Size: 30 gal. **Temperature:** 22 to 28°C (72 to 82°F).
Aquarium Suitability Index: 5.
Remarks: The Barred Snake Moray has many rows of needle-sharp teeth, the anterior nostril is tubular, there are two lines that extend back from the posterior edge of the eye, and the body has wavy, narrow black lines. This species is synonymous with *Uropterygius goslinei*.

Uropterygius macrocephalus (Bleeker, 1865)

Common Name: Largehead Snake Moray.
Maximum Length: 40 cm (15.7 in.).
Distribution: Christmas Island, Indian Ocean to Panama, north to southern Japan and the Hawaiian Islands, and south to the Society Islands.
Biology: The Largehead Snake Moray occurs on reef flats, reef faces, and fore-reef slopes at depths of less than 1 up to at least 14 m (3.3 to 46 ft.). This species feeds heavily on gastropods, but also eats crabs. In the case of snails, it apparently grasps the operculum in its jaws and rips the body from the shell.
Captive Care: This species will do well in the home aquarium as long as it is provided with plenty of hiding places in which to shelter. It is very secretive and will spend most of the daylight hours hidden. It may also require live foods such as grass shrimp when first introduced to the aquarium, but will readily accept pieces of fresh fish, clam, or shrimp from a feeding stick once it has fully acclimated. Its smaller size makes it more vulnerable to being preyed upon by larger moray tankmates.
Aquarium Size: 20 gal. **Temperature:** 22 to 28°C (72 to 82°F).
Aquarium Suitability Index: 5.

References

Abrams et al. (1983), E. Böhlke (personal communications), Böhlke & McCosker (1997), Chave & Randall (1971), Danemann (1992), Diamant & Shpigel (1985), C. Evans (personal communication), Ferraris (1985), Fishelson (1990, 1992, 1996), Francis-Floyd et al. (1992), Hatooka (1986), Hemdal (1986), Hiatt & Stratsburg (1960), Hobson (1974), Humann (1994), Kuiter & Debelius (1994), Lieske & Myers (1994), McCosker & Randall (1977), Miller (1987), Moyer & Zaiser (1982), Myers (1989), Randall (1967, 1968, 1985), Randall & Golani (1995), Schroeder (1980), Thomson et al. (1979), J. Walters (personal communication), Young (1992), Yukihira et al. (1994).

Family Heterocongridae
Conger and Garden Eels

Many seasoned aquarists regularly prowl the display tanks of their local marine shops in a continual search for rare, unusual, or especially interesting specimens. The conger eel family has the ability to excite these advanced fishkeepers, and an aquarium that contains a colony of garden eels can provide a spectacular display. These marvelous members of the Family Heterocongridae are familiar to any diver who has strayed from the reef and explored the adjacent sandy expanses. From a distance, the garden eels look like a field of seagrass. But as you draw nearer, the "seagrass" miraculously disappears. In most cases, these eels are quite shy and rarely allow a human to approach closer than 1 or 2 m (3.3 to 6.5 ft.) before they vanish into their burrows. Although they have some specific husbandry needs, a colony of garden eels makes a unique aquarium presentation.

Classification and Biology

The Family Heterocongridae is comprised of 42 genera and about 110 species, which can be classified into four subfamilies—the Bathymyrinae, or short congers; the Muraenesocinae, or pike congers; the Congrinae, or conger eels; and the Heterocongrinae, or garden eels. We will concern ourselves with the latter two subfamilies, as they are more likely to be encountered by aquarists and divers. The members of these two groups differ more in their behavior than they do in their morphology. Both conger and garden eels have elongate bodies with small gill openings, a caudal fin that is continuous with the dorsal and anal fins, and bodies that are round in cross section—as opposed to the compressed bodies of most morays. Garden eels differ from the congers in having tiny (or no) pectoral fins, upturned mouths, and extremely elongate bodies (the length of their bodies can be divided by the width over 60 times). There are 25 conger eel genera and 2 garden eel genera. The garden eel genera, *Heteroconger* and *Gorgasia*, contain about 25 species.

Conger eels behave much like the morays. Most are nocturnal predators that feed on fishes and crustaceans. Congers conceal themselves during the day among rocky and coral reefs, or burrow in soft substrate. Garden eels, in contrast, use the rigid tips of their tails to burrow into the sand, where they spend their days and nights. They extend their heads and bodies from the substrate to capture zooplankton carried by ocean currents. Garden eels usually live in colonies, which can consist of thousands of individuals. Conger eels are also commonly found in temperate and/or deep water, ranging to depths of at least 500 m (1,625 ft.).

When constructing a burrow, a garden eel will shove its hard-tipped tail into the substrate and flex its muscular body to drive its posterior end deep into the sand or mud. Collagen in the dermis of the tail tip forms a rigid structure to facilitate this tail-

Heteroconger polyzona, Striped Garden Eel: strikingly handsome and an unusual aquarium subject, but one with specialized husbandry needs.

Unidentified conger eel buries itself with only its head exposed. Provide these eels witth a deep layer of substrate in which to bury.

first entry. After the tail is positioned deep in the substrate, the garden eel will undulate its dorsal fin, causing the disturbed substrate to be carried away by the current. Mucus, exuded by secretory cells in the skin, helps to cement the grains of substrate together and reinforce the burrow walls. The diameter of Red Sea Garden Eel (*Gorgasia sillneri*) holes can range from 1 to 13 mm.

When a garden eel feeds, it extends about three-quarters of the anterior portion of its body out of its burrow, bends its head into the current, and sways to and fro as it picks off individual plankters that pass by. Although the dietary habits of only two garden eels have been examined (Atlantic Garden, *Heteroconger longissimus*, and Hawaiian Garden, *Gorgasia hawaiiensis*), it is likely that they all have similar food habits. These species feed mainly on a variety of copepods (80% by volume in the Hawaiian form), but also ingest solitary eggs, egg masses, pelagic tunicates, pteropods, ostracods, shrimp larvae, amphipods, tanaids, ostracods, euphausids, mysid shrimp, radiolarians, and gastropod larvae. The stomach of an adult Atlantic Garden Eel may contain as many as 600 copepods at any one time, ranging in size from 0.4 to 2.1 mm. For the aquarist, this observation indicates that these eels require frequent feeding. The Hawaiian Garden Eel feeds on prey items ranging from 100 microns (eggs) to 3 mm (calanoid copepods) in length.

As mentioned earlier, some garden eels form large colonies. A colony of Red Sea Garden Eels (*Gorgasia sillneri*) was reported to cover an area of about 6,000 m^2 (64,560 ft.^{2}) and was comprised of an estimated 10,000 individuals. In this colony, larger, more dominant males occupied burrows in the center, where current velocities were greater and the sand was deeper. Juveniles, who were only found at depths greater than 25 m (81 ft.), could reach densities of 14 individuals per square meter (10.76 ft.^{2}). Although young Red Sea Garden Eels are often found on the edges of a colony in deep water, an occasional juvenile may succeed in constructing a burrow within the territory of a large male. Population densities in smaller colonies ranged from 0 to 7 adults per square meter, with the territory of adults being directly correlated to the size of the individual (larger eels occupied larger territories). The number of individuals in a colony was a function of sand depth, current velocities, and possibly the presence of site-attached predators like crocodile snake eels (*Brachysomophis* spp.).

Garden eels are targeted by a number of predators. In the Red Sea, Crocodile and Stargazer Snake Eels (*Brachysomophis crocodilinus* and *B. cirrocheilos*), the Marbled Snake Eel (*Callechelys marmorata*), and the Saddled Snake Eel (*Leiuranus semicinctus*) feed on garden eels, stalking them under the sand and capturing them in their burrows. Lizardfishes, lethrinids (emperor snappers), adult Pavo Razorfish (*Xyrichtys pavo*), and some of the larger triggerfishes either dig these eels out of the sand or sneak up and capture them when the eels extend from their burrows.

At least one species of garden eel is sexually dimorphic: in the Red Sea Garden Eel, males have longer jaws, a more pointed caudal fin, and are larger than females. During the breeding season, male and female garden eels will move their burrows closer to each other—burrows that were approximately 20 cm (8 in.) apart will be moved to about 3 cm (1 in.) apart. The male defends the female from potential mates at this time. It will strike at rivals with its head, perform lateral displays (erecting the dorsal fin), and even bite encroaching competitors behind the head. The male will extend from its burrow to approach the female and will rub its head over the female's body. If the female is not sex-

Brachysomophis crocodilinus, Crocodile Snake Eel: a Red Sea Garden Eel predator that can stalk and devour prey hidden in under-sand burrows.

ually receptive, she will withdraw into her burrow. If she is ready to spawn, she will wrap her body around the male so that their urogenital pores are close together. The pair will remain in this position for up to 9½ hours and apparently release their pelagic gametes into the water column. Actual spawning, however, has never been observed.

Captive Care

Conger eels are much like morays in their husbandry requirements. They need suitable hiding places and should be placed in a tank that has a tight-fitting top to prevent them from jumping out. Live food may be required to initiate feeding in these fishes, but they will usually switch to fresh or frozen pieces of seafood—squid, strips of fish flesh, and chunks of scallop are all appropriate. They will eat any tankmate that is small enough to swallow whole and may even harass and nip at larger fishes when hungry or stimulated by the odor of food.

Garden eels require more care than conger eels or morays. Although a huge tank is not required for most species, if you are going to keep a colony, you need to provide enough space so that individuals can spread out. The depth of the substrate is extremely important. Red Sea Garden Eels will not burrow in sand of less than 20 cm (7.9 in.) in depth, and are most often found in areas where the sand is 35 to 135 cm (14 to 53 in.) deep. However, keep in mind that the Red Sea species attains a maximum length of 42 cm (17 in.), while the species most commonly seen in aquarium stores (Spotted Garden Eel, *Heteroconger hassi*) is smaller. If the aquarium substrate is too shallow, garden eels may damage the tips of their tails. The average adult may extend 30 cm (12 in.) or more into the sand, but in an aquarium they will usually curve their bodies horizontally in response to the tank bottom. Nevertheless, the substrate in the aquarium should be at least 15 cm (6 in.) deep.

A garden eel aquarium should also have a gentle current that blows along the bottom of the tank to bring the eels their food. One of the best ways to meet this requirement is to run a pipe down the back of the aquarium so that it is 7.5 to 10 cm (3 to 4 in.) above the bottom. Connect the pipe to a pump that returns water from a sump or powerhead in the tank, and attach a spray bar to the outflow pipe. The spray bar should extend from the back of the tank to the front glass along one end. The spray bar should have ¼-inch holes drilled every 3 inches in a line that will direct water across, but not into, the substrate. This will ensure that food is washed the length of the tank, past the relatively stationary eels. The pump can be placed on a timer so that you can observe the difference in the eels' behavior during the different "tidal phases." Rigged with a rheostat, the pump and its flow rate could be adjusted to mimic the gradual changes in current flow found in the eels' natural habitat.

These fishes should be fed live brine shrimp initially, but can usually be switched to substitute foods, such as frozen brine shrimp, finely chopped fresh or frozen seafoods, and frozen *Mysis* shrimp. They will also eat baby livebearers, free-swimming copepods, and live mysid shrimp. A relatively constant supply of the latter could be provided by connecting an internal or external refugium to your aquarium (for more details on refugiums, see "Keys to Successful Anthias Husbandry.", page 548).

Garden eels are often shy, especially when first introduced to the aquarium, retracting into their burrows as the aquarist approaches. If you sit still in front of the tank for a long enough period of time, they will usually extend from their holes again. One way to prevent these eels from retracting every time you approach the tank is to build a tank using one-way glass for the front panel. This way, the eels can't see out and the aquarist can observe them without affecting their behavior. By placing a mirror on the back of the tank, you can create the illusion that there are twice as many garden eels in the aquarium.

Garden eels are best displayed in a taller tank. In most cases, aquarists prefer aquariums with greater surface area (this would apply to most other eels), but the garden eel tank needs to be high enough to accommodate a deep sand bed and still allow the eels to extend out of their burrows and into the water column. For example, a 45-gallon tank (which is 23 inches tall) is a better choice than a 30-gallon aquarium (16 inches tall). (The footprint of these two tanks is exactly the same.) Decor should be kept to a minimum in the garden eel tank, or if the aquarium is long enough, a vertical reef could be constructed at one end of the

Xyrichtys pavo, Pavo Razorfish: garden eel predators include this species, along with lizardfishes, emperor snappers, and some larger triggerfishes.

tank. If you create a high-profile reef, be sure the rocks are securely attached to each other with cable ties or underwater epoxy. Some calcareous macroalgae (e.g., *Halimeda*) or even seagrass could be included in a realistic garden eel aquarium. (A low-growing member of the genus *Halophila* is sometimes found among garden eel colonies in Indonesia.) There are no special lighting requirements for the garden eel tank, although those species from shallow water may be more inclined to extend further from their burrows in brighter conditions, while the opposite may be true for deep-water forms. The glitter lines produced by a point source of light, like a metal halide lamp, create a very pleasing effect in a garden eel aquarium.

Several garden eels can be kept together in the same tank, but care should be taken when placing them. The adult males of some species are territorial and will fight if there is an insufficient distance between them. It is also important to choose eel tankmates carefully. Avoid any fish species that may behave aggressively toward them, as well as vigorous substrate sifters (like sleeper gobies, *Valenciennea* spp.) and diggers (like goatfishes) that may disturb their burrows. Table 21 lists some fish species that occur in garden eel habitat and are less likely to pester them. Note that some larger razorfish species (*Xyrichtys* spp.) may feed on juvenile garden eels. If these special requirements are met, the eels will do fairly well in a home aquarium. In at least one species, juveniles (less than 10 cm [4in.]) do better than adults.

Some garden eels develop a condition known as blisterhead, a blisterlike swelling under the skin on the head giving the eel a puglike appearance. It is not fatal and affects a relatively small number of individuals in a population. Only 3 to 4% of one large sample of Atlantic Garden Eels had blisterhead, with slightly more adults suffering from the condition than smaller specimens. Fortunately for aquarists, garden eels do not appear to be susceptible to parasitic infections—they should not be exposed to copper sulfate, malachite green, or organophosphates.

TABLE 21

Suitable Garden Eel Tankmates

Indo-West Pacific

Oriental Helmut Gurnard	(*Dactyloptena orientalis*)
Sand divers	(*Trichonotus* spp.)
Pearlstreaked Spinecheek	(*Scolopsis xenochrous*)
Blue Whiptail	(*Pentapodus* sp.)
Schauinsland's Sand Perch	(*Parapercis schauinslandi*)
U-marked Sand Perch	(*Parapercis snyderi*)
Melanopus Razorfish	(*Xyrichtys melanopus*)
Black Razorfish	(*Xyrichtys niger*)
Fivefinger Razorfish	(*Xyrichtys pendactylus*)
Sand gobies	(*Istigobius* spp.)

Tropical Western Atlantic

Flying Gurnard	(*Dactylopterus volitans*)
Tobacco Fish	(*Serranus tabacarius*)
Clown Wrasse	(*Halichoeres maculipinna*)
Rainbow Wrasse	(*Halichoeres pictus*)
Green Razorfish	(*Hemipteronotus niger*)
Bluehead Wrasse	(*Thalassoma bifasciatum*)
Rosy Razorfish	(*Xyrichtys martinicensis*)
Pearly Razorfish	(*Xyrichtys novacula*)
Bridled Goby	(*Coryphopterus glaucofraenum*)
Orangespotted Goby	(*Nes longus*)
Seminole Goby	(*Microgobius carri*)
Blue Goby	(*Ptereleotris calliurus*)
Hovering Goby	(*Ptereleotris helenae*)

Heteroconger hassi, Spotted Garden Eel: an appropriate aquarium setting for these species includes a deep sand bed and minimal aquascaping.

Conger and Garden Eel Species

Genus *Conger*

Conger cinereus Rüppell, 1830
Common Name: Mustache Conger.
Maximum Length: 1.3 m (4.2 ft.).
Distribution: Red Sea to Hawaiian, Marquesas, and Easter Islands, north to southern Japan, and south to Lord Howe Island.
Biology: The Mustache Conger occurs on reef flats, in lagoon seagrass beds, reef faces, and on fore-reef slopes, at depths from less than 1 up to 80 m (3.3 to 260 ft.). This species feeds mainly at night, on crustaceans (including shrimps and crabs) and bony fishes (including surgeonfishes and filefishes). It will capture torpid fishes as they sleep.
Captive Care: *Conger cinereus* must be housed in a large tank with numerous hiding places. Initially, it is likely to spend more time in the open in a tank that is dimly lit. As it becomes accustomed to its new living conditions, it will become quite bold. Often, individuals will learn to recognize their keeper as a source of food and will come out to greet the aquarist as he or she approaches the tank.
Aquarium Size: 180 gal. **Temperature:** 21 to 27°C (70 to 80°F).
Aquarium Suitability Index: 4.
Remarks: The population from the Hawaiian Islands represents a valid subspecies, known as *Conger cinereus marginatus*. The Mustache Congers from the rest of the Pacific and Indian Oceans are known as *Conger cinereus cinereus*. Humans consider this eel good to eat. The **Barred Conger** (***Poeciloconger fasciatus***) **Günther, 1871** is a more attractive species that has been reported from Madagascar, Indonesia, the Marshall Islands, Hawaii, and Tahiti. It can burrow backward into the sand with its stiff tail tip and attains a maximum length of 60 cm (23.6 in.).

Genus *Gorgasia*

Gorgasia maculatus Klausewitz & Eibl-Eibesfeldt, 1959
Common Name: Whitespotted Garden Eel.
Maximum Length: 70 cm (27.6 in.).
Distribution: Maldives to the Solomon Islands, north to the Philippines.
Biology: This species occurs on sand slopes and lives in small to large colonies.
Captive Care: For details on the husbandry of this species, see the Captive Care section in the family account, page 289.

Conger cinereus, Mustache Conger: may become a keeper's pet.

Conger cinereus, Mustache Conger: adult length demands a large aquarium.

Poeciloconger fasciatus, Barred Conger: small, attractive Indo-Pacific species.

Gorgasia maculatus, Whitespotted Garden Eel: may gather in large colonies.

Gorgasia preclara, Splendid Garden Eel: attractive species for smaller tanks.

Gorgasia sp., Speckled Garden Eel: rather pale species rarely collected.

Aquarium Size: 55 gal. **Temperature:** 23 to 27°C (74 to 80°F).
Aquarium Suitability Index: 3.
Remarks: This extremely elongate eel has white spots around the pore on the head and on the anterior portion of the lateral line. The **Red Sea Garden Eel** (*Gorgasia sillneri*) **Klausewitz, 1962** and the **Hawaiian Garden Eel** (*G. hawaiiensis*) **Randall & Chess, 1979** are two very similar species. The Hawaiian Garden Eel occurs in small- to moderate-sized colonies, with densities reaching up to 26 eels in 16 m². The holes average 20 to 30 cm (7.9 to 12 in.) apart and measure 5 to 9 mm in diameter.

Gorgasia preclara Böhlke & Randall, 1981
Common Names: Splendid Garden Eel, Orangebarred Garden Eel.
Maximum Length: 38 cm (15.0 in.).
Distribution: Maldives, Indonesia, Philippines, Ryukyus, Marianas, and possibly Fiji.
Biology: This beautiful garden eel occurs on sand and rubble slopes. Although it can occur at depths as shallow as 15 m (50 ft.), smallcolonies of *G. preclara* are usually found at depths greater than 30 m (98 ft.). Solitary individuals are occasionally observed.
Captive Care: For details on the husbandry of this species, see the Captive Care section in the family account, page 289. This is not a common species in the aquarium trade. It is one of the smallest *Gorgasia* species, and it is better suited for the home aquarium than most other members of the genus because less substrate is needed to provide it with an adequate burrow. It is also one of the most attractive members of the family.
Aquarium Size: 45 gal. **Temperature:** 23 to 27°C (74 to 80°F).
Aquarium Suitability Index: 3.
Remarks: *Gorgasia preclara* has alternating orangish brown and white bars.

Gorgasia sp.
Common Name: Speckled Garden Eel.
Maximum Length: 46 cm (18.1 in.).
Distribution: Great Barrier Reef and Coral Sea north to Guam and the Marshall Islands.
Biology: This species is found on sand slopes adjacent to coral reefs at depths greater than 18 m (59 ft.).
Captive Care: For details on the husbandry of this species, see the Captive Care section in the family account, page 289. This species is rarely, if ever, collected for the aquarium trade.
Aquarium Size: 45 gal. **Temperature:** 23 to 27°C (74 to 80°F).
Aquarium Suitability Index: 3.
Remarks: The Speckled Garden Eel is pale gray with small yellowish brown speckles.

Genus *Heteroconger*

Heteroconger hassi (Klausewitz & Eibl-Eibesfeldt, 1959)
Common Name: Spotted Garden Eel.
Maximum Length: 35 cm (13.8 in.).
Distribution: Red Sea to Line Islands, north to the Ryukyus, and south to New Caledonia and Tonga.
Biology: Colonies of these eels are found on sandy slopes exposed to moderate or strong currents. They are occasionally found in seagrass beds. They occur at depths of 7 to 45 m (23 to 146 ft.). Eel density in a colony can be as many as 15 per m^2 (10.76 ft.^{2}), with 20 to 60 cm (7.9 to 24 in.) separating each eel.
Captive Care: For details on the husbandry of this species, see the Captive Care section in the family account, page 289. This is the most common species in the aquarium trade; its small size makes it better suited for the home aquarium than some of its larger relatives. Up to 12 eels can be kept in a 180-gallon tank.
Aquarium Size: 45 gal. **Temperature:** 22 to 27°C (72 to 80°F).
Aquarium Suitability Index: 3.
Remarks: This species has small black speckles and three black spots on the body—one surrounding the gill opening, one on the side of the trunk, and one around the anus. The **Freckled Garden Eel** (*Heteroconger lentiginosus*) **Böhlke & Randall, 1981** is closely related but can be distinguished by its color pattern (it lacks the three black spots) and the position of its dorsal fin (the origin is farther back in *H. lentiginosus*). This eel has only been reported from the Marquesas and Society Islands on sand and rubble bottoms at depths greater than 30 m (98 ft.).

Heteroconger longissimus Günther, 1870
Common Name: Atlantic Garden Eel.
Maximum Length: 51 cm (20.1 in.), but usually under 35 cm (13.8 in.). In Bermuda, this species is larger on average, commonly attaining 45 cm (17.7 in.).
Distribution: Bermuda, south Florida, and the Bahamas to the Lesser Antilles.
Biology: This species occurs on sandy expanses near fringing and fore-reef slopes at depths from 4.6 to 60 m (15 to 195 ft.). In Bermuda, adults occur in male-female pairs, while in other localities, the sexes are randomly spaced in colonies.
Captive Care: For details on the husbandry of this species, see the Captive Care section in the family account, page 289.
Aquarium Size: 55 gal. **Temperature:** 22 to 27°C (72 to 80°F).
Aquarium Suitability Index: 3.
Remarks: This species is synonymous with *Nystactes hallis*. Another garden eel from the Atlantic is the **Yellow Garden Eel** (*Heteroconger luteolus*) **Smith, 1995**.

Heteroconger hassi, Spotted Garden Eel: groups make an arresting display.

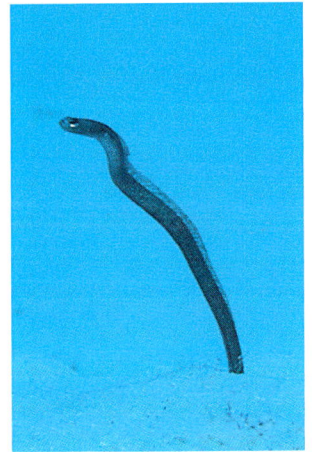 
Atlantic eels: *Heteroconger longissimus* (left); *Heteroconger luteolus* (right).

Heteroconger perissodon Böhlke & Randall, 1981
Common Names: Manytoothed Garden Eel, Black Garden Eel.
Maximum Length: 51 cm (20.1 in.).
Distribution: Indonesia and the Philippines.
Biology: This species occurs on sand and mud flats and slopes, near fringing reefs, at depths from 1 to 35 m (3.3 to 114 ft.). In shallow water, these eels are often found in small groups, while on deep slopes they usually occur in large colonies.
Captive Care: For details on the husbandry of this species, see the Captive Care section in the family account, page 289.

Heteroconger perissodon, Manytoothed Garden Eel: note white head blotch.

Heteroconger polyzona, Striped Garden Eel: distinguished by brown striping.

Heteroconger taylori, Leopard Garden Eel: juvenile at left, adult at right.

Aquarium Size: 55 gal. **Temperature:** 23 to 27°C (74 to 80°F).
Aquarium Suitability Index: 3.
Remarks: *Heteroconger perissodon* has a white blotch on the side of the head and is usually dusky gray to brown overall with light flecks on the body and white-edged median fins.

Heteroconger polyzona Bleeker, 1868
Common Name: Striped Garden Eel.
Maximum Length: 40 cm (15.7 in.).
Distribution: Indonesia to southern Japan.
Biology: The Striped Garden Eel is usually found on sand and mud flats, typically in water less than 6 m (20 ft.) in depth, in small or large colonies. It sometimes occurs in the same area as the Leopard Garden Eel (*Heteroconger taylori*) and the Whitespotted Garden Eel (*Gorgasia maculatus*).
Captive Care: For details on the husbandry of this species, see the Captive Care section in the family account, page 289. Although handsome, this species is infrequently available.
Aquarium Size: 45 gal. **Temperature:** 22 to 27°C (72 to 80°F).
Aquarium Suitability Index: 3.
Remarks: The Striped Garden Eel is unique in having dark brown stripes on the back and sides. The **Cobra Garden Eel (*Heteroconger cobra*) Böhlke & Randall, 1981** is an attractive species known from deep water (over 30 m [98 ft.]) around New Guinea and the Solomon Islands. *Heteroconger cobra* is easily recognized by its unique markings—dark brown blotches with white centers on the head and trunk.

Heteroconger taylori Castle & Randall, 1995
Common Names: Leopard Garden Eel, Taylor's Garden Eel.
Maximum Length: 40 cm (15.7 in.).
Distribution: Indonesia (Bali and Flores), Mabul, and Papua New Guinea.
Biology: The Leopard Garden Eel lives on black or white sand slopes at depths from 8 to 35 m (26 to 114 ft.), usually adjacent to coastal reefs. It often lives singly or in small colonies, rather than in large groups.
Captive Care: For details on the husbandry of this species, see the Captive Care section in the family account, page 289.
Aquarium Size: 45 gal. **Temperature:** 22 to 27°C (72 to 80°F).
Aquarium Suitability Index: 3.
Remarks: Young of this species are often yellowish overall, with less numerous and larger dark spots. Adults are creamy white.

References
Böhlke & Randall (1981), Clark et al. (1990), Randall & Chess (1979), Tyler & Luckhurst (1994).

Family Ophichthidae
Snake Eels

Brachysomophis crocodilinus, Crocodile Snake Eel: an ambush predator that can explode from the sand to grab passing prey—or aquarists' hands.

Although sharing a similar serpentine appearance, the snake eels are very different from the morays (Muraenidae), both in habitat preferences and behavior. Most snake eels are common on sand, mud flats, and seagrass beds, spending much of their time living a subterranean lifestyle. Some snake eels explode from their sand homes to capture passing prey, others leave the substrate to explore holes and rubble in search of their quarry. These latter snake eels are often followed by opportunistic carnivores.

Classification and Biology

The Family Ophichthidae is a large group that includes some of the most evil-looking fish in the sea, as well as some that are ornately patterned. It is comprised of approximately 55 genera and more than 250 species, which are difficult to characterize because they are so diverse. Several features that most species possess include a posterior nostril that opens either inside the mouth or through a valve in the upper lip, a fixed tongue, no palatine teeth, and a lateral line that extends onto the head. The Family Ophichthidae is comprised of two subfamilies, the Myrophinae (commonly known as worm eels) and the Ophichthinae (commonly known as snake eels). The worm eels have a tail with a flexible tip and a short caudal fin. The snake eels have a tail with a hard or fleshy tip and no caudal fin. Although not uncommon where they occur, the worm eels spend their lives under the sand and are rarely encountered by divers or aquarists. For this

Unidentified snake eels, possibly *Ichthyapus vulturis*, Vulture Eels: note gashes on head, which may result from individuals biting each other.

reason, we will limit our examination of the snake eels to the Subfamily Ophichthinae. Although many snake eels are also secretive, a handful of species often move about the reef or the surrounding seagrass, rubble, or sand. Some of these eels regularly make it into the aquarium trade.

Snake eels are found in temperate and tropical seas around the world. Although not all members associate with reefs—either coral or rocky—many do live adjacent to these biomes. Members of the family have been reported at depths from less than 1 up to 1,418 m (3.3 to 4,609 ft.).

The rigid tip of the snake eel's tail enables it to slide tailfirst into the substrate. Many species spend most of their time "underground," and some can even move freely around under the sand or mud. For this reason, they are often referred to as "indwellers." Some snake eels are nocturnal, emerging from the substrate to hunt at night, while others are frequently observed foraging during the day as well as after dark. One species common in the aquarium trade, the Pacific Spotted Snake Eel (*Myrichthys maculosus*), actively forages during the day.

The diets of most of the coral reef-associated snake eel species are poorly known, but a comprehensive study on a species from the Mediterranean (*Ophichthus rufus*), demonstrated that there was a difference between the diets of males and females. The males fed more on krill and decapod crustaceans, while females (which attain a greater length than males) consumed larger numbers of teleosts. The number of different prey items consumed was greatest in medium-sized individuals. The primary prey items were snapping shrimps (e.g., *Alpheus glaber*), processid shrimps (e.g., *Processa caniliculata*), and dragonets (e.g., *Callionymus maculatus*). Food habit studies on reef-associated species have shown that they have a "preference" for crustaceans and fishes, but also consume cephalopods and polychaete worms.

Most snake eels actively hunt their prey, either by grubbing in cracks and crevices or under the sands. Two genera of snake eels, however, *Brachysomophis* and *Ophichthus*, ambush passing prey. The *Brachysomophis* have eyes located toward the tip of the snout. This enables them to conceal their entire body and most of their head under the substrate and still see prey items that move past. Their jaws also have an enormous gape, enabling them to swallow larger prey. When a cephalopod, crustacean, or fish comes too close, these eels lunge from the substrate to capture them. The *Ophichthus* species also hide their bodies under the substrate, leaving their heads protruding from the sand or mud. Members of both genera may completely hide under the substrate during the day.

Snake eels fall prey to large predatory fishes and sea snakes. Some species apparently mimic these venomous reptiles and

Myrichthys maculosus, Pacific Spotted Snake Eel: this specimen actively probes reef crevices in search of prey.

Myrichthys breviceps, Sharptail Snake Eel, being followed by opportunistic predators feeding on prey it flushes from the sand.

Snake Eel Associates

If you are diving in the Caribbean and encounter a foraging snake eel, it will likely be escorted by an entourage of opportunistic predators. It has been my experience that snake eels attract a wider range of "followers" than any other fish species. I once observed a Sharptail Snake Eel (*Myrichthys breviceps*) foraging on Bonaire's reef flat late one afternoon. It was probing the rubble in search of small sea bass, gobies, and shrimps that refuge in nooks and crannies. This eel was being followed by no less than ten fish species, including a large terminal-phase Spanish Hogfish (*Bodianus rufus*), a large Bar Jack (*Caranx ruber*), several Coneys (*Epinephelus fulva*), a Rock Hind (*Epinephelus adscensionis*), a Greater Soapfish (*Rypticus saponaceus*), and several snappers (*Lutjanus* spp.). The attendant species were jockeying for a position near the snake eel's head in order to be the first to get a shot at any fish or crustacean flushed out of hiding. The most aggressive attendant, the Greater Soapfish, swam alongside the anterior end of the snake eel so that their heads were next to each other. When the snake eel stopped to explore an interstice, the Greater Soapfish lay on its side with its head near the opening. At one point, I saw the Bar Jack race after, and capture, a small fish flushed by the snake eel's probing activities. I followed the feeding party for nearly an hour, at which time my efforts to get more photographs scared the snake eel off the reef flat into the deeper water of the fore-reef slope. About 45 minutes later, I encountered what appeared to be the same snake eel. This time it was being followed by four Coneys. I saw numerous Sharptail Snake Eels foraging during my stay at Bonaire, and on every occasion one or more predators followed them.

may be avoided by some fishes and birds as a result of this resemblance.

Snake eels occur singly during most of the year, but some species are thought to migrate and aggregate in specific locations to breed. Some spawn near the ocean's surface. Courtship behavior has been observed in at least one species—the Saddled Snake Eel (*Leiuranus semicinctus*). Three of these individuals were encountered at the water's surface and were collected and placed in a tank. The male bit the female behind the head and remained in this position for hours. When the male's hold was broken by the observer, the male immediately seized the female again, but this time he bit her ventral surface so that the two eels were belly-to-belly. While in this position, the male emitted a cloud of sperm, after which he released his grip and ignored the female. Although the female released no eggs, slight palpitations of the abdomen by the observer encouraged the ova to be expelled. In this species, there is sexual dimorphism in the dentition, possibly related to the biting behavior observed during courtship.

Captive Care

Although many members of this family can be successfully housed in the home aquarium, they do require special care and attention. Most snake eels will not accept food in captivity unless they are provided with plenty of swimming room, an appropriate amount of substrate, and live prey. Unlike morays, which spend much of their time peering out from coral crevices, snake eels often move about the tank—when they are not buried under the substrate. In fact, they often swim incessantly along the front of the aquarium glass and up the sides of the tank. Therefore, it is important to provide a snake eel with more room than you would give a moray of equal size. Most snake eels live in areas that are relatively devoid of reef structure, so tank decor should be kept to a minimum.

Snake eels require a thick layer of fine substrate on the aquarium bottom under which to hide. Although it depends on the size of the eel, a minimum substrate depth of 7.5 to 10 cm (3 to 4 in.) is recommended. If the sand is not properly agitated, however, it could become anaerobic and possibly lead to the production of poisonous hydrogen sulfide. To avoid this problem, manually stir the sand several times a week, either with your hand or with a piece of clear rigid tubing. (The tubing is preferable, as it is less likely to startle your eel and you won't risk having your hand bitten.) If the eel is very active and its frequent swimming bouts and digging are already stirring up the substrate, it may not be necessary to do any manual agitation.

Having little in the way of decor will facilitate feeding, as potential prey items won't have as many places to hide from the snake eel. Live fiddler crabs, grass shrimps, or livebearers (e.g., guppies or mollies) are often required to induce these finicky fishes to feed. It may also help if these food items are introduced to the aquarium after dark, when many snake eels feed more actively. You can use a red light (either incandescent or fluorescent) to observe their behavior at this time. Once a snake eel is enticed to eat in captivity, it may be possible to use a feeding stick and switch them to chunks of seafood like clams, scallops, shrimps, or squids. If your snake eel does not eat, it will often take many months before it starves to death.

Snake eels are also very effective at escaping from the aquarium. For this reason, it is essential to have a tight-fitting cover on the tank. A top made from eggcrate material or fiberglass screen will permit gas exchange at the water's surface. If you use eggcrate material, make sure it is weighted down so that the eel can't push it up and get out. Some eels will swim frantically about the tank and attempt to leap out if disturbed by the aquarist, so it is best to work in the aquarium as little as possible. When intrusion is necessary, move very slowly and stay clear of the eel.

Brachysomophis crocodilinus, Crocodile Snake Eel: species-tank candidate.

Snake eels rarely suffer from parasitic infections. Be careful when treating a tank that contains a snake eel; they may react negatively to copper sulfate, malachite green, and organophosphates.

Snake eels typically do best if kept either in a specimen tank or with other eels. However, large morays may eat smaller snake eels. The smaller eels are also prone to be picked on by fishes that feed on sessile invertebrates—typical examples being the angelfishes, triggerfishes, filefishes, puffers, tobies, and porcupinefishes. Avoid placing aggressive feeders in a tank with a snake eel; otherwise, the eel may never have a chance to get enough to eat. Although most snake eels will not eat a fish tankmate unless it is small and bottom-dwelling (e.g., dartfishes and gobies), there are exceptions. The snake eels of the genus *Brachysomophis* have massive jaws. They can and will ingest large prey items. Members of the genus *Ophichthus* also eat fishes. If you are willing to devote a large tank to one or more snake eels and you want to keep something else in the aquarium with them, try a few goatfishes, a school of monos, a sand perch, a flying gurnard, or some spine cheeks. All of these fishes occur in the same habitat (open sand or mud slopes) as most snake eels and will not harm them. However, some of these fishes will compete with them for food, so they should not be added until the snake eels are acclimated and feeding. Any fish kept with a snake eel should be large enough to avoid being swallowed. Snake eels might also be eaten by larger snappers, emperor snappers, and groupers. For example, a Dog Snapper (*Lutjanus jocu*) of about 60 cm (24 in.) was recorded to have eaten a *Myrichthys* snake eel of about the same length.

Snake eels are not suitable for the reef tank because too little of the bottom is usually devoted to open substrate and they will be too difficult to feed in this setting.

Brachysomophis cirrocheilos, Stargazer Snake Eel: massive predatory jaws.

Snake Eel Species

Genus *Apterichthus*

Apterichthus klazingai (Weber, 1913)
Common Name: Sharpsnout Snake Eel.
Maximum Length: 40 cm (15.7 in.).
Distribution: East Africa to the Marshall Islands, south to the Great Barrier Reef.
Biology: The Sharpsnout Snake Eel is a very secretive species that spends most of its time buried under the sand. It occurs on sand slopes near coral reefs. It has been reported from depths of 5 to 20 m (16 to 65 ft.).
Captive Care: This is not a highly desirable aquarium species because it hides most of the time and is difficult to feed. Provide it with a thick layer (15 cm [6 in.]) of fine sand substrate.
Aquarium Size: 75 gal. **Temperature:** 23 to 28°C (74 to 82°F).
Aquarium Suitability Index: 2.
Remarks: *Apterichthus klazingai* is white with light brown spots, a pointed snout, no fins, and minute papillae on the snout and head. There are currently nine species recognized in the genus *Apterichthus*, but a revision of the group is greatly needed.

Genus *Brachysomophis*

Brachysomophis cirrocheilos (Bleeker, 1857)
Common Name: Stargazer Snake Eel.
Maximum Length: 1.25 m (4.1 ft.).
Distribution: Red Sea to Indonesia, south to Papua New Guinea, north to Japan.
Biology: The Stargazer Snake Eel is most commonly observed in sand and mud, near coastal reefs, at depths of 1 up to at least 10 m (3.3 to 33 ft.). I once observed a larger individual under a pier in Indonesia on several consecutive nights. Only its head was visible, emerging from the mud, leaf litter, and tree branches. The Stargazer Snake Eel will burrow into the sand tailfirst until only its eyes and the top of its snout are visible. At night, its entire head—and in some cases the anterior portion of its body—will protrude from the substrate. It has been reported to feed on fishes and cephalopods. In the areas where I have seen this species, cuttlefish, crabs, flatheads, cardinalfishes, and flatfishes move over the substrate at night and are probably ambushed by the Stargazer. When a prey item is captured in the eel's tooth-studded jaws, it is pulled beneath the substrate. In the Red Sea, *B. cirrocheilos* has been reported to feed on garden eels, approaching them under the sand and capturing them in their burrows.

Apterichthus klazingai, Sharpsnout Snake Eel: difficult-to-feed species.

Apterichthus klazingai, Sharpsnout Snake Eel: rarely collected.

Brachysomophis cirrocheilos, Stargazer Snake Eel: note tooth-studded jaws.

Captive Care: The Stargazer Snake Eel should be housed in a large tank, with at least 15 cm (6 in.) of fine substrate (live sand) to burrow under. This fish is best kept on its own, as it is likely to grab any fish or crustacean that moves too close. Aquarists should also be wary of where they place their hands when working in a tank with this species.
Aquarium Size: 180 gal. **Temperature:** 22 to 28°C (72 to 82°F).
Aquarium Suitability Index: 3.
Remarks: This species differs from the Crocodile Snake Eel (*Brachysomophis crocodilinus*) in the length of its pectoral fins (the pectoral fin length can be divided into the head length about 4 to 5 times in *B. cirrocheilos*; 10 to 12 times in *B. crocodilinus*), the number of vertebrae (136 to 139 for *B. cirrocheilos*; 114 to 130 for *B. crocodilinus*), and the coloration. Most Stargazer Snake Eels are light brown overall, with irregular lighter patches on the back and sides. The belly is dark yellow, the head has fine black spots, there is a line of white spots on the back of the head, and there are dark spots evenly spaced on the nape and along the lateral line. The median fins are dark brown with black edges.

Brachysomophis crocodilinus (Bennett, 1833)
Common Name: Crocodile Snake Eel.
Maximum Length: 1.1 m (3.6 ft.).
Distribution: Mauritius to Tahiti.
Biology: The Crocodile Snake Eel is most commonly found in sand or mud, near coastal reefs, at depths of less than 1 to 12 m (3.3 to 39 ft.). Small juveniles can be observed in the same habitat occupied by adults and may fall prey to them on occasion. Often, more than one Crocodile Snake Eel is encountered in the same area, along with other snake eels such as Bonapart's Snake Eel (*Ophichthus bonaparti*) and the Stargazer Snake Eel (*B. cirrocheilos*). At night, the Crocodile Snake Eel is frequently observed with its head, and even the anterior portion of its body, protruding from the substrate. During the day, it will often bury with only the tip of its snout and the top of its head projecting from the sand or mud.
Captive Care: *Brachysomophis crocodilinus* is rarely seen in the aquarium trade. Its husbandry needs are similar to those of the Stargazer Snake Eel.
Aquarium Size: 180 gal. **Temperature:** 22 to 28°C (72 to 82°F).
Aquarium Suitability Index: 3.
Remarks: This snake eel is white to tan overall. Henshaw's Snake Eel (*Brachysomophis henshawi*), from the Hawaiian Islands, is reported to be synonymous with this species. The Reptilian Snake Eel (*Brachysomophis sauropsis*) may also be a synonym. Much work needs to be done on the taxonomy of the members of this genus, but relatively few specimens are available for examination. Some individuals (which are thought to be this species) have pink heads and white lines on the edge of the lower jaw.

Genus *Callechelys*

Callechelys marmorata (Bleeker, 1853)
Common Name: Marbled Snake Eel.
Maximum Length: 87 cm (34.3 in.).
Distribution: East Africa and the Red Sea to the Society Islands, south to Lord Howe Island.
Biology: The Marbled Snake Eel is most common on sand or mud flats in protected bays or near coastal reefs. It has also been reported from loose gravel substrates. This snake eel occurs at a depth of 1 to at least 10 m (3.3 to 33 ft.). It burrows in the sand

Brachysomophis crocodilinus, Crocodile Snake Eel: seldom-collected species.

Brachysomophis crocodilinus, Crocodile Snake Eel: yellow color variant.

it is to acclimate successfully. Live food will be required to catalyze a feeding response. While the newly acquired Marbled Snake Eel may pull its head into the substrate when the aquarist approaches the tank, with time and patience it will become more bold. However, you should always approach the tank very slowly.
Aquarium Size: 180 gal. **Temperature:** 22 to 28°C (72 to 82°F).
Aquarium Suitability Index: 2.
Remarks: The **Freckled Snake Eel** (*Callechelys luteus*) Snyder, 1904 is a very similar species that is endemic to the Hawaiian Islands. The **Darkline Snake Eel** (*Callechelys catostomus*) (Bloch & Schneider, 1801) is a related species that is easily recognized by the broad lateral lines that run down both sides of the body. This latter species is distributed from Indonesia to the Society Islands.

Genus Leiuranus

Leiuranus semicinctus (Lay & Bennett, 1839)
Common Names: Saddled Snake Eel, Culverin.
Maximum Length: 60 cm (23.6 in.).
Distribution: East Africa to the Hawaiian, Marquesas, and Mangareva Islands, north to southern Japan, and south to New South Wales.
Biology: The Saddled Snake Eel is most common in sandy areas, in lagoons, or near coastal reefs, at depths of less than 1 to at least 10 m (3.3 to 33 ft.). It spends much of its time hiding under the sand, but occasionally emerges to feed during both the day and night, consuming small fishes, crustaceans, and polychaete worms. In the Red Sea, it has also been reported to feed on garden eels—approaching them under the sand and capturing them in their burrows. This eel is often mistaken for the Banded

Callechelys marmorata, Marbled Snake Eel: a rarity requiring special care.

or mud, like other members of the family, and usually leaves its head protruding from the substrate both night and day. If threatened, it will withdraw its head. It probably feeds on small fishes and crustaceans that swim past. In the Red Sea, it is reported to prey on garden eels.
Captive Care: Although this eel is rare in the aquarium trade, it is found in areas where fish collecting is common. It will require a large tank with a deep substrate bed (at least 20 cm [8 in.]) if

Leiuranus semicinctus, Saddled Snake Eel: resembles Banded Sea Snake.

Sea Snake (*Laticauda colubrina*), although it is not as similar-looking as the Banded Snake Eel (*Myrichthys colubrinus*). In areas where the Banded Sea Snake is common, the Saddled Snake Eel may derive some protection from predators (mainly predatory fishes and birds) because of its resemblance to the venomous reptile. Sea snakes often eat snake eels. By resembling the Banded Sea Snake, the Saddled Snake Eel may also be able to avoid being eaten by these reptilian predators.
Captive Care: See the Captive Care section for *Myrichthys colubrinus*, below.
Aquarium Size: 135 gal. **Temperature:** 22 to 28°C (72 to 82°F).
Aquarium Suitability Index: 1.
Remarks: Unlike the Banded Snake Eel (*M. colubrinus*), the bars of the Saddled Snake Eel are incomplete, there is no stripe over the eye, and it has a longer snout.

Genus *Myrichthys*

Myrichthys breviceps (Richardson, 1844)
Common Name: Sharptail Snake Eel.
Maximum Length: 102 cm (40.2 in.).
Distribution: South Florida and Bermuda, south to Brazil.
Biology: The Sharptail Snake Eel lives in lagoons, on reef flats, and on fore-reef slopes at depths of less than 4.5 to over 185 m (15 to over 601 ft.). This species often forages on rubble bottoms and seagrass beds at night, but will also hunt during the daylight hours. Other predatory fishes will follow the Sharptail Snake Eel and feed on prey items that it flushes out as it probes holes and crevices with its snout. This eel feeds mainly on crabs (including *Mithrax sculptus*), but also eats mantis shrimps and sea urchins.

Captive Care: The Sharptail Snake Eel is a difficult species to feed in captivity. Live foods, such as grass shrimps and fiddler crabs, are most effective for catalyzing a feeding response. Some individuals can be trained to take shrimps, squids, and fish flesh from a feeding stick after they have fully acclimated to captive life. It is not uncommon for a Sharptail Snake Eel to swim along and up the aquarium glass when the tank lights are on. It may ingest fish tankmates that are small enough to swallow whole, but it can be kept with larger fishes and other eels—including members of its own species. However, the Sharptail Snake Eel should be the first fish in the tank, and any potential food competitors should be introduced only after it is feeding.
Aquarium Size: 180 gal. **Temperature:** 22 to 28°C (72 to 82°F).
Aquarium Suitability Index: 2.
Remarks: This species differs from the sympatric Goldspotted Snake Eel (*Myrichthys ocellatus*) in having light spots without dark rings around them. In the past, the Sharptail Snake Eel was referred to as *Myrichthys acuminatus*.

Myrichthys colubrinus (Boddaert, 1781)
Common Names: Banded Snake Eel, Harlequin Snake Eel.
Maximum Length: 88 cm (34.6 in.).
Distribution: Red Sea to the Society Islands, north to the Ryukyus, and south to Queensland.
Biology: The Banded Snake Eel lives on sand and mud bottoms adjacent to coastal reefs, in seagrass beds, and on reef flats. It occurs at depths of less than 1 to 25 m (3.3 to 81 ft.) and feeds on small bony fishes, crustaceans, and polychaete worms. This eel hunts on open sand or mud bottoms both day and night. It is similar in appearance to, and is often mistaken for, the Banded Sea Snake (*Laticauda colubrina*). In areas where the Banded Sea

Myrichthys breviceps, Sharptail Snake Eel: a challenge to feed in captivity.

Myrichthys colubrinus, Banded Snake Eel (variant): sea snake mimic.

Myrichthys colubrinus, Banded Snake Eel: one of many color variants.

Myrichthys maculosus, Pacific Spotted Snake Eel: may require live foods.

Snake is common, the Banded Snake Eel may derive some protection from predators as a result of the similarities between it and the venomous reptile. It has been suggested that by resembling the Banded Sea Snake, the snake eel may be able to avoid being eaten by these reptilian piscivores. However, the Banded Sea Snake has been seen eating this snake eel in Japanese waters.

Captive Care: A tank containing a Banded Snake Eel should have at least 5 cm (2 in.) of fine coral sand on the bottom, as this eel often buries itself. When released from a shipping bag, it is not uncommon for this species to lie on the bottom with parts of its body rigid and curled up off the substrate. The biggest problem in keeping the Banded Snake Eel is that it often proves difficult to feed. Live grass shrimps or small benthic fishes (gobies) provide the best chances of success. Be careful when choosing tankmates for this species, as many fish are inclined to nip at it. I have seen juvenile tobies (*Canthigaster* spp.) bite the eel's tail, irritating it and forcing it to swim about the tank.

Aquarium Size: 180 gal. **Temperature:** 22 to 28°C (72 to 82°F).
Aquarium Suitability Index: 1.

Remarks: *Myrichthys colubrinus* is highly variable in color pattern. This variation has resulted in ten different species names being applied to this one eel. The three most commonly recognized ones are *M. colubrinus*, *Myrichthys bleekeri*, and *Myrichthys elaps*. Individuals from Japan, the Philippines, Belau, Guam, and Indonesia have wide bands that encircle the body, similar to the Banded Sea Snake.

In areas where the Banded Sea Snake does not occur (Indian Ocean, Red Sea, Polynesia), the color is more variable and includes individuals with narrow bands that do not completely encircle the body ("*bleekeri*" phase) and specimens that have complete stripes with black spots between them ("*elaps*" phase).

Myrichthys maculosus (Cuvier, 1817)
Common Name: Pacific Spotted Snake Eel.
Maximum Length: 1 m (3.3 ft.).
Distribution: Red Sea to the Marquesas and Society Islands, north to southern Japan, south to Lord Howe and Rapa Islands.
Biology: The Pacific Spotted Snake Eel occurs on coastal reefs and reef flats at depths of less than 1 up to 262 m (3.3 to 852 ft.). It actively moves about the reef, probing crevices, holes, and rubble interstices in search of crustaceans and small fishes on which to feed. This eel will also move over the sand with its nostrils close to the substrate surface. Occasionally it will stop and plunge its head into the sand or a hole, then begin whipping its body frantically to and fro. It has been reported to feed on shrimp gobies and their crustacean associates by using this technique. This eel hunts both in the day and at night.

Captive Care: *Myrichthys maculosus* should be housed in a tank with plenty of surface area and a relatively thick layer (at least 7.5 cm [3 in.] deep) of fine substrate. It can be difficult to feed and will do best if not housed with overly aggressive eaters or fishes that may nip at it. Live grass shrimps and adult mollies are most effective for catalyzing a feeding response.

Aquarium Size: 135 gal. **Temperature:** 22 to 28°C (72 to 82°F).
Aquarium Suitability Index: 2.

Remarks: The spotting pattern of this eel changes as it grows. Juveniles of less than 25 cm (10 in.) have a single row of spots above the midline and lack spots on the chin, throat, and ventrum. Individuals between 30 to 50 cm (12 to 20 in.) have larger spots equally spaced along the midline that alternate with pairs of spots that meet along the middle of the dorsal surface. Finally, specimens exceeding 50 cm (20 in.) have two to three rows of large, ovoid spots above the midline and two to three rows of smaller

Myrichthys ocellatus, Goldspotted Snake Eel: nocturnal Caribbean species.

Ophichthus bonaparti, Bonapart's Snake Eel: beautiful but rarely collected.

spots on the ventrum. Spots extend onto the dorsal fin (but not onto the anal fin), and there are spots on the chin and throat.

This species is replaced in the Hawaiian Islands and Johnston Island by the **Magnificent Snake Eel** (*Myrichthys magnificus*) (**Abbott, 1861**). The Magnificent Snake Eel has fewer vertebrae (177 to 183, compared to 185 to 199) and larger individuals (over about 70 cm [28 in.]) have smaller (diameter less than snout length) and rounder spots on the head and flanks, and fewer and smaller (diameter less than that of the eye) spots on the chin and throat than *M. maculosus*. This species differs from the **Tiger Snake Eel** (*Myrichthys tigrinus*) **Girard, 1859**, of the Eastern Pacific, and the **Clipperton Snake Eel** (*Myrichthys pantostigmius*) **Jordan & McGregor, 1899**, of Clipperton and the Revillagigedo Islands, in the total number of vertebrae (149 to 156 and 158 to 168, respectively).

Myrichthys ocellatus (Lesueur, 1825)
Common Name: Goldspotted Snake Eel.
Maximum Length: 102 cm (40.2 in.).
Distribution: Southern Florida, Bahamas, and Bermuda to Brazil.
Biology: The Goldspotted Snake Eel occurs on reef flats, lagoons, and fore-reef slopes at depths of less than 1 to over 12 m (3.3 to 39 ft.). It is often found in seagrass beds. This species usually hunts at night, spending most of the time during the day under the sand. It feeds mainly on crabs (including xanthid, swimming, and majid crabs), but also eats mantis shrimps, decapod shrimps, fishes, and polychaete worms.
Captive Care: See the Captive Care section in the *Myrichthys breviceps* account, page 302.

Aquarium Size: 180 gal. **Temperature:** 22 to 28°C (72 to 82°F).
Aquarium Suitability Index: 2.
Remarks: In younger specimens, the lower spots are mostly brown with small gold centers.

Genus *Ophichthus*

Ophichthus bonaparti (Kaup, 1856)
Common Names: Bonapart's Snake Eel, Brownsaddled Snake Eel.
Maximum Length: 75 cm (29.5 in.).
Distribution: South Africa to Indonesia, including the Maldives.
Biology: Bonapart's Snake Eel is found near coastal reefs and fore-reef slopes, on sand and mud bottoms, at depths of 1.5 to 20 m (5 to 65 ft.). In certain places, a number of these eels can be found living in the same area with at least 2 m (7 ft.) between specimens. *Ophichthus bonaparti* is sometimes seen with its head sticking out from the substrate during the day, but more individuals are observed at night. It is rarely observed moving about in the open and probably feeds on cuttlefishes, crabs, cardinalfishes, and soles that move past their burrows.
Captive Care: This beautiful snake eel is rarely encountered in the aquarium trade, but it would make a fascinating display animal for a species tank. It would need to be housed in a larger tank, with a layer of fine sand at least 15 cm (6 in.) deep. This species will eat smaller fishes and motile invertebrates.
Aquarium Size: 100 gal. **Temperature:** 23 to 28°C (74 to 82°F).
Aquarium Suitability Index: 3.
Remarks: Bonapart's Snake Eel has 18 to 27 saddles, golden marbling, and spots on its snout and head.

Ophichthus bonaparti, Bonapart's Snake Eel: color variant.

Ophichthus bonaparti, Bonapart's Snake Eel: color variant.

Ophichthus cephalozona (Bleeker, 1864)
Common Names: Blacksaddle Snake Eel, Onebanded Snake Eel.
Maximum Length: 1.12 m (3.6 ft.).
Distribution: East Indies to the Society Islands, north to the Marianas, and south to Queensland.
Biology: The Blacksaddle Snake Eel occurs on or near coastal reefs, where it inhabits reef crevices, coral rubble, and holes in areas with large rocks. It also buries in the sand. It occurs at depths of 8 to at least 26 m (26 to 85 ft.). Although they are usually solitary animals, I have seen two of these snake eels within 1 m (3.3 ft.) of each other. Initial observations also suggest that they may remain in the same area for days or even months. The Blacksaddle Snake Eel has been observed feeding in the open at night. It may also eat fishes and crustaceans that share its daytime shelter sites.
Captive Care: *Ophichthus cephalozona* is rarely encountered in the aquarium trade, but it would be an excellent candidate for a species tank. It should be housed in a larger tank, with a layer of fine sand at least 15 cm (6 in.) deep. During the day, it will bury in the sand with only its head sticking out of the substrate, and it will usually eat live grass shrimps. Like all snake eels, it is adept at finding small holes to jump out of—cover the aquarium accordingly.
Aquarium Size: 180 gal. **Temperature:** 23 to 28°C (74 to 82°F).
Aquarium Suitability Index: 3.
Remarks: The Blacksaddle Snake Eel has a gray or black head. It also has a black saddle behind the eyes, surrounded by a white band, which extends from behind the jaw to the end of the pectoral fin. The rest of the body is brown, shading to white ven-

Ophichthus cephalozona, Blacksaddle Snake Eel: adept escape artist.

trally. The dorsal and anal fins are white-edged with a black submarginal line. The lateral line pores appear as black dots.

Ophichthus melanochir Bleeker, 1865
Common Name: Blackfinned Snake Eel.
Maximum Length: 80 cm (31.5 in.).
Distribution: Thailand to Indonesia south to northwestern Australia, and north to the Philippines.
Biology: The Blackfinned Snake Eel burrows in sand and mud bottoms, usually near protected coastal coral reefs, at depths of 1 to 10 m (3.3 to 33 ft.). It spends the day with its head sticking up from the substrate. Occasionally, a species of cleaner shrimp can be observed sitting on the tip of the eel's snout. The

Ophichthus melanochir, Blackfinned Snake Eel: common but seldom caught.

Ophichthus melanochir, Blackfinned Snake Eel: note cleaner shrimp on snout.

shrimp will display to passing fish and will occasionally leave its living perch for a short time and then return to the eel's nose. Although no food habit data exists for this species, it probably feeds on cephalopods, crustaceans, and small fishes like the cardinalfishes that move over the sand surface at night. It has also been observed to leave its sand burrow at night, possibly to hunt for food or relocate to a better ambush site.

Captive Care: This species is rare in the aquarium trade, but is distributed in areas where a great deal of fish collecting occurs. Its care requirements are similar to *O. cephalozona*.

Aquarium Size: 180 gal. **Temperature:** 23 to 28°C (74 to 82°F).
Aquarium Suitability Index: 3.

Remarks: The Blackfinned Snake Eel is common over certain parts of its range. It is tan or golden in color with a dark dorsal fin and black pectoral fins. It has large eyes and pebblelike teeth adapted to crushing hard-shelled invertebrates. The upper jaw extends past the lower jaw, making the eel look as if it has an overbite. The dorsal fin origin is either above or behind the gill opening, and the pectoral fin is at least twice as long as the eye diameter.

Ophichthus ophis (Linnaeus, 1758)
Common Name: Spotted Snake Eel.
Maximum Length: 1.4 m (4.6 ft.).
Distribution: South Florida and Bermuda, south to Brazil, east to Ascension Island in the Eastern Atlantic.
Biology: The Spotted Snake Eel is found on sand flats near the reef, or areas with mixed sand, gravel, and rubble. It burrows into the substrate during the day, often with its head protruding from the bottom. From this position, it captures passing octopuses and fishes. It sometimes comes out of hiding at night, but

Ophichthus ophis, Spotted Snake Eel: widespread tropical Atlantic species.

Ophichthus ophis, Spotted Snake Eel: large and piscivorous.

Echiophis intertinctus, Spotted Spoonnose Eel: can inflict painful bite.

can also move under the sand. This eel tends to be quite bold and will not withdraw into the sand when approached.
Aquarium Size: 180 gal. **Temperature:** 22 to 28°C (72 to 82°F).
Aquarium Suitability Index: 3.
Captive Care: The Spotted Snake Eel will require an extra-large tank, with 15 to 20 cm (6 to 8 in.) of substrate. It will spend its days buried in the substrate with only its head showing, and will readily eat any fish tankmates that are small enough to swallow whole.
Remarks: The Spotted Snake Eel has a broad, dark collar that crosses the nape and "cheeks" and two rows of large black spots running down the body. This species is superficially similar to the **Spotted Spoonnose Eel** (*Echiophis intertinctus*). The Spotted Spoonnose has a stout body, a short, V-shaped snout, a large mouth with strong canine teeth along the front of the jaws as well as on the roof of the mouth, a pale yellowish body with numerous spots of varying sizes on the body, and small spots on the head. It attains a maximum length of 1.2 m (3.9 ft.) and ranges from North Carolina and the northern Gulf of Mexico south to Brazil. A warning to the aquarist: this eel is capable of inflicting a painful bite.

Ophichthus polyophthalmus Bleeker, 1864
Common Name: Manyeyed Snake Eel.
Maximum Length: 50 cm (19.7 in.).
Distribution: Southern Africa east to Hawaii.
Biology: I have observed this species inhabiting burrows in rubble and gravel bottoms at a depth of about 20 m (65 ft.). During the day, it often hides in its burrow with only its head protruding, while it may move into the open to hunt at night. It probably feeds on crustaceans and fishes.

Captive Care: The captive care of this species is similar to that of other *Ophichthus* species.
Aquarium Size: 100 gal. **Temperature:** 22 to 28°C (72 to 82°F).
Aquarium Suitability Index: 3.
Remarks: This handsome species is a pale salmon color overall, with yellow spots on its head, yellowish ocelli on the body, and dark margins on the median fins.

References
Casadevall et al. (1994), Deraniyagala (1930), Humann (1994), Kuiter & Debelius (1994), McCosker & Rosenblatt (1993), Nemtzov et al. (1986-1987), Randall (1967).

Ophichthus polyophthalmus, Manyeyed Snake Eel: typical hiding behavior.

Family Plotosidae
Eel Catfishes

Plotosus lineatus, Striped Eel Catfish: typical balling behavior of juveniles, possibly from a single brood, that form dense schools for protection from predators.

WHILE FRESHWATER AQUARISTS HAVE A WEALTH OF catfishes from which to choose, the marine aquarium trade has but one species, a member of the Plotosidae. This family is comprised of 9 genera and approximately 32 species.

Plotosus lineatus (Thünberg, 1787)
Common Names: Striped Eel Catfish, Coral Catfish.
Maximum Length: 32 cm (12.6 in.).
Distribution: Red Sea to Samoa, north to South Korea, and south to Lord Howe Island.
Biology: The Striped Eel Catfish is most often observed in coastal bays and estuaries, but also occurs in reef lagoons. Juveniles and subadults are found among pier pilings, in seagrass beds, or over open mud or sand flats—often in areas where debris such as coconuts, sticks, palm fronds, or trash is strewn over the bottom. In contrast, larger adults live under ledges and in reef crevices. This species occurs at a depth range of less than 1 to at least 45 m (3.3 to 146 ft.).

Juveniles and subadults form large, tight schools that move like one massive, undulating ball near the substrate. These groups are thought to consist of the progeny of a single brood. Smell plays an important role in the maintenance of these schools. The catfish apparently release pheromones that attract conspecifics. These pheromones seem to be released from a gland on each side of the genital pore. As these fish grow larger, they tend to form smaller, looser groups, and many break from the ranks to lead solitary lives. It has been demonstrated that adult females are less attracted to the pheromones released by conspecifics and are more likely to leave the group than adult males. The dispersal of larger individuals from these schools suggests that predation pressures decrease as the size of these fish increase.

Juvenile Striped Eel Catfish feed mainly on crustaceans, including shrimps and crabs. Adults will also eat small fishes. Although some larger predators prey upon Striped Eel Catfish, their sharp fin spines with associated venom glands can deliver a painful and potentially dangerous sting. People who have been stung by more than one of these fish simultaneously have died from the venom. Being stuck by the spine of a smaller fish, however, has been compared to the sting of a wasp. If a Striped Eel Catfish stings you, either immerse the wound site immediately in hot water or direct hot air at it with a hair dryer. These fish are so undesirable to most predators that juveniles of an unrelated species, the Convict Blenny (*Pholidichthys leucotaenia*), mimic the appearance and behavior of young Striped Eel Catfish. It is difficult to distinguish a juvenile Convict Blenny, which does not have the toxic armament of the *Plotosus* species, from a juvenile Striped Eel Catfish. This is a perfect example of Batesian mimicry, in which a harmless species resembles a harmful one.

Reproduction of the Striped Eel Catfish has been observed both in captivity and in the wild. Males dig a hole under a rock or a piece of debris. The female deposits her eggs, which the male fertilizes and then defends until they hatch. The eggs are about 3 mm in diameter, while the newly hatched larvae are approximately 7 mm long. The larva has a large yolk sac at hatching, which is absorbed in about 10 days. After the yolk sac is gone, the young fish begins swimming about and feeding. When it is 15 mm long, the juvenile has the form of the adult catfish, but lacks stripes. Female Striped Eel Catfish are reported to reach sexual maturity at 1 to 3 years, and at a maximum length of as little as 14 cm (5.5 in.). The maximum lifespan is about 7 years.

Captive Care: Juvenile *P. lineatus* make interesting additions to a marine aquarium. A small- to medium-sized group of youngsters is especially entertaining to watch as it moves about the tank and forages off the substrate. They are very effective scavengers, grubbing in the sand and around the aquarium decor to get at any food that hits the bottom. The biggest drawback to keeping them is that they transform from cute little fish into less attractive big fish. While a small group of juveniles may not tax a tank, as adults they will take up a huge amount of room and place a significant burden on the biological filter. Adults are also a threat to any fish or motile invertebrate they can catch and fit into their mouths. Larger specimens tend to be secretive, hiding in and around the aquarium decor. One advantage to keeping juveniles is to see the interactions of a schooling species. Within the school, all individuals are equal and there is little or no display of aggression—either toward each other or unrelated species. Juveniles do best when kept in groups and may hide constantly and stop eating if kept on their own. The school is a form of protection for them; they seem to lose this sense of security when alone.

These fish are not finicky and will eat almost any food particles that land on the aquarium bottom. They will occasionally succumb to parasitic infections, and caution must be exercised when treating them with copper-based medications or organophosphates. They can be treated with freshwater dips.

The Striped Eel Catfish has spawned in public aquariums. The larvae should be easy to raise, as they are large enough after absorbing their yolk sacs to ingest newly hatched brine shrimp.

Aquarium Size: 75 gal. **Temperature:** 22 to 28°C (72 to 82°F).
Aquarium Suitability Index: 5.
Remarks: The color of the Striped Eel Catfish changes as it grows. Small juveniles are entirely black; as they grow, white or yellow lines develop on the body, and the body becomes a dark brown overall. As the intensity of the color fades, larger adults tend to look washed out.

References
Kajikawa (1993), Moriuchi & Dotsu (1973), Myers (1989).

Plotosus lineatus, Striped Eel Catfish: boldy colored juveniles feeding.

Plotosus lineatus, Striped Eel Catfish: somewhat drab adult coloration.

Family Synodontidae
Lizardfishes

Although from a distance they look rather benign when spotted at rest by snorkelers and divers, members of the Family Synodontidae are some of the quickest and most voracious predators on the reef.

The lizardfishes are javelinlike in shape and can erupt from the bottom with incredible speed to capture small fishes that swim past. On closer inspection, their toothy grin is more apparent and very formidable. Their jaws are lined with numerous sharp, inwardly depressible teeth that are perfect for grasping small, slippery prey items. Other characteristics of this family are large scales and an adipose fin.

The family Synodontidae encompasses 5 genera and approximately 55 species. Many of these species are found in deep water on soft substrate. The three genera most often encountered on or near coral reefs are *Synodus* (25 Indo-Pacific species, 3 in the tropical Western Atlantic), *Saurida* (11 Indo-Pacific species), and *Trachinocephalus* (1 species). Some authors elevate the Subfamily Harpadontinae, which includes the genus *Saurida*, to family status (Family Harpadontidae).

Biology

Lizardfishes that are associated with coral reefs can be found on sand, mud, or hard substrate, with their microhabitat preferences varying between species. Some lizardfishes found on soft substrate bury themselves—either totally or partially—under the sand or mud surface. Others frequent hard substrate and regularly move from one ambush site to another.

The lizardfishes are daytime hunters—sit-and-wait predators that dart off the bottom to capture passing prey items. Some species sit on rocks or coral heads to scan the surrounding water column for potential victims. They usually limit their attacks to prey species less than 1.2 m (4 ft.) above the seafloor. The lizardfishes can consume relatively large prey items. For example, a 16.5-cm (6.5-in.) Graceful Lizardfish (*Saurida gracilis*) contained the partially digested remains of a Pacific Trumpetfish (*Aulostomus chinenis*) that would have measured about 9 cm (3.5 in.) when intact. Lizardfishes are also cannibals, feeding on smaller members of their own species. Some lizardfishes prefer small,

Synodus variegatus, Variegated Lizardfish: a formidable predator allows itself to be worked on by a pair of *Periclimenes* cleaner shrimp.

silver schooling fishes like anchovies and will follow these fishes as they move to different locations on the reef. Other species prey more heavily on nonschooling fishes. An extensive study conducted on one species (Variegated Lizardfish, *Synodus variegatus*) reported that this species attacks a fish every 35 minutes, with 11% of these attacks resulting in successful prey capture. *Synodus variegatus* normally eats approximately two prey items per day, which is equal to about 12% of the lizardfish's total body weight. In this study, two unusual feeding situations were reported. In one, a Variegated Lizardfish sat near a crevice opening and repeatedly attacked a shoal of juvenile cardinalfishes for 55 minutes. In another, a lizardfish preyed upon members of a large school of baitfish for over 90 minutes. In these unusual feeding circumstances, the attack (5.5 and 15.7 attacks per hour, respectively) and success (25% and 45%, respectively) rates differed significantly from that under normal feeding situations. Not all lizardfishes are exclusively piscivorous. Some also eat invertebrates, such as crabs, shrimps, annelid worms, and even spatangoid sea urchins.

While lizardfishes are ignored or avoided by some reef fishes, similar-sized piscivores and larger individuals of potential prey species will chase or harass them. Small groupers, or hinds, of

Synodus variegatus, Variegated Lizardfish (adult): an active daytime hunter that typically perches until a prey item passes within striking range.

Synodus variegatus, Variegated Lizardfish eating a filefish: a highly distensible stomach enables these lizardfish to eat large prey items.

the genus *Cephalopholis* have been observed chasing the Variegated Lizardfish, while larger damselfishes will slap them in the face with their tails. The Batu Coris (*Coris batuensis*) and the Tailspot Wrasse (*Halichoeres melanurus*) have been observed to bite resting lizardfishes. Other species observed disturbing lizardfishes include the Cheekline Maori Wrasse (*Cheilinus diagrammus*), Green Razorfish (*Xyrichtys splendens*), Yellowsaddle Goatfish (*Parupeneus cyclostomus*), Manybar Goatfish (*Parupeneus multifasciatus*), and Cylindrical Sand Perch (*Parapercis cylindrica*).

The mating system of one species, the Sand Lizardfish (*Synodus dermatogenys*), has been studied in detail. Males of this species form leks (an aggregation of males at a common courtship area) just before sunset, at specific locations. Males behave aggressively toward one another before, during, and after courtship. When a male and female engage in a spawning ascent, other males (from two to seven individuals) join them. Females mate from one to three times a night when visiting leks, but if they are part of a spawning pair (consisting of only one male and one female), they mate only once a night.

Captive Care

For the most part, the lizardfishes are relatively easy to keep. Since they can vary greatly in size, the volume of the aquarium used to house a lizardfish will depend on the species you are interested in keeping. Because these fishes spend most of their time in repose on the aquarium bottom, the surface area of the tank is more important than the actual volume. In selecting a tank for a lizardfish, length and width are more important considerations than height. Many lizardfishes will require some open areas on the aquarium bottom on which to lie and possibly bury. A sand substrate at least 2.5 to 5 cm (1 to 2 in.) deep is important for those species that like to bury. A darker substrate, such as black sand, may help intensify the coloration of your lizardfish. Individuals found on light sand bottoms have more muted colors than those from mud or dark sand substrates.

When it comes to feeding, lizardfishes are often reluctant to ingest anything but live food. They readily eat live grass shrimp and feeder fishes, and some individuals can be tricked into taking dead food if it is placed in the outflow of a powerhead or pulled through the water on a piece of fishing string. If you attempt the latter technique, be sure the food is loosely tied so that it separates from the string easily. Try cutting pieces of marine fish flesh, table shrimp, or scallop flesh. Smaller specimens will also eat live adult brine shrimp. Studies of food intake indicate that these fishes should be fed at least one larger or several smaller prey items per day.

Only one lizardfish should be kept per tank, unless you can acquire a male-female pair. These fishes are territorial and may fight in the confines of the aquarium. This not only applies to members of the same species, but also holds true for lizardfishes of different species. As previously mentioned, lizardfishes are also cannibals, feeding on smaller members of their own and related species. A lizardfish should be considered an extreme threat

Synodus sp., unidentified lizardfish eating a grass shrimp: with patience, these fishes may be weaned onto a diet of fresh and frozen marine foods.

Trachinocephalus myops, Snakefish: typical burying behavior that calls for a bed of aquarium substrate. Black sand may bring out more intense colors.

to any fish tankmate that can fit into its mouth—and its gape can be quite large. It is not uncommon to see a synodontid in the wild with a fish that is almost too large for it to ingest protruding from its mouth. I have even seen them trying to swallow inflated pufferfishes. Keep a lizardfish with tankmates that are at least equal to it in length. On the other end of the spectrum, lizardfishes can fall prey to moray eels, frogfishes, scorpionfishes, and groupers.

Lizardfishes are capable jumpers that might leap out of the aquarium if the tank is left open. These aerial acrobatics are most likely to occur if the fishes are harassed by a tankmate or startled by an aquarium net or an aquarist's hand. They can also sustain injuries by hurling themselves against a glass aquarium top.

Although members of this family can suffer from protozoan infections such as ich (*Cryptocaryon irritans*), they are not particularly susceptible to them. A number of lizardfishes have been reported to have copepod parasites living in their gills. A cleaner wrasse will help rid the lizardfish of gill parasites, as long as the lizardfish does not eat the wrasse before it can provide its useful service. It is best to introduce the cleaner wrasse to the tank before the lizardfish, but even then the voracious synodontid may eat its potential benefactor. If necessary, lizardfishes can be treated with the more commonly used antiparasitics.

LIZARDFISH SPECIES

Genus *Saurida*

The members of the genus *Saurida* are easily distinguished from the *Synodus* species by their teeth and the number of pectoral rays. In the *Saurida* species, there are several rows of villiform teeth visible on the lips, and they have nine pectoral rays. In contrast, the teeth of *Synodus* species are contained within the mouth, and they have eight pectoral rays.

Saurida gracilis (Quoy & Gaimard, 1824)
Common Names: Graceful Lizardfish, Slender Grinner.
Maximum Length: 32 cm (12.6 in.).
Distribution: Eastern Africa north to the Red Sea, east to French Polynesia, north to southern Japan, and south to the Great Barrier Reef.
Biology: The Graceful Lizardfish is found in mangrove swamps, on fringing reefs, in lagoons, on reef flats, and on sand slopes at depths of 2 to 135 m (7 to 438 ft.). It is typically seen resting on mud, sand, rubble, rock, or coral substrates, and often sits adjacent to rocks or coral heads that shelter small fishes. Its mottled coloration helps it blend with the substrate, and on rare occasions it will enhance its camouflage by partially burying itself under the sand. It darts from its seafloor cover to capture passing fishes, including cardinalfishes and rabbitfishes.
Captive Care: See the Captive Care section in the family account, page 312.
Aquarium Size: 55 gal. **Temperature:** 23 to 28°C (74 to 82°F).
Aquarium Suitability Index: 3.
Remarks: This species is similar to the **Nebulous Lizardfish or Blotched Grinner** (*Saurida nebulosa*) (Valenciennes, 1849).

Saurida gracilis, Graceful Lizardfish: note the highly expansible jaws.

However, the Nebulous Lizardfish has slightly shorter pectoral fins (the tip extends to within four to six predorsal scales from the dorsal origin in *S. nebulosa* and two or three predorsal scales in *S. gracilis*). *Saurida nebulosa* also has a shorter upper jaw and usually 12 pectoral rays (*S. gracilis* typically has 13). The Nebulous Lizardfish attains a maximum length of 16 cm (6.3 in.) and ranges from Mauritius to the Society Islands, north to the Hawaiian Islands, and south to Queensland, Australia. It occurs in estuaries, mangrove swamps, seagrass beds, and on sand or mud slopes near coastal reefs. In Micronesia, this species is also seen resting on hard substrates like live stony corals, rocks, and green calcareous algae (e.g., *Halimeda*). It occurs at depths of 0.5 to 100 m (1.6 to 325 ft.) on mud, sand, and rubble substrates, and often rests adjacent to rocks or coral heads that shelter small fishes.

Genus *Synodus*

Synodus binotatus Schultz, 1953
Common Name: Twospot Lizardfish.
Maximum Length: 18 cm (7.0 in.).
Distribution: Gulf of Aden east to the Hawaiian and Mangareva Islands, north to Taiwan, and south to Tonga.
Biology: The Twospot Lizardfish usually resides on hard substrates, at depths of 1 to 30 m (3.3 to 98 ft.), but it is most common at depths of less than 10 m (33 ft.). It is most abundant on coastal reefs, where it occurs on the reef face.
Captive Care: See the Captive Care section in the family account, page 312.
Aquarium Size: 55 gal. **Temperature:** 23 to 28°C (74 to 82°F).
Aquarium Suitability Index: 3.
Remarks: *Synodus binotatus* has two black spots on the tip of its snout and long pectoral fins that extend beyond the origin of both the dorsal and pelvic fins.

Synodus dermatogenys Fowler, 1912
Common Names: Sand Lizardfish, Clearfin Lizardfish.
Maximum Length: 23 cm (9.1 in.).
Distribution: Red Sea to the Hawaiian, Marquesas, and Tuamotu Islands, north to the Ryukyus, and south to Lord Howe Island.
Biology: The Sand Lizardfish occurs on reef flats where it rests on coral rubble, sand, or coral-encrusted reef pavement. It is found on both protected and exposed reefs, at depths ranging from 1 to 20 m (3.3 to 65 ft.). It will rest on the sand or bury under it with only its eyes exposed. Just before nightfall, male Sand Lizardfish form leks (breeding colonies) at specific sites. Sexually receptive females visit these sites and spawn with solitary males or multi-male groups.
Captive Care: See the Captive Care section in the family account, page 312.
Aquarium Size: 75 gal. **Temperature:** 23 to 28°C (74 to 82°F).
Aquarium Suitability Index: 3.
Remarks: The Sand Lizardfish has a row of eight or nine dark blotches—often with light centers—along the lateral line and six small spots on the end of the snout. It is often confused with the Variegated Lizardfish (*Synodus variegatus*).

Synodus intermedius (Spix, 1829)
Common Name: Sand Diver.
Maximum Length: 45 cm (17.7 in.).
Distribution: North Carolina, Bermuda, and north Gulf of Mexico, south to Brazil and the Guineas.
Biology: The Sand Diver is usually found in clear water on sand, rock, or coral substrate at depths from 3 to 320 m (10 to 1,040 ft.). However, it is most common at depths of less than 12 m (39 ft.). It usually sits with the anterior part of its body propped up on its pelvic fins, but will also bury under the sand. This species feeds almost entirely on fishes, including silversides,

Synodus binotatus, Twospot Lizardfish: attractive and widespread species.

Synodus dermatogenys, Sand Lizardfish: note small spots on end of snout.

anchovies, herrings, small jacks, grunts, small groupers, sea basses, and Blue Chromis (*Chromis cyanea*). It also captures and ingests squid and shrimp on occasion. It has been observed resting near shrimp cleaning stations, being groomed by the Pederson's Cleaner Shrimp (*Periclimenes pedersoni*). It may also feed on smaller fishes that come to visit these cleaners.
Captive Care: See the Captive Care section in the family account, page 312.
Aquarium Size: 135 gal. **Temperature:** 22 to 28°C (72 to 82°F).
Aquarium Suitability Index: 3.
Remarks: This species has a black blotch behind the upper edge of the gill cover, with thin gold stripes running down the body. When the dorsal fin is depressed, the anterior dorsal rays do not extend past the ends of the posterior rays.

Synodus jaculum Russell & Cressey, 1979
Common Names: Blackblotch Lizardfish, Tailblotch Lizardfish.
Maximum Length: 14 cm (5.5 in.).
Distribution: East Africa to the Marquesas and Society Islands, north to the Izu Islands, and south to southeast Australia.
Biology: This species is most often found on light or dark sand flats or slopes adjacent to patch reefs or coral heads. It occurs at depths of 2 to 100 m (6.5 to 325 ft.) and is most common in deeper water (greater than 50 m [163 ft.]). It is sometimes found in pairs or small aggregations, and individuals often bury under the substrate. This species is unusual in that it will swim in the water column for prolonged periods of time when hunting its prey.
Captive Care: *Synodus jaculum* is better suited to smaller aquariums than many of the other members of its genus. See the Captive Care section in the family account, page 312, for more information.
Aquarium Size: 30 gal. **Temperature:** 23 to 28°C (74 to 82°F).
Aquarium Suitability Index: 3.
Remarks: This species is easily recognized by the dark patch on the caudal peduncle.

Synodus rubromaculatus Russell & Cressey, 1979
Common Name: Redmarbled Lizardfish.
Maximum Length: 12 cm (4.7 in.).
Distribution: Malaysia to Taiwan, north to the Philippines, and south to northern Australia and the Great Barrier Reef.
Biology: *Synodus rubromaculatus* is found on protected coastal reefs, on reef slopes, or at the base of dropoffs. It occurs at depths of 1 to 50 m (3.3 to 163 ft.), but is more common at depths in excess of 15 m (49 ft.). It will rest on coral rubble and sand, but is most often seen perched on rocks or stony corals.

Synodus intermedius, Sand Diver: large species that often buries.

Synodus jaculum, Blackblotch Lizardfish: juvenile specimen.

Synodus jaculum, Blackblotch Lizardfish: note patch just in front of tail.

Captive Care: The Redmarbled Lizardfish is not common in nature or in the aquarium trade, but its small size and chromatic attire make it a desirable captive species. See the Captive Care sec-

Synodus rubromaculatus, Redmarbled Lizardfish: colorful but uncommon.

Synodus ulae, Ulae: commonly seen lizardfish of the Hawaiian Islands.

Synodus synodus, Red Lizardfish: note spot on snout.

Synodus variegatus, Variegated Lizardfish: widespread on West Pacific reefs.

tion in the family account, page 312, for more information.
Aquarium Size: 30 gal. **Temperature:** 23 to 28°C (74 to 82°F).
Aquarium Suitability Index: 3.
Remarks: In the Redmarbled Lizardfish, the end of the pectoral fin does not extend to a line that would run from the origin of the dorsal fin down to the origin of the pelvic fins. In most other lizardfishes associated with reefs, the pectoral fin tip reaches beyond this line. This lizardfish is mottled with bright red, making it one of the most colorful members of the genus.

Synodus synodus (Linnaeus, 1758)
Common Names: Red Lizardfish, Rockspear.
Maximum Length: 33 cm (13.0 in.). Rarely reaches over 15 cm (5.9 in.). The largest specimen was taken at St. Helena.
Distribution: Northern Gulf of Mexico to Uruguay, east to Madeira, the Canary Islands, Ascension, and St. Helena.
Biology: The Red Lizardfish is common in certain parts of the Caribbean, where it resides in protected bays, coves, and on patch reefs and coral heads at depths from less than 1 up to 90 m (3.3 to 293 ft.). It is most common at depths of 5 to 20 m (16 to 65 ft.) and is more frequently found resting on hard reef substrate than on sand or mud. It feeds almost exclusively on small fishes.
Captive Care: See the Captive Care section in the family account, page 312.
Aquarium Size: 75 gal. **Temperature:** 22 to 28°C (72 to 82°F).
Aquarium Suitability Index: 3.
Remarks: This species usually has a small black spot just behind the tip of the snout and red or brown bars on the body.

Synodus ulae Schultz, 1953
Common Name: Ulae.
Maximum Length: 33 cm (13.0 in.).
Distribution: Hawaiian Islands and Japan.
Biology: *Synodus ulae* occurs on sand bottoms at depths from less than 1 up to 122 m (3.3 to 397 ft.). The Ulae spawns in pairs just before sunset. The pair's spawning ascent takes them as high as 4 m (13 ft.) off the seafloor. This is one of the most common members of the family around the Hawaiian Islands.

Captive Care: See the Captive Care section in the family account, page 312.
Aquarium Size: 75 gal. **Temperature:** 22 to 27°C (72 to 80°F).
Aquarium Suitability Index: 3.
Remarks: The Ulae has a series of eight pale-centered, dark blotches along the lateral line and small spots on the head.

Synodus variegatus (Lacépède, 1803)
Common Names: Variegated Lizardfish, Reef Lizardfish.
Maximum Length: 27 cm (10.6 in.).
Distribution: Red Sea to the Hawaiian, Marquesas, and Ducie Islands, north to the Ryukyus, and south to Lord Howe Island.
Biology: The Variegated Lizardfish is found in lagoons—where it usually associates with patch reefs—or on the reef face or fore-reef slope, at depths from 3 to 40 m (9.8 to 130 ft.). Although it will sometimes rest on, or bury under, the sand adjacent to reefs, it is more often found perched on hard substrate (stony corals, rocks) than any other lizardfish. From this position, it scans the surrounding water column in search of potential prey and rival conspecifics.

This species feeds primarily on fishes, including small groupers, dottybacks, cardinalfishes, goatfishes, damselfishes, wrasses, gobies, dartfishes, and blennies (including the Gosline's Scale Eating Blenny, *Plagiotremus goslinei*). It is reported to change position once every 4 minutes and attack a prey item once every 35 minutes. Although it does most of its hunting during the day, it has also been reported to attack prey items at night. The Variegated Lizardfish often occurs in pairs, with individuals lying alongside or even on top of each other. This is the most common lizardfish on Western Pacific coral reefs. *Synodus variegatus* is often host to copepod parasites, which infest the gill filaments.
Captive Care: See the Captive Care section in the family account, page 312.
Aquarium Size: 75 gal. **Temperature:** 23 to 28°C (74 to 82°F).
Aquarium Suitability Index: 3.
Remarks: The Variegated Lizardfish has an orangish red to greenish gray stripe running down the middle of each flank, which contains seven or eight darker spots. *Synodus englemani* is a junior synonym of this species.

Genus *Trachinocephalus*

Trachinocephalus myops (Forster & Schneider, 1801)
Common Names: Snakefish, Painted Lizardfish.
Maximum Length: 33 cm (13.0 in.), but usually under 20 cm (7.9 in.).

Trachinocephalus myops, Snakefish: elusive and a poor aquarium candidate.

Distribution: Circumglobal in warm temperate and tropical seas.
Biology: The Snakefish is found on sand, mud, shell, or rock bottoms, at depths from less than 1 to 400 m (3.3 to 1,300 ft.). During the day, it is usually buried with only its eyes exposed. It erupts from the sand when prey organisms pass overhead, but will immediately bury itself again after making the strike. At night, the Snakefish is often encountered lying on the substrate, and may also hunt at this time on nocturnal cephalopods, crustaceans, and small fishes. It is often found in loose, buried aggregations. Adult individuals often chase one another. If disturbed, it will swim away at an incredible speed and then rapidly bury itself when it comes to a stop.
Captive Care: *Trachinocephalus myops* is not as well suited to aquarium living as most of the other lizardfish species. This is because it is more secretive and is easy to startle. When disturbed, it may launch itself into the side of the tank or the aquarium cover. If the tank is uncovered, it will jump out. All of these potential reactions can result in injury. The Snakefish should be housed in a larger tank with little, if any, decor to ensure that there is plenty of swimming space on the bottom. The tank should also have a deep sand substrate (about 5 to 13 cm [2 to 5 in.] deep). For more details on the general husbandry requirements of these lizardfishes, see the Captive Care section in the family account, page 312.
Aquarium Size: 135 gal. **Temperature:** 22 to 28°C (72 to 82°F).
Aquarium Suitability Index: 3.
Remarks: The Snakefish is unique with its very short snout and its yellow and pale blue stripes along the length of the body.

References
Cressey (1981), Donaldson (1990), Hiatt & Stratsburg (1960), Hobson (1974), Kuiter (1992, 1993), Kuiter & Debelius (1994), Myers (1989), Randall (1985), Sweatman (1984).

Family Bythitidae
Livebearing Brotulas

Dinematichthys riukiuensis, Yellow Brotula: attractive but so cryptic that it typically disappears into the rockwork of an aquarium, never to reappear.

Some coral reef fishes receive little attention from aquarists or scuba divers, usually because they are not brightly colored or they lack an unusual or elegant form. But other species go unnoticed because of their cryptic behaviors. These are the indwellers, fishes that make their homes in the "bowels" of the reef or deep within the extensive beds of coral rubble that often fringe the reef.

One of these groups is the Family Bythitidae, commonly called the livebearing brotulas. Divers rarely observe these fishes, but there is at least one species frequently encountered in the aquarium trade. Although these fishes are uncommon, and interesting, their surreptitious tendencies make them unsuitable aquarium display animals.

Biology

The Family Bythitidae contains 2 subfamilies, 31 genera, and over 90 named (as well as many undescribed) species. Both subfamilies are represented in the aquarium trade. The Subfamily Bythitinae has 14 genera and about 55 species. These have a dorsal and anal fin that is continuous with the caudal fin. The Black Brotula (*Stygnobrotula latebricola*), which is occasionally encountered in aquarium stores, belongs to this subfamily. The livebearing brotula most often seen in the aquarium trade belongs to the Subfamily Brosmophycinae, which has 17 genera and about 35 species. Members of this subfamily have a caudal fin that is not united with the dorsal and anal fins.

The members of the Family Bythitidae possess a broad head,

a tapering body, and long dorsal and anal fins. They propel themselves both backward and forward by undulating their dorsal and anal fins. Many of them have scales, although they can be deeply embedded in the skin. All species have a swim bladder (this organ is lacking in some related families in the Order Ophidiiformes). In most species, there is also a pronounced preopercular spine, while the pelvic fins are comprised of simple, elongate filaments. Although the eyes of livebearing brotulas can vary in size, in most they are well developed. Some, however, have either minute or vestigial eyes, or the eyes are covered with skin. Unlike their relatives the cusk eels, the livebearing brotulas lack barbels on the chin. Some fishes in this family produce copious amounts of slime that may protect their skin from injury as they wiggle through reef interstices. The slime may also function to make them less appetizing to crevice-dwelling piscivores.

The majority of livebearing brotulas occur in marine environments, although a handful of species live in either brackish water or freshwater. Some members of the Family Bythitidae are quite abundant on coral reefs, but are rarely observed because of their cryptic habits. They live deep in reef crevices or in the catacombs that exist in coral rubble beds. Those species with larger eyes may leave their diurnal hiding places at night, while those with tiny or vestigial eyes appear to be banished to the "underworld" for most, if not all, of their lives.

As the common name implies, livebearing brotulas are ovoviviparous, which means that the eggs hatch within the female and she gives birth to live young. In some species, males have an intromittent organ, or penis, which transfers sperm into the female's reproductive tract. This organ is located in front of the anal fin and behind the anus. The male copulatory apparatus of some species (e.g., the *Dinematichthys* spp.) consists of a fleshy hood, a pair of pseudoclaspers (made up of external and internal lobes), and the penis itself. Instead of a copulatory organ, females have a genital pore. At least one species of brotula displays size dimorphism, with females tending to be larger than males. Because of their secretive lifestyle, the actual mating behavior of the livebearing brotulas has never been described. It has been suggested, however, that the male curls its body around the female, inserts the penis, and pumps sperm into her genital pore by flexing his body. In most livebearing brotulas, the eggs hatch in the female's ovaries and remain there, feeding on yolk reserves in a yolk sac, until parturition. In one species, the young are reported to place their mouths around a bulb that grows from the oviduct wall and are thought to "suckle" fluid from the mother. The young of one reef-dwelling species are born at a length of about 6 mm, while in others, the newborns are up to 12 mm long. After they are born, the juveniles of most species enter the plankton, but in at least one species, the young remain and may be cared for by a parent.

Captive Care

Because these fishes are so secretive, they are not highly desirable aquarium inhabitants. If you want to keep and observe a livebearing brotula, it is best to house it in a small tank (10 to 30 gallons) with limited aquascaping. One or two desirable hiding places are necessary, but too much rock may allow the specimen to disappear permanently from your sight. In a setting with limited cover, you will increase both the chance of catching a glimpse of this fish and the ability to see if it is eating. Other ways to increase viewing opportunities are to use dim lighting or to observe them at night by placing a red bulb, either incandescent or fluorescent, over the tank. Even with these tactics, however, it is entirely possible that you will never see your specimen.

Livebearing brotulas will eat any animal life small enough to be ingested. In a tank with live rock, they will prey on secretive invertebrates like snapping shrimps, small crabs, isopods, and amphipods. Crustacean lovers beware—they will also eat ornamental shrimps. You can feed them live brine shrimp, grass shrimp, frozen mysid shrimp, and frozen brine shrimp, but it is best to introduce the food after dark (use a red light to be sure they are eating) or ensure that the food gets behind the rockwork where the fish lives.

Apparently, livebearing brotulas are quite resistant to disease, and most individuals ship well. However, an occasional specimen may abrade the skin on its rostrum while in transit. This occurs when the fish swims constantly up against the shipping bag in an attempt to escape.

LIVEBEARING BROTULA SPECIES

Genus Dinematichthys (Free-tailed Brotulas)

This genus contains one species that occurs in the Western Atlantic and six species found in the Indian and Pacific Oceans. In all, the anterior nostrils are positioned well above the upper lip, and the caudal fin is not connected to the dorsal and anal fins. One species is common in the aquarium trade, although it is possible that several other species might be encountered, including the **Large-eye Brotula (*Dinematichthys iluocoeteoides*) Bleeker, 1855** from the Indo-Pacific and **Randall's Brotula (*Dinematichthys randalli*) Machida, 1994** from Micronesia. In the

Large-eye Brotula, the head length can be divided by the eye diameter about five times, while Randall's Brotula has a smaller eye (divides into head length more than nine times). Randall's Brotula has scales on the cheek and operculum and there are no cirri on the head. Because of their secretive habits, the free-tailed brotulids are almost always collected with chemicals (e.g., cyanide). Members of this genus occur in reef crevices and deep in coral rubble (individuals have been collected as much as 1 m [3.3 ft.] under the rubble).

Dinematichthys riukiuensis Aoyagi, 1952
Common Names: Yellow Brotula, Lycopod Goby, Yellow Eel Goby.
Maximum Length: 10 cm (3.9 in.).
Distribution: Okinawa, the Philippines, Queensland, and the Fijian Islands.
Biology: The Yellow Brotula occurs in tidepools, in crevices and caves found in patch reefs and coral heads, and under coral rubble. It is most common in shallow water, having been reported from depths of 0.5 to 3 m (19 in. to 10 ft.). This species is reported to be a voracious predator that captures both crustaceans and small fishes.
Captive Care: *Dinematichthys riukiuensis* is probably one of the most secretive fishes available to marine aquarists, which does not make it a desirable display animal. It has a relatively large mouth and is capable of ingesting ornamental shrimps and small fishes. Although it is an unlikely threat to most sessile invertebrates, a friend of mine had a specimen that bit the mantle of a clam. The undulating fins of this species are sometimes ripped and damaged by aggressive fish tankmates. A specimen could be kept in a reef tank, but it is likely that you would never see it.
Aquarium Size: 10 gal. **Temperature:** 23 to 28°C (74 to 82°F).
Aquarium Suitability Index: 1.
Remarks: *Dinematichthys riukiuensis* is usually yellow or yellowish orange overall, although it can be pale brown. The posterior nostril is not tubelike, there is a patch of scales just above the opercular spine, and it has small cirri on top of its head. This species is synonymous with *Brotulina fusca* (a name often used in the aquarium literature).

Genus *Stygnobrotula* (Tailless Brotulas)

Stygnobrotula latebricola Böhlke, 1957
Common Names: Black Brotula, Black Widow.
Maximum Length: 7 cm (2.8 in.).
Distribution: Southern Florida and the Bahamas south to Curacao.
Biology: The Black Brotula occurs in patch reef crevices, in coral head hollows, and in inshore caves, at depths of 1.2 to 22 m (4 to 70 ft.). It is a secretive species that swims deep in crevices or along the ceiling or walls of reef caves. This species rarely swims in open water or near the substrate, even in caves. It tends to remain in the same "home" cave for days or even weeks, although it may leave its diurnal shelter to hunt on dark nights. It often shares its cave with other nocturnal fishes like morays, other brotulids, squirrelfishes, soldierfishes, and cardinalfishes.
Captive Care: Although it is a remarkable fish, the Black Brotula (along with the other members in this family) is poorly suited for captivity because it is so reclusive. If possible, create a large cave with a wide opening that will allow you to see inside the chamber. If you are lucky, the Black Brotula will settle in the cave where you can observe it (or at least catch an occasional glimpse) in its daytime hiding place. Occasionally, you can use a flashlight to see within the cave and get a better look. If you do this too often, however, the fish will probably move to a more private hiding place. You may want to keep this fish with a few cardinalfishes, such as the sympatric Flamefish (*Apogon maculatus*) and the Twospot Cardinalfish (*Apogon pseudomaculatus*).
Aquarium Size: 10 gal. **Temperature:** 23 to 28°C (74 to 82°F).
Aquarium Suitability Index: 1.
Remarks: The body and head of the Black Brotula are dark brown to black, while the median fins are jet black. It has a shorter body and a more rounded head than most of the other bythitids. It also has a rounded lower jaw. The peritoneum that surrounds the viscera is black.

References
Böhlke & Chaplin (1993), Longley & Hildebrand (1941), Machida (1994), Myers (1989), Saurez (1975), Turner (1946), Wourms & Bayne (1973).

Stygnobrotula latebricola, Black Brotula: remarkable but extremely cryptic.

Family Batrachoididae
Toadfishes

Batrachomoeus trispinosus, Threespined Toadfish: capable of producing "love songs" and bred in captivity, toadfishes are underappreciated by aquarists.

The Family Batrachoididae is an odd group whose members are known for their ability to produce a wide range of unusual sounds. They have long antagonized houseboat owners along the west coast of the United States—at certain times of the year, nocturnal toadfish love songs echo through the bottoms of these floating homes, often waking up the people inside. Toadfishes exhibit other interesting behaviors as well. Although they are not terribly popular with marine aquarists, a handful are found in aquarium stores.

Biology

The toadfishes have large heads with relatively big eyes, which are as much on top of the head as they are on the side. Most have cylindrical bodies, a long dorsal fin with two or three short spines at the anterior end, a sizable mouth adorned with small conical teeth, a gill opening that is present just in front of the pectoral fin base, thick slimy skin that is loosely attached to the body, three to four stout spines on the operculum (which are usually hidden under the skin), and a rounded tail. Many also have skin flaps and barbels around the mouth, giving them a bearded appearance. Toadfishes produce sounds by resonating their air bladders. These sounds, which can include grunts, hums, croaks, and whistles, are employed by males to attract females to their nesting sites.

The Family Batrachoididae is comprised of 3 subfamilies, 24 genera, and 71 species. The majority of the toadfishes occur in the Western Atlantic (3 or more of the 27 species in this region are found in freshwater). The second most specious region (with 15 species) is the Eastern Pacific, while approximately 8 species occur in South Africa and 9 are known in the Indo-West Pacific.

Most species are not extremely colorful, displaying various shades of browns, grays, and greens with a lot of mottling and markings. But several species in the Caribbean do sport dramatic color patterns. One of these, aptly named the Splendid Toadfish (*Sanopus splendidus*), has zebra stripes on its head, with bright yellow fin margins. Another species, the Reticulate Toadfish (*Sanopus reticulatus*), has a reticulate network of white lines on the head and body.

All the toadfishes are benthic and relatively sluggish, and most occur on rocky areas, coral reefs, or in seagrass beds. At least one species, *Batrachoides manglae*, is a resident of high salinity mangrove swamps, while others are known to live in freshwater creeks and brackish estuaries. During the day, many of these toadfishes live in reef crevices, caves, hollows under coral heads, empty shells, human refuse (like cans), sponge lumens, under overhangs, among tunicate colonies, and in holes that they dig under rocks or rubble. Some toadfishes live on open sand or mud substrates. Many of these resilient fishes can live for a considerable period of time out of water, and have been observed to "crutch" across exposed mud flats at low tide using their paired fins.

Burrowing, Antipredation, and Feeding Behavior
Some toadfishes excavate their own burrows under coral heads or at the edge of a reef. They dig these burrows by scooping sand up in their mouths and spitting it out away from the entrance. In two toadfish species studied, the burrows extended from 10 to 25 cm (3.9 to 9.8 in.) under the sand surface, were up to 1 m (3.3 ft.) in length, and had an average burrow entrance size of 24 cm (9.4 in.) wide and 11 cm (4.3 in.) high. The burrows usually have one opening, but in some cases they have as many as three. Toadfishes do not usually reside in the same burrow for more than three days, although some will stay for months—one species was reported to occur in the same burrow for 134 consecutive days. Certain toadfishes will relocate when food supplies become limited.

Toadfishes have a number of adaptations to avoid predators and capture prey. For example, the dorsal and opercular spines of members of the Subfamily Thalassophryninae are venomous. Although being "stung" by one of these toadfishes is rarely (if ever) lethal, it can cause severe pain. The members of this subfamily are commonly called the venomous toadfishes.

One species of toadfish uses mimicry to dissuade potential predators. The Twofaced Toadfish (*Batrachoides lacinia*) has flaps of skin on the sides of its head, each of which is adorned with a black spot. The flaps extend out laterally and give the impression that the Twofaced Toadfish is much larger when viewed head-on. This apparently is less appealing to piscivores.

The Twofaced Toadfish also has toxic mucus on its body (possibly from glandular tissue around the pectoral fins). This mucus may function to deter the attacks of moray eels that share its cracks and crevices. Although the Twofaced Toadfish is unlikely to enter the aquarium trade, if you happen to purchase one, place it in its own aquarium. The toxins it exudes are capable of killing other fishes and at least some invertebrates (e.g., sea stars).

Toadfishes are voracious predators whose stomachs can expand to accommodate large prey items. The diets of most species are quite varied and include polychaete worms, crabs, shrimps, octopuses, bivalves, snails, sand dollars, urchins, and fishes (including spiny boxfishes, *Chilomycterus* spp.). Not even the long, needlelike spines of the Longspine Sea Urchin (*Diadema antillarum*) can deter a hungry toadfish. In fact, two toadfish species in the Caribbean feed almost exclusively on these spiny invertebrates: the Cryptic Toadfish (*Amphichthys cryptocentrus*) and the Barbeled Toadfish (*Sanopus barbatus*). These two toadfishes are well equipped to feed on urchins. Both have a solid skull, a bony palate, thick skin in the mouth, a mouth with a broad gape, and large peglike teeth. When an urchin moves past the burrow of one of these toadfishes, the fish lunges out and grasps the urchin in its mouth, then proceeds to masticate it. In some cases, a toadfish's burrow can be located by broken urchin spines and pieces of shell lying near its entrance. These toadfishes eat an average of one urchin per day. Although they appear to prefer urchins, they are opportunistic and do not depend on the urchins for survival. When the urchin population was nearly decimated by a mass mortality in the Caribbean, these two toadfish species exhibited a dietary shift. The Cryptic Toadfish began feeding on crabs, snails, hermit crabs, octopuses, scallops, lobsters, and fishes, while the Barbeled Toadfish switched to small fishes, hermit crabs, small scallops, and shrimps. These reef-dwelling toadfishes feed during both the day and at night, with the food taking about 12 hours to pass through the gut.

The majority of toadfishes capture active prey by employing a sit-and-wait feeding strategy. However, certain species may lure their prey. The fringed lips and chins of certain toadfishes may act as passive lures to attract small algae-eating or shelter-seeking fishes or crustaceans. An even more compelling case of toadfish luring involves the Barbeled Toadfish (*S. barbatus*). Its tail exhibits an array of small eyespots. In the early morning, the Barbeled Toadfish has been observed lying on exposed sand patches close to its diurnal sanctuary with its tail curled forward near its mouth. The anterior portion of the body becomes pale and blends in perfectly with the sand, while the slender posterior portion is darker than normal and the eyespots on the tail become conspicuous. Robertson (1987) suggested that this behavior, along with the associated color changes and the eye-

Batrachoides lacinia, Twofaced Toadfish: a toxic species with protruding flaps on the sides of its head to make it appear larger to would-be predators.

spots, might function to attract potential prey items. The posterior portion of the Barbeled Toadfish resembles the head of a moray eel, and this may attract fishes into striking range of the toadfish's camouflaged head. But why would reef fishes be attracted to a moray eel? A number of predators follow the morays to take advantage of prey items flushed from hiding by the eel's foraging activities.

Members of the Subfamily Porichthyinae (the luminous toadfishes) may also use mimicry to attract potential prey. These toadfishes have photophores on the head and body. It has been suggested that these light organs may mimic the photophores of ctenophores (comb jellies) and may serve to lure the fishes that feed on the comb jellies into striking range.

Reproduction

Reef-dwelling toadfishes lay their eggs in crevices, under overhangs, or in burrows dug under coral heads. They typically deposit the eggs on the roof of the cavity. In some species, both parents guard the developing eggs; in others, only the male tends the nest. The tending parent is very aggressive and will chase away potential predators. This parent also fans the eggs with its pectoral fins to waft debris off them and to aerate them. In some species—including some of the reef-dwelling forms—the males guard the newly hatched, free-swimming juveniles. The young toadfishes (which can number up to at least 60 in one reef-dwelling species) will gather around the adult male—even sitting on, or hiding under, its head. When they are able to fend for themselves, the juvenile toadfishes leave the nest and "Dad's" watchful eye. The males of some reef-dwelling forms will mate more than once a year. In at least one species (Oyster Toadfish, *Opsanus tau*), more than one female may lay eggs in one male's nest.

Captive Care

Although some of the toadfishes available in the aquarium trade can reach over 30 cm (12 in.) in length, they do not require a lot of swimming room. In fact, the largest species covered in this book can be kept in a tank as small as 55 gallons. Most of the other species will do fine in aquariums as small as 15 gallons. Because the toadfishes are so secretive, it is important that the tank be furnished with a suitable cave, crevice, or overhang for the fish to refuge in or under. Your toadfish may not spend a lot of time in the open at first, but it will eventually start to come out when the aquarium is illuminated. If it rarely makes an appearance when the tank lights are on, you may have to employ a red light to observe its nocturnal activities. Place the red light over the tank and turn it on after all the other lights—both on the aquarium and in the room—are extinguished.

Toadfishes should be offered a varied diet that includes crustacean and/or mollusk flesh. Initially, some individuals may not be eager to ingest nonliving food, but with the aid of a feeding stick, most will learn to accept these offerings. Some will even snatch nonliving food as it falls to the bottom of the aquarium. Finicky toadfishes can be enticed with live grass shrimps and small livebearers. Toadfishes will also consume any tankmate that can fit into their capacious jaws, including crabs, shrimps, clams, snails, urchins, brittle stars, and smaller fishes. For this reason, tankmates must be carefully selected.

Toadfishes will often behave aggressively toward each other, especially during the mating period. Fights can lead to torn fins and cuts on the head and body. In some cases, if the individuals are not separated, one will be killed. It is best to keep only one individual per tank, unless you can acquire a male-female pair. A toadfish may also behave aggressively toward any fish that tries to enter its favorite hiding place, while males with eggs or offspring will attack any fish that ventures too close. Toadfishes can be kept with a wide range of other fish species, as long as they are not small enough for the toadfish to swallow.

Members of this family are skilled diggers that will excavate burrows under the aquarium decor. This can lead to the toppling of precariously balanced rocks and coral and could result in damage to tankmates or to the toadfish itself. Therefore, it is best to secure rockwork together with cable ties or to at least make sure that the decor is fixed in place.

Toadfishes rarely succumb to parasites that inflict most reef fishes, like *Cryptocaryon* and *Amyloodinium*. However, nematode worms frequently parasitize the alimentary tracts of these fishes. If you have a specimen that is feeding but losing weight, it may be necessary to give it a dewormer like fenbendazole. For more information on how to use this drug, see the Captive Care section in the walking batfish family account, page 359.

While toadfishes can be kept in reef tanks because they are not a threat to sessile invertebrates, they are a threat to algae-eating snails, ornamental crustaceans, and echinoderms. Toadfishes will "appreciate" the many hiding places that are typically characteristic of a reef aquarium, but in a large reef tank, they may be hard to find because of their reclusive habits. This can present feeding challenges. They will also dig in under the live rock if sand is present in the tank, and may cause structural instability. One positive attribute of keeping toadfishes in a reef aquarium is that they will consume small mantis shrimps and fireworms.

Toadfishes have been called "perhaps the easiest saltwater fishes to raise in the aquarium." Although the eggs and young are simple to "raise," getting them to breed is not simple. Try placing an amorous pair of toadfishes in a tank on their own with a suitable nesting site (e.g., a jar or a ceramic flowerpot). How to tell the sexes apart? Unfortunately, there are no known sexual dimorphisms described in the toadfish species. To find a pair, you will need to place two conspecific toadfish in the same tank. Then observe their behavior. If the individuals fight, they are probably the same sex and will need to be separated. If they do not behave aggressively toward each other, they may be a heterosexual pair.

The eggs of most toadfish species are quite large. In the most common aquarium species (Gulf Toadfish, *Opsanus beta*) they are 3.9 to 4.4 mm in diameter, while the eggs of *Opsanus tau* average about 5 mm. The eggs are adhesive and are described as looking like tapioca pudding. The newly hatched young of some species are large enough to eat vitamin-fortified brine shrimp and are soon able and willing to ingest finely chopped table shrimp. However, the pieces of shrimp will need to be moving in order for the juveniles to be interested. This can be accomplished by creating currents with an airstone or water pump. The young fish should be fed at least three times a day and can either be removed or left with their parents—the adults rarely eat them if they are kept well fed. Aquarists beware: nest-guarding toadfishes can be aggressive and will readily bite the hand that feeds them.

TOADFISH SPECIES

Genus *Batrachoides* (Scaly Toadfishes)
This genus contains nine species. At least one of these occurs on coral reefs, while some of the others inhabit rocky reefs.

Batrachoides gilberti Meek & Hildebrand, 1928
Common Name: Large-eye Toadfish.

Opsanus pardus, Leopard Toadfish: easily kept Gulf of Mexico species.

Batrachoides gilberti, Large-eye Toadfish: often migrates into freshwater.

Maximum Length: 26 cm (10.2 in.).
Distribution: Caribbean, from the Yucatan Peninsula south to the Panama Canal.
Biology: The Large-eye Toadfish is often found in freshwater. It enters tidal creeks (it was reported 32 km [20 mi.] up the Temash River in Nicaragua) and mangrove areas in lagoons. It feeds on crabs (including xanthid and swimming crabs), shrimps, snails, and fishes. *Batrachoides gilberti* often hides among rocks or rubble or in reef crevices. It will sometimes rest with its head protruding from its sanctuary. One female specimen was reported to contain 398 eggs.
Captive Care: See the Captive Care section in the family account, page 323.
Aquarium Size: 30 gal. **Temperature:** 23 to 28°C (74 to 82°F).
Aquarium Suitability Index: 5.
Remarks: *Batrachoides gilberti* has large eyes, scales on the body but few on the head, usually 25 dorsal fin rays, and 22 to 23 anal fin rays. The skin tabs present along the lateral line have pointed (rather than rounded) tips.

Genus *Opsanus* (Common Toadfishes)

Opsanus beta (Goode & Bean, 1879)
Common Names: Gulf Toadfish, Orange Toadfish.
Maximum Length: 30 cm (11.8 in.).
Distribution: Atlantic and the Gulf Coast of Florida and the Bahamas (where it is rare), south to Campeche, Mexico. There is a report of a single specimen from Belize.
Biology: The Gulf Toadfish occurs in bays and lagoons, where it is found at depths of less than 1 to 12 m (3.3 to 39 ft.). It usually resides on oyster reefs, around jetties, or in seagrass beds, where it lives among rubble and human refuse. *Opsanus beta* often shelters in discarded cans and jars, and will use this debris for both an ambush and breeding site. Some individuals rarely leave these shelter sites. Instead, they ambush prey items that wander into their lair. These specimens may actually grow too large to get out of the jar or bottle opening and end up spending the rest of their lives trapped in their man-made homes. The Gulf Toadfish feeds mainly on crabs (including hermit crabs), but it will also eat snails and small fishes. On the west coast of Florida, *O. beta* spawns in February and March at a water temperature of 16.7 to 19.4°C (62 to 67°F). Males are sexually mature at lengths greater than 9 cm (3.5 in.). The Gulf Toadfish lays its eggs in old conch shells, clam shells, tin cans, jars, and sponge cavities, and the male protects the eggs. It fans the eggs with its pectoral fins, increasing the frequency of nest-tending activities at night. The male does not feed during the egg-guarding period.
Captive Care: The Gulf Toadfish is the only member of this genus regularly encountered by aquarists, with most individuals being collected by live rock farmers along the Gulf Coast of Florida. It is a durable fish that fares well in captivity. In the wild, it is often found in polluted water and can tolerate suboptimal conditions in captivity. *Opsanus beta* rarely succumbs to disease, even when other fish in the aquarium are infected. It is a voracious predator that will consume smaller fishes and crustaceans. It will burrow under aquarium decor and hide much of the time. When food is added to the tank, the Gulf Toadfish will dash from its refuge to claim it and then quickly return to the safety of its shelter. See the Captive Care section in the family account, page 323, for more details about its husbandry.
Aquarium Size: 30 gal. **Temperature:** 17 to 28°C (62 to 82°F).
Aquarium Suitability Index: 5.

Opsanus beta, Gulf Toadfish: commonly seen orange color form.

Opsanus beta, Gulf Toadfish: mottled color variant.

Remarks: The color of this species can vary, but most that enter the aquarium trade are orange overall with lighter mottling on the body. They can also be dark overall with green, gray, or brown mottling and have diagonal bars on both the median and pectoral fins. *Opsanus beta* has large eyes, and the chin is not heavily whiskered.

Opsanus tau (Linnaeus, 1766)
Common Names: Oyster Toadfish, Atlantic Toadfish.
Maximum Length: 38 cm (15.0 in.).
Distribution: Cape Cod to Florida (as far south as Miami in cold years).
Biology: The Oyster Toadfish is most common in inshore habitats like rocky bottoms and jetties, and on shipwrecks. It seems to have a special predilection for trash and is often found in polluted conditions. *Opsanus tau* feeds most heavily on xanthid and hermit crabs, while mollusks and fishes are a minor part of its diet. In more northern climates, this fish spawns in the summer (June and July). In the south, they breed from April to October. The adhesive eggs average 5 mm in diameter and are deposited in a variety of natural and human-made cavities. In 1899, one naturalist penned, "The toadfish seems to prefer the debris of civilization to nesting beneath the rock—for example, tin cans, old boots, broken jugs, etc." It is also reported to nest on waterlogged boards, mollusk shells, and in burrows. The nest site is cleaned by the male, which involves removing substrate and debris from the deposition site. The male's nest may contain from 22 to 723 eggs—larger clutches result from several females laying their eggs in the nest of a single male. The male guards the eggs until they hatch, which takes 10 to 25 days. The males continue to feed during nest tending, but consume less during this period.

Opsanus tau, Oyster Toadfish: often found amidst underwater trash items.

Captive Care: This species is easy to keep. Provide it with several caves in which to hide and do not keep it with small fishes or ornamental crustaceans. *Opsanus tau* will eat chunks of table shrimp, marine fish flesh, and scallops either from a feeding stick or as the food sinks toward the substrate. See the Captive Care section in the family account, page 323, for more details about its husbandry.
Aquarium Size: 30 gal. **Temperature:** 18 to 27°C (64 to 80°F).
Aquarium Suitability Index: 5.
Remarks: The Oyster Toadfish is light brown overall with darker mottling on the body and bars composed of individual markings on the pectoral and caudal fins.

The **Leopard Toadfish** (*Opsanus pardus*) **Goode & Bean, 1879** is a similar species that replaces the Oyster Toadfish in the Gulf of Mexico (see photograph, page 324). This species differs from the Oyster Toadfish in color (the Leopard Toadfish is tan to yellowish brown overall, with dark brown spots and irregular blotches on the fins) and in the structure of the dermal appendages both on the lower jaw and behind the mouth (they are well developed). It is more common in deeper water on offshore reefs than the sympatric Gulf Toadfish (*O. beta*).

Genus *Sanopus* (Coral Toadfishes)
The five species in this genus occur on coral reefs. *Sanopus* is placed in the Subfamily Batrachoidinae, whose members lack venomous spines and photophores. These fishes also lack scales on the body and glands on the posterior surface of the pectoral fins. They have longer bodies than the *Opsanus* species, and have papillae along the dorsal and ventral lateral lines. Some sport striking color patterns.

Sanopus astrifer Robins & Starck, 1965
Common Name: Whitespotted Toadfish.
Maximum Length: 28 cm (11.0 in.).
Distribution: Belize, in the Caribbean.
Biology: This species is found in caves and hollows under coral heads (e.g., *Montastrea*) at depths of 3 to 31 m (9.8 to 100 ft.). It will usually rest on the sand, but will also lie on stony corals.
Captive Care: See the Captive Care section in the family account, page 323, for more details about its husbandry.
Aquarium Size: 55 gal. **Temperature:** 23 to 28°C (74 to 82°F).
Aquarium Suitability Index: 3.
Remarks: The body of *S. astrifer* is dark brown overall with many small white spots. It has long, unbranched barbels on the chin and side of the head. The barbels on the side of its mouth are similar in size to those on the chin. This toadfish also has a very broad head.

Sanopus johnsoni Collette & Starck, 1974
Common Name: Johnson's Toadfish.
Maximum Length: 25 cm (9.8 in.) (only one specimen has ever been measured).
Distribution: Cozumel, Mexico (probably more wide-ranging).
Biology: This species lives in lagoons and on the reef face at depths to at least 8 m (26 ft.). It is found in small caves under coral heads and in reef crevices. It comes out at night and feeds on the Longspine Sea Urchin (*Diadema antillarum*).
Captive Care: See the Captive Care section of the family account, page 323, for information about the husbandry of this species.
Aquarium Size: 55 gal. **Temperature:** 22 to 29°C (74 to 82°F).
Aquarium Suitability Index: 3.
Remarks: Johnson's Toadfish is brown overall with a reticulated pattern on its belly. It has cirri on the head between the eyes. The **Barbeled Toadfish** (*Sanopus barbatus*) (**Meek & Hildebrand, 1928**) is a similar species from Panama, Costa Rica, and Honduras. Both of these species have well-developed, branching chin barbels. There are fewer branches in Barbeled Toadfish of less than 25 cm (10 in.), while large individuals usually have ocelli on the caudal fin. The Barbeled Toadfish also feeds on *D. antillarum*, but will eat shrimps, scallops, hermit crabs, crabs, and snails. It attains a maximum length of 43 cm (16.9 in.) and thus is a greater threat to tankmates than most other toadfishes.

Sanopus splendidus (Collette, Starck & Phillips, 1974)
Common Name: Splendid Toadfish.
Maximum Length: 20 cm (7.9 in.).
Distribution: Cozumel, Mexico.
Biology: The Splendid Toadfish is common in small caves on sand substrates at depths of 10 to 25 m (33 to 81 ft.), although it occurs in water as shallow as 4 m (13 ft.). It remains in hiding during the day, but often rests partly out of its refuge at night. This toadfish feeds on fishes, snails, and polychaete worms.
Captive Care: *Sanopus splendidus* rarely, if ever, makes it into the aquarium trade because it is illegal to collect fishes around Cozumel. If you encounter one, you should not purchase it.
Aquarium Size: 30 gal. **Temperature:** 23 to 28°C (74 to 82°F).
Aquarium Suitability Index: 4.
Remarks: This species exhibits a striking color pattern that consists of light bars with dark borders across the head, and yellow or yellowish orange margins on the median and pectoral fins.

References
Breder (1941), Breder & Rosen (1966), Collette (1974), Collette & Russo (1981), Hoffman & Robertson (1983), Robertson (1987), Straughan (1970).

Sanopus astrifer, Whitespotted Toadfish: dramatic species from Belize.

Sanopus johnsoni, Johnson's Toadfish: note cirri between eyes.

Sanopus splendidus, Splendid Toadfish: illegal to collect in its native waters.

Family Antennariidae
Frogfishes

MOTHER NATURE HAS EQUIPPED HER SUBJECTS WITH A variety of anatomical and behavioral features to aid them in capturing prey. Lionfishes, groupers, barracudas, and sharks all come to mind as reef fishes "blessed" with predatory prowess. But after 12 years of keeping and observing members of the Family Antennariidae, I am convinced that they are the most gifted predators on the reef, having a bizarre appendage that they skillfully flick, dangle, or cast to lure prey fishes into their striking zone.

These lumpish creatures, commonly known as frogfishes, are a favorite with underwater photographers and aquarists who specialize in the rare and unusual. They were also a favorite of Louis Renard, a French book dealer to King George I of England. In 1719, he wrote, "I caught it [a frogfish] on the sand and kept it alive in my house [out of water!] for three days; it followed me everywhere with great familiarity; much like a little dog." Although this story is highly suspect, frogfishes have captured human imagination for centuries.

Classification and Biology

There are about 43 species of frogfishes currently recognized that make up 12 different genera. Most of the species encountered in the aquarium trade belong to the genus *Antennarius*, which contains 24 valid species. This genus can be broken down further into six smaller "groups" of closely related species.

All frogfishes are globular in form, have modified leglike pectoral fins complete with "feet" and "toes," small gill openings that are not covered by bony plates, and a first dorsal spine that is an important component in the acquisition of nutrients. This spine, called the illicium, is elongate. In most species, the end is adorned with a fleshy tip known as the esca. The esca comes in a variety of different shapes and sizes. Its form, to some degree, is species specific. For example, in the Striated Frogfish (*Antennarius striatus*) it is wormlike, while in the Wartskin Frogfish (*Antennarius maculatus*) it is often shaped and marked like a small fish (complete with an eyespot). In members of the genus *Antennatus*, the esca is so small that it is barely visible.

Antennarius commerson, Giant Frogfish: a true marine oddity and a long-time favorite of naturalists, divers, and aquarists who seek out uncommon and strange specimens. Note white esca, or lure, dangling above fish's mouth.

Antennarius pictus, Painted Frogfish: wrapped around a coral skeleton, it flashes an amazingly fishlike lure, while a small goby observes, at top.

Feeding Behavior

What is the function of the modified spine? When a frogfish sees a fish of edible size, it will often erect the spine and move it about. The esca, dangling on the end of the spine, acts as a lure to attract prey within striking distance. The way the rod and associated lure are "cast" depends in part on the frogfish species doing the angling. The Striated Frogfish, with its artificial worm, jerks the bait around so that it looks like a writhing polychaete, while the Wartskin Frogfish moves its spine in a circular motion that causes the esca to undulate as if it were a small fish swimming.

Although the "casting" method used is somewhat stereotypical within a species, individuals of some species may vary their angling technique. In a study I conducted on the luring behavior of the Coinbearing Frogfish (*Antennarius nummifer*), I found

Antennarius maculatus, Wartskin Frogfish: mimicking a piece of reef substrate encrusted with yellow sponge and flashing a fishlike lure.

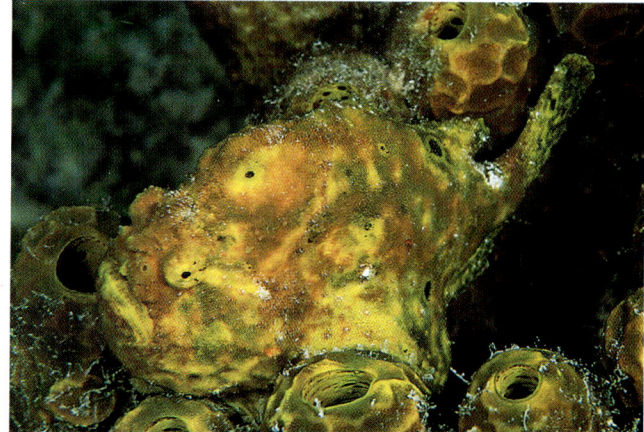

Antennarius commerson, Giant Frogfish: a perfect sponge replica, complete with apparent oscula (the excurrent openings of true sponges).

that an individual frogfish may use three or more different luring patterns. On some occasions, this frogfish would lift the illicium off the head slightly and then vibrate the esca. In other instances, the same individual would throw the illicium forward and hold the esca still in front of the mouth, sometimes for over 1 minute. In a third pattern, the fish would throw the illicium forward and backward very rapidly, much like a fly fishermen casting a nymph to a wily trout (I call this the "quick flick").

Luring also varied in its frequency. In my study, I found that frogfishes would engage in more luring bouts of shorter duration (average bout duration: 12 seconds) if novel prey fish were added to the aquarium. If an individual had been in an aquarium with prey species for some time, it would lure less frequently, but each bout would last longer (average duration: 26 seconds).

The most interesting finding of the study was that frogfishes will even lure in the dark. I used a red fluorescent light to observe the nocturnal behavior of my antennariids and found that *A. nummifer* will fish for nocturnal species, such as cardinalfishes, under the cover of darkness. Even more fascinating was the type of luring behavior most often seen at different times: the quick flick was the method most often used at night, and vibration of the esca was also more common at night than during the day. While visual cues may not be important in attracting prey at night, the movement of the esca in the noncompressible water medium transmits a signal to the pressure sensors in the prey fish's acoustico-lateralis system. Although a hungry cardinalfish or squirrelfish may not see the lure, it can feel it. So a dynamic luring pattern like the quick flick is more likely to be sensed by potential prey than one in which less movement of the bait is involved.

What happens if a prey fish succeeds in biting off the frogfish's esca? Unlike the fisherman who loses his prize lure to an elusive "lunker," the frogfish can regenerate a new lure. The new esca, which can take from 120 to 240 days to fully form, is usually a close replica of the lost member. If the illicium is damaged behind the lure, with the original esca still intact, an individual may grow a second esca. When not in use, the fishing apparatus is laid back along the second dorsal spine. In some species, it is covered either by this spine or by the skin between the spine and the head.

Not only do these cunning anglers attract food with their specialized spines, many frogfishes are camouflaged to look like sponges, aquatic plant life, or rubble covered with encrusting invertebrates. The large spots on some frogfishes (Giant Frogfish, *Antennarius commerson*, and the Longlure Frogfish, *Antennarius multiocellatus*) appear to mimic the oscula (the openings through which water is passed) of the sponges that they live among. These frogfishes usually select sponges that match their body color, or will change their hue to match that of their invertebrate perch. Occasionally, they will even hide in the sponge's lumen. Other frogfishes (Hispid Frogfish, *Antennarius hispidus*; Striated Frogfish, *Antennarius striatus*; and Threespot Frogfish, *Lophiocharon trisignatus*) have skin flaps on the head and body that look like algal growth. These appendages often become more numerous and grow longer if the individual lives in an environment where filamentous algae are prevalent. To enhance their camouflage even further, many frogfishes move their dorsal fin—or their entire body—from side to side like debris waving in the current when approached by either their prey or a predator. Fishes that feed on sessile invertebrates or algae could easily be duped into mis-

Antennarius striatus, Striated Frogfish: unadorned specimen found in an area of relatively open substrate with no algal growth present.

Antennarius striatus, Striated Frogfish: same species as at left, with modified skin flaps resembling algal patches in the habitat where it was photographed.

taking the body of a frogfish for their normal bill of fare. This can be problematic in the aquarium if a frogfish is kept with fishes that eat encrusting organisms.

Frogfishes might also attract small reef animals looking for places to hide. The mimicry of a shelter site by a predator is known as protective resemblance and is not a phenomenon limited to this family. Certain scorpionfishes and wobbegong sharks, for example, also depend on this form of mimicry to aid in the acquisition of prey. But frogfishes are not totally dependent on luring to capture prey—they are also excellent stalkers. Frogfishes methodically sneak up on their quarry by crawling over the substrate with their leglike pectoral fins.

When a frogfish succeeds in bringing a small fish or crustacean into the strike zone, its true gift becomes apparent. In as little as 6 milliseconds, the jaws can project forward and engulf its quarry, while at the same time the mouth cavity can expand up to 12 times its normal size. The prey animal vanishes so fast that other animals in the area do not even have time to recognize the frogfish as a threat.

These fishes also possess the incredible ability to ingest prey items longer than themselves. I once extracted a Pacific Goldeneyed Tilefish (*Caulolatilus affinis*) from a Bloody Frogfish (*Antennarius sanguineus*); the tilefish was slightly longer than the frogfish. The stomach of the frogfish was greatly distended, with the tilefish curled up neatly within. Even more astonishing is the report of a Longlure Frogfish with a squirrelfish in its stomach that had a body length almost 25% longer than that of the antennariid. This form of gluttony may be the undoing of some frogfishes, both on the reef and in the aquarium. For example, a Giant Frogfish was discovered floating at the surface with an inflated porcupinefish in its stomach. (See Captive Care, page 335.)

Frogfishes eat a wide variety of sea life. Not even venomous reef fishes are safe from antennariid attack. For example, the Striated Frogfish consumes Mushroom Scorpionfish (*Scorpaena inermis*): one 64-cm (25-in.) specimen had the remains of a 61-cm (24-in.) scorpionfish in its stomach, and I once watched a Coinbearing Frogfish slurp up a Spotfin Lionfish (*Pterois antennata*), which did not appear to cause the frogfish any discomfort or health problems. Frogfishes also consume shrimp, crabs, and mantis shrimp that approach too closely.

Antennarius striatus, Striated Frogfish: a yawn that displays the prodigious mouth cavity and jaws that can project outward with blinding speed.

Antennarius maculatus, Wartskin Frogfish: color change series, starting as black with orange spots.

Antennarius maculatus, Wartskin Frogfish: same specimen, in transition to color at right.

Antennarius maculatus, Wartskin Frogfish: near-complete reversal of colors from photo at far left.

Antipredation Behavior

Although frogfishes look unpalatable, they do not have sharp spines, long pointy teeth, or distasteful slime to deter potential predators. Instead, their main form of defense is being inconspicuous. Not only does their mimicry of sessile invertebrates and plants attract potential prey, it also helps them avoid potential predators. Frogfishes can change color in order to blend with their surroundings. This goes beyond simply changing from dark brown to tan (which they indeed can do)—they can accomplish radical color shifts. I had a Wartskin Frogfish change from black with orange spots to orange with black spots over a 1-month period (photographs above). Frogfish buyers beware—you may purchase a bright red frogfish only to have it turn brown.

One way to prevent chromatic change from occurring is to provide ambush sites that are the same color as the frogfish. For example, a red Wartskin Frogfish in a tank with artificial or live red sponge to perch upon is much more likely to retain its coloration. Be aware that your specimen may not use the ambush site if you put it in a place where conditions are not conducive to frogfish perching (an area with too much water flow, or at the front of a tank in a room with a lot of human activity).

Some frogfish species also discourage potential predators by mimicking things that are not good to eat. For example, juvenile Wartskin Frogfish and Painted Frogfish (*Antennarius pictus*) undulate their dorsal fins as they slowly crawl over the bottom. The movement of the fins, and their coloration, resembles that of a flatworm—many of which are distasteful and not eaten by predators.

Frogfishes also possess the ability to distend their stomachs with water or air in a manner similar to the pufferfishes. I have witnessed this behavior in several species (Hispid, Giant, Coin-bearing, and Wartskin Frogfishes), but in only one incident was the cause of inflation obvious. In this case, a Wartskin Frogfish inflated when attacked by a larger Giant Frogfish. The attacker could not swallow the smaller fish due to its increased girth. After floating around in the tank for a few minutes with the bloated Wartskin sticking out of its mouth, the attacker spit it out. In the other inflation events I have observed, the frogfish did not appear threatened in any way. Frogfishes might also swallow air at the water's surface to facilitate relocation: floating can provide a way for these relatively poor swimmers to get from one reef to another.

Reproduction

Frogfish reproduction is as fascinating as their feeding behavior. The reproductive act follows the same general pattern in all the species in which it has been observed. From several days to 8 hours prior to the act of spawning, the female's abdomen begins

Antennarius maculatus, Wartskin Frogfish: juvenile mimicking a distasteful flatworm, complete with undulating dorsal fin to simulate the crawling worm.

Antennarius striatus, Striated Frogfish: a pair engaged in courtship; the smaller male, at rear, follows and gropes the expectant female.

to swell with the ripening ova. During this period, the courting male begins visiting her—often under the cover of darkness—and displays by convulsing and spreading his fins. He also makes physical contact with his potential mate, often nibbling her and touching her with his handlike pectoral fins. As spawning nears, the female—with her distended belly—begins to signal the male by erecting all her fins and vigorously undulating her body. The male approaches her and follows as she begins to swagger along the seafloor, her tail lifted, exposing her swollen abdomen. Suddenly, the female shoots into the water column trailed by the male. At the top of her ascent, she ejects a large scroll-shaped egg mass from her cloaca in as little as 0.4 seconds, which is immediately fertilized by her suitor. This unusual structure, reminiscent of the egg case of a nudibranch, is known as an egg raft. Its form is an exact model of the female's ovaries. The shape and size can vary somewhat from one species to the next. In some frogfishes, the unrolled egg raft can measure 16 cm (6.3 in.) wide and over 2.7 m (9 ft.) long, but in most it is considerably smaller. There is some evidence that in certain species, the male grasps the end of the egg raft in his mouth and jerks it from the female's cloaca at the top of the spawning ascent. After ejecting her gametes, the exhausted female returns to the ocean or aquarium bottom.

The egg raft is positively buoyant, and it has been estimated that it can contain from 48,000 to over 280,000 eggs—depending on its size. As the hours pass, the raft begins to unroll and expand. After 2 to 5 days, depending on the water temperature, the eggs hatch. The larvae spend the first 1 or 2 months of their lives floating in the plankton before settling onto the reef.

Several frogfish species take their parental duties more seriously. In the Threespot Frogfish (*Lophiocharon trisignatus*), the

Antennarius maculatus, Wartskin Frogfish: female swollen with eggs, which may number from 48,000 to 280,000 in larger individuals and species.

FROGFISHES 333

Antennarius nummifer, Coinbearing Frogfish: courting pairs with huge female and small male below.

Antennarius maculatus x *A. commerson*: newly released egg case. Captive spawning does occur.

Antennarius maculatus x *A. commerson*: egg case after 48 hours. Fry are relatively large at hatching.

600+ eggs adhere, by means of short threads, to one side of the male's body. Eggs with the same threadlike structure were also taken from the ovaries of the Marblemouthed Frogfish (*Lophiocharon lithinostomus*), suggesting that this species displays a similar form of parental care. Not only does riding along on the male give the developing eggs a better chance at survival, it is another way for the hungry parent to lure prey into the range of his capacious jaws. In other frogfish species, the female takes care of the eggs. For example, in the Cryptic Frogfish (*Histiophryne cryptacanthus*), the female creates a hiding place for her clutch of eggs by wrapping her tail and body around them. Female Tasseled Anglerfish (*Rhycherus filamentosus*) and Prickly Anglerfish (*Echinophryne crassispina*), both of which occur in temperate Australian waters, fan the eggs and cover them with their bodies to conceal them.

It is not rare for antennariids to spawn in the confines of an aquarium. On numerous occasions, I have had solitary females eject infertile egg rafts. The biggest problem with breeding these animals is in acquiring a pair. Unfortunately, few of the antennariids are known to display permanent sexual dimorphism, so finding a male and female requires more luck than skillful selection. Cannibalism is also quite common in antennariids, so putting two individuals together may result in the demise of the smaller one. The best way to breed frogfishes is to place them in a small aquarium that has an acrylic divider with ¼-inch holes drilled in it. Be sure that water readily diffuses from one side to the other, in case any pheromones are present that may elicit a reproductive response in one or both members. For example, if you use an outside filter, place the siphon in one section and have the water returned on the other side. If one individual is a female and begins to swell with eggs, remove the divider and see what happens. If the other individual is a male, it should begin engaging in the behaviors described above. If it does not, you will have to find another potential mate. Even if a pair of frogfish should breed, one may still make a meal out of the other.

Frogfish species will also crossbreed in the aquarium. For example, the Striated Frogfish was reported to hybridize with either the Giant or Painted Frogfish (the identity of the second fish was uncertain), although Pietsch and Grobecker (1987) suggest it was aggressive, and not reproductive, behavior. I kept a male Giant Frogfish and a female Wartskin Frogfish, which regularly crossbred both before and after I purchased them.

Habitat and Social Behavior

Frogfishes occur in a variety of different habitats. Although most species live in tropical marine environments, at least one species, the Twinspot Frogfish (*Antennarius biocellatus*), also occurs in brackish or freshwater. On coral and rocky reefs, some species are most common in crevices, caves, and under overhangs. The Tuberculated Frogfish (*Antennatus tuberosus*) is extremely cryptic, hiding and hunting in reef crevices and among the branches of

Antennarius biocellatus, Twinspot Frogfish: this species is found in freshwater as well as in marine environments.

hard corals. Larger frogfishes are more mobile and frequently occupy more exposed resting sites than their smaller counterparts. At Cocos Island, Costa Rica, large Giant Frogfish can be seen resting in shallow depressions on the sides of cliffs or large boulders. Likewise, the Ocellated Frogfish (*Antennarius ocellatus*), is often found on open sand or mud bottoms. One of the most unique antennariid habitats is within the floating masses of brown algae known as sargassum. The Sargassum Frogfish (*Histrio histrio*) resides on these great algae rafts. Its color pattern and the skin flaps that cover its body help it to blend with the plant's fronds.

As long as food supplies are present, frogfishes will stay at the same location for extended periods of time. Individuals are often observed in the same general area for months and have been observed to oust intruding conspecifics aggressively from a preferred site. These fights usually consist of the resident frogfish performing lateral displays (in which it spreads its dorsal, anal, and tail fins; its color intensifies; and it undulates its body) between the intruder and the frogfish's ambush site. The modified pectoral fins also come in handy during these slow-motion melees. I have observed combatants put their "hands" on the face or body of the other frogfish and push each other away. I have also observed that resident frogfishes often lure when an intruder approaches, possibly to communicate a threat. If aggression escalates, individuals may bite each other. Most frogfishes change ambush sites at night, when they are less likely to be eaten by diurnal piscivores.

Frogfishes employ several modes of locomotion. They either "walk" over the bottom on their pectoral and pelvic fins, or they rhythmically eject streams of water out of their gill slits to pro-

Frogfishes in the Field

Recording good frogfish images on film is relatively easy—if you can find them. Because frogfishes are so cryptic, they are often overlooked by even the most observant diver. One of the best places to look is among encrusting sponges on pier pilings. The Lembeh Straits in Indonesia are a prime site for observing and photographing (but not collecting) frogfishes. Here one can commonly see as many as seven species on the coastal reefs and macroalgae-sponge beds. On our last trip to this area, my wife and I observed over 30 individual frogfishes. Other good sites in the Western Pacific to view these interesting creatures include the coastal reefs around Ambon and Bali (Indonesia), the reefs of Sipadan (Borneo), Batangas (Philippines), and the Izu Peninsula (Japan). The Caribbean also has some frogfish hot spots, including St. Croix, Dominica, St. Lucia, Barbados, and Bonaire.

Frogfishes are best photographed with a housed camera, using a 60 or 105 mm macro lens, but portraits can also be taken with an older Nikonos system using extension tubes or a close-up kit. Unfortunately in many cases, when framers are placed around a frogfish it becomes stressed. This may cause it to relocate if the site is visited by numerous Nikonos-wielding divers. You should never move a frogfish, even if it means getting a better photograph. The frogfish will perceive you as a potential predator—not as an underwater photographer with good intentions. When you handle or prod a frogfish, its respiration rate will increase and it will burn valuable calories. These fishes have no sharp or poisonous spines, nor do they exude any distasteful toxins. They rely completely on camouflage to avoid becoming a meal; therefore, if they are cast into the water column or displaced to a less suitable shelter site by a diver or photographer, they may end up as fish fodder.

Histrio histrio, Sargassum Frogfish: exceptionally well camouflaged for its habitat, this species resides in great floating rafts of brown algae.

pel themselves along the substrate. When a sudden burst of speed is required, a frogfish will rapidly beat its caudal fin.

Captive Care

One of the great things about frogfishes is that they do well in smaller aquariums. I have housed single specimens for long periods of time in tanks as small as 5 gallons. Of course, with a small aquarium you have to monitor water parameters more closely because changes occur much faster. A 10-gallon aquarium, with either an undergravel filter or just several pieces of conditioned live rock with an airstone for aeration and circulation, will work well for a lone frogfish. Frogfishes do not appreciate being buffeted by a strong current, so make sure that there are places in

Antennarius multiocellatus pair: orange specimen exhibits aggressive display.

Antennarius commerson, Giant Frogfish: may perch on corals in a reef tank.

Antennarius striatus, Striated Frogfish eats a seahorse: predation in action.

the tank sheltered from direct water flow. This is especially true if you have a small aquarium equipped with powerheads.

If you are not interested in keeping small fishes or shrimps, a frogfish is a great choice for the reef aquarium. The only problem with putting them in an aquarium replete with live rock and coral is that they will hide so successfully—especially the more cryptic species—that they go unnoticed. If you want to buy a frogfish for your reef aquarium, try a Wartskin, Painted, or Giant Frogfish. These species tend to be more active and spend more time in the open.

These fishes do not contribute greatly to the nitrogenous load of the reef aquarium, because they do not have to be fed frequently. They ingest all the food you put into the aquarium and their feces are large and solid so they can be easily recognized and removed. The only drawback to keeping them with sessile invertebrates is that they sometimes perch on hard or soft corals (leather corals, *Sarcophyton* spp.) and cause their polyps to stay retracted. This can be problematic if the frogfish remains on the same coral for long periods of time. If this happens, carefully push the frogfish off its preferred spot with a piece of rigid tubing. If you do this every time you see it perching there, it will move to a new site. Feeding is usually not a problem in the reef aquarium—if you are feeding live food, the net method (described on page 337) works particularly well.

Compatibility

Frogfishes should not be kept with invertebrates that have a potent sting, such as Elegance Corals (*Catalaphyllia jardinei*), carpet anemones (*Stichodactyla* spp.), or fire anemones (*Actinodendron* spp.), as these animals can damage the frogfish's skin if they should come in contact.

Antennariids are best kept in an aquarium without other fish species. If you decide to house them with other fishes, tankmate selection must be done carefully. Because frogfishes can eat incredibly large prey items, any fish kept with them should be at least 2 times longer than the frogfish if they are of slender build (e.g., wrasses), or slightly longer than the frogfish if they are deep-bodied species (e.g., *Dascyllus* damselfishes).

A frogfish can also be injured by its tankmates. Fish that browse on sessile invertebrates, such as sponges or tunicates, may mistake a frogfish for a natural grazing surface. I have had angelfishes, butterflyfishes, surgeonfishes, and triggerfishes persistently nip at frogfishes. In at least one case, the antennariid died as a result of injuries that an angelfish inflicted to its lower jaw. Although these species may not always pester your frogfish, it is not worth the risk of having an individual maimed (see Tables 22 and 23 for suitable and unsuitable frogfish tankmates).

TABLE 22

Potential Frogfish Tankmates

Following are some of the fishes that can be kept with antennariids. These include species that will not nip at your frogfish, as well as those that are not as easy for the frogfish to eat. But always remember that any fish you keep with an antennariid should be at least 2 times the total length of the frogfish.

Soldierfishes (Myripristinae)
Squirrelfishes (Holocentrinae)
Scorpionfishes (Scorpaenidae)*
Groupers (Serranidae)*
Larger hawkfishes (*Paracirrhites* spp.)*
Snappers (Lutjanidae)*
Grunts and Sweetlips (Haemulidae)
Swallowtail angelfishes (*Genicanthus* spp.)
Pyramid butterflyfishes (*Hemitaurichthys* spp.)
Monos (*Monodactylus* spp.)

* These fishes may eat a frogfish that can be swallowed whole.

TABLE 23

Unsuitable Frogfish Tankmates

Members of the following fish families are most likely to harm frogfishes. Although some representatives may not always bother their antennariid tankmates, you are taking a risk if you house them in the same aquarium—especially if the tank is not large or is devoid of hiding places. While less of a threat, herbivores like surgeonfishes, rabbitfishes, and blennies are also potential frogfish nippers.

Batfishes (Ephippidae)
Angelfishes (Pomacanthidae)*
Butterflyfishes (Chaetodontidae)*
Surgeonfishes (Acanthuridae)*
Triggerfishes (Balistidae)*
Filefishes (Monocanthidae)
Trunkfishes (Ostraciidae)
Pufferfishes (Tetraodontidae)
Porcupinefishes (Diodontidae)

* The species in these families that eat zooplankton are of little or no threat to frogfishes.

Different species of frogfishes can be kept in the same tank, as long as the tank is large enough and the specimens are similar in size. But if there is enough size disparity between the individuals, large specimens will not hesitate to eat their smaller relatives. Pietsch and Grobecker (1987) report having had a Striated Frogfish (*Antennarius striatus*) eat another of nearly equal size. One way to curb frogfish cannibalistic tendencies is to keep them well fed. Frogfishes may behave aggressively toward each other, but—with the exception of the Sargassum Frogfish (*Histrio histrio*)—they rarely inflict serious harm unless the aquarium is too small.

Feeding

Frogfishes have a low metabolic rate and are extremely efficient at assimilating nutrients from their food. Therefore, it is only necessary to feed the adults twice a week, unless you are keeping more than one in the same aquarium. If so, feed them three or four times a week. It is not uncommon for adult frogfishes to consume two or three small feeder fish a day, but it is not necessary and may be harmful to feed them this much. Juvenile frogfishes should be fed three or four times a week because of the greater metabolic demands associated with growth. Although it is entertaining to watch them eat live food, it is best to convert your frogfish to a varied seafood diet, since a diet consisting only of freshwater fish will not provide all the nutrients needed by marine piscivores (like omega-3 fatty acids). Although most frogfishes can be switched to "dead" food if you are patient and persistent, an occasional individual will refuse such offerings. If this is the case, feed your frogfish live grass shrimp and an occasional feeder fish.

If you use fresh or frozen foods, the best way to feed your frogfish is to impale the food on the end of a feeding stick. This makes it easier to present food directly, although you may have to fend off hungry tankmates to keep them from stealing it. To entice a frogfish to eat off the stick, try to mimic the movement of living prey by slowly moving it back and forth about one body length away from the frogfish. If the frogfish begins to lure, carefully move the food into its strike zone. Don't be too aggressive in presenting food (sticking it right in the fish's face) because the frogfish will then feel threatened, not hungry.

Frogfishes are quite methodical in their feeding behavior, often stalking prey for some time before ingesting it. If you are keeping them with aggressive feeders like groupers or snappers, it can be difficult to feed them—especially if you are simply dumping live food into the aquarium. The best way to feed your frogfishes live fare in a tank that contains food competitors is to place the prey organism in a net and gradually move it toward the antennariid (keeping a grass shrimp, molly, or guppy in a net is

Antennarius commerson, Giant Frogfish: this football-sized animal could eat a wide array of tankmates, including prey too large for it to digest.

easy if you move the net slowly). Position the net several body lengths from the frogfish and watch what happens. In most cases, the frogfish will "walk" over to the net, crawl in, and capture the prey item. Soon the frogfish will learn to associate the net with food and will begin moving toward it as soon as it enters the tank. I have seen frogfish that lure when you put the net up to the front glass (one individual was dubbed "Pavlov's frogfish" because it would lure frenetically anytime someone walked past the tank with a net). The net method is a great way to feed frogfishes in a reef aquarium.

When feeding your antennariid, it is extremely important not to give it prey items any longer than half of its total body length. It is better to feed it several smaller prey items than one large one. If a frogfish ingests a fish that is too large, the food may decay faster than it can be digested. The gas produced during decomposition often becomes trapped in the alimentary tract causing the overfed frogfish to float like a cork. Death typically occurs in two to three days after floating begins. I have tried either purging their stomachs with a syringe full of seawater or pulling the decaying prey item out of the digestive tract with tweezers, but have rarely succeeded in removing it. Even if you are able to remove the decaying food, the episode may still result in the death of the frogfish. On several occasions, I have had individuals die hours after regurgitating an oversized food item.

Most of the frogfishes that I have seen suffering in this way ingested a tankmate that was thought to be too big to swallow. I had a Hispid Frogfish eat a Comet (*Calloplesiops altivelis*) that was 3 cm (1 in.) longer than the antennariid. Within 24 hours, the frogfish was floating around the aquarium. The next day, it was dead. The fish species that are most frequently housed with, eaten by, and end up killing frogfishes are wrasses and gobies. This is because these fishes are elongate and flexible, making them easy to swallow and roll up within the frogfish's stomach. Other fishes I have seen or heard of being consumed by frogfishes (even though they were considerably longer than the frogfish) include: bamboo sharks, certain anthias, dottybacks, tilefishes, blennies, and sand perches. In the case of the bamboo shark, the shark was at least twice as long as the frogfish. When the antennariid died 24 hours later, the tail and part of the body of the shark was still sticking out of its mouth.

Disorders and Diseases

Frogfishes have the potentially suicidal habit of ingesting air, especially during shipping or when they are lifted from the water. For this reason, it is extremely important to keep them submerged. If you need to transfer an individual from one tank to another, use a specimen container—not a net—to catch and move it. If they are being transported from the store to your home, the water and frogfish should be carefully poured from the specimen container into a plastic fish bag. When you get home, acclimate the fish, discard some of the water in the bag, then submerge the bag opening and release the frogfish into the aquarium. Although I usually do not recommend adding water from a dealer's aquarium to your own, in the case of a frogfish it is warranted. If your frogfish ingests air during the transfer, there is not much you can do. They will often succeed in expelling the air on their own, but it is not uncommon for specimens to float around until they die.

Antennarius commerson, Giant Frogfish: protozoan infections can plague frogfishes, but spotting the parasites on a fish such as this takes a trained eye.

Occasionally, a frogfish will damage the anterior edge of its lower jaw by rubbing up and down against the side of its plastic bag during shipping. This can abrade its skin, causing redness and possible blistering. Although these wounds often heal without treatment, there is some risk of bacterial infection. One way collectors and wholesalers may be able to prevent this from occurring during transport is to place something that sinks but is lightweight into the bag so that the frogfish can perch on it. A small piece of PVC pipe large enough for the frogfish to perch inside will work. For smaller frogfish, a plastic drinking cup (it should be large enough in diameter so that it fits snugly in the bag) with the top third cut off can be submerged in the bag (the top edge should be about 1 inch below the water level). Place the frogfish in the cut-down cup and hope that it will stay inside it while being transported. Placing newspaper or black plastic around the outside of the bag may also help reduce stress and prevent the frogfish from injuring itself.

One unusual malady I have heard of but have never seen is bubbles developing under the skin and on the edges of the fins and body. It has been suggested (not proved) that this may result from being exposed to excessive amounts of UV light or from an air embolism, which results from small air bubbles being injected into the tank at high pressure. There is no known treatment for this disorder, and the fish usually dies a slow death.

Another thing to consider when shipping frogfishes is that they should not be fed for at least 1 week before they are shipped. I have seen specimens regurgitate a meal up to 5 days after ingesting it and have had several specimens die in transit as a result. In most cases, the wholesaler was not aware that the antennariid had eaten a fish that had been placed in the same holding tank with it.

Frogfishes are very susceptible to protozoan and dinoflagellete infections. I have had them succumb to both *Cryptocaryon* and *Amyloodinium*. Because frogfishes are often covered with spots, numerous scablike growths, and filamentous appendages, these parasites (especially *Amyloodinium*) can be difficult to detect unless you examine your frogfish very carefully. A frogfish that is suffering from a heavy infestation of parasites will look "puffy" (the body will look like a blob and have no contours), the eyes will look sunken in and cloudy, and the respiration rate will increase dramatically. If a skin parasite is detected, treat your frogfish immediately. I have successfully used copper to treat parasite-ridden antennariids, but lowering the specific gravity to 1.014 for about 1 week may be a more effective treatment for *Cryptocaryon*. I have never used this treatment on a frogfish, but it has been employed to control parasites in numerous other reef fish species.

Frogfish Species

Photographs are often of little use when separating frogfish species. To make it easier to identify a particular form, I have listed them in species groups and/or genera as suggested by Pietsch and Grobecker (1987). The species groups consist of closely related forms that are named after the species in the assemblage that was first ascribed a scientific name. Some frogfishes are difficult to tell apart because there can be considerable morphological variation within each species. Although it may not always be possible to identify an individual down to the species level, you should at least be able to narrow it down to two or three possible species. The characteristics that can facilitate identification include esca form, illicium length, second dorsal spine shape, the presence or absence of warts on the body, the presence or absence of a caudal peduncle, the position of the gill opening, and, to some degree, fin ray counts. One thing that may make frogfish taxonomy even more confusing is that some species will interbreed. The overall coloration of a frogfish is typically not useful for identification, but the presence or placement of spots can help to separate some species.

Antennarius biocellatus Group

This group contains a single species.

Antennarius biocellatus (Cuvier, 1817)
Common Names: Twinspot Frogfish, Brackishwater Frogfish.
Maximum Length: 14 cm (5.5 in.).
Distribution: Philippines to Indonesia, New Guinea, and the Solomon Islands.

Antennarius biocellatus, Twinspot Frogfish: "colored anglerfish" to many.

Biology: This species occurs at depths as shallow as 1 m and up to 73 m (3.3 to 237 ft.), but most individuals are found in less than 9 m (29 ft.) of water. What is truly unique about this frogfish is that it frequently lives in brackish water, or even freshwater, in mangrove swamps or streams.

Captive Care: This species is sporadically available in the aquarium trade, and the price varies considerably, depending on the color of the individual. I have seen bright orange specimens that were selling for $300, and small, more drably colored individuals that cost less than $30. Most Twinspot Frogfish are sold under the generic labels of "common," "assorted," or "colored anglerfish."
Aquarium Size: 20 gal. **Temperature:** 23 to 27°C (74 to 80°F).
Aquarium Suitability Index: 4.
Remarks: This is an attractive frogfish with a rather unique appearance. It has bold ocelli (eyespots) on each side of the body, a short illicium (less than the length of the second dorsal spine) whose base originates well behind the upper jaw, one or more well developed "whiskers" on its chin, 12 dorsal rays with as many as 4 of the posterior-most rays being bifurcate, 7 anal rays (rarely 6) that are all bifurcate, and 9 pectoral rays (rarely 8 or 10), all of which are simple rays. The Twinspot Frogfish can be yellow, brick red, bright orange, chocolate brown, gray, or black overall with darker markings.

Antennarius nummifer Group

There are nine species in this group, but only six are encountered in the aquarium trade. In all nine species, the second dorsal spine is not connected to the head by a membrane, the base of the illicium sits distinctly behind the symphysis of the upper jaw, and there are 8 to 12 simple pectoral rays. Many of these species also have a spot at the base of the dorsal fin, but they are usually not encircled by a light ring.

These fishes occur in the Atlantic, Pacific, and Indian Oceans and are some of the most common antennariids in the aquarium trade. They are often sold under the broadly used name "common anglerfish."

Antennarius coccineus, Scarlet Frogfish: a cryptic species that may virtually disappear from sight in a large aquarium heavily aquascaped with live rock.

Antennarius coccineus, Scarlet Frogfish: green color form with white lure.

Antennarius dorehensis, New Guinean Frogfish: small, reclusive species.

Antennarius coccineus (Cuvier in Lesson, 1831)
Common Names: Scarlet Frogfish, Freckled Frogfish.
Maximum Length: 13 cm (5.1 in.).
Distribution: Red Sea and East African coast to several islands in the Eastern Pacific.
Biology: The Scarlet Frogfish occurs near coastal reefs, in lagoons, and on the outer-reef slope, at depths of less than 1 to over 75 m (3.3 to 244 ft.). It is most common in less than 9 m (29 ft.) of water. It is a cryptic species, hiding in reef crevices, alongside rocks on sand bottoms, or among coral rubble. I have also encountered a number of these frogfish among encrusting invertebrates on pier pilings. Some of these individuals had unicellular algae growing on their bodies.
Captive Care: The Scarlet Frogfish is quite cryptic, spending most of its time hiding among the aquarium decor. For this reason, it is a poor choice for tanks containing large quantities of live rock. It readily accepts live foods and can be trained to take fresh seafood from a feeding stick.
Aquarium Size: 20 gal. **Temperature:** 22 to 28°C (72 to 82°F).
Aquarium Suitability Index: 4.
Remarks: This is one of the most common species in aquarium stores. Most individuals that enter the trade are small and dark brown, tan, or green. However, they can be bright red, orange, black, or gray. The Scarlet Frogfish can be separated from its nearest relatives by its lack of a caudal peduncle (the dorsal and anal fin end right at the base of the tail), the absence of an ocelli under the dorsal fin (if present, it is usually not well developed), a lack of large spots on the belly, 12 dorsal fin rays, and 10 pectoral fin rays. The illicium is short—barely half the length of the second dorsal spine—with a small filamentous esca. When this frogfish lures, it simply erects its illicium and holds it in this position or moves it back and forth. This species is very similar to the **Hawaiian Freckled Frogfish** (*Antennarius drombus*) **Jordan & Evermann, 1903**, and is considered by some authors to be synonymous with this species. *Antennarius drombus* differs from *A. coccineus* in having 12 pectoral rays. The Hawaiian Freckled Frogfish is endemic to the Hawaiian Islands and attains a maximum length of 11.5 cm (4.5 in.). It is often gray to brown with dark spots on the body and fins. There are possibly several other forms considered to be synonymous with *A. coccineus* that may actually be valid species.

Antennarius dorehensis Bleeker, 1859
Common Name: New Guinean Frogfish.
Maximum Length: 7.5 cm (3.0 in.). Most specimens are less than 5 cm (2.0 in.) in total length.
Distribution: East Africa east to Tahiti, north to southern Japan, and south to New Guinea.
Biology: This species occurs in shallow water, having been reported from near the surface to a depth of 2.5 m (8 ft.). Of 46 specimens examined by Pietsch and Grobecker (1987), 76% were collected in water less than 1 m (3.3 ft.) deep. Like many other small frogfish species, this fish tends to be reclusive, hiding in cracks and crevices.
Captive Care: This frogfish will spend much of its time hiding among the aquarium decor. It readily accepts live foods and can be trained to take fresh seafood from a feeding stick.
Aquarium Size: 20 gal. **Temperature:** 23 to 28°C (74 to 82°F).
Aquarium Suitability Index: 4.
Remarks: This species is often confused with *A. coccineus*. The best way to tell the two species apart is the caudal peduncle: *A. dorehensis* has one, *A. coccineus* does not. The New Guinean Frog-

Antennarius nummifer, Coinbearing Frogfish: orange variant.

Antennarius nummifer, Coinbearing Frogfish: common brown variant.

Antennarius nummifer, Coinbearing Frogfish: yellow variant.

Antennarius nummifer, Coinbearing Frogfish: pink and red variant.

fish has a short illicium (less than or equal to the length of the second dorsal spine), no spot at the base of the dorsal fin (if it has one it is not very conspicuous), and it usually has 9 pectoral fin rays (rarely 8 or 10). It differs from *Antennarius sanguineus*, the Bloody Frogfish, in lacking spots on its belly. The New Guinean Frogfish can be maroon, dark violet, white, or gray overall with white or black spots and patches.

Antennarius nummifer (Cuvier, 1817)
Common Names: Coinbearing Frogfish, Whitefingered Frogfish.
Maximum Length: 13 cm (5.1 in.).
Distribution: East Africa and the Red Sea to Indonesia, south to Australia and New Zealand, north to southern Japan, and east to Hawaii. Small populations of this species have also been reported from the Eastern Atlantic, where it is typically found at greater depths (usually deeper than 91 m [296 ft.]).
Biology: The Coinbearing Frogfish is most commonly encountered on rocky and coral reefs, but it also has been reported from river mouths. It is found in water from less than 1 to over 176 m (3.3 to 572 ft.) in depth, but is most common at depths less than 50 m (163 ft.). It perches under overhangs, behind sponges, in holes, crevices, and caves, and among macroalgae. In southern Japan, this species breeds in July and August, when females become swollen with eggs and are accompanied by smaller males. A pair of what was thought to be Coinbearing Frogfish were observed to spawn as frequently as every 3 days in an aquarium. The egg raft of this species is like a "perforated balloon with a single entrance for water at its base" and has been estimated to contain over 48,000 eggs, which are about 0.7 mm in diameter. In captivity, this species spawns at night.

Captive Care: The Coinbearing Frogfish spends more time in full view than some of its cryptic relatives. It is not an extremely popular species because most specimens that enter the hobby are tan or brown in color. However, some specimens display extravagant pigmentation. This species, like all frogfishes, is a glutton. I once had a specimen eat a Spotfin Lionfish (*Pterois antennata*) nearly as long as it was. Some specimens can be trained to take pieces of seafood from a feeding stick, but live food is often necessary to induce a feeding response.
Aquarium Size: 20 gal. **Temperature:** 22 to 28°C (72 to 82°F).
Aquarium Suitability Index: 4.
Remarks: The Coinbearing Frogfish is commonly seen in aquarium stores and is often confused with its close relative, the Scarlet Frogfish (*A. coccineus*). It differs from this species in having a caudal peduncle. This frogfish almost always has a well-developed ocellus at the base of its dorsal fin, no spots on its belly, an illicium that is shorter than or equal to the length of the second dorsal fin, 10 to 11 pectoral rays (rarely 9 to 12), and 12 dorsal fin rays. It can be beige, light brown, black, yellow, brownish orange, orange, pink, or red. The **Rosey Frogfish (*Antennarius rosaceus*) Smith & Radcliffe, 1912**, is a similar species that may be encountered in the aquarium trade on occasion. Unlike the Coinbearing Frogfish, this species has a very long illicium that is distinctly longer than its second dorsal spine—which also is much longer than that of *A. nummifer*. The Rosey Frogfish occurs from the Red Sea to Samoa, north to Japan, and south to Lord Howe Island and is a smaller species, growing to about 5 cm (2 in.) in total length.

Antennarius sanguineus Gill, 1863
Common Names: Bloody Frogfish, Sanguine Frogfish.
Maximum Length: 14 cm (5.5 in.).
Distribution: Eastern Pacific from the southern Gulf of California to Chile, including the Galapagos Islands.
Biology: *Antennarius sanguineus* is a cryptic species that hides in shallow crevices or depressions, in rocky reef walls, or under overhangs. It has been reported from depths of less than 1 to 40 m (3.3 to 130 ft.). Of 45 specimens examined by Pietsch and Grobecker, the average depth of capture was 9 m (29 ft.).
Captive Care: The Bloody Frogfish is a secretive species that will spend much of its time tucked away under ledges and in holes. It is rarely seen in the aquarium trade because limited collecting occurs over its range.
Aquarium Size: 20 gal. **Temperature:** 20 to 27°C (68 to 80°F).
Aquarium Suitability Index: 4.
Remarks: This species is almost identical to the Scarlet Frogfish (*A. coccineus*) but it has large dark spots on its ventrum and usu-

Antennarius sanguineus, Bloody Frogfish: seldom-collected species.

Antennarius sanguineus, Bloody Frogfish: bright orange variant

ally has 13 or 14 dorsal fin rays (the Scarlet Frogfish usually has 12). This species can be yellow, red, orange, cream, brown, reddish brown, lavender, or purple, with dark irregularly shaped blotches on the head and body and small spots on the fins.

Antennarius ocellatus Group
There are six species in this group. All are characterized by having an illicium about equal to the length of the second dorsal spine, the second dorsal spine attached to the head by a membrane, 1 to 3 distinct spots on the side of the body surrounded by a light ring, 12 to 14 pectoral rays (on rare occasions 11), usually all of the pectoral rays being bifurcate, 8 to 10 anal rays (rarely 7), and all the rays of the pelvic fins being bifurcate. This group is represented in the Atlantic, Pacific, and Indian Oceans. Only two species, *Antennarius indicus* and *Antennarius ocellatus*, are seen in the aquarium trade.

Antennarius indicus, Indian Frogfish: bold species with unusual esca (lure).

Antennarius ocellatus, Ocellated Frogfish: often by-catch from crab fishermen.

Antennarius ocellatus, Ocellated Frogfish: large species from Gulf of Mexico.

Antennarius indicus Schultz, 1964
Common Name: Indian Frogfish.
Maximum Length: 25 cm (9.8 in.).
Distribution: Zanzibar and the Seychelles, north to the Arabian Gulf, Sri Lanka, and India.
Biology: Little is known about the biology of this rare species, but two individuals have been collected at depths between 15 and 29 m (49 and 94 ft.).
Captive Care: I have encountered this species in the marine fish trade on rare occasions. These individuals acclimate quickly to their captive homes and spend much of their time sitting in the open at the base of live rock. They readily accept live feeder fish and grass shrimp.
Aquarium Size: 20 gal. **Temperature:** 22 to 28°C (72 to 82°F).
Aquarium Suitability Index: 4.
Remarks: This species has two or three eyespots (ocelli) on the body, one in the middle of the side, one at the base of the dorsal fin, and the third ocellus, if present, is usually above the base of the anal fin. The esca consists of "a number of flattened leaflike appendages." In the specimens I had, the esca was fluorescent orange in color. Most specimens are brown to yellow-brown in overall coloration, with darker spots and blotches.

Antennarius ocellatus (Bloch & Schneider, 1801)
Common Name: Ocellated Frogfish.
Maximum Length: 38 cm (15.0 in.).
Distribution: Eastern Gulf of Mexico and North Carolina south to Venezuela.
Biology: The Ocellated Frogfish is typically collected on rubble, mud, or sand bottoms, but is also commonly encountered on rocky reefs in the eastern Gulf of Mexico. It occurs at depths of 1 to 145 m (3.3 to 471 ft.) and is most common at depths greater than 24 m (78 ft.).
Captive Care: Many of the Ocellated Frogfish that show up in aquarium stores are incidentally captured by crab fishermen, who then sell them to marine fish wholesalers. This species often performs an exaggerated side-to-side rocking motion (much like the Leaf Scorpionfish, *Taenianotus triacanthus*) when you approach the aquarium or when it moves along the bottom. It may be that *A. ocellatus* relies on mimicking bottom debris more than other species because it spends more time in areas devoid of structures (hiding places). Its larger size makes it a threat to its fish tankmates, but it does not appear to be a particularly aggressive species. I have kept as many as three individuals in the same tank without having them fight.
Aquarium Size: 20 gal. **Temperature:** 22 to 26°C (72 to 78°F).
Aquarium Suitability Index: 4.

Remarks: The Ocellated Frogfish, one of the largest members of the antennariid family, shows up sporadically in aquarium stores. It is easily recognized by the three ocelli on each side of the body—one just under the dorsal fin, one in the center of the body, and one on the caudal fin (on rare occasions this ocellus may not be present). This species also has numerous small spots on the head, the chin, and the ventrum. The overall color can be beige, yellowish brown, brown, gray, or brick red. These colors are especially common on specimens captured on sand or mud bottoms; those taken on rocky or coral reefs are often multicolored. They can be lemon yellow or light brown overall, with brown and pink patches that look like coralline algae. Some individuals have many filamentous skin appendages, while others do not; their presence is probably a function of the habitat where the frogfish was collected.

Antennarius pauciradiatus Group

This group contains two species. In each, a second dorsal fin is connected to the head and the base of the third dorsal spine, the third dorsal spine is long and connected by a membrane to the soft dorsal fin, a caudal peduncle is present, the illicium is shorter than the second dorsal spine, and there is a small spot at the base of the dorsal fin. These two species are also small, attaining maximum lengths of less than 4.3 cm (1.7 in.).

Antennarius randalli Allen, 1970
Common Name: Randall's Frogfish.
Maximum Length: 4.3 cm (1.7 in.).
Distribution: Indonesia east to the Hawaiian Islands, north to the Philippines, and south to Easter Island.
Biology: This species occurs on rocky and coral reefs at depths of 8 to 30 m (26 to 98 ft.), but it is most often found at depths less than 18 m (59 ft.). Around Easter Island, this species was found in rocky areas with stands of brown macroalgae (e.g., *Sargassum*).
Captive Care: Randall's Frogfish is a secretive species that will rarely sit in the open when the lights are on, making it a poor display specimen. Because of its small size, you must be careful not to feed it oversized prey items. Initiate feeding with baby guppies and live grass shrimp, then try to switch it to small pieces of marine fish flesh and table shrimp. This diminutive frogfish is vulnerable to being preyed upon by other frogfishes.
Aquarium Size: 20 gal. **Temperature:** 22 to 27°C (72 to 80°F).
Aquarium Suitability Index: 4.
Remarks: Randall's Frogfish can be yellow, reddish brown, beige, or brown to almost black overall, with a dark spot at the base of the dorsal fin. It usually has two white spots on the caudal fin. The Atlantic counterpart of this species, the **Dwarfed Frogfish** (*Antennarius pauciradiatus*) **Schultz, 1957**, has a pair of skin flaps arising from the tip of the second dorsal fin spine and from the membrane connecting the second and third dorsal spines. The Dwarfed Frogfish is usually yellow or beige overall with dark bars radiating from the eyes, a dark spot at the base of the dorsal fin, and scattered dark spots on the body and fins. I have never encountered *A. pauciradiatus* in the trade, but it is likely that it is occasionally collected from Florida and the Caribbean.

Antennarius pictus Group

This species group is comprised of five frogfishes, all but one of which are encountered in the aquarium trade. Members of this group have an illicium that is usually twice the length of the second dorsal spine (this may not be the case in juvenile specimens); a second dorsal spine that is attached to the head by a membrane; 10 or 11 pectoral rays that are never bifurcate; frequent dark, circular spots on the head, body, and fins; and (often) three spots—spaced in the form of a triangle—on the caudal fin. Some of these species are difficult to distinguish from each other unless closely examined. This group is represented in the Atlantic, Pacific, and Indian Oceans and is frequently encountered in the aquarium trade. Most frogfishes labeled as "colored anglerfish" in retail stores are members of this group.

Antennarius commerson (Latreille, 1804)
Common Names: Giant Frogfish, Commerson's Frogfish.
Maximum length: 30 cm (11.8 in.).
Distribution: Southern Africa and the Red Sea to the tropical Eastern Pacific, north to southern Japan, and south to Lord Howe Island.

Antennarius randalli, Randall's Frogfish: a tiny, secretive species.

Antennarius commerson, Giant Frogfish: large adult female.

Antennarius commerson, Giant Frogfish: juvenile.

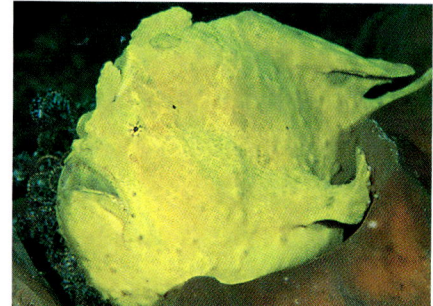
Antennarius commerson, Giant Frogfish: large green variant.

Antennarius commerson, Giant Frogfish: pink variant.

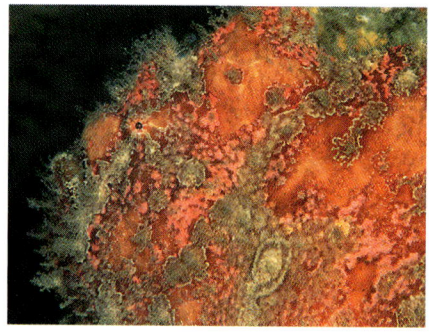
Antennarius commerson, Giant Frogfish: reddish orange variant.

Antennarius commerson, Giant Frogfish: tan variant.

Antennarius commerson, Giant Frogfish: yellow variant.

Antennarius commerson, Giant Frogfish: white variant with scablike patches.

Antennarius commerson, Giant Frogfish: deep orange variant.

Biology: The Giant Frogfish occurs at a depth range of 1 to 50 m (3.3 to 163 ft.), but is most common at depths greater than 13 m (42 ft.). It resides on shallow fringing and coastal reefs, on fore-reef slopes, in lagoons and ship wreckage, and on pier pilings. The Giant Frogfish is often found in association with sponges and typically adopts the color of its invertebrate perch to enhance its camouflage. It will often sit in a larger sponge or hang upside down beneath a ledge. It occurs singly, in pairs, or in trios. Although not yet confirmed by field studies, my observations suggest that this species forms long-term pair bonds. This would decrease the time and risk necessary for this uncommon fish to locate a mate. This species has been observed to take advantage of the presence of scuba divers to capture its prey. In the Lembeh Straits off Sulawesi, house-cat-sized Giant Frogfish will approach the nests of egg-guarding Indo-Pacific Sergeant Majors (*Abudefduf vaigiensis*) to feed on Klein's Butterflyfish

(*Chaetodon kleini*). When the adult sergeants retreat at the approach of a diver, the opportunistic butterflyfish move in to feed on the eggs. In response to this, the Giant Frogfish move close to the nests and attempt to consume the inattentive butterflies. One large frogfish was observed ingesting 7 Klein's Butterflyfish in less than 10 minutes time.

Captive Care: This is one of the larger frogfishes, and as it grows it will become a greater threat to a wider range of tankmates. Like other frogfishes, this species is susceptible to *Cryptocaryon* and *Amyloodinium*. Dr. Bruce Carlson, of the Waikiki Aquarium, told me that they have had specimens succumb to a strange infection, which may be bacterial in origin. Carlson explained that after being held in captivity for a while, large boil-like sores often appear all over the bodies of *A. commerson*. Soon after, the frogfish die. In spite of these disease problems, this larger frogfish is well suited for the reef aquarium, because it often spends the daylight hours in full view. They are known to spawn in captivity.

Aquarium Size: 30 gal. **Temperature:** 22 to 27°C (72 to 80°F).
Aquarium Suitability Index: 4.

Remarks: This is a common, colorful frogfish that is often seen in the aquarium trade. It is also one of the largest frogfishes observed in North American aquarium stores. The only frogfish species that grow larger are the Roughjaw Frogfish (*Antennarius avalonis*), which attains 34 cm (13.4 in.), and the Ocellated Frogfish (*A. ocellatus*).

The Giant Frogfish was originally described by the eminent scientist Philibert Commerson 200 years ago from a specimen collected near the Indian Ocean island of Mauritius. It has been described under numerous scientific names since that time; one synonym that is relatively well known is *Antennarius moluccensis*.

Giant Frogfish can be distinguished from other members of the *Antennarius pictus* Group by having 8 anal rays, 13 dorsal rays (rarely 11 or 12), and 11 pectoral rays (rarely 10). Also, the second dorsal spine becomes wider toward the end and has a thick membrane that nearly reaches the spine tip and extends to the base of the third dorsal spine. The third dorsal spine is also long and very thick toward the end.

Giant Frogfish come in a rainbow of colors, with white, yellow, brown, green, red, orange, pink, and black color phases all having been reported. Like most frogfishes, they can change from one color to another. Pietsch & Grobecker (1987) report that a specimen they kept changed from lemon yellow to brick red in 3 weeks. Often, these fish are mottled with scablike pink patches or irregular blue, brown, white, or black markings. This frogfish is typically peppered with small dark spots or with larger, irregularly shaped spots on the body and fins.

Antennarius maculatus (Desjardins, 1840)
Common Names: Wartskin Frogfish, Warty Frogfish, Clown Frogfish.
Maximum Length: 10 cm (3.9 in.).
Distribution: Mauritius to the Solomon Islands, north to Ryukyus, and south to the Great Barrier Reef.
Biology: The Wartskin Frogfish is a shallow-water species that has been reported from water depths of less than 1 up to 15 m (3.3 to 49 ft.). It is often found on coastal, low-profile reefs consisting mainly of macroalgae, sponges, soft coral, and the occasional large-polyped stony coral. Adults apparently spend more time hiding in reef interstices or among benthic debris, while juveniles are often seen in the open. When these frogfish move, sinusoidal waves travel down the edge of the dorsal fin, and they

Antennarius maculatus, Wartskin Frogfish: note large warts.

Antennarius maculatus, Wartskin Frogfish: mottled variant luring.

Antennarius maculatus, Wartskin Frogfish: a species highly sought-after by aquarists that is very similar to *Antennarius pictus*, Painted Frogfish.

Antennarius maculatus, Wartskin Frogfish: white with a hint of yellow.

Antennarius maculatus, Wartskin Frogfish: more yellow, several days later.

move the erect second dorsal spine and the associated membrane from side to side. This species is usually found on its own.

Captive Care: Because of its propensity to spend more time in full view, the Wartskin Frogfish is one of the best frogfish species for a reef aquarium. It may behave aggressively toward other frogfish, especially members of its own species or closely related forms. These agonistic encounters usually consist only of lateral displays—pushing with the pectoral fins and tail-slapping. Like most frogfishes, this species will ingest slender fishes much longer than itself.

Aquarium Size: 20 gal. **Temperature:** 23 to 27°C (74 to 80°F).
Aquarium Suitability Index: 4.
Remarks: Those individuals seen in aquarium stores are usually lemon yellow or creamy white with pink, white, or reddish brown saddles and patches on the body. But they can also be greenish yellow, dark brown, light brown, black (sometimes this color phase has yellow or orange spots), or red overall. I have had white individuals change to yellow or pinkish purple overall. The Wartskin Frogfish often has black spots surrounded by lighter borders on the head and fins (with fewer on the body), most of which are larger than the eye and all of them are roughly the same size. The esca sometimes looks like a small fish, with an eyespot and vertical bands. In most specimens, however, the esca consists of numerous filaments connected by a common base, rather than one flattened fishlike appendage. In older aquarium literature, this species is often referred to as *Antennarius phymatodes*, which is a junior synonym. This species is very similar to the Painted Frogfish (*Antennarius pictus*).

Antennarius multicellatus (Valenciennes, 1837)
Common Name: Longlure Frogfish.
Maximum Length: 20 cm (7.9 in.), but most do not exceed 12.5 cm (4.9 in.).
Distribution: Western Atlantic, from Bermuda and Florida south to Brazil. It has also been reported from Ascension Island in the Eastern Atlantic.
Biology: This species occurs at depths of less than 1 to more than 61 m (3.3 to 198 ft.), but is most common in water less than 7.5 m (24 ft.) deep. It is found on fringing reefs, reef faces, on fore-reef slopes, and frequently occurs among encrusting invertebrates on pier pilings. I observed six of these frogfish on the pilings of a pier in the U.S. Virgin Islands. They most frequently associate with sponges and tunicates (they will even hide in the lumen of a larger tube sponge), but they also occur in exposed areas on sandy bottoms. Breder (1949) suggested that black specimens, observed on open sand bottoms, may mimic loggerhead sponges. Barbour (1942) remarked that they look like gastropods as they slowly glide over the sand and sway their second and third dorsal spines from side to side. I have seen both solitary individuals and pairs; in the pairs, one individual was always significantly larger than the other. This species eats scorpionfishes, grunts, squirrelfishes, clinid blennies, gobies, and other reef fishes, as well as mantis shrimps and crabs.
Captive Care: The Longlure Frogfish is occasionally available from wholesale operations on the East Coast. It is a good display animal because it will spend a considerable amount of time in exposed portions of the tank.

Antennarius multicellatus, Longlure Frogfish: distended from a recent meal.

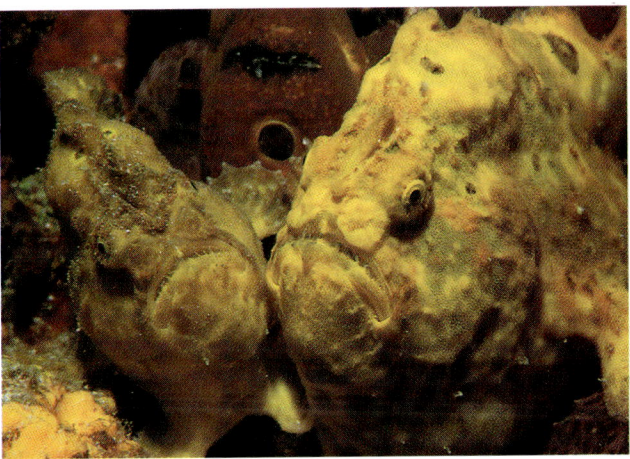
Antennarius multicellatus, Longlure Frogfish: sometimes found in pairs.

Antennarius multicellatus, Longlure Frogfish: common Caribbean species.

Antennarius multiocellatus, Longlure Frogfish: white form.

Antennarius multiocellatus, Longlure Frogfish: pink form.

Antennarius multiocellatus, Longlure Frogfish: yawning behavior.

Antennarius multiocellatus, Longlure Frogfish: gray form.

Aquarium Size: 30 gal. **Temperature:** 21 to 27°C (70 to 80°F).
Aquarium Suitability Index: 4.
Remarks: This is the most common frogfish in the Caribbean. It can be distinguished from other members of its species group by the membrane behind the second dorsal spine—which is not well developed and ends well before the third dorsal spine. It also has a relatively short third dorsal spine, the second dorsal spine is slightly tapered from the base, and it may have bumps (but not large warts like *A. maculatus*). This species can be white, yellow, orange, bright red, brick red, pink, tan, dark green, or black overall, with white saddles on the caudal peduncle and shoulder region and eyespots (ocelli) on the unpaired fins and at the dorsal fin base. The Longlure Frogfish often has three ocelli on the tail, and some individuals have pink or reddish brown irregularly shaped patches on the body and head.

Antennarius pictus (Shaw & Nodder, 1794)
Common Name: Painted Frogfish.
Maximum Length: 10 cm (3.9 in.).
Distribution: Mozambique to the Hawaiian Islands (where it is rare), north to southern Japan, and south to New South Wales, Australia.
Biology: The Painted Frogfish occurs in water less than 1 to over 73 m (3.3 to 237 ft.) deep and is found on coastal reefs, in lagoons, and on the seaward reef face or slope. It usually associates with sponges, coral rubble, macroalgae, or live corals during the day, but often moves into more exposed areas on sand and

mud at night. It has also been found among floating algae.
Captive Care: *Antennarius pictus* is regularly seen in the aquarium trade. It is a good display animal, spending much of its time in full view, and has spawned in captivity. Although more than one individual can be kept in the same tank, they may display at and fight with one another in smaller tanks.
Aquarium Size: 20 gal. **Temperature:** 22 to 27°C (72 to 80°F).
Aquarium Suitability Index: 4.
Remarks: *Antennarius pictus* is similar to *A. maculatus*; in fact, it can be difficult to tell the two species apart. The most recognizable characteristic of the *A. maculatus* is the large warts on the fins and body (although these may not be present in juveniles). The Painted Frogfish (*A. pictus*) may have bumps and smaller warts, but they are not nearly as conspicuous as those of an adult *A. maculatus*. The shape of the second dorsal spine and the development of the membrane that connects it to the head can also help in separating these two fishes. In *A. maculatus*, the spine is more club-shaped—it has a narrow base that is very swollen to-

Antennarius pictus, Painted Frogfish: nine examples of the same species demonstrating its remarkable ability to adapt its appearance to different surroundings, including the specimen, top left, that has taken on the waffled pattern of a nearby white bryozoan (moss animal) colony. This species is a fine choice for aquarists.

Antennarius hispidus, Hispid Frogfish: note esca (lure) and illicium (rod).

Antennarius hispidus, Hispid Frogfish: some have bioluminescent lures.

Antennarius hispidus, Hispid Frogfish: often sold as "Sargassum Anglerfish."

ward the end. In *A. pictus*, the spine is more tapered from the base to the tip. The membrane in *A. maculatus* is slightly larger than in *A. pictus*, extending from the second dorsal spine tip to the base of the third dorsal spine. To make identification matters more difficult, the Painted Frogfish often displays color patterns common to the Wartskin Frogfish, including yellow with pink or lavender saddles and white with rust-colored markings. The Painted Frogfish can be dark blue or black (sometimes this color phase has orange spots), yellow, yellowish green, dark green, orange, dark brown, tan, bright red, or brick red. Darker individuals often have white-tipped pectoral rays, and all color forms regularly have dark spots of varying size. This species can be separated from the Giant Frogfish (*A. commerson*) by the presence of 6 or 7 anal rays (8 in *A. commerson*); usually 10 pectoral rays, although on rare occasions it can have 9 or 11 (usually 11, rarely 10 in *A. commerson*); and 12 dorsal rays, rarely 11 or 13 (usually 13, but on rare occasions 11 or 12 in *A. commerson*). There are also differences described in the *A. commerson* species account.

Antennarius striatus Group

This group contains two very similar species, both of which are encountered in the aquarium trade. Both typically have a distinct color pattern, consisting of dark streaks on the body and fins. They also have an illicium that is about twice the length of the second dorsal spine, a second dorsal spine that is attached to the head by a membrane, and an illicium that extends beyond the symphysis of the upper jaw. The two species in this group can be differentiated by the form of the esca.

Antennarius hispidus (Bloch & Schneider, 1801)

Common Names: Hispid Frogfish, Shaggy Frogfish.
Maximum Length: 20 cm (7.9 in.).
Distribution: East Africa to Fiji, north to Taiwan, and south to northern Australia.
Biology: The Hispid Frogfish occurs at depths of 1 to 69 m (3.3 to 224 ft.), but is most common in water deeper than 30 m (98 ft.). In coastal bays, it often refuges among leaf litter that has accumulated on the sandy bottom. When luring, the esca is moved erratically in a triangular pattern and looks like the tentacles of tubeworms waving in the current. Recently, Hispid Frogfish collected in 45 m (146 ft.) of water off Bombay were discovered to harbor bioluminescent bacteria in their esca. These microorganisms produce a greenish light that causes the "bait" to glow in the dark.
Captive Care: *Antennarius hispidus* is a good display animal that will spend much of its time in the open. It has a ravenous appetite and will often swim, by jet propulsion, around the tank.

Aquarium Size: 30 gal. **Temperature:** 22 to 27°C (72 to 80°F).
Aquarium Suitability Index: 4.
Remarks: This is an attractively marked species that is often misidentified as the unrelated Sargassum Frogfish (*Histrio histrio*), possibly because it has stripes and skin appendages like the Sargassum. Otherwise, they are very different from each other. The Hispid Frogfish can be distinguished from the closely related Striated Frogfish by its esca. In *Antennarius striatus*, the lure has wormlike appendages, while in the Hispid Frogfish, the esca is shaped like a pom-pom. The Hispid Frogfish can be black, beige, yellow, white, or orange overall, with dark stripes on the body and lines radiating from the eyes.

Antennarius striatus (Shaw & Nodder, 1794)
Common Names: Striated Frogfish, Striped Frogfish.
Maximum Length: 22 cm (8.7 in.).
Distribution: The Striated Frogfish is widespread in its distribution—Western Atlantic (from New Jersey to Brazil), Eastern Atlantic and Indo-Pacific (from South Africa to the Society Islands, north to Japan, and south to New Zealand and Australia).
Biology: This is one of the most fascinating members of the antennariid family. Like the Hispid Frogfish, it is truly a master angler, having evolved more sophisticated ways of attracting prey. The esca of the Striated Frogfish has secretory cells that release an olfactory stimulus that is attractive to other fishes, and the esca enlarges by as much as 35% when it is in use. The fact that it emits an odor allows this frogfish to lure prey in deeper, darker water than its congeners. This may explain why it is often found at greater depths: *A. striatus* has been reported at depths from near the surface to as deep as 218 m (709 ft.). Over 86% of 92 specimens examined by Pietsch and Grobecker (1987) were collected in over 33 m (107 ft.) of water. In tropical seas, the Striated Frogfish may be encountered at more shallow depths during the winter months, when water temperatures are cooler.

This species is found on coral or rocky reefs, but in many areas it is most abundant on sand or mud substrates where it often sits alongside sponges or macroalgae. The frogfish will often position themselves so that their heads are facing downcurrent, which may facilitate the broadcasting of the scent associated with their esca. Scorpionfishes and sea basses have been reported from the stomachs of Caribbean specimens, but a Striated Frogfish will eat any fishes or crustaceans small enough to ingest.
Captive Care: The Striated Frogfish makes an interesting addition to a species tank or even a reef aquarium. Unlike some members of the genus, it will spend most of its time in full view, rather than hiding amid the aquarium decor. There are a number of reports documenting captive spawning in this species.

Antennarius striatus, Striated Frogfish: note trident lure.

Antennarius striatus, Striated Frogfish: not prone to hiding in the aquarium.

Antennarius striatus, Striated Frogfish: type found with filamentous algae.

The reproductive behavior closely follows that described in the Reproduction section (page 332). Most of the courtship activity takes place in midwater or near the surface of the aquarium.
Aquarium Size: 30 gal. **Temperature:** 22 to 26°C (72 to 78°F).
Aquarium Suitability Index: 4.
Remarks: Even though it is quite widespread, *A. striatus* is not common in aquarium stores—possibly because it occupies deeper water. It shows some geographical variation in pectoral fin counts and in the number of tentacles on the esca (which can range from two to seven) and, like most frogfishes, it comes in a variety of different colors, including light yellow, fluorescent yellow, orange, green, gray, brown, and white with dark stripes and blotches. On rare occasions, individuals will either lack or have few markings on the body. This seems to be especially true for Japanese specimens. In the aquarium, the black color phase often changes to light yellow or gray in as little as two weeks. Individuals that have been associating with filamentous or macroalgae may develop numerous long filaments on the body, fins, and dorsal fin spines and rays.

Many of the variants of *A. striatus* have been described as distinct species—no less than 28 scientific names have been ascribed to this species. One of the most common is *Antennarius scaber*, which was used for individuals from the Western Atlantic population. It is still thought to be a valid species by some ichthyologists. Individuals from this area have 11 or 12 pectoral rays and a bifid esca. There may be other valid species (such as *Antennarius tridens* from Japan) that have been erroneously linked with *A. striatus* as well.

Genus *Antennatus*

There are three described, and possibly one undescribed, species in this genus, all of which are recognized by the presence of closely spaced dermal spinules all over the body, an illicium that tapers toward its tip so that it forms a fine point, a very small esca or no esca, an immobile third dorsal spine that is connected by skin over its entire length to the skull, no caudal peduncle in most species, and bifurcate caudal fin rays. The members of this genus are also smaller, cryptic fishes that are known from the Indo-Pacific and tropical Eastern Pacific Oceans, and possibly the Western Atlantic. One of the known *Antennatus* species was recently described from two individuals collected off southern Japan. This species, the **Flagellated Frogfish** (*Antennatus flagellatus*) **Ohnishi, Iwata & Hiramatsu, 1997**, has an incredibly long illicium that is 3.6 times the length of the second dorsal spine (or over 40% of the standard length of the fish) and a caudal peduncle. These two specimens were collected from under a rock ledge in 45 m (146 ft.) of water.

Antennatus strigatus, Bandtail Frogfish: small, cryptic Eastern Pacific fish.

Antennatus strigatus (Gill, 1863)
Common Name: Bandtail Frogfish.
Maximum Length: 8 cm (3.1 in.).
Distribution: Eastern Pacific, from the southern part of the Gulf of California to Colombia and some of the offshore islands, including the Galapagos and Clipperton Islands.
Biology: This is a cryptic species that occurs in water of less than 1 up to 38 m (3.3 to 124 ft.) deep, but is most common in depths of less than 15 m (49 ft.). It occurs on rocky reefs, especially dropoffs, and spends most of its time deep in cracks and crevices. The Bandtail Frogfish is thought to mimic tubeworm snails and sponges in order to ambush its prey.
Captive Care: The husbandry requirements of this species are similar to those of the Tuberculated Frogfish (*Antennatus tuberosus*).
Aquarium Size: 20 gal. **Temperature:** 20 to 26°C (68 to 78°F).
Aquarium Suitability Index: 4.

Antennatus sp.: undescribed frogfish collected in the Western Atlantic.

Remarks: In the Bandtail Frogfish, the esca is present, although it is very small. This fish is less common in the trade than *A. tuberosus* because relatively little collecting occurs over its range. I have run across a member of this genus that may be undescribed. This individual was reportedly collected in the Atlantic, an area where no *Antennatus* species have yet been discovered. It was yellow in color and had no distinct markings on the fins.

Antennatus tuberosus (Cuvier, 1817)
Common Names: Tuberculated Frogfish, Pygmy Frogfish.
Maximum Length: 7 cm (2.8 in.).
Distribution: East Africa to the Hawaiian, Line, and Pitcairn Islands, south to Samoa.
Biology: The Tuberculated Frogfish associates with coral reefs, in water as shallow as 1 m (3.3 ft.) to as deep as 73 m (237 ft.). It is most prevalent at depths of less than 20 m (65 ft.). It often hides among the branches of hard corals.
Captive Care: *Antennatus tuberosus* is a very cryptic species—once you place it in a larger aquarium with lots of hiding places, you may never see it again. At night, it will seek out holes, crevices, or the backside of a rock to hide in or behind. I once placed a specimen in a smaller tank, only to have it disappear. I finally decided it must have died and been consumed by the scavengers associated with my live rock. Time passed, until one day I added a Sunrise Dottyback (*Pseudochromis flavivertex*) and it mysteriously disappeared within 10 minutes of being placed in the tank. I noticed some commotion behind a rock and lifted it up to find the long-lost Tuberculated Frogfish with the tail of the much longer dottyback sticking out of its mouth.
Aquarium Size: 20 gal. **Temperature:** 22 to 26°C (70 to 78°F).
Aquarium Suitability Index: 4.
Remarks: This species is infrequently seen in the trade, although it is not as popular due to its more subdued color pattern and reclusive behavior. It has no esca—instead, the illicium tapers to a point. Although it may not be as effective at attracting prey as its well-endowed cousins, it will still lift its illicium when hunting. Most specimens I have seen in fish stores are a cream color overall with brown marbling and a dark band on the tail. Some individuals may have patches of lavender that look like coralline algae. It can also be creamy yellow with little or no darker marbling, and a distinct band on the tail. This frogfish has been observed to change from dark gray to light cream in captivity.

Genus *Histrio*
This genus contains one highly specialized frogfish.

Histrio histrio (Linnaeus, 1758)
Common Names: Sargassum Frogfish, Sargassumfish.
Maximum Length: 19 cm (7.5 in.).
Distribution: All tropical seas, except the Eastern Pacific.
Biology: Adults of this species are almost always found near the surface, but the larval and postlarval specimens, up to 4 mm in length, have been reported at depths from 50 to 600 m (163 to 1,950 ft.). In the wild, Sargassum Frogfish hunt during the day. In the Atlantic, individuals feed mainly on the sargassum shrimp *Latreutes fucorum* and *Leander tenuicornis*, but also eat fishes, polychaete worms, and crabs. Individuals from the Indo-Pacific, in contrast, feed primarily on fishes (including conspecifics, blennies, damselfishes, filefishes, chubs, and jacks) and to a lesser degree on polychaete worms, planktonic crustaceans, and shrimps. As far as potential tankmates are concerned, these frogfish are more voracious than their cousins. Straughan (1954) reported seeing this species attempting to ingest a fish twice its own length. As suggested by stomach content analysis, this species is also more likely to eat members of its own kind: the stomach of a large Sargassum Frogfish has contained as many as 12 smaller individuals. This voracity may be due to the fact that they live in an environment where food is not as plentiful; therefore, they cannot be as selective about when and what they eat.

Although they blend in well with the *Sargassum* macroalgae beds in which they live, Sargassum Frogfish are occasionally preyed upon by other fishes. They have been taken from the stomachs of Dolphinfish (*Coryphaena hippurus*), tuna, and Night Sharks (*Carcharhinus signatus*). One strategy they use to elude predators is to leap out of the water onto the top of the *Sargassum* bed and remain there for a time before flipping back into the water. Cover your aquarium in case your Sargassum Frogfish decides to try this in its new home. This fish will also inflate its stomach with water so that certain predators (including con-

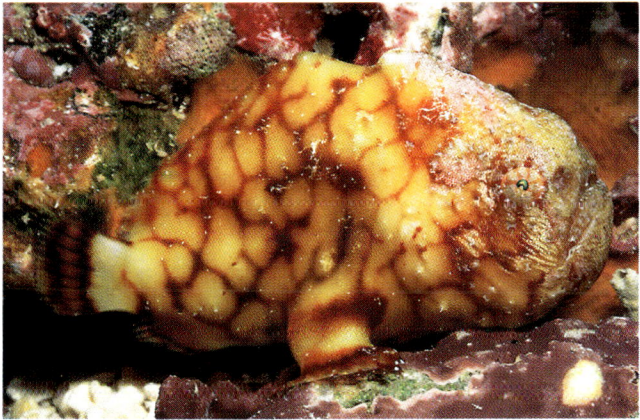
Antennatus tuberosus, Tuberculated Frogfish: a small, very reclusive species.

Histrio histrio, Sargassum Frogfish: will breed in captive conditions.

specifics) cannot to swallow it.

Captive Care: Even though the Sargassum Frogfish is always found in association with *Sargassum* macroalgae in the wild, it can be kept without it in the aquarium. But it does like to perch between coral branches, rocks, *Caulerpa* fronds, highly branching artificial plants (which can be anchored to the bottom or left to float), the undergravel uplift tube, and the aquarium glass. These fish tend to have an affinity for the surface of the water, so it is best to position a resting site in the upper part of the tank. The Sargassum Frogfish is more aggressive than other antennariids. Adults of the same species will not tolerate each other in the confines of a tank, except during courtship and mating. After mating, females are best removed because fights can result in serious injuries. Individuals will bite each other—ripping their fins and skin flaps to shreds—and smaller specimens will end up dead. Because of their violent nature, adult Sargassum Frogfish cannot be trusted with other frogfish species either.

Sargassum Frogfish can be bred in captivity, but sexing specimens is difficult. The only way to tell if you have a pair is to place two adults together and closely observe their behavior. If they do not attack each other, there is a chance that they are opposite sexes. If courtship displays ensue, you have a pair. It may be necessary to separate the couple between spawning bouts if you keep them in a smaller aquarium (less than 55 gallons), because males have a tendency to harm the females. If no aggressive behavior is noted, it is best not to isolate them as the male's presence may induce the female to produce eggs more rapidly.

For the most part, Sargassum Frogfish breed in a similar manner to other antennariids. Courtship typically includes the male circling, nudging, and pushing the female with his pectoral fins, with the frequency of these behaviors increasing just before spawning. However, some of these reproductive bouts can become more bellicose, with males chasing, vigorously butting, and even biting and shaking their mates. When courtship commences, males become darker in color (chocolate brown). About 8 hours after the first signs of abdominal expansion are noticed, the now turgid, heavily respiring female leaves her perch and begins the prespawning march along the bottom of the aquarium. As the female walks along the bottom on her pectoral fins, with her tail positioned higher than her head, the male follows with his snout near her cloaca and pushes her toward the surface. This promenade lasts about 3 minutes. Then the male suddenly shoots past the female and the gametes are expelled. There is some evidence to indicate that when the male dashes past the female, he grasps the end of the partially protruding egg raft in his jaws and jerks it from the female's oviduct. On rare occasions, the female may have difficulty ejecting the egg raft and will return to the aquarium bottom with this structure still hanging from her cloaca. In these cases, the male usually does not fertilize the eggs and it may take the female several hours or longer to expel the raft. The pair will spawn every 3 to 39 days, with these events typically occurring at about the same time (plus or minus 1 hour) every evening. Eggs hatch in 4 to 5 days, at a water temperature of 22°C (72°F), and the larvae are about 1.4 mm at this time. The yolk sac disappears about 11 days after the hatch; after this time, if adequate prey organisms are not present, the larvae will die.

Aquarium Size: 30 gal. **Temperature:** 22 to 27°C (72 to 80°F).
Aquarium Suitability Index: 4.

Remarks: This species is regularly available in the hobby, although two other antennariids (the Hispid and the Striated Frogfish) are commonly misidentified as *H. histrio*. What makes the Sargassum Frogfish unique is that it lives among the fronds of floating *Sargassum* algae. Its color pattern and the skin flaps that cover its body help it to blend with its natural surroundings. The color typically consists of brown stripes and blotches on a tan background, but is highly variable and can suddenly fade or intensify to match the surroundings or communicate the fish's mood. Juveniles can be entirely black with white-tipped pectoral fins.

Genus *Lophiocharon*

This genus contains three species, two of which I have encountered in the trade. Characteristics include one or two transparent eyespots between each ray of the caudal fin, an illicium with an upturned base, a second dorsal spine connected to the base of the third dorsal spine, a third dorsal spine connected to the soft dorsal fin by skin, bifurcate rays in the caudal and soft dorsal fins, caudal peduncle absent, and nine pectoral rays. These species are found from the Philippines to tropical Australia.

Lophiocharon lithinostomus, Marblemouthed Frogfish: hardy but rarely seen.

Lophiocharon trisignatus, Threespot Frogfish: produces large eggs and fry.

Lophiocharon lithinostomus (Jordan & Richardson, 1908)
Common Name: Marblemouthed Frogfish.
Maximum Length: 12 cm (4.7in.).
Distribution: Philippines and Borneo.
Biology: The only specimen where depth information is available was taken in less than 1 m (3.3 ft.) of water.
Captive Care: This is a relatively rare species and thus is infrequently encountered in aquarium stores. It is hardy in captivity, but is a voracious predator. A Marblemouthed Frogfish at a local fish store ingested a Convict Surgeonfish (*Acanthurus triostegus*) that was about its same length, an adolescent Rockmover Wrasse (*Novaculichthys taeniourus*) that was longer than itself, and a smaller Zebra Lionfish (*Dendrochirus zebra*). This species will lie up against rocks and coral and wait for its quarry to swim past, or it will actively stalk its prey if nothing comes within striking distance. The luring technique of *L. lithinostomus* consists of simply throwing the illicium and tiny esca forward and holding it steady.
Aquarium Size: 20 gal. **Temperature:** 22 to 27°C (72 to 80°F).
Aquarium Suitability Index: 4.
Remarks: This species has a greatly reduced esca and a long illicium. The fish is usually green with darker mottling and blotches and has been described as resembling "an algae-covered rock."

Lophiocharon trisignatus (Richardson, 1844)
Common Name: Threespot Frogfish.
Maximum Length: 18 cm (7.1 in.).
Distribution: Philippines to the northern and western coasts of Australia.
Biology: No information exists on its depth distribution or its habitat preferences, but its unusual reproductive mode is well known. The eggs—which measure about 2 mm in diameter—are attached by threads to the side of the male. The young are miniature versions of their parents at hatching. Because the fry are relatively large and well developed, this species would be an ideal candidate for captive propagation.
Captive Care: This species is infrequently encountered in aquarium stores.
Aquarium Size: 20 gal. **Temperature:** 22 to 27°C (72 to 80°F).
Aquarium Suitability Index: 4.
Remarks: The Threespot Frogfish shows up in aquarium stores on occasion as a "colored" or "assorted frogfish." The easiest way to identify members of this genus is by the ocelli that occur between the rays of the caudal fin and the illicium, which is distinctly curved toward its base. This species differs from the other described member of the genus, the Marblemouthed Frogfish, in having a well developed esca. In the Marblemouthed Frogfish, the esca is extremely small. The Threespot Frogfish can be brown, reddish brown, or light green overall, with a cream-colored belly and chin; black reticulations on the head, body, and fins; and ocelli on the tail.

References
Barbour (1942), Breder (1949), Breder & Rosen (1966), Friese (1973, 1974), Hornell (1921), Humann (1994), Hutchins & Swainston (1986), K. Imai (personal communication), Kuiter (1993, 1996), B. Nagerda (personal communication), Mosher (1954), Ohnishi et al. (1997), Pietsch & Grobecker (1980, 1987), Randall (1967), Randall & Randall (1960), Randall et al. (1990), Ray (1961), L. Smith (personal communication), Straughan (1954), C. Stillwell (personal communication), Thresher (1984).

Family Ogcocephalidae
Walking Batfishes

Ogcocephalus darwini, Redlip Batfish: highly unusual fishes that prefer walking to swimming, the batfishes have a lure located in a depression under their snout.

Looking less like fishes than like amphibians that have been flattened by a truck, the walking batfishes are oddities that never fail to amaze underwater photographers and aquarists. They can make endearing aquarium residents, but they do require special care and attention.

Biology

The Family Ogcocephalidae contains 62 species and 9 genera, all of whose members have a broad, flat body and modified pelvic and pectoral fins similar to those of the frogfishes (Family Antennariidae). These modified fins are used to walk across the seafloor. Their gaits have been described as rabbitlike, toadlike, or doglike. On rare occasions, they will swim in a cumbersome fashion, using their caudal fin to thrust them forward and off the seafloor. The batfishes also have a modified first dorsal spine, usually tucked into a depression between the rostrum and the mouth. This spine has a long rod, the illicium, with an attachment, the esca, at its free end. The illicium and esca are thought to be used like a fishing rod and lure. The illicium is projected from the depression and the esca is vigorously wriggled at potential prey. It has been suggested that individuals tend to wiggle the esca to one side or the other, which would be analogous to being either right- or left-handed. It is not known how frequently the lure is successful in attracting prey, but the few food habit studies available suggest that it actually would not be very effective at attracting many of their target species. Walking batfishes lure infrequently in captivity, although they occasionally engage in this behavior if small fishes are added to the aquarium.

Members of this family have a small protrusible mouth that is effective for plucking prey items off the substrate. Although they lack scales, some have tubercles, bucklers (cone-shaped scales covered with spinules), or hairlike cirri, as well as small gill openings situated at the posterior base of the pectoral fins. When identifying a walking batfish, remember that there is an allometric change in rostrum (snout) length as these fish age—young specimens often have longer rostrums than older individuals.

This family is represented in tropical and temperate waters all around the world. In most areas, they live on mud or clay bottoms in deep water. The tropical Western Atlantic and Caribbean is the only region where several of these fishes can be observed regularly in nearshore waters adjacent to reefs. Those batfishes found near reefs usually choose sand, rubble, or rocky bottoms. Walking batfishes may also be encountered in relatively shallow depths off the Galapagos and Cocos Islands. The Redlip Batfish (*Ogcocephalus darwini*) has been reported at depths of less than 1 up to 1,818 m (3.3 to 5,909 ft.).

Several of the walking batfishes are euryhaline, which means that they can withstand a wide range of salinity levels. For example, the Oval Batfish (*Ogcocephalus notatus*) has been reported from estuaries and tidal creeks, while the South American Batfish (*Ogcocephalus vespertilio*) has been collected more than 1,300 km (806 mi.) up the Amazon River. The *Ogcocephalus* species are those most likely to be encountered by aquarists, as members of this genus tend to occupy shallower waters where they are more easily collected. Ten of these species occur in the Western Atlantic; two in the Eastern Pacific.

Although the batfishes do not look edible, sharks occasionally eat them. One Galapagos Hornshark (*Heterodontus quoyi*) was found to have a Redlip Batfish in its stomach, and Tiger Sharks (*Galeocerdo cuvier*) have also been reported to consume these fishes. When threatened, walking batfishes either remain motionless or throw sand over their bodies to hide.

Captive Care
Much of what we know about walking batfish husbandry is the result of detailed observations and studies conducted by Dr. David Schleser at the Dallas Aquarium and Bronson Nagreda, a serious fishkeeper from Hawaii. A large part of the information presented here is the result of their research efforts.

Batfishes are sensitive aquarium inhabitants that require special care in order to thrive, or even survive, in captivity. For example, it is important to house your batfish in a tank with little or no decor and a soft substrate on the aquarium bottom. Live sand is a great bottom material because it is fine enough for the batfish to bury under and the microfauna and macrofauna it con-

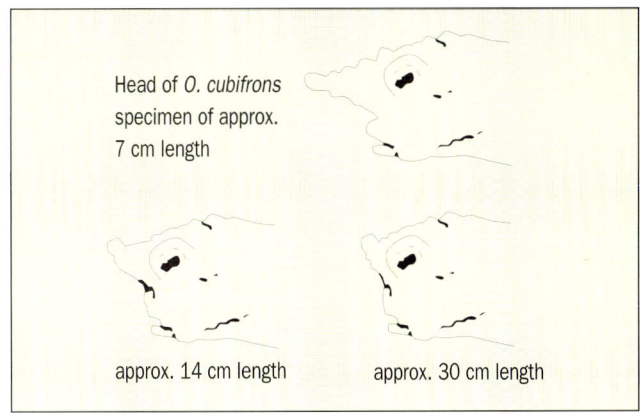

As a walking batfish grows, its rostrum (snout) often decreases in length and becomes more knoblike in shape. This characteristic can help determine the approximate age of an individual. (Adapted from Bradbury, 1980.)

tains will help maintain good water quality while providing a natural source of food (e.g., annelid worms). When selecting a tank in which to house your batfish, the more surface area the better. For example, a standard 30-gallon tank (36 x 13 x 17 in.) would be better than a 29-gallon tank (30 x 12 x 19 in.).

Batfishes often damage their rostrums by either swimming or walking into the aquarium glass. This damage can lead to bacterial infections and subsequent death. To help prevent a new batfish from engaging in this behavior, place a 15-cm (6-in.) wide piece of black plastic or paper around the outside bottom of all four sides of the tank. (Although this will work for most individuals, some will continue to engage in this behavior, especially if the tank is small or there is little uncluttered substrate.) After the batfish fully acclimates, the black plastic can be removed. Batfishes can also injure their snouts by swimming against the sides of the plastic shipping bag during transport.

The batfishes that make it into the aquarium trade are often collected incidentally by shrimp trawlers, and the specimens are usually in bad shape when they arrive at your local aquarium store. If possible, try to order your batfish from a collector. This may cost more, but it will increase the likelihood of keeping the fish successfully. Batfishes often develop skin lesions due to bacterial infections. Although insensitive to most of the antibiotics normally sold at aquarium stores, the infections can be effectively treated by adding chloramphenicol succinate to the quarantine tank at a concentration of 1 gm per 200 liters (this drug can only be obtained from a veterinarian). For minor infections, some positive results have been achieved using Furanace and neomycin for about 1 week. It can take up to 6 weeks for an infected rostrum or fins to heal.

Batfishes are also susceptible to infestations of external flukes from the genus *Neobenedenia*. To prevent fluke problems, it is highly recommended that all batfishes be quarantined for at least 2 weeks. During the quarantine process, treat the batfish with praziquantel by administering a 1- or 2-hour bath at a concentration of 10 to 15 parts per million. Obtaining praziquantel will also require the assistance of a veterinarian.

Other parasites that batfishes often succumb to in the aquarium are nematodes and pinworms. These animals live in the intestines and can cause ulcerations and perforations in stressed captive batfishes. Individuals suffering from heavy infestations often refuse to feed. The drug fenbendazole can be used to eradicate these parasites. It should be given orally, at a dosage of 100 mg/kg of batfish body weight. In order to weigh the fish, it is best to anesthetize it by placing it into some aquarium water that contains MS-222 at a concentration of 100 to 200 mg/liter. Alter a hypodermic syringe by removing the needle and replacing it with a piece of plastic tubing that has an inside diameter of 3 mm. Then place the appropriate amount of fenbendazole in the syringe and slide the tube into the batfish's mouth until it reaches the stomach. You can then inject the drug into the alimentary tract and place the batfish back into the tank. Over the next two days, you will find nematodes on the aquarium substrate. If the batfish is going to recover, it will begin to feed. Batfishes can also contract saltwater ich (*Cryptocaryon irritans*), which can easily be treated with copper.

Because batfishes have tubercles and bucklers that are easily entangled in nets, you should always catch your batfish with a specimen container. But avoid moving and disturbing these fishes unless absolutely necessary as they may go into shock.

Walking batfishes can be trained to take small pieces of fresh fish, scallop, shrimp, or squid from a feeding stick. Their mouths are small, so the food should be cut into small pieces. These fishes will also eat live brine shrimps, live black worms, and baby livebearers (e.g., guppies). If feeding live food like baby guppies, it is important that there be no places for these prey items to hide. When batfishes become fully accustomed to their new surroundings, they may start recognizing the aquarist as the food provider, moving to the front of the tank and taking food from his or her fingers.

Batfishes are best housed with other batfishes or with placid, slow-moving species. Angelfishes, butterflyfishes, puffers, and triggerfishes—groups that feed on benthic invertebrates—should never be kept with batfishes, as they are likely to nip at and damage them. Walking batfishes may also have a difficult time competing for food with more voracious predators like morays, groupers, snappers, hawkfishes, and wrasses. There are reports of batfishes living as long as 3 years in a public aquarium.

WALKING BATFISH SPECIES

Genus *Halieutichthys*

Halieutichthys aculeatus (Mitchill, 1818)
Common Names: Pancake Batfish, Spiny Batfish.
Maximum Length: 10 cm (3.9 in.).
Distribution: North Carolina, Bahamas, and northern Gulf of Mexico to northern South America.
Biology: The Pancake Batfish occurs at depths of less than 1 to 120 m (3.3 to 390 ft.). Around the Dry Tortugas, it is most common at depths of greater than 270 m (878 ft.). This fish occurs on open sandy bottoms and often covers itself with a thin layer of sand by the movements of its pectoral fins. At night, it emerges from the sand and actively hunts prey, moving forward by alternating motions of the pectoral fins.
Captive Care: As for all members of the genus, this species is reported to be more active either in a dimly lit tank or when all the lights are extinguished. For more information, see the Captive Care section in the family account, page 359.
Aquarium Size: 30 gal. **Temperature:** 21 to 26°C (70 to 78°F).
Aquarium Suitability Index: 2.
Remarks: The front margin of the Pancake Batfish's body is rounded and the pectoral fin bases are broad. The pectoral fins are often bright yellow; in young specimens, there are distinct black bars on these fins.

Halieutichthys aculeatus, Pancake Batfish: small species preferring dim light.

Ogcocephalus cubifrons, Polkadot Batfish: deworming may be needed.

Ogcocephalus cubifrons, Polkadot Batfish: color variant.

Ogcocephalus nasutus, Shortnose Batfish: will feed on fauna in live sand.

Ogcocephalus nasutus, Shortnose Batfish: rostrum shortens with age.

Genus *Ogcocephalus*

Ogcocephalus cubifrons (Richardson, 1836)
Common Name: Polkadot Batfish.
Maximum Length: 38 cm (15.0 in.).
Distribution: North Carolina to the northern Bahamas and northwest Florida, and south to Yucatan.
Biology: The Polkadot Batfish occurs on sand, mud, or rocky bottoms at depths of less than 1 to 70 m (3.3 to 228 ft.), but is common at depths of less than 10 m (33 ft.).
Captive Care: See the Captive Care section in the family account, page 359.
Aquarium Size: 75 gal. **Temperature:** 22 to 27°C (72 to 80°F).
Aquarium Suitability Index: 2.
Remarks: The Polkadot Batfish has a short rostrum and either large brown spots or a netlike pattern on the pectoral fins. Some individuals have reddish orange or yellowish orange areas on the dorsum. The **Spotted Batfish** (*Ogcocephalus pantostictus*) **Bradbury, 1980** is a similar species known only from the north and western Gulf of Mexico. Its color pattern is like *O. cubifrons*, but there are some slight morphological differences (e.g., the head depth is more than 1.7 times the mouth width in *O. cubifrons*, and less than 1.7 times the mouth width in *O. pantostictus*). In the past, the Polkadot Batfish has been referred to as *Ogcocephalus radiatus*.

Ogcocephalus nasutus (Cuvier & Valenciennes, 1837)
Common Name: Shortnose Batfish.
Maximum Size: 38 cm (15.0 in.).
Distribution: South Florida and the Bahamas south to the mouth of the Amazon River.
Biology: The Shortnose Batfish occurs in lagoons and on fore-

reef slopes, at depths of less than 1 up to 275 m (3.3 to 894 ft.). It lives on sand and coral rubble, in seagrass meadows, and in turbid water on mud flats. In some areas, *O. nasutus* is reported to be most common on open bottoms with scattered shells and sparse vegetation. It often partially covers its body with substrate. Its diet consists primarily of bivalves, gastropods, and crabs (including *Emerita portoricensis*, parthenopids, and gonoplacids). It will also feed on polychaetes, barnacles, fishes (including juvenile pufferfishes), and bubble algae (*Valonia* spp.)—possibly mistaking the algae for snails. Their mollusk prey consists of small snails (including *Haminoea elegans, Mitrella nitens, Olivella* sp., and *Sinum perspectivum*) and bivalves (including *Corbula contracta* and *Tellina* sp.) that can be swallowed whole. The Shortnose Batfish has a lure, but stomach content analysis suggests that it is rarely if ever used for attracting prey; the majority of food items they ingest are algae, detritus, and filter feeders.

Captive Care: See the Captive Care section in the family account, page 359.
Aquarium Size: 75 gal. **Temperature:** 22 to 27°C (72 to 80°F).
Aquarium Suitability Index: 2.
Remarks: The color of *O. nasutus* varies from black to dark brown or grayish olive green overall, often with black spots on each shoulder. Some individuals have a red ventral surface and red lips. This species is most similar to *O. cubifrons* and *Ogcocephalus vespertilio*. *Ogcocephalus nasutus* differs from *O. cubifrons* in lacking the bright spots on the pectoral fins and from *O. vespertilio* in having a shorter rostrum, a narrower interorbital distance, and a lower modal count of pectoral rays (usually 12 to 13 in *O. nasutus*; 14 in *O. vespertilio*).

The **South American Batfish** (*Ogcocephalus vespertilio*) **Linnaeus, 1758** occurs on the coast of Brazil and Uruguay, from the Amazon River south to the La Plata River. It is an inshore species that has been collected as far as 1,300 km (2,080 mi.) up the Amazon River, suggesting that it could be kept in a freshwater aquarium. It is occasionally imported for the aquarium trade from Brazil. The **Oval Batfish** (*Ogcocephalus notatus*) (**Cuvier & Valenciennes, 1837**) is another endemic South American species that has been observed in river mouths, tidal creeks, and swamps and is reported from depths of 1.8 to 64 m (5.9 to 208 ft.). It is easily identified by its oval pupils (these structures are kidney-shaped in all other batfishes) and its lack of opercula over the gill openings.

Ogcocephalus parvus Longley & Hildebrand, 1940
Common Name: Roughback Batfish.
Maximum Length: 10 cm (3.9 in.).
Distribution: South Carolina south to Brazil, including the eastern Gulf of Mexico.
Biology: The Roughback Batfish is found at depths of less than 1 to 126 m (3.3 to 410 ft.), although it is most abundant at depths in excess of 29 m (94 ft.). It has been reported from sand, mud, and rocky substrates.
Captive Care: See the Captive Care section in the family account, page 359.
Aquarium Size: 75 gal. **Temperature:** 22 to 27°C (72 to 80°F).
Aquarium Suitability Index: 2.
Remarks: The Roughback Batfish has a short rostrum that projects upward and a rough body surface with prominent bucklers and a lumpy integument. The mouth is small relative to the head depth, the ends of the pectoral rays have fleshy, thickened pads on the bottoms of the fins, and the fin membranes are thick and opaque. This species usually has red lips. It is closely related to the **Gulf Batfish** (*Ogcocephalus declivirostris*) **Bradbury, 1980** from the Gulf of Mexico. The Gulf Batfish also has a short rostrum, but it slopes downward. In addition, the body contours of *O. declivirostris* are smoother, the mouth is wider, there are no fleshy pads on the ends of the pectoral fin rays, and the membrane between these rays is thin and transparent. *Ogcocephalus declivirostris* occurs at depths of 3.5 to 388 m (11 to 1,261 ft.).

References
Bradbury (1980), Humann (1994), Schleser (1994), Straughan (1970).

Ogcocephalus parvus, Roughback Batfish: note rough body surface.

Family Anomalopidae
Flashlight Fishes

Photoblepharon palperbratus, Onefin Flashlight Fish: a special-needs species with the ability to blink light from a bioluminescent organ beneath the eye.

In 1900, a scientist named Vordermann witnessed a fascinating phenomenon. He observed an unusual fish, which belonged to the Family Anomalopidae, produce a greenish light with an enigmatic organ. This organ was not new to science—it had been recognized and described on a member of this family in 1781, and was thought to protect the fish's eye from coral cuts. But until Vordermann described it, no one knew that the organ produced light. The light organ, called a photophore, is bean-shaped and occurs below each eye. Depending on the species, the fish can turn the photophore "off" or "on" either by raising or lowering a black membrane that veils the organ or by rotating the organ in its socket so that the light is no longer visible.

The light itself is produced by billions of luminescent bacteria that live in the photophore. The emitted light is apparently used by the fishes to aid in prey capture, to navigate, to communicate with conspecifics in the dark, and to deter or confuse would-be predators. What do the bacteria receive in return for brightening the lives of these fishes? They are supplied with nutrients—oxygen and sugar—present in the fishes' blood.

These fishes, commonly called flashlight or lantern fishes, are used by native fishermen and seafarers. In the Banda Sea, for example, fishermen catch flashlight fishes, then remove the photophores to use as fishing lures. In the Cook Islands, seafarers follow the eerie glow produced by shoals of flashlight fishes to navigate through reef passes at night. In a dimly lit tank of their own or among a community of other nocturnal species, the flashlight fishes can make an unforgettable aquarium display.

Biology

The fishes of the Family Anomalopidae, which contains five genera and six species, are coal black overall, with relatively large mouths and deeply incised, or forked, tails. They are gregarious, with most forming shoals in caves and shipwrecks during the day. For example, the Red Sea Flashlight Fish (*Photoblepharon steinitzi*) is reported to occur in groups numbering up to 200 individuals, with these groups typically refuging in caves on steep reef fronts during the day. Some members of the family inhabit deep water and may migrate into shallower depths under the cover of darkness. The flashlight fishes that inhabit shallow depths stray further from their diurnal haunts on moonless or cloudy nights, when ambient light levels are reduced.

The on-and-off blinking of the photophore may be used by these fishes to communicate with members of their own species. They have been observed to change their blinking rate when they encounter each other. For example, male-female pairs of Red Sea Flashlight Fish maintain small territories at night. When a conspecific approaches a territory, the female pair member extinguishes her light, swims toward the interloper, then suddenly uncovers her photophore when positioned right next to the intruding fish. Invariably, the intruding fish leaves the area in response to this display.

The light organ also functions to help a flashlight fish avoid becoming a predator's meal. A study of the Red Sea Flashlight Fish showed that the rate of blinking was normally around 2 to 3 blinks per minute, but increased to about 75 blinks per minute when the fish was agitated. This sudden increase in blinking may act to deter predators by startling or confusing them. These fishes have also been reported to engage in a behavior called the "blink and run." When a flashlight fish encounters a potential predator, it will swim off with its light on, then abruptly cover its photophore and dart off in another direction. When it is some distance from its original position, it will stop swimming and put its light "on" again. Imagine a group of 20 to 200 flashlight fishes doing this all at once. It would confuse any nocturnal predator. Also, an aggregation of these glowing fishes would provide a nocturnal predator with a very confusing target: it would be difficult for a piscivore to select a single fish from the glowing mass. This antipredation behavior seems to work, as the flashlight fishes are rarely found in the stomachs of piscivorous fishes.

If you have ever been night diving, you know what happens when an underwater light is turned on: all kinds of zooplankters are attracted to the source of illumination, swarming around the light like moths around a campfire. Likewise, the light produced by a group of flashlight fishes may attract the zooplankters on which these fishes feed.

Captive Care

The flashlight fishes vary in their ability to acclimate to aquarium life. The members of the genus *Photoblepharon* do reasonably well in captivity if certain requirements are met, while the more readily available members of the genus *Anomalops* are difficult to maintain for any length of time.

The flashlight fishes should be kept in medium to large tanks (a minimum size of 55 gallons). Because these fishes are very sensitive to light, it is imperative that they be provided with one or more dark hiding places in which to seek refuge. They are best housed in aquariums with reduced lighting. If both the tank and the room are always dark, it is possible to keep them in a tank with limited shelter. The flashlight fishes will have a more difficult time adjusting if the tank is in a high traffic area. The aquarium or room lights should never be turned on suddenly when the fishes are in total darkness. This will cause them to dash about the tank and possibly injure themselves.

These fishes are rarely aggressive toward each other and acclimate more readily if housed in small groups. Although they are best kept on their own, select nocturnal and nonaggressive species if you choose to place other fishes in an aquarium with them. You could include pinecone fishes, soldierfishes, certain cardinalfishes, and bigeyes. However, the flashlight fish should always be the first introduced to the nocturnal community tank and should be feeding and well acclimated before other tankmates are added.

One of the biggest challenges faced by the flashlight fishkeeper is getting them to feed. In most cases, live foods are necessary to catalyze a feeding response. These can include live brine shrimp, black worms, and baby guppies and mollies. If they begin to accept these foods, you can often switch them to pieces of krill, frozen brine shrimp, and frozen *Mysis* shrimp. It is not uncommon for the light emitted by the photophores to become dimmer after the fishes have been in captivity for some time. The health of the fish apparently affects the well-being of the bacteria. A vitamin supplement like Selco may reduce the likelihood that the light will lose intensity.

Although propagating flashlight fishes in captivity is a difficult task, there is a report of a pair of flashlight fishes having spawned soon after they were collected.

Flashlight Fish Species

Anomalops katoptron Bleeker, 1856
Common Names: Twofin Flashlight Fish, Great Flashlight Fish.
Maximum Length: 28 cm (11.0 in.).
Distribution: Indonesia, Malaysia, and the Philippines, east to the Tuamotus, north to southern Japan, and south to the Great Barrier Reef.
Biology: *Anomalops katoptron* is most often found on deep forereef slopes and in reef passes at depths of 20 to 400 m (65 to 1,300 ft.), but it has also been reported from tidepools. During the day, it is found in aggregations at the back of caves or in deep water. There are two forms of this fish—a shallow-water form (attains 10 cm [3.9 in.]) and a deep-water form (attains 28 cm [11.0 in.]). The shallow-water form has been reported at depths from 20 to 50 m (65 to 163 ft.), while the deep-water form occurs at a depth range of 200 to 400 m (650 to 1,300 ft.).

The Twofin Flashlight Fish is found in shallow, inshore waters around the Philippines during the cooler months of the year. At night, this species often occurs in schools of 20 to 50 individuals. It spends more time in the open on moonless nights or before the moon is out, and blinks its lights rapidly as it swims.
Captive Care: The Twofin Flashlight Fish is seen in the aquarium trade more often than any other member of its family. Unfortunately, it also tends to be more difficult to keep than members of the genus *Photoblepharon*. This may be the result of improper handling of *A. katoptron* during collection in the Philippines. For a better chance of keeping this species successfully, follow the suggestions in the Captive Care section in the family account, page 364.
Aquarium Size: 55 gal. **Temperature:** 22 to 26°C (72 to 78°F).
Aquarium Suitability Index: 2.
Remarks: This species is easily recognized by its two dorsal fins. It rotates its photophores within their sockets to "turn them off."

Kryptophanaron alfredi Silvester & Fowler, 1926
Common Name: Atlantic Flashlight Fish.
Maximum Length: 13 cm (5.1 in.).
Distribution: Cayman Islands, Jamaica, Puerto Rico, and Barbados.
Biology: The Atlantic Flashlight Fish lives along steep dropoffs, at depths of 18 to 200 m (59 to 650 ft.), migrating into shallower water on cloudy or moonless nights to feed. They move close to the substrate, using their photophores to locate the shrimps and small fishes on which they feed. Groups of these fish have been

Anomalops katoptron, Twofin Flashlight Fish: photophore turned "on."

Anomalops katoptron, Twofin Flashlight Fish: photophore turned "off."

Anomalops katoptron, Twofin Flashlight Fish: pelagic stage.

Kryptophanaron alfredi, Atlantic Flashlight Fish: rarely collected species.

Photoblepharon palperbratus, Onefin Flashlight Fish: good choice if available.

observed swimming around each other, with their light organs flashing, in what may be courtship behavior.
Captive Care: This species is reported to be more durable than its close relative, *Anomalops katoptron*, but it is rarely available to aquarists.
Aquarium Size: 55 gal. **Temperature:** 22 to 26°C (72 to 78°F).
Aquarium Suitability Index: 3.
Remarks: This species was originally described in 1907, with a second specimen not being collected until 1978. It has two dorsal fins and a line of reflective scales along the base of the dorsal and anal fins and along the lateral line. The photophore of *K. alfredi* can be rotated slightly and covered by a flap of skin, which prevents the light from being emitted.

Photoblepharon palperbratus (Boddaert, 1791)
Common Names: Onefin Flashlight Fish, Small Flashlight Fish, Le Petit Peugeot.
Maximum Length: 11 cm (4.3 in.).
Distribution: Philippines to the Society Islands, north to the Marshall Islands, south to the Great Barrier Reef and Rarotonga.
Biology: The Onefin Flashlight Fish is found on steep fore-reef dropoffs that have numerous caves and in reef passes at depths of 5 to 50 m (17 to 163 ft.). They live in groups, secreting themselves deep in these caves during the day and venturing out to feed on dark nights. When they leave the sanctuary of their diurnal hideouts, the aggregations disperse. On cloudy or moonless nights, individuals move up into shallow water to feed. The closely related Red Sea Flashlight Fish (*Photoblepharon steinitzi*) will form pairs in the intertidal area at high tide. They will defend a territory from conspecifics, driving off intruders. This species also occurs in small or large shoals and as solitary individuals at night. When groups meet one another along the reef face, the leading members of each group race towards each other and the groups intermingle, forming one large shoal.
Captive Care: This species is moderately hardy if the requirements listed in the Captive Care section in the family account (page 364) are met. These include a tank that is both outfitted with a large cave and dimly lit, or one that is in complete darkness all the time. Researchers studying the behavior of *Photoblepharon palperbratus* in the field and the laboratory reported that they "were maintained [in aquariums] without difficulty." (Of course, unlike those fishes available to North American hobbyists, the fish in this laboratory study did not have to deal with any shipping stress or improper handling by collectors, wholesalers, or retailers.)
Aquarium Size: 55 gal. **Temperature:** 22 to 26°C (72 to 78°F).
Aquarium Suitability Index: 3.
Remarks: *Photoblepharon palperbratus* has a single dorsal fin and a skin membrane that covers the eye. It is very similar to the **Red Sea Flashlight Fish (*Photoblepharon steinitzi*) Abe & Haneda, 1973**, which occurs in the Red Sea, southern Oman, the Comoro Islands, and the Maldives. The Onefin Flashlight Fish has one more pelvic fin ray, some differences in the form of the head bones, and an obvious white spot on the upper corner of the operculum. The Red Sea form is reported from shallower depths than *P. palperbratus* and is known to be sexually dimorphic, with the female in a pair being larger than the male. The females in territorial pairs are more aggressive than the males.

References
Kuiter & Debelius (1994), Hemdal (1992), McCosker & Rosenblatt (1987), Morin et al. (1975), Randall (1995).

Family Monocentridae
Pineapple Fishes

Cleidopus gloriamaris, Pineapple Fish: given a quiet and dimly lit setting, these unusual cave dwellers can make highly appealing aquarium specimens.

HANDSOMELY ARMORED AND BEARING BIOLUMINESCENT markings on their jaws, members of the Family Monocentridae, the pineapple fishes, are uniquely designed denizens of the ocean that can make a remarkable aquarium display.

Biology

This family is comprised of two genera and three species of very unusual fishes. They are residents of coral and rocky reefs in the warm temperate and tropical waters of the Indo-Pacific. The body of a pineapple fish is covered with heavy scales that are adorned with a central spine directed towards the tail. Each scale is trimmed in black. The pineapple fishes have large, stout fin spines that can be locked in an erect position. These characteristics make the members of this family unappetizing to all but the most voracious piscivores. One of their most interesting features is a patch of skin near the edge of each side of the mouth. This skin acts as a growing substrate for bioluminescent bacteria. The bacteria glow green in the dark and are used to help locate food at night and, possibly, to communicate with conspecifics.

During the day, pineapple fishes live in caves and under ledges. They often occur in small aggregations, but at night they disperse over the surrounding sandy bottoms to feed.

Pineapple Fish Species

Cleidopus gloriamaris, Pineapple Fish (juvenile): long-lived with the right care; best kept in small groups and fed live foods, at least when first acquired.

Captive Care

A tank with a group of pineapple fishes makes an excellent display for both day and night viewing. Two of the three members of this family show up in the trade on occasion and can be successfully maintained in the home aquarium if several requirements are met. The most important of these is that they be housed with passive tankmates. In fact, they do best when they are the only species kept in the tank. Although they are not normally a threat to their tankmates, adult individuals might eat small heterospecifics. They may have difficulty competing for food with aggressive feeders like groupers, snappers, and wrasses. And they should not be kept with cleaner fishes, which tend to annoy pineapple fishes by persistently picking at them.

If possible, pineapple fishes should also be provided with a sizable cave or ledge for shelter during the day, with plenty of swimming room around the entrance of the hiding place. If you can't provide a suitable hiding place, make sure the tank has a low light level. Finally, live foods may be needed to elicit a feeding response.

The large fin spines of pineapple fishes will often puncture shipping bags and may pierce the skin of a careless aquarist. The spines are also prone to becoming entangled in mesh nets.

Genus *Cleidopus*

Cleidopus gloriamaris De Vis, 1882
Common Name: Pineapple Fish.
Maximum Length: 22 cm (8.7 in.), more commonly attain a length of 8 to 12 cm (3.1 to 4.7 in.).
Distribution: Western and eastern Australia.
Biology: The Pineapple Fish is usually found in warm temperate water on rocky reefs, but can also occur on coral reefs. It is most common on coastal reefs and in estuaries, where it is found at depths that range from 20 to 250 m (65 to 813 ft.). This species hunts on open sandy bottoms at night and feeds mainly on small, swarming shrimps. Its light organs may enable it to locate food in the dark or allow individuals to communicate with each other and coordinate their movements. Even the smallest juveniles reported to date already have light organs. This species occurs singly or in small groups.
Captive Care: *Cleidopus gloriamaris* can be successfully kept if it is fed live shrimps—including small grass, mysid, and brine shrimps—and kept in an aquarium that contains other peaceful fish species. Some individuals will also accept baby livebearers (e.g. guppies) and live blackworms, and can even be switched to chopped frozen seafoods once they have fully adjusted to aquarium life. One way to switch these fish to nonliving foods is to mix the two kinds of food. In its excitement to capture the live prey, a Pineapple Fish will often ingest the nonliving food. Over time, you should be able to wean them off live food. If you are having difficulty tempting Pineapple Fish to feed during the day, try adding their food when the lights are extinguished.

These fish are inactive during the day, spending most of their time in a corner of the tank or slowly moving around the aquarium. If provided with a large enough cave, they will hang inside it. This species has been kept as long as 10 years in captivity and is reported to do best when kept in small groups.
Aquarium Size: 55 gal. **Temperature:** 20 to 24°C (68 to 76°F).
Aquarium Suitability Index: 4.
Remarks: The Pineapple Fish can be yellow or yellowish orange overall. Its light organ is on the side of the lower jaw that is not visible when the mouth is closed. The *C. gloriamaris* population from western Australia is distinct from the eastern Australia population; they may represent two species. Individuals from western Australia have 10 midline scales (there are 11 in the eastern form) and smaller spines.

Adult *Monocentris japonicus*, Pinecone Fish: somewhat uncommon in the aquarium trade, but a good choice for a passive species tank with a large cave.

Genus *Monocentris*

Monocentris japonicus (Houttuyn, 1782)
Common Names: Pinecone Fish, Japanese Pineapple Fish.
Maximum Length: 17 cm (6.7 in.).
Distribution: Red Sea and East Africa to the Pitcairn group, north to southern Japan, and south to Lord Howe and Rapa Islands. It is common in southern Japan.
Biology: The Pinecone Fish is most often found on rocky reefs, at depths of 20 to 200 m (65 to 650 ft.). The young, which occur singly and are very secretive, can be found at depths as shallow as 3 m (10 ft.). Juveniles hide in crevices and under ledges. Adult Pinecone Fish usually occur singly or in pairs, but there is one location in Japan where they can be found in large aggregations of up to 100 individuals. Adults are inactive during the day, hiding in caves or near soft corals. The Pinecone Fish and Pineapple Fish occur together off the coast of eastern Australia.
Captive Care: Although not as common in the aquarium trade as *C. gloriamaris*, this species is equally suited to captivity. It should be kept in a species tank that has a large cave in which it can hide. It is not aggressive toward other fishes—or even members of its own species—and does best if kept in small groups.
Aquarium Size: 55 gal. **Temperature:** 18 to 24°C (64 to 76°F).
Aquarium Suitability Index: 4.

Remarks: The color of the Pinecone Fish varies from pale to dark yellow, and it has a light organ at the corners of its mouth. It can be separated easily from *C. gloriamaris* by its profile—*M. japonicus* is more rounded.

References
K. Imai (personal communication), Kuiter (1992, 1993), Randall (1995).

Monocentris japonicus, Pinecone Fish: juvenile specimen from Japan.

SUBFAMILY HOLOCENTRINAE
SQUIRRELFISHES

During the day, the coral reef teems with an immense variety of fish species that display a variety of lifestyles. As dusk approaches, many of these fishes disappear into the sanctuary of the reef and are replaced by a different set of species. Some of the most ubiquitous members of the night shift are from the Family Holocentridae, known commonly as squirrelfishes (Subfamily Holocentrinae) and soldierfishes (Subfamily Myripristinae). These fishes also show up in aquarium stores, but are often passed over by the uninitiated hobbyist because they will hide both when newly introduced to a tank and when there is a lot of commotion in the room—as in a retail store. Many species will lose this shyness in the home aquarium, becoming bolder and adding an unusual splash of crimson to the tank.

Although not as ornately colored as other members of the reef fish community, the holocentrids are mainly red—a color that is relatively rare in other fishes from this biome. In the majority of squirrelfishes, red is the most important component of their chromatic attire. Although it is a bold, conspicuous color under aquarium lights, the red spectrum in their natural habitat is filtered out by the dense water medium at relatively shallow depths, making it less obvious as one moves down the reef. In fact, if you get deep enough, a red squirrelfish actually looks gray, not red. Many red fishes are also most active after dark. One other interesting holocentrid trait is that they produce audible clicking and grunting noises when they interact with conspecifics or other fish species. These noises are produced by the swim bladder and associated muscles.

Classification and Biology

The subfamily Holocentrinae is comprised of 4 genera and approximately 30 species. When it comes to nomenclature, the squirrelfishes have gone through a number of years of taxonomic flux. This may lead to confusion if you examine the genus names used in identification guides that have not been recently updated. At one time, most of the squirrelfishes were placed in the genus *Holocentrus*. Subsequently, many of these species were moved to the genus *Adioryx*, but all the members of this genus have since been moved to the genus *Sargocentron*. In older books, you will also see the genus *Flammeo*, rather than the genus *Neoniphon*, which is currently in use.

The squirrelfishes spend their days hiding within the holes, caves, overhangs, and crevices that pervade the reef. They do vary in how secretive they are, ranging from those that hide deep in the reef to those that often hang near the entrance or even make short excursions away from their sanctuaries. When the sun begins to set, the squirrelfishes begin to leave their homes and hunt in the surrounding environs—including both soft and hard substrates. Some species also feed on the invertebrates that share their diurnal haunts. The most important components of squirrelfish diets are crustaceans, although other motile invertebrates and fish are minor constituents. Although most of their prey is taken from the substrate, they also capture larger zooplankton near the ocean floor.

Squirrelfish species vary in their social structure. Some species occur singly during both the night and day, while others are more commonly observed in aggregations—at least when refuging during the day. Individuals that comprise these groups usually disperse onto the reef at night. Although these fishes are common on coral reefs around the world, there is a paucity of information available on their reproductive behavior.

Holocentrus rufus, Longspine Squirrelfish: a larger species that will do best in a reasonably spacious system with places where it can seek refuge.

Holocentrus rufus, Longspine Squirrelfish: unusual daytime aggregation in a Caribbean crevice. The group will emerge at dusk to begin feeding.

Captive Care

Squirrelfishes need to be housed in medium- to large-sized tanks, depending on the species you intend to keep. Because these fishes are nocturnal, they need plenty of good shelter sites in which to hide when the lights are on. For some species, a large cave or overhang should be created to insure that their refuging needs are met. The majority of species will adjust to being fed during the day and will begin spending more time in the open as they habituate to their new home; in time, some squirrelfishes can become great pets. Some members of this subfamily, however, are more secretive and will hide incessantly when the lights are on, no matter how long they have been in the aquarium. For example, the Reef Squirrelfish (*Sargocentron coruscum*) and the Fineline Squirrelfish (*Sargocentron microstoma*) are both very secretive species.

Squirrelfishes are usually not very selective when it comes to their aquarium diets. They will eat a wide-range of food items, including any chopped fresh or frozen seafood, live and frozen brine shrimp, small feeder fish, live grass shrimp, and frozen preparations. Usually squirrelfishes will race out to grab passing food particles, quickly returning to their hideouts after ingesting a morsel. It may take a week or more before they come out to feed when the lights are on, but most do so eventually. If an individual refuses food when the tank is illuminated, try adding it when the lights are off. It may help to place a red light, either incandescent or fluorescent, over the tank when all other lights are extinguished, to see if a shy squirrelfish comes out to feed. Often, nonliving food introduced to the tank must be moving in the water column in order for a squirrelfish to ingest it. Any food items that come to rest on the bottom will usually go unnoticed and uneaten.

These fishes are usually not aggressive towards heterospecifics, with the possible exception of fishes that attempt to enter one of their preferred refuges or a nearby hole or crevice. Some squirrelfishes actively defend their hiding places from intrusion. Squirrelfish of the same species may "bicker" amongst themselves if placed in a smaller tank or in an aquarium with limited hiding places. They may also dominate their close relatives, the soldierfishes. Larger squirrelfishes may prey on fishes that are small enough to be swallowed whole, although such predation events are relatively rare.

Although squirrelfishes are not a threat to sessile invertebrates, they will feed on a variety of motile invertebrates like worms, crustaceans, and serpent stars. If kept in a brightly lit reef aquarium, these fishes are also likely to spend almost all of their time under cover.

Many squirrelfishes have spines on their heads and gills that can easily become entangled in aquarium nets; use plastic specimen containers when capturing one of these fishes. The aquarist should exercise special care when handling those squirrelfishes that have a large preopercular spine. Not only can this ornamentation produce a nasty puncture wound, in some species there is also venom associated with the spine that will cause intense pain.

SQUIRRELFISH SPECIES

Genus *Holocentrus*

Holocentrus ascensionis (Osbeck, 1765)
Common Name: Squirrelfish.
Maximum Length: 30 cm (11.8 in.).
Distribution: New York, Bermuda, and northern Gulf of Mexico to Brazil, to St. Paul's Rocks, Ascension, and St. Helena in the Eastern Atlantic.
Biology: The Squirrelfish occurs on patch reefs, the reef flat, the reef face, and at the top of reef walls at depths of 1 to 175 m (3.3 to 569 ft.). This species feeds primarily on crabs, including clinging crabs, clown crabs, and swimming crabs. To a lesser degree, it feeds on snapping shrimp, penaeid shrimp, polychaetes, gastropods, and isopods. It apparently feeds more in seagrass habitats than other squirrelfishes in the tropical Atlantic. This species occurs singly or in small- to medium-sized groups that are often seen during the day at the entrances of crevices or at the base of gorgonians. At about 6:00 P.M., Squirrelfish aggregations disperse and individuals move out over the adjacent sand flats to feed. These individuals return to their daytime haunts at about 6:30 A.M. The Squirrelfish is sometimes host to parasitic isopods, which attach to their heads.

Holocentrus ascensionis, Squirrelfish: will eat ornamental shrimp and crabs.

Captive Care: The Squirrelfish is relatively common in the aquarium trade. It can be kept in small groups in larger tanks and usually will not bother fish tankmates—unless they are significantly smaller in size. This species will eat motile invertebrates, including ornamental crustaceans. It can be kept in a shallow-water or deep-water reef tank, if provided with suitable hiding places. It will spend more time in the open if the tank has subdued lighting.
Aquarium Size: 100 gal. **Temperature:** 22 to 27°C (72 to 80°F).
Aquarium Suitability Index: 4.
Remarks: The spinous dorsal fin of this species is yellow, especially the anterior portion. When aggregating during the day, *H. ascensionis* often adopts a blotched color pattern.

Holocentrus rufus (Walbaum, 1792)
Common Name: Longspine Squirrelfish.
Maximum Length: 28 cm (11.0 in.).
Distribution: South Florida and Bermuda south to Venezuela.
Biology: The Longspine Squirrelfish is found on rocky and coral reefs, typically on the reef face and fore-reef slopes, at depths of 1 to 125 m (3.3 to 406 ft.). It hangs near crevice entrances or hides in holes during the day. At night, it forages on nearby sand and reef substrates. It feeds mainly on crabs—including clinging crabs, swimming crabs, porcelain crabs, and xanthid crabs—gastropods, serpent stars, and shrimps—including snapping and penaeid shrimps. The sound production of this fish (clicking and grunting) peaks at dusk and dawn. This is typically a solitary species that will defend its diurnal hiding place(s) aggressively from conspecifics and other fish species.
Captive Care: The Longspine Squirrelfish needs adequate cover and will be a more conspicuous member of the fish community if kept in a dimly lit tank. It will feed on fresh and frozen pieces of seafood, frozen brine shrimp, *Mysis* shrimp, and even pellet foods as they fall to the bottom or are transported around the tank by water currents. More than one Longspine can be kept in the same tank, as long as the aquarium is of substantial size with numerous hiding places. Although they can be housed with similar-sized fishes, they will eat smaller tankmates, including ornamental crustaceans. They can be kept in a reef tank if provided with enough swimming space and shelter sites. In shallow-water reef aquariums, they are likely to spend more time in or near their preferred hiding places.
Aquarium Size: 100 gal. **Temperature:** 22 to 27°C (72 to 80°F).
Aquarium Suitability Index: 4.
Remarks: This species has white triangles on the tips of the spinous dorsal fin.

Genus *Neoniphon*

Neoniphon argenteus (Valenciennes, 1831)
Common Name: Clearfin Squirrelfish.
Maximum Length: 22 cm (8.7 in.).
Distribution: East Africa to the Marquesas, north to the Ryukyus, south to Samoa and the Tuamotus.
Biology: The Clearfin Squirrelfish is most frequently found on reef flats and fore-reef slopes at depths of less than 1 to at least 50 m (3.3 to 163 ft.)—it is most common at depths greater than 15 m (49 ft.). This species is often found hanging within and above thickets of branching staghorn corals (*Acropora* spp.). It usually occurs in small groups and often forms heterospecific aggregations with the Bloodspot Squirrelfish (*Neoniphon sammara*).

Holocentrus rufus, Longspine Squirrelfish: displays best in subdued lighting.

Neoniphon argenteus, Clearfin Squirrelfish: stunning metallic coloration.

Neoniphon aurolineatus, Goldlined Squirrelfish: a rarely seen beauty.

Neoniphon marianus, Longjaw Squirrelfish: small, colorful Caribbean fish.

Captive Care: Although this species is not beautifully marked, its metallic silver coloration is quite stunning under aquarium lighting. The Clearfin Squirrelfish will readily acclimate to captivity. It can be housed in a dimly lit tank or an aquarium with bright illumination. It should be provided with appropriate hiding places—a stand of faux or live staghorn corals will provide a natural-looking microhabitat. The Clearfin Squirrelfish can be kept in groups with conspecifics or with the Bloodspot Squirrelfish (*N. sammara*) in a larger aquarium.
Aquarium Size: 75 gal. **Temperature:** 22 to 27°C (72 to 80°F).
Aquarium Suitability Index: 4.
Remarks: The dorsal fin membrane of this species lacks black markings and is mainly clear (there are some red markings toward the outer edge of the fin).

Neoniphon aurolineatus (Liénard, 1839)
Common Name: Goldlined Squirrelfish.
Maximum Length: 23 cm (9.1 in.).
Distribution: Comoro Island east to the Hawaiian Islands, north to southern Japan, and south to the Great Barrier Reef (mainly around islands).
Biology: The Goldlined Squirrelfish is found on deep fore-reef slopes. It is most often encountered at depths in excess of 30 m (98 ft.) and has been observed as deep as 160 m (520 ft.). No data is available on its food habits, although it probably feeds principally on crustaceans.
Captive Care: *Neoniphon aurolineatus* is rarely seen in the aquarium trade, but is one of the most desirable members of the subfamily to display because of its pleasing color pattern. It should be housed in a dimly lit tank and provided with numerous hiding places.

Aquarium Size: 75 gal. **Temperature:** 22 to 27°C (72 to 80°F).
Aquarium Suitability Index: 4.
Remarks: This is the only member of this genus that is pinkish silver overall with gold stripes, having a last dorsal spine that is shorter than the one before it. The Goldlined Squirrelfish was once referred to as *Flammeo scythrops*.

Neoniphon marianus (Cuvier, 1829)
Common Name: Longjaw Squirrelfish.
Maximum Length: 17 cm (6.7 in.).
Distribution: Florida Keys and Bahamas south to Venezuela and Trinidad.
Biology: The Longjaw Squirrelfish occurs on reef faces and fore-reef slopes at depths of 1 to 120 m (3.3 to 390 ft.), but is most common at depths greater than 30 m (98 ft.). For example, in the U.S. Virgin Islands, it is the most common member of the family at depths of 33 to 66 m (107 to 215 ft.). It is usually solitary and will hang under helmet-shaped Boulder Star Coral (*Montastrea annularis*) or between coral colonies during the day, but it never strays far from a hiding place at this time. At about 6:30 P.M., this species moves out over nearby sand flats or sand patches, where it feeds mainly on shrimps and crabs. It also eats mantis shrimp larvae and copepods. At about 6:00 A.M., the Longjaw returns to its diurnal shelter site.
Captive Care: *Neoniphon marianus* is one of the most colorful squirrelfishes. It does best if housed in a dimly lit tank and provided with several good crevices in which to hide. Only one Longjaw Squirrelfish should be kept per tank. Although they will rarely bother fishes of their own size, they have been known to pester smaller tankmates. They will eat ornamental crustaceans and some other motile invertebrates, but can be kept with corals.

Neoniphon opercularis, Blackfin Squirrelfish: large, handsome species.

Neoniphon sammara, Bloodspot Squirrelfish: better choice for well-lit tanks.

Aquarium Size: 75 gal. **Temperature:** 22 to 27°C (72 to 80°F).
Aquarium Suitability Index: 4.

Neoniphon opercularis (Valenciennes, 1831)
Common Name: Blackfin Squirrelfish.
Maximum Length: 35 cm (13.7 in.).
Distribution: East Africa to the Tuamotus, north to the Ryukyus, and south to New Caledonia.
Biology: The Blackfin Squirrelfish occurs on subtidal reef flats and lagoon reefs, back reefs, reef faces, and outer-reef slopes at depths of 6 to 50 m (20 to 163 ft.). It is most abundant at depths greater than 20 m (65 ft.). This species occurs singly or in small loose groups, usually in areas with rich coral growth. The dorsal fin is black with white-tipped spines and white spots at the base of the fin. It has been suggested that when the fin is suddenly erected it may resemble the mouth of a large fish. This display may be used to startle potential predators.
Captive Care: *Neoniphon opercularis* is not common in the aquarium trade. It should be housed in a dimly lit tank with long overhangs under which it can hide. It will eat ornamental crustaceans and small fishes.
Aquarium Size: 100 gal. **Temperature:** 22 to 27°C (72 to 80°F).
Aquarium Suitability Index: 4.

Neoniphon sammara (Forsskål, 1775)
Common Names: Bloodspot Squirrelfish, Blooddrop Squirrelfish.
Maximum Length: 32 cm (12.6 in.), usually less than 26 cm (10.2 in.).
Distribution: Red Sea to the Marquesas and Ducie Islands, north to southern Japan and the Hawaiian Islands, south to Lord Howe Island.
Biology: The Bloodspot Squirrelfish occurs on coastal reefs, patch reefs in the seagrass meadows of sheltered lagoons, back reefs, subtidal reef flats, reef faces, and fore-reef slopes, at depths of 2 to 46 m (7 to 150 ft.). It feeds almost exclusively on benthic crustaceans, hunting isopods near its diurnal shelter sites during the day and dispersing over the nearby reef at dusk to hunt snapping and caridean shrimps and swimming and xanthid crabs. Fishes, polychaetes, and small snails have also been found in their stomachs. The Bloodspot Squirrelfish also incidentally ingests small pieces of coral as it attempts to extract coral crabs (*Trapezia* sp.) from between the scleractinian branches. Although it mainly feeds at night, it will also consume isopods and small crabs during the day. One study reported that the average number of prey consumed per day was 5.2, while an average of 9.5 prey was consumed at night. This species occurs singly or in small aggregations during the day, at which time it usually hangs in the water near branching corals, crevices, or a cave. It tends to be less secretive than the Blackfin Squirrelfish (*N. opercularis*).
Captive Care: *Neoniphon sammara* is better suited for brightly lit tanks, as it tends to spend more time in the open. It should be provided with a crevice or cave to hide in and can be kept in small groups if your tank is large enough. It will eat crustacean tankmates and small fishes. It might also wrest the coral crabs from stony coral colonies. On the positive side, this species will consume small mantis shrimp and may eat undesirable bristleworms.
Aquarium Size: 100 gal. **Temperature:** 22 to 27°C (72 to 80°F).
Aquarium Suitability Index: 4.
Remarks: The Bloodspot Squirrelfish has a red blotch on the front of the spinous dorsal fin. After dark, the color of this species changes—it adopts dark bars on the upper part of the sides and the lines become less distinct.

Sargocentron caudimaculatum, Tailspot Squirrelfish: note preopercular spine.

Sargocentron cornutum, Threespot Squirrelfish: a noted daytime recluse.

Genus *Sargocentron*

Sargocentron caudimaculatum (Rüppell, 1838)
Common Name: Tailspot Squirrelfish.
Maximum Length: 25 cm (9.8 in.).
Distribution: Red Sea to the Line, Marquesas, and Tuamotu Islands, north to southern Japan and Marcus Island, and south to the southern Great Barrier Reef.
Biology: The Tailspot Squirrelfish is found on lagoon patch reefs, reef faces, fore-reef slopes, and dropoffs at depths of 5 to over 40 m (16 to 130 ft.). It occurs singly or in small to large groups and stays under ledges or in caves during the day. When it moves from cover to feed at night, the white caudal peduncle and tail become red like the rest of the body.
Captive Care: This is not an overly secretive species, making it a suitable choice for a large fish tank. It should be provided with a large cave or overhang for shelter. The Tailspot Squirrelfish will eat small fishes and crustaceans, including ornamental shrimps.
Aquarium Size: 100 gal. **Temperature:** 22 to 27°C (72 to 80°F).
Aquarium Suitability Index: 4.
Remarks: The Tailspot Squirrelfish has a long preopercular spine. Unlike the Giant Squirrelfish (*Sargocentron spiniferum*), which has a similar spine, the posterior part of the body and tail of the Tailspot is white during the day.

Sargocentron cornutum (Bleeker, 1853)
Common Name: Threespot Squirrelfish.
Maximum Length: 17 cm (6.7 in.).
Distribution: Indonesia to the Solomon Islands, north to the Philippines, and south to the Great Barrier Reef.
Biology: This species occurs on reef faces, outer-reef slopes, and dropoffs, often in areas of rich hard coral growth, at depths of 6 to at least 40 m (20 to 130 ft.). It occurs singly or in small groups, refuging among the branches of stony corals or in crevices during the day.
Captive Care: This is a secretive species that will spend most of its time hiding among the reef decor when the tank is illuminated. It is more likely to venture into the open in a dimly lit tank, making it unsuitable for the shallow reef aquarium. This species will eat smaller ornamental crustaceans.
Aquarium Size: 75 gal. **Temperature:** 22 to 27°C (72 to 80°F).
Aquarium Suitability Index: 4.
Remarks: *Sargocentron cornutum* has a dark brown to black spot on the base of the caudal, soft dorsal, and anal fins (the spot on the anal base may be quite small). It also has an elongate white spot on the membranes between most of the spines, and white triangles near the tips of each dorsal spine.

Sargocentron coruscum (Poey, 1860)
Common Name: Reef Squirrelfish.
Maximum Length: 13 cm (5.1 in.).
Distribution: Florida and Bermuda south to Venezuela.
Biology: The Reef Squirrelfish lives on rocky and coral reefs, in patch reef habitats, on reef faces, and on fore-reef slopes at depths of 1 to 30 m (3.3 to 98 ft.). It is often observed in tight groups, hovering between coral heads during the day. If threatened, it will dart into a nearby hiding place. At night, it disperses over the nearby sand flats to hunt shrimps and a variety of crabs, including clinging and swimming crabs.
Captive Care: If your tank is large enough, this species can be kept either in small groups or on its own. Its diminutive proportions mean that it is better suited to smaller aquariums. Pro-

vide the Reef Squirrelfish with a ledge or cave and do not keep it with overly aggressive fish species. It can be kept in a shallow-water or deep-water reef aquarium, but will spend more time in full view in the latter setting. This holocentrid is not common in the aquarium trade.
Aquarium Size: 55 gal. **Temperature:** 22 to 27°C (72 to 80°F).
Aquarium Suitability Index: 4.
Remarks: This species has a black blotch on the dorsal fin that starts near the first spine and extends to the third or fourth spine.

Sargocentron diadema (Lacépède, 1801)
Common Name: Crown Squirrelfish.
Maximum Length: 17 cm (6.7 in.).
Distribution: Red Sea to the Hawaiian, Marquesas, and Tuamotu Islands, north to the Ryukyus, and south to Lord Howe Island.
Biology: The Crown Squirrelfish is a resident of lagoon reefs, subtidal reef flats, the reef face, fore-reef slopes, and dropoffs at depths of less than 2 to over 30 m (7 to 98 ft.). It typically occurs in clear water, in areas with either rich coral growth or scattered coral heads. It is found singly or in small groups, and often swims near a hiding place. It will sometimes mix with other members of its family, including the Blackspot Squirrelfish (*Sargocentron melanospilos*).

The Crown Squirrelfish feeds on gastropods and polychaete worms, but it also consumes crustaceans—including xanthid crabs, hermit crabs, isopods, and snapping shrimps, as well as coral-dwelling bivalves. Although it mainly feeds under the cover of darkness, it will also ingest prey during the day. One study found that it consumed an average of 4.5 prey items during the day and 10.8 at night.

Captive Care: This attractive squirrelfish is relatively common in the aquarium trade. It is usually shy at first, but with time it will become bolder and spend more time in the open when the lights are on. It can be kept in a reef tank, although it will be a more conspicuous part of the fish community in a tank with less lighting. Provide it with good hiding places and do not keep it with ornamental shrimp. The Crown Squirrelfish will eat bristleworms, including the notorious Fireworm (*Hermodice carunculata*).
Aquarium Size: 75 gal. **Temperature:** 22 to 27°C (72 to 80°F).
Aquarium Suitability Index: 4.
Remarks: The Crown Squirrelfish is very similar to the Samurai Squirrelfish (*Sargocentron ittodai*) and the Hawaiian Squirrelfish (*Sargocentron xantherythrum*), but can be separated by the color of its spinous dorsal fin. In the Crown Squirrelfish, it is dark red to almost black, with white-tipped spines and a white line running through the middle of the fin.

Sargocentron coruscum, Reef Squirrelfish: nocturnal coloration.

Sargocentron coruscum, Reef Squirrelfish: daytime coloration.

Sargocentron diadema, Crown Squirrelfish: will eat bristleworms.

Sargocentron ensiferum, Yellowstriped Squirrelfish: deep-water species.

Sargocentron ittodai, Samurai Squirrelfish: very similar to Crown Squirrelfish.

Sargocentron ensiferum (Jordan & Evermann, 1903)
Common Name: Yellowstriped Squirrelfish.
Maximum Length: 25 cm (9.8 in.).
Distribution: Hawaiian Islands, Japan, South China Sea, New Caledonia, and the Pitcairn Group.
Biology: The Yellowstriped Squirrelfish is found on the reef face and fore-reef slopes from 18 m (59 ft.) to depths greater than 40 m (130 ft.). It is usually found in aggregations under ledges, in caves, and among stony corals. In certain locations, it can be found in the same habitat with the similar Goldlined Squirrelfish (*Neoniphon aurolineatus*).
Captive Care: This squirrelfish should be housed in a dimly lit tank provided with numerous hiding places. It is a larger species that will consume a wide range of ornamental crustaceans and fishes small enough to be ingested whole. It should not be housed in a shallow-water reef aquarium because of the bright lighting associated with this type of tank.
Aquarium Size: 75 gal. **Temperature:** 22 to 27°C (72 to 80°F).
Aquarium Suitability Index: 4.
Remarks: *Sargocentron ensiferum* has a yellow spinous dorsal fin with a red margin. There are narrow yellow lines on the side of the body that become white as they move toward the ventrum; the first dorsal spine is about the same length as the second; and there is a stout spine along the edge of the operculum, just behind the eye.

Sargocentron ittodai (Jordan & Fowler, 1903)
Common Name: Samurai Squirrelfish.
Maximum Length: 20 cm (7.9 in.).
Distribution: Red Sea to the Marquesas Islands and Great Barrier Reef, north to southern Japan (where it is common).
Biology: The Samurai Squirrelfish is most often found on outer lagoon reefs, reef faces, and outer-reef slopes. Although it has been recorded at depths of 5 to 70 m (16 to 228 ft.), it usually occurs deeper than 16 m (52 ft.). This is a solitary species that spends the days under ledges and in caves.
Captive Care: The Samurai Squirrelfish is not as common in the aquarium trade as the closely related Crown Squirrelfish (*S. diadema*). Only one specimen should be housed per tank, and it should not be trusted with very small fishes. It is also a threat to ornamental shrimps. The Samurai can be kept in a shallow-water or deep-water reef tank, but will spend more time in the open in an aquarium with reduced lighting.
Aquarium Size: 75 gal. **Temperature:** 21 to 27°C (70 to 80°F).
Aquarium Suitability Index: 4.
Remarks: This species is most similar to the Fineline Squirrelfish (*Sargocentron microstoma*), but differs in having a slightly deeper body and in the coloration of the spinous dorsal fin. *Sargocentron ittodai* has a white band in the middle of the spinous dorsal fin, with white tips on the spines and a dark blotch on the membranes between the first and second spines.

Sargocentron melanospilos (Bleeker, 1858)
Common Name: Blackspot Squirrelfish.
Maximum Length: 25 cm (9.8 in.).
Distribution: South Africa to Samoa, north to the Ryukyus, and south to New Caledonia.
Biology: The Blackspot Squirrelfish is found at the base of large lagoon patch reefs and clear coastal reefs at depths of 3 to at least 33 m (7 to 107 ft.). It usually occurs in areas with rich coral growth. This species is usually solitary, although it may occur in pairs or mix with other holocentrid species. It is often seen hang-

ing near the entrance of a crevice during the day, but moves out over the sand or reef to feed at night.

Captive Care: This species is uncommon in nature, so it is not often seen in the aquarium trade. It should be kept singly in a tank with plenty of suitable cover. It can be kept in a deep-water reef tank, but it will consume ornamental crustaceans.

Aquarium Size: 75 gal. **Temperature:** 22 to 27°C (72 to 80°F).

Aquarium Suitability Index: 4.

Remarks: *Sargocentron melanospilos* has three black spots—one on the caudal fin base, one on the anal fin base, and one on the dorsal fin base. It also has a very small spot on the pectoral fin base.

Sargocentron microstoma (Günther, 1859)

Common Name: Fineline Squirrelfish.

Maximum Length: 20 cm (7.9 in.).

Distribution: Chagos and Maldives, east to the Hawaiian Islands, Marquesas, and Tuamotu Islands, north to the southern Ryukyus, and south to Austral Island.

Biology: The Fineline Squirrelfish occurs on lagoon reefs, reef flats, reef faces, and fore-reef slopes at depths of less than 1 to 183 m (3.3 to 595 ft.). It feeds mainly on crustaceans, including crabs, shrimps, and mantis shrimps. It also eats small bony fishes (including *Chromis* damsels), gastropods, and polychaete worms.

Captive Care: *Sargocentron microstoma* is occasionally encountered in the aquarium trade. It is a shy species, but will spend more time in the open if kept in a tank with reduced illumination. It should not be housed with overly aggressive species. It can be kept in a deep-water reef tank. Provide the Fineline Squirrelfish with good hiding places, and do not keep it with ornamental shrimps or very small fishes.

Aquarium Size: 75 gal. **Temperature:** 22 to 27°C (72 to 80°F).

Aquarium Suitability Index: 4.

Remarks: The Fineline Squirrelfish differs from similar species in that the inner part of the spinous dorsal fin is clear with white vertical lines, red near the fin's distal edge and base, and white on the spine tips. The operculum has an orange tip.

Sargocentron punctatissimum (Cuvier, 1829)

Common Names: Speckled Squirrelfish, Peppered Squirrelfish.

Maximum Length: 20 cm (7.9 in.).

Distribution: Red Sea to Easter Island, north to southern Japan, and north to the southern Great Barrier Reef and the Austral Islands.

Biology: The Speckled Squirrelfish occurs on rocky and coral reefs, occupying coastal reefs, reef crests, reef faces, and fore-reef slopes, at depths of 1 to 183 m (3.3 to 595 ft.). However, this is the most

Sargocentron melanospilos, Blackspot Squirrelfish: uncommon species.

Sargocentron microstoma, Fineline Squirrelfish: deep-water reef tank choice.

Sargocentron punctatissimum, Speckled Squirrelfish: pretty but secretive.

common member of the family in very shallow water—often occurring in the surge zone and rarely seen at depths in excess of 30 m (98 ft.). It feeds over open sand bottoms at night, consuming crabs, shrimps, mantis shrimps, snails, and polychaete worms. During the day, it will occasionally capture small fishes like *Chromis* damselfishes.
Captive Care: The Speckled Squirrelfish is a secretive species that will need plenty of suitable hiding places. It will spend much of its time hiding in a brightly lit aquarium, and will be more inclined to swim in the open in a tank with less illumination.
Aquarium Size: 75 gal. **Temperature:** 22 to 27°C (72 to 80°F).
Aquarium Suitability Index: 4.
Remarks: *Sargocentron punctatissimum* is silvery red, often with narrow red stripes and fine black spots and silver flecks on its sides.

Sargocentron rubrum (Forsskål, 1775)
Common Name: Redcoat Squirrelfish.
Maximum Length: 27 cm (10.6 in.).
Distribution: Red Sea to New Caledonia, north to Japan, and south to the southern Great Barrier Reef.
Biology: The Redcoat Squirrelfish occurs on coastal reefs, reef flats, lagoon patch reefs, and on gently sloping fore reefs at depths of 6 to over 50 m (20 to 163 ft.). It usually lives in caves or under overhangs, where it forms small to large aggregations.
Captive Care: This is a hardy aquarium species that can be kept singly or in small groups if the tank is of substantial size (100+ gallons). It feeds on most aquarium fare and will also eat small fishes and ornamental shrimps. The Redcoat Squirrelfish is often sold as an "assorted squirrelfish" or even as a "Hawaiian squirrelfish," even though it is not found around these islands. It is suitable for a shallow- or deep-water reef aquarium, but should always be provided with adequate sanctuaries in which to refuge.
Aquarium Size: 75 gal. **Temperature:** 22 to 27°C (72 to 80°F).
Aquarium Suitability Index: 4.
Remarks: *Sargocentron rubrum* is very similar to the **Darkstriped Squirrelfish** (*Sargocentron praslin*) (**Lacépède, 1802**), which differs from *S. rubrum* in lacking a red band in the middle of the dorsal fin and in having more brownish red stripes. The Darkstriped Squirrelfish is more common around islands, where it is usually found on dead sections of the reef, while the Redcoat Squirrelfish is a continental species.

Sargocentron spiniferum (Forsskål, 1775)
Common Names: Giant Squirrelfish, Longjawed Squirrelfish, Duckbilled Squirrelfish.
Maximum Length: 45 cm (17.7 in.).
Distribution: Red Sea to the Hawaiian and Ducie Islands, north to southern Japan and southern New South Wales.
Biology: The Giant Squirrelfish occurs on lagoon reefs, reef flats, reef faces, and fore-reef slopes at depths of 6 to 122 m (20 to 397 ft.). Juveniles occur on more protected, shallow reefs. During the day, it resides in caves, under ledges and table corals, or in the open near the entrance of a hiding place. At night, it forages in surrounding reef habitats. Individuals tend to return to the same shelter site before sunrise. This species feeds on crabs—including xanthid, swimming, and clinging crabs—mantis shrimps, decapod shrimps, slipper lobsters, and small fishes. It occurs singly, in pairs, or in small groups.
Captive Care: *Sargocentron spiniferum* gets too big for many home aquariums, but is a great pet for the owner of a very large tank. It will spend most of its time in the open and will approach the

Sargocentron rubrum, Redcoat Squirrelfish: found near islands.

Sargocentron praslin, Darkstriped Squirrelfish: too large for many aquariums.

Sargocentron spiniferum, Giant Squirrelfish: can become a great pet for the aquarist with a large tank, but note the long, venomous preopercular spine.

front of the tank to check out activity in the room. Although its larger size would apparently make it a greater threat to smaller fishes, it rarely bothers fish tankmates once it gets accustomed to taking food from the water's surface. It will even take food right from its owner's fingers. Even though it is a bolder species, it must still be provided with a large cave or overhang for shelter. It gets too large for most reef aquariums, but it can be kept with sessile invertebrates.

Aquarium Size: 180 gal. **Temperature:** 22 to 27°C (72 to 80°F).
Aquarium Suitability Index: 4 (**Venomous**).
Remarks: The Giant Squirrelfish is easily recognized by its very high body and long preopercular spine. This long spine is venomous, so the fish must be handled with great care.

Sargocentron tiere (Cuvier, 1829)
Common Names: Blueline Squirrelfish, Tahitian Squirrelfish.
Maximum Length: 33 cm (13.0 in.).
Distribution: Aldabra to Hawaiian, Marquesas, and Ducie Islands, north to southern Japan, and south to Austral Islands.
Biology: The Blueline Squirrelfish is most common around islands, where it inhabits fringing reefs, reef faces, and outer-reef slopes at depths of 5 to 183 m (16 to 595 ft.). It hides deep in reef caves and crevices during the day, but at night it leaves these hiding places and moves to exposed areas along reef ledges. It feeds both off the substrate and in the water column. Xanthid

Sargocentron tiere, Blueline Squirrelfish: develops a white band in the dark.

SQUIRRELFISHES 381

Sargocentron tieroides, Pink Squirrelfish: secretive and rarely encountered.

Sargocentron vexillarius, Dusky Squirrelfish: may starve in some systems.

crabs, caridean shrimps, and crab megalops comprise the bulk of its diet. However, it will also consume small fishes, polychaetes, and peanut worms.

Captive Care: *Sargocentron tiere* is a large species that needs a concomitantly large aquarium. It is also fairly reclusive, so it must be provided with suitable hiding places. Because it is of larger proportions, the Blueline Squirrelfish is a greater threat to fish tankmates and motile invertebrates. However, like all other holocentrids, it can be housed with sessile invertebrates. It will spend more time in full view in a dimly lit tank.

Aquarium Size: 135 gal. **Temperature:** 22 to 27°C (72 to 80°F).
Aquarium Suitability Index: 4.

Remarks: The color of this species is very distinctive: at night, its chromatic attire changes and a white band develops in the middle of the body.

Sargocentron tieroides (Bleeker, 1853)

Common Name: Pink Squirrelfish.
Maximum Length: 17 cm (6.7 in.).
Distribution: East Africa to the Line and Society Islands, north to the Ryukyus, and south to the Great Barrier Reef.
Biology: The Pink Squirrelfish occurs on lagoon reefs, reef faces, and fore-reef slopes at depths of 15 to 36 m (49 to 117 ft.). It lives deep in reef caves and crevices during the day, and hunts along coral or rock faces at night.
Captive Care: *Sargocentron tieroides* is not common in the wild or in the aquarium trade. Its highly secretive nature makes it a less desirable display animal. Provide it with deep hiding places and keep it in a dimly lit tank.
Aquarium Size: 75 gal. **Temperature:** 22 to 27°C (72 to 80°F).
Aquarium Suitability Index: 3.

Remarks: The dorsal fin of *S. tieroides* is light red to almost clear, with a deep red band along the fin margin and a white spot on the spines.

Sargocentron vexillarius (Poey, 1860)

Common Name: Dusky Squirrelfish.
Maximum Length: 18 cm (7.1 in.).
Distribution: Florida and Bermuda south to Venezuela.
Biology: The Dusky Squirrelfish is found on rocky shorelines (where it is most common) and on coral reefs. It occurs in tidepools, on patch reefs, reef faces, and on fore-reef slopes at depths of less than 1 up to 20 m (3.3 to 65 ft.). It lives in small holes or among the branches of Elkhorn Coral (*Acropora palmata*) during the day and feeds on nearby reef areas and on the sand at night. This species consumes zooplankters that live near the bottom, as well as benthic invertebrates. Although its diet consists mainly of crabs, crab larvae, gastropods, and shrimps, it will also eat chitons, barnacle appendages, small octopuses, brittle stars, isopods, larval fishes, polychaete worms, and copepods.
Captive Care: Although abundant over much of its range, *S. vexillarius* is not commonly encountered in the marine aquarium trade. It is a secretive species that will hide among the aquarium decor when the lights are on. It will be seen more frequently in a tank with dim lighting. It also appreciates conditions similar to those in the surge zone, with strong, oscillating water movement. Keeping this fish with more aggressive feeders can be problematic, as the Dusky Squirrelfish may not get enough to eat. It can be kept with sessile invertebrates, but as the list above suggests, it will eat many types of motile invertebrates.
Aquarium Size: 75 gal. **Temperature:** 22 to 27°C (72 to 80°F).
Aquarium Suitability Index: 4.

Sargocentron violaceum (Bleeker, 1853)

Common Name: Violet Squirrelfish.
Maximum Length: 25 cm (9.8 in.).
Distribution: East Africa to the Line and Society Islands, north to the Ryukyus, and south to the Great Barrier Reef.
Biology: The Violet Squirrelfish is found on lagoon reefs, on reef flats, reef faces, outer-reef slopes, and dropoffs at depths of 6 to 30 m (20 to 98 ft.). During the day, it hangs in caves and narrow crevices, while at night it moves onto the reef to feed. It is usually a solitary fish.
Captive Care: This attractive holocentrid is a secretive species that will need a deep crevice or cave to hide in when the lights are on. It will tend to spend more time at the entrance of a preferred shelter site if the tank has low illumination, and therefore is not a great choice for the shallow-water reef aquarium. It will also ingest smaller fishes and motile invertebrates.
Aquarium Size: 100 gal. **Temperature:** 23 to 27°C (74 to 80°F).
Aquarium Suitability Index: 4.
Remarks: *Sargocentron violaceum* is similar to *S. spiniferum*, but the Violet Squirrelfish's body has a distinctive violet tinge, the head is red, and the dorsal fin spines are white-tipped.

Sargocentron xantherythrum, Hawaiian Squirrelfish: nice, smaller species.

Sargocentron xantherythrum (Jordan & Evermann, 1903)

Common Name: Hawaiian Squirrelfish.
Maximum Length: 17 cm (6.7 in.).
Distribution: Johnston and Hawaiian Islands.
Biology: The Hawaiian Squirrelfish is found on basalt reefs, where it aggregates in caves and under ledges. It occurs at depths of less than 1 to 100 m (3.3 to 325 ft.), but it is most common at depths greater than 20 m (65 ft.). At night, it moves out from its hiding places to feed over rock, coral, and sand pockets. Its diet is comprised of large zooplankters and benthic invertebrates, including xanthid crabs, crab megalops, caridean shrimps, prosobranch gastropods, mantis shrimps, opisthobranch gastropods, peanut worms, bivalves, krill, and mysid shrimps.
Captive Care: This squirrelfish is commonly collected for the aquarium trade. It is best kept in small groups and provided with adequate hiding places. This species is rarely aggressive toward heterospecifics and is less of a threat to fish tankmates than many of its larger relatives. It will eat a wide variety of motile invertebrates.
Aquarium Size: 75 gal. **Temperature:** 22 to 27°C (72 to 80°F).
Aquarium Suitability Index: 4.
Remarks: The spinous dorsal fin of the Hawaiian Squirrelfish is red with white tips and there is a dark spot at the inner axil of the pectoral fin.

References

Hiatt & Stratsburg (1960), Hobson (1968, 1974), Kuiter & Debelius (1994), Myers (1989), Randall (1967, 1983), Sano et al. (1984), Vivien & Peyrot-Clausade (1974).

Sargocentron violaceum, Violet Squirrelfish: usually a solitary fish.

Subfamily Myripristinae
Soldierfishes

Myripristis vittata, Whitetip Soldierfish: similar to the squirrelfishes, but with larger eyes, deeper bodies, a blunt snout, and an upturned "frowning" mouth.

Although often confused with their close relatives the squirrelfishes (Subfamily Holocentrinae), the soldierfishes, Subfamily Myripristinae, are easily distinguished, both by appearance and behavior. The soldierfishes have larger, more bulbous eyes; an upturned mouth that appears to be frowning; a blunt snout; and a deeper body. Some of these differences are related to their feeding behavior. The soldierfishes feed primarily on nocturnal zooplankton in the water column, rather than foraging for crustaceans and other bottom-dwelling prey. The position of their mouth and their large eyes enable them to capture small, free-floating prey more effectively after dark. Their eyes are sensitive enough to function with the diminished ambient light available at night. Their shorter snout enables them to see an approaching prey item with both eyes, increasing their depth perception. Some soldierfishes make interesting and attractive aquarium subjects, especially if provided with a cave or rocky overhang mimicking their natural habitat.

Classification and Biology

This subfamily is comprised of five genera—*Corniger, Myripristis, Ostichthys, Plectrypops,* and *Pristilepis.* Two of these genera, *Myripristis* and *Plectrypops,* are frequently encountered in aquarium stores. *Myripristis* is the most specious genus, with 26 species—22 in the Indo-Pacific, 3 endemic species in the Eastern Pacific, and 1 species in the Atlantic. These fishes are usually sold in the aquarium trade as "bigeye squirrelfish."

The *Myripristis* species are zooplanktivores that hide by day and feed at night. The most important food in their diets is crustacean larvae, especially crab megalops. These are larger than most zooplankton fed upon by diurnal planktivores. Some *Myripristis* species will also capture benthic invertebrates (including polychaete worms and gastropods) and small fishes.

Soldierfishes typically feed about 3 m (9.8 ft.) above the substrate. The color of most species changes at night, when the ventrum and the lower portion of the sides become silvery. On dark nights, they stray farther from the reef and disperse over a larger area than on nights when moonlight is present. When they are threatened, individuals move closer together, and if pressed, will dart toward shelter. At the signs of first light, these fish take shelter in caves and crevices. In the wild, the soldierfishes are preyed upon by sharks, morays, trumpetfishes, groupers, snappers, and jacks.

Captive Care

Soldierfishes are not difficult to maintain in the home aquarium. Because most species are nocturnal, spending their days in reef caves and interstices, it is important to construct overhangs, caves, and large crevices when aquascaping your tank. They are rarely aggressive toward other fishes, and can even be kept with members of their own kind in more spacious tanks that have plenty of hiding places. In some cases, these fishes may acclimate more readily if kept in small groups. Occasionally, a dominant individual will pester subordinates and may have to be removed from the tank.

If fed when the lights are on, soldierfishes will dash out from their shelters to capture food blown past by water currents and are usually not reluctant to consume chopped fresh or frozen seafoods, live or frozen brine shrimp, mysid shrimp, and frozen preparations. Some individuals will also eat flake food, while an occasional specimen will refuse food altogether. They will rarely take nonliving food off the substrate. A finicky soldierfish will not be able to refuse an offering of live brine shrimp or baby guppies, and once they start feeding on live foods, they can usually be switched to other types of fare. Individuals that refuse food when the lights are on may be fed once the tank is darkened for the night. Some individuals will fade in color after they have been kept in captivity for some time. Soldierfishes should be captured in a specimen container instead of a net, as their large eyes can be easily damaged by abrasive net material.

Although not aggressive, soldierfishes may consume very small fish and crustacean tankmates. Soldierfishes are usually ignored by most other fish tankmates, although they may be bullied by larger, more aggressive species that occupy reef caves and crevices. For example, in a small- to medium-sized tank, large dottybacks such as the Red, Lined, or Australian Dottybacks (*Labracinus cyclophthalmus, Labracinus lineatus,* and *Ogilbyina novaehollandiae*) may continually evict soldierfishes from shelter sites. The evicted fishes will usually huddle in the upper corners of the tank and may refuse to feed. Soldierfish relatives, the squirrelfishes, tend to be more aggressive and may bully them if space is limited. Smaller individuals are also potential prey for morays, frogfishes, groupers, and snappers.

The members of the genus *Plectrypops* are more aggressive than the *Myripristis* species and should be kept singly. They are also likely to pick on other members of this subfamily, and the problem is compounded if they are housed together in a smaller tank. I have even seen *Plectrypops* species evict *Myripristis* species from crevices in larger tanks. These fishes are also more likely to eat small fish tankmates and ornamental crustaceans.

It is possible to maintain some of the *Myripristis* species in shallow-water reef aquariums, but they must be provided with dark recesses in which to refuge. A tank with subdued lighting, such as a deep-water reef tank or a fish-only aquarium, is better suited for those species that live at greater depths. All members of the genus will spend more time in the open if housed in a dimly lit tank. If you want to view the activity of these fishes at night, place a red incandescent or fluorescent light over the tank. Soldierfishes can startle easily if there is sudden movement in

Myripristis jacobus, Blackbar Soldierfish: easily bullied by aggressive species.

the room or a light is suddenly turned on when the tank is dark. At least some species provide a valuable service in the reef aquarium, feasting on undesirable polychaetes like fireworms. Some species may also feed on small ornamental shrimp and crabs.

One member of the genus, the Red Soldierfish (*Myripristis murdjan*), has spawned in a large public aquarium. Prior to spawning, the male and female swam in circles, which became smaller and smaller until the pair suddenly dashed up in the water column and expelled their gametes. The eggs of all members of this genus are pelagic.

SOLDIERFISH SPECIES

Genus *Myripristis*

Myripristis adusta Bleeker, 1853
Common Name: Bronze Soldierfish.
Maximum Length: 32 cm (12.6 in.).
Distribution: East Africa to the Society Islands, Tuamotus, and Line Islands, north to the Ryukyus, and south to the Great Barrier Reef.
Biology: The Bronze Soldierfish is found in exposed reef flats, lagoon reefs, and bays, but is most abundant in coral-rich steep channels on fore-reef slopes at depths of 2 to 25 m 7 to 81 ft.). It often occurs in caves or beneath ledges during the day, but will occasionally venture out into the open—although it never strays far from shelter. This species typically occurs singly or in pairs, but also forms small groups in some oceanic locations.
Captive Care: This is a sizable species that will need to be housed in a large tank with plenty of swimming room. Because of its larger size, it is also a greater threat to fish tankmates and ornamental crustaceans. It will spend time in the open when the lights are on, especially in a dimly lit aquarium.
Aquarium Size: 100 gal. **Temperature:** 22 to 27°C (72 to 80°F).
Aquarium Suitability Index: 4.
Remarks: The Bronze Soldierfish is readily recognized by the broad black margins on its median fins.

Myripristis amaena (Castelnau, 1873)
Common Names: Brick Soldierfish, Black Soldierfish.
Maximum Length: 26 cm (10.2 in.).
Distribution: Philippines and Indonesia to the Hawaiian and Ducie Islands, north to the Ryukyus.
Biology: The Brick Soldierfish lives on reef flats, the reef face, and fore-reef slopes, often in areas exposed to open-ocean swell. It occurs at depths of 2 to 52 m (7 to 169 ft.), but in certain areas it is most common in less than 9 m (30 ft.) of water. During the day, small aggregations of Brick Soldierfish inhabit large caves, hide among boulders, or shelter under ledges. It often shares its diurnal refuge with other congeners, like the Bigscale Soldierfish (*Myripristis berndti*). About 30 minutes after sunset, Brick Soldierfish leave their shelter sites. On moonless nights, they often move offshore to feed. This species feeds only at night, mainly on crab megalops, larval hermit crabs, and larval snapping shrimp. Polychaetes and stomatopod larvae also make up a minor part of its diet. This species reaches maturity at about 6 years of age and can live for a maximum of 14 years.
Captive Care: *Myripristis amaena* is often collected for the aquarium trade in Hawaiian waters. It is a hardy fish that requires care similar to that of other soldierfishes. See the Captive Care section in the subfamily account, page 385.

Myripristis adusta, Bronze Soldierfish: large fish requiring ample space.

Myripristis amaena, Brick Soldierfish: hardy fish often collected in Hawaii.

Aquarium Size: 100 gal. **Temperature:** 22 to 27°C (72 to 80°F).
Aquarium Suitability Index: 4.
Remarks: The median fins of the Brick Soldierfish are uniformly red. It lacks a white spot in front of its pectoral fin axil, the third anal spine is shorter than the fourth spine, and the front of the lower jaw does not fit into a deep notch on the upper jaw.

Myripristis berndti Jordan & Evermann, 1903
Common Name: Bigscale Soldierfish.
Maximum Length: 30 cm (11.8 in.).
Distribution: East Africa to the Line and Tuamotu Islands and the Eastern Pacific, north to the Ryukyus, and south to Norfolk Island.
Biology: The Bigscale Soldierfish is found on back reefs, in channels, on subtidal reef flats, the reef face, and fore-reef slopes at depths of less than 1 to 159 m (3.3 to 517 ft.). It also occurs on rocky reefs in the Eastern Pacific. It is often found along dropoffs, where it inhabits caves or shelters under ledges. This species occurs singly or in loose aggregations. The Bigscale Soldierfish feeds on shrimps and zooplankton. It has been suggested that *M. berndti* may hybridize with the Red Soldierfish (*Myripristis murdjan*) in certain locations, with the resulting progeny displaying characteristics indicative of both species.
Captive Care: This wide-ranging species is fairly common in the aquarium trade. See the Captive Care section in the subfamily account, page 385, for more information on its husbandry.
Aquarium Size: 100 gal. **Temperature:** 22 to 27°C (72 to 80°F).
Aquarium Suitability Index: 4.
Remarks: The spiny portion of the dorsal fin is yellowish orange and the median and pelvic fins are edged with white. It also has a dark bar on the edge of the operculum.

Myripristis botche Cuvier, 1829
Common Name: Finspot Soldierfish.
Maximum Length: 30 cm (11.8 in.).
Distribution: East Africa to New Caledonia, north to the Ryukyus, and south to the southern Great Barrier Reef.
Biology: The Finspot Soldierfish is often found on protected, silty reefs, usually at depths in excess of 25 m (81 ft.) and to a maximum depth of at least 64 m (208 ft.). It has also been reported from deep lagoons, where it hangs near large coral heads. If threatened, it seeks shelter in caves or crevices. The Finspot Soldierfish occurs singly, in pairs, or in small aggregations.
Captive Care: The Finspot Soldierfish is rare both in the wild and in the aquarium trade. It will acclimate more readily if placed in an aquarium with reduced lighting.
Aquarium Size: 100 gal. **Temperature:** 22 to 26°C (72 to 78°F).
Aquarium Suitability Index: 4.
Remarks: *Myripristis botche* has distinct black blotches on the tips of the median fins and white body scales. Melanistic individuals have been reported that have dark blotches on their fins and bodies. *Myripristis melanosticta* is a synonym of this species.

Myripristis chryseres Jordan & Evermann, 1903
Common Name: Yellowfin Soldierfish.
Maximum Length: 25 cm (9.8 in.).
Distribution: East Africa to the Hawaiian Islands and Samoa, north to southern Japan, and south to the Great Barrier Reef.
Biology: This handsome species is found on deep fore-reef slopes, usually at depths greater than 30 m (98 ft.), although it has been reported at a depth range of 12 to 240 m (39 to 780 ft.). This species occurs singly or in small groups. It is sometimes found with aggregations of Brick Soldierfish (*M. amaena*).

Myripristis berndti, Bigscale Soldierfish: large, commonly seen species.

Myripristis botche, Finspot Soldierfish: rare; prefers reduced lighting.

Myripristis chryseres, Yellowfin Soldierfish: lovely deep-water fish.

Myripristis hexagona, Doubletooth Soldierfish: not common in the fish trade.

Captive Care: This is one of the most attractive members of the subfamily. Unfortunately, because of its preference for deeper water, it is not commonly seen in the aquarium trade.
Aquarium Size: 100 gal. **Temperature:** 22 to 26°C (72 to 78°F).
Aquarium Suitability Index: 4.
Remarks: All the fins of *M. chryseres* are yellow, and it has a dark bar at the edge of the operculum.

Myripristis hexagona (Lacépède, 1802)
Common Name: Doubletooth Soldierfish.
Maximum Length: 20 cm (7.9 in.).
Distribution: East Africa to Samoa, north to the Ryukyus, south to the southern Great Barrier Reef.
Biology: The Doubletooth Soldierfish is found in lagoons, on reef faces and fore-reef slopes, usually in caves or large crevices, at depths of 15 to 40 m (49 to 130 ft.). It usually occurs in relatively calm water and often on reefs that are near silt or mud bottoms.
Captive Care: *Myripristis hexagona* is occasionally found in the aquarium trade. See the Captive Care section in the subfamily account, page 385, for more on the husbandry of this fish.
Aquarium Size: 75 gal. **Temperature:** 22 to 26°C (72 to 78°F).
Aquarium Suitability Index: 4.
Remarks: As the common name suggests, the Doubletooth Soldierfish has two pairs of tooth patches at the front of the lower jaw. In larger specimens, the tooth patches are visible when the jaws are closed. This species is similar to the Yellowfin Soldierfish (*M. chryseres*) but it lacks yellow on the fin tips.

Myripristis jacobus Cuvier & Valenciennes, 1829
Common Name: Blackbar Soldierfish.
Maximum Length: 20 cm (7.9 in.).
Distribution: North Carolina and northern Gulf of Mexico, south to Brazil, east to the Eastern Atlantic, including St. Paul's Rocks, Ascension, and St. Helena Islands.
Biology: The Blackbar Soldierfish is found under piers, hiding among man-made refuse (tires and shipwrecks), and on back reefs, patch reefs, reef faces, and fore-reef slopes at depths of 5 to 50 m (16 to 163 ft.). It lives in caves and under ledges and is found singly or in loose aggregations that can number up to 30 or more individuals. At approximately 5:30 to 6:30 P.M., these fish move up to 3 m (10 ft.) over the reef and into the water column to feed primarily on planktonic organisms—especially shrimp, stomatopod, and crab larvae. At about 7:00 A.M., they return to their daytime shelter sites. The Blackbar Soldierfish is often parasitized by gnathid isopods.
Captive Care: *Myripristis jacobus* is one of the most common species in the U.S. aquarium trade. It is a durable aquarium fish that can be kept singly or—if you have a larger tank—in small groups. Although typically nonoffensive toward heterospecifics, this species may ingest smaller crustaceans.
Aquarium Size: 75 gal. **Temperature:** 22 to 26°C (72 to 78°F).
Aquarium Suitability Index: 4.
Remarks: This is the only member of the genus *Myripristis* known from the Atlantic Ocean.

Myripristis kuntee Cuvier, 1831
Common Name: Pearly Soldierfish.
Maximum Length: 19 cm (7.5 in.), usually less than 15 cm (5.9 in.).
Distribution: East Africa to the Line and Tuamotu Islands, north to southern Japan and Hawaii, south to Lord Howe Island.
Biology: The Pearly Soldierfish occurs on subtidal reef flats, lagoon patch reefs, reef faces, and fore-reef slopes at depths of 1 to 26 m

(3.3 to 85 ft.). In the Hawaiian Islands, it inhabits small crevices during the day. Just after sunset, it moves out of its hiding place and aggregates fairly close to the substrate. It returns to its diurnal haunt about 30 minutes before sunrise. In Micronesia, this species is less secretive during the day, often forming large aggregations over areas of rich coral growth. The Pearly Soldierfish is often observed associating with other members of the genus. It feeds mainly on crab megalops, but also consumes shrimp larvae, copepods, mysid shrimp, polychaete worms, and small fishes.

Captive Care: *Myripristis kuntee* is occasionally found in the aquarium trade. See the Captive Care section in the subfamily account, page 385, for more on the husbandry of this fish.
Aquarium Size: 55 gal. **Temperature:** 22 to 26°C (72 to 78°F).
Aquarium Suitability Index: 4.
Remarks: This species has smaller scales and a lighter opercular bar than similarly colored species. It is, however, very similar to the **Scarlet Soldierfish** (*Myripristis pralina*) (**Cuvier, 1829**), which has a preopercular bar that is very short and does not extend down as far as the pectoral fin axil. The Scarlet Soldierfish attains a maximum length of 20 cm (7.9 in.) and ranges from East Africa to the Line and Society Islands, north to the Ryukyus, and south to the Great Barrier Reef. It occurs on subtidal reef flats, the reef face, and fore-reef slopes at depths of 1 to 40 m (3.3 to 130 ft.), but it is most often found at shallow depths. The Scarlet Soldierfish occurs in loose aggregations, refuging under reef ledges during the day and moving out to feed on zooplankton in the water column after dark.

Myripristis murdjan (Forsskål, 1775)
Common Names: Red Soldierfish, Crimson Soldierfish.
Maximum Length: 27 cm (10.6 in.).
Distribution: Red Sea to Samoa, north to the Ryukyus, and south to the southern Great Barrier Reef.
Biology: The Red Soldierfish occurs on silty coastal reefs, on subtidal reef flats, and on fore-reef slopes at depths of 1 to 50 m (3.3 to 163 ft.). It aggregates in shipwrecks, caves, and under overhangs during the day. Between 30 and 50 minutes after the sun sets, the Red Soldierfish ascends into the water column and may even move offshore, especially on moonless nights. This species feeds mainly at night on crab megalops and polychaete worms, as well as shrimp larvae, mysid shrimp, mantis shrimp larvae, krill, small cephalopods, amphipods, prosobranch gastropods, and copepods. Although it feeds mainly at night, it will consume crab larvae and the occasional shrimp, small fish, polychaete, or isopod during the day. This species apparently feeds on benthic polychaetes as they move over hard and soft substrates at night, and even on infaunal forms. About 30 minutes before

Myripristis jacobus, Blackbar Soldierfish: the only Atlantic soldierfish.

Myripristis kuntee, Pearly Soldierfish: will mix with others of its genus.

Myripristis murdjan, Red Soldierfish: can be kept singly or in groups.

Myripristis violacea, Violet Soldierfish: note cleaner wrasse nearby.

Myripristis vittata, Whitetip Soldierfish: lacks opercular bar.

sunrise, Red Soldierfish return to their shelter sites.
Captive Care: *Myripristis murdjan* can be kept singly or in small groups. They will spend more time in the open in a tank with reduced lighting. Although they can be successfully housed in a shallow-water reef tank, Red Soldierfish should be provided with suitable dark hiding places. They will eat noxious polychaete worms, such as the Fireworm (*Hermodice carunculata*), when both come out to forage at night. It has also been observed to feed on polychaetes of the genera *Ceratonereis*, *Eunice*, *Glycera*, *Lysidice*, *Nematonereis*, *Nereis*, and *Platynereis*. One Red Soldierfish may eat as many as 20 worms per night.
Aquarium Size: 100 gal. **Temperature:** 22 to 26°C (72 to 78°F).
Aquarium Suitability Index: 4.
Remarks: The lower jaw of *M. murdjan* projects in front of the upper jaw, except in juveniles. The soft dorsal, anal, and tail fin leading edges are white and it has a red spiny dorsal fin.

Myripristis violacea Bleeker, 1851
Common Names: Violet Soldierfish, Orangefin Soldierfish.
Maximum Length: 20 cm (7.9 in.).
Distribution: East Africa to the Tuamotus, north to the Ryukyus, and south to New Caledonia and Austral Island.
Biology: The Violet Soldierfish occurs on lagoon reefs, on the reef face, and on fore-reef slopes at depths of 4 to 25 m (13 to 81 ft.), but it is more common in protected areas at depths of less than 8 m (26 ft.). It resides in caves, under overhangs (often with rich soft coral growth), or among branching or laminar stony corals. It often occurs singly and feeds most heavily on zooplankton—including crustacean larvae—as well as benthic invertebrates like portunid crabs, alpheid shrimps, and sand-dwelling polychaetes. In one food habit study, a Violet Soldierfish's stomach was full of hundreds of polychaetes, which it apparently pulled out of their membranous tubes that are formed under the sand.
Captive Care: *Myripristis violacea* is one of the most common members of the *Myripristis* genus in the aquarium trade. See the Captive Care section in the subfamily account, page 385, for more on the husbandry of this fish.
Aquarium Size: 75 gal. **Temperature:** 22 to 27°C (72 to 80°F).
Aquarium Suitability Index: 4.
Remarks: The body of *M. violacea* has a distinctive violet cast, a dark red opercular bar, and orange-tipped dorsal, anal, and caudal fin lobes. Some individuals have been reported with black blotches on the body and fins.

Myripristis vittata Valenciennes, 1831
Common Name: Whitetip Soldierfish.
Maximum Length: 20 cm (7.9 in.).
Distribution: East Africa to the Marquesas and the Tuamotus, north to southern Japan, and south to New Caledonia.
Biology: The Whitetip Soldierfish resides on coral-rich reef faces and fore-reef dropoffs at depths of 3 to 80 m (10 to 260 ft.), although it is most common at depths greater than 20 m (65 ft.). It is usually found singly, in pairs, or in large aggregations, often with other soldierfish species (e.g., *M. adusta*, *M. berndti*). Aggregations are usually observed under large overhangs, where the fishes often swim upside down along the ceiling. Solitary individuals are often observed in the open during daylight hours, but never stray far from shelter.
Captive Care: This handsome fish is not a common species in the aquarium trade. Its husbandry requirements are similar to those of other soldierfishes.

Aquarium Size: 75 gal. **Temperature:** 22 to 27°C (72 to 80°F).
Aquarium Suitability Index: 4.
Remarks: *Myripristis vittata* has no opercular bar, is red overall, and has white-tipped dorsal spines, white at the base of the dorsal fin, and white leading edges on all the fins.

Myripristis xanthacara Randall & Guézé, 1981
Common Name: Yellowtip Soldierfish.
Maximum Length: 20 cm (7.9 in.).
Distribution: Central Red Sea to the Gulf of Aden.
Biology: The Yellowtip Soldierfish occurs on reef flats, the reef face, and fore-reef slopes at depths of 1 to 18 m (3.3 to 59 ft.).
Captive Care: *Myripristis xanthacara* is rarely observed in the aquarium trade. See the Captive Care section in the subfamily account, page 385, for more on the husbandry of this fish.
Aquarium Size: 55 gal. **Temperature:** 22 to 27°C (72 to 80°F).
Aquarium Suitability Index: 4.
Remarks: This fish is easily recognized by the yellow tips present on the dorsal, anal, and caudal fins.

Genus *Plectrypops*

Plectrypops lima (Valenciennes, 1831)
Common Name: Roughscale Soldierfish.
Maximum Length: 16 cm (6.3 in.).
Distribution: East Africa to the Hawaiian and Easter Islands, north to the Ryukyus, and south to Lord Howe.
Biology: This unusual fish is found on reef flats, reef faces, and fore-reef slopes at depths of less than 1 to 25 m (3.3 to 81 ft.). It is very secretive, living deep in reef interstices during the day. It does move out into the open to feed at night, but never ranges too far from a shelter site. It feeds mainly on caridean shrimps and xanthid crabs, but will also eat crab megalops, fishes, and amphipods. Although it feeds mainly off the bottom, it will also ingest larger zooplankton near the seafloor.
Captive Care: The Roughscale Soldierfish is quite secretive in captivity, and is usually only seen peering from a crevice or cave—or when food is introduced to the tank. As soon as food is added, this fish will dash out to capture any morsels as they float past. It acclimates quickly to aquarium living. Although it will never be a fish that spends a lot of time in the open, it makes more frequent brief appearances as its time in captivity goes on. It will often hang behind or next to aquarium decor with its head down and its large eyes rolled forward, looking toward any observer. In this posture, it appears to have binocular vision. *Plectrypops lima* may display aggression toward smaller tankmates and will eat any fishes or crustaceans that it can ingest whole. As they are likely to fight, only one Roughscale Soldierfish should be housed per tank. It may also squabble with other holocentrids.
Aquarium Size: 55 gal. **Temperature:** 22 to 27°C (72 to 80°F).
Aquarium Suitability Index : 4.
Remarks: The Roughscale Soldierfish is closely related to the **Cardinal Soldierfish** (*Plectrypops retrospinis*) **(Guichenot, 1853)** of the tropical Western Atlantic. The natural history and husbandry of the two species are very similar. Limited food habitat data shows that the Cardinal Soldierfish eats xanthid crabs and polychaete worms.

References
Dee (1986), deGraaf (1973), Hobson (1968, 1974), Kuiter & Debelius (1994), Myers (1989), Randall (1967, 1983b), Randall et al. (1990), Vivien & Peyrot-Clausade (1974).

Myripristis xanthacara, Yellowtip Soldierfish: uncommon Red Sea species.

Plectrypops lima, Roughscale Soldierfish: secretive and somewhat scrappy.

Family Aulostomidae
Trumpetfishes

Carnivorous reef fishes employ a variety of different strategies to capture their prey, but few are as cunning as the trumpetfishes. These masters of predation display an astounding array of hunting techniques to get into striking range of their quarry. Although the trumpetfishes are not suitable additions to the average home aquarium, they make unique and interesting display animals in a larger tank. They will become very tame and are extremely personable pets.

Classification and Biology

The trumpetfishes belong to the Family Aulostomidae. This is a very small family, containing one genus and three species—all of which associate with coral and rocky reefs. All three trumpetfish species have elongate, laterally compressed bodies, short dorsal spines, tubelike snouts with tiny teeth, and a small chin barbel. They are most closely related to the cornetfishes (Family Fistulariidae). The trumpetfishes usually propel themselves forward by undulating their transparent dorsal and anal fins, but when they need to move quickly, they will employ their small caudal fin.

The trumpetfishes are found on both coral and rocky reefs and generally occupy a variety of different reef zones and habitats. They feed heavily on fishes and crustaceans, employing various strategies for prey capture. These hunting methods include ambushing, stalking, "hunting by riding," associating with schooling fish, and following other fishes.

In order to be successful at ambushing, a predator must go undetected until the prey fish or crustacean is within striking range. Trumpetfishes will hide by hanging vertically among soft corals and gorgonians, or by lying alongside boulders and coral heads. From this position, they are able to ambush fishes that move past.

Trumpetfishes also stalk prey, moving slowly along and among the structure of the reef as they make their approach. When they are within striking range, they dart forward and attempt a capture. I observed an Atlantic Trumpetfish (*Aulostomus maculatus*) near a rocky jetty that would advance slowly between boulders or near the edge of the jetty. When it spotted

Aulostomus chinensis, Pacific Trumpetfish: these masters of predatory stalking shadow a Leather Bass, *Epinephelus dermatolepis*, in search of prey.

a fish (usually a small wrasse) out over the sand, the trumpetfish would increase its speed, gliding directly toward its prey like an amphibious arrow. When it closed to within about 1 m (3.3 ft.), it would move its snout from side to side, then shoot forward and try for a strike.

In its approach, the trumpetfish draws very little attention to itself. Its movements are inconspicuous. It propels itself by beating its transparent dorsal and anal fins, which are probably almost invisible to its prey. Also, by approaching its prey head-on, the trumpetfish considerably decreases its apparent size. For instance, a 1-m (3.3-ft.) trumpetfish may only be 5 cm (2 in.) in diameter and a fish may be less likely to flee when seeing this smaller form approach. The head-on perspective is different from most other ocean carnivores, and the peculiar movement of the trumpetfish's snout as it makes its final approach may serve to distract its prey. Another trumpetfish approach is to hang in open water with its head directed toward the seafloor. When a fish or crustacean moves below, the trumpetfish lunges down to capture the unwary prey.

One of the most deceptive hunting strategies the aulostomids employ is hunting by riding, or shadow stalking. In this method, the trumpetfish uses another fish, either a large herbivore or carnivore, as a moving blind. The trumpetfish positions itself along

Aulostomus maculatus, Atlantic Trumpetfish, riding *Mycteroperca tigris*, Tiger Grouper, ready to dart forward and catch any appropriate fish or crustacean.

Aulostomus maculatus, Atlantic Trumpetfish, rides a Queen Parrotfish (*Scarus vetula*): the trumpetfish requires a very large aquarium.

the back of the fish that it "rides," often placing its lower jaw on the dorsum or along one side so that it is leaning on the base of the pectoral fin of the fish. Aulostomids ride a variety of different fish species, including groupers, goatfishes, angelfishes, wrasses, parrotfishes, puffers, and filefishes. When the species that is being ridden moves over a potential prey item, the trumpetfish moves to one side or the other and then darts forward to strike the unsuspecting fish or crustacean. If a trumpetfish is riding a herbivore, it will typically leave its position along the fish's back or side when the fish begins to graze. The trumpetfish then takes up a position near the mouth of the feeding fish and searches for small prey items disturbed by the fish's grazing activities. When the herbivore stops feeding and begins to move on, the trumpetfish assumes its original position along the fish's back. Some fishes (notably certain parrotfishes) regularly chase hitchhiking trumpetfishes, possibly because the aulostomid makes it more difficult for them to swim. To enhance their camouflage, trumpetfishes can quickly change color to match the fish they are riding. I once saw an Atlantic Trumpetfish (*A. maculatus*) turn from brown to yellow when it began riding a male Whitespotted Filefish (*Cantherhines macrocerus*).

Trumpetfishes will swim among shoaling or schooling fishes and feed on territorial species that attempt to drive these groups of invaders away. They also capture prey disturbed by the feeding activities of these foraging "herds." Sometimes more than one trumpetfish will associate with a shoal or school of fish.

For example, as many as three Atlantic Trumpetfish have been observed in a single shoal of surgeonfish. As in hunting by riding, a trumpetfish will often change its color to blend in better with the members of the group. I have seen Pacific Trumpetfish (*Aulostomus chinensis*) assume a very pale color overall while associating with Convict Surgeonfish (*Acanthurus triostegus*), and the Atlantic Trumpetfish has been observed to change its hue when the surgeonfish with which it was swimming became darker overall. When Atlantic Trumpetfish move among aggregations of Blue Chromis (*Chromis cyanea*) their bodies turn gray while their snouts become bright blue. I have seen this species slip through these moving curtains of zooplankton-feeding damselfishes to attack Masked Gobies (*Coryphopterus personatus*) and juvenile wrasses. I have even seen them attempting to feed on the Blue Chromis themselves.

I have also witnessed the Atlantic Trumpetfish following hunting Sharptail Snake Eels (*Myrichthys breviceps*) and roving bands of predators, including Rock Hinds (*Epinephelus adscensionis*), Conies (*Epinephelus fulva*), large Spanish Hogfish (*Bodianus rufus*), and Yellow Goatfish (*Mulloidichthys martinicus*). These foraging groups always included at least one species that was proficient at exposing buried prey (goatfishes). In some cases, several trumpetfish will join these feeding aggregations. As the predators mill around the "grubbing" species, the trumpetfish assume a vertical position above the group and wait for any potential prey species to attempt an escape.

The aulostomids are one of the few piscivores that will eat

Aulostomus chinensis, Pacific Trumpetfish, with a huge shoal of *Acanthurus triostegus*, Convict Surgeonfish, which allows it to approach prey unnoticed.

cleaner fishes; for example, the Atlantic Trumpetfish has been observed stalking juvenile Spanish Hogfish as they cleaned other fishes.

Although the trumpetfish's mouth appears quite small, these fishes can consume relatively large prey. For example, a 59-cm (23.2-in.) Atlantic Trumpetfish had a 13-cm (5.1-in.) squirrelfish in its stomach, while a 64-cm (25.2-in.) Pacific Trumpetfish had a damselfish in its stomach that was 10 cm (3.9 in.) long and 5 cm (2.0 in.) deep. How can trumpetfishes eat prey items that appear too large to swallow? The floor of the trumpetfish's narrow snout is expandable, enabling it to distend so that larger prey can pass into the stomach.

Trumpetfishes also have their own enemies. They frequently fall victim to morays, groupers, and snappers. Many of these predators readily consume trumpetfishes that are longer than themselves. One 28-cm (11.0-in.) Schoolmaster (*Lutjanus apodus*) had a 30-cm (11.8-in.) trumpetfish in its stomach. When larger trumpetfishes are ingested, they are folded over in the stomach of the predator.

Not much is known about the social organization of trumpetfishes. However, anecdotal observations suggest that they may be territorial. On several occasions, Collette and Talbot (1972) reported observing one Atlantic Trumpetfish chase another, and then return to its original spot.

Trumpetfishes are pelagic spawners. Gronell (in Thresher 1984) described their courtship and spawning behavior. Two pale gray Pacific Trumpetfish (apparently males) were observed chasing a larger, yellow conspecific with a distended abdomen (most likely the female) just before dusk. The two smaller fish were fighting each other as they pursued the female. One male apparently gave up and departed, while the female held a position a few meters above the substrate. The male moved toward the female, at which time its ventral surface became pinkish and its overall color became darker. As the pair started to swim off, the male began swimming back and forth in front of the female. The pair then made an apparent spawning ascent, about 8 m (26 ft.) off the bottom, but no gametes were observed.

Captive Care

Trumpetfishes make wonderful aquarium fish if you have a large enough tank in which to keep them. Although young individuals can be kept in tanks as small as 55 gallons, adults need to be housed in aquariums of 200+ gallons. It is important to give the trumpetfish plenty of swimming room (unobstructed with decor) and some structure to hang in or alongside. This could be either live or artificial gorgonians, long-bladed algae (e.g., *Caulerpa prolifera*), long pieces of PVC, or other long plastic

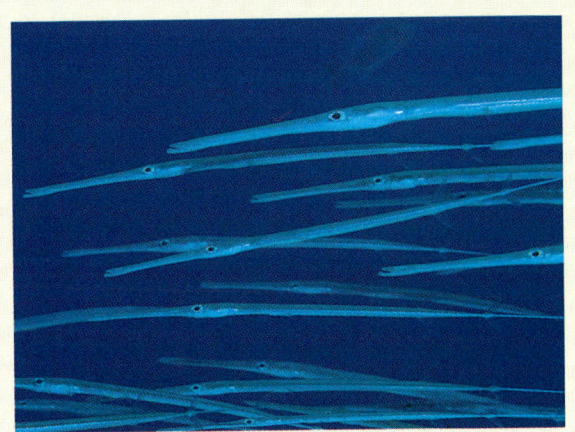

Fistularia commersonii, Smooth Cornetfish

Family Fistulariidae: Cornetfishes

The cornetfishes, or flutemouths, are very closely related to the trumpetfishes. Both species are extremely elongate with long, tubelike snouts. The easiest way to tell members of the two families apart is by the presence of a long filament extending from the middle of the tail in the cornetfishes. This was once thought to act as a stinger that these fishes would use against unwary fishermen. There is one genus in the family and four species, all of which live in tropical and warm temperate seas around the world.

Like their close relatives, the cornetfishes are voracious predators that feed almost exclusively on fishes. They even use some of the same hunting tactics to capture their prey. For example, these fishes have been observed to "hunt by riding," although they apparently engage in this behavior much less often than trumpetfishes. Cornetfishes can quickly alter their color, often changing from a plain to a barred color pattern when moving near the bottom. They often occur singly, but at least some cornetfishes form small aggregations. They are most often found in shallow seagrass beds and on coral reefs, although one species (*Fistularia corneta*) lives over open bottoms at depths greater than 30 m (98 ft.). Some also inhabit rocky reefs.

These fishes are rarely available to aquarists. They are large (up to 2 m [7 ft.] in length), active fishes that require a very large tank in order to be kept successfully. The tank should also be devoid of aquascaping material, which reduces swimming space. A coral head or ledge for them to shelter behind or under should be provided. They are more skittish than trumpetfishes and are more likely to dash into the side of the tank or try to launch themselves out if startled. In captivity, cornetfishes rarely eat anything but live feeder fish.

objects. These fishes may hide behind decor, but are more likely to hang in the upper corners of the aquarium if suitable hiding places are not present.

Although somewhat shy at first, trumpetfishes quickly learn to associate their keeper with food. Initially, live food may be necessary to get them started, but they rarely refuse feeder fish or live grass shrimp. Smaller individuals will also eat live adult brine shrimp. In time, they can be coaxed into ingesting strips of fish flesh or pieces of squid and shrimp. They will also eat any fish or crustacean tankmates small enough to fit into their (expandable) mouths.

Although juvenile trumpetfishes can be kept together, adults (especially males) may quarrel. It is important that you select their tankmates carefully. A number of piscivorous fishes will eat them—even if they are similar to the trumpetfish in total length. Potential predators include sharks, morays, lizardfishes, frogfishes, scorpionfishes, groupers, soapfishes, and snappers. Other fishes, such as large damselfishes, certain wrasses, triggerfishes, and some puffers, may pester and/or injure juvenile trumpetfishes.

Because trumpetfishes like to hang along a vertical structure, any intake siphons for pumps or filters must have strainers on them to prevent the trumpetfishes from being sucked in and damaged. Trumpetfishes are also likely to jump out of a tank, and often succeed in getting through relatively small openings. They are most likely to leap when the lights are turned off or when being chased by a fish or a fishkeeper's net.

Because of their large size at sexual maturity, it is not likely that trumpetfishes will ever be bred in home aquariums. It may be possible, however, for them to spawn successfully in large public aquariums.

TRUMPETFISH SPECIES

Aulostomus chinensis (Linnaeus, 1758)
Common Name: Pacific Trumpetfish.
Maximum Length: 90 cm (35.4 in.), but usually does not exceed 60 cm (23.6 in.).
Distribution: East Africa to Panama, north to the Ryukyus, and south to the Great Barrier Reef.
Biology: The Pacific Trumpetfish occurs near rocky and coral reefs, in almost all reef habitats, at depths of 5 to 122 m (16 to 397 ft.). It is often found among branching stony corals, black corals, soft corals, and seagrass. Fishes—including bigeyes, goatfishes, cardinalfishes, damselfishes, surgeonfishes, and tobies—and shrimps, including *Saron* species, comprise its diet. It is interesting to note that in a study of its food habits, all but 2 of 27 specimens with food in their stomachs had consumed either shrimp or fish—not both—suggesting that individuals adopt a narrow search image. This species has been observed hunting by riding, but does not appear to engage in this behavior as often as its Atlantic counterpart. The species it has been observed riding include coral groupers (*Plectropomus* spp.), Leather Bass (*Epinephelus dermatolepis*), large goatfishes, Blueface Angelfish (*Pomacanthus xanthometopon*), Foxface Rabbitfish (*Siganus vulpinus*), and the Map Puffer (*Arothron mappa*).
Captive Care: See the Captive Care section in the family account, page 395.
Aquarium Size: 180 gal. **Temperature:** 21 to 27°C (70 to 80°F).
Aquarium Suitability Index: 4.
Remarks: The Pacific Trumpetfish displays two different color forms—a reddish or gray-brown morph and a bright yellow

Aulostomus chinensis, Pacific Trumpetfish: small juvenile with soft coral.

Aulostomus chinensis, Pacific Trumpetfish: often hangs among gorgonians.

form. It has less chromatic plasticity than its Atlantic relative (*Aulostomus maculatus*). While individuals can become lighter or darker, they cannot undergo the more drastic color changes seen in *A. maculatus*. For example, the yellow coloration seen in some Pacific Trumpetfish is a permanent chromatic characteristic, not something that can be turned on and off. All of the different color forms have two black spots on the caudal fin, one black spot on the base of each pelvic fin, and a black streak on the lower jaw. In addition, the gray-brown color form is darker toward the posterior part of the body.

Aulostomus maculatus Valenciennes, 1842

Common Name: Atlantic Trumpetfish.
Maximum Length: 1.0 m (39.4 in.).
Distribution: South Florida and Bermuda and northern Gulf of Mexico, south to northern South America.
Biology: Adult Atlantic Trumpetfish are found around rocky shorelines, on reef flats, on the reef crest, reef face, and on forereef slopes at depths of less than 1 to at least 25 m (3.3 to 81 ft.). Juveniles usually hang vertically among the branches of large gorgonians. I have seen as many as five small trumpetfish lying vertically along an old rope attached to a buoy and numerous juveniles refuging at night among a framework of pipe. Young individuals also have been found hiding in floating masses of *Sargassum* algae. This species has been reported to feed on caridean shrimps, larval surgeonfishes, cardinalfishes, blennies, clinids, chromis, grunts, squirrelfishes, soldierfishes, damselfishes, goatfishes, gobies, and wrasses. It does most of its hunting at dusk and early in the morning. In one study, 17% of the Atlantic Trumpetfish observed were either hunting by riding or associating with schools of herbivores. They will ride Graysbys (*Epinephelus cruentatus*), Tiger Groupers (*Mycteroperca tigris*), Spanish Hogfish (*Bodianus rufus*), many parrotfishes, and Whitespotted Filefish (*Cantherhines macrocerus*). Individuals have been observed to adopt a bright blue snout while following shoals of Blue Chromis (*Chromis cyanea*) and Creole Wrasses (*Clepticus parrae*). If they get close enough to one of these fishes, they lunge forward and attempt to eat it. It has been suggested that by assuming the blue snout color, the trumpetfish confuses the *Chromis*, which use visual cues to maintain their shoals.
Captive Care: See the Captive Care section in the family account, page 395.
Aquarium Size: 200 gal. **Temperature:** 22 to 27°C (72 to 80°F).
Aquarium Suitability Index: 4.
Remarks: This species is replaced by *Aulostomus strigosus* Wheeler, 1955 in the Eastern Atlantic, and Ascension and St. Helena Islands.

Aulostomus maculatus, Atlantic Trumpetfish: for large aquariums only.

Aulostomus maculatus, Atlantic Trumpetfish: yellow variant.

Aulostomus maculatus, Atlantic Trumpetfish: blue-snouted variant.

References

Aronson (1983), Collette & Talbot (1972), Kaufman (1976), Randall (1967), Thresher (1984).

Family Pegasidae
Sea Moths

While some of the unexpected adaptations found on the reef include fishes that glow in the dark, others that live most of their lives under the sand, or families that fish for their food with a rod and bait, still others are absolute masters of camouflage. The Family Pegasidae is one of these bizarre families, containing a number of fish species that look like creatures from mythology.

Eurypegasus draconis, Dragon Sea Moth: mated pair viewed from above. The larger-bodied female is being followed by her male mate. Both are masters at camouflage.

Classification and Biology

Pegasidae is comprised of two genera (*Eurypegasus* and *Pegasus*) and five species. All of them are smaller fishes, attaining maximum lengths of less than 18 cm (7.1 in.). They are found in warm temperate and tropical areas of the Indo-Pacific, where they inhabit protected inshore waters. They are usually found on sand, coral gravel, rubble, and mud bottoms. Although most often found on slopes adjacent to coastal reefs, some species also inhabit seagrass beds and estuaries.

These fishes are true camouflage artists. They sport earthy colors, which they can change to better match the seafloor, and they will remain motionless on the substrate when threatened. The body is encased in a carapace that also provides some protection from predators. It has been suggested that the sea moths masquerade as pieces of debris, like broken seashells or dead plant material. Some species will also partially bury under the substrate. Sea moths move slowly, using their tentacle-like pelvic fins to walk over the substrate. If disturbed, they can move at greater speeds by beating the caudal fin.

The sea moths feed on small invertebrates that live on the substrate. They bring their mouths near their prey, then move their jaws forward and down to suck up small crustaceans, isopod eggs, crustacean larvae, fish eggs, worms, and foraminiferans. The sea moths stop crawling soon after the sun sets, and remain inactive until sunrise.

At least one species is known to be monogamous, with pair members forming long-lasting bonds. This mating system appears to maximize reproductive efficiency, especially for fishes like sea moths that occur at low densities and may otherwise have difficulty locating mates. The Dragon Sea Moth (*Eurypegasus draconis*) spawns at dusk and is a broadcast spawner, releasing its eggs into the water column where they enter the plankton. This species is also sexually dimorphic, with females having a larger carapace than males. Color differences between the sexes have been noted in at least one nonreef species.

Sea moths shed their skin to rid themselves of fouling organisms. One species (Dragon Sea Moth) has been reported to engage in skin shedding every 1 to 5 days, with the skin sloughing off in a single piece.

At least one species is collected and used for medicinal purposes in Hong Kong. The dead sea moth is placed in boiling water and the resulting broth is given to patients with throat problems.

Captive Care

The two sea moths that are available to aquarists have been successfully kept in tanks ranging in size from 5 to 220 gallons. However, adult individuals should be housed in tanks of at least 30 gallons. Because these fishes do not use the upper levels of the aquarium—with the exception of their spawning ascent—a tank with greater surface area is a better choice than an aquarium with more height. If you want to attempt to spawn sea moths, select a tank at least 61 cm (24 in.) high.

These fishes are not suitable for most reef aquariums because the tank bottoms do not offer the open expanse they need. Large individuals, especially Dragon Sea Moths, should be housed in aquariums with little, if any, live rock or other decor. If the aquarium is 100 gallons or more, a small patch reef composed of live rock and soft corals, stony corals, or corallimorpharians could be placed in one corner or along the back of the tank. You could also add some *Caulerpa* or *Halimeda* to the tank, but do not let the former take over as it may make it more difficult for the sea moth to find introduced food. Algal growth can be beneficial because it encourages the growth of amphipods, a valuable natural food source for sea moths. Sand, preferably of the live variety, should be used on the bottom of the tank, although the substrate depth is not critical.

Sea moths will not eat nonliving foods, but will take adult brine shrimp and their nauplii, *Mysis* shrimp, and other small benthic crustaceans (e.g., amphipods, isopods). They feed off the bottom—if the food is not lying on the substrate, they will not eat it. They should be fed four or five times a day to ensure they get enough to eat.

Sea moths should be housed with extremely passive tankmates. These fishes are slow and methodical when it comes to locating and ingesting their food. If they are kept with more active fishes, they may never get enough to eat. Potential tankmates include seahorses, pipefishes, gobies, and dragonets. They are also potential targets of sessile invertebrate feeders like angelfishes, triggerfishes, and puffers.

SEA MOTH SPECIES

Genus *Eurypegasus*

Eurypegasus draconis (Linnaeus, 1758)
Common Names: Dragon Sea Moth, Little Dragonfish.
Maximum Length: 7 cm (2.8 in.).
Distribution: East Africa north to the Red Sea, east to French Polynesia, north to southern Japan, and south to Lord Howe Island.
Biology: *Eurypegasus draconis* occurs on sand and mud slopes, often near coastal reefs, at depths of less than 1 to 91 m (3.3 to 296 ft.). One study reports that it is most abundant at 37 to 91 m (120 to 296 ft.), while another study regularly encountered this fish at a range of 1 to about 18 m (3.3 to 59 ft.). The Dragon Sea Moth is typically found on sand, mud, shell rubble, and fine to coarse pebble substrate. It is occasionally found in areas with isolated coral heads or small patch reefs, and sometimes occurs in seagrass or *Caulerpa* beds. In a study conducted in an area of suitable habitat in the northern Red Sea, it was estimated that the Dragon Sea Moth population density was one pair in every 325 to 477 m^2 (3,497 to 5,133 ft.^{2}). The most important components of the Dragon Sea Moth's diet are isopods, isopod eggs, copepods, copepod larvae, decapod larvae, and goby eggs. This species also consumes polychaetes, nematodes, trematodes, and

Eurypegasus draconis, Dragon Sea Moth: walking on leglike pelvic fins.

Eurypegasus draconis, Dragon Sea Moth: note pectoral fin patterns.

SEA MOTHS

Pegasus volitans, Slender Sea Moth: the most common sea moth in the aquarium trade.

Pegasus volitans, Slender Sea Moth: note lighter coloration to match the substrate below.

Pegasus volitans, Slender Sea Moth: a dark form typical of those from black sand or muddy areas.

pistol shrimps (*Alpheus* spp.) and will regularly ingest small stones (up to 1 mm in diameter). These fish live in pairs, with the male typically following close behind the female. Pairs have overlapping home ranges. A male will protect its mate from a consexual by placing itself between the intruding male and its female partner. The male will sometimes even cover the female with the front of his body and vibrate his pectoral fins when a consexual rival approaches.

Captive Care: Dragon Sea Moths will spend a lot of time moving about the tank and must be provided with plenty of room. More than one can be kept in the same tank as they rarely, if ever, display conspecific aggression. There have been reports of breeding in captivity, with aquarium spawnings taking place at water temperatures of around 27°C (81°F) in tanks with a minimum height of 61 cm (24 in.). It should be noted that the individuals that spawned were collected as pairs and housed in aquariums very near the collection site. Unfortunately, the Dragon Sea Moth often suffers from shipping stress and may take weeks before it fully acclimates. It is also inclined to damage its rostrum during transport by rubbing it against the plastic shipping bag. This fish should not be kept in a reef tank.

Aquarium Size: 55 gal. **Temperature:** 23 to 28°C (74 to 82°F).
Aquarium Suitability Index: 2.
Remarks: The Dragon Sea Moth is sexually dimorphic. The female has a larger carapace (it is appreciably wider), a shorter rostrum, and a shorter tail than the male. Some individuals have a light blue or white band along the outer margin of the pectoral fin. The only other member of this genus is the **Hawaiian Dragonfish** (*Eurypegasus papilio*) **(Gilbert, 1905)**. This species is more colorful than *E. draconis*, being olive green overall with white spots and orange mottling. It lacks the reticulated color pattern characteristic of *E. draconis* and occurs at greater depths (usually at 80 to 115 m [260 to 374 ft.]). It is rarely, if ever, available in the aquarium trade.

Genus *Pegasus*

Pegasus volitans Linnaeus, 1758
Common Names: Slender Sea Moth, Volitans Sea Moth, Slender Dragonfish.
Maximum Length: 11 cm (4.3 in.).
Distribution: East Africa north to the Arabian Gulf, east to eastern Australia, north to southern Japan.
Biology: The Slender Sea Moth occurs in bays, tidal channels, and estuaries, often in seagrass beds. It has been reported at depths of 1 to 73 m (3.3 to 237 ft.), although it is most common in the shallow part of this range (3 to 6 m [9.8 to 20 ft.]). Little is known about its natural history. The closely related Sculptured Sea Moth (*Pegasus lancifer*) forms aggregations in estuaries, where they spawn in pairs. Courtship includes raising the dorsal fin and spreading the pectoral fins; the male and female assume a vent-vent orientation and make a spawning ascent 1 m (3.3 ft.) over the seafloor. Gametes are released at the apex of this ascent. The Slender Sea Moth may bury under the substrate and is capable of rapid color changes to match its surroundings. It is reported to emit a strong odor when taken from the water.
Captive Care: This is the most common sea moth in the aquarium trade. It needs live food and peaceful tankmates. See the Captive Care section in the family account.
Aquarium Size: 30 gal. **Temperature:** 23 to 27°C (74 to 80°F).
Aquarium Suitability Index: 2.
Remarks: The coloration of Slender Sea Moths can vary appreciably. Those found on black sand or mud are often very dark, almost black; those from lighter substrates are pale. This species is not known to display any sexual dimorphism.

References
Herold & Clark (1993), Kuiter (1993), Palsson & Pietsch (1989).

Family Solenostomidae
Ghost Pipefishes

Although requiring an expert's care to survive in captivity, the ghost pipefishes seem to have universal appeal to reef naturalists. Members of the Family Solenostomidae are uncommon in most areas, but are probably sought after by more photographers and underwater observers than any other family of bony fishes.

Classification

Although there has been controversy over the actual number of species in Solenostomidae (ten nominal species were recognized until 1993), it is now thought that this family contains a single genus comprised of three described species, and three forms that are apparently undescribed (based on Orr & Fritzsche, 1993). One characteristic of the group that has caused some taxonomic confusion is that certain body proportions change as these fishes age. For example, an older specimen will have a thicker caudal peduncle, a deeper midbody, and a deeper snout than a juvenile.

All representatives of the family are limited in distribution to the Indo-west-Pacific and are characterized by a short body, long snout, two dorsal fins, a large anal fin, and large pelvic fins. The female's pelvic fins are larger than the male's and are connected to her body, forming a pouch. The ghost pipefish's body is enclosed by a series of stellate-shaped plates that form both incomplete and complete rings (defined as "interconnecting with all plates in the same vertical plane") of plates around the body. The characteristics that are most helpful in separating adult individuals of the various species are: the depth of the snout; the length and depth of the caudal peduncle; the presence of spines, spinules, and dermal appendages; the number of body and caudal peduncle plates; and the morphology of the nasal cavity. Unfortunately, young individuals are difficult to differentiate.

Biology

The ghost pipefishes inhabit calm coastal reefs, bays, and lagoon areas. They typically associate with sponges, gorgonians, soft corals, crinoids, algae, and seagrass. They often adopt the color, and sometimes the texture, of their hiding places in order to enhance their camouflage. The relatively small, pipettelike mouth is used to suck up small decapod shrimp and swarming mysid shrimp. Ghost pipefishes use sight to fixate on their prey. Once they do so, they stop moving, then dart forward to suck the prey into their small mouths. They ingest their prey at a maximum distance of about 1 cm.

The ghost pipefishes often occur in pairs as adults, and display size dimorphism, with females becoming larger than males.

Solenostomus paradoxus, Ornate Ghost Pipefish: typically found in pairs, as here with a large female, bearing eggs, and her much smaller mate.

Females are also easily recognized by their modified pelvic fins, which are joined together along the anterior edge and united along the rear margin by a membrane. There is a small opening on the right side of the brood pouch, between the uppermost pelvic fin ray and the "belly." The female is also more "girthy" than the male. Although quantitative studies are lacking on ghost pipefish social organization, it appears that they are monogamous, forming pair bonds for the reproductive season and possibly longer. These pairs are fairly site specific, being found in the same crinoid or gorgonian for days, weeks, or even months. At certain times of year, it is possible to encounter aggregations of ghost pipefishes in some areas. For example, more than 12 Ornate Ghost Pipefish (*Solenostomus paradoxus*) have been observed at the same time on a medium-sized patch reef near northeastern Sulawesi. At night, the color patterns of ghost pipefishes fade as they rest among algae, seagrasses, or the invertebrates with which they associate.

In courtship, the male approaches the female, swims back and forth, and circles her. While doing this, he raises and lowers his dorsal fin. In at least some species, the coloration of the male intensifies during these displays. The female adopts a head-down posture and directs the side of her body toward the male. This courtship can last for as long as three days and consummates with the two fish pressing their venters together as the female contracts and expands the pelvic "pouch" in order to draw sperm to the eggs.

Unlike the pipefishes of the Family Syngnathidae (whose males hold the eggs in a brood pouch), female ghost pipefishes carry the fertilized eggs and the embryos in a pouch formed by their modified pelvic fins. The brood pouch of the ghost pipefishes is also more structurally complex: unique branching stalks develop from the epidermis on the inside of the female's pelvic fins. These structures, known as cotylephores, are only present in brooding females and apparently appear when the eggs are deposited in the brood pouch. The cotylephore branches have a wide end, called the apical calyx, to which the eggs adhere. The cotylephores contain blood vessels that extend through these structures up into the apical calyx of each branch. It has been speculated that the capillary system present in the cotylephores may facilitate gas exchange, with oxygen entering and carbon dioxide exiting via the mother's bloodstream. In order to help oxygenate the brood pouch—and possibly also to reduce the ammonia level—the female expands and contracts the pelvic fins, ventilating the pouch. By adhering to the cotylephores, the eggs

Solenostomus paradoxus, Ornate Ghost Pipefish: the same fish or pair will often associate with the same crinoid or gorgonian for long periods of time.

Solenostomus armatus, Longtailed Ghost Pipefish (or possibly an undescribed species): a perfect *Halimeda* mimic.

Solenostomus paradoxus, Ornate Ghost Pipefish: camouflaging itself in a mass of black coral branches to avoid predation.

are prevented from being flushed out of the pouch.

The eggs are quite small, measuring about 1 mm in diameter, and hatch in 10 days to 3 weeks. The larvae are discharged from the dorsal slit of the pouch by sudden contractions of the pelvic fins. During each contraction, two to four larvae are expelled, which then enter the plankton. One captive Robust Ghost Pipefish (*Solenostomus cyanopterus*) was observed expelling 80 larvae. The fish was anesthetized and her brood pouch examined; it contained 70 more larvae and 200 eggs in various stages of development. This indicates that ghost pipefishes engage in multiple matings with the same partner. Egg clutch size in seven pregnant Ornate Ghost Pipefish ranged from 37 to 151 eggs and embryos, and may be as high as 350. When they settle out of the plankton, ghost pipefish young are transparent and quite large; in fact, they are almost sexually mature at this time. Soon after settling out, the transparent juveniles also begin changing to the adult coloration.

Captive Care

Ghost pipefishes do not do well in most home aquariums, and for this reason are best left in the ocean. The biggest problem they present is related to feeding. They typically ignore most aquarium fare, with the exception of live mysid shrimp, live brine shrimp, and small crustaceans associated with live rock. Large individuals may also consume small grass shrimp on occasion. The ghost pipefishes should be fed four or five times a day, or provided with a continuous source of food, to meet their nutritional needs.

Some aquarists have succeeded in maintaining these spectacular fishes in reef aquariums or tanks with lots of live rock, filamentous algae, and macroalgae. But even when housed in this setting, it is essential that food competitors (such as small wrasses, gobies, and dragonets) be excluded from the aquarium. They might thin out the populations of small crustaceans often associated with live rock that would serve as ghost pipefish fare.

If you are going to attempt to keep one of these fishes, it is best to house it in a smaller tank filled with live rock, either on its own or with a conspecific. They are relatively inactive fishes and can be housed in tanks as small as 20 gallons. Make sure you provide ghost pipefishes with adequate shelter. This can include live gorgonians or other soft corals, sponges (live or artificial), live rock, macroalgae, live seagrass, and artificial plants. Avoid live crinoids because they are very difficult to maintain for extended periods of time.

If you keep a ghost pipefish in a community aquarium with peaceful tankmates like seahorses, pipefishes, dragonets, and dart gobies, it is a good idea to set up a refugium—a separate tank with live rock and algae but no predators. A population of small crustaceans like amphipods can be encouraged to grow in this tank. About once a week, you can take pieces of live rock from the refugium and put them in the display tank to reinoculate the main aquarium with the ghost pipefish's natural prey. Larvae of ornamental shrimp, like those of the Peppermint Shrimp (*Lysmata wurdemanni*), also make excellent ghost pipefish food and can be produced in a refugium tank by a population of adult shrimp.

An external or internal refugium that slowly pumps water into the display aquarium, along with small crustaceans, is probably the most effective way to provide a ghost pipefish with enough to eat (for more information on refugiums, see "Keys to Successful Anthias Husbandry," page 548).

It is important not to house them with invertebrates that pack a potent sting like carpet anemones (*Stichodactyla* spp.), Elephant Ear Anemones (*Amplexidiscus fenestrafer*), and Elegance Coral (*Catalaphyllia jardinei*), or with large, potentially dangerous crustaceans like boxer shrimps, arrow crabs, large hermit crabs, and other large crab species. They will also feel more at home if kept in a tank with relatively little water flow, although the water should be well oxygenated. It is possible that bubbles produced by airstones may stick to these fishes and cause irritation.

GHOST PIPEFISH SPECIES

Solenostomus armatus Weber, 1913
Common Name: Longtailed Ghost Pipefish.
Maximum Length: 10 cm (3.9 in.).
Distribution: New South Wales, Australia, north to southern Japan.
Biology: The Longtailed Ghost Pipefish is a resident of coastal reefs—often in protected bays—where it lives over mud, sand, rubble, macroalgae, and sponge substrates. It has been reported from depths of 15 to 95 m (49 to 309 ft.). This species usually swims horizontally, with its tail slightly higher than its head.
Captive Care: See the Captive Care section in the family account, at left.
Aquarium Size: 20 gal. **Temperature:** 20 to 27°C (68 to 80°F).
Aquarium Suitability Index: 2.
Remarks: The Longtailed Ghost Pipefish is typically brown, greenish brown, or yellow overall. This species has a longer caudal peduncle, its length can be divided four to five times by its depth, the deepest part of the snout is equal to the eye orbit width, and the posterior margin of the brood pouch is concave.

Solenostomus armatus, Longtailed Ghost Pipefish (male): difficult to keep.

Adult *Solenostomus armatus*, Longtailed Ghost Pipefish: rubble dweller.

Solenostomus cyanopterus, Robust Ghost Pipefish: seagrass mimic.

Solenostomus cyanopterus Bleeker, 1854

Common Name: Robust Ghost Pipefish.
Maximum Length: 15 cm (5.9 in.).
Distribution: In the Indian Ocean from southern Africa, Réunion and Mauritius Islands, north to the northern Red Sea, and east to Christmas Island and western Australia. In the Western Pacific from Indonesia east to Fiji Islands, north to Japan, and south to New South Wales, Australia.
Biology: The Robust Ghost Pipefish occurs in coastal bays, in river mouths or estuaries, and on protected fringing reefs, where it usually associates with seagrass, macroalgae, and macroalgae/sponge beds. In the Red Sea, it has been reported living around macroalgae and seagrasses of the genera *Cytoseira*, *Halimeda*, *Halophila*, and *Sargassum*. When threatened, this fish will move in among the plant life. It feeds on crustaceans that swarm near, or live on, this plant material. This pipefish is found near the surface to a depth of 25 m (81 ft.). The Robust Ghost Pipefish usually hangs vertically in the water column, with its head toward the bottom, but often adopts a horizontal orientation when it moves. It feeds on small crustaceans and often occurs in pairs.
Captive Care: See the Captive Care section in the family account, page 404. This species has been reported to breed in captivity and will eat small crustaceans like live brine shrimp, small isopods, and amphipods.
Aquarium Size: 20 gal. **Temperature:** 21 to 27°C (70 to 80°F).
Aquarium Suitability Index: 2.
Remarks: This species is bright green, greenish brown, pale brown, reddish brown, gray, or yellow. Some darker individuals have yellow to orange blotches, while others have pink splotches that look like encrusting coralline algae. In certain habitats, such as among rocks and macroalgae, these fish assume a blotched color pattern. The Robust Ghost Pipefish is easily distinguished from other members of the genus by the short caudal peduncle (about equal to the depth of the caudal peduncle), a deep snout (the depth is greater than the width of the eye orbit), and a convex posterior brood pouch margin. Its body is often covered with small filaments.

Solenostomus cyanopterus, Robust Ghost Pipefish: a pair among seagrass.

Solenostomus paradoxus (Pallas, 1870)
Common Name: Ornate Ghost Pipefish.
Maximum Length: 10 cm (3.9 in.).
Distribution: East Africa north to the northern Red Sea, south to New South Wales, Australia, and north to Japan.
Biology: The Ornate Ghost Pipefish is found on coastal coral and rocky reefs. It occurs on patch reefs in sheltered bays, on fringing reef faces, and on dropoffs. This species is usually found at a depth range of 3 to 30 m (10 to 98 ft.), hanging vertically in the arms of crinoids or amid the branches of gorgonians and black coral. Adults of this species form pairs, but occasionally they may form temporary groups. Even where this fish is common, it is often overlooked because of its effective camouflage.

Captive Care: See the Captive Care section in the family account, page 404.
Aquarium Size: 20 gal. **Temperature:** 20 to 27°C (68 to 80°F).
Aquarium Suitability Index: 2.
Remarks: *Solenostomus paradoxus* comes in a rainbow of hues, including white, black, or transparent body and fins, with yellow, red, or orange blotches. There are two large spots on the first dorsal fin, which in some color morphs look like fried eggs (white with yellow centers).

This species apparently displays sexual dimorphism, with females attaining a larger size than males. Unlike the other ghost pipefishes, this species has deeply incised membranes between the caudal fin rays.

Solenostomus paradoxus, Ornate Ghost Pipefish: male.

Solenostomus paradoxus, Ornate Ghost Pipefish: female.

Solenostomus paradoxus, Ornate Ghost Pipefish: black and yellow variant.

Solenostomus paradoxus, Ornate Ghost Pipefish: from Northern Sulawesi.

Solenostomus sp. 1, Hairy Ghost Pipefish: a bizarre, undescribed species that often occurs among red filamentous algae or soft corals.

Solenostomus sp. 1
Common Names: Hairy Ghost Pipefish, Irish Setter.
Maximum Length: 12 cm (4.7 in.).
Distribution: Indonesia and the Solomon Islands.
Biology: This rare, bizarre-looking creature usually associates with colorful soft corals. The specimen in the photograph above was found at a depth of 12 m (39 ft.).
Captive Care: See the Captive Care section in the family account, page 404.
Aquarium Size: 20 gal. **Temperature:** 24 to 28°C (76 to 82°F).
Aquarium Suitability Index: 2.
Remarks: This species is pink or reddish orange with long dermal appendages. It has a deep snout (wider than the eye orbit) and photographs show it to have a short caudal peduncle. It is possible that the Hairy Ghost Pipefish is a rare morph of *S. paradoxus*.

Solenostomus sp. 2
Common Name: Filamented Ghost Pipefish.
Maximum Length: 9 cm (3.5 in.).
Distribution: Indonesia and the Philippines.
Biology: This is another rare ghost pipefish that occurs on shallow sand flats near clumps of macroalgae. I observed several of these fishes (one adult pair and one juvenile) in approximately 4 m (13 ft.) of water.
Captive Care: See the Captive Care section in the family account, page 404.
Aquarium Size: 20 gal. **Temperature:** 24 to 28°C (76 to 82°F).
Aquarium Suitability Index: 2.
Remarks: This species is pale green with brown and white patches and filaments. There are also two white spots on the first dorsal fin membrane. The Filamented Ghost Pipefish has a deep snout (wider than the eye orbit), a long caudal peduncle (three or four

Solenostomus sp. 2, Filamented Ghost Pipefish: lives among macroalgae.

Solenostomus sp. 2, Filamented Ghost Pipefish: displaying.

Solenostomus sp. 3, Velvety Ghost Pipefish: female with damaged tail.

Solenostomus sp. 3, Velvety Ghost Pipefish: smaller male.

times the depth of the caudal peduncle), and is covered with short filaments. Although not greatly incised, the membranes between the rays of the caudal fin are concave.

Solenostomus sp. 3
Common Name: Velvety Ghost Pipefish.
Maximum Length: 10 cm (3.9 in.).
Distribution: Sulawesi, Indonesia.
Biology: The Velvety Ghost Pipefish is a spectacular fish found on coastal reefs to depths of at least 9 m (29 ft.). It occurs in pairs and often hangs near the sponges it appears to mimic. Swims head down. This species appears to be sexually dimorphic, with females being larger than males.

Captive Care: See the Captive Care section in the family account, page 404.
Aquarium Size: 20 gal. **Temperature:** 24 to 28°C (76 to 82°F).
Aquarium Suitability Index: 2.
Remarks: The body texture of this pipefish looks like velvet, hence the common name. It can be pink to deep red in color. It has a short caudal peduncle (about equal to the caudal peduncle depth) and a deep snout (depth greater than the width of the eye orbit).

References
Fishelson (1966), Kuiter (1996), Kuiter & Debelius (1994), Orr & Fritzsche (1993), Wetzel & Wourms (1995), Wilder & Fritzsche (1993).

Family Syngnathidae
Seahorses and Pipefishes

For millennia, the ocean's inhabitants have captured the imagination of humankind. Giant squids, sharks, and moray eels, for example, have long been depicted as oceanic villains that would devour any hapless human (or in the case of the giant squid, any ship) that entered their domain. Although not cast in the role of the rogue, the seahorse has also been the subject of numerous myths and tales that amplified its rather humble size and unusual anatomy.

The genus name, *Hippocampus*, comes from the Greek, *hippo*, meaning horse, and *kampos*, a sea monster. In ancient times, the seahorse was considered an oceanic freak, composed of the forequarters of a horse and the hindquarters of a dolphin. This thought may have been at the root of the fanciful notion that mythical gods and superheroes used the seahorse for transportation. Although his views are not as sensationalistic, in 1810, the Italian naturalist M. Rafinesque suggested that the seahorse was not a "true fish" at all, but was more likely a "marine insect."

While aquarists are aware of their true piscine status, the seahorses still generate fascination among hobbyists. Their equally odd family mates, the pipefishes, are also of interest. Although both groups are considered difficult to keep, seahorses and pipefishes can be successfully maintained in a home aquarium with proper care and careful tankmate selection. Some species are actually easy to breed, and the offspring can be raised in captivity.

The Family Syngnathidae is comprised of 52 genera and approximately 200 species. It is divided into two subfamilies—the Hippocampinae (seahorses) and the Syngnathinae (pipefishes). All the syngnathids have elongate bodies encased in a series of body rings. Pipefishes swim in the more conventional fishlike fashion (i.e., with their bellies oriented toward the substrate), while seahorses swim upright with their tails down and their heads up. Most family members have one dorsal fin and a small anal fin. They have small pectoral fins, no pelvic fins, and a caudal fin that is either small or absent. In the Subfamily Hippocampinae, and in a few pipefish species, the caudal peduncle is prehensile and can bend ventrally, which is unique among fishes. This prehensile peduncle enables these fishes to remain stationary by holding onto benthic structures. All members of the family have small gill openings, while some have cirri and skin flaps to accentuate their camouflage. They have relatively small mouths located on the end of a long snout, no teeth, and very simple stomachs. Like the Old World chameleons, the syngnathids can also move their eyes independently. One naturalist penned, "One eye may roll towards you, while the other may be passive, or look backward, or the opposite direction."

The most peculiar characteristic of this family is their reproductive mode. In all the syngnathids, it is the adult male that gets pregnant; that is, the males brood the developing eggs in an abdominal pouch until they hatch. The morphology of the brood pouch differs between seahorses and pipefishes and can vary from one genus to the next within the the pipefish subfamily.

Most members of this family inhabit marine environments, although some also occur in brackish and/or freshwater. They reach their apex of diversity in relatively shallow-water habitats like seagrass beds and mangrove swamps and on coral reefs. Some species are limited in distribution to temperate seas, including the spectacular Weedy Seadragon (*Phyllopteryx taeniolatus*) and the Leafy Seadragon (*Phycodurus eques*), which are found among macroalgae on rocky reefs in Australia. The seadragons are protected by law and can only be imported by collectors with special permits.

Hippocampus ingens, Pacific Seahorse: engaging inshore creatures that are attracting new attention from marine biologists and serious aquarists.

SUBFAMILY HIPPOCAMPINAE (SEAHORSES)

Biology

The Subfamily Hippocampinae currently contains a single genus with 30 recognized species, although it is widely accepted that this subfamily is in need of taxonomic revision. Seahorse species can be difficult for the untrained ichthyologist to differentiate. The characteristics most useful in separating them include the number of trunk and tail rings, the presence or absence of spines or thorns on the body ring ridges, the length of the snout, and the color pattern (although this can be quite variable). The morphology of certain species varies greatly from one location to the next, and these disparate populations may actually represent distinct species.

Habitat, Predators, and Prey

The majority of seahorses occur in marine environments, although one has been reported to live in a freshwater river in Vietnam. Seahorses are most often encountered in protected habitats where water movement is reduced, including coastal bays and lagoons. They often associate with seagrass meadows or pier pilings, where they attach to sessile invertebrates like sponges and gorgonians that grow on the submerged structures. At least some species stay within a relatively small home range, especially when pregnant. For example, in one species, it is not uncommon for a gravid male to remain in an area of less than 1 m (3.3 ft.) and stay on the same blade of seagrass for over half of its pregnancy.

The seahorses rely on crypsis and—to a lesser degree—their bony armor to avoid being eaten. Although they are often well camouflaged, seahorses are still eaten by predatory fishes (e.g., frogfishes, remoras, and tunas) and may also fall prey to large crustaceans. Sea turtles, including the Ridley Turtle (*Lepidochelys olivacea*), Kemp's Turtle (*Lepidochelys kempi*), and Loggerhead Turtle (*Caretta caretta*), are also seahorse predators. Seahorses feed on small crustaceans—both swarming varieties (like mysid shrimp and copepods) and benthic forms (like amphipods and small shrimps). Most employ a sit-and-wait feeding strategy, remaining stationary and snapping up prey items that come near. When capturing prey, they quickly throw open their small toothless jaws, creating a vacuum that draws the prey item into the mouth. Instead of being masticated, the food goes straight into the alimentary tract. The seahorse stomach is very simple—it consists of a slight widening of the intestine—and is not very efficient at absorbing nutrients from the food that passes through. As a result, these fishes have to eat a lot to meet their nutritional needs.

Seahorses are capable of rapid color transformations, which they employ to blend with their surroundings and to communicate with conspecifics. Color change is also an important component of courtship and mating. These quick changes consist of a modification of the hue—either a lightening or darkening of the skin or the development of brighter highlights. Drastic chromatic alterations take longer and can be a function of the seahorse's diet. For example, individuals that have consumed prey rich in carotenoids may turn orange. In other cases, a seahorse's color appears to be genetically controlled.

Reproduction

To date, all of the seahorses studied in the wild are monogamous (although they don't always maintain pair bonds in captivity). This is a rare mating system in the coral reef fish community. One behavior that apparently facilitates their monogamous mating system is the morning greeting. Each morning, even during the nonmating period, the male and female seek each other out, then engage in "dancing" and color changes. Even during the male's pregnancy, the pair continues to perform these communication ceremonies—although the duration of the bouts is shorter. Greeting behavior apparently functions to synchronize reproductive readiness in both sexes and may also be important in establishing and maintaining pair bonds (see the Biology section on pipefishes, page 427, for more details).

It appears that males compete for females with several stereotypical behaviors. In snapping behavior, one seahorse will lower its head and flick its snout against the pectoral or gill area of a competitor. If the snap is well placed, it will actually launch the rival up to 10 cm (3.9 in.) away from the individual that delivered the blow. Males also exhibit wrestling behavior, in which one male grasps the other with its prehensile tail.

During the mating period, pair members engage in lengthy bouts of courtship behavior. Individuals change color (e.g., black individuals lighten and develop a red color along the dorsal ridge and the margin of the dorsal fin) and display (e.g., erect all fins, snap, chase, nip, and wrestle). Males initiate reproduction in the wild, while multiple males have been observed to solicit a single female in captivity.

Courtship may last up to 3 days before mating actually takes place. On the second day of courtship, the female's eggs start to become hydrated and her abdomen becomes noticeably swollen. If a female is separated from a male after the eggs become hydrated, she will expel the unfertilized clutch. Males will indicate

Hippocampus erectus, Lined Seahorse: although fascinating and often brightly colored, members of this family demand specialized aquarium care and ideally should be housed in a simple system devoted to seahorses.

Hippocampus bargabanti, Pygmy Seahorse: male seahorses carry fertilized eggs in a brood pouch, giving birth to between 10 and 150 fully formed fry.

their readiness to mate by flexing their tail up and down against the trunk, which pumps water in and out of the pouch. A receptive female will respond to the males pumping by pointing. She does this by directing her snout upward so that it forms an oblique angle with her body axis.

When seahorses mate, the pair members intertwine and begin to rise off the substrate. While in the water column, the female inserts her ovipositor into the male's pouch opening and deposits her clutch of eggs. Fertilization takes place in the brood pouch, which becomes spongy, heavily vascularized, and distended during the mating period. This unique compartment provides the developing eggs with nourishment, oxygen, protection, and a suitable osmotic environment. The pregnancy lasts for about 10 to 21 days, and development is highly dependent on temperature. Males usually give birth in the early morning, expelling an estimated 10 to 150 "baby" seahorses. After a male liberates his young, courtship and mating begins again. In pairs that have already spawned, the duration of courtship is usually shorter. Even if a female encounters other sexually receptive males, she will usually wait for her original partner to give birth and then mate with him again.

Captive Care

There are two schools of thought regarding captive care of seahorses. Some hobbyists suggest they are very difficult to keep, while others feel they are well suited to aquarium living. Actually, both groups are right. If you can acquire healthy individuals, know their specific needs, and are willing to meet them, seahorses can be successfully maintained in the home aquarium. However, if you purchase unhealthy individuals and do not have either the time or desire to give them the attention they deserve, you are bound to fail. Before you plunge into seahorse keeping, please read "Seahorses in Trouble," page 413, and consider the potential ecological consequences that collecting seahorses can have on wild stocks.

The Aquarium, Water Conditions, and Aquascaping

Seahorses can be kept in smaller aquariums; in fact, they often do better in a more restricted setting. It is actually easier to feed seahorses in a smaller volume of water, because food densities will be higher and they will have to swim a shorter distance to capture the food. A 10-gallon aquarium is suitable for as many as 6 or 8 adult seahorses and could house as many 20 Dwarf Seahorses (*Hippocampus zosterae*). Remember, however, that the more seahorses you have, the more time and effort will be required to care for these needy creatures. You would be better off starting with a solitary individual or a pair. If a seahorse is kept in a larger aquarium (especially if the tank contains more active food competitors), you can remove the seahorse from the more spacious tank at feeding time and place it in a smaller container, such as a 1-gallon glass jar, with some plastic plants. Wait 10 or 15 minutes for the seahorse to settle down, then add the live food. The drawback to this method is that capturing and relocating the fish may reduce its likelihood of eating and may cause stress and/or physical damage to the specimen.

Seahorses are not very particular about water conditions. A specific gravity of 1.020 to 1.025 will suffice (some species, like the Dwarf Seahorse, *H. zosterae*, can be kept in more hyposaline

Seahorses in Trouble

While no other reef fishes kept by aquarists appear to be threatened, endangered, or in trouble from overcollection, the state of the world's seahorses is of growing concern to a number of biologists. Before purchasing seahorses for an aquarium, you should know that populations of these remarkable creatures are declining at a rapid rate in many areas. For example, reports indicate that the *Hippocampus* populations in the central Philippines have diminished by 70% between 1985 and 1995. Preliminary data also suggests that seahorse numbers have dropped by 50% in five seahorse exporting countries in the last 5 years. Two questions immediately come to mind: Why are seahorse numbers declining at such a rapid rate? Are we marine aquarists responsible for the potential demise of these marvelous animals?

Unfortunately, the ornamental fish trade must take some of the blame, because a substantial number (possibly hundreds of thousands) of seahorses are imported to North America, Europe, Taiwan, and Japan every year for sale as live pets. (Sadly, most are purchased by children or beginning hobbyists who are woefully unaware of how to keep them alive.) However, the biggest consumer of the various *Hippocampus* species is traditional Chinese, Japanese, and Korean medicine. Dried seahorses are used to treat a wide range of illnesses and conditions, including asthma, arteriosclerosis, thyroid disorders, skin diseases, heart disease, sexual dysfunction, lethargy, and general pain. The annual consumption by Asian nations of dried seahorses has been estimated at 45 tons, which equates to about 16 million individuals. Global consumption of seahorses for medicinal purposes, for curios (dried seahorses are still being sold as decorations) and for the aquarium trade is probably around 20 million individuals a year, with Thailand, Vietnam, India, and the Philippines exporting most of these seahorses. However, a total of 39 countries are involved in the buying and selling of seahorses. (In the United States, around 112,000 seahorses were collected in Florida in 1994).

If you've ever searched for seahorses in the wild, you know that they are not easy to find. The densities of most species are naturally low, while the demand is high. As a result, there are many fishermen who go after seahorses, with each individual catching relatively few. However, within any given area, seahorses are susceptible to overfishing, because: 1) they have a low fecundity (producing relatively few young); 2) they have a lengthy parental-care period; 3) they are monogamous, and their social structure can be easily disrupted when adult individuals are removed; and 4) it is difficult for them to recolonize an area because they are not extremely mobile and thus occupy relatively small home ranges.

The other significant problem that seahorses face is the destruction of their habitat. Many seahorses live in seagrass beds and mangrove swamps, two inshore ecosystems that are under worldwide pressure from development and population growth. For example, the Dwarf Seahorse (*Hippocampus zosterae*) is declining in southern Florida because of the decimation of favorable habitat (collection for the aquarium trade has no doubt contributed to their scarcity here as well).

Overcollection and habitat destruction threaten wild stocks.

Dr. Amanda Vincent, the world's leading authority on the Hippocampinae, is spearheading the effort to save the seahorses. She works closely with the Philippine and Vietnamese governments in an attempt to preserve their shrinking seahorse populations. In Vietnam, Dr. Vincent is helping to set up captive-breeding programs, while in the Philippines she works with the Haribon Foundation for the conservation of natural resources encouraging local fishermen to place any juvenile seahorses they capture into "grow-out cages" for 5 months so that they can mature and produce some progeny (which can swim through the mesh netting of the cage) before they are removed from the wild.

As aquarists, we can be part of the solution. Given the threat to wild populations and the healthy market for these animals, here is a clear opportunity for competent seahorse keepers: establish breeding populations of these animals so that hobbyist's demands can be met with captive-raised individuals. This will help take some of the pressure off wild stocks and will also provide a *Hippocampus* repository in case the populations of some seahorse species are totally wiped out.

Consumers can also help by supporting captive-breeding programs and exercising care when buying these fishes. Fish collectors, wholesalers, retailers, and hobbyists can all make a difference by only picking adult individuals. Younger seahorses should be left in the wild and given an opportunity to reproduce. I would also encourage beginning aquarists should start with a hardier group of fishes that is not in potential ecological peril. Finally, you may wish to visit Dr. Amanda Vincent's Web site (**www.anyware.co.uk/seahorses**) to learn more about the seahorse trade or how to support her conservation efforts.

conditions), with an alkalinity of 175 to 200 ppm, and no ammonia or nitrites. Seahorses do not seem to be overly sensitive to the buildup of nitrates, although biweekly or monthly water changes (totaling about 20 to 25% of water volume per month) are recommended. Because these fishes require frequent feeding, it is also a good idea to use a protein skimmer to reduce the level of dissolved organics in the aquarium water. This is not essential, but if you do offer frozen mysid shrimp—which are very oily—a protein skimmer will be necessary to remove the slick that will form on the water's surface. In order for a seahorse to maintain a healthy body armor, it must have enough calcium. Either calcium levels in the water should be maintained at higher levels (300 to 400 mg/L or more), or the fish's diet should be supplemented with calcium (one researcher used Kalkwasser in the diet of Dwarf Seahorses).

Try to avoid excessive water flow in a seahorse aquarium. These fishes are poor swimmers and will have difficulty pursuing food or changing position if strong currents buffet them. A seahorse will also need to expend large amounts of energy during daily activities in a tank with swirling currents. This could lead to a caloric deficit and its eventual demise. Remember that these fishes are mainly found in bays and protected coastal reefs, not in areas prone to excessive or constant currents. If you do keep them in a tank with heavy currents, like a reef aquarium, the pumps should be on a timer. This will allow for periods of time when water movement is reduced. Seahorse holdfasts should also be placed in areas of the tank that are not subjected to too much current. One advantage of some water movement is that it moves nonliving food particles around the aquarium, making them more attractive to your seahorses.

It is very important to provide seahorses with stationary objects around which they can wrap their prehensile tails when at rest. These can include macroalgae, like *Caulerpa* or *Gracilia*, plastic plants, bleached hard or faux corals (especially branching forms like staghorn coral), tubular sponges, dried (make sure they're treated) and live gorgonians, as well as plastic gorgonian replicas. Calcareous macroalgae, like *Halimeda*, *Penicillus*, and *Udotea*, also make great "hitching posts."

It is possible for captive seahorses to become wedged in rock crevices and need the aquarist to liberate them. Avoid placing rockwork too close to the front of the tank; the seahorse may get stuck between the decor and the aquarium glass. This is not usually a fatal problem if the seahorse is released, but it may expend a considerable amount of energy trying to get free.

Seahorses can be kept in a reef aquarium, as they are of little or no threat to desirable invertebrates, but they are often more difficult to feed in this venue—especially if it is a large tank—and they could be stung by some large-polyped stony corals (e.g., Elegance Coral, *Catalaphyllia jardinei*). One advantage of reef aquariums is that populations of small crustaceans, which often grow profusely in tanks that lack microcrustacean predators, can provide a supplementary seahorse food source. Although seahorses will not pick at corals, they have been known to cause damage to gorgonians, especially in a tank that contains few

Hippocampus reidi, Longsnout Seahorse: seahorses require suitable holdfasts. This pregnant male grasps a sponge.

Hippocampus kuda, Common Seahorse: hitching themselves to live corals can cause problems, and they are often difficult to feed in a reef tank.

suitable attachment sites. They often use gorgonians as holdfasts, wrapping their tails around the branches. This usually causes the gorgonian to retract its tentacles, which interferes with its ability to feed. If the seahorse consistently uses the gorgonian as a hitching post, it could cause long-term health problems for the invertebrate.

Nutrition and Feeding

One of the biggest obstacles in the long-term maintenance of seahorses is proper feeding and nutrition. The most popular foods given to pet store seahorses are live brine shrimp and baby livebearers (e.g., guppies, mollies). While in most cases seahorses may do well for up to six months on such a diet, they will gradually become malnourished and die. If you offer a diet consisting mainly of live brine shrimp, it is important to fortify them with vitamins. For example, you can place the shrimp in a gallon jar with some seawater, then add liquid vitamin supplement. One of the best products is Selco, a nutritional supplement fortified with omega-3 fatty acids and stabilized vitamins C and B_{12}. Add approximately 1.0 ml of Selco for every 6 oz. of brine shrimp. Let the shrimp soak in the fortified medium for 12 to 24 hours, rinse them with seawater, then feed them to your seahorses. The shrimp will have ingested the extra nutrients, making them a more complete food source for your seahorses. You can also feed the adult brine shrimp a food that has been soaked in a nutritional additive.

The best source of nutrition for captive seahorses is mysid shrimp. Seahorses fed exclusively on frozen mysid shrimp have been reported to live for over 18 months, as well as to engage in reproductive behavior. You can feed either live or frozen mysids, although frozen mysids are easier to obtain and maintain. When thawed, the mysid shrimp should be whole specimens—not an enormous mass of appendages and body parts. It is also best to choose a brand enriched with omega-3 fatty acids (the only supplier I know of is Piscine Energetics Inc., RR #2 S11 C5, Enderby, BC, V0E 1V0, Canada).

Healthy seahorses will usually accept thawed mysid shrimp without much coaxing. Others will need to be duped into ingesting this nonliving diet. Placing the shrimp in the current, which pushes the small dead mysids around the tank, is one effective way to do this. Another is to introduce the shrimp along with live prey (i.e., live brine shrimp or baby livebearers). Finicky seahorses are often catalyzed to feed by the presence of baby guppies or mollies and will usually suck up the thawed mysids as well as the livebearers.

Live mysid shrimp cultures are also currently available and can be raised in a refugium attached to the display tank. In most refugiums, mysids and other small crustaceans are slowly introduced to the tank with a water pump—which can damage the shrimp as they pass through the pump. In internal refugiums, the mysids are carried over an overflow into the tank (for more information on refugiums and their use for fish feeding, see "Keys to Successful Anthias Husbandry," page 548). Mysids and other crustaceans can also be cultured in a totally separate aquarium. To do this, set up a 20-gallon tank and put plenty of light over the aquarium (e.g., two 20-watt fluorescent lights). Add a few pieces of live rock and some macroalgae, like *Caulerpa*. Occasionally add a little fish food, like sinking pellets. In a setup like this, you should be able to farm a healthy population of amphipods, copepods, and mysids. Occasionally, you can scoop up some of these crustaceans with a small brine shrimp net and add them to the seahorse display tank.

Although less desirable than mysids, another readily available seahorse food item is the grass shrimp. These are often sold for freshwater tanks, and small, live specimens make an adequate starter food or dietary supplement for larger seahorses. The only problems with feeding grass shrimp are that they may carry seahorse parasites and disease. Freshwater or saltwater amphipods (like *Grammarus*) are also suitable seahorse fodder, but are often more difficult to obtain.

The hobbyist who lives near a coast could acquire a plankton net and capture zooplankton to feed his or her *Hippocampus*. Other possible foods include *Daphnia* and mosquito larvae, although neither of these organisms will live long in saltwater.

Seahorses require frequent feeding. In the wild, a seahorse will consume hundreds or even thousands of small crustaceans in a single day. In captivity, you should feed them a minimum of three times a day. Because these fishes are inefficient at extracting nutrients from their food, are slow-moving, and have a difficult time chasing their prey (they are ambush predators), it is important to add enough food to the tank for them to get enough to eat. In order to avoid fouling the aquarium with uneaten, rotting food, remove perishable foods after the seahorse has had about 30 minutes to feed. One of the advantages to adding adult brine, grass, and mysid shrimps or baby livebearers is that they will continue as a live food source for a while in the saltwater aquarium. For more details on seahorse feeding, see Giwojna (1996a, 1996b, 1996c).

Seahorse Tankmates

Great care should be exercised when selecting tankmates for your seahorses. They should never be housed with aggressive feeders, which will snap up any available food before the seahorses have a chance to feed. Some groups that fall into this category are anthias, dottybacks, grammas, hawkfishes, damselfishes, and wrasses. These fishes will also eat any small crustaceans that may be naturally reproducing in the aquarium, which could otherwise provide a supplementary source of natural fare for your seahorses.

It is possible to keep seahorses with potential competitors if you are willing to take the extra time to make sure the seahorses have access to enough food. There are several ways to do this. One is to remove the seahorse from the tank and feed it in a separate container; however, there are problems inherent with this feeding method. A more desirable technique is to train your seahorses to take food from a large eyedropper or a turkey baster with a piece of air line tubing connected to the end. Just suck up some frozen mysids or fortified live brine shrimp and place the air line tubing into the tank. Move the tubing slowly and deliberately toward the seahorse until the opening is 3 or 4 cm (1.2 to 1.6 in.) away from the fish's head, then gently squeeze the bulb until a couple of shrimp are expelled. If the seahorse eats these, push out several more. Continue to do this until the fish loses interest (i.e., is satiated). The seahorse will learn to recognize the feeding instrument as a source of food and will move toward it when it is placed in the aquarium.

Slow-moving seahorses can fall victim to nipping species, like wrasses, blennies, and tobies. For example, cleaner wrasses (*Labroides* spp.) will irritate seahorses by doggedly picking at them; blennies, like the Jeweled Rockskipper (*Salarias fasciatus*), will persistently gnaw at their body surfaces; and small tobies (*Canthigaster* spp.) will bite off their undulating fins. Fortunately, if the guilty fin-nipper is removed from the tank, a seahorse can regenerate its fins in about 2 weeks. Even though they are armor-plated, seahorses still fall prey to other fishes. For example, large pufferfishes, triggerfishes, and porcupinefishes will eat seahorses like hard candy; while frogfishes, scorpionfishes, and groupers will swallow them whole (see photograph, page 336).

There are also some invertebrates that are not suitable seahorse tankmates. These include reef lobsters, larger anemones with a more potent sting (especially the carpet anemones), and large crabs, including hermit crabs. Seahorses may collide with stinging anemones, which might eat or at least sting and damage them, while predatory crustaceans are not above capturing and eating the less nimble seahorse.

The most suitable tankmates are nonaggressive, slow-moving fishes like ghost pipefishes, shrimpfishes, dragonets, some smaller gobies, and the seahorse relatives, the pipefishes.

Diseases, Parasites, and Other Maladies

Unfortunately, like any marine fishes, seahorses are not immune to an array of parasites and diseases. One of the most lethal is white boil disease. This ailment, which is almost always fatal, is caused by the microsporidian (fungus) *Glugea heraldi*. This fungus infects the external body surface as well as the internal organs (e.g., liver, connective tissue, and musculature). It first appears as white boil-like cysts on the head and body. Individuals with this disease often continue to breed and feed, although as the disease progresses they become lethargic and anorexic. In the latter stages, whitish gray ulcerations begin to appear on the body surface, swimming ability becomes impaired, and death usually follows soon after. *Glugea* is difficult to treat and is highly infectious. Therefore, the best way to prevent your seahorse colony from being wiped out is to quarantine all new specimens for at least 2 weeks and to promptly remove any individual within the "herd" that shows signs of this fungus. The most common source of *Glugea* is seahorses collected from Florida—these animals should never be introduced to an existing colony without long and careful observation. White boil disease can also be easily transmitted from one tank to another via cleaning sponges, filter equipment, and any substrate (including invertebrates). It is important, therefore, to disinfect any equipment that has been used in the infected tank and to avoid introducing substrate from an aquarium known to contain *Glugea*. There are no known treatments for this disease, although some have reported success with malachite green and metronidazole. In most cases, however, it is best to euthanize any seahorse that comes down with this disease. Tear down and bleach any tank that contained a *Glugea*-infected seahorse and either throw away or sterilize the substrate that was in it.

Young seahorses have also been reported to succumb to other fungal infections. In these individuals, massive amounts of mucus are produced, their integument sloughs off, and fungus covers the fins and tail. Seahorses exhibiting these symptoms should be treated by swabbing the body and fins with Betadine (10% povidone-iodine), then giving a 1-minute freshwater bath. This treatment regime should be performed for 5 consecutive days.

Another parasite that affects seahorses is *Brooklynella hostilis*, often called anemonefish disease. This ciliated protozoan infects the gills and skin of its fish host, causing the fish to become lethargic and anorexic. Lesions appear on the body and epithelial layer of the skin and later slough off. *Brooklynella* infections if left untreated typically result in the death of the seahorse. This parasite is most often encountered in aquariums that are overcrowded or where water conditions have deteriorated. Fortunately, *Brooklynella* can be effectively eradicated by treating with formalin and malachite green (available in several aquarium medications). Freshwater dips can also bring about some immediate relief, although this can also increase a fish's stress level. Copper is ineffective against this parasite.

Newly collected seahorses may host parasitic copepods and/or isopods, which are best removed with a pair of tweezers. Seahorses can also be infected by monogenetic trematodes (flukes). Trematodes usually do not have a deleterious impact on their seahorse host unless the fish's immune system has been compromised as a result of poor water quality or inadequate nutrition. If a seahorse is respiring rapidly and flaring its gill covers, it may be necessary to treat for flukes. The two compounds most commonly employed to kill these parasites are trichlorfon (Dylox) and praziquantel. You can add trichlorfon to the aquarium (at a concentration of 0.4 to 0.6 ppm) or immerse the fish in a praziquantel bath (leave the individual in a bath that contains 10 mg of praziquantel per liter of seawater for no less than 3 hours). A freshwater dip (of about 3 minutes) can impede the reproduction of some flukes, although it won't eradicate them. Liver flukes are a more serious seahorse plague that is not detectable until a necropsy is done on the dead fish. There is nothing you can do to prevent or treat this condition, but it does not appear to be contagious.

The notorious protozoan *Uronema marinum* can also infect and kill seahorses. It is difficult to diagnose, unless you take a skin smear and look at some slime under the microscope. *Uronema* infestations typically manifest as lesions or reddened areas (resulting from secondary bacterial infections) on the body surface.

Hippocampus reidi, Longsnout Seahorse: this family is not immune to diseases and parasites, and the keeper must be alert to developing problems.

Seahorses are also host to the ciliated protozoan *Licnophora hippocampi*. Protozoans are best treated with formalin.

One final note about seahorse parasite treatment: Although commonly used to treat parasitic infections in many other fishes, copper sulfate is not always well-tolerated by seahorses. Therefore, this medication should only be used as a last resort and only at low treatment concentrations (less than 0.15 mg/L).

Gas bubble disease is a common malady that most often affects adult male seahorses (although females may also develop gas bubbles beneath the skin). This disease usually occurs when a male's pouch fills with gas, making the fish positively buoyant. In courting males, where pumping water into the pouch is part of the precopulatory repertoire, this disease apparently results from the collection of small air bubbles in the brood pouch. In pregnant or postpartum males, it is thought to result from the decomposition of nonviable eggs in the brood pouch. In order to liberate the gas that has built up in the male's brood pouch, hold the seahorse under the water's surface, insert a blunt-ended probe into the pouch opening, and palpate the pouch as you pull the probe out. Unfortunately, gas buildup often continues to plague these individuals. There is strong evidence that suggests that this is a stress-induced illness, hence its prevalence in males that have been reproductively active (which is a very stressful activity). It was reported that injecting one male's brood pouch with streptomycin resulted in the elimination of gas buildup, which suggests that the problem (at least in this individual) was caused by the presence of a pathogen.

Another potential seahorse problem is the ingestion of small bubbles, which affects a fish's buoyancy. In most cases the air is expelled, but some individuals have difficulty purging the air and may become distressed or expend large amounts of energy trying to maintain their balance. To reduce the likelihood that seahorses will ingest air bubbles, use airstones that generate large bubbles, gravity-fed power filters, or small powerheads. Be aware, however, that seahorses are not strong swimmers and have been sucked into filter intake tubes. It is very important that any intake tube or opening has a strainer on it (or in the case of smaller seahorses, a nylon or fiberglass mesh) to prevent this from occurring.

One thing the aquarist should know before attempting to keep seahorses is that they do not have a long life span. For example, most Dwarf Seahorses (*Hippocampus zosterae*) live no longer than 1 year in the wild (there are reports of this fish living longer in captivity), while the larger forms (like the Lined Seahorse, *Hippocampus erectus*) are reported to live 2 to 3 years. Of course, you never know how old a fish is when you acquire it, so it is possible that an adult specimen may die a natural death in less than a few months in your aquarium.

Selecting Healthy Seahorses

To ensure success with seahorses, you need to select healthy specimens. This is easier said than done, because many of the seahorses that come into the aquarium trade—especially those from the Western Pacific—are in bad condition when they arrive at the retail store. Often, they have not been fed for days or even weeks and have been kept in small containers or crowded into larger tanks, subjected to deteriorating water conditions, and jostled about in a shipping bag for extended periods of time. It is no wonder that Indo-Pacific seahorses are very stressed or near death by the time they arrive in a Midwestern pet store.

Look for individuals that seem alert and are moving about the aquarium. Ask the retailer to feed them so you can see if they will eat. In addition, steer clear of individuals that display white nodules or spots on the body, tail, or fins; skin sloughing off the body; listlessness; difficulty swimming; or aimless floating about the aquarium. If an aquarium contains a seahorse that has white boils or cysts on the body (indicative of white boil disease), do not purchase any seahorses from that tank. Because this disease is so contagious, it would be prudent to avoid any syngnathids in the entire store, unless you know that the employees carefully sterilize specimen containers or nets before they catch fish from different tanks.

When you need to catch a seahorse, use an appropriately sized specimen container. These fishes often have spiny protuberances that can get entangled in a net, which can cause both stress and physical damage to the animal. Open abrasions resulting from such injuries not only provide a site for secondary bacterial infections, they also afford an entrance for small bubbles to get between the seahorse's skin and its bony armor.

As previously mentioned, seahorses can and will engage in drastic color changes. For example, a black seahorse can turn gold

Hippocampus histrix, Thorny Seahorse: selecting healthy specimens is key. This male with its distended brood pouch is obviously carrying young.

Hippocampus erectus, Lined Seahorse (small juvenile): biologists are urging aquarists to initiate captive-breeding programs to take pressure off wild populations.

or orange, and an orange or red seahorse may assume drabber chromatic attire. So if you select a brightly colored specimen, don't be surprised if you end up with a less spectacular individual in your tank later on. Placing decorations in the tank similar in color to your seahorse may encourage it not to change colors, but even this technique is not foolproof. Feeding foods high in certain carotenoids (e.g., table shrimp, krill, mysid shrimp) may help an orange or red seahorse maintain its color.

Reproduction in Captivity

Seahorses are not hard to breed in aquarium confines, and raising the fry is not as difficult as it is with many other marine fishes. It is also easy to distinguish the sexes, as the male has a prominent brood pouch. There is no real trick to getting these fishes to breed, although at least one researcher suggests including a dawn and dusk photoperiod. To do this, have only half the lights come on in the morning before giving them full light, then have half the lights go off in the evening before giving them complete darkness. Some species may also breed more frequently at specific temperatures and salinities. Occasionally, gravid male seahorses will show up in the aquarium trade. Sometimes these individuals will hold their young in the pouch until term, while others abort them prematurely and the larvae die.

Although many seahorse breeders keep more than one pair in the same aquarium, individuals can interfere with the courtship and mating of another pair, or they can cause the female to prematurely expel her eggs. If you have multiple males in with a female, the males often compete with each other to mate with the female. If a female has hydrated eggs and 1) is separated from her mate; 2) her mate has accepted eggs from another female; or 3) courtship has been prolonged by a competing male, she may either expel or drop her clutch. On rare occasions, conspecific females will engage in courtship with each other and end up dropping their eggs.

When the time comes to give birth, the male seahorse may expel the young on several consecutive days, with the greatest number of young being released on the second day in at least one species. Seahorses will breed continuously if the environmental parameters of their aquarium remain constant. This can be lethal to some males because of the high energy cost involved in maintaining the osmotic environment present in the brood pouch. Even though some brooding males may continue to feed, they will become emaciated and die. To discourage continuous breeding, it is best to replicate the natural seasonal changes that a seahorse is exposed to.

When a male expels young seahorses, it is important to separate the adults from the newborns immediately. Otherwise, the parents will feed on the progeny. Newborn seahorses can be fed newly hatched brine shrimp nauplii that have been soaked in Selco or Selcon (omega-3 enriching supplements for fishes) for 24 hours and then rinsed with seawater. The growing young have a huge appetite and must be provided with food almost constantly throughout the day. In some cases, the growing young may begin to ignore the nauplii and may require subadult (5- to 8-day-old) brine shrimp, amphipods (e.g., *Gammarus*), or similar-sized crustaceans. After 2 weeks or so, adult brine shrimp can be substituted for these other food sources. These fishes will grow rapidly in captivity. For example, young Lined Seahorses (*H. erectus*) may grow 13 to 14 cm (5.1 to 5.5 in.) in 10 months.

One problem with raising the young of seahorses is that they are prone to being sucked up in aquarium filters. One way to deal with this is to create a nursery tank that has a compartmentalized filter. You can section off about one-quarter or one-half of an aquarium with a tight-fitting aquarium divider that has holes in it too small for the young seahorses to swim through. Place the filtration equipment (whether an internal filter or the siphon or overflow of an external filter) in this section of the tank and keep the young seahorses on the other side of the divider. Restricting the young to a smaller volume of water will also increase the chances that they will encounter and capture food items.

A simpler but less effective way to stop the baby seahorses from being sucked up or damaged by external filters is to place nylon or plastic screening over the intake of a siphon tube. A sponge filter and air pump can also be used to filter a nursery tank, but the bubbles produced should be too large to be consumed by the young seahorses. Water exchanges are also important, with their frequency depending on the filter's effectiveness. If the tank is heavily loaded, you should siphon the feces off the bottom of the aquarium either every day or every other day.

It is not only important to provide attachment sites for adult seahorses, but newborns also need suitable holdfasts. If these are not provided, young *Hippocampus* individuals have been observed to wrap their tails around each other and form "chains," which inhibit locomotion and feeding and cause juveniles to die of exhaustion (this unfortunate phenomenon was reported as early as 1953 by David Graham). Plastic plants (thin-bladed grasslike forms) or a heavy monofilament line weighted to the aquarium bottom with stainless steel weights can provide suitable attachment sights.

Seahorse Species

Genus *Hippocampus*

Hippocampus bargabanti Whitley, 1970
Common Name: Pygmy Seahorse.
Maximum Length: Reported to reach 5 cm (2.0 in.), but those I have seen, including pregnant males, were less than 1 cm (0.4 in.).
Distribution: New Caledonia, Great Barrier Reef, and Indonesia.
Biology: The Pygmy Seahorse is found on coastal reefs and fore-reef slopes. It usually occurs at depths in excess of 30 m (98 ft.), clinging to the branches of a gorgonian of the genus *Muricella*. From one to dozens of these tiny syngnathids may be found residing on an individual gorgonian. They apparently feed on tiny zooplankton entrapped in the gorgonian's polyps or slime.
Captive Care: The minute size of the Pygmy Seahorse (and the associated difficulties involved in feeding them) and their strong dependence on their gorgonian host, which is difficult to acquire and keep, makes them an unsuitable addition to the home aquarium. They should be left in the wild to be enjoyed by eagle-eyed divers (they are extremely difficult to see).
Aquarium Size: 20 gal. **Temperature:** 22 to 27°C (72 to 80°F).
Aquarium Suitability Index: 1.
Remarks: A similar species (or possibly a morph of this animal) has been found off northern Sulawesi; it lacks the polyplike bumps on the body surface.

Hippocampus bargabanti, Pygmy Seahorse: marvelous mimics.

Hippocampus erectus, Lined Seahorse: can thrive and breed in captivity.

Hippocampus erectus Perry, 1810
Common Name: Lined Seahorse.
Maximum Length: 15 cm (5.9 in.).
Distribution: Nova Scotia south to Argentina—including the Gulf of Mexico and the east coast of Africa in the Eastern Atlantic.
Biology: The Lined Seahorse is found in bays, lagoons, and brackish estuaries, where it typically associates with seagrass beds. It occurs at depths of less than 1 to at least 46 m (3.3 to 150 ft.), although it is most common in water less than 10 m (33 ft.) deep. Those individuals that live in *Sargassum* rafts have fleshy tabs of skin on the body and bony protuberances that help them blend with their surroundings. *Hippocampus erectus* lives for two or three years in the wild. It is eaten by sea turtles, such as young Ridley, Kemp's, and Loggerhead Turtles, and piscivorous fishes (e.g., a 16-cm [6.3-in.] Barbfish, *Scorpaena brasiliensis*, contained a Lined Seahorse that was 6 cm [2.4 in.] from the top of its head to the bottom of its coiled tail).
Captive Care: The Lined Seahorse will thrive and reproduce in captivity if provided with a nutritionally complete diet (e.g., mysid shrimp). It will grow quickly—juveniles will attain a length of 13 cm (5.1 in.) in as little as 10 months. This species has bred in captivity at water temperatures of 24 to 28°C (75 to 82°F). It may succumb to monogenetic trematodes if it becomes stressed (i.e., the immune system is suppressed). This can occur if the seahorse is being picked on by tankmates, being malnourished, or kept in deteriorating water conditions. This species, especially individuals from Florida, are frequent carriers of *Glugea*.
Aquarium Size: 20 gal. **Temperature:** 21 to 28°C (70 to 82°F).
Aquarium Suitability Index: 2.
Remarks: The color of this species can be orange, yellow, olive-brown, or black, with pale blotches and dark lines on the neck and back. It has 18 to 21 dorsal fin rays and is more robust, has a shorter snout, and does not have dark spots when compared to the Longsnout Seahorse (*Hippocampus reidi*). The morphology of *H. erectus* can vary considerably from one geographical location to the next, and these populations may represent distinct species. For example, the Lined Seahorse populations around southern Florida are very different from those found off eastern Virginia. *Hippocampus hudsonius* and *Hippocampus punctulatus* are synonymous with *H. erectus*.

Hippocampus histrix Kaup, 1856
Common Names: Thorny Seahorse, Spiny Seahorse.
Maximum Length: 17 cm (6.7 in.).
Distribution: Red Sea to Hawaiian and Society Islands, north to southern Japan, and southwest to Papua New Guinea.
Biology: The Thorny Seahorse occurs on shallow sheltered bays, in estuaries, mangrove swamps, and reefs, where it is usually found in association with seagrass or macroalgae beds. In the latter habitat, it often associates with small finger sponges. Larger individuals have been observed hanging onto floating debris. *Hippocampus histrix* has been reported at depths of 1 to at least 34 m (3.3 to 111 ft.). It is often found in pairs, which typically stay relatively close to each other.
Captive Care: This species is not as common in the aquarium

Hippocampus histrix, Thorny Seahorse: large species with elongate snout.

Hippocampus histrix, Thorny Seahorse: red variant; note long snout.

Hippocampus histrix, Thorny Seahorse, or possibly *Hippocampus jayakarai*.

trade as the sympatric *Hippocampus kuda*. Its husbandry is similar to that of the other larger seahorse species (e.g., the Lined Seahorse, *H. erectus*, and the Common Seahorse, *H. kuda*). For more information, see the Captive Care section in the Subfamily Hippocampinae account, page 412.
Aquarium Size: 20 gal. **Temperature:** 22 to 28°C (72 to 82°F).
Aquarium Suitability Index: 2.
Remarks: The Thorny Seahorse has 33 to 34 tail rings and 11 trunk rings. There are sharp spines (often with black tips) on the ridges between the trunk rings, a crown of five short spines, and spines above and just before the eyes. The snout is as long or slightly longer than the head length behind the eyes. This seahorse can be brown, white, yellow, or yellowish brown. Some individuals have a shorter snout (it goes approximately twice into the head length), and the snout is banded. They may represent a valid species known as *Hippocampus jayakarai* **Boulenger, 1900**. However, these two species are considered to be synonyms by some ichthyologists.

Hippocampus ingens Girard, 1858
Common Name: Pacific Seahorse.
Maximum Length: 28 cm (11.0 in.).
Distribution: San Diego, California, south to northern Peru, also the Galapagos Islands and the entire Gulf of California.
Biology: *Hippocampus ingens* is usually found associating with seagrass meadows and beds of gorgonians, black coral trees, and branching sponges on offshore patch reefs or rocky dropoffs. It is usually observed with its tail wrapped around the seagrass blades or the gorgonian branches, but it will also float over or lie on sand substrates. It occurs at the water's surface, but is most common at depths in excess of 10 m (33 ft.)—it has been reported as deep as 18.5 m (60 ft.).
Captive Care: The Pacific Seahorse is rarely available to marine aquarists. For details on its requirements, see the Captive Care section in the Subfamily Hippocampinae account, page 412.
Aquarium Size: 30 gal. **Temperature:** 16 to 26°C (60 to 78°F).
Aquarium Suitability: 2.

Remarks: The color of this species varies considerably, but includes shades of red, yellow, gold, tan, brown, gray, black, and green. It often has thin white lines on the head and body as well as black and white spots. It has 11 or 12 body rings, 38 to 40 tail rings, and 19 to 21 dorsal rays. This is the only seahorse in the Eastern Pacific.

Hippocampus kuda Bleeker, 1852
Common Names: Common Seahorse, Spotted Seahorse, Yellow Seahorse, Black Seahorse.
Maximum Length: 30 cm (11.8 in.).
Distribution: Red Sea to the Hawaiian and Society Islands, north to southern Japan, and south to the Great Barrier Reef.
Biology: The Common Seahorse occurs in protected coastal bays, where it often associates with seagrass beds or is found hanging on the sponges attached to pier pilings. It has also been reported from estuaries and is occasionally observed hanging on free-floating macroalgae, like *Sargassum* spp. *Hippocampus kuda* is found at depths of less than 1 up to 40 m (3.3 to 130 ft.).
Captive Care: This is probably the most frequently encountered seahorse in the aquarium trade, with most individuals originating from Indonesia and the Philippines. The Common Seahorse is often less hardy than its Eastern Atlantic counterparts, because the latter are usually treated with greater care and experience less shipping stress. For this reason, it is important to be very selective when choosing Common Seahorses. If possible, purchase only *H. kuda* that are active and already feeding. If good specimens are acquired, they will do well in captivity. As many as five generations of the Common Seahorse have been kept and raised in one public aquarium. Its care requirements are similar to those of other seahorses (see the Captive Care section in the Subfamily Hippocampinae account, page 412).
Aquarium Size: 20 gal. **Temperature:** 22 to 28°C (72 to 82°F).
Aquarium Suitability Index: 2.
Remarks: The name *Hippocampus kuda* apparently includes several "good" or valid species. For example, the Hawaiian "*H. kuda*" is probably a distinct species. The "true" *H. kuda* has 34 to 37 tail rings, 11 trunk rings, and 15 to 18 dorsal rays. The coronet on top of the head consists of five tubercles that project backward at oblique angles. Tubercles on the body ridges may be well developed or small and blunt. There is a short spine above each eye, and tubercles both on the snout and below the base of the dorsal fin. The snout is as long as, or slightly longer than, the head length behind the eyes.

The Common Seahorse can be black, yellow, or orange, and some individuals have irregular white bars. Lighter color forms usually have small dark spots.

Hippocampus ingens, Pacific Seahorse: rarely seen Eastern Pacific species.

Hippocampus kuda, Common Seahorse (juvenile): select specimens with care.

Hippocampus kuda, Common Seahorse: note algae on body.

Hippocampus kuda, Common Seahorse (?): Indian Ocean variant.

Hippocampus kuda, Common Seahorse (?): Indian Ocean variant.

Hippocampus trimaculatus, Longnose Seahorse: note upcurved snout.

The **Longnose Seahorse (*Hippocampus trimaculatus*) Leach, 1814** is similar to *H. kuda* but the snout is longer and is curved slightly upward. The tubercles present on the body and tail ring ridges are prominent and conical with a rounded top. The Longnose Seahorse has 38 to 42 tail rings, 11 trunk rings, and 19 to 21 dorsal rays. This species ranges from East Africa east to Indonesia, and north to southern Japan. It attains a maximum length of at least 20 cm (7.9 in.).

Hippocampus reidi Ginsburg, 1933
Common Names: Longsnout Seahorse, Giant Brazilian Seahorse.
Maximum Length: 15 cm (5.9 in.).
Distribution: North Carolina south to northern South America, including Bermuda and the Gulf of Mexico.
Biology: The Longsnout Seahorse is often found in seagrass beds, on pier pilings, and on the reef face. It will hang on seagrass, sponges, and gorgonians. An occasional specimen may associate with floating rafts of *Sargassum*. This species occurs at depths of less than 1 to over 15 m (3.3 to 49 ft.) and is sometimes found swimming in the open over very deep water. Although information is lacking on its food habits, they are probably similar to those of the sympatric Lined Seahorse (*H. erectus*). During courtship, this species often exhibits neon highlights.
Captive Care: For information on the husbandry of this species, see the Captive Care section for *H. erectus*, page 421.
Aquarium Size: 20 gal. **Temperature:** 22 to 28°C (72 to 82°F).
Aquarium Suitability Index: 2.
Remarks: The color of the Longsnout Seahorse ranges from yellow to reddish orange, brown, and black, and it usually has small dark spots evenly scattered over its head and body. The snout is long, and individuals have 16 to 19 dorsal fin rays.

Hippocampus reidi, Longsnout Seahorse: white variant on gorgonian.

Hippocampus reidi, Longsnout Seahorse.

Hippocampus reidi, Longsnout Seahorse.

Hippocampus reidi, Longsnout Seahorse.

Hippocampus zosterae Jordan & Gilbert, 1882
Common Name: Dwarf Seahorse.
Maximum Length: 5 cm (2.0 in.).
Distribution: Bermuda to the Bahamas and southern Florida, and the entire Gulf of Mexico.
Biology: The Dwarf Seahorse is most often found in estuaries and bays, where it inhabits shallow seagrass beds, namely Turtle Grass (*Thalassia testudinum*). It is most commonly found at depths of less than 1 m (3.3 ft.). The bulk of this fish's diet consists of copepods (mainly harpacticoid copepods), which are small, swarming crustaceans that live near the substrate. The stomach of an adult Dwarf Seahorse may contain as many as 200 copepods at any one time. Larger individuals may also consume amphipods, while ostracods and minute caridean shrimp are eaten infrequently. When this fish feeds, it attaches to a grass blade with its prehensile tail and captures prey organisms that live on, or swim near, the vegetation. These tiny syngnathids are, in turn, eaten by a number of predaceous fishes, like stingrays and pufferfishes, as well as by crustaceans like the Blue Crab (*Callinectes sapidus*).

The Dwarf Seahorse is monogamous, with a male and female remaining together and breeding repeatedly over the reproductive period (although captive observations suggest that some males may accept eggs from more than one female). Courtship in this species can be broken down into phases. Phase 1 occurs in the morning for 1 to 2 days before copulation and consists primarily of side-by-side quivering. Males usually initiate quivering and often brighten in color during this phase. The female responds to the male's quivering and chromatic alterations by brightening her color. Males may also engage in pumping behavior during Phase 1. Phase 2 occurs early on the day of mating and is characterized by female pointing (that is, she raises her head to form an oblique angle with the body axis). The male typically responds by leaning toward the female and quivering. Males often pump during this phase as well—opening the brood pouch and flexing the tail. The frequency of this behavior varies from 8 to 30 pumps. During a latency period that occurs between Phases 2 and 3, the orange eggs become hydrated and are visible through the female's abdominal wall. In Phase 3, the male points in response to the female, with both males and females initiating this behavior equally and brightening in color simultaneously. During Phase 4, the pair rises up into the water column 5 to 44 times until the eggs are transferred from female to male during the final rise. (In some cases, females do not respond to the approach and mating does not occur.) The entire contents of the female's ovaries—an average of 12 viable eggs and, in some cases, dead eggs and other ovarian tissue—are transferred into the male's brood pouch. Within about 10 days, the eggs hatch and

Hippocampus zosterae, Dwarf Seahorse: durable fish for small aquariums.

from 3 to 16 fully developed young are liberated from the pouch. The pair mates again within 4 to 20 hours after the male releases its brood. The breeding season occurs from mid-February to the end of October. At water temperatures of 29.4°C (85°F), males may have as many as two broods a month during the reproductive season. Juveniles reach sexual maturity in 2 to 3 months, with as many as three generations being produced in one year. There is an uneven sex ratio, with females outnumbering males in Floridian populations.

In the wild, the life span of this fish is very short, with few individuals reaching 1 year in age, and no specimens ever having been reported to live for 2 years. In captivity however, there are reports of specimens living over 3 years.

Captive Care: The Dwarf Seahorse is a durable aquarium fish that will readily reproduce in captivity, which is why it has been referred to as the "saltwater guppy." They are also less likely to contract the diseases and parasites that regularly inflict their larger cousins. These seahorses can be kept in very small aquariums; as many as 20 adults can be successfully kept in a tank as small as 10 gallons if suitable biological filtration is present. One advantage in housing Dwarf Seahorses in smaller aquariums is that food densities can be maintained at a high level and you can ensure that they get enough to eat. A problem presented by their small size is that they are prone to being sucked up by external filters or going over overflow boxes. One way to protect them from this fate is by placing the siphon of the external filter into the uplift tube of a functioning undergravel filter. You can also place nylon or plastic screening over the intake of a siphon tube or overflow box (in the latter case, be careful that the screen does not get clogged and cause the tank to overflow). It is risky to keep live rock with these miniature seahorses, as many of the hitchhikers that frequently come in on live rock (e.g., glass anemones, mantis shrimp, and crabs) can and will eat these seahorses. Do not keep seahorses in a tank with strong water movement; they do best in environments with minimal current.

The Dwarf Seahorse is found at a range of salinities and temperatures; they can occur in water with a specific gravity of 1.006 to 1.025 and at a water temperature of 16.7 to 32.2°C (62 to 90°F). However, in the aquarium, *H. zosterae* are best kept at a specific gravity of 1.016 to 1.021 and at water temperatures of 20 to 28°C (68 to 82°F). This fish does best if kept in a tank on its own. If you do choose to keep other fishes in the aquarium, select tankmates very carefully. The best tankmates are dragonets—like mandarin or scooter dragonets—or pipefishes (the Gulf Pipefish, *Syngnathus scovelli*, is a sympatric species). *Hippocampus zosterae* will require live brine shrimp that are either newly hatched or up to about 4 days old (these seahorses feed mainly on prey items less than 1 mm in length). In one study, the *Artemia* fed to Dwarf Seahorses was supplemented with calcium in the form of Kalkwasser. Because these fishes eat a lot, it is best to keep some brine shrimp in the aquarium at all times.

Newly born seahorses should be fed rotifers, newly hatched brine shrimp, or a similar-sized microcrustacean, and these should all be fortified with Selco. You can also add some *Chlorella*, a unicellular alga sometimes sold as "greenwater," to the tank containing the young seahorses. This will help in culturing a population of microcrustaceans for the young seahorses to eat.

Aquarium Size: 5 to 20 gal. **Temperature:** 20 to 28°C (68 to 82°F).
Aquarium Suitability Index: 3.
Remarks: The Dwarf Seahorse is usually tan, with no pattern on the body—although it does have a submarginal stripe. This species has 11 to 13 dorsal fin rays and can be bright green, gold, yellow, brown, black, or white overall. When placed in a tank with white coral and a light substrate, its color will often lighten. If you keep brightly colored attachment sites (e.g., green plants or colorful gorgonians), the seahorses are more likely to maintain more pleasing colors. The number of dermal appendages also varies from one specimen to the next, and individuals are capable of losing or developing them depending on their surrounding habitat.

SUBFAMILY SYNGNATHINAE (PIPEFISHES)

Even to the untrained eye, members of the Subfamily Syngnathinae appear anatomically linked to the seahorses, with the pipefishes swimming in the more "normal" horizontal position and their seahorse relatives assuming a slower, much more unusual vertical orientation. The majority of pipefishes lack a prehensile tail (*Acentronura*, the pipehorses, are one exception). Pipefishes have slender, elongate bodies and either slink over the bottom on their bellies or hover just above it. Members of this subfamily are often distinguished by their configuration of ridges—which are present on the dorsal and ventral surface of the body, as well as on the sides (the latter are known as the lateral ridges).

Biology

There are 51 genera and about 190 species in the pipefish subfamily. At least 17 species occur in freshwater, another 35 species are euryhaline, and the rest live in seawater habitats. A number of members of the latter group are found on or near coral reefs. One of the largest reef-dwelling genera is the genus *Corythoichthys*. Some of the other genera, like the *Syngnathus* species, are more often found in protected seagrass meadows. Few pipefishes occur in extremely deep water, although some species have been reported from depths to 30 m (98 ft.).

Like the seahorses, pipefishes feed on small crustaceans, including swarming mysid shrimp, isopods, copepods, amphipods, and crustacean larvae. A couple of pipefish species are known to clean other fishes. However, unlike most of the other teleost cleaners of the reef, they tend to more secretive clients, like moray eels and cardinalfishes.

The reef-associated pipefishes studied (e.g., *Corythoichthys* spp.) engage in greeting behavior (described by the first four courtship action patterns explained below). Greeting behavior takes place early in the morning (usually 5 minutes before sun-

Halicampus sp.: closely related to the seahorses, the pipefishes are a challenge for aquarists, demanding quiet conditions and a diet of live foods.

rise) year round, with all pair members—whether they are carrying eggs or not—participating. It has not been determined how individual pipefishes recognize their mates. The functions of greeting may include maintaining contact between pair members during the nonreproductive period, increasing spawning synchrony between the mates, reinforcing mate fidelity, and alerting a pair member that their mate has disappeared.

In many species, courtship is quite long and appears to play an important part in preparing the male pipefish's brood pouch for egg transfer. Courtship in at least some of the *Corythoichthys* species takes place early in the morning (at sunrise). While courting, the female genital papillae become noticeably swollen, the eggs become hydrated, and the abdomen swells. Males often change color during courtship. The spawning behavior of one reef-dwelling species, the Messmate Pipefish (*Corythoichthys intestinalis*), was well documented by Gronell in 1984. Courtship in this species consists of nine different fixed-action patterns, including: 1) approach; 2) parallel swimming; 3) arch ("quick arching of the body from a level position"); 4) cross (one individual crosses over the back of its partner); 5) rising up (both individuals lift the anterior part of the body off the substrate as they move parallel to one another over the bottom); 6) entwine (individuals briefly twist around each other); 7) position (the pair members become rigid, maintaining a vertical, parallel orientation in the water column with the brood pouch held slightly below the female's ovipositor); 8) spawning; and 9) wiggle dance (after spawning occurs, both individuals pause and then begin vigorously wiggling while still in the water column). During spawning, the female extrudes the eggs and the male accepts them into his pouch (in one study this transfer lasted 3.8 to 6.8 seconds). Egg transfer typically occurs within 2 or 3 hours of the beginning of courtship.

In the *Corythoichthys* species, the eggs are forced out as a single flat sheet. The brood pouch provides the developing eggs with an osmoregulated environment during gestation and with nutrients and oxygen via a structure analogous to a placenta. When brooding eggs, food intake and activity are reduced. The length of incubation is greatly affected by water temperature. For example, in one study, it was shown that a change in temperature of only 1°C could increase the brooding period by as much as 2 days. In *Corythoichthys*, it takes about the same time for the ova of the female to mature as it does for the eggs to hatch. In at least some species of this genus, all the eggs hatch at dusk on the same day. The eggs hatch in the male's pouch, and the young pipefishes are released when the pouch splits open several days later. The newly hatched pipefishes are free-swimming and have small yolk sacs.

While the most ubiquitous genus of coral-reef-associated pipefishes is monogamous, other genera exhibit polygamy: a female may deposit eggs in the brood pouch of more than one male, while males may accept eggs from more than one female. In these pipefishes, most of the eggs in a male's brood pouch are at the same stage of development, although they may vary in size. The number of viable eggs often decreases as the brood develops (this is known as brood loss). It has been suggested that there is competition between the developing eggs for brood pouch resources, with larger eggs apparently having a competitive edge. Larger eggs also produce larger young, which are more likely to survive than their smaller cohorts. Because egg size is a function of the female's size, males tend to prefer larger females for mates. In this way, they ensure that their brood contains more "healthy" eggs and that their young are more "fit."

Captive Care

The husbandry requirements of pipefishes are very similar to their close relatives the seahorses. Read the Captive Care section in the seahorse subfamily account, page 412, as well as the following information on pipefishes.

Like the seahorses, the pipefishes can be kept in smaller aquariums, and are often easier to feed in more confined spaces. Pipefishes are less susceptible to being blown about the aquarium

Syngnathoides biaculeatus, Alligator Pipefish: note egg mass on abdomen.

by strong water currents than the seahorse species, although many are more commonly found in the calm waters of protected bays or lagoons.

Tankmates, Nutrition, and Disease

One of the biggest challenges facing the pipefish keeper is providing adequate nutrition. Pipefishes are often reluctant to accept anything but live foods when initially introduced to the aquarium, and require frequent feedings (they have an inefficient alimentary tract, much like the seahorses). Many pipefishes will accept live adult brine shrimp, *Daphnia*, mosquito larvae, baby guppies and mollies, and live grass shrimp. In time, pipefishes can be coaxed into eating frozen mysid shrimp and frozen brine shrimp, but these are typically eaten only if they are being moved by the current. A refugium is a great addition to an aquarium that contains pipefishes. They will benefit from the small, live crustaceans that can be cultured in a small aquarium that slowly supplies water into the display aquarium.

Pipefish tankmates should be carefully selected. Avoid those species that are likely to pick at them, like blennies, wrasses, tobies, triggerfishes, and porcupinefishes. Also, they will not do well if housed in a tank full of fleet-finned food competitors. If you are counting on the live rock or the crustaceans from a refugium to provide them with enough to eat, all food competitors should be excluded—unless the tank is very large with an ample supply of live rock or the refugium is extremely productive. Although it is often said that pipefishes and seahorses make suitable tankmates, pipefishes tend to be more efficient predators, and seahorses may not get enough to eat if food is limited.

Less is known about pipefish diseases than about those that afflict seahorses, but pipefishes are susceptible to at least some of the same maladies (see page 416). They should be quarantined and, when necessary, treated in a similar manner.

Reproduction in Captivity

Several pipefish species have been bred in captivity, although they do so less commonly than the seahorses. Many of the same problems and procedures described for the seahorses apply to the pipefishes. The narrow diameter of the baby pipefish's body does present special problems when it comes to suitable filtration. Newborn pipefishes are more likely to be drawn through screens placed around filter siphons and overflow boxes. Sponge filters are best employed in the nursery tank to avoid this problem. Newborn pipefishes will also require smaller food items than their seahorse counterparts. Rotifers, or similar-sized planktonic crustaceans, are the best first foods. As the pipefishes age, they can be switched to Selco-enriched baby brine shrimp.

PIPEFISH SPECIES

Genus *Corythoichthys* (Dragon Pipefishes)

This common reef-dwelling genus contains ten species that move by crawling over the substrate. Members of this genus have a brood pouch under the tail that protects the dorsal surface and sides of the egg mass, but the ventral surface is exposed.

Corythoichthys amplexus Dawson & Randall, 1975

Common Name: Brownbanded Pipefish.
Maximum Length: 9.5 cm (3.7 in.).
Distribution: East Africa to Samoa, north to the Ryukyus, and south to the Great Barrier Reef.
Biology: This species is found in deeper water than many of its congeners, occurring at depths to 31 m (101 ft.) but it can also be found in water as shallow as 0.2 m (8 in.). It is more common on the fore-reef slope than in lagoons. When observed in lagoons, the Brownbanded Pipefish is usually found in small groups near cave entrances. It is also more secretive than many other species in this genus, refuging in caves and crevices, and often associating with flat sponges. Like all *Corythoichthys*, this species is monogamous, with the brood pouch of the male containing an average of 90 eggs. Males reach sexual maturity and begin brooding eggs at a length of 5.7 cm (2.2 in.).
Captive Care: The Brownbanded Pipefish is one of the least common members of this genus in the aquarium trade. When available, it is sold under the generic name "banded pipefish." It is a reclusive fish that will require a cave or crevice in which to shelter. Otherwise, its care requirements are similar to those of other pipefishes.

Corythoichthys amplexus, Brownbanded Pipefish: secretive and uncommon.

Corythoichthys flavofasciatus, Network Pipefish: widespread species.

Corythoichthys haematopterus, Yellowstreaked Pipefish: common in lagoons.

Corythoichthys intestinalis, Messmate Pipefish: possible reef tank candidate.

Aquarium Size: 20 gal. **Temperature:** 22 to 27°C (72 to 80°F).
Aquarium Suitability Index: 2.
Remarks: The Brownbanded Pipefish has a pale or reddish snout with very small red spots; the body has reddish brown bands with pale interspaces.

Corythoichthys flavofasciatus (Rüppell, 1838)
Common Name: Network Pipefish.
Maximum Length: 12 cm (4.7 in.).
Distribution: Red Sea to the Tuamotus, north to the Ryukyus, south to the Great Barrier Reef and Austral Island. (It is the most widely distributed member of this genus.)
Biology: The Network Pipefish is found on lagoon patch reefs, the reef face, and fore-reef slopes at depths of less than 1 up to 25 m (3.3 to 81 ft.). It is most common on stony corals and algae-covered rocks, although it can also be found on reef pavement, rubble, and sand. Copepods are major contributors to its diet, but it also eats small isopods and ostracods. The males reach sexual maturity and begin brooding eggs at a length of 7.2 cm (2.8 in.).
Captive Care: See the Captive Care section in the Subfamily Syngnathinae account, page 428, for husbandry information.
Aquarium Size: 20 gal. **Temperature:** 22 to 27°C (72 to 80°F).
Aquarium Suitability Index: 2.
Remarks: This species has red spots on its snout, with reddish bars and narrow yellow lines on the body. Males larger than 5 cm (2.0 in.) have a blue spot around the anus.

Corythoichthys haematopterus (Bleeker, 1851)
Common Name: Yellowstreaked Pipefish.
Maximum Length: 9.5 cm (3.7 in.).
Distribution: East Africa to Vanuatu, north to southern Japan.
Biology: The Yellowstreaked Pipefish is most common in shallow lagoons and on reef flats in water less than 1 m (3.3 ft.) deep, but also occurs on fore-reef slopes to depths of 21 m (68 ft.). Its most important food is planktonic copepods that form swarms in crevices, caves, or reef interstices during the day. It also feeds on cumaceans, amphipods, isopods, tanaids, barnacle larvae, and ostracods. Males reach sexual maturity and begin brooding eggs at a length of 9.4 cm (3.7 in.).
Captive Care: See the Captive Care section in the Subfamily Syngnathinae account, page 428, for husbandry information.
Aquarium Size: 20 gal. **Temperature:** 22 to 27°C (72 to 80°F).
Aquarium Suitability Index: 2.
Remarks: The snout of *C. haematopterus* has dark spots, the head has dark stripes, and the body is pale with dark blotches consisting of reticulate black lines.

Corythoichthys intestinalis (Ramsay, 1881)
Common Names: Messmate Pipefish, Dragon Pipefish.
Maximum Length: 17 cm (6.7 in.).
Distribution: Borneo to Samoa and Rapa Island, north to the Marshall and Marianas Islands, and south to New Caledonia and Tonga.
Biology: The Messmate Pipefish occurs in shallow waters (from less than 5 cm [2 in.] to 6 m [20 ft.] deep) in lagoons. It is most often found on rubble bottoms or in *Acropora* beds, and feeds on small animals that refuge in the algae at the base of these corals. The most important food of these pipefish is planktonic copepods that form swarms in crevices, caves, or reef interstices during the day. However, they also feed on cumaceans, amphipods, isopods, tanaids, barnacle larvae, and ostracods. Male and female Messmate Pipefish are strongly site-attached, but do not defend a territory. Instead, they occur in broadly overlapping home ranges. The male occupies a smaller home range than the female, and typically doesn't leave its home coral patch. Females, in contrast, regularly move between coral patches and may cover a linear distance of 20 m (65 ft.) in a day. Spawning begins in early spring and ends in early autumn; pairs repeatedly use the same spawning site. Males become sexually mature at a length of 7.1 cm (2.8 in.).
Captive Care: This is one of the most common pipefishes in the aquarium trade and does well in the reef aquarium if its nutritional needs are met. See the Captive Care section in the Subfamily Syngnathinae account, page 428, for husbandry information.
Aquarium Size: 20 gal. **Temperature:** 22 to 27°C (72 to 80°F).
Aquarium Suitability Index: 2.
Remarks: This species has a banded snout and the body color pattern is quite variable.

Corythoichthys nigripectus Herald, 1953
Common Name: Blackbreasted Pipefish.
Maximum Length: 11 cm (4.3 in.).
Distribution: Red Sea to the Society Islands, north to the Marianas Islands.
Biology: The Blackbreasted Pipefish is found on sand, rubble, and patch reefs in lagoons, on the reef face, and on the fore-reef slope at depths of 4 to 28 m (13 to 91 ft.). It is often found under overhangs and in caves. Males mature at 9.1 cm (3.6 in.).
Captive Care: See the Captive Care section in the Subfamily Syngnathinae account, page 428, for husbandry information.
Aquarium Size: 20 gal. **Temperature:** 23 to 27°C (74 to 80°F).
Aquarium Suitability Index: 2.
Remarks: This species is easily recognized by the black area on the chest that begins under the pectoral fin. The **Insular Pipefish** (*Corythoicthys insularis*) **Dawson, 1977** is a similar species from the Western Indian Ocean. It is often found in caves and under ledges at depths of 15 to 40 m (49 to 130 ft.).

Corythoichthys schultzi Herald, 1953
Common Name: Guilded Pipefish.
Maximum Length: 15 cm (5.9 in.).
Distribution: Red Sea to the Society Islands, north to the Ryukyus, and south to Rowley Shoals and Tonga.
Biology: The Guilded Pipefish occurs in lagoons, on reef flats, reef faces, and fore-reef slopes at depths of less than 1 up to 30 m (3.3 to 98 ft.). It lives on rocks, sand, rubble, coralline algae, and

Corythoichthys nigripectus, Blackbreasted Pipefish: often found over rubble.

Corythoichthys insularis, Insular Pipefish: Western Indian Ocean species.

Corythoichthys schultzi, Guilded Pipefish: note pink tail.

Corythoichthys schultzi, Guilded Pipefish: sometimes found in groups.

Doryrhamphus dactyliophorus, Banded Pipefish: male with eggs.

live coral substrate (e.g., gorgonians) and is sometimes observed in small groups. Males are sexually mature at 9.4 cm (3.7 in.).
Captive Care: See the Captive Care section in the Subfamily Syngnathinae account, page 428, for husbandry information.
Aquarium Size: 20 gal. **Temperature:** 23 to 27°C (74 to 80°F).
Aquarium Suitability Index: 2.
Remarks: The Guilded Pipefish has spots on the snout, the tail is pink with light margins, and there are orange dashes and spots on the body.

Genus *Doryrhamphus* (Hovering Pipefishes)
Unlike members of the genus *Corythoichthys*, the *Doryrhamphus* species hover over the bottom (rather than crawl over it) and often occur in pairs. Most of these pipefishes sport striking color patterns, and several are known to engage in cleaning behavior.

Doryrhamphus dactyliophorus (Bleeker, 1853)
Common Names: Banded Pipefish, Ringed Pipefish.
Maximum Length: 20 cm (7.9 in.).
Distribution: Red Sea to the Austral Islands, north to the Izu Islands, and south to New Caledonia.
Biology: The Banded Pipefish inhabits patch reefs in nutrient-rich bays and lagoons. It is also found on the reef flat, reef face, and on outer-reef slopes at depths of less than 1 up to 56 m (3.3 to 182 ft.). *Doryrhamphus dactyliophorus* feeds on swarming and benthic crustaceans and is found singly, in pairs, or in small groups. Males begin brooding eggs at around 9.6 cm (3.8 in.) in length.
Captive Care: This species is common in the aquarium trade but individuals should only be purchased by those aquarists willing to spend the time and money to maintain them. Provide them with suitable shelter sites, like an overhang or a cave, and choose their tankmates carefully. The Banded Pipefish will typically consume only live food, such as brine shrimp. If possible, these fishes should be switched over to frozen mysid shrimp, which are more nutritionally complete. They will ingest nonliving food only if it is pushed through the water column by currents. If you cannot get your pipefish to accept frozen mysid shrimp, feed it live brine shrimp that have been soaked in Selco. *Doryrhamphus dactyliophorus* is better suited for the reef aquarium than most of its congeners because of its less reclusive nature.
Aquarium Size: 20 gal. **Temperature:** 22 to 27°C (72 to 80°F).
Aquarium Suitability Index: 2.
Remarks: This handsome pipefish has white or cream-colored bands alternating with red to black bands, and a red tail trimmed with white. Some authors place this species in the genus *Dunkerocampus*.

Doryrhamphus excisus, Bluestripe Pipefish: beautiful reef tank species.

Doryrhamphus excisus, Bluestripe Pipefish: Eastern Pacific color variant.

Doryrhamphus excisus Kaup, 1856
Common Name: Bluestripe Pipefish.
Maximum Length: 7.0 cm (2.8 in.).
Distribution: East Africa to Mexico, north to the Ryukyu and Hawaiian Islands, and south to the Tuamotus and southern Great Barrier Reef.
Biology: The Bluestripe Pipefish is a reclusive species often found in caves and crevices at depths of less than 1 up to 45 m (3.3 to 146 ft.). Some individuals are found swimming upside down under overhangs, while others associate with long-spined sea urchins (*Diadema* spp.). Like other members of this genus, the Bluestripe Pipefish hovers above the substrate, often bobbing up and down as it swims. It has been observed cleaning other secretive species, especially moray eels. Myers (1989) suggested that the colorful tail and peculiar swimming behavior may advertise the fact that the Bluestripe Pipefish engages in cleaning. This species often occurs in male-female pairs, and will defend its "home" crevices from intruders. Males have an abdominal brood pouch. The brood pouch of a 5.6-cm (2.2-in) male was reported to contain 137 eggs, which were 1.2 mm in diameter. Males begin brooding eggs at a length of approximately 3.6 cm (1.4 in.). Although its reproductive behavior has not been described, captive observations suggest that courtship is brief.
Captive Care: This beautiful little pipefish is a spectacular addition to the reef aquarium. It will benefit from being in this type of tank because of its proclivity for caves and crevices. Unfortunately, it is often finicky and usually requires live feedings of brine shrimp, amphipods, or other minute crustaceans. This fish may do better in a tank full of live rock because of the small crustaceans that often associate with this substrate, or in a tank with a thick filamentous algal bed. Often, small amphipods thrive in this type of environment if other microcrustacean predators are not present. The only problem with keeping the Bluestripe Pipefish in a tank full of live rock is that it may spend a considerable amount of time in hiding. Do not house this pipefish with food competitors or aggressive species (e.g., dottybacks, angelfishes, wrasses, triggerfishes, or pufferfishes).
Aquarium Size: 20 gal. **Temperature:** 22 to 27°C (72 to 80°F).
Aquarium Suitability Index: 2.
Remarks: The color of the Bluestripe Pipefish varies. Some individuals can be yellow overall with a dark or blue stripe that does not extend all the way down the body, while most are orange with a blue stripe that runs from the tip of the snout to the beginning of the caudal fin. There are three subspecies of the Bluestripe Pipefish. *Doryrhamphus excisus abbreviatus* occurs in the Red Sea, while *D. excisus paulus* is found around the Revillagigedo Islands. The third subspecies is found over the rest of the range and is referred to as *D. excisus excisus*. The subspecies may differ in the number of body rings, coloration, and the size at which males start brooding eggs. The **Negros Pipefish** (*Doryrhamphus negrosensis*) **Herre, 1934** is a smaller species (it attains a maximum length of 5.1 cm [2.0 in.]) that is orangish brown overall, with bluish brown on the dorsum and a darker head and snout. There is also a blue line behind the eye, and the tail has a yellow central spot and a white margin. The Negros Pipefish ranges from Borneo to Vanuatu, north to the Yaeyamas, and south to Rowley Shoals.

Doryrhamphus janssi (Herald & Randall, 1972)
Common Name: Janss's Pipefish.
Maximum Length: 13 cm (5.1 in.).
Distribution: Gulf of Thailand to the Solomon Islands, north to

Doryrhamphus janssi, Janss's Pipefish: cardinalfish cleaner.

Doryrhamphus multiannulatus, Multibar Pipefish: Indian Ocean species.

the Philippines, and south to Queensland.

Biology: Janss's Pipefish occurs on coastal reefs and in tidepools on the reef flat, at depths of less than 1 up to 35 m (3.3 to 114 ft.), where it is often found among sponges or under table corals. It is sometimes found occupying the same crevices used by cleaner shrimps. Like these crustaceans, it also picks parasites off fishes and is reported to specialize in cleaning cardinalfishes in the genus *Cheilodipterus* and damselfishes in the genus *Neopomacentrus*. This species occurs singly or in pairs. Males begin brooding eggs at about 8.7 cm (3.4 in.).

Captive Care: *Doryrhamphus janssi* is a secretive fish that should be provided with plenty of crevices or, preferably, an overhang or a table coral under which to hide. Live food, like brine shrimp or other minute crustaceans, is usually required to initiate feeding and may be needed as long as you have the fish. As with the Bluestripe Pipefish, populations of small crustaceans that are sometimes found on live rock or live sand may provide a supplemental food source. This is a great reef aquarium fish, but it may not be the best display animal as it is a recluse. Janss's Pipefish may spend more time in the open if the aquarium is dimly lit.

Aquarium Size: 20 gal. **Temperature:** 22 to 27°C (72 to 80°F).
Aquarium Suitability Index: 2.

Doryrhamphus multiannulatus (Regan, 1903)
Common Name: Multibar Pipefish.
Maximum Length: 18 cm (7.1 in.).
Distribution: Red Sea to Chagos, the Maldives, and Sumatra, and south to southern Africa.
Biology: The Multibar Pipefish is most often found under overhangs and in crevices at depths of less than 2 up to 75 m (7 to 244 ft.). Like other members of the genus, it hovers off the substrate and is often found in pairs.

Captive Care: This species should be provided with an overhang or crevice to hide under or in. It will sometimes feed on frozen mysid or brine shrimp, but will usually require live food. The Multibar Pipefish, along with most other members of this family, does best if kept in a tank attached to a productive refugium. Make sure to exclude potential food competitors from a tank that contains this pipefish. It is also more likely to thrive if placed in a tank with a rich crop of filamentous algae or in a reef aquarium with plenty of live rock (all of which are potential sources of small crustaceans).

Aquarium Size: 20 gal. **Temperature:** 22 to 27°C (72 to 80°F).
Aquarium Suitability Index: 2.

Remarks: This species is often misidentified as the Yellowbanded Pipefish (*Doryrhamphus pessuliferus*). The Multibar Pipefish has 60 or more red or reddish brown bands on a whitish body, the tail is red with a white margin and a white spot in the middle, and it is limited in distribution to the Indian Ocean. *Doryrhamphus multiannulatus* is not encountered in the aquarium trade as often as the similar *D. dactyliophorus* or *D. pessuliferus*.

Doryrhamphus pessuliferus (Fowler, 1938)
Common Name: Yellowbanded Pipefish.
Maximum Length: 15 cm (5.9 in.).
Distribution: North Sulawesi, Indonesia, and the Philippines.
Biology: The Yellowbanded Pipefish is found on coastal patch reefs at depths of at least 25 m (81 ft.). Here it is often found hovering in the open, just in front of a hole or crevice. It occurs singly or in pairs.

Captive Care: The care requirements of this species are the same as for the Multibar Pipefish (*D. multiannulatus*). *Doryrhamphus pessuliferus* is more often encountered in the aquarium trade than *D. multiannulatus* and is often confused with it.

Aquarium Size: 20 gal. **Temperature:** 22 to 27°C (72 to 80°F).
Aquarium Suitability Index: 2.
Remarks: The Yellowbanded Pipefish is most similar to the Banded Pipefish, but is easily recognized by its orange background color (it is white or cream-colored in *D. dactyliophorus*). The tail of the Yellowbanded Pipefish is mostly red with a yellow spot in the center and white markings on the margin.

Genus *Dunkerocampus*

Dunkerocampus baldwini Herald & Randall, 1972
Common Name: Redstripe Pipefish.
Maximum Length: 14 cm (5.5 in.).
Distribution: Hawaiian Islands.
Biology: The Redstripe Pipefish is found on the reef face and fore-reef slopes at depths of 6 to 128 m (20 to 416 ft.). It lives under ledges, in crevices, and in caves and is known to clean other fishes. This species hovers above the substrate, like the members of the genus *Doryrhamphus*.
Captive Care: The care requirements of this species are the same as for the members of the genus *Doryrhamphus*, page 432.
Aquarium Size: 20 gal. **Temperature:** 22 to 27°C (72 to 80°F).
Aquarium Suitability Index: 2.
Remarks: The Redstripe Pipefish has a red stripe along the sides of the body that becomes darker on the snout. It also has a red tail with white on all but the posterior margin, which is black.

Genus *Halicampus*
This genus contains a number of little known pipefish species that occur on coral reefs, as well as nearby habitats. All have a ridge down the middle of the snout that is not concave in profile and is often elevated and spiny. They also have a lateral ridge or spine on the snout and often have dermal appendages over the eye. Many species have similar appendages along the back.

Halicampus brocki (Herald, 1953)
Common Names: Brock's Pipefish, Tasseled Pipefish.
Maximum Length: 11.5 cm (4.5 in.).
Distribution: Philippines east to the Marshall and Mariana Islands, south to northwestern Australia and Queensland, north to southern Japan.
Biology: *Halicampus brocki* is found on rocky and coastal coral reefs, in lagoons and on the reef face, at depths of 2 to 23 m (7 to 75 ft.). It is often found in protected areas among macro-

Doryrhamphus pessuliferus, Yellowbanded Pipefish: male with eggs.

Dunkerocampus baldwini, Redstripe Pipefish: Hawaiian endemic species.

Halicampus brocki, Brock's Pipefish: often found in clumps of macroalgae.

Halicampus macrorhynchus, Ornate Pipefish: a gorgeous species for the reef aquarist willing to provide a habitat with macroalgae and live crustacean foods.

algae. Males begin brooding eggs at a length of 9 cm (3.5 in.).
Captive Care: See the Captive Care section in the Subfamily Syngnathinae account, page 428.
Aquarium Size: 55 gal. **Temperature:** 23 to 28°C (74 to 82°F).
Aquarium Suitability: 2.
Remarks: The color of this species is usually a pale brown. Its head is adorned with filamentous appendages, and there are often dermal flaps present along the dorsum. There are usually three brown bars on the snout and under the eye and 10 to 11 faint bars on the body.

Halicampus macrorhynchus Bamber, 1915
Common Name: Ornate Pipefish.
Maximum Length: 16 cm (6.3 in.).
Distribution: Red Sea to the Solomon Islands, south to the Great Barrier Reef.
Biology: The Ornate Pipefish occurs on reef flats and coastal reefs at a depth range of 1 to 25 m (3.3 to 81 ft.), but is most common at depths of less than 10 m (33 ft.). It is often found among macroalgae, as its skin flaps help it to blend in with plant materials.
Captive Care: This uncommon species will acclimate most readily to a macroalgae-filled aquarium. It can be difficult to feed, but usually cannot resist live mysid or brine shrimp (the latter should be soaked in Selco if used as a staple food). See the Captive Care section in the Subfamily Syngnathinae account, page 428, for husbandry information.
Aquarium Size: 20 gal. **Temperature:** 22 to 27°C (72 to 80°F).
Aquarium Suitability Index: 2.
Remarks: Smaller Ornate Pipefish (under 10 cm [3.9 in.]) have winglike appendages that extend out laterally along the upper surfaces of the body. Although these lateral projections are lost as this pipefish gets larger, adults retain some tassels and dermal appendages on the head and body.

Genus *Siokunichthys* (Commensal Pipefishes)

This genus contains five species, several of which associate with cnidarians. For example, *Siokunichthys breviceps* is often referred to as the Soft Coral Pipefish because it usually lives among the branches of soft corals. All of the members of the genus have a short snout and are plain in color.

Siokunichthys nigrolineatus Dawson, 1983
Common Name: White Pipefish.
Maximum Length: 8 cm (3.1 in.).
Distribution: Indonesia, Philippines, and New Guinea.
Biology: The White Pipefish is found only among the tentacles of the anemone-like Longtentacled Plate Coral (*Heliofungia actiniformis*) and occurs at a depth range of 7 to 20 m (23 to 65 ft.). It rarely, if ever, leaves the sanctuary of its host's tentacles and probably feeds on organisms that become trapped in the coral's mucus. The White Pipefish does occur singly, but is most often found in small groups. These aggregations often include several different age classes. Male *S. nigrolineatus* start brooding eggs when they are as small as 4.5 cm (1.8 in.).
Captive Care: Although the White Pipefish is not regularly collected, it is possible that a specimen may show up in an imported Longtentacled Plate Coral. If you happen to acquire one of these fish, it is essential that it be kept with its scleractinian host. The White Pipefish will rarely accept regular aquarium foods, although it may eat small plankters (e.g., baby brine shrimp) that adhere to the plate coral's tentacles.
Aquarium Size: 20 gal. **Temperature:** 22 to 27°C (72 to 80°F).
Aquarium Suitability Index: 1.
Remarks: This species is white with a thin diagonal line that runs through the eye.

Genus *Syngnathoides*

Syngnathoides biaculeatus (Bloch, 1785)
Common Names: Alligator Pipefish, Double-ended Pipefish.
Maximum Length: 28 cm (11.0 in.).
Distribution: Red Sea to the Samoas, north to southern Japan and New South Wales.
Biology: The Alligator Pipefish is found in protected bays and lagoons where it associates with seagrass beds, macroalgae stands, or floating plant debris (including *Sargassum* rafts). It has occasionally been observed to leap up onto the floating plant material if threatened. This species is found at depths of less than 1 up to 10 m (3.3 to 33 ft.). The eggs are exposed on the undersurface of the male's body, and the male starts brooding eggs when it reaches sexual maturity, which occurs at a length of 18 cm (7.1 in.).
Captive Care: *Syngnathoides biaculeatus* is occasionally available in the aquarium trade and is best kept in a tank with seagrasses or macroalgae, such as *Caulerpa*. It can be difficult to feed, but will usually accept live mysid or brine shrimp (the latter should be soaked in Selco if used as a staple food). The Alligator Pipefish will also eat small live grass shrimp. It is most likely to thrive in captivity if not housed with aggressive feeders, and it should not be kept with fishes that might harass it (e.g., pufferfishes, spiny boxfishes).
Aquarium Size: 30 gal. **Temperature:** 22 to 27°C (72 to 80°F).
Aquarium Suitability Index: 3.
Remarks: This species has a prehensile tail, which it uses to hold onto plant material, and no caudal fin. It is typically green or yellowish green overall. In the Philippines, the Alligator Pipefish is roasted and eaten.

Siokunichthys nigrolincatus, White Pipefish: note plate coral tentacles.

Syngnathoides biaculeatus, Alligator Pipefish: prefers seagrass habitats.

Syngnathus scovelli, Gulf Pipefish: hardy seagrass dweller.

Trachyrhamphus bicoarctatus, Short-tailed Pipefish: larger tank required.

Genus *Syngnathus* (Seagrass Pipefishes)

This is a specious genus that is most abundant in shallow bays, where members usually inhabit seagrass meadows. All fishes in this genus have an anal fin, no ridge over the operculum, a ridge on each side of the snout, no dermal flaps, and a moderately long snout.

Syngnathus scovelli (Evermann & Kendall, 1896)
Common Name: Gulf Pipefish.
Maximum Length: 18 cm (7.1 in.).
Distribution: Northeast Florida and the northern part of the Gulf of Mexico to the northern part of South America.
Biology: The Gulf Pipefish is found in protected bays and estuaries, and it will even enter freshwater (a breeding population occurs in a freshwater lake in Louisiana that is 240 km [150 mi.] inland). It often lives among seagrasses, over mud and sand, and is sympatric with the Dwarf Seahorse (*Hippocampus zosterae*) in many locations. *Syngnathus scovelli* occurs at depths of less than 20 cm to at least 6 m (7.9 in. to 20 ft.). The most frequently consumed prey of this species include harpacticoid, cyclopoid, and calanoid copepods. Larger individuals also consume amphipods, shrimps, ostracods, and crustacean eggs. This species often adopts a vertical position in the seagrass so that it blends in better with the plant material. It has been reported at water temperatures as high as 32°C (90°F).
Captive Care: This species is relatively hardy, but it may initially require live foods like brine shrimp, amphipods, and small grass shrimp. However, the Gulf Pipefish should be switched to frozen mysid shrimp after a while. Provide this pipefish with live or artificial seagrass or long-bladed macroalgae like *Caulerpa prolifera*. It should be housed with peaceful tankmates and is often kept with seahorses like the Dwarf (*H. zosterae*) and Lined (*H. erectus*) Seahorses. The Gulf Pipefish could be kept in a reef tank, but "prefers" less turbulent conditions than are typically present in many of these systems. It is most secure among seagrasses.
Aquarium Size: 10 gal. **Temperature:** 17 to 28°C (62 to 82°F).
Aquarium Suitability Index: 3.
Remarks: This species is usually tan overall. There are a number of representatives of the *Syngnathus* genus in Floridian and Caribbean waters, and some of these other species could show up in the aquarium trade. The Gulf Pipefish has a moderately long snout, 25 to 37 dorsal fin rays, 16 trunk rings, and 28 to 34 tail rings. The males have a flat belly and are plain in color, while females are deeper bodied, the belly is V-shaped in cross section, and they are banded.

Genus *Trachyrhamphus* (Stick Pipefishes)

This genus contains three species that resemble a soggy stick resting on the seafloor (hence the common name). They attain large sizes (up to 40 cm [15.7 in.]), and during their planktonic lives they have elongate dermal flaps on the dorsum of the trunk and tail. The brood pouch is located under the tail.

Trachyrhamphus bicoarctatus (Bleeker, 1857)
Common Names: Short-tailed Pipefish, Stick Pipefish.
Maximum Length: 40 cm (15.7 in.).
Distribution: Red Sea to New Caledonia, north to south Japan.
Biology: The Short-tailed Pipefish most often inhabits coastal bays, estuaries, and lagoons. It resides in a number of different microhabitats, including mud flats, seagrass, or macroalgae. *Trachyrhamphus bicoarctatus* is also found on reef slopes on sand or rubble substrates. On reef slopes, it is often found lying ex-

Trachyrhamphus bicoarctatus, Short-tailed Pipefish: note snout length.

Trachyrhamphus longirostris, Longsnout Pipefish: compare with *T. bicoarctatus*.

posed on the featureless bottom. It occurs at a depth range of 1 to 42 m (3.3 to 137 ft.), and can be found singly or in pairs. In strong currents, Short-tailed Pipefish use the end of their tails to grip the substrate, which may lead to abrasion and loss of the tail as they grow larger. This pipefish often raises its head into the water column (with its head facing into the current), balancing itself on the posterior portion of its body. From this position, *T. bicoarctatus* captures zooplankton that float past. These pipefish are slow moving and typically remain still when approached, as if to mimic bottom debris (such as seagrass blades, sticks, or stony coral branches).

Males begin brooding eggs at a length of 26 cm (10.2 in.). The newly hatched specimens and planktonic juveniles have elongate dermal appendages on the back of the body that may function to buoy the pelagic young. The young have been reported in the plankton at an approximate length of 10 cm (3.9 in.).

Captive Care: This pipefish will require a larger aquarium than many of its more diminutive relatives and is best kept in a tank containing some macroalgae as well as an open sand or rubble bottom. *Trachyrhamphus bicoarctatus* could be housed in a reef tank if plenty of open bottom space is provided. It will eat live adult brine and frozen mysid shrimp swept past by water currents.

Aquarium Size: 55 gal. **Temperature:** 22 to 27°C (72 to 80°F).
Aquarium Suitability Index: 3.
Remarks: The color of this species is highly variable, but the body is the same color overall (either white, yellow, brown, or black). Sometimes there are small dark spots present. Juveniles possess a small caudal fin, which is absent or almost nonexistent in adults.

The **Longsnout Pipefish** (*Trachyrhamphus longirostris*) **Kaup, 1856** is a similar species that ranges from Madagascar and Zanzibar east to New Hebrides, north to the Red Sea and Japan, and south to the east coast of Australia. It can be distinguished from *T. bicoarctatus* by the length and width of its snout: the snout length of the Short-tailed Pipefish can be divided 1.5 to 2.0 times into the head length, and the snout depth can be divided about 7.5 times into the snout length; in the Longsnout Pipefish, the snout length can be divided into the head length 1.9 to 2.8 times, and the snout depth can be divided about 6 or less times into the snout length.

Trachyrhamphus longirostris can also be separated from *T. bicoarctatus* by the number of tail rings—*T. bicoarctatus* has 55 to 63 tail rings, while *T. longirostris* has 41 to 53.

It has also been reported that the Longsnout Pipefish does not hold its body off the substrate like its close relative, suggesting that it might feed more on small benthic crustaceans (e.g., amphipods) rather than on planktonic forms. This would reduce competition between these two similar-sized, sympatric pipefishes. The Longsnout Pipefish ranges from Madagascar to Indonesia, north to Japan, and south to the east coast of Australia.

References
Ahnesjö (1996), Burke et al. (1993), Campson & Paleudis (1995), Dawson (1977, 1982), J. Forshey (personal communication), Giwojna (1996a, 1996b, 1996c, 1997), Gronell (1984), Hemdal (1987), Hueter (1998), Masonjones & Lewis (1996), Myers (1989), G. Paleudis (personal communication), Randall (1995), Sano et al. (1984), Scarratt (1996), Strawn (1958), Tipton & Bell (1988), Vincent (1994a, 1994b, 1995) Vincent & Sadler (1995).

Family Centriscidae
Shrimpfishes

Centriscus scutatus, Rigid Shrimpfish: with razor-thin bodies and a habit of swimming head down in groups, shrimpfishes are an impressive aquatic sight.

Swimming in perfectly synchronized groups, floating with heads-down and tails straight up and with bodies resembling suspended blades of seagrass, the shrimpfishes present a rather amazing spectacle—both in the wild or in quiet species tanks and reef aquarium settings.

The shrimpfish family consists of two genera and four species. All have razor-thin bodies (an attribute that has led to their being dubbed razorfishes by some authors), extremely long snouts, well-developed ventral keels, and median fins located at the ends of their bodies. The shrimpfish's body is also encased in a series of bony plates that are actually expansions of the vertebrae. The two genera are easily separated by the morphology of the first dorsal spine. In members of the genus *Aeoliscus*, the posterior portion of the spine is jointed and usually leans to one side or the other. In the genus *Centriscus*, the first dorsal spine is rigid.

Biology

All the shrimpfishes are residents of the Indo-Pacific. One species is limited in distribution to the Indian Ocean and Red Sea, while the other two reef-associated forms are found in both the Indian Ocean and the Western Pacific. They are often found in shallow, inshore habitats and more commonly associate with coastal reefs, as opposed to oceanic islands or reefs.

The behavior of shrimpfishes is as unusual as their appearance. They live their lives in a vertical position with their heads oriented toward the seafloor. It is an unusual sight to see large schools of these fish drifting over the bottom in this head-down posture. They swim in a synchronous fashion, with individuals turning in unison and moving as a single unit. Their forward movement is achieved by paddling with the pectoral fins. They can move surprisingly fast when threatened. The reproductive behavior of the shrimpfishes has not been observed, but they are assumed to be pelagic spawners.

Captive Care

Shrimpfishes can be kept in aquariums as small as 30 gallons and will thrive in captivity if their dietary needs are met. This requires providing a source of minute, living crustaceans like brine shrimp, amphipods, copepods, and shrimp larvae. These fishes tend do better in tanks with plenty of live rock and/or a tank that is connected to a refugium. A colony of Peppermint Shrimp (*Lysmata wurdemanni*)—although not sympatric with these fishes—will add food items by breeding and producing larvae. Healthy growths of filamentous algae, which can harbor dense amphipod populations, may be another source of foods. Shrimpfishes will also eat newborn guppies or mollies. Any food competitors in the tank that are likely to thin out the small crustacean stocks will interfere with the successful maintenance of these animals.

Shrimpfishes should not be housed with belligerent fishes like pygmy angelfishes, damsels, larger wrasses, triggerfishes, and puffers. In addition, large crustaceans should not be kept with them, as they might catch and consume the shrimpfishes. Some fish species that may be suitable tankmates for shrimpfishes include seahorses, pipefishes, ghost pipefishes, anthias, chromis, flasher wrasses, pygmy gobies, wormfishes, dart gobies, dragonets, and fang blennies. However, some of these fishes are potential food competitors and should not be added to the tank until the shrimpfishes are feeding and you are sure you can provide adequate food.

You are likely to have better success with shrimpfishes if they are kept in their own specimen tank. They are not aggressive towards each other and do best if kept in groups. A school of these fishes makes an eye-catching display in a reef tank, especially a stony coral display. Long-spined sea urchins (*Diadema* spp.) are an interesting addition to a shrimpfish home, although they are not the best invertebrates to keep in a reef aquarium because they will eat coralline algae and can damage large-polyped stony corals.

Shrimpfishes can suffer from parasitic infection and are reported to be sensitive to copper-based medications, although they can withstand lower doses.

SHRIMPFISH SPECIES

Genus *Aeoliscus*

Aeoliscus punctulatus (Bianconi, 1855)
Common Names: Speckled Shrimpfish, Spotted Shrimpfish.
Maximum Length: 15 cm (5.9 in.).
Distribution: East Africa north to the Red Sea.
Biology: The Speckled Shrimpfish is found in inshore waters, often near coastal reefs. It occurs in lagoons and bays and often resides in seagrass meadows at a depth of 1 to 17 m (3.3 to 55 ft.). Although these fish can be found singly, they more frequently occur in large schools, which can number over 100 individuals. They drift over the substrate and are sometimes found among the swarms of small crustaceans on which they feed. Their nearly transparent bodies, covered with black speckles, may help them blend in with these crustacean aggregations.
Captive Care: See the Captive Care section at left.
Aquarium Size: 30 gal. **Temperature:** 22 to 28°C (72 to 82°F).
Aquarium Suitability Index: 3.
Remarks: As the name implies, the Speckled Shrimpfish has small black spots scattered on the body and lacks a midbody stripe. It has a hinged or movable posterior dorsal spine.

Aeoliscus punctulatus, Speckled Shrimpfish: can occur in large schools.

Aeoliscus strigatus (Günther, 1860)
Common Names: Coral Shrimpfish, Striped Shrimpfish, Razorfish.
Maximum Length: 15 cm (5.9 in.).
Distribution: Aldabra and the Seychelles, east to New Caledonia, north to southern Japan, and south to southeast Australia.

Aeoliscus strigatus, Coral Shrimpfish: school of juveniles.

Aeoliscus strigatus, Coral Shrimpfish: adults hovering over corals.

Centriscus scutatus, Rigid Shrimpfish: can be kept singly, in pairs, or in groups.

Biology: The Coral Shrimpfish inhabits clear coastal reefs and leeward fringing reefs around offshore islands. It occurs in lagoons, on reef flats, the reef face, and the fore-reef slope at depths of 1 to at least 30 m (3.3 to 98 ft.). It is found singly and in pairs, but is most often seen in small to very large schools. These groups often dwell among whip corals, seagrasses, or long-spined sea urchins (*Diadema* spp.), or over branching acroporid corals. Even tiny Coral Shrimpfish have an affinity to sea urchins, often seeking them out when they settle from the plankton. It is not uncommon to find young Coral Shrimpfish floating along with bits of seagrass. Adults are sometimes observed hanging among the branches of *Ctenocella* gorgonians. This soft coral is bright red, but looks brown or black at depth, enabling the Coral Shrimpfish with its black stripe to blend in. It is reported to feed on small benthic crustaceans, swarming *Mysis* shrimp, and zooplankton.

Captive Care: See the Captive Care section in the family account, page 441.

Aquarium Size: 30 gal. **Temperature:** 22 to 28°C (72 to 82°F).
Aquarium Suitability Index: 3.

Remarks: The Coral Shrimpfish is white overall with a dark stripe running down the middle of the body, through the eye, and down the snout. This stripe can fade or darken. This species has a hinged or movable posterior dorsal spine.

Genus *Centriscus*

Centriscus scutatus Linnaeus, 1758
Common Names: Rigid Shrimpfish, Grooved Shrimpfish.
Maximum Length: 15 cm (5.9 in.).
Distribution: Red Sea and the Arabian Gulf east to Indonesia and Malaysia, north to southern Japan, and south to Queensland.
Biology: This species tends to live in muddy habitat near coastal reefs from depths of 3 to over 100 m (10 to 325 ft.) and will shelter near sessile invertebrates like sea pens, gorgonians, or whip corals, or vegetation like seagrass. The Rigid Shrimpfish occurs singly, in pairs, or in groups that can be quite large.
Captive Care: See the Captive Care section in the family account, page 441.
Aquarium Size: 30 gal. **Temperature:** 22 to 28°C (72 to 82°F).
Aquarium Suitability Index: 3.
Remarks: The Rigid Shrimpfish is silvery or silvery pink overall with a dark gray abdomen and a bronze stripe running down the middle of the body, through the eye, and down the snout. The posterior dorsal spine is rigid.

References
Debelius (1993), Kuiter & Debelius (1994), Randall (1995).

Family Caracanthidae
Coral Crouchers

Branching stony coral colonies provide sanctuaries for numerous invertebrates and bony fishes. Some animals rely on these calcareous structures as temporary hiding places during the day or places to refuge at night. Others spend their entire lives among the coral's branches. The coral crouchers, or orbicular velvetfishes, are a specialized group of obligatory coral dwellers that are so secretive that aquarists and divers only rarely see them.

The Family Caracanthidae is comprised of one genus and four species. Because they are small and live deep within ramose coral heads, they are very difficult to observe. Stubby fishes that are laterally compressed and oval in shape, they have short, stout pectoral fins that are used to brace themselves between coral branches. These fishes also flare their opercula—which have associated spines—when disturbed, making them even more difficult to extract from the coral. Like their cousins the scorpionfishes, the coral crouchers have venomous dorsal spines—remember to take care when capturing or transporting them. They also have small papillae on their bodies that give them a velvety appearance, hence one common name, velvetfishes.

The coral crouchers are found in the tropical waters of the Indian Ocean and the West, South, and Central Pacific Ocean. They live among the branches of live stony corals in the genera *Acropora*, *Pocillopora*, and *Stylophora*. There they hunt snapping shrimps (*Alpheus* spp.) and zooplankton that either hide in the coral or float past with the current. The stomach contents of at least one coral croucher also contained coral tissue, indicating that these fishes feed to some degree on their hosts (whether incidentally or intentionally). Although a typical coral head may contain only one or two coral crouchers, a single football-sized colony can yield as many as four (one social grouping of four individuals consisted of one male and three females). The social and mating system of these fishes has not been studied, so it is not known whether males exclude consexuals from their "home" coral head or whether they tolerate each other.

Captive Care

Coral crouchers are not ideal aquarium inhabitants because they spend almost all of their time in hiding. However, if you really want to keep one of these unique creatures, the first step is to set up a tank with live ramose stony corals. It is best to house

Caracanthus maculatus, Spotted Coral Croucher: living among the branches of acroporid corals, these fishes present special challenges to the aquarist.

the coral croucher in a small tank (10 to 20 gallons) with one or two coral colonies. This in itself will be a challenge, as most stony coral aquariums are much larger, but the small tank will make it much easier to feed the fish and monitor its health. The best way to view the fish is by looking down between the coral branches. To do this, either position the coral colony so that it is leaning toward the front of the aquarium or mount a pendant light over the tank so that you can remove the aquarium cover and look down. You could also mount a mirror above the tank to see the reflection of the view from the top.

Although a tank with one coral croucher may lose its appeal, a stony coral microhabitat tank can provide a unique display. Before attempting to maintain this type of aquarium, however, be sure you have the equipment and knowledge to care for stony corals. The aquarium's centerpiece should be a colony of branching *Acropora* or *Pocillopora*. Place at least 5 cm (2 in.) of live sand on the aquarium bottom and set the coral colony on a base constructed of live rock. Then add a coral croucher, some *Trapezia* crabs (these often come in with the corals), and a pair of coral gobies (*Gobiodon* spp.). If the coral colony is large enough, you might include a few species that are less dependent on stony corals, such as a Blue Green Chromis (*Chromis viridis*) or Blue-lined Dottyback (*Pseudochromis cyanotaenia*). Colonies of obligatory coral dwellers could be set up in a larger tank, but it would be hard to observe them.

Coral crouchers have spines along the edge of their gill covers that can easily become entangled in a small mesh net. A much better way to catch one is in a specimen cup. To get a coral croucher out of a coral head, lift the coral head from the water and try to shake the fish into a specimen cup or bag. If this proves too difficult, you might try to chase the fish from the coral with a piece of rigid tubing.

Coral Croucher Species

Caracanthus maculatus (Gray, 1831)
Common Name: Spotted Coral Croucher.
Maximum Length: 5 cm (2.0 in.).
Distribution: Indonesia to the Line Islands, north to southern Japan, and south to Austral Island and the Great Barrier Reef.
Biology: The Spotted Coral Croucher is most often found among the branches of larger stony corals, such as *Pocillopora eydouxi*, *Stylophora mordax*, and some *Acropora* species. It feeds on snapping shrimps.
Captive Care: See details in the Captive Care section in the family account, page 443.
Aquarium Size: 10 gal. **Temperature:** 23 to 28°C (74 to 82°F).
Aquarium Suitability Index: 2 (Venomous).
Remarks: The Spotted Coral Croucher is light gray with small red spots and has a deeply notched dorsal fin. There are two species similar to *C. maculatus*. One of them, the **Hawaiian Coral Croucher (*Caracanthus typicus*) Kroyer, 1845,** is endemic to the Hawaiian Islands. The other, the **Madagascar Coral Croucher (*Caracanthus madagascariensis*) (Guichenot, 1869),** is found in the Western Indian Ocean and has red dashes instead of red spots.

Caracanthus unipinna, Pygmy Coral Croucher: these fishes have a distinct preference for live foods, such as grass shrimp and adult brine shrimp.

Caracanthus unipinna (Gray, 1831)
Common Name: Pygmy Coral Croucher.
Maximum Length: 5 cm (2.0 in.).
Distribution: East Africa to the Tuamotus, north to southern Japan, and south to the Great Barrier Reef.
Biology: The Pygmy Coral Croucher is known to inhabit heads of *Acropora humilis*, *Acropora corymbosa*, *Pocillopora* spp., and *Stylophora mordax*. It seems to prefer stony corals with stubbier branches that provide narrow spaces for it to wedge between. Up to four of these fish have been found in a single coral head that was 20 cm (7.9 in.) in diameter. The Pygmy Coral Croucher sometimes shares its coral head with coral, or clown, gobies (*Gobiodon* spp.).
Captive Care: See details in the Captive Care section in the family account, page 443.
Aquarium Size: 10 gal. **Temperature:** 23 to 28°C (74 to 82°F).
Aquarium Suitability Index: 2 (Venomous).
Remarks: *Caracanthus unipinna* is a uniform brown or gray on the back and lighter on the ventrum; its dorsal fin is not deeply notched.

References
Patton (1994), Randall (1996), Tyler (1971).

Family Tetrarogidae
Waspfishes

The waspfishes are somewhat of an enigma to taxonomists and—with a potent sting and the habit of mimicking dead leaves and sunken debris— little more than a strange curiosity to most aquarists.

Ichthyologists disagree as to the family status of the waspfishes and some place them in Family Scorpaenidae, the scorpionfishes. The biggest difference between the two is that the dorsal fin of the waspfishes originates above—or in front of—the eyes, while that of the scorpionfishes begins well behind the eyes. In addition, waspfishes have small scales embedded in their skin and are typically more laterally compressed than most scorpaenids (except the Leaf Scorpionfish, *Taenianotus triacanthus*). Finally, although separated, the dorsal and anal fins of the waspfishes are contiguous with the caudal fin and can be partially joined in some species. After considering these differences, ichthyologists must decide whether or not the waspfishes belong in their own family. This author agrees with Myers (1989) and Kuiter and Debelius (1994), and recognizes the waspfishes in their own family, the Tetrarogidae.

Biology

There are approximately 11 genera and 35 species in the Family Tetrarogidae (although this family is in need of serious revision). Most occur in the Indo-Pacific, but many are found in the warm temperate waters around southern Australia and Japan. Like their relatives the scorpionfishes, the waspfishes are benthic predators that feed mainly on crustaceans and polychaete worms. Small bottom-dwelling fishes are a less important component of their diets. When in repose on the seafloor, waspfishes often both look and act like algal debris. Some species are known to sway from side to side; in fact, they often lie almost flat on the bottom like a piece of flotsam in the surge. This behavior helps waspfishes to catch—and to avoid becoming—food. Prey species, like small crustaceans, do not perceive this swaying piece of debris as a threat, while fish-eating predators do not recognize the waspfish as something edible. In at least one species, filamentous green algae grows on the skin, further enhancing the fish's camouflage. The algae may actually serve to attract small algae-eating crustaceans within striking range.

Many scorpionfishes shed their outer layer of skin (the cuticle) to rid their bodies of algae and sessile invertebrates that grow on them. Although I have never seen a waspfish do this, and there are no reports of it in the literature, it is likely that waspfishes shed this cuticle as well.

Waspfishes are highly venomous, delivering a painful and potentially lethal sting. Special care is required when working in a tank that contains a waspfish, because it is easy to overlook and bump into these cryptic fishes when you are cleaning the glass or rearranging the decor. If you do get stung, immediately immerse the wound site in very hot water to help dull the pain, and seek the attention of a physician (for more on treating envenomization, see "When a Lion Strikes," page 491).

Ablabys taenianotus, Cockatoo Waspfish: note algae on body surface.

Richardsonichthys sp.: some waspfishes require a sand substrate.

Captive Care

Because of their relatively small size and inactive lifestyle, adult waspfishes can be housed in tanks as small as 20 gallons. They are relatively easy to keep if you provide them with live black worms and grass shrimp. Some individuals might also ingest small feeder fish, but they often have difficulty catching them. Smaller specimens will eat live brine shrimp. On rare occasions, waspfishes can be trained to take pieces of fresh seafood from a feeding stick. These fishes are nocturnal hunters; if you find that your specimen does not eat, try adding some live food—like grass shrimp—after you turn the lights off over the tank.

Like many bottom-dwelling predators, waspfishes are often mistaken for food-encrusted substrate by those fishes that eat sessile invertebrates—including butterflyfishes, angelfishes, pufferfishes, triggerfishes, and porcupinefishes. Because the waspfishes look like plant material, large herbivores may also pick at them. Waspfishes are apt to miss out at feeding time if kept with more aggressive food competitors like groupers and snappers. Therefore, it is best to keep waspfishes in a small-species aquarium or with slow-moving carnivores like frogfishes and scorpionfishes. If you decide to house a waspfish with a frogfish, make sure that the waspfish's body length is at least 1½ times that of the antennariid. Waspfishes pose little threat to tankmates except very small benthic fishes (like certain gobies) and ornamental crustaceans.

A waspfish needs suitable places to hide during the day. These can be caves, crevices, or a large stand of long-bladed macroalgae like *Caulerpa prolifera* or *Caulerpa sertularoides*. Some waspfishes (like the Whiteface Waspfish, *Richardsonichthys leucogaster*) prefer to bury under the substrate. These species should be provided with 5 to 10 cm (2 to 4 in.) of fine coral sand. They can be kept in a reef aquarium, but are sensitive to the stings of corals or anemones with more potent nematocysts. Waspfishes can suffer from parasitic infections, but the resulting cysts can be difficult to detect because the fishes are naturally mottled and/or have prickles on the skin. If you cannot locate the cysts visually, two other signs of parasitic infection are an increased respiration rate and cloudy eyes. The common antiparasitics (e.g., copper) can be used successfully. If you need to transfer a waspfish from one tank to another, use a specimen container or a fine mesh net to prevent the dorsal and cheek spines from becoming entangled.

At least one member of the family, *Hypodytes rubripinnis*, has been reported to spawn in captivity. One of the biggest tricks in breeding these fishes is to acquire both a male and female. At least some species are sexually dichromatic.

Ablabys taenianotus, Cockatoo Waspfish: ideal subject for a small species aquarium or a quiet system without aggressive food competitors.

Waspfish Species

Genus *Ablabys*

Ablabys macracanthus (Bleeker, 1852)
Common Name: Spiny Waspfish.
Maximum Length: 18 cm (7.1 in.).
Distribution: Indonesia to the Philippines.
Biology: The Spiny Waspfish is found at a depth range of 10 to 50 m (33 to 163 ft.) on coastal sand and mud slopes, often adjacent to deep water. These fishes often rest on exposed sand or mud bottoms.
Captive Care: This species is less common in the aquarium trade than its close relative the Cockatoo Waspfish (*Ablabys taenianotus*). Their husbandry is similar (see the Captive Care section in the following species account).
Aquarium Size: 20 gal. **Temperature:** 22 to 27°C (72 to 80°F).
Aquarium Suitability Index: 3 (**Highly Venomous**).
Remarks: The Indian Ocean Waspfish (*Ablabys binotatus*) (Peters, 1855) is very similar to this species, but differs in having 5 rays in the anal fin (*A. macracanthus* has 7 to 8 anal rays).

The Spiny Waspfish can be separated from the Cockatoo Waspfish (*Ablabys taenianotus*) by the number of dorsal spines (*A. macracanthus* has 15; *A. taenianotus* has 17), and the number of anal rays (*A. macracanthus* has 7 to 8; *A. taenianotus* has 5). The origin of the dorsal fin in these species is also a distinguishing characteristic. It starts well in front of the eyes in *A. macracanthus*; but over the eyes in *A. taenianotus*.

Ablabys macracanthus, Spiny Waspfish: to encourage an initial feeding response, offer live grass shrimp after aquarium lights have been dimmed.

Ablabys macracanthus, Spiny Waspfish: note origin of dorsal fin.

Ablabys taenianotus, Cockatoo Waspfish: sways like plant debris.

Ablabys taenianotus (Cuvier, 1829)
Common Name: Cockatoo Waspfish.
Maximum Length: 15 cm (5.9 in.).
Distribution: Andaman Sea to Fiji, north to southern Japan, and south to Australia.
Biology: In some areas, this is a very cryptic fish often found among stands of macroalgae like *Padina* and *Gelidium*. The Cockatoo Waspfish seems to prefer protected areas of the reef where there is limited wave action, as well as a lot of algal debris and rubble on the bottom. In other locations, this waspfish sits in more exposed positions during the day—often lying against rocks, rubble, or algae. *Ablabys taenianotus* occurs at depths of less than 1 up to 20 m (3.3 to 65 ft.). It feeds primarily during the day and at dusk on bottom-dwelling invertebrates (like shrimps and crabs) and small fishes. Each specimen occupies an exclusive home range of about 10 x 14 m (33 x 46 ft.) or larger, but they have never been observed to evict intruding conspecifics. Instead, Cockatoo Waspfish just seem to avoid each other. Their home ranges do not overlap, and they patrol them throughout the day. Females in spawning condition will change color from brown to jet black by the middle of the day and begin to swell with eggs by late afternoon. As sunset approaches, the ripe female will move into the male's home range and rest near the spawning site. The male and female will lie next to each other just before courtship takes place. The male will move past her and brush her side with one of his pectoral fins and occasionally circle in front of her, making more tactile contact with his dorsal and paired fins. As passions rise, he moves alongside her and remains motionless, with his body touching hers. After a minute or more, the mating march begins; the female begins to move forward along the bottom, closely followed by the male. During this procession, the male may circle her until she begins to swim up into the water column (this is known as the upward rise). The male will swim beside her into the water column until they are about 1 m (3.3 ft.) above the bottom. At this point, they perform a loop-the-loop, shedding their gametes when upside down and at the apex of the loop. The eggs, which are spherical, buoyant, and about 1.2 mm in diameter, are broadcast into the water column and carried away as part of the plankton.
Captive Care: It is advisable to keep only one Cockatoo Waspfish per tank, unless you want to add a male and female to a larger aquarium and try to induce spawning behavior. If you have more active carnivores in the aquarium, it may be difficult to feed your *A. taenianotus*, as they hunt by ambush or slowly stalk their quarry and are not quick to get to, and ingest, food items. Although you should provide these fishes with a place to hide, they often sit in exposed portions of the tank.
Aquarium Size: 20 gal. **Temperature:** 20 to 27°C (68 to 80°F).
Aquarium Suitability Index: 3 (**Highly Venomous**).
Remarks: The color pattern of the Cockatoo Waspfish is highly variable, with no two individuals sharing the same number and shape of white blotches and spots. However, the blotches and spots are consistent enough in placement that they can be used to distinguish the sex of an individual, at least in those specimens from Japanese waters. Females have single white spots or blotches above and below the lateral line on each side of the body, while males lack those above the lateral line on one or both sides. Males also have one or two white spots on the distal margin of the operculum on one or both sides.

Genus *Paracentropogon*

This genus contains several described forms and some species that are apparently undescribed (the genus appears to be in need of taxonomic revision). Most of the *Paracentropogon* species occur on or near coastal reefs, often in macroalgae beds.

Paracentropogon longispinus (Cuvier & Valenciennes, 1829)

Common Name: Longspine Waspfish.
Maximum Length: 12 cm (4.7 in.).
Distribution: India to China, south to Australia, and north to the Philippines.
Biology: The Longspine Waspfish is found in silty, coastal habitats on mud flats, in estuaries, and among sponges and macroalgae on sand and mud slopes. In Northern Sulawesi, I have observed *P. longispinus* at depths between 10 and 30 m (33 to 98 ft.). However, it is also trawled in deeper water. Although no information is available on the feeding habits of this species, I have seen them capture errant polychaete worms at night. A related waspfish from Japan and Korea feeds mainly on small crustaceans like isopods, grammarids, and caprellids, as well as polychaete worms and shrimps. The Longspine Waspfish is cryptic during the day—hiding among the macroalgae—but moves into more exposed areas to hunt after dark. I have seen males display at the smaller females by raising all their fins and undulating their bodies.
Captive Care: See the Captive Care section in the family account, page 447.
Aquarium Size: 20 gal. **Temperature:** 23 to 27°C (74 to 80°F).
Aquarium Suitability Index: 3 (**Highly Venomous**).
Remarks: The color of this species is variable, although most that

Paracentropogon longispinus, Longspine Waspfish: variant.

Paracentropogon longispinus, Longspine Waspfish: variant.

Paracentropogon longispinus, Longspine Waspfish: variant.

Paracentropogon longispinus, Longspine Waspfish: variant.

Paracentropogon longispinus, Longspine Waspfish: variant.

Paracentropogon longispinus, Longspine Waspfish: variant.

Paracentropogon sp., Sailfin Waspfish: note distinctive dorsal fin.

Paracentropogon sp., Sailfin Waspfish: variant.

enter the aquarium trade are brown overall with a white face and have a spot or patch below the tenth dorsal spine just above the lateral line.

In Northern Sulawesi, individuals living in sponge and macroalgae beds are often mottled with what looks like pink and red calcareous algae and may have a white face. I have also observed females that were orange overall with a distinct white spot. This species is sexually dimorphic—in males, the dorsal spines are long (shorter in females) and the membrane between them is deeply incised (not deeply incised in females).

Paracentropogon sp.
Common Name: Sailfin Waspfish.
Maximum Length: approx. 7.5 cm (3.0 in.).
Distribution: Sulawesi, Indonesia.
Biology: I have observed this apparently undescribed form on coastal reefs, among sponges and macroalgae, at depths of 4.5 to 6 m (15 to 20 ft.).
Captive Care: See the Captive Care section in the family account, page 447.
Aquarium Size: 20 gal. **Temperature:** 23 to 28°C (74 to 82°F).
Aquarium Suitability Index: 3 (**Highly Venomous**).
Remarks: The dorsal membrane placement easily distinguishes this waspfish from others in the genus: the membrane between the second and third dorsal spines begins at the distal end of the second spine and ends a short way below the tip of the third; the membrane between the third and fourth dorsal spines begins near the tip of the third, but attaches to near the base of the fourth spine. This species does not have a distinct white spot on the side, but has light and dark mottling. Some individuals have a white face.

Richardsonichthys leucogaster, Whiteface Waspfish: secretive species.

Richardsonichthys leucogaster, Whiteface Waspfish: variant.

Genus *Richardsonichthys*

Richardsonichthys leucogaster (Richardson, 1848)
Common Name: Whiteface Waspfish.
Maximum Length: 10 cm (3.9 in.).
Distribution: India to Melanesia, south to northern Australia.
Biology: The Whiteface Waspfish is found on mud or sand flats at depths of 3 to 18 m (10 to 59 ft.). It hides under the substrate during the day, emerging at night to feed on small crustaceans and errant polychaetes. It usually occurs singly, although several individuals may be observed within a few meters of each other. In Indonesia, this species occupies the same habitat as the Black-finned Snake Eel (*Ophichthus melanochir*), the Striated Frogfish (*Antennarius striatus*), numerous species of flatheads (Platycephalidae), the Ambon Scorpionfish (*Pteroidichthys amboinensis*), and the Shortfin Lionfish (*Dendrochirus brachypterus*).
Captive Care: This secretive species will spend much of the day hiding and can present feeding problems. Use live grass shrimp and small livebearers to stimulate feeding before trying to switch over to fresh seafood like shrimp, squid, scallops, and fish.
Aquarium Size: 20 gal. **Temperature:** 20 to 27°C (68 to 80°F).
Aquarium Suitability Index: 3 (**Highly Venomous**).
Remarks: Many individuals in the *Paracentropogon* genus are mistaken for this waspfish, but the Whiteface Waspfish is not as laterally compressed. I have seen what appears to be an undescribed species of *Richardsonichthys* on coastal sand flats off North Sulawesi. It has a white face and a white saddle on the nape.

References
Baba & Sano (1987), R. Kuiter (personal communication), Kuiter & Debelius (1994), Moyer et al. (1985), Myers (1989).

Richardsonichthys leucogaster, Whiteface Waspfish: variant.

Richardsonichthys sp.: an apparently undescribed species.

Family Scorpaenidae
Scorpionfishes

A NUMBER OF REEF FISHES MAKE THEIR LIVING BY SITTING on the bottom and waiting for unwary fish or crustaceans to happen by. This sit-and-wait strategy requires the hunter to blend in with its surroundings and go unnoticed by its prey, or to possess something to attract its quarry into striking range. The frogfishes (Antennariidae), for example, not only look like reef substrate, they also have a modified dorsal spine that they use to entice their prey. Other groups of fishes also use deception and crypsis in order to fill their bellies. These include the Subfamilies Apistinae, Minoinae, Scorpaeninae, Synanceinae, and Choridactylinae, all of which belong to the scorpionfish family, Scorpaenidae. Some of these fishes look like medieval dragons, while others resemble algae-encrusted stones. While near-perfect camouflage and venomous spines make them a hazard for swimmers, snorkelers, and divers in shallow waters, the unusual appearances and predatory prowess of the scorpionfishes attract many aquarists to these odd creatures. In the next account (page 491), we examine another group within this family, the Subfamily Pteroinae, whose members are commonly called lionfishes. They have diverged from the other scorpaenids, and some ichthyologists have even suggested that the subfamily be elevated to family status.

Classification and Biology

The Family Scorpaenidae is a large group that contains an estimated 388 species and 45 genera. Family members have large heads, mouths, and eyes, and a bony ridge running from the eye across the cheek (the supraorbital stay). They have spines on the gill cover and head, and stout fin spines—which in most species are venomous. The spines responsible for delivering the venom are associated with the dorsal, anal, and pelvic fins. In some species, there is glandular tissue on each side of the spine that produces the venom; in others, there is a gland that secretes the venom into a duct running through the spine. The toxicity of venom varies from one species to the next, but in some forms, like the Reef Stonefish (*Synanceia verrucosa*), it can produce excruciating pain or even death. In most species, however, the venom causes swelling and temporary irritation. If you are stung,

Scorpaenopsis papuensis, Papuan Scorpionfish: typically seen in Indonesian waters, reposing among branches of soft corals (North Sulawesi).

follow the treatment procedures listed in the section on lionfishes (page 491). Unfortunately, placing the sting site in hot water or heating the area with a hair dryer, as suggested for lionfish stings, may not provide as much relief for scorpionfish stings (especially for stings caused by members of the stonefish subfamily). But by administering this treatment, you still may be able to denature some of the venom protein. A scorpionfish sting may take weeks, or even up to a month, to heal. Apply topical antiseptic to the wound site until it heals. For a stonefish sting, an antivenin is available from physicians.

For identification purposes, some scorpionfishes can be difficult to differentiate. Characteristics useful in separating these species include: the length of the first three dorsal spines relative to each other, the number and shape of the dermal appendages on the head, the number of pectoral rays, the coloration on the inside of the pectoral fins, eye size, snout length, the presence or absence of tentacles over the eyes, and the overall color pattern. But even within some species these characteristics can vary. For example, many scorpionfishes can change their color to better match their surroundings. In addition, in some species the snout length relative to the eye diameter changes as the fish grows.

Distribution and Habitat

Scorpionfishes are found in all the world's oceans, but unlike most of the families associated with coral reefs, scorpionfishes reach their apex of diversity on rocky reefs in temperate seas. For example, the coral reefs of Micronesia are home to approximately 24 species of scorpionfishes from the Subfamilies Scorpaeninae, Synanceinae, and Choridactylinae, while in cool water along the California coast, at least 57 species of a single scorpionfish genus (*Sebastes* spp., known commonly as rockfishes) occur.

Scorpionfishes live on both hard and soft substrates. On coral reefs they lie in crevices, in caves, and under overhangs. Most possess dermal flaps, tassels, and reef-tone colors that help them blend in with their surroundings. Some of the smaller species are especially secretive; for example, the Speckled Scorpionfish (*Sebastapistes coniorta*) is found among the branches of *Pocillopora* corals during the day. Some other diminutive forms live among coral rubble, while some larger species lie in exposed areas. Because of their cryptic coloration and sedentary behavior, however, even the exposed species are often overlooked by divers and potential prey alike.

Not all scorpionfishes live on calcareous substrate. Some live in sand, mud, or seagrass beds adjacent to the reef. For example, most devilfishes (*Inimicus* spp.) bury in the soft substrate in lagoons and near coastal reefs, while the Reef Stonefish is often found buried in sand patches on the reef itself.

Feeding and Antipredation Behavior
The behavior of scorpionfish species also helps enhance their camouflage. For example, the Leaf Scorpionfish (*Taenianotus triacanthus*) sways its body from side to side so that it looks like a piece of debris, while the Weedy Scorpionfish (*Rhinopias frondosa*) rocks back and forth to achieve a similar effect. Most species, however, go unnoticed by remaining motionless. Even when disturbed, they may only move a short distance.

In some of these sedentary fishes, plants and sessile invertebrates actually grow on their bodies. Consider the Reef Stonefish. In the Red Sea, this species is often covered with a dense coating of hydroids of the genus *Podocorella*. Many stonefishes are used as a growth substrate by green filamentous algae, golden diatoms, and cyanobacteria (blue-green algae). It has been suggested that stonefishes exude a white, milky substance over their bodies and that this substance encourages plant growth. Not only do these plants help the stonefish blend in with its surroundings, they may even act as a passive lure to attract herbivorous fishes close enough for the stonefish to eat. Herbivores, such as parrotfishes, have been found in stonefish stomachs. These scorpionfishes may not only lure herbivores looking for food, they may also attract fishes searching for a place to hide by resembling a shelter site. This is known as protective resemblance. Reef Stonefish look so much like reef substrate that mollusks and shrimps have been observed climbing over or sitting on them. Not all scorpionfishes rely on passive luring to attract their prey. The Decoy Scorpionfish (*Iracundus signifier*), for example, uses its fishlike dorsal fin to entice fish into striking range. The fish are probably drawn to the lure out of aggression rather than hunger.

Although some species may lure—either passively or actively—most scorpionfishes rely on concealment to ambush their food. Like other ambush predators, they have an incredibly fast feeding mechanism. When a fish or shrimp moves close enough to the mouth of the scorpionfish, its jaws are projected forward rapidly and its mouth cavity expands. This creates a vacuum, drawing in the prey with lightning speed. Although they are not quite as fast as the frogfishes, scorpionfishes like the Reef Stonefish have been documented extending the mouth to full gape in as little as 15 milliseconds.

The diets of the reef-dwelling scorpionfishes vary somewhat between species. Some larger species (e.g., *Scorpaenopsis gibbosa*) feed exclusively on fishes, while others of similar size (e.g., *Scorpaenopsis oxycephala*) have a wider dietary breadth, feeding on invertebrates like shrimps, crabs, and squids, as well as bony fishes. Some smaller scorpionfishes feed heavily on annelid worms and small crustaceans, while others feed almost exclusively on crabs.

Like their cousins the lionfishes, most scorpionfishes in the Subfamilies Scorpaeninae, Synanceinae, and Choridactylinae hunt mainly at night. However, they will feed whenever the opportunity arises. On the reef, they usually feed on one or two organisms in a day—and those that feed on larger prey may not eat for several days between meals. Both juvenile scorpaenids and those species that feed on diminutive prey—like smaller crustaceans—may ingest a higher number of prey items more often.

The scorpionfish's cryptic nature is also one of its primary defenses against predators. If a scorpionfish is threatened, it will erect its dorsal spines. If danger persists, it may flee—which usually consists of swimming a short distance, quickly settling back on the bottom, and then "freezing." A number of species also have bright colors on the inner surfaces of their pectoral fins. These colors are not visible when the fish is in repose on the ocean bottom (if they were, they would make the fish more conspicuous and could interfere with food acquisition). But if the

Scorpaenopsis sp.: algae and parasitic isopods on the fish's skin may serve to attract prey fishes.

Scorpaenopsis diabola, Devil Scorpionfish: flashing bright warning colors.

Scorpaena plumieri, Spotted Scorpionfish: flash-flight warns off predators.

scorpionfish moves or rolls these fins forward, there is a sudden flash of color (these are sometimes called flash colors). These markings may warn larger piscivores that these fish are not good to eat. For example, a Humpback Scorpionfish (*Scorpaenopsis gibbosa*), was observed to display these colors when a large jack was swimming near it. The sudden display of the brilliant fin surface may also startle a potential predator. The combination of the flash of color and the quick relocation to another spot is referred to as flash-flight.

Reproduction and Social Organization

The Scorpaeninae, Synanceinae, and Choridactylinae, like their relatives the lionfishes, reproduce by producing a floating, gelatinous mass in which the eggs are embedded. In these species, fertilization occurs outside the female's body. (Some species from temperate waters practice internal fertilization and bear live young.) There is little information available on the reproductive behavior, mating systems, and social organization of reef-dwelling scorpionfishes. I did witness courtship behavior in the Leaf Scorpionfish (*Taenianotus triacanthus*) off the island of Ambon in Indonesia (see page 487). Although some temperate species aggregate, most tropical forms are solitary. Occasionally, however, species such as the Reef Stonefish are found in pairs, and the Leaf Scorpionfish is commonly found in pairs or trios. Combat has been observed between individuals of some species, suggesting that they defend either a territory or possibly a preferred ambush site. Some scorpionfishes, such as the Devil Scorpionfish (*Scorpaenopsis diabola*), will perform jaw gaping when approached by a conspecific. The skin between the jaw elements is bright yellow, making the threat display even more conspicuous to the scorpionfish's potential rival.

"Skin" Shedding

Shedding of the cuticle (which is a product of the skin) has been documented in numerous scorpionfishes, including the lionfishes (Pteroinae), *Taenianotus triacanthus*, *Rhinopias* spp., *Inimicus* spp., and at least some of the *Scorpaenopsis*. The cuticle is tissue-like and is typically opaque or whitish in color. In some species, like *Rhinopias aphanes*, it is shed as often as once a week; in others it occurs less frequently. The shedding process can take from a few minutes to several hours. Some scorpaenids (e.g., *Rhinopias* spp.) facilitate the separation of the cuticle from the body by exhaling rapidly, which inflates the cuticle like a balloon. Then they

Scorpaenopsis diabola, Devil Scorpionfish: threatening gape offers dramatic display of bright yellow jaw skin that may drive away potential rivals.

Synanceia horrida, Horrid Stonefish: scruffy specimen preparing to shed.

Synanceia verrucosa, Reef Stonefish: freshened appearance after shedding.

Scorpaenopsis oxycephala, Tasseled Scorpionfish: resting on leather coral.

shake their bodies until the cuticle breaks off into smaller pieces. The function of this shedding is to rid the skin of organisms—like hydroids, algae, and cyanobacteria—that grow on these fishes as a result of their sedentary lifestyles, as well as ridding them of parasites. In fact, the cuticle is often shed more frequently if the fish is suffering from a severe protozoan infection, reducing the chances that it will succumb to these parasites. After the skin is shed, the fish's appearance may change drastically. For example, some Reef Stonefish turn vivid pink after they shed their encrusted cuticle.

Captive Care

Because most of their time is spent in repose on the aquarium substrate, scorpionfishes are not for everyone. Like a peculiar work of art, they are oddities that are appreciated most by the collector of the unusual. In addition, the fact that they are venomous means that they bring with them the inherent risk of stinging the aquarist. For this reason, they should never be kept in a home where small children have access to the tank. One beneficial aspect of their sluggishness is that they can be kept in smaller aquariums without any ill effects. For example, I have kept a single medium-sized scorpionfish species in a 10-gallon aquarium. If you want to keep more than one scorpionfish in the same tank, of course, it should be larger. A standard 30- or 55-gallon tank will provide a suitable home for several medium-sized species.

When planning your aquascaping, provide those species that live on hard substrates with ledges and caves in which to refuge. Most of the small *Parascorpaena* and *Sebastapistes* species live among coral rubble and should be provided with a similar microhabitat in the aquarium. If you are keeping those scorpionfishes that bury in softer bottom materials, the substrate should be covered with at least 2.5 cm (1 in.) of sand or crushed coral. If you are keeping larger specimens, increase the depth of the substrate so that the fish can bury itself almost completely.

Scorpionfishes can be kept in reef aquariums if you are not interested in housing shrimps or small fishes in the same tank. You should probably select species that spend more time in the open. These would include the Tasseled Scorpionfish (*Scorpaenopsis oxycephala*), the Devil Scorpionfish (*S. diabola*), and the Humpback Scorpionfish (*S. gibbosa*). If you add one of the more secretive forms—like the smaller *Parascorpaena* species—to a large tank full of live rock, you may never see it. Like some of the other ambush predators, a scorpionfish may choose a stony or soft coral colony as an ambush site. If the fish remains on the coral for long periods of time (days), it could cause damage to the coral colony. When working in a tank with a scorpionfish, remember to be vigilant to avoid contact with its venomous spines.

Most scorpionfishes require live prey to induce a feeding response and may prove difficult to switch to "dead" foods. There are several tricks to entice your scorpionfish into eating nonliving foods. The first, and easiest, is to cut a fresh marine fish filet into strips and impale one of these on the end of a feeding stick. Then pull the fish flesh through the water, as if it were swimming, past the head of your scorpionfish. Another method is to loosely tie a piece of string to the end of the fish strip and pull it through the water to achieve the same effect. It is important that the string not be tied tightly around the food or it may be ingested and difficult to retrieve without distressing the scorpionfish.

Avoid feeding your scorpionfish a diet consisting only of feeder goldfish. Raw goldfish flesh contains thiaminase, an enzyme that causes the breakdown of thiamin. With a goldfish-only diet, the scorpionfish may become thiamin-deficient, which can result in feeding cessation, clamped fins, and loss of nervous coordination. The best way to ensure that your scorpionfish stays healthy is to feed it a varied diet of fresh and frozen seafoods. You can also include some live foods like grass shrimp, fiddler crabs, and small crayfishes.

Hepatic lipidosis—fatty degeneration of the liver—has been reported in a Reef Stonefish that was fed only fresh hake. This condition can cause liver failure, which leads to suppression of the immune system, hemorrhaging, and anemia. Lipidosis is best avoided by giving your scorpionfish as varied a diet as possible and by not overfeeding it. I recommend feeding your scorpionfish to satiation twice a week.

Most scorpionfishes are solitary animals. Although it is possible to keep members of different species together in the same aquarium, conspecifics—especially two males—may fight. These battles begin with lateral displays and may culminate in head biting, in which one animal engulfs the other's head in its mouth and shakes it vigorously. If fighting escalates to this point, it is important to separate the dueling fish. Some species are more prone to behave aggressively than others. For example, more than one Leaf Scorpionfish can be kept in the same tank without aggression problems, but two male Decoy Scorpionfish are likely to fight—especially if they are housed in a smaller aquarium. Large scorpionfishes will also eat smaller members of their own, or related, species.

I have never seen or heard of a scorpionfish behaving aggressively toward an unrelated fish species. However, they will eat any fish or crustacean they can fit into their mouths—which are often larger than many aquarists anticipate. I once placed an unusual anemonefish and an Eschmeyer's Scorpionfish (*Rhinopias eschmeyeri*) in the same quarantine aquarium. The next morning the anemonefish was gone, and the belly of the scorpaenid

Synodus synodus, Red Lizardfish, eating scorpionfish: proof that venomous spines do not offer absolute protection from determined predators.

was conspicuously distended. In this case, the anemonefish—which was a deep-bodied species—was about half the length of the *Rhinopias*. Even more amazing, a friend and fellow rare fish lover, Jeff Voet, told me that his Reef Stonefish ate a parrotfish that was nearly equal to it in length. Larger scorpionfishes have even been known to eat lionfishes. Any tankmate should be at least the same length as your scorpionfish and, if of a lesser girth, at least 1½ times the scorpaenid's length. Those species with smaller mouths relative to their body size (e.g., *Choridactylus multibarbus*) can be kept with smaller tankmates.

Many aquarists believe that because scorpionfishes are venomous, other fishes will not bother them. But this is far from the truth. Wobbegongs, morays, lizardfishes, frogfishes, and even other scorpionfishes will swallow them whole. Because scorpionfishes often mimic reef substrate, fishes that feed on encrusting invertebrates—such as angelfishes, triggerfishes, and pufferfishes—may nip at, and damage, them.

Scorpionfishes can contract common saltwater parasites, but they tend to be less susceptible to them than many other fishes. This may be due in part to their ability to shed their cuticle. If they do come down with *Cryptocaryon* or *Amyloodinium*, the standard copper and/or formaldehyde treatments can be employed to eradicate these pests. Scorpionfishes occasionally suffer from intestinal worms like cestodes and nematodes. These specimens may lose weight even though they eat frequently. Schleser (1994) suggests treating fish suffering from such infestations with fenbendazole. This is administered orally at a dosage of 100 mg/kg of fish. To estimate the correct dosage, the fish needs to be weighed. To do this, capture the fish in a soft, small-meshed net, place another net over it so the fish cannot flip out, and place the nets with the fish on a scale. (Care must be taken when netting scorpionfishes because their spines can get tangled in any net with a coarse mesh.) After you weigh the fish and subtract the weight of the nets, you can figure out the amount of drug needed. If the scorpionfish will accept nonliving food, the medication can be placed in a piece of fish. If not, and you have access to a fish tranquilizer (e.g., tricaine methane-sulfate, MS222), you can anesthetize the fish so the drug can be delivered down the gullet and into the alimentary tract with a syringe. Remember to avoid the fish's venomous spines.

SCORPIONFISH SPECIES

SUBFAMILY APISTINAE (LONGFIN WASPFISHES)

This subfamily includes several unusual fish species, but only, the **Longfin or Bearded Waspfish** (*Apistus carinatus*) (**Bloch & Schneider, 1801**) occurs in the right places and at the right depths to make it into the aquarium trade. It ranges from the east coast of Africa and the Red Sea, east to the Indo-Malayan region, north to Japan, and south to Queensland. The Longfin Waspfish occurs on soft bottoms as shallow as 6 m (20 ft.) to depths of at least 60 m (195 ft.). It is typically found on open silty sand and mud plains where it spends its days buried under the substrate. It has one big ocellus on each side of the spiny dorsal fin that may function to deter potential predators, and black reticulations on the median fin. The greatly elongated pectoral fins may be dragged over the substrate to flush out animals hiding just under the sand or mud surface. These fins are also used to block the escape of small benthic fishes or crustaceans that the waspfish is stalking. The three barbels under the chin are probably used to locate potential prey items or test their palatability. The Longfin Waspfish reaches a maximum length of 18 cm (7.1 in.).

The husbandry of this species is similar to that of the devilfishes, Genus *Inimicus* (see the Captive Care section for *Inimicus didactylus*, page 461). The Longfin Waspfish should be provided with a large tank that has an open sand or mud bottom and no decoration. It is an active fish at night and requires plenty of swimming space, so select a tank with a large surface area (e.g., 75 gallons). The substrate should be at least 5 cm (2.0 in.) in depth. Feed this fish live black worms, live grass shrimp, and small polychaete worms either taken from live rock or purchased from a bait shop. Unfortunately, live food will probably be required to meet its nutritional needs, but try to entice the fish to take food from a feeding stick.

SUBFAMILY CHORIDACTYLINAE (STINGFISHES AND DEVILFISHES)

This subfamily contains the genera *Choridactylus* and *Inimicus*, which are characterized by having two or three free pectoral fin rays; that is, they are not connected to the rest of the fin by a membrane. These fin rays can be moved independently from the rest of the fin and are used in locomotion. They function as "legs," enabling these fish to walk on the ocean bottom, and may also aid in locating buried prey, as in the case of *Choridactylus*. The inner surfaces of the pectoral fins are brightly colored in many species and are quickly spread outward and forward when the fish is threatened. This may serve either to startle potential predators or to warn them of the fish's sharp, venomous spines.

Apistus carinatus, Longfin Waspfish: aposematic (warning) display.

Choridactylus multibarbus, Many-barbed Stingfish: variant.

Choridactylus multibarbus, Many-barbed Stingfish: a rare color variant of a species that occasionally appears in the aquarium trade and is sold as a "sea goblin."

Genus *Choridactylus* (Stingfishes)

This genus contains two species, both of which have three free pectoral fin rays and a round head profile. Only one of these, the **Many-barbed Stingfish, (*Choridactylus multibarbus*) Richardson, 1848**, makes it into the aquarium trade on occasion. Because it is not pictured in popular aquarium books, it is rarely identified properly and is usually sold as a "sea goblin" (a name most often applied to members of the genus *Inimicus*). The color of this species varies from mottled brown with irregular dark markings to bright orange overall. The fins of brown specimens may be orange and the body may have small yellow patches and white spots. All specimens have a dark band on the base of the tail. This species has been reported from the Red Sea, Persian Gulf, Gulf of Oman, Pakistan, India, the Gulf of Thailand, and the Philippines. Most specimens in the aquarium trade come from the Philippines. It is typically found on sand or mud bottoms, and sometimes adjacent to coral reefs, at depths as great as 40 m (130 ft.).

The Many-barbed Stingfish is an interesting addition to a home aquarium. It should be kept in a tank with a finely crushed coral or sand bottom so that it can bury in the substrate. This species rarely eats anything but live shrimp, live black worms, or baby livebearers. Smaller specimens can be fed live brine shrimp, while larger individuals will consume grass shrimp. It may also eat annelid worms present in live sand. Be careful when selecting tankmates for this fish. Food competitors will often prevent it from getting enough to eat, while sessile invertebrate feeders (e.g., large angelfishes, triggerfishes, pufferfishes, and porcupinefishes) may nip at and damage its skin. A final caution regarding *C. multibarbus*: this fish can deliver an extremely painful sting.

Genus *Inimicus* (Devilfishes)

The genus *Inimicus* is the other group in Subfamily Choridactylinae. *Inimicus* species are commonly referred to by the colorful names devilfishes, sea goblins, bearded ghouls, or demon stingers. There are at least eight species in this genus, several of which can be found in aquarium stores. These fish differ from the *Choridactylus* species in having two free pectoral rays and a flattened snout with eyes situated high on the head. They are limited in distribution to the Central and Western Pacific Ocean and

Inimicus didactylus, Spiny Devilfish: typical position, buried in substrate.

Inimicus caledonicus, Caledonian Devilfish: note white spots and band.

the Indian Ocean. Devilfishes occur on sand and mud bottoms, adjacent to reefs, in seagrass meadows, and in estuaries. They have been reported from depths of less than 1 up to 90 m (3.3 to 293 ft.).

The *Inimicus* species often bury themselves in the substrate with only the dorsal fin and top of the head exposed. In the more "advanced" forms of *Inimicus*, the eyes are higher on the head and the mouth is more upturned so that they can bury deeper in the substrate and still catch fish that swim past. When buried, the devilfish will place its free pectoral rays in front of its body so that it can quickly pull forward to capture prey. In nature, they feed mainly on small fishes; in the aquarium, they also relish grass shrimp. In most cases, live food is necessary to induce feeding. They will either use an ambush strategy to capture their prey or will stalk their quarry by slowly moving toward it on their leglike free pectoral rays. Like the stingfishes, devilfishes should be housed with less aggressive eaters so that they have a chance to compete for food. Although I find this difficult to believe, one species has been reported "to have attacked underwater photographers." Even though that may be an exaggeration, devilfishes can inflict excruciatingly painful stings. In certain locations, scuba divers regularly, and inadvertently, kneel on buried devilfishes when they come to rest on mud or sand bottoms.

Captured devilfishes will swim frantically against the side of a shipping bag, which often results in damage to the tip of the lower jaw. Collectors and wholesalers may discourage this behavior by placing a layer of fine coral sand in the bottom of the bag. I would not purchase specimens with an abraded lower jaw until the wound is healed and the fish is eating. Often, a nodule will develop where the wound was, and although the jaw may not look as good as it does in an undamaged specimen, this bony protuberance will not interfere with maintaining the fish.

Inimicus caledonicus (Sauvage, 1878)
Common Names: Caledonian Devilfish, Caledonian Stinger.
Maximum Length: 25 cm (9.8 in.).
Distribution: Andaman Sea to Australia and New Caledonia.
Biology: The Caledonian Devilfish is found on sand and mud substrate at depths of 15 to 60 m (49 to 195 ft.).
Captive Care: See the Captive Care section for *Inimicus didactylus*, below.
Aquarium Size: 30 gal. **Temperature:** 22 to 28°C (72 to 82°F).
Aquarium Suitability Index: 3 (**Highly Venomous**).
Remarks: This species is very similar to *I. didactylus*, but differs in pectoral fin coloration: in *I. caledonicus*, the inner surface of the pectoral fin has a dark band running through the middle and a dark region at the inner axil of the fin. In addition, *I. caledonicus* often has white spots in front of the eyes and a band on the tail.

Inimicus didactylus (Pallas, 1769)
Common Names: Spiny Devilfish, Sea Goblin.
Maximum Length: 18 cm (7.1 in.).
Distribution: Thailand to Vanuatu, north to southeast China and Micronesia.
Biology: The Spiny Devilfish is most often found on sand, mud, and mixed sand and rubble bottoms at depths of 5 to over 40 m (16 to 132 ft.). In some areas, it is also observed among macroalgae and sponges. In the daytime, it either buries in soft bottom materials or sits on the substrate. From these positions, it captures small fishes that swim nearby. At night, it emerges

from the substrate to hunt for food. When it displays at a rival or a potential predator, it spreads its pectoral fins down and forward, curls its caudal peduncle to the side, and expands its tail. The coloration on the inner pectoral fin can be white or yellow, with black markings. The Spiny Devilfish is typically a solitary species.

I have seen specimens behaving aggressively toward conspecifics, or possibly courting, in the wild. In one incident I watched an individual chase a larger specimen across the sand. As it moved closer, the smaller specimen displayed at the larger. On another occasion, I was photographing a Spiny Devilfish when I accidentally disturbed another individual that emerged from the sand and rubble. The specimen flushed out of hiding was larger, with a broader snout and a greatly distended abdomen, suggesting that it might be a female ripe with eggs. The pair moved slowly over the bottom, with the smaller animal moving alongside and trying to cut in front of the larger conspecific. Occasionally, as it moved alongside the larger fish, the smaller fish would display. The larger fish did not respond, but slowly lumbered forward in an apparent attempt to escape the aggressor (or possible suitor).

Captive Care: The Spiny Devilfish should be kept in a tank with at least 5 cm (2.0 in.) of fine coral sand on the bottom. When initially placed in an aquarium, some specimens may continually swim with their snouts pressed up against the aquarium glass. This is particularly true if the tank is very small, if there is no sand on the bottom for it to bury in, if there is excessive water movement, or if it is being picked on by its tankmates. This behavior can cause damage to the fish's lower jaw. One way to curb this undesirable behavior is to tape some black plastic, about 25 cm (10 in.) wide, along the outside bottom of all four sides of the aquarium. Live foods—like grass shrimp or small feeder fish—are usually necessary to elicit a feeding response. An occasional specimen will even refuse to eat live food, while others can be enticed into taking strips of fresh marine fish flesh from a feeding stick. I would only keep one Spiny Devilfish per aquarium.

Aquarium Size: 30 gal. **Temperature:** 22 to 28°C (72 to 82°F).
Aquarium Suitability Index: 3 (**Highly Venomous**).
Remarks: In this species, the overall coloration can vary greatly—brown, chocolate brown, pink, red, and even bright orange. The inner surface of the pectoral fin can be yellow or white with a black region beginning at the axil and extending to the middle of the fin. This dark area has white streaks. There is also a dark band, broken up by light color spots, bordering the fin margin. Juveniles of this species may have one or two filamentous rays extending from the upper margin of the pectoral fins, but these disappear as the fish grows.

Inimicus didactylus, Spiny Devilfish: stings can bring excruciating pain.

Inimicus didactylus, Spiny Devilfish: full-flared pectorals issue a warning.

Inimicus didactylus, Spiny Devilfish: unusual red color variant.

Inimicus didactylus, Spiny Devilfish: a male fish attempts to excavate a female buried in substrate (see photograph at right). Note sexual dimorphism.

Inimicus didactylus, Spiny Devilfish: flushed out by the male, the female devilfish emerges from the substrate.

Inimicus filamentosus, Filamented Devilfish: Red Sea and Indian Ocean fish.

Minous trachycephalus, Blue-eyed Stingfish: often mistaken for a sea robin.

Inimicus filamentosus (Cuvier, 1829)

Common Names: Filamented Devilfish, Filament-finned Stinger.
Maximum Length: 25 cm (9.8 in.).
Distribution: Red Sea to the Maldives, south to Madagascar and Mauritius.
Biology: This species occurs on sand and mud bottoms, sometimes seagrass beds, at depths of 10 to 55 m (33 to 179 ft.).
Captive Care: See the Captive Care section for *I. didactylus*, page 461.
Aquarium Size: 30 gal. **Temperature:** 22 to 28°C (72 to 82°F).
Aquarium Suitability Index: 3 (**Highly Venomous**).
Remarks: The Filamented Devilfish differs from the Spiny Devilfish and the Caledonian Devilfish by the presence of two filamentous rays on the upper part of each pectoral fin that are present in individuals of all sizes, and in having more elevated eyes that are joined together at their bases. In the other two species, the bases of the eyes are far apart, although they are connected by a bony ridge.

SUBFAMILY MINOINAE (STINGFISHES)

This subfamily consists of one genus and ten unusual species that are often mistaken for sea robins (Family Triglidae). Like the sea robins, they have large pectoral fins. Rather than having three modified pectoral rays, however, they only have one. All stingfishes have 12 rays in the pectoral fins, the lowest ray on each fin is separated from the other rays; together they function like "legs" that the fish use to walk over the substrate. Some species have barbels on the chin (sea robins do not) that are probably used to help locate their prey. Other distinguishing characteristics found in most stingfishes include 8 to 12 dorsal spines, 10 to 14 dorsal soft rays, 1 pelvic fin spine, and 5 pelvic soft rays that are unbranched. Some of these fishes have bright colors on the inner surface of the pectoral fins, which are displayed when they are threatened. These fishes are found in the Western Pacific Ocean and the Indian Ocean, and the largest member of the genus attains a maximum length of 15 cm (5.9 in.). The stingfishes are found on sand, clay, or mud bottoms at depths of 5 to 420 m (16 to 1,365 ft.). Although they are not found on coral reefs, they sometimes venture near these structures in the coastal waters of Indonesia. Although very rare in the aquarium trade, individuals may be collected on occasion in the Philippines and Indonesia. The **Blue-eyed Stingfish** (*Minous trachycephalus*) (**Bleeker, 1845**) is a shallow-water form (depth range 11 to 46 m [36 to 150 ft.]) distributed from the South China Sea and Indonesia to Sri Lanka. The care requirements are similar to that of the members of the Subfamily Choridactylinae, page 458.

Iracundus signifier, Decoy Scorpionfish: note dorsal fin that lures prey.

SUBFAMILY SCORPAENINAE (SCORPIONFISHES)

The Scorpaeninae, comprised of about 15 genera and approximately 150 species, is the largest of the Scorpaenidae subfamilies. This is a diverse group, and many of its members are found in aquarium stores.

Genus *Iracundus*

Iracundus signifier Jordan & Evermann, 1903
Common Name: Decoy Scorpionfish.
Maximum length: 13 cm (5.1 in.).
Distribution: Mauritius, Taiwan, Society, Pitcairn, and Hawaiian Islands.
Biology: The Decoy Scorpionfish lives on mixed sand and rubble bottoms, usually near the mouths of caves or ledges. It will also refuge among macroalgae and ship wreckage. This species is unique in that the spinous portion of its dorsal fin resembles a small fish and is used to attract potential prey. The space between the first and second spines looks like a mouth, while the elongate fourth dorsal spine resembles the anterior portion of the dorsal fin. When a small fish is detected, the color of the dorsal fin becomes more intense, and a dark eyespot, located between the third and fourth dorsal spines, becomes more pronounced. The lure is then snapped from side to side, starting with the front of the fin and progressing to the posterior region. As the sine wave moves down the fin, the first and second dorsal spines

Dorsal fin detail from specimen above: note apparent mouth and eye.

separate and then come together again, giving the appearance that the mouth is being opened and closed as if the lure were respiring. When hunting, this fish (as well as some other scorpaenids) will respire in a slightly different fashion. Normally, the gill cover and the branchiostegal membrane—which is located under the operculum—are expanded and contracted during respiration. But when stalking or luring its prey, this fish uses only the branchiostegal membrane to move water over the gills. The operculum is held open and not moved. This type of respiration is known as camouflage breathing, because the lack of movement makes the predator less conspicuous to its prey.

When one considers the size of the lure relative to the size of the scorpionfish's body, it seems likely that the lure functions not only to attract hungry predators, but also to attract potential mates and elicit aggression or curiosity. Food habit studies

Rhinopias Species and Their Kin

The members of the genus *Rhinopias* have to be some of nature's most exquisite creations. To the diver and aquarist alike, they are the Holy Grail of the scorpionfish clan. Divers pay incredible amounts of money to find and photograph them, and aquarists pay high prices to keep one in an aquarium. The genus contains only six species, none of which are considered to be common. However, their apparent rareness may be due to their cryptic behavior, excellent camouflage, and the fact that some species live in habitats that are not readily explored. The species that comprise the genus are: the **Lacey or Merlet's Scorpionfish (*Rhinopias aphanes*) Eschmeyer, 1973**, the **Easter Island Scorpionfish (*Rhinopias cea*) Randall & DiSalvo, 1997**, the **Japanese Scorpionfish (*Rhinopias argoliba*) Eschmeyer, Hiroski & Abe, 1973**, **Eschmeyer's Scorpionfish (*Rhinopias eschmeyeri*) Conde, 1977**, the **Weedy Scorpionfish (*Rhinopias frondosa*) (Günther, 1891)**, and the **Strange-eyed Scorpionfish (*Rhinopias xenops*) (Gilbert, 1905)**.

All *Rhinopias* have deep, laterally compressed bodies and eyes set high on top of their heads. Some species have dermal appendages above the eyes, on the jaws, and on the body surface. As with other scorpionfish species, *Rhinopias* are known to shed their cuticle. This is a normal process that helps rid the animal's body of algae, parasites, or encrusting organisms. In some individuals, shedding can occur quite often. For example, in a specimen of *R. eschmeyeri*, shedding was reported to occur every 12.6 days.

These fishes rarely swim, but move about by "crutching" along the bottom on their pectoral and pelvic fins. When hunting, they either remain motionless and wait for their prey to approach within striking distance, or they slowly stalk their quarry. When a specimen is very hungry and accustomed to being fed in the aquarium, it may "hop" rapidly toward an offered prey item, rather than approach it slowly. When a *Rhinopias* gets close enough to its prey, it will lunge forward and suck in its victim. Although the mouth does not look very capacious, *Rhinopias* species can ingest relatively large prey items. *Rhinopias* will also rock to and fro in order to mimic a piece of debris sitting on the ocean bottom.

Two of the most beautiful members of the genus are the Weedy Scorpionfish (*R. frondosa*) and the Lacey Scorpionfish (*R. aphanes*). These species often differ in their color patterns, but some individuals are indistinguishable chromatically. *R. aphanes* often has dark reticulations on its body, head, and fins, while *R. frondosa* has round and oblong pale spots and blotches. *Rhinopias frondosa* has a longer caudal fin, some longer anal and dorsal spines, slightly larger eyes, a shorter snout, and tentacles above the eyes that are thicker and less branched than those of *R. aphanes*. In some cases, these tentacles are flattened and leaflike. *Rhinopias frondosa* can be separated from *R. eschmeyeri* by its incised dorsal fin membrane.

***Rhinopias aphanes*, Lacey Scorpionfish: variant. (Milne Bay, Papua New Guinea)**

The Weedy Scorpionfish is usually considered the rarer of the two species. It is a wide-ranging species that occurs from East Africa to the Caroline Islands, north to Japan, and south to Mauritius. This scorpaenid attains a maximum length of 23 cm (9.1 in.). It has been reported at depths from 10 to 297 m (33 to 965 ft.) on bottoms consisting of macroalgae, rocks, and stony corals. I kept my specimen in a small tank full of live rock, and it adapted quickly to its new home.

The Lacey Scorpionfish has been reported from northeast Australia, New Guinea, New Caledonia, and southern Japan. It is found on coral reefs and rocky substrates at depths from 5 to 30 m (16 to 98 ft.) and often associates with crinoids, which it is thought to mimic. It is site specific, remaining in the same area or spot for long periods of time (weeks or even months). If you want to see one of these fish in their natural habitat, go diving in Milne Bay, Papua New Guinea. Rob Vanderloos, the owner of the live-aboard dive boat the *Chertan*, is a great *Rhinopias* hunter and will assist you in locating a specimen to observe and photograph.

Eschmeyer's Scorpionfish (*R. eschmeyeri*) has been reported from Mauritius to Sri Lanka, but I once received a specimen that was supposedly collected in the Philippines. This species differs from its congeners in having a more uniform body color and unbranched, flattened skin appendages. It comes in a variety of bright colors, including light blue, lilac, yellow, orange, or brick red and attains a maximum length of 19 cm (7.5 in.). It is reported to occur on open sand bottoms at depths from 2 to 40 m (7 to 130 ft.). It has also been observed in beds of macroalgae. I kept mine in a tank with crushed coral substrate and a few medium-sized pieces of bleached coral; it spent most of its time sitting in exposed portions of the tank.

Rhinopias frondosa, Weedy Scorpionfish: red color variant.

Rhinopias frondosa, Weedy Scorpionfish: lilac color variant.

Rhinopias frondosa, Weedy Scorpionfish: greenish tan variant.

Rhinopias aphanes, Lacey Scorpionfish: brown and tan variant.

Rhinopias aphanes, Lacey Scorpionfish: dark variant.

R. eschmeyeri, Eschmeyer's Scorpionfish: brick-red variant.

The Japanese Scorpionfish (*R. argoliba*), as the common name suggests, has only been reported from Japanese waters. It is unlikely that it will ever make it to North American aquarium stores. This species has no dermal appendages on its lower jaw and few on its body. The closely related Strange-eyed Scorpionfish (*R. xenops*) has been reported from the Hawaiian Islands, where it is typically found in water between 60 to 100 m (198 to 325 ft.) deep. It has also been reported from Japan. I have never seen or heard of either of these species entering the North American aquarium trade, although *R. xenops* has been kept on display at the Waikiki Aquarium.

The Easter Island Scorpionfish (*R. cea*) is known from a single specimen collected from the island for which it is named. This is one of the least spectacular members of the genus, and is most similar to the Japanese Scorpionfish. It is distinct in having 18 pectoral rays and no dermal flaps on the lower jaw or tentacles above the eye. This species is orangish red with pale brown markings and two dark blotches above the pectoral fin.

All the *Rhinopias* readily adapt to captivity and, because they are relatively inactive, can be kept in smaller aquariums. Because they are prone to bacterial infections, aquarists should keep them only if they have experience in the diagnosis and treatment of marine fish diseases. These fishes are great additions to a reef aquarium that does not contain small fishes or ornamental shrimps. Although live foods (like grass shrimp, mollies, and guppies) may be necessary to initiate feeding, these fishes can be trained to take pieces of shrimp, squid, and fish from a feeding stick. They can be housed with other fishes, but I would avoid keeping them with species that eat encrusting invertebrates as they may mistake the *Rhinopias* for a rock covered with food. Although such tankmates may not harm your *Rhinopias*, it is not worth the risk. You should also be careful when putting them in tanks with other predatory fishes. Although the deep body and venomous spines of the *Rhinopias* may dissuade most predators, smaller specimens may be eaten by frogfishes, other scorpionfishes, or large groupers.

My Eschmeyer's Scorpionfish met a tragic end when its head was engulfed by a smaller Striated Frogfish (*Antennarius striatus*). I had placed several feeder fish in the tank and was watching these two fishes stalk them. The *Rhinopias* was moving around a piece of coral when the frogfish decided to try to eat it. I quickly grabbed the frogfish by the tail and it released the *Rhinopias*, but the eye of the scorpionfish was damaged and became infected. It died several days later. I had another *Rhinopias* that abraded the tip of its lower jaw by swimming up and down against its bag during the shipping process. This wound gradually healed, but for a while it was raw and

(continued on next page)

Rhinopias xenops, Strange-eyed Scorpionfish.

Pteroidichthys amboinensis, Ambon Scorpionfish.

Pteroidichthys amboinensis, Ambon Scorpionfish.

bloody and I was concerned that it might get infected. These animals are also susceptible to being injured by larger crustaceans.

Although not a member of the genus *Rhinopias*, the **Ambon Scorpionfish (*Pteroidichthys amboinensis*) Bleeker, 1865** is a close relative that is more frequently encountered in aquarium stores. This little-known species is similar in its appearance and behavior to the *Rhinopias* species. It ranges from southern Japan to New Guinea and has been reported at depths of 3 to 182 m (10 to 592 ft.). I have encountered a number of Ambon Scorpionfish on open dark sand bottoms—and sometimes in areas with lush filamentous algae growth—off northeast Sulawesi. There, they are often encountered in pairs or trios, with one individual being significantly larger than the other(s), suggesting possible sexual dimorphism. I have seen specimens that were golden brown, rusty orange, or maroon overall. The horns above the eyes and the "mustache" extending from the jaw can vary in length. In some specimens, the horns—or supraorbital tentacles—are extremely long and resemble rabbit ears. In others, the horns are branched. Some individuals are also adorned with more dermal appendages. For example, the Ambon Scorpionfish I observed associating with beds of filamentous algae had numerous skin flaps and tassels on the body and head. Fish expert Rudie Kuiter reports observing a pair of these fish in an estuary on the west coast of Bali. They were slowly moving along the bottom—the larger individual was feeding on mysid shrimps, while the smaller individual was following behind. Both of these fish were yellow.

I have had the good fortune of acquiring several *Rhinopias* species for my home aquariums. They eat small livebearers and grass shrimp and spend most of their time in the open. When they move, they crutch on their enlarged pectoral fins and rock back and forth in an exaggerated manner to mimic plant debris.

Although I do not encourage the collecting of these relatively rare fishes, if you see one in an aquarium store and decide to purchase it, make sure you provide it with adequate housing and care.

Pteroidichthys amboinensis, Ambon Scorpionfish: with "horns" and "mustache" mimicking plant debris, it disguises a lethal presence.

Parascorpaena mossambica, Mozambique Scorpionfish: dark variant.

Parascorpaena mossambica, Mozambique Scorpionfish: light variant.

show that this fish feeds heavily on other scorpionfishes, which may see the lure as a potential mate. The Decoy Scorpionfish also eats other teleosts, like cardinalfishes, most of which are not piscivorous and are too small to consume a prey item as large as the lure. Curiosity may be the undoing of these species, or they may see the lure as a territorial intruder. While the dorsal fin of *I. signifier* may function as an active lure, the skin itself may passively attract prey: the dermal flaps look like fronds of coralline algae and may serve to attract certain herbivores.

When undisturbed, a healthy *I. signifier* will respire at a rate of 20 gill movements per minute. When agitated or unhealthy, this rate can rise to 38 movements per minute.

Captive Care: The Decoy Scorpionfish is a hardy aquarium species whose behavior and bright coloration make it a desirable addition to either a fish-only tank or a reef aquarium. One habit that makes it appropriate for a reef aquarium is that it often sits in the open. Like most scorpionfishes, it is a threat to ornamental crustaceans or small fishes. *Iracundus signifer* can eat prey up to one half of its total length and may consume six smaller fishes in one feeding episode. Although I have never had the good fortune of keeping more than one specimen at a time, I kept a larger individual that responded aggressively toward its reflection in a small mirror placed in the tank. This suggested that they may fight conspecifics if housed together. However, Schallenberger and Madden (1973) did not observe any aggressive interactions between specimens kept in large fiberglass tanks without substrate or hiding places. I have kept this species, without incident, with other scorpaenids. Although this fish is typically bright red with white mottling, the color will blanch if the fish is placed on a light substrate or if it is disturbed. Aquarium observations of this fish suggest that it prefers soft substrates.

Aquarium Size: 20 gal. **Temperature:** 22 to 26°C (72 to 78°F).
Aquarium Suitability Index: 4 (Venomous).

Genus *Parascorpaena*

Parascorpaena mossambica (Peters, 1855)
Common Name: Mozambique Scorpionfish.
Maximum Length: 10 cm (3.9 in.).
Distribution: South Africa to the Society Islands, north to southern Japan, and south to Australia.
Biology: The Mozambique Scorpionfish is a smaller species that occurs in lagoons, on reef flats, and in reef channels at depths of less than 1 up to 18 m (3.3 to 59 ft.). It typically lives on mixed sand and rubble substrates, among which it hides during the day. At night, it moves into more exposed areas to feed.
Captive Care: *Parascorpaena mossambica* readily adapts to aquarium life. It does best if housed in a tank with coral rubble or pieces of live rock on the bottom. It often sits up against rocks and rubble and can be observed in full view. This species will eat feeder fish and grass shrimp. In time, it can be trained to take fresh bits of seafood from a feeding stick.
Aquarium Size: 20 gal. **Temperature:** 22 to 27°C (72 to 80°F)
Aquarium Suitability Index: 4 (Venomous).
Remarks: Along with several other scorpionfishes that associate with coral reefs, this species has large tentacles over its eyes. However, the rear spine of the preorbital is hooked forward in *P. mossambica*. Another species that has well-developed tentacles above the eyes is the Barchin Scorpionfish (*Sebastapistes strongia*). The **Ocellated Scorpionfish** (*Parascorpaena mcadamsi*) (Fowler, 1938) is similar to the Mozambique Scorpionfish but lacks the supraocular tentacles, or, if present, they are very small.

Parascorpaena mossambica, Mozambique Scorpionfish: greenish variant.

Parascorpaena mossambica, Mozambique Scorpionfish: red-white variant.

Parascorpaena mossambica, Mozambique Scorpionfish: red variant.

Parascorpaena mcadamsi, Ocellated Scorpionfish: lacks above-eye tentacles.

The males of *P. mcadamsi* have a dark spot between the eighth and tenth dorsal spines. Larger male Ocellated Scorpionfish have canine teeth, while the teeth in the Mozambique Scorpionfish are undifferentiated.

Genus *Scorpaena*

Scorpaena brasiliensis Cuvier & Valenciennes, 1829
Common Names: Barbfish, Orange Scorpionfish.
Maximum Length: 23 cm (9.1 in.).
Distribution: Virginia to Brazil.
Biology: The Barbfish occurs on coral reefs, rubble, and sand, where it often sits near fronds of macroalgae. It occurs at depths ranging from 1.5 to 91 m (5 to 296 ft.). It feeds primarily on crustaceans, like shrimps, mantis shrimps, and crabs; however, one specimen's stomach was reported to contain a seahorse.
Captive Care: The Barbfish is common in the North American aquarium trade. It is a durable aquarium species, but should not be housed with fishes that feed on encrusting invertebrates or algae. For example, I have seen pygmy angelfishes persistently pick at the skin of smaller Barbfish. Provide them with plenty of hiding places, especially smaller individuals. Like most scorpionfishes, they may need to be offered live food to initiate a feeding response. In the aquarium, the Barbfish will readily eat small fishes and crustaceans.
Aquarium Size: 20 gal. **Temperature:** 21 to 26°C (70 to 78°F).
Aquarium Suitability Index: 4 (Venomous).

Scorpaena brasiliensis, Barbfish: attractively colored variant of the commonly seen and hardy Barbfish from the Western Atlantic and Caribbean.

Scorpaena brasiliensis, Barbfish: drab variant.

Scorpaena brasiliensis, Barbfish: yellow variant.

Scorpaena grandicornis, Plumed Scorpionfish: seagrass dweller.

Remarks: This species is separated from other Atlantic species by the presence of a dark spot above the pectoral fin, three dark spots inside the same fin, and two dark bars on the tail. The abdomen and ventral surfaces are often peppered with dark spots, and some specimens have tentacles over the eyes. The overall color of this fish can range from orange or yellow to red or brown.

Scorpaena grandicornis Cuvier & Valenciennes, 1829
Common Names: Plumed Scorpionfish, Grass Scorpionfish.
Maximum Length: 17 cm (6.7 in.).
Distribution: Florida and Bermuda to southern Brazil.
Biology: The Plumed Scorpionfish occurs at depths of 1 to 15 m (3.3 to 49 ft.) among macroalgae, seagrass, or in the open on sandy bottoms. Its coloration, numerous dermal flaps, and frond-like tentacles give this fish the appearance of a piece of rock covered with algae. It feeds mainly on snapping shrimps, panaeid shrimps, mantis shrimps, swimming crabs, brachyuran crabs, hermit crabs, and fishes.
Captive Care: This species readily adapts to aquarium life and can be kept with slightly smaller fishes than many of its larger relatives. It can be housed in a reef aquarium, but will make short work of ornamental shrimps. Larger fishes that feed on encrusting invertebrates, like angelfishes, triggerfishes, and pufferfishes, should not be kept with this fish as they may nip at its skin.
Aquarium Size: 20 gal. **Temperature:** 22 to 27°C (72 to 80°F)
Aquarium Suitability Index: 4 (**Venomous**).
Remarks: The Plumed Scorpionfish has greatly exaggerated tentacles, or horns, over its eyes. It is typically brown overall with darker mottling and small white spots at the axil of the pectoral fins, the pectoral fin bases, the chest, and the ventral part of the head. The **Goosehead Scorpionfish** (*Scorpaena bergi*) **Evermann & Marsh, 1900** is similar in having tentacles over the eyes, although they are not as well developed. The Goosehead Scorpionfish has 17 pectoral fins (18 or 19 in *S. grandicornis*) and a dark spot in the middle of the spinous dorsal fin. Both of these species have bands on the caudal fin.

Scorpaena inermis Cuvier & Valenciennes, 1829
Common Name: Mushroom Scorpionfish.
Maximum Length: 7.5 cm (3 in.).
Distribution: Florida, Bahamas, and the Yucatan, and south to Curacao.
Biology: The Mushroom Scorpionfish is typically found on rubble bottoms or in seagrass meadows at depths of less than 40 cm up to 72 m (16 in. to 234 ft.)—although it is most common at depths of less than 9 m (30 ft.). It sometimes forms small aggregations under rocks and rubble. It feeds primarily on shrimps,

but on occasion it will also eat mantis shrimps, fishes, and crabs. It will ingest a surprisingly large number of prey items during a hunting bout; for example, a 6-cm (2.4-in.) specimen whose stomach contents were examined contained 11 small shrimps, a swimming crab, and fish remains. This species has been reported in the stomach of the Striated Frogfish (*Antennarius striatus*).

Captive Care: The Mushroom Scorpionfish is a secretive species that should be provided with plenty of rubble or pieces of live rock to hide among. It will hide most of the time, which can present difficulties in feeding, especially if it is housed with more aggressive food competitors. Live grass shrimp are a good starter food. In time, you may get it to take fresh seafood from a feeding stick.

Aquarium Size: 20 gal. **Temperature:** 22 to 27°C (72 to 80°F).
Aquarium Suitability Index: 4 (Venomous).

Remarks: This species is usually red or brown with lighter mottling on the body. It has two ill-defined bands on the caudal fin, a fleshy growth resembling an inverted mushroom extending onto the upper portion of each eye, no markings on the pectoral fins, and seven to eight segmented soft rays in the dorsal fin. This species is similar to the **Smoothhead Scorpionfish (*Scorpaena calcarata*) Goode & Bean, 1882.** The Smoothhead is reddish overall with no distinctive markings on its body and fins—except for dark shading on the upper pectoral fins, a small cirrus over each eye, and usually nine segmented rays in the soft dorsal fin. *Scorpaena calcarata* replaces *S. inermis* along continental coastlines; *S. calcarata* is not found around most islands in the Caribbean.

Scorpaena plumieri Bloch, 1789

Common Name: Spotted Scorpionfish.
Maximum Length: 36 cm (14.2 in.).
Distribution: New York and Bermuda to Brazil, and east to the eastern coast of Africa. In the tropical Eastern Pacific, it ranges from Baja California to Peru, including the Revillagigedos and Galapagos Islands (the Eastern Pacific form was once known as *S. mystes* and is now considered a subspecies, *S. plumieri mystes*).
Biology: The Spotted Scorpionfish occurs at depths of 1 to 55 m (3.3 to 179 ft.) on rocky and coral reefs as well as pier pilings, seagrass beds, and rubble bottoms. It resides on reef flats, reef faces, and fore-reef slopes. In some areas, it is commonly found lying on sand bottoms next to coral boulders—often in shallow areas with heavy surge. Juveniles are more common in seagrass habitats. This species feeds mainly on fishes, but also eats crabs, snapping shrimps, panaeid shrimps, mantis shrimps, porcelain crabs, swimming crabs, and octopuses. It is usually solitary, but may aggregate in preferred habitats.

Scorpaena inermis, Mushroom Scorpionfish: cryptic and difficult to feed.

Scorpaena plumieri, Spotted Scorpionfish: good reef aquarium specimen.

Scorpaena plumieri, Spotted Scorpionfish: mimicking corraline algae.

Scorpaena plumieri, Spotted Scorpionfish: Eastern Pacific variant.

Scorpaena plumieri, Spotted Scorpionfish: rests among sponges.

Scorpaenodes caribbaeus, Reef Scorpionfish: common but often in hiding.

Captive Care: Although this larger scorpionfish is a good aquarium species, it should not be kept with any fish that is less than three-quarters of its total body length. In the wild, it has been reported to eat deep-bodied species like surgeonfishes, as well as long, slender forms like conger eels. It is a good scorpionfish for the reef aquarium because of its less cryptic nature and because it tends to spend more time on sand bottoms near the base of any live rock, rather than on the soft or hard corals. This habitat makes it less likely to cause mechanical damage to reef tank invertebrates.
Aquarium Size: 30 gal. **Temperature:** 22 to 27°C (72 to 80°F).
Aquarium Suitability Index: 4 (Venomous).
Remarks: *Scorpaena plumieri* has three dark bands on its tail, and the axil of the pectoral fins has a black patch with brilliant white spots. The inner pectoral surface has flash colors that are exposed either when the fish is threatened or when it swims. This species has numerous dermal flaps on the chin and head and often has large tentacles over the eyes. It is usually brown, gray, or pink, with dark and light mottling of various colors.

Genus *Scorpaenodes*

Scorpaenodes caribbaeus Meek & Hildebrand, 1928
Common Name: Reef Scorpionfish.
Maximum Length: 10 cm (3.9 in.).
Distribution: Florida and the Bahamas to Panama and northern South America.
Biology: This is a common species but it is rarely seen due to its secretive nature. It occurs in tidepools to depths of 15 m (49 ft.) on the reef face and fore-reef slopes. The Reef Scorpionfish will drift over, or sit on, rubble, hard reef substrate, or sponges. It will also perch upside down on the ceilings of caves and under ledges. It feeds mainly on shrimps, but also eats small xanthid and porcelain crabs.
Captive Care: The Reef Scorpionfish should be provided with plenty of hiding places, such as overhangs, caves, and coral rubble. Live foods like grass shrimp will be necessary to catalyze a feeding response. This species may prove difficult to feed if kept with aggressive feeders like groupers, soapfishes, snappers, or triggerfishes. It is also a potential prey item for morays, frogfishes, and larger groupers.
Aquarium Size: 20 gal. **Temperature:** 22 to 27°C (72 to 80°F)
Aquarium Suitability Index: 4 (Venomous).
Remarks: *Scorpaenodes caribbaeus* has spotted pectoral, dorsal, and caudal fins; some spots on the opercle and cheeks; and 18 to 20 pectoral rays. Young specimens have two bands on the pectoral fins and a faint broad band on the caudal peduncle.

Scorpaenodes guamensis, Guam Scorpionfish: widespread species often found in rubble, among live coral colonies or hanging upside down under ledges.

Scorpaenodes guamensis (Quoy & Gaimard, 1824)
Common Name: Guam Scorpionfish.
Maximum Length: 14 cm (5.5 in.).
Distribution: Red Sea to Pitcairn Island, north to southern Japan, and south to New South Wales, Australia.
Biology: This is a secretive species that occurs among rubble, rocks, or live hard coral on the reef flat, in lagoons or channels, or under ledges—where it often hangs upside down. It hides during the day and comes out at night to feed. It mainly eats shrimps, while crabs, amphipods, and polychaete worms are consumed much less frequently.
Captive Care: The reclusive Guam Scorpionfish needs a lot of hiding places and live food in order to acclimate to captivity. It will spend much of its time out of sight—behind rocks or other aquarium decor. It will readily accept live grass shrimp and feeder fish. It should not be kept with more aggressive carnivores until it is fully acclimated, as it might have difficulty getting enough to eat.
Aquarium Size: 20 gal. **Temperature:** 22 to 27°C (72 to 80°F).
Aquarium Suitability Index: 4 (Venomous).
Remarks: There are two forms of the Guam Scorpionfish, which may represent two distinct species. The first dorsal spine of the *guamensis* form is equal to the greatest diameter of the eye, and the blotch on the gill cover is clear. The first dorsal spine of the *scabra* form is greater than the maximum diameter of the eye, and the blotch on the gill cover is indistinct (this is not to be confused with *Scorpaenodes scaber*, the Pygmy Rockcod, which is a valid species).

Scorpaenodes guamensis, Guam Scorpionfish: variant on pier piling.

Scorpaenodes parvipinnis, Lowfin Scorpionfish (juv.): emerges after dark.

S. parvipinnis (adult): note antennae of just-caught Banded Coral Shrimp.

Scorpaenodes tredecimspinosus, Deepreef Scorpionfish: tiny Caribbean fish.

Scorpaenodes parvipinnis (Garrett, 1864)
Common Names: Lowfin Scorpionfish, Shortfin Scorpionfish, Coral Scorpionfish.
Maximum Length: 13 cm (5.1 in.).
Distribution: East Africa and Red Sea to the Marquesas and the Tuamotus, north to the Ryukyus, and south to Queensland.
Biology: The Lowfin Scorpionfish is a secretive species that occurs in lagoons and on both the inner- and outer-reef slopes. It is found among rich coral growth on patch reefs, sponges, and among encrusting invertebrates on pier pilings. At night, it is often seen on the side of large sponges, such as the Barrel Sponge (*Xestospongia testudinaria*). It occurs at depths of less than 1 to 49 m (3.3 to 159 ft.) and feeds almost entirely on shrimps.
Captive Care: Like the Guam Scorpionfish (*S. guamensis*), this species needs plenty of hiding places and live food in order to acclimate to captivity. It will spend much of its time out of sight—behind rocks or other aquarium decor. The Lowfin Scorpionfish will readily accept live grass shrimp and small fiddler crabs. Although it is less of a threat to fish tankmates than many other members of its family, the Lowfin Scorpionfish may eat small damselfishes, blennies, and gobies and is a definite threat to ornamental crustaceans. It will do well in a reef aquarium, but rarely comes out into the open before the lights are turned off for the night. The best way to observe the Lowfin Scorpionfish is by installing a red fluorescent or incandescent bulb over the tank at night or by using a flashlight with a red filter.
Aquarium Size: 20 gal. **Temperature:** 22 to 27°C (72 to 80°F).
Aquarium Suitability Index: 4 (**Venomous**).
Remarks: The color of this species is highly variable. Overall coloration is usually salmon pink, gray, or brown; some individuals (especially smaller specimens), have a broad white saddle on the anterior and middle portion of the body. This species has a very short dorsal fin (longest spine is usually less than the eye diameter), 13 dorsal spines, 9 dorsal rays, and 17 to 19 pectoral rays.

Scorpaenodes tredecimspinosus (Metzelaar, 1919)
Common Names: Deepreef Scorpionfish, Spotfin Scorpionfish.
Maximum Length: 7 cm (2.8 in.).
Distribution: Florida and the Bahamas south to northern South America.
Biology: *Scorpaenodes tredecimspinosus* occurs on the reef face and fore-reef slopes at depths of 4.5 to at least 83 m (15 to 270 ft.) in areas with rich stony coral growth as well as among coral rubble. It is one of many smaller fishes that utilize the rubble mounds constructed by the Sand Tilefish (*Malacanthus plumieri*) as a place to refuge. At the shallow end of its depth range, it is sometimes found in association with *S. caribbaeus*.

Captive Care: This diminutive scorpionfish is best displayed in a smaller aquarium. It is so secretive that you may never see it if you place it in a larger tank with many hiding places. It can be kept in a reef tank—because of its small size, it is less of a threat to other fishes and ornamental shrimps (although it will eat any crustacean that fits into its mouth). This species is potential prey for lizardfishes, frogfishes, and other scorpionfishes. More than one individual can be housed in the same tank.
Aquarium Size: 10 gal. **Temperature:** 21 to 27°C (70 to 80°F).
Aquarium Suitability Index: 4 (Venomous).
Remarks: *Scorpaenodes tredecimspinosus* is usually red overall, with 16 or 17 pectoral rays (*S. caribbaeus* has 18 to 20) and only one row of suborbital spines (*S. caribbaeus* adults have two rows). There is often a dark spot on the dorsal fin. Young specimens have no markings on the pectoral fins and no bands on the caudal peduncle.

Scorpaenodes varipinnis, Blotchfin Scorpionfish: hanging upside down.

Scorpaenodes varipinnis Smith, 1957
Common Name: Blotchfin Scorpionfish.
Maximum Length: 7 cm (2.8 in.).
Distribution: East Africa to Guam.
Biology: The Blotchfin Scorpionfish occurs on coastal reefs, the reef face, and the outer-reef slope at depths of 3 to 20 m (10 to 65 ft.). It feeds on shrimps and small crabs, typically consuming two to four prey items in a day. This species does most of its hunting at night, when it leaves reef crevices.
Captive Care: *Scorpaenodes varipinnis* needs a lot of hiding places and live food in order to acclimate to captivity. It will spend much of its time out of sight—behind rocks or other aquarium decor. It will readily accept live grass shrimp and feeder fish, but should not be kept with more aggressive carnivores as it might have difficulty getting enough to eat.
Aquarium Size: 20 gal. **Temperature:** 22 to 27°C (72 to 80°F).
Aquarium Suitability Index: 4 (Venomous).
Remarks: This species has red markings around the eyes and usually along the base of the dorsal fin, 13 dorsal spines, 8 dorsal rays, 17 to 18 pectoral rays, and few skin flaps on the body. It sometimes has a dark spot on the rear of the spinous dorsal fin.

Genus *Scorpaenopsis*

Scorpaenopsis brevifrons Eschmeyer & Randall, 1975
Common Names: Shortsnout Scorpionfish, Bigmouth Scorpionfish.
Maximum Length: 15 cm (5.9 in.).
Distribution: East Africa and the Red Sea, east to Samoa and the Hawaiian Islands.
Biology: This species occurs on coastal reefs composed of either

Scorpaenodes varipinnis, Blotchfin Scorpionfish: nocturnal hunter.

Scorpaenopsis brevifrons, Shortsnout Scorpionfish: often collected in Hawaii.

Scorpaenopsis fowleri, Dwarf Scorpionfish: extremely cryptic habits.

Scorpaenopsis fowleri, Dwarf Scorpionfish: red variant among macroalgae.

coral or rock at depths of less than 1 up to 35 m (3.3 to 114 ft.). It is found on hard substrates or in the open on sand bottoms. Other fishes that share the sand habitat with the Shortsnout Scorpionfish include the Blackblotch Lizardfish (*Synodus jaculum*), the Oriental Helmut Gurnard (*Dactyloptena orientalis*), the Spiny Devilfish (*Inimicus didactylus*), and the Banded Sole (*Soleichthys heterorhinos*).

Captive Care: Care requirements of the Shortsnout Scorpionfish are similar to those of the Tasseled Scorpionfish (*Scorpaenopsis oxycephala*). Those individuals that enter the trade most often originate from the Hawaiian Islands.

Aquarium Size: 20 gal. **Temperature:** 21 to 27°C (70 to 80°F).
Aquarium Suitability Index: 4 (Venomous).
Remarks: The Shortsnout Scorpionfish has a short snout with a steep profile (the eye diameter is slightly longer than the snout length). It has 18 to 20 pectoral rays, and the first three dorsal spines gradually increase in length. This species does not have the large number of dermal appendages on its jaws and chin that the Tasseled Scorpionfish (*Scorpaenopsis oxycephala*) has.

Scorpaenopsis fowleri (Pietschmann, 1934)
Common Name: Dwarf Scorpionfish.
Maximum Length: 4 cm (1.6 in.).
Distribution: Maldives to Oeno, north to the Philippines and Hawaiian Islands.
Biology: The Dwarf Scorpionfish occurs on sand and rubble and among hard corals or rocks to depths of at least 27 m (88 ft.). This tiny scorpionfish attains sexual maturity at less than 2.4 cm (0.9 in.) in total length. It probably feeds most on small crustaceans and annelid worms.
Captive Care: *Scorpaenopsis fowleri* is very cryptic, spending most of the daylight hours hiding among rubble and the aquarium decor. As a result, it is often difficult to find and feed. It will eat baby livebearers (e.g., guppies) and live grass shrimp. The Dwarf Scorpionfish is potential prey for morays, groupers, and other scorpionfishes.
Aquarium Size: 20 gal. **Temperature:** 21 to 27°C (70 to 80°F).
Aquarium Suitability Index: 4 (Venomous).
Remarks: This diminutive scorpaenid probably belongs in a different genus.

Humpbacked Scorpionfish Species Group
There are three species in this group, all of which have a back with a distinct arch (especially pronounced in *Scorpaenopsis diabola* and *Scorpaenopsis gibbosa*), and bright colors on the inner surfaces of the pectoral fins. Although concealed when the fish is at rest, the bright inner pectoral fin surfaces are exposed when

Scorpaenopsis diabola, Devil Scorpionfish: amazing coralline-algae mimicry.

Scorpaenopsis diabola, Devil Scorpionfish: same species clad in pale green.

the fish is threatened or when it is swimming. These colors have an aposematic function—they warn potential predators that these fishes are spiny and venomous. Any fish that has survived contact with a scorpionfish's spines learns to associate this flashing behavior with discomfort. All three of these species are often sold erroneously as "stonefish."

The humpbacked scorpionfishes are easy to keep, although you may have a difficult time getting them to accept nonliving food. They are all fish-eaters with large mouths, so be careful when selecting tankmates. Although they can be housed with other scorpionfishes, they will eat smaller specimens. I have seen at least one of these species (*Scorpaenopsis diabola*) shed its cuticle. I have also had specimens in which cyanobacteria grew on their body surface. All three are good reef aquarium fishes because they spend most of their time in the open and rarely roost on hard and soft corals. A humpbacked scorpionfish will sometimes rub the tip of its lower jaw against its plastic bag during shipping, which can result in a bacterial infection that is difficult to treat. However, the fish will often continue to eat even when its lower jaw is inflamed and swollen. I would not purchase a specimen exhibiting this condition.

Scorpaenopsis diabola Cuvier, 1829
Common Names: Devil Scorpionfish, False Stonefish.
Maximum Length: 30 cm (11.8 in.).
Distribution: Red Sea to the Hawaiian Islands, north to southern Japan, and south to the Great Barrier Reef and Tonga.
Biology: The Devil Scorpionfish occurs in shallow water on the reef flat and reef crest and to depths of 70 m (228 ft.) on the fore-reef or soft-substrate slopes. It is found in protected habitats and areas with heavy surge—among macroalgae, on sand or rubble, and sometimes either on or among live corals. Its color varies in order to enhance its camouflage, and filamentous green algae often grow on its skin. This not only facilitates its resemblance to reef substrate, but also acts to attract herbivores into striking range. I once encountered a pink specimen, resting amid coralline encrusted coral rubble, that was barely discernible from the substrate. This species feeds on fishes, including small parrotfishes and wrasses.
Captive Care: See the introduction to the Humpbacked Scorpionfish Species Group, page 476.
Aquarium Size: 30 gal. **Temperature:** 22 to 28°C (72 to 82°F).
Aquarium Suitability Index: 4 (Venomous).
Remarks: The Devil Scorpionfish can be separated from closely related forms by the coloration on the inside of its pectoral fins, which consists of orange and white bands, with several black spots. The Devil Scorpionfish differs from the Flasher Scorpionfish (*Scorpaenopsis macrochir*) in having a smaller eye, and a longer snout. The inner surface of the pectoral fins of *S. diabola* is yellow, orange, and black (see photograph, page 455).

Scorpaenopsis gibbosa (Bloch & Schneider, 1801)
Common Name: Humpback Scorpionfish.
Maximum Length: 15 cm (5.9 in.).
Distribution: Red Sea and Western Indian Ocean.
Biology: The Humpback Scorpionfish is found on sand or rubble bottoms. Like the Devil Scorpionfish and Reef Stonefish, it often has green filamentous algae growing on its body surface.

SCORPIONFISHES 477

Scorpaenopsis gibbosa, Humpback Scorpionfish: algae grows over its skin.

Scorpaenopsis macrochir, Flasher Scorpionfish: yellow variant.

Scorpaenopsis macrochir, Flasher Scorpionfish: drab variant.

Scorpaenopsis macrochir, Flasher Scorpionfish: gray variant.

Scorpaenopsis macrochir, Flasher Scorpionfish: mottled green variant.

Scorpaenopsis macrochir, Flasher Scorpionfish: brown variant.

It feeds on fishes during the day and at night.
Captive Care: See the introduction to the Humpbacked Scorpionfish Species Group, page 476.
Aquarium Size: 20 gal. **Temperature:** 22 to 28°C (72 to 82°F).
Aquarium Suitability Index: 4 (Venomous).
Remarks: This species is very similar to the Devil Scorpionfish in overall appearance, but the inner surface of the pectoral fin is yellow with a complete band of black spots near the edge of the fin.

Scorpaenopsis macrochir Ogilby, 1910
Common Name: Flasher Scorpionfish.
Maximum Length: 13 cm (5.1 in.).
Distribution: Philippines to Marquesas and Society Islands, north to the Ryukyu Islands, and south to northwest Australia and Tonga.
Biology: The Flasher Scorpionfish occurs on reef flats, on coastal reefs, and in shallow lagoons on sand, mixed sand and rubble, mud, and among macroalgae and sponges. It occurs at depths of less than 1 up to at least 15 m (3.3 to 50 ft.). Although no stomach-content data is available, this species probably feeds primarily on bony fishes, similar to the other humpbacked scorpionfishes. One Flasher Scorpionfish was observed eating a male Goldbar Sand Diver (*Trichonotus halstead*). I once saw an individual in the wild with a clump of green filamentous algae growing on the middle of its lower jaw, which may have served to attract small herbivores into striking range.
Captive Care: See the introduction to the Humpbacked Scorpionfish Species Group, page 476. *Scorpaenopsis macrochir* is the most common member of the humpbacked group in the aquarium trade.
Aquarium Size: 20 gal. **Temperature:** 22 to 27°C (72 to 80°F).
Aquarium Suitability Index: 4 (Venomous).
Remarks: The Flasher Scorpionfish differs from the two preceding species in having a slightly larger eye and a shorter snout; the back is also humped to a lesser degree. The coloration of the inner surface of the pectoral fins is most similar to *S. gibbosa*, but the two are not sympatric. The **Bandtail Scorpionfish** (*Scorpaenopsis neglecta*) Heckel, 1837 is even more similar to the Flasher Scorpionfish. It differs from *S. macrochir* in having serrations on the ridge above its eye (the ridge is not serrated in *S. macrochir*), and it is more commonly found on soft bottoms (e.g., mud and sand) than on reefs. The overall coloration of the Flasher Scorpionfish varies, but some common base colors include white, gray, brown, and even bright yellow. Darker specimens may have white patches on the head and body that look like encrusting sponges.

Scorpaenopsis neglecta, Bandtail Scorpionfish: resembles *S. macrochir*.

Possible variant of *Scorpaenopsis macrochir* or undescribed species.

Possible variant of *Scorpaenopsis macrochir* or undescribed species.

Tasseled Scorpionfish Species Group

There are several closely related scorpionfishes in the genus *Scorpaenopsis* that are difficult for the fish enthusiast with an untrained eye to separate. As the name implies, all members of this group have numerous dermal flaps on the jaws and head. None of these are common in the aquarium trade, which is unfortunate because they are some of the most unusual and attractive members of the family. Smaller individuals tend to be more cryptic than adult specimens. The juveniles tend to hide in and among coral branches or in reef crevices. The substrate that a tasseled scorpionfish chooses to sit upon can greatly affect its coloration. I once observed a tasseled scorpionfish displaying a lovely pink hue as it perched on a lavender sponge. This color then changed to a less appealing brownish cast when it moved to a nearby patch of coral pavement. You can encourage your captive *Scorpaenopsis* specimen to maintain a more pleasing hue by placing colorful substrate in the tank.

Scorpaenopsis barbatus, Bearded Scorpionfish: perching on leather coral.

Scorpaenopsis barbatus (Rüppell, 1838)
Common Name: Bearded Scorpionfish.
Maximum Length: 25 cm (9.8 in.).
Distribution: Red Sea, Gulf of Aden, and Arabian Gulf.
Biology: This species is usually found on hard substrate (including hard and soft corals). Food habit details are not available.
Captive Care: The Bearded Scorpionfish is a good aquarium species. It will accept most live foods (e.g., feeder fish and grass shrimp), but you should try to feed it fresh seafoods like squid, fish, and shrimp. It will eat small tankmates, both fishes and crustaceans, but is otherwise appropriate for the reef tank. It often positions itself in full view, occasionally perching on soft or hard corals.
Aquarium Size: 30 gal. **Temperature:** 21 to 27°C (70 to 80°F).
Aquarium Suitability Index: 4 (Venomous).
Remarks: The Bearded Scorpionfish has 17 to 19 (usually 18) pectoral rays, the snout is short (equal to or slightly longer than the eye diameter), and the first three dorsal spines increase gradually in length as you move from the first to the third. There is a deep depression between the eyes and snout that is visible when the fish is viewed from the side. The Bearded Scorpionfish is also "stubbier," with a deeper body, than most of the other tasseled scorpionfishes. Its color is variable, but it is often brown to reddish brown overall with pale mottling. Some individuals have patches of orange coloration that resemble encrusting sponge.

Scorpaenopsis cacopsis Jenkins, 1901
Common Name: Titan Scorpionfish.
Maximum Length: 50 cm (19.7 in.).
Distribution: Hawaiian Islands.
Biology: The Titan Scorpionfish usually sits in the open—either on sand substrates or live coral—at depths of 4 to 60 m (13 to 195 ft.). It feeds during the day on small fishes, including damselfishes, squirrelfishes, surgeonfishes, trumpetfishes, and octopuses.
Captive Care: This species will quickly acclimate to captivity if provided with live food. Feeder fish, fiddler crabs, small freshwater crayfishes, and grass shrimp are voraciously accepted, but every attempt should be made to switch the scorpionfish to fresh seafoods like squid, fish, and shrimp. The Titan Scorpionfish will ingest any fish tankmate small enough to fit into its cavernous mouth. (It has a ravenous appetite.) It is rare in the aquarium trade, partly because of its highly palatable flesh, which makes it a primary target for spear fishermen. *Scorpaenopsis cacopsis* is a great fish for the reef tank because it will spend much of its time in the open either on live rock or at its base on the sand.
Aquarium Size: 55 gal. **Temperature:** 22 to 27°C (72 to 80°F).

Scorpaenopsis cacopsis, Titan Scorpionfish: excellent aquarium species.

Juvenile *Scorpaenopsis oxycephala*, Tasseled Scorpionfish: light variant.

S. oxycephala, Tasseled Scorpionfish: note first three dorsal spines.

Scorpaenopsis oxycephala, Tasseled Scorpionfish: note many dermal flaps.

Aquarium Suitability Index: 4 (**Venomous**).
Remarks: The Titan Scorpionfish has 17 to 19 pectoral rays (usually 18), the snout is considerably longer than the eye diameter, and the first dorsal spine is about one-third the length of the second dorsal spine (which is slightly shorter than the third spine).

Scorpaenopsis oxycephala (Bleeker, 1849)
Common Names: Tasseled Scorpionfish, Smallscale Scorpionfish.
Maximum Length: 36 cm (14.2 in.).
Distribution: Red Sea to the Mariana Islands, north to Taiwan, and south to the Great Barrier Reef.
Biology: The Tasseled Scorpionfish occurs at depths of 1 to 35 m (3.3 to 114 ft.) on coastal reefs, in reef channels, on the reef face, and on fore-reef slopes. It is usually found sitting motionless on hard substrates like coralline boulders, coral rubble, or live stony corals. This species will also lie on or amid soft corals like *Xenia, Sinularia,* and *Sarcophyton,* or in the lumen of the Barrel Sponge (*Xestospongia testudinaria*). It is more likely to be found in clear water amid living substrate than its close relative, the Raggy Scorpionfish (*Scorpaenopsis venosa*). The Tasseled Scorpionfish eats fishes, crustaceans, and the occasional squid, with adults feeding more heavily on fishes than juveniles do. Although this fish is usually a solitary species, two or three may be found in close proximity on occasion, and many individuals may occur on the same patch reef.
Captive Care: This gorgeous scorpionfish makes a great addition to a fish-only or reef aquarium, as long as smaller fishes or ornamental crustaceans are not housed in the same tank. They usually stay out in full view, so they are one of the more desirable species

Scorpaenopsis oxycephala, Tasseled Scorpionfish: extravagant color variant.

Scorpaenopsis papuensis, Papuan Scorpionfish: note supraorbital tentacles.

Scorpaenopsis cirrhosa, Bearded Scorpionfish: found in Southern Japan.

Scorpaenopsis papuensis, Papuan Scorpionfish: variant.

for a tank heavily decorated with live rock. The Tasseled Scorpionfish will sometimes perch on soft corals, which may cause the polyps to close up. If a scorpionfish stays on the same soft coral for extended periods of time, it could be deleterious to the invertebrate. Because they have so many dermal flaps on their head and body, Tasseled Scorpionfish are often picked at by fishes that feed on coralline algae, such as triggerfishes and pufferfishes. Live shrimp and feeder fish may be necessary to induce a feeding response, but they can be trained to take food like strips of fish or squid from a feeding stick.

Aquarium Size: 30 gal. **Temperature:** 22 to 27°C (72 to 80°F).
Aquarium Suitability Index: 4 (**Venomous**).
Remarks: *Scorpaenopsis oxycephala* is one of the most attractive scorpionfish species, usually sporting bright colors and numerous skin flaps on the lower jaw and sides of its head. It usually has 20 pectoral rays, the first dorsal spine is about half the length of the second dorsal spine (which is almost the same length as the third dorsal spine), and the snout is considerably longer than the orbit length. This species is often misidentified as the **Bearded Scorpionfish** (*Scorpaenopsis cirrhosa*) (**Thunberg, 1793**), which is only found in southern Japan and probably never makes it into the aquarium trade.

Scorpaenopsis papuensis (Cuvier, 1829)
Common Name: Papuan Scorpionfish.
Maximum Length: 20 cm (7.9 in.).
Distribution: Indonesia and the Philippines, east to the Society Islands, north to the Ryukyus, and south to the Great Barrier Reef.
Biology: The Papuan Scorpionfish is found on fringing reefs, reef faces, and fore-reef slopes, at depths of 1 to 40 m (3.3 to 130

Scorpaenopsis papuensis, Papuan Scorpionfish: highly variable in color.

Scorpaenopsis papuensis, Papuan Scorpionfish: rests on hard corals.

Scorpaenopsis papuensis, Papuan Scorpionfish: color variant.

Scorpaenopsis venosa, Raggy Scorpionfish: often sits in the open.

ft.). I have seen individuals on hard corals, in the lumens of large sponges, and on coral rock. In the Fiji Islands, it often rests on the sides or tops of large coral heads in clear lagoons. During the day, it rests motionless in exposed areas, in crevices, under overhangs, or on top of coral rock or live hard corals. At night, those individuals that are hiding often come out into the open.

Captive Care: See the Captive Care section for *Scorpaenopsis oxycephala*, page 481.
Aquarium Size: 20 gal. **Temperature:** 22 to 27°C (72 to 80°F).
Aquarium Suitability Index: 4 (**Venomous**).
Remarks: This species has 18 to 20 pectoral spines (usually 19), the snout is noticeably longer than the orbit, and there is often a dark purplish blotch on the rear part of the spinous dorsal fin. The overall color is highly variable. It sometimes has well-developed supraorbital tentacles.

Scorpaenopsis venosa (Cuvier, 1829)
Common Name: Raggy Scorpionfish.
Maximum Length: 22 cm (8.7 in.).
Distribution: East Africa and Arabian Gulf to the Fiji Islands, north to the Philippines, and south to the Great Barrier Reef.
Biology: In Indonesia, the Raggy Scorpionfish is most common on rubble, sand, or mud slopes and among sponges or macroalgae, often in turbid water. I have also observed it on shipwrecks. It occurs at depths of 3 to 25 m (10 to 81 ft.) and is a solitary species.
Captive Care: See the Captive Care section for *Scorpaenopsis oxycephala*, page 481. Field observations suggest that this species may be less likely to sit on soft corals in a reef aquarium than *S. oxycephala*, as it is most often found in repose on sand or mud substrate. Its smaller maximum length makes it a more suitable

Scorpaenopsis sp., Spinycrown Scorpionfish: Red Sea specimen.

Scorpaenopsis sp., Spinycrown Scorpionfish: variant from Sulawesi.

Scorpaenopsis sp., Spinycrown Scorpionfish: variant.

Scorpaenopsis sp., Spinycrown Scorpionfish: juvenile from Sulawesi.

addition for a smaller home aquarium.
Aquarium Size: 20 gal. **Temperature:** 22 to 27°C (72 to 80°F).
Aquarium Suitability Index: 4 (Venomous).
Remarks: *Scorpaenopsis venosa* has 16 to 17 pectoral rays (usually 17). It often has a dark spot on the soft portion of the dorsal fin, and the snout is usually the same length or shorter than the orbit length. The first three dorsal spines increase gradually in length as you move from the first to the third.

Scorpaenopsis sp.
Common Name: Spinycrown Scorpionfish.
Maximum Length: 20 cm (7.9 in.).
Distribution: Red Sea to the Marquesan and Pitcairn Islands, north to the Ryukyus.
Biology: I have observed this species lying on coralline-encrusted boulders in exposed areas on offshore reef slopes and among sponges, coral rock, and stony corals on coastal reefs. It occurs at depths of 4.5 to at least 21 m (15 to 68 ft.).
Captive Care: See the Captive Care section for *Scorpaenopsis oxycephala*, page 481.
Aquarium Size: 20 gal. **Temperature:** 22 to 27°C (72 to 80°F).
Aquarium Suitability Index: 4 (Venomous).
Remarks: The Spinycrown Scorpionfish has 17 to 18 pectoral rays (usually 18), its snout length is less than the orbit diameter in small specimens and slightly greater in larger individuals, the length of the first dorsal spine is about one-third the length of the second spine, and the first three spines gradually increase in length. Although well known in the ichthyological community, the Spinycrown Scorpionfish is awaiting formal description and naming.

Genus *Sebastapistes*

Sebastapistes ballieui (Sauvage, 1875)
Common Name: Spotfin Scorpionfish.
Maximum Length: 11 cm (4.3 in.).
Distribution: Hawaiian Islands.
Biology: Little is known about the biology of this relatively common fish. It is reported to be quite numerous in inshore areas, hiding among rocks and rubble.
Captive Care: The Spotfin Scorpionfish is a secretive species that will spend its time in cracks and crevices or at rest at the base of the aquarium decor. It may have a difficult time getting enough to eat if kept with more aggressive feeders like groupers and wrasses.
Aquarium Size: 20 gal. **Temperature:** 22 to 28°C (72 to 82°F).
Aquarium Suitability Index: 4 (**Venomous**).
Remarks: *Sebastapistes ballieui* has numerous small dark spots on the body, while larger individuals often have a large black spot between the seventh and tenth spines of the spinous dorsal fin.

Sebastapistes ballieui, Spotfin Scorpionfish: small, shy Hawaiian species.

Sebastapistes coniorta Jenkins, 1903
Common Name: Speckled Scorpionfish.
Maximum Length: 10 cm (3.9 in.).
Distribution: Hawaiian, Wake, and Line Islands.
Biology: During the day, individuals more than 5 cm (1.9 in.) in length reside deep in coral crevices, while smaller fish live among the branches of the hard coral *Pocillopora meandrina*. At night, some Speckled Scorpionfish leave their refuges and rest in exposed positions on rocks, corals, or the sandy seafloor. From these nocturnal resting sites, they capture xanthid crabs, shrimps, and small fishes. In the daytime, they hunt crustaceans that are found among *Pocillopora* branches.
Captive Care: *Sebastapistes coniorta* is secretive during the day, spending most of its time hiding under or among the aquarium decor. It will eat live fishes or shrimps.
Aquarium Size: 20 gal. **Temperature:** 21 to 28°C (70 to 82°F).
Aquarium Suitability Index: 4 (**Venomous**).
Remarks: The Speckled Scorpionfish has dark spots scattered over its body and fins. These spots help it blend in with the hard coral in which in it lives.

Sebastapistes coniorta, Speckled Scorpionfish: often hides in deep crevices.

Sebastapistes cyanostigma (Bleeker, 1856)
Common Name: Yellowspotted Scorpionfish.
Maximum Length: 8 cm (3.1 in.).
Distribution: Red Sea to the Line Islands, north to the Ryukyus, and south to the Great Barrier Reef and Samoa.

Sebastapistes cyanostigma, Yellowspotted Scorpionfish: unique coral dweller.

Biology: The Yellowspotted Scorpionfish is an obligatory hard coral dweller that often limits its movements to within a single coral colony. It feeds on fishes (e.g., dottybacks) and crustaceans that live among the branches. In many areas, this species is found among the branches of hard corals in the genus *Pocillopora*, but I have also observed it living among the more leaflike branches of *Pavona* sp. This Yellowspotted Scorpionfish would emerge at night and sit, exposed, on the coral's "fronds," possibly waiting for errant polychaete worms or small fishes to swim past. It occurs at a depth range of 2 to 15 m (7 to 49 ft.).

Captive Care: In the aquarium, it is best to provide the Yellowspotted Scorpionfish with a piece of live *Pocillopora* coral or, if this is not available, with a bleached skeleton of a branching coral. It will often, but not always, take up residence in these corals. If not, it will sit on some other hard substrate. A voracious feeder, it will shoot forward to snatch any small fish or shrimp that has moved too close. This species has a special fondness for grass shrimp, but will also eat feeder fish. Occasionally, it can be coaxed into accepting nonliving food impaled on a feeding stick.

Its small size means it can be kept with a wider range of fish tankmates, but you need to be careful if you are keeping it with other large predators (including other scorpaenids). The diminutive size of the Yellowspotted Scorpionfish makes it more vulnerable to these piscivores. I once had a juvenile Yellowmargin Moray (*Gymnothorax flavimarginatus*) bite a small Yellowspotted Scorpionfish in half.

Aquarium Size: 20 gal. **Temperature:** 22 to 28°C (72 to 82°F).
Aquarium Suitability Index: 4 (**Venomous**).
Remarks: *Sebastapistes cyanostigma* is a smaller, attractive species that occasionally shows up in aquarium stores. Its large, bright yellow spots make it more appealing than some of its less colorful relatives.

Sebastapistes strongia (Cuvier, 1829)
Common Name: Barchin Scorpionfish.
Maximum Length: 10 cm (3.9 in.).
Distribution: Red Sea to the Society Islands, north to Taiwan, and south to the Great Barrier Reef.
Biology: The Barchin Scorpionfish is found on reef flats, in channels, and in lagoons at depths of less than 1 to over 18 m (3.3 to 59 ft.). Although stomach-content information is not available on this species, closely related forms feed on shrimps, crabs, and small fishes.
Captive Care: *Sebastapistes strongia* is a hardy aquarium inhabitant. Provide it with plenty of hiding places, including scattered pieces of coral rubble. It will often lie up against the rubble in full view. This species readily consumes live grass shrimp and feeder fish, and can also be coaxed into accepting nonliving foods.
Aquarium Size: 20 gal. **Temperature:** 22 to 27°C (72 to 80°F).
Aquarium Suitability Index: 4 (**Venomous**).
Remarks: *Sebastapistes strongia* has well-developed tentacles over the eyes, and the eyes have orangish red spokes radiating from the pupil. There are dark bars on the lower jaw, and a dark spot is often present at the anterior base of the dorsal fin.

The **Mauritius Scorpionfish** (*Sebastapistes mauritiana*) (Cuvier, 1829) is similar but lacks supraorbital tentacles, usually has three lacrymal spines (*S. strongia* typically has two), and has a distinct occipital pit. It ranges from East Africa to the Marquesas and Rapa Islands and is often found in the intertidal zone.

Sebastapistes mauritiana, Mauritius Scorpionfish: no tentacles over eyes.

Sebastapistes strongia, Barchin Scorpionfish: good aquarium species.

Genus *Taenianotus*

Taenianotus triacanthus Lacépède, 1802
Common Names: Leaf Scorpionfish, Leaf Fish, Paper Fish.
Maximum Length: 10 cm (3.9 in.).
Distribution: East Africa to the Galapagos Islands, north to the Ryukyus, and south to New South Wales, Australia.
Biology: The Leaf Scorpionfish occurs at depths of less than 1 to over 134 m (3.3 to 436 ft.) on reef flats, reef channels, reef faces, and fore-reef slopes, or on lagoon reefs, in areas protected from strong water movement. It will often sit at the mouth of caves or crevices or between columnar corals. If threatened, it will duck into the cave or disappear among the coral branches. The Leaf Scorpionfish regularly occurs in pairs. In the East Banda Sea, I have observed three pairs (one pink, one white, and one maroon pair) at different dive sites. In most pairs, one individual is larger than the other, suggesting size-related sexual dimorphism. Occasionally, the Leaf Scorpionfish can be found in aggregations numbering up to eight individuals.

On a dive in Ambon, Indonesia, I once observed *Taenianotus triacanthus* courtship behavior and males competing for a mate. It began about 30 minutes before sunset. A white individual, presumably a male, followed a pink specimen, presumably a female, as she slowly "crutched" her way over the substrate. In about 15 to 20 minutes, the male proceeded to chase off several rival males and continued to follow and court the female. The original male also bit one of the consexuals that moved close to the female. Unfortunately, I ran out of air before spawning took place.

Captive Care: The Leaf Scorpionfish is a great aquarium fish, but it should not be placed in a tank with more aggressive feeders or any fish that might nip at its leaflike body. A small tank with several pieces of live rock and two or three Leaf Scorpionfish would make an attractive display. I have never had them behave aggressively—either toward each other or other fish species—but sexually active males may fight in smaller aquariums. The Leaf Scorpionfish will rarely accept anything but live food like small feeder fish or grass shrimp. It has a small mouth for a scorpionfish, so potential prey items should be chosen accordingly. This species is an excellent choice for the reef aquarium because it spends much of its time on exposed perches. The best way to feed a Leaf Scorpionfish in a reef tank is to place its food in a net and slowly move it toward the fish. It can even be taught to jump into the net to capture its live food.
Aquarium Size: 20 gal. **Temperature:** 22 to 27°C (72 to 80°F).
Aquarium Suitability Index: 4 (Venomous).
Remarks: The Leaf Scorpionfish gets its name from its unusual

Taenianotus triacanthus, Leaf Scorpionfish: great aquarium fish.

Taenianotus triacanthus, Leaf Scorpionfish: brown variant.

Taenianotus triacanthus, Leaf Scorpionfish: yellow variant.

Taenianotus triacanthus, Leaf Scorpionfish: red variant.

Taenianotus triacanthus, Leaf Scorpionfish: dark marbled variant.

Synanceia horrida, Horrid Stonefish: may cause human fatalities. (Deadly.)

form. With its laterally compressed body and high dorsal fin, it resembles a leaf or a macroalgae frond. It also mimics bits of plant debris by rocking back and forth or swaying from side to side. Its overall coloration can be black, maroon, red, pink, brown, tan, bright yellow, or white, with dark or light mottling. I have seen photographs of a pair of bicolored specimens from the Fijian Islands; they were orange overall with bright yellow backs and dorsal fins. Coloration can change slightly as a result of cuticle shedding—which is quite common in this fish—or being moved from a lighter to a darker background, or vice versa. Small juveniles are nearly transparent and are rarely encountered in the aquarium trade.

SUBFAMILY SYNANCEINAE (STONEFISHES)

This subfamily contains ten species, five of which belong to the genus *Synanceia*. Although none of these are common in the aquarium trade, the species that the marine hobbyist is most likely to encounter is the Reef Stonefish (*Synanceia verrucosa*). This is the most venomous fish in the world, having been responsible for numerous human fatalities. Wholesalers have told me that it is illegal to sell this stonefish to private individuals in the United States because of its potentially lethal sting, but they still show up on occasion.

Synanceia horrida (Linnaeus, 1766)
Common Names: Horrid Stonefish, Estuarine Stonefish.
Maximum Length: 30 cm (11.8 in.).
Distribution: India to Australia, north to China.
Biology: The Horrid Stonefish is commonly found in coastal bays, in lagoons, on fringing coral reefs, on rocky reefs, and in estuaries, sometimes in brackish conditions. Near Exmouth, in northwestern Australia, this fish is regularly encountered under a large naval pier, sitting in the open on the sand or among man-made debris. In other areas, it is commonly found among coral rubble and rocks. It is difficult to see in this habitat. To make its presence even less conspicuous, it will often bury most of its body under the sand so that only the top of the head is exposed. The Horrid Stonefish often occurs in the shallow intertidal zone and, on occasion, it is left partially exposed to the air when the tide recedes. If kept moist, this species can live up to 24 hours without being totally immersed in water. It has also been reported at depths of 40 m (130 ft.). The Horrid Stonefish is very sluggish, moving little—if at all—during the course of the day. When in repose on the substrate, it will often curl its tail to one side.
Captive Care: Because the sting of this scorpionfish has been reported to cause human fatalities, I would not recommend it to

any home aquarist. Even at small sizes (e.g., 8 cm [3 in.]), the venom glands and spines are fully formed. If you do decide to keep one, you should know that it is a hardy aquarium species that needs a small-grained substrate in which to bury. Blue-green algae, golden diatoms, and filamentous green algae will grow on its body and head. Before it sheds its cuticle, its body surface takes on a pale appearance. This species is disease-resistant, but it will occasionally float upside down at the surface of the aquarium, with its tail curled up against its side—as if feigning death. The Horrid Stonefish will readily accept live grass shrimp and feeder fish. Wrasses, surgeonfishes, pufferfishes, and triggerfishes will nip at the skin and lips of this species and could cause permanent damage.

Aquarium Size: 20 gal. **Temperature:** 22 to 28°C (72 to 82°F).
Aquarium Suitability Index: 4 (**Highly Venomous**).
Remarks: *Synanceia horrida* has prominent warts on the sides of its body and a bony ridge above and between the eyes. It can be dark brown, tan, gray, or pink overall. In the **Dwarf Stonefish** (*Synanceia nana*) **Eschmeyer & Rama-Roa, 1973**, the mouth is directed upward and the top of the head is flat, with a deep depression between the eyes, but there is no deep pit below the eyes. The dorsal spines are also short, while the edges of the anal and paired fins are black, flecked with white.

Synanceia verrucosa Bloch & Schneider, 1801
Common Names: Reef Stonefish, Common Stonefish.
Maximum Length: 35 cm (13.8 in.).
Distribution: Red Sea to Mangareva, north to southern Japan, and south to New Caledonia and Austral Island.
Biology: The Reef Stonefish occurs on shallow reef flats, where it may be partially exposed at ebb tide, to depths of at least 20 m (65 ft.) on reef faces and fore-reef slopes. It is often found sitting among coral rubble (with which it blends incredibly well), under ledges, or buried in the sand with only the top of its head exposed. The color of most specimens ranges from black or dark brown to tan, and they can change their hue depending on the color of the substrate on which they are resting. Some specimens have orange spongelike growths on their bodies and heads, making them look even more like coral rubble. An occasional individual that has just shed its cuticle may be pink, resembling a coralline-algae-encrusted rock. The Reef Stonefish is a patient hunter that will remain motionless for long periods of time, even when prey species are nearby. It may orient toward its prey by moving its body slightly up, down, or to the side, or it may twist its head slightly to one side or the other. If a fish is positioned behind the head, the Reef Stonefish may scare it into the strike zone by raising its dorsal fin. When prey is in the strike zone,

Synanceia verrucosa, Reef Stonefish: world's most venomous fish. (Deadly.)

the Reef Stonefish throws its jaws out and upward; the mouth cavity expands, creating a vacuum, and the small prey fish disappears. Algae (including macroalgae, such as *Padina*) and sessile invertebrates often grow on the Reef Stonefish's body surface and may actually attract potential prey. This is one of the few gregarious scorpionfishes; it is often seen in pairs or even in small groups. If enough food is present, this sluggish creature will stay in the same general area of the reef for months or even years.

Captive Care: Because of the severe nature of stonefish stings, I cannot recommend these fish to the home aquarist. However, they do acclimate readily to captivity. If kept, they need a varied diet and must not be overfed. Otherwise, they may suffer from fatty infiltration of the liver. A Reef Stonefish will eat any fish or crustacean that will fit in its mouth. More than one specimen can be kept in a tank as long as the fish are similar in size (they are cannibals and will eat other scorpionfishes). Some individuals will move about when they are hungry, while others rarely move at all. Although I have not had much difficulty keeping these fishes, I did hear of a public aquarium that lost several Reef Stonefish to unknown causes over a period of about 3 months.

Aquarium Size: 30 gal. **Temperature:** 22 to 28°C (72 to 82°F).
Aquarium Suitability Index: 4 (**Highly Venomous**).

References
Atiya (1991), Dinesen & Nash (1982), Endean (1961), Eschmeyer et al. (1973, 1979a, 1979b), Grieg & Gnaedinger (1971), Grobecker (1983), Harmelin-Vivien & Bouchon (1976), Howe et al. (1988), Lieske & Myers (1994), Myers (1989), Penrith et al. (1994), Randall (1995, 1996), Randall & DiSalvo (1997), Schallenberger & Madden (1973), Schleser (1994).

SUBFAMILY PTEROINAE
LIONFISHES

There are few experiences as thrilling as encountering one's first lionfish underwater. Aquarium specimens can provide a mesmerizing show, of course, but the spectacle these majestic creatures provide in their natural habitat is unforgettable. The lionfishes are some of the most ornate and attractive fishes on Indo-Pacific coral reefs. They possess greatly elongated—and venom-loaded—dorsal fin spines and large pectoral fins that resemble Oriental fans in some species and party streamers in others. Their dramatic color patterns typically consist of alternating bands of contrasting hues, making them look more like a float from a Chinese parade than a predatory reef animal. This spectacular appearance has made the lionfishes a perennial favorite with both the neophyte and the well-seasoned aquarist. An equally alluring trait is the ease with which most individuals adapt to life in the home aquarium.

Classification and Biology

Lionfishes are members of the Family Scorpaenidae and the Subfamily Pteroinae. There are 5 genera in this subfamily and approximately 16 species. Two of these genera and at least 11 species make it into the aquarium trade. The two genera encountered by aquarists—*Dendrochirus* and *Pterois*—are easily separated by the form of their pectoral fins. In *Dendrochirus* species, the pectoral fin rays do not reach the base of the caudal fin, they are branched and are connected by a membrane over much of their length. The two genera also differ somewhat in their behavior.

Lionfishes are found in the Indian Ocean—including the Red Sea—and the Western and Central Pacific. Most have a wide range, but several species display limited distributions. For example, the Hawaiian Lionfish (*Pterois sphex*) and the Green Lionfish (*Dendrochirus barberi*) are endemic to the Hawaiian Islands (these are the only two species known from this archipelago). And the Japanese Lionfish (*Pterois lunulata*) is only found around Japan. Most lionfish species associate with coral or rocky reefs in tropical and subtropical waters, but some are found on open sand or mud bottoms. Russell's Lionfish (*Pterois russelli*) commonly occurs on soft substrates devoid of structure.

Pterois antennata, Spotfin Lionfish: like a float from a Chinese parade, the lionfishes sports lovely fluttering finnage—some mounted on needle-sharp, venom-loaded spines. Many species make excellent captive specimens.

Lionfish Stings

Like all the other members of the Family Scorpaenidae, the lionfish's dorsal, anal, and pelvic spines are armed with venom glands. These weapons are used for defense against predators and to fend off rival conspecifics. How bad is a lionfish sting? The severity of the pain can vary and is probably a function of how much venom is injected, which may or may not be a function of the size of the lionfish. While in many episodes the pain is relatively minor and short-lived, in other cases it is reported to be extremely painful. The following is a quote from H. Steinitz, a zoologist who was stung in the forefinger by a juvenile (10-cm [3.9-in.]) *Pterois volitans*.

"I was tortured by pains beyond measure, and yet the pain was still growing more intense. It sent me running. I tried to sit down, to lie on the ground, to stand still. The pain would not let me. I had to move on, to run about. It is a strange experience recognizing quite lucidly that nothing fatal has happened to

> **When a Lion Strikes**
>
> If you are stung by your lionfish, immediately immerse the wound in hot—but not scalding—water (from 43.3 to 45°C, or 110 to 113°F, for 30 or 40 minutes or until pain has diminished) or heat it with a hair dryer. The heat will denature the protein that constitutes the venom, preventing it from spreading through your body. (Don't panic and make the mistake of treating a lionfish wound with scalding water: the burn can prove worse than the venom.) The most common symptom of a lionfish sting is intense pain in the affected extremity and swelling. Nausea, vomiting, delirium, chest and abdominal pain, difficulty breathing, fainting, and fever may also occur. It is advisable to seek medical attention immediately after being stung if the victim appears intoxicated, weak, short of breath, begins to vomit, or becomes unconscious. In rare cases, cardiovascular collapse, respiratory distress, and even death have occurred as a result of a lionfish envenomization. But in most cases, pain is the only major symptom and this subsides relatively quickly. In 35 lionfish envenomization incidents studied, the pain was entirely gone in 24 hours in all cases, although four of these patients reported numbness in the affected extremity for some time.

oneself, and feeling at the same time that this was much worse than anything previous. In fact, it is just short of driving oneself completely mad."

Although a lionfish will not race across the aquarium to impale an aquarist, it will raise and direct its spines toward a potential threat, such as a hand moving in the aquarium. The majority of aquarists are stung by lionfishes while cleaning their tanks. An aquarist preoccupied with the task at hand may accidentally bump or brush into the lionfish's needle-sharp dorsal spines. To prevent this, always be vigilant when working in a lionfish's aquarium. Many lionfishes hide behind pieces of aquarium decor and can easily go unnoticed. It is a good idea to locate these fishes before starting the cleaning process to prevent accidental contact. Also, never place your hand or arm too near a lionfish's dorsal spines. If it perceives you as a threat, it can arch its back and thrust its dorsal armament forward to jab you.

The second activity that most commonly results in envenomization is transferring a lionfish. When the fish is captured in a net or plastic container and lifted from the water, it may struggle, stabbing the careless aquarist with its spines. To minimize this danger, always place a net over the container you are using for transfer—a large specimen container is ideal. Simply herd the fish into the submerged container with a net, then place the net over the opening. A deep, fine-mesh net with a long handle can be used to catch larger specimens, but be sure to cover the net when the fish is lifted from the water.

Pterois russelli, Russell's Lionfish: imposing, flared pectoral fins can be used both as a threat and as a barrier to herd prey items and block their escape.

The primary function of these spines is to dissuade potential predators. But some fishes will consume lionfishes, despite their venomous arsenal. For example, a juvenile Volitans Lionfish (*Pterois volitans*) was recovered from the stomach of a Smooth Cornetfish (*Fistularia commersonii*.), and I have had captive frogfishes ingest their lionfish tankmates on several occasions—with no ill effects to the antennariid.

Octopus sp., Mimic Octopus, thought to mimic *Pterois* sp.

A Lionfish Look-Alike?

The octopuses are some of the most behaviorally complex of all the invertebrates. They are adept predators and masters of camouflage. Many octopuses can change their color, as well as the texture of their integument, to blend in better with their surroundings. Although many of these cephalopods are masters of masquerade, the most incredible "actors" in the group are the mimic octopuses.

The mimic octopus subgroup consists of at least two undescribed, long-armed species that are known to inhabit reefs in the Western Pacific. Both have banded arms and mantles. One species (pictured here) displays a more striking color pattern than the other, although it does not engage in mimicry as often. These two species apparently mimic a variety of marine creatures (both harmless and harmful forms), possibly to confuse the search image of potential predators, or to dissuade them by looking like something inedible. The creatures they are thought to mimic include a jellyfish, a sea snake, a crinoid, and a flatfish. In some instances, these octopuses assume a posture (throwing their striped arms up and to the side) wherein they appear to be mimicking a venomous lionfish. The lionfishes are indeed worthy models for defensive mimicry, considering that they are unattractive prey to most predators.

Pterois volitans, Volitans Lionfish, lurking among feather star crinoids and using them to camouflage its presence, encouraging potential targets to approach.

Feeding Behavior

One of the most attractive anatomical features of the lionfishes is their enlarged pectoral fins. They vary in size from one species to the next, reaching their most flamboyant display in the Volitans and Russell's Lionfishes. In these species, the upper pectoral rays have a membrane hanging down that looks like the plumage of a bird (hence the common name "turkeyfish," often used to refer to these species). But what function do these attractive appendages serve? They have apparently evolved, at least in part, to aid the lionfish in capturing prey. Watch a lionfish stalk and ingest live food, and you may notice that when it approaches its prey, it spreads its fins to the side and slightly forward. This makes its approach less distracting, preventing the prey from seeing the movement of the tail and median fins and allowing the lionfish to move closer without startling its quarry. The expanded finnage also acts as a barrier to cut off the escape path of the victim or to corner it against the reef or in a crevice. Large Volitans Lionfish have been observed dragging the trailing ends of their pectoral rays over the algal mat or sand as they move, possibly to flush out refuging crustaceans.

The elaborate finnage of some lionfishes may even enhance their camouflage when light levels are low (at dusk). A shrimp, which has poor visual acuity, could easily mistake a resting Volitans Lionfish for a striped crinoid. Crinoids, or feather stars, pose no threat to crustaceans and are even utilized as shelter by some species. Therefore, a lionfish that looks like a crinoid is less likely to be avoided by potential prey and may even attract them. The Clearfin Lionfish (*Pterois radiata*) enhances this mimicry by utilizing crinoid aggregations as an ambush sight, sitting motionless among these echinoderms until a prey item comes within striking range. The related Lacey Scorpionfish (*Rhinopias aphanes*) also associates with crinoids and, like the lionfish, may derive a hunting advantage by doing so. More quantitative field observations are necessary to determine whether there is a mimetic relationship between crinoids and the *Pterois* species. It may be that coloration similar to that of the lionfishes has evolved

Dendrochirus zebra, Zebra Lionfish: juvenile specimen bears eye spots to confuse predators. These will fade as it grows and becomes less vulnerable.

in some crinoid species to deter potential predators.

Lionfishes possess other adaptations to facilitate prey capture. For example, some members of the genus *Dendrochirus* move their dorsal spines from side to side as they stalk their prey. In the Twinspot Lionfish (*Dendrochirus biocellatus*), this motor pattern is highly exaggerated—the spines are snapped from side to side down the length of the dorsal fin. Certain species, such as the Shortfin Lionfish (*Dendrochirus brachypterus*), may employ this behavior during hunting bouts. The movement may either attract or distract potential prey and enhance the lionfish's predatory efficiency. One member of the Family Scorpaenidae, the Decoy Scorpionfish (*Iracundus signifer*), has taken this luring method a step further. Not only is the dorsal fin moved from side to side, it is also adorned with markings that resemble an eye and a mouth.

Most lionfishes are brightly colored, at least under aquarium lighting. In low-light conditions, such as at depth or at dusk, the characteristic red-and-white or brown-and-white stripes serve as disruptive camouflage that makes them less conspicuous to their prey.

When threatened by a predator, lionfishes will either spread their pectoral fins open and direct their dorsal spines toward their adversary or swim for shelter. In several species, the inner pectoral fin surfaces have spots or are boldly marked, which may serve to warn potential predators that they are venomous. In juveniles of the Zebra Lionfish (*Dendrochirus zebra*), the markings on the inner pectoral fins are reminiscent of eyespots. When displayed suddenly, these markings may frighten off an approaching piscivore.

Reproductive Behavior

Lionfishes are typically solitary predators and occupy a home range that overlaps that of other conspecifics. However, it is not uncommon for them to aggregate in a suitable cave, crevice, or overhang. Courting and spawning occur at specific rendezvous sites about 20 to 40 minutes after the sun sets. Males are aggressive prior to spawning and will bite and ram each other with their dorsal spines to gain access to sexually receptive females. Subordinate males are typically lighter in color than dominant consexuals, and all the species studied thus far display temporary sexual dichromatism during reproductive bouts, with males adopting a darker hue than females. When a male encounters a potential mate, he will circle around or swim beside her. He will then swim up into the water column in an attempt to elicit spawning. The pair may undertake several ascents before spawning actually occurs. Immediately before the spawning act, the female's genital pore enlarges. Then she expels two mucous sacs, or egg balls, that contain from 2,000 to 15,000 eggs, which the male fertilizes. These structures are apparently unappetizing to planktivores, which protect the eggs from being eaten.

Like many of the other scorpionfishes, lionfishes will occasionally shed their cuticle to rid themselves of fouling organisms such as algae and parasites. The cuticle sloughs off the body and often appears as a transparent membrane hanging from the fins.

Captive Care

The size of the aquarium needed to house one or more lionfishes comfortably will depend on the species you choose to keep. Members of the genus *Dendrochirus*, which attain smaller sizes than most of the *Pterois* species, can be kept in aquariums as small as 30 gallons. Because they usually hide during the day, they should be provided with a suitable overhang, cave, or crevice.

Members of *Pterois* do best if kept in aquariums of 30+ gallons. Adults of the larger species, such as the Volitans Lionfish, should be kept in tanks no smaller than the standard 55 gallons. Although the *Pterois* species can be kept in smaller tanks temporarily, be prepared to move them to larger living quarters as they grow.

Aquascaping requirements for the *Pterois* species vary between species; for example, the Spotfin (*Pterois antennata*) and Clearfin (*P. radiata*) need good hiding places to shelter in during the day, while the Volitans (*P. volitans*) and Russell's (*P. russelli*) spend most of their time in the open and readily acclimate even if hiding places are not provided. However, juveniles of the latter species will more readily adapt if provided with a cave or crevice in which to refuge.

Lionfishes are ideal candidates for the reef aquarium, as long as you do not intend to keep small fishes and ornamental shrimps. Some species, like the Volitans and the Russell's Lionfish, spend more time in the open when the lights are on, while other *Pterois* and *Dendrochirus* species usually hide among the live rock during the day.

Nutrition

One of the biggest challenges faced by lionfish owners is providing a nutritious diet. Most specimens readily accept live feeder fish, such as goldfish, but this is not a recommended staple food for a captive scorpaenid. The best way to ensure that a lionfish remains fit is to give it a varied diet of fresh and frozen seafoods. This is where potential problems can arise. Most lionfishes need to have the food "look" alive before they ingest it. Wiggling a piece of shrimp on a feeding stick will often tempt a reluctant feeder. With time, a lionfish may be trained to come to the surface and take pieces of seafood out of your fingers. Although this makes feeding simpler, on rare occasions it has resulted in the aquarist being accidentally jabbed by a venomous dorsal spine. Use caution if you choose to feed your lionfish in this manner. If you want to continue offering live foods, choose grass shrimp, fiddler crabs, small crayfish, and live brine shrimp (even larger specimens will eat these minute crustaceans), as these animals are most similar to their normal prey. In addition, it is usually easier to get a younger fish to switch to nonliving foods than an older specimen.

Dendrochirus species are more secretive than *Pterois* species, spending most of the daylight hours hiding beneath reef structure or hanging upside down behind pieces of coral. They will come out to feed, but live food is usually necessary to elicit a feeding response. With time and patience, they can be trained to accept pieces of fresh seafood moving in the current or on the end of a feeding stick. It is often more difficult to feed the *Dendrochirus* in this manner than the *Pterois* species. Keeping a *Dendrochirus* species with more voracious predators, such as groupers and snappers, can present a problem. The lionfish may have difficulty getting anything to eat when competing with these more aggressive gluttons. You may have to present feeder fish or shrimp to the slower *Dendrochirus* in a fine-meshed fish net. This method is also effective for feeding a lionfish in a reef aquarium.

It is important not to offer your lionfish large prey items. Although the problem is less common in lionfishes than in frog-

Pterois sphex, Hawaiian Lionfish: open mouth and spread gill covers make for an aggressive display meant to intimidate rivals.

fishes (probably because the antennariids are capable of ingesting larger prey relative to their body size), lionfishes will occasionally kill themselves by overeating. Offer several smaller prey items rather than one large morsel. In the wild, a lionfish will consume from 1 to 11 small- to medium-sized prey items per day. I recommend feeding your lionfish to satiation two or three times a week, depending on the temperature of your aquarium (at lower water temperatures, you will not need to feed them as much). If you are trying to encourage your lionfish to spawn, feed it more frequently.

I once observed an unusual malady in which a lionfish's jaws became locked in an extended position when they were rapidly protruded during a feeding episode. Although the jaws eventually returned to their proper position, they became dislocated again during subsequent attempts to capture food.

Compatibility
Frequently, more than one lionfish is kept in the same aquarium. Although there is usually no problem housing two or more of these fishes together, conspecifics and closely related forms (e.g., the Zebra Lionfish, *D. zebra*, and the Shortfin Lionfish, *D. brachypterus*) will occasionally fight. This is especially true if, 1) both individuals are male and one specimen is placed in the aquarium after the other or, 2) there is a sexually receptive female present. Although these encounters are usually limited to lateral displays, gill cover flaring, and head shaking, the fishes may bite each other if one of the individuals does not back down. A Shortfin Lionfish will grasp the head of an opponent in its mouth and vigorously shake it from side to side. This behavior can result in damage to the victim's jaws. Individuals may also bite the flank of a conspecific or ram their opponent with their venomous dorsal spines. Although a lionfish stung by a conspecific will not usually die as a result, the sting can cause temporary distress, including an increased respiration rate (as much as three times its normal rate) and decreased swimming activity. If one lionfish persistently attacks another, they should be separated or the subordinate individual may cease feeding and die. Another thing to be aware of when keeping more than one lionfish in the same aquarium is that larger lionfishes have been known to prey on smaller members of their own species. The stomachs of larger Volitans Lionfish in the wild occasionally contain the remains of smaller conspecifics.

Special consideration needs to be used when selecting tankmates for your lionfishes. They will eat any fish or crustacean that can fit in their large mouths, although they rarely behave aggressively toward unrelated species. And even though they are venomous, lionfishes are not immune to being preyed upon by other marine organisms. Large eels, frogfishes, other scorpionfishes, and octopuses are all predators known to eat lionfishes. Of these predators, the frogfishes are especially notorious, even when the lionfish is the same length or slightly longer. Large angelfishes, pufferfishes, and triggerfishes have also been known to harass and damage lionfishes. I have had a Passer Angelfish (*Holacanthus passer*) nip the dorsal spines off a Spotfin Lionfish; a Clown Triggerfish (*Balistoides conspicillum*) kill a Volitans Lionfish; and an Orangehead Filefish (*Pervagor melanocephalus*) nip the pectoral fins of a Spotfin Lionfish. In the latter interaction, the lionfish fought back and attempted to bite the filefish.

Lionfishes have also been known to jab tankmates with their venomous spines. This is more likely to occur in a crowded aquarium. The fishes targeted by lionfishes are usually slow moving or sedentary (e.g., other scorpionfishes or porcupinefishes). Envenomization can occur in one of two ways: the lionfish may make aggressive advances toward a tankmate and intentionally impale it, or a fish may accidentally swim into the lionfish's spines when startled or pursuing food. When struck by a lionfish's spines, a fish will usually develop lesions in the impaled area, and these may appear inflamed and reddened. The tissue around the wounds may then die and slough off. Other symptoms of lionfish stings include an increased respiration rate, color loss, jerky swimming movements, and inactivity in fish species that are normally active. In many instances, death is the end result. Most fishes (including squirrelfishes, groupers, goatfishes, and damselfishes) injected with a large dose of lionfish venom (more than that delivered by one normal sting) die within 10 to 30 minutes.

Parasites and Diseases
Although they can suffer from protozoan and dinoflagellate infections, lionfishes are less likely to contract these diseases than many other marine fishes. If a lionfish does develop a parasite problem, copper-based medications can be used to treat it. Freshwater dips and formaldehyde baths may also prove helpful in eradicating these pests. Lionfishes occasionally suffer from fin rot, which can be treated with antibiotics (nitrofurazone). This bacterial infection is especially common in specimens that have just been shipped or those kept in a poorly maintained aquarium.

When selecting a lionfish for your aquarium, make sure it is eating and that the muscles above the lateral line do not look atrophied. Also check for fin rot—especially on the tail—and skin parasites. In addition, the respiratory rate of a healthy lionfish is quite slow (usually less than 30 operculum movements per minute) and shallow, so avoid individuals that are breathing heavily.

Lionfish Species

Genus *Dendrochirus*

Dendrochirus barberi (Steindachner, 1900)
Common Names: Green Lionfish, Hawaiian Lionfish.
Maximum Length: 16 cm (6.3 in.).
Distribution: Hawaiian Islands.
Biology: The Green Lionfish is found in turbid lagoons and clear fore-reef areas at depths of 1 to 45 m (3.3 to 146 ft.). It is typically secretive during the day, hiding in reef holes and crevices. On occasion, it will sit in the open at the base of a coral head. Although food habit data is lacking for this species, it probably feeds primarily on crustaceans.
Captive Care: *Dendrochirus barberi* is rarely encountered in aquarium stores, possibly because of its less attractive appearance and more restricted distribution. It is a hardy aquarium species that should be provided with plenty of hiding places. Although it may eat only live food initially, it can be trained to take pieces of fish flesh, table shrimp, and squid either off a feeding stick or out of the aquarist's fingers. Larger specimens may behave aggressively toward members of their own species or other *Dendrochirus* species. Aggression problems are more likely to occur if a conspecific is added to a small tank that already contains a larger Green Lionfish.
Aquarium Size: 30 gal. **Temperature:** 21 to 27°C (70 to 80°F).
Aquarium Suitability Index: 4 (**Venomous**).
Remarks: The Green Lionfish is greenish brown or reddish brown overall and lacks the elongate white pectoral rays present in the other Hawaiian pteroine, *Pterois sphex*.

Dendrochirus biocellatus (Fowler, 1934)
Common Names: Twinspot Lionfish, Ocellated Lionfish, Fu Manchu Lionfish.
Maximum Length: 10 cm (3.9 in.).
Distribution: Mauritius to the Society Islands, north to Japan, and south to Australia.
Biology: The Twinspot Lionfish occurs at depths of 1 to 40 m (3.3 to 130 ft.) on reef faces and fore-reef slopes—typically in areas with rich coral growth. This is a solitary, secretive fish that often hangs upside down in deeper crevices and caves during the day. At night, it moves into open areas to hunt. The Twinspot Lionfish will snap its dorsal spines and shake its head from side to side as it approaches its prey. This behavior may serve to distract, or possibly attract, the prey item. It often stalks its quarry by slinking along the bottom or around the reef structure like a cat, and moves forward either by "hopping" on its pelvic fins or by undulating its caudal fin. When it is about half a body length away from its prey, it lunges forward with amazing speed to ingest it. The ocelli on the soft portion of the dorsal fin can be black or fade to gray. In agonistic interactions, the ocelli will typically fade in the dominant individual. During courtship, the spots fade in males.
Captive Care: *Dendrochirus biocellatus* is considered to be the most problematic member of the subfamily to maintain, because an occasional specimen will refuse to eat (most specimens, however, cannot resist live grass shrimp). This species will be more difficult to feed if it is kept with aggressive carnivores. Potential competitors like groupers, soapfishes, snappers, and triggerfishes do not make good tankmates, and large angelfishes, triggerfishes, pufferfishes, and porcupinefishes may nip at a Twinspot Lionfish's fins. It is imperative to provide this fish with caves, crevices,

Dendrochirus barberi, Green Lionfish: hardy but drab, seldom collected.

Dendrochirus barberi, Green Lionfish: variant with reddish highlights.

Dendrochirus biocellatus, Twinspot Lionfish: note pale soft-dorsal eye spots.

Compare "switched on" eye spots to those at left—visual signs at work.

and overhangs in order for it to acclimate properly. I have even had specimens hang upside down under the heads of large leather corals. Adult Twinspot Lionfish will eat smaller members of their own species, and larger specimens (presumably males) will behave aggressively toward conspecifics. When displaying, the fan-like pectoral fins are extended forward, the dorsal spines are erected, and the body quivers. Smaller individuals will usually flee when a larger individual displays, but threats may escalate into fighting if both fish are similar in size and one specimen does not back down. In this case, biting and dorsal fin jabbing may occur, which can result in torn fins, scale loss, damaged eyes, and death if the fish are not separated. If you keep more than one Twinspot Lionfish in a larger aquarium (70+ gallons), they will usually avoid each other. However, dominant specimens in smaller aquariums often stalk and injure subordinate conspecifics. Like all the lionfishes, this species is suitable for a reef tank if you are not interested in keeping shrimps and smaller fishes—especially benthic species like gobies. The Twinspot Lionfish is less of threat to more active fish species than its relatives due to its slightly smaller mouth and unique hunting behavior. Do not expect to see your Twinspot Lionfish much if your aquarium is replete with live rock. Smaller specimens tend to be more secretive than adults, and some larger individuals will come out into the open as they become more accustomed to aquarium life. The best way to view these fish in a reef aquarium is to place a red fluorescent or incandescent bulb over the tank at night.

Aquarium Size: 20 gal. **Temperature:** 22 to 27°C (72 to 80°F).
Aquarium Suitability Index: 3 (Venomous).
Remarks: This is a magnificent little fish that is less frequently seen in aquarium stores than many of the other lionfishes. The two barbels on the upper jaw and pair of ocelli on the soft dorsal fin set it apart from all of its relatives.

Dendrochirus brachypterus (Cuvier, 1829)
Common Names: Shortfin Lionfish, Dwarf Lionfish, Fuzzy Dwarf Lionfish.
Maximum Length: 17 cm (6.7 in.).
Distribution: Red Sea to Samoa, north to southern Japan, and south to Lord Howe Island.
Biology: Over most of its range, the Shortfin Lionfish species is common on reef flats, in shallow lagoons, and on coastal reefs. It lies on sand bottoms near isolated rocks, coral fragments, and small coral heads, often near dense coral growth. In some locations (e.g., northern Red Sea) it is abundant close to shore, on muddy substrates, where other lionfishes are seldom seen. In other areas (e.g., Madagascar and Papua New Guinea), it frequents seagrass beds on inner-reef flats. It occurs at depths of 2 to 30 m (7 to 98 ft.).

During the day, the Shortfin Lionfish hangs upside down under ledges or rests among boulders, rubble, and soft corals (*Sinularia* spp., *Sarcophyton* spp.). At dusk, Shortfin Lionfish disperse from their daytime shelter sites to court, mate, and hunt. They will, however, also prey on animals that share their diurnal hiding places. They feed primarily on crabs and shrimps, but occasionally supplement their diet with isopods and polychaete worms. Rather than ingesting one large food item, *D. brachypterus* usually consumes a larger number of smaller items (individuals may ingest up to 11 prey items in a single night). In the Red Sea, this lionfish has been observed to sit next to aggregations of *Diadema* sea urchins and capture small cardinalfishes that stray too far from their spiny refuges.

Dendrochirus brachypterus, Shortfin Lionfish: may require live foods.

Dendrochirus brachypterus, Shortfin Lionfish: brown variant.

Dendrochirus brachypterus, Shortfin Lionfish: rare yellow variant.

Dendrochirus brachypterus, Shortfin Lionfish: reddish yellow variant.

The Shortfin Lionfish occurs singly or in small groups of three to ten individuals. These social units typically consist of a larger dominant male, several females, and one or more smaller males. This fish has been reported to spawn in aquariums of 60 to 200 gallons at water temperatures ranging from 23 to 26°C (74 to 78°F). Courtship and spawning occur 20 to 30 minutes before dark and are initiated by the male. The mating ritual begins when the male visits sexually receptive females. He ascends into the water column until the female joins him. This behavior may be repeated numerous times for 10 to 15 minutes before spawning takes place. When the fish are ready to spawn, they swim near the water's surface. With the male positioned under the female, he pushes her upward with his head and nips at the white skin flaps on her chin. The genital pore of the female enlarges at this time and she exudes two egg balls that the male fertilizes. The egg balls swell with water until they are 2 to 5 cm (0.7 to 2 in.) in diameter. At 26°C (78°F), the eggs hatch in 36 hours. The larvae are just over 1 mm at hatching and begin feeding four or five days later when they are about 2 mm in length.

Captive Care: The Shortfin Lionfish should be kept in an aquarium with plenty of places for it to hide. If you want to keep more than one specimen per aquarium, purchase one larger individual and one or more smaller specimens. A larger aquarium (75+ gallons) with numerous hiding places will also allow you to keep a group of these fish. If you notice any antagonism between specimens, they will have to be separated. This species is often reluctant to eat anything but live food. If more boisterous eaters are present, the Shortfin Lionfish may be difficult to feed. It is more likely to spend time in the open in the reef aquarium than its close relative the Zebra Lionfish.

Dendrochirus zebra, Zebra Lionfish: hunting at night.

Dendrochirus zebra, Zebra Lionfish: in repose during the day.

Dendrochirus zebra, Zebra Lionfish: requires hiding places and a varied diet.

Aquarium Size: 30 gal. **Temperature:** 21 to 27°C (70 to 80°F).
Aquarium Suitability Index: 4 (**Venomous**).
Remarks: Most Shortfin Lionfish are reddish or purplish brown in color with dark bars on the body, but some individuals sport varying amounts of yellow on the body and fins. The sexes are reported to differ in both form and coloration. Males have larger heads than females and their pectoral fins are longer, extending back to the middle of the caudal peduncle (in females, the pectorals reach only to the base of the caudal peduncle). The coloration of their pectoral fins also differs: in males, there are six to ten bands, while females typically have four to six. During courtship, males become darker overall and are often one uniform color, especially the anterior part of the body. The belly of a "ripe" female becomes silvery white, as does the gill and mouth region, and it develops a white line from the eye to the skin flap on the chin. Females swell with eggs just prior to spawning.

Dendrochirus zebra (Quoy & Gaimard, 1825)
Common Names: Zebra Lionfish, Dwarf Lionfish.
Maximum Length: 18 cm (7.1 in.).
Distribution: South Africa and the Red Sea to Samoa, north to southern Japan, and south to Lord Howe Island.
Biology: The Zebra Lionfish occurs in lagoons, on reef flats, and on fore-reef slopes at depths of 1 to 35 m (3.25 to 114 ft.). It resides among coral and volcanic rubble, among small- to medium-sized coral boulders, or on patch reefs with sponges. It prefers areas that are sheltered from wave action, with moderate to no current. This species feeds mainly on crabs and shrimps, although they may occasionally eat small fishes like damselfishes and cardinalfishes. An individual may make as many as four or five attacks on potential prey within an hour, but usually only two or three of these attempts are successful. It may ingest as many as ten small items in a single night. Although this lionfish is primarily nocturnal, males may attempt to locate females in spawning condition during the day and females may feed at this time—especially during peak reproductive periods. However, most specimens begin hunting about 3 hours before sunset.

The social organization of this species varies from one location to the next and may be a function of population densities. In Indonesia, small groups of Zebra Lionfish—three or four individuals of varying sizes—associate with large lavender Barrel Sponges (*Xestospongia testudinaria*). These lionfish hang on the sides of the sponge or live in the sponge's lumen. In other areas, like southern Japan, this species lives as a solitary fish that occupies a large home range covering an area of up to 115 by 75 m (373 by 244 ft.). This home range overlaps with those of other males and females. When females meet, they do not behave aggressively toward each other. Males, however, almost always fight when they cross paths. These battles result in broken dorsal spines, ripped fins, and other wounds. When a larger, dominant male encounters a subordinate member of the same sex, the dominant individual will darken in color and move toward its opponent. The color of the subordinate individual will fade and this fish will usually flee. Sometimes, the dominant individual will chase an opponent over a considerable distance. One Zebra Lionfish was reported to have chased another individual a distance of over 30 m (98 ft.). Within the male's home range, males and females visit specific areas, with as many as two or three females in spawning condition aggregating at a rendezvous site. Spawning takes place any time from 30 minutes before to 55 minutes after sunset.

Captive Care: The Zebra Lionfish is a commonly kept species whose husbandry requirements are similar to that of the Shortfin Lionfish (*D. brachypterus*). The most important prerequisites for keeping this fish are to provide it with plenty of good hiding places and to give it a varied diet. The Zebra Lionfish may behave aggressively toward conspecifics or other lionfishes in the genus *Dendrochirus*. It can be kept in a shallow-water or deep-water reef aquarium, but will spend much of its time out of sight. It is more likely to spend time in the open in the deep-water reef aquarium because of the reduced light levels.

Aquarium Size: 30 gal. **Temperature:** 18 to 29°C (64 to 84°F).
Aquarium Suitability Index: 4 (**Venomous**).

Remarks: *Dendrochirus zebra* is one of the most common pteroines in the marine aquarium trade. It is characterized by the dark spot on the lower part of the operculum and conspicuous concentric bands that are present on the inner part of the pectoral fins. As in all the members of this genus, the membranes between the pectoral rays extend almost all the way to the tips. This species displays subtle sexual dimorphism. Males are generally larger than females and have a slightly more robust head. Just before spawning, females change color, with the head, gill cover, facial appendages, and the tips of the first four dorsal spines becoming a brilliant white. The abdomen also swells with eggs at this time and becomes pale near the vent.

Genus *Pterois*

Pterois antennata (Bloch, 1787)
Common Names: Spotfin Lionfish, Antennata Lionfish, Raggedfinned Firefish.
Maximum Length: 20 cm (7.9 in.).
Distribution: East Africa to the Marquesas and Mangareva Islands, north to southern Japan, and south to the Great Barrier Reef and Austral Island.
Biology: The Spotfin Lionfish occurs in water as shallow as 1 m (3.3 ft.) on the reef flat to depths of 50 m (163 ft.) on the fore reef. During the day, it hides in caves, holes, and under overhangs. Occasionally, two to six individuals will occupy the same hiding place, which they may share with the Volitans (*Pterois volitans*) and Clearfin (*Pterois radiata*) Lionfishes. In the late afternoon and at night, the Spotfin Lionfish emerges to hunt shrimps and crabs. During the day, it will also feed on crustaceans that share its diurnal hiding places. It will consume as many as four prey items during a single hunting bout.
Captive Care: *Pterois antennata* is a durable aquarium fish that readily adapts to captive life if provided with adequate hiding places. If you keep more than one specimen, provide each individual with its own shelter site. It will readily accept grass shrimp

Pterois antennata, Spotfin Lionfish: commendable aquarium fish.

Pterois antennata, Spotfin Lionfish: compare pectoral spots to image at left.

and feeder fish, and can be switched to nonliving food. Although it feeds on crustaceans in the wild, it will eat any fish in the aquarium that is small enough to fit into its mouth.
Aquarium Size: 30 gal. **Temperature:** 22 to 28°C (72 to 82°F).
Aquarium Suitability Index: 5 (Venomous).
Remarks: The color of *P. antennata* is somewhat variable. Some individuals have bright red body stripes, while in others they are brownish red. Some individuals might also have fewer spots on the pectoral fins.

Pterois mombasae (Smith, 1957)
Common Names: Deep-water Lionfish, Deep-water Firefish, African Lionfish, Mombasa Turkeyfish.
Maximum Length: 16 cm (6.3 in.).
Distribution: East Africa to Papua New Guinea, north to Sri Lanka, and south to South Africa and northwestern Australia.
Biology: The Deep-water Lionfish occurs on offshore reefs and fore-reef slopes, usually at depths in excess of 40 m (130 ft.). It has been reported as shallow as 15 m (49 ft.). It is usually found in habitats with rich soft coral and sponge growth. This fish feeds almost entirely on brachyuran crabs, consuming approximately three small specimens during each feeding session.
Captive Care: This species is usually identified incorrectly as a "Spotfin Lionfish" in the aquarium trade. The Deep-water Lionfish is similar in its husbandry requirements to the other medium-sized *Pterois* species. It should be provided with plenty of hiding places and is best kept in a dimly lit aquarium.
Aquarium Size: 30 gal. **Temperature:** 22 to 26°C (72 to 78°F).
Aquarium Suitability Index: 4 (Venomous).
Remarks: *Pterois mombasae* is recognized by its lack of a series of dark spots on the pectoral fins (as in *P. antennata*), short pectoral fin filaments, the complex barring pattern on the caudal peduncle, and large eyes.

Pterois radiata Cuvier, 1829
Common Names: Clearfin Lionfish, Radiata Lionfish.
Maximum Length: 24 cm (9.4 in.).
Distribution: Red Sea to the Society Islands, north to the Ryukyu Islands, and south to New Caledonia. This species is very common in the Red Sea.
Biology: *Pterois radiata* occurs at depths of 1 to 15 m (3 to 49 ft.). Occasionally seen in coral head caves, on reef flats, or in lagoons, it also occurs on reef faces and fore-reef slopes with rich hard coral growth. In certain locations, it is abundant on rocky reefs with sparse coral growth and numerous sea urchins. This lionfish hides in crevices, under overhangs, or in caves during the day. Although it is usually solitary, two or three specimens may share the same shelter site. Occasionally, it refuges with the Spotfin Lionfish (*P. antennata*). At night, the Clearfin Lionfish leaves its hiding place to search for food, often invading flooded reef flats. When hunting, it moves slowly over and between coral heads, with its body pitched slightly forward and its pectoral fins spread to the side. It will also use groups of feather stars as an ambush site to capture passing prey. This lionfish feeds almost exclusively on crabs. It will, however, eat the occasional shrimp—including the Banded Coral Shrimp (*Stenopus hispidus*). Like most other lionfishes, it typically ingests several small- to medium-sized crustaceans, rather than one larger specimen.
Captive Care: The Clearfin Lionfish is not as common in aquarium stores as the Spotfin Lionfish, and commands a much higher

Pterois mombasae, Deep-water Lionfish: often confused with *P. antennata*.

Pterois mombasae, Deep-water Lionfish: variant photographed in Oman.

price. Like *Pterois antennata*, this species should be provided with a place to hide—either a cave or an overhang—and should not be kept with overly aggressive tankmates that might interfere with feeding. Initially, it can be difficult to feed and usually requires live food to start the feeding process. Grass shrimp, small freshwater crayfish, and fiddler crabs are good live foods for this species if you cannot get it to accept fresh or frozen substitutes (marine fish flesh, fresh shrimps, scallops, clams). Although it feeds almost entirely on crustaceans in the wild, it will eat small fishes in the aquarium.
Aquarium Size: 30 gal. **Temperature:** 22 to 28°C (72 to 82°F).
Aquarium Suitability Index: 4 (Venomous).
Remarks: This species is easily recognized by the white horizontal lines on the caudal peduncle and the lack of spots on the pectoral fin membranes.

Pterois sphex Jordan & Evermann, 1903
Common Names: Hawaiian Lionfish, Hawaiian Turkeyfish.
Maximum Length: 20 cm (7.9 in.).
Distribution: Hawaiian Islands.
Biology: The Hawaiian Lionfish occurs at depths of 3 to 120 m (10 to 390 ft.) in lagoons and fore-reef slopes. It hides under ledges during the day and hunts at night. It feeds mainly on shrimps, but also eats xanthid crabs and small hermit crabs.
Captive Care: This is a good aquarium fish whose husbandry needs are similar to those of *Pterois antennata* (see page 501). It can be aggressive toward conspecifics or congeners, especially if they are housed in a smaller tank.
Aquarium Size: 30 gal. **Temperature:** 22 to 27°C (72 to 80°F).
Aquarium Suitability Index: 5 (Venomous).
Remarks: *Pterois sphex* is similar to *P. antennata*, but often lacks spots on the pectoral fin membrane. It is not nearly as common in the marine trade as *P. antennata*.

The Volitans Group
There are four closely related species of lionfishes that comprise this group—two of which are commonly encountered in the aquarium hobby. The four species are: the Japanese Lionfish, Miles's Lionfish, Russell's Lionfish, and the Volitans Lionfish. Miles's Lionfish is a poorly known species that rarely shows up in aquarium stores and is frequently misidentified. The Japanese Lionfish is also rare in the aquarium trade, but is often confused with Russell's Lionfish by saltwater hobbyists. One thing that all four of these fishes have in common is that they become heavier-bodied as they grow, and the length of their pectoral rays relative to their body length shortens as they mature.

Pterois radiata, Clearfin Lionfish: groups of 2 or 3 make an impressive sight.

Pterois radiata, Clearfin Lionfish: hunting over rubble at night.

Pterois sphex, Hawaiian Lionfish: good fish for medium-sized aquariums.

Pterois russelli, Russell's Lionfish (juvenile): often sold as the "Red Volitans," it has pale red or rusty brown bands on the body and is a durable aquarium fish.

Pterois russelli Bennett, 1828
Common Names: Russell's Lionfish, Spotless Lionfish, Red Volitans Lionfish, Soldier Lionfish, Plaintail Firefish, Largetail Turkeyfish, Military Turkeyfish.
Maximum Length: 30 cm (11.8 in.).
Distribution: East Africa to tropical Australia—including New South Wales—north to India.
Biology: This lionfish usually resides on silty, coastal reefs or on sand or mud flats in estuaries. Where the water is clear, Russell's Lionfish tends to occur in deeper water than the Volitans Lionfish (*P. volitans*). It can also be common in shallow water in more turbid conditions. It has been reported from depths of 10 to 100 m (33 to 325 ft.), but is most common at depths greater than 20 m (65 ft.)—except in muddy, estuarine conditions, where it is regularly encountered at depths between 3 to 5 m (10 to 16 ft.). Little information is available on the diet of this species, but it probably feeds on fishes, crabs, and shrimps.
Captive Care: This is a durable aquarium species that will spend much of its time in full view. It can be trained to eat pieces of fresh seafood, but live feeder fish or grass shrimp may be necessary to entice a finicky newcomer. Like its relatives, it is typically not aggressive toward other fish, with the possible exception of other lionfishes. It does well in both shallow-water and deep-water reef aquariums.
Aquarium Size: 55 gal. **Temperature:** 22 to 28°C (72 to 82°F).

Pterois russelli, Russell's Lionfish (large adult): often occurs in the open.

Pterois lunulata, Japanese Lionfish (juvenile): this the true *P. lunulata*.

Pterois lunulata, Japanese Lionfish (adult): seldom seen outside of Japan.

Aquarium Suitability Index: 5 (**Venomous**).
Remarks: *Pterois russelli*, which is sold in the aquarium trade under the confusing name "Red Volitans Lionfish," has few or no spots on the dorsal, anal, and tail fins and no bands on the dorsal spines. The bands on the body tend to be pale red or rusty brown in color. In large adults, there is a conspicuous dark spot over the pectoral fin base. The **Japanese Lionfish (*Pterois lunulata*) Temminck & Schlegel, 1843** is similar, but individuals from clear water have fewer spots on the base of the median fins and broad bands on the dorsal fin spines. As the common name implies, *P. lunulata* is known only from Japan. Many aquarists use the name *P. lunulata* incorrectly when referring to *P. russelli*.

Pterois volitans (Linnaeus, 1758)
Common Names: Volitans Lionfish, Common Lionfish, Turkeyfish, Red Firefish, Butterfly Cod, Devilfish.
Maximum Length: 38 cm (15.0 in.).
Distribution: In the Pacific, *P. volitans* is found from Malaysia and western Australia to the Pitcairn Group, north to southern Japan, and south to Lord Howe, Kermadec, and the Austral Islands. It is also found in the Indian Ocean from the Red Sea to Sumatra, north to the Persian Gulf, and south to South Africa. One specimen has also been reported from the Mediterranean.
Biology: This species is found in clear and turbid water, estuaries, lagoons, and fore-reef slopes at depths of 1 to 50 m (3 to 163 ft.). In the Red Sea, it is typically found on the reef face and fore reef, although at flood tide it may enter back-reef areas and lagoons to hunt. Adult Volitans Lionfish often occur in the open during the day, usually hovering near cave entrances, reef ledges, or ship wreckage (the latter seems to be a preferred habitat) However, they are also found perched upside down—under overhangs, on cave ceilings, and on pier pilings.

Adults occur singly or in aggregations. In some cases, these animals will gather in huge numbers, especially around shipwrecks. For example, near the wreck of the *Mawali*, off Sulawesi, Indonesia, groups of adult Volitans Lionfish numbering in excess of 80 individuals can be found hanging near, and perched on, the wreck's superstructure. The Volitans Lionfish sometimes shares a cave or crevice with the Zebra Lionfish (*Dendrochirus zebra*) or the Clearfin Lionfish (*P. radiata*). Juveniles tend to be more secretive and solitary than larger specimens, spending most of their time in reef crevices, under ledges, in large Barrel Sponges (*Xestospongia testudinaria*), or among the spines of sea urchins in reef crevices. Although these fish will feed to some extent during the day, they do most of their hunting at dusk and after dark. Adult Volitans Lionfish feed more heavily on fishes than most other members of the genus, but crabs (including protunid or "swimming" crabs) and shrimps (including the Banded Coral Shrimp, *Stenopus hispidus*) are also important in their diet. Juveniles consume more crustaceans than adults. This species hunts near the bottom, often dragging the lower pectoral fin rays along the sand or algal mat to disturb refuging crustaceans. It will also feed on schooling fishes in the upper water column. At dusk, some individuals ascend into open water and position themselves just beneath the surface. They watch patiently until schools of baitfishes are chased by other predators, like needlefishes, into striking range. In the Red Sea, the Volitans Lionfish also hunts in groups of up to five individuals. These hunting bands herd baitfishes into a tight mass, then take turns attacking them. The Volitans Lionfish will associate with foraging eels like the Gray Moray (*Siderea grisea*), as well as octopuses. The lionfish follows these animals in order to capture small fishes and crustaceans that

Pterois volitans, Volitans Lionfish (juvenile): a bold, beautiful aquarium fish.

Pterois volitans, Volitans Lionfish (small adult): a varied diet is recommended.

Pterois volitans, Volitans Lionfish (large adult): will eat smaller fishes.

Pterois volitans, Volitans Lionfish: venomous spines command respect.

are flushed out from between coral branches and reef crevices.

Captive Care: The Volitans Lionfish is a great aquarium species that spends most of its time in the open. It should be provided with plenty of space to hover in the water column or sit in repose on the substrate. Its large size makes it a greater threat to tankmates, so choose them accordingly. On rare occasions, a Volitans Lionfish may behave aggressively toward a conspecific or another member of the genus *Pterois*. Because of its boldness, it is one of the best species of this subfamily for both shallow-water and deep-water reef aquariums. However, it will eat ornamental shrimps, including dancing shrimps, cleaner shrimps, and Banded Coral Shrimp. *Pterois volitans* can withstand water temperatures as cold as 14°C (58°F).

Aquarium Size: 55 gal. **Temperature:** 17 to 28°C (62 to 82°F).
Aquarium Suitability Index: 5 (Venomous).

Remarks: The coloration of the Volitans Lionfish can vary, with the bands on the body and fins ranging from red to black. In this species, as well as some of its close relatives, the pectoral fins become shorter as the fish grows, and the tentacle above each eye shrinks and may disappear entirely. There has been some confusion when it comes to the taxonomy of this species and the **Miles's Lionfish (*Pterois miles*) Bennett, 1828**. In 1986, Schultz suggested that the "Volitans-type" Lionfish found in the Western Indian Ocean and the Red Sea were *P. miles* and that *P. volitans* was restricted in its distribution to the Eastern Indian and Pacific Oceans. He stated that the Volitans Lionfish normally has one more dorsal and anal fin spine, longer pectoral fins (which are significantly longer in specimens larger than 8.5 cm,

Pterois volitans, Volitans Lionfish: a pride of lions hunts a deep reef in Bali.

Japanese Lions

The subtropical reefs off southern Japan have a unique ichthyfauna, which includes several interesting lionfishes. One of these species is Bleeker's Lionfish (*Ebosia bleekeri*). In this species, there are two large crests on the parietal bones of the skull, which are much more pronounced on larger males than on females or juveniles. This species occurs from southern Japan to Hong Kong and is most commonly observed on open sand or mud slopes. The Blackfin Lionfish (*Parapterois heterura*) is unique in having elongate upper caudal rays (the first and sometimes the second), two spines in the anal fin (three in *Pterois*), and a truncate caudal fin (rounded in *Pterois*). They also have dermal appendages on each side of the upper jaw, like those of the Twinspot Lionfish (*Dendrochirus biocellatus*). The adults of this species have beautiful blue broken bands on the inner surfaces of the pectoral fins. The Blackfin is found in a habitat similar to that of Bleeker's Lionfish. Two other species endemic to Japan are the Bellus Lionfish (*Dendrochirus bellus*) and the Japanese Lionfish (*Pterois lunulata*). The Bellus Lionfish is similar to the Shortfin Lionfish (*D. brachypterus*) and is found on sand, mud, or gravel substrates at a depth of 15 to 200 m (50 to 660 ft.). The reefs of southern Japan are also home to several other species with broader distributions, including the Zebra Lionfish (*D. zebra*), Shortfin Lionfish (*D. brachypterus*), Twinspot Lionfish (*D. biocellatus*), Spotfin Lionfish (*P. antennata*), Clearfin Lionfish (*P. radiata*), and the Volitans Lionfish (*P. volitans*). This makes the reefs of Japan one of the best places in the world for observing and photographing members of the lionfish subfamily.

Ebosia bleekeri, Bleeker's Lionfish

Parapterois heterura, Blackfin Lionfish

Dendrochirus bellus, Bellus Lionfish

Pterois volitans, Volitans Lionfish: unusual Red Sea color variant.

3.3 in.), and larger spots on the median fins than *P. miles*. But according to Rudie Kuiter, a fish expert from Australia, the true *P. miles* is a coastal species from the Indian Ocean (the type specimen is from Sri Lanka) that is typically found in muddy habitats, not in the clear water characteristic of most offshore coral reefs. The true *P. miles* differs from *P. volitans* in having numerous close-set tubercles on the cheek. Spotting in all the members of the Volitans Group can be misleading, because individuals of any of these species taken from more turbid water tend to have more spotting on the median fins.

References

Bernadsky & Goulet (1991), Doubilet (1987), Harmelin-Vivien & Bouchon (1976), Fishelson (1975), Hiatt & Stratsburg (1960), Hobson (1974), K. Imai (personal communication), Kizer et al. (1985), R. Kuiter (personal communications), Kuiter (1993), Kuiter & Debelius (1994), Moyer & Zaiser (1981), Myers (1989), Schultz (1986), Steinitz (1959).

Family Platycephalidae
Flatheads

Sorsogona welanderi, Welander's Flathead: popularly known as "crocodilefishes," these ambush predators make for a highly unusual aquarium display.

With eerily crocodilian looks, veiled eyes, and predatory maws, the flatheads have everything it takes to appeal to aquarists and underwater observers who seek the strange and slightly sinister. Although quite different in overall appearance, the flatheads are closely related to the scorpionfishes (Family Scorpaenidae). Unlike their venomous relatives, the flatheads have elongate bodies, a dorso-ventrally compressed head, and two dorsal fins. In addition, most of the flatheads lack a swim bladder and all lack venomous spines. Members of Family Platycephalidae have an iris lappet, a specialized structure that hangs over the eye, expanding or contracting to control the amount of light entering the iris. This structure may also serve to hide the eye from potential prey.

Biology

Family Platycephalidae is comprised of approximately 19 genera and 60 species, most found in the Indo-Pacific. Many of the flatheads are more abundant on soft substrate, in mangroves, or in seagrass beds. They are best represented in warm-temperate to temperate seas (e.g., southeastern and southern Australia).

All flatheads are bottom dwellers whose muted attire helps them blend in with their natural surroundings. They occur at depths ranging from less than 1 m (3.3 ft.) up to about 300 m (975 ft.), but most are found in less than 100 m (325 ft.) of water. The flatheads seen in the aquarium trade either associate with soft bottoms or coral rubble on or near the reef. They rely on ambush to capture squids, polychaete worms, crabs, shrimps (including the Banded Coral Shrimp, *Stenopus hispidus*), serpent stars, and small fishes. Flatheads have large mouths that enable them to ingest relatively large prey and are opportunistic predators that feed both during the day and at night. Many species hide just under the sand or mud during the day, but emerge from the substrate at night to move to a new ambush site or hunt nocturnal prey. They may also court and reproduce at night.

Captive Care

Flatheads are great aquarium candidates for the hobbyist looking for something new and unusual. The size of the tank depends on the species, as they range in size from 14 to 100 cm (5.5 to 39 in.). They are not active fishes, but they need to be provided with plenty of open space on the aquarium bottom on which to lie. Most species prefer a layer of sand 5 to 7.6 cm (2 to 3 in.) in depth, but a few species—such as Beaufort's Crocodilefish (*Cymbacephalus beauforti*)—will be fine if the aquarium bottom is covered with coral rubble.

Flatheads require live foods like grass shrimp, feeder fish, or live brine shrimp (for very small specimens). It is difficult to get them to switch to nonliving foods, but it can be done with a feeding stick and a strip of marine fish flesh or a piece of table shrimp. Care should be taken when removing flatheads from a tank, as their head spines can easily get caught in the mesh of aquarium nets. It is best to use a large specimen container rather than a net. Although not highly adept at aerial acrobatics, these fishes might jump out of an open tank when disturbed by an aquarist or tankmate.

Flatheads will eat smaller fishes and crustaceans, so choose their tankmates carefully. Their capacious jaws are able to engulf fairly large prey items. Like most predators, flatheads can swallow elongate fishes (e.g., gobies) with greater ease than deep-bodied forms (e.g., butterflyfishes). Flatheads may be nipped at by more aggressive tankmates like damselfishes and triggerfishes. Adults may quarrel if they are housed together in smaller tanks; it is best to keep only one flathead per tank unless the aquarium is extra large (180+ gallons).

Flatheads are not particularly susceptible to any skin parasites, although if they do show signs of such an infestation, they can be successfully treated with copper.

Flathead Species

Genus *Cymbacephalus*

Cymbacephalus beauforti (Knapp, 1973)

Common Names: Beaufort's Crocodilefish, Crocodilefish.
Maximum Length: 54 cm (21.3 in.).
Distribution: Singapore and the Philippines, south to New Caledonia.
Biology: The Beaufort's Crocodilefish occurs in seagrass meadows, mangrove swamps, and near coastal reefs—where it often occurs on reef flats. It is found at depths of less than 1 to at least 30 m (3.3 to 98 ft.).
Captive Care: This is a larger species that will need to be housed in tanks with plenty of surface area and open substrate. It is not well suited for reef tanks, as uncluttered bottom space is often unavailable and the flathead will eat small fishes and crustaceans.
Aquarium Size: 135 gal. **Temperature:** 22 to 27°C (72 to 80°F).
Aquarium Suitability Index: 3.
Remarks: What differentiates Beaufort's Crocodilefish from most of the other flatheads is that adult specimens have a distinct pit behind the eye, and the sides of the head behind the eyes are concave when viewed from above. The **Mangrove Crocodilefish** (*Cociella punctata*) is a similar species, although its iris lappet is a simple lobe as opposed to the complex iris lappet in *C. beauforti*.

Cymbacephalus beauforti, Beaufort's Crocodilefish: growing large, it demands an open bottom and care in choosing suitable tankmates.

Genus *Onigocia*

Onigocia spinosa (Temminck & Schlegel, 1844)
Common Name: Spiny Flathead.
Maximum Length: 10 cm (3.9 in.).
Distribution: Northwest and eastern Australia and Indonesia.
Biology: The Spiny Flathead is found on sand or mud flats, often in protected bays, at depths of 4 to at least 15 m (13 to 49 ft.). It buries deep under the substrate during the day and emerges to feed at night. It is sometimes found in caves. I have seen it consume errant polychaete worms; it probably eats crustaceans and small nocturnal fishes as well.
Captive Care: This small, attractively marked species should be kept in a tank with at least 2.5 cm (1 in.) of sand on the bottom. Although it can be kept with a wide range of crustaceans and fishes, the Spiny Flathead will eat them if they are small enough to fit into its sizable mouth. Its smaller dimensions make it well suited for a reef aquarium, although it needs to be provided with enough open bottom space to hide and hunt.
Aquarium Size: 20 gal. **Temperature:** 22 to 27°C (72 to 80°F).
Aquarium Suitability Index: 4.
Remarks: *Onigocia spinosa* has a broad head adorned with numerous spines. The dorsal fin has a dark outer half, the pelvic fins are dark with a white margin, and both the body and caudal peduncle have dark bars. The overall color of this flathead can be brown or red.

Onigocia spinosa, Spiny Flathead: emerges from the sand at night.

Genus *Papilloculiceps*

Papilloculiceps longiceps (Cuvier, 1829)
Common Names: Tentacled Flathead, Tentacled Crocodilefish.
Maximum Length: 70 cm (27.6 in.).
Distribution: South Africa north to the Red Sea and Oman.
Biology: The Tentacled Flathead is found on sand and rubble bottoms near coral reefs or on reef flats, at depths of 1 to 15 m (3.3 to 49 ft.).
Captive Care: This is a larger species that will need to be housed in tanks with plenty of surface area and open substrate. It is not well suited for reef tanks because not enough uncluttered bottom space is available, and the Tentacled Flathead will eat any fish or crustacean that will fit into its sizable mouth.
Aquarium Size: 135 gal. **Temperature:** 22 to 27°C (72 to 80°F).
Aquarium Suitability Index: 3.
Remarks: *Papilloculiceps longiceps* has a short dermal appendage—or tentacle—over each eye. There is a bony ridge with a single spine below the eye, a dark brown bar below each eye, and both the pelvic and pectoral fins are spotted.

Papilloculiceps longiceps, Tentacled Flathead: large and predatory.

Papilloculiceps longiceps, Tentacled Flathead: note tentacle above eye.

Sorsogona welanderi, Welander's Flathead: modestly sized species.

Thysanophrys arenicola, Broadhead Flathead: widespread species.

Thysanophrys celebica, Sulawesi Flathead: nocturnal hunter.

Genus *Sorsogona*

Sorsogona welanderi (Schultz, 1966)
Common Name: Welander's Flathead.
Maximum Length: 13 cm (5.1 in.).
Distribution: Indonesia to Samoa.
Biology: Welander's Flathead is found in coastal bays, in lagoons, on the edge of the reef slope, and on sand or mud flats at depths of 3 to 12 m (10 to 39 ft.). It hides under the substrate during the day and comes out to feed at night.
Captive Care: This is a more diminutive species that is well suited to smaller aquariums. Provide it with at least 2.5 cm (1 in.) of sand and plenty of open substrate to rest on and move over. It is not appropriate for most reef aquariums due to a lack of open bottom space and the fact that it is a threat to small crustaceans and any benthic fishes it can swallow whole.
Aquarium Size: 30 gal. **Temperature:** 22 to 27°C (72 to 80°F).
Aquarium Suitability Index: 4.
Remarks: In this species, the ridge under the eye is finely serrated, the iris lappet is bilobed, and the distance between the eyes (the interorbital width) is 5.5 to 6.0 times the eye diameter.

Genus *Thysanophrys*

Thysanophrys arenicola (Schultz, 1966)
Common Names: Broadhead Flathead, Sand Flathead.
Maximum Length: 26 cm (10.2 in.).
Distribution: East Africa to the Marshall Islands, north to Taiwan and the Ryukyus.
Biology: The Broadhead Flathead is most often found either partially buried or resting on the surface of sand substrate. It occurs at depths of less than 1 to at least 15 m (3.3 to 49 ft.). This ambush predator feeds on crabs (including xanthid and protunid crabs), shrimps, and small fishes that venture past. It sometimes forms large aggregations on shallow intertidal sand flats.
Captive Care: See the Captive Care section in the subfamily account, page 510.
Aquarium Size: 30 gal. **Temperature:** 22 to 27°C (72 to 80°F).
Aquarium Suitability Index: 4.
Remarks: In *T. arenicola*, the interorbital width is 1.1 to 2.0 times the eye diameter, and the snout is broad and round.

Thysanophrys celebica (Bleeker, 1854)
Common Name: Sulawesi Flathead.
Maximum Length: 17 cm (6.7 in.).
Distribution: East Africa and Arabian Gulf east to Indonesia, north to southern Japan, and south to Queensland.

Thysanophrys chiltonae, Longsnout Flathead: an appealing, modestly sized flathead species that does require a particularly large aquarium.

Biology: This species occurs on sand or mud bottoms in protected bays and lagoons, usually adjacent to coral reefs, at depths of less than 1.8 to at least 12 m (6 to 39 ft.). It will bury during the day and emerge from the substrate at night to feed and spawn.
Captive Care: See the Captive care section in the family account, page 510.
Aquarium Size: 30 gal. **Temperature:** 22 to 27°C (72 to 80°F).
Aquarium Suitability Index: 4.
Remarks: The body of *Thysanophrys celebica* is flecked with dark brown and white, and there are small black spots on all fins (except the anal fin). Some individuals have a thick white band on the back behind the head, a darker bar on the dorsum below the base of each dorsal fin, and a saddle on the caudal peduncle. The interorbital width is 3.9 to 4.5 times the eye diameter.

Thysanophrys chiltonae Schultz, 1966
Common Name: Longsnout Flathead.
Maximum Length: 25 cm (9.8 in.).
Distribution: Red Sea to the Marquesas and Line Islands.
Biology: The Longsnout Flathead occurs on sand bottoms, in protected bays and lagoons, on coastal reef flats, and in reef passes at depths of less than 1 to 80 m (3.3 to 260 ft.). It often buries under the substrate.
Captive Care: See the Captive Care section in the family account, page 510.
Aquarium Size: 30 gal. **Temperature:** 22 to 27°C (72 to 80°F).
Aquarium Suitability Index: 4.
Remarks: In this species, the interorbital width is 5 to 6 times the eye diameter. There is a ridge on the dorsal surface of the head with well-developed spines and a ridge under the eye with four or more spines. The iris lappet has slender lobes. The **Fringelip Flathead** (*Thysanophrys otaitensis*) (**Cuvier, 1829**) is another species that is often found near coastal reefs. It is easily recognized by the presence of skin flaps on the lips. The interorbital width is 2.1 to 2.9 times the eye diameter, and in many individuals, the pectoral fins have a checkered appearance. The Fringelip Flathead attains a maximum length of 25 cm (9.8 in.) and ranges from East Africa to the Tuamotus, north to Taiwan, and south to Queensland.

References
Hiatt & Stratsburg (1960), Kuiter (1996), Kuiter & Debelius (1994), Myers (1991), Randall (1995), Randall et al. (1990).

Family Dactylopteridae
Helmut Gurnards

With pelvic fin rays that allow them to "walk" and anterior pectoral rays that they use either as fingerlike tools or as winglike defensive devices, the helmut gurnards are a pleasure to encounter on the reef, but somewhat of a challenge for interested aquarists. Along with the scorpionfishes and several other families, the helmut gurnards are members of the Order Scorpaeniformes. Unlike the scorpionfishes, however, the helmut gurnards lack both head spines and venomous fin spines. Their most notable features are large pectoral fins that resemble wings when they swim over the substrate. It was once thought that helmut gurnards could use these fins—the way flying fishes do—to leap from the water and glide over the ocean's surface. However, the fins lack the rigidity needed to allow this. The helmut gurnards are relatively slow-moving and spend their lives near the seafloor. They are closely related, and somewhat similar in appearance, to the sea robins (Family Triglidae), although the helmut gurnards have two separate dorsal fins, a bulbous head, a rounded snout, and a shoulder girdle that extends backward and ends in a sharp spine.

Classification and Biology

The Family Dactylopteridae is comprised of two genera and seven species. Two species are commonly found around coral reefs and both of these are occasionally encountered in the aquarium trade. Several forms also occur in deep water. For example, Tilton's Helmut Gurnard (*Dactyloptena tiltoni*) is found on mud bottoms at a depth range of 119 to 565 m (387 to 1,836 ft.). The majority of species, however, live in shallow water and do not associate with coral reef habitats.

The pelvic fin rays of the helmut gurnards are similar to legs and are used to move—both forward and backward—over the bottom. The first three anterior pectoral rays are used like fingers to probe the substrate and turn over rubble to locate food items. Helmut gurnards have fairly large mouths and feed on amphipods, crabs, mantis shrimp, small bivalves, and small benthic fishes. Most of this feeding apparently occurs after dark, although they also feed during the day.

During the day, helmut gurnards are often found sitting on

Dactylopterus volitans, Flying Gurnard: gliding over Caribbean seagrass with its winglike pelvic fins, it offers a rewarding sight for divers and snorkelers.

the seafloor. When alarmed, they spread their pectoral fins, displaying the colorful markings on the upper surface of the fins. This also increases the fish's apparent size by about five times, which makes it a more formidable target to predators. If pressed, a helmut gurnard will try to swim away with rapid beats of the tail, and may do so with the pectoral fins either open or closed. When pursued, they often swim in circles. Helmut gurnards are capable of producing sounds by using the hyomandibular arch.

Although the reproductive behavior of these fishes has yet to be described, they are apparently broadcast spawners, with pelagic eggs and larvae. Prejuveniles are also pelagic and can be attracted to a light after dark.

Captive Care

Young helmut gurnards are occasionally encountered in the aquarium trade. Although they can be successfully kept in the home aquarium, they are not suitable for all aquariums nor every aquarist. Even a small specimen needs at least a 75-gallon tank with plenty of open, sandy bottom. Decor should be kept to a minimum. A few small mounds of live rock or other aquascaping material could be used, but should cover a minimal amount of the aquarium bottom. Decorations should not be placed close to the aquarium glass, as an agitated helmut gurnard could become wedged between the decorations and the glass.

Helmut gurnards are best kept in a tank away from high traffic areas, where they may become agitated and collide with or rub up against the sides of the tank. If a helmut gurnard does begin swimming against the glass, a 3- or 4-inch-wide piece of black plastic should be placed along the bottom of the aquarium (as described for walking batfishes, page 359). This should discourage the fish from engaging in this behavior.

Helmut gurnards are not easy to feed. They are most likely to accept live foods like marine worms (e.g., bristleworms), black worms, brine and mysid shrimp (they will only pick these off the substrate), amphipods, and grass shrimp. In time, they can be enticed into taking small pieces of shrimp or fish from a feeding stick.

These fishes should not be housed with aggressive tankmates like angelfishes, large damselfishes, hawkfishes of the genus *Paracirrhites*, puffers, porcupinefishes, or triggerfishes. On the other hand, the helmut gurnards have relatively large mouths and will eat small bottom-dwelling fishes like gobies. They might also consume small ornamental shrimps. Do not keep this fish with stinging invertebrates, particularly carpet anemones, as they often collide with and will be stung by these noxious creatures.

These fishes are not suitably housed in most reef tanks because they need more open bottom space than can usually be provided in that setting.

HELMUT GURNARD SPECIES

Dactyloptena orientalis (Cuvier, 1829)
Common Name: Oriental Helmut Gurnard.
Maximum Length: 38 cm (15.0 in.).
Distribution: East Africa to the Hawaiian, Marquesas, and Tuamotu Islands, north to southern Japan, and south to New Zealand.
Biology: The Oriental Helmut Gurnard lives on shallow sand flats and sand slopes with scattered coral heads. It most often occurs at depths of 1 to 45 m (3.3 to 146 ft.), but has been taken in trawls as deep as 100 m (325 ft.). These fish typically occur singly, but occasionally are observed in pairs. It either swims near or sits on the substrate, and will partially bury itself. *Dactyloptena orientalis* feeds on sand-dwelling crustaceans, mollusks, worms, and bottom-dwelling fishes.
Captive Care: See the Captive Care section in the family account, page 515.
Aquarium Size: 180 gal. **Temperature:** 22 to 28°C (72 to 82°F).

TABLE 24
Possible Tankmates for the Oriental Helmut Gurnard*

Sand Lizardfish	(*Synodus dermatogenys*)**
Blackblotch Lizardfish	(*Synodus jaculum*)
Redmarbled Lizardfish	(*Synodus rubromaculatus*)
Dragon Sea Moth	(*Eurypegasus draconis*)
Devilfishes	(*Inimicus* spp.)
Longsnout Flathead	(*Thysanophrys chiltonae*)
Fringelip Flathead	(*Thysanophrys otaitensis*)
Indian Goatfish	(*Parupeneus indicus*)
Sidespot Goatfish	(*Parupeneus pleurostigma*)
Yellowblotch Razorfish	(*Xyrichtys aneitensis*)**
Pavo Razorfish	(*Xyrichtys pavo*)**
Knife Razorfish	(*Cymolutes praetextatus*)**
Finescale Razorfish	(*Cymolutes torquatus*)**
Fingered Dragonet	(*Dactylopus dactylopus*)
Steinitz's Shrimp Goby	(*Amblyeleotris steinitzi*)
Yellow Shrimp Goby	(*Cryptocentrus cinctus*)
Banded Goby	(*Amblygobius phalaena*)
Orangespotted Sleeper Goby	(*Valenciennea puellaris*)
Filament Dartfish	(*Ptereleotris hanae*)
Spottail Dartfish	(*Ptereleotris heteroptera*)
Green Dartfish	(*Ptereleotris microlepis*)
Sand divers	(*Trichonotus* spp.)
Soles	(Soleidae)
Lefteye flounders	(Bothidae)

* Large helmut gurnards may consume fishes they can swallow whole.
** Large lizardfishes may attempt to eat juvenile helmut gurnards.
*** As adults, razorfishes can be aggressive toward helmut gurnards and other fishes.

Dactyloptena orientalis, Oriental Helmut Gurnard: requires room to roam.

Aquarium Suitability Index: 3.
Remarks: All of the *Dactyloptena* species have one or two dorsal spines separated from the rest of the spiny portion of the dorsal fin. *Dactyloptena orientalis* has two. Other distinguishing characteristics of this species include dark spots on the pectoral fins (which are more distinct in individuals over 15 cm [5.9 in.] Standard Length), a dark ocellus on the pectoral fin in smaller specimens (5 to 6 cm [2.0 to 2.4 in.] SL), and large spots on the upper portion of the head (noted in specimens over 10 cm [3.9 in.] SL). At night, the Oriental Helmut Gurnard becomes orange overall.

TABLE 25

Possible Tankmates for the Flying Gurnard*

Inshore Lizardfish	(*Synodus foetens*)
Shortnose Batfish	(*Ogcocephalus nasutus*)
Polkadot Batfish	(*Ogcocephalus cubifrons*)
Bandtail Sea Robin	(*Prionotus ophryas*)
Tobacco Fish	(*Serranus tabacarius*)
Sand Tilefish	(*Malacanthus plumieri*)
Mojarra	(*Gerres* spp.)
Yellow Goatfish	(*Mulloidichthys martinicus*)
Spotted Goatfish	(*Parupeneus maculatus*)
Pearly Razorfish	(*Xyrichtys novacula*)
Rosy Razorfish	(*Xyrichtys martinicensis*)
Green Razorfish	(*Xyrichtys splendens*)
Pudding Wife	(*Halichoeres radiatus*)
Slippery Dick	(*Halichoeres bivittatus*)
Yellowhead Jawfish	(*Opistognathus aurifrons*)
Spotfin Jawfish	(*Opistognathus* sp.)
Blue Goby	(*Ptereleotris calliurus*)
Hovering Goby	(*Ptereleotris helenae*)
Orangespotted Goby	(*Nes longus*)
Lefteye flounders	(Bothidae)

* Large helmut gurnards may consume fishes they can swallow whole.

Dactyloptena orientalis, Oriental Helmut Gurnard: juvenile specimen.

Dactyloptena orientalis, Oriental Helmut Gurnard: adult at night.

Dactylopterus volitans (Linnaeus, 1758)

Common Names: Flying Gurnard, Atlantic Helmut Gurnard.
Maximum Length: 45 cm (17.7 in.).
Distribution: Massachusetts and Bermuda to Argentina, east to Ascension Island and the Eastern Atlantic.
Biology: The Flying Gurnard lives on sand flats or slopes at the edge of the reef and in seagrass beds, at depths of 1 to 12 m (3.3 to 39 ft.). It feeds mainly on crabs (including decorator and swimming crabs), but also eats mantis shrimps, penaeid shrimps, small benthic fishes, and amphipods. It usually occurs singly.
Captive Care: See the Captive Care section in the family account, page 515.
Aquarium Size: 180 gal. **Temperature:** 22 to 28°C (72 to 82°F).
Aquarium Suitability Index: 3.
Remarks: This is the only species in the genus *Dactylopterus*. It is unique in that the first two dorsal spines are equal in length, right next to each other, and connected to the rest of the dorsal fin.

References
Eschmeyer (1997), Randall (1967), Randall et al. (1990).

Dactylopterus volitans, Flying Gurnard: usually occurs singly in nature.

SUBFAMILY SERRANINAE
DWARF SEABASSES AND HAMLETS

FROM ENCOUNTERS ON SALTWATER FISHING TRIPS, AT SEAFOOD markets and restaurants, or during visits to public aquariums, many people have come into contact with the Family Serranidae. Depending where you are in the world, members of the Family Serranidae are referred to by a throng of common names, including seabass, grouper, coral trout, coral cod, rock cod, groper, hind, graysby, scamp, and rockfish. There are nearly 400 species in this family, which range in size from 5 cm (2 in.) Lilliputians that barely tip the scales at several ounces, to piscine mammoths that grow to over 3 m (9.8 ft.) in length and weigh over 409 kg (900 lbs.). Many members of this family get too large and are too predatory for the average home aquarium—making great subjects for seafood chefs as well as underwater photographers. However, several subfamilies of the Serranidae include highly desirable and exceptionally attractive specimens for the marine aquarist, among them the dwarf seabasses, hamlets, anthias, grammas, a number of smaller groupers, and the reef basslets. In this section, we will cover the Subfamily Serraninae (dwarf seabasses and hamlets), and in the next section we discuss the Subfamily Anthiinae (the anthias). The Subfamily Epinephelinae, which includes the Tribes Epinephelini (groupers), Liopropomini (reef basslets), and Diploprionini and Grammistini (soapfishes), will appear in Volume 2 of this series.

Many members of the Subfamily Serraninae are especially well suited to the home aquarium. This subfamily contains 13 genera and 75 species, with the dwarf seabasses (genus *Serranus*) and the hamlets (genus *Hypoplectrus*) both well known to many aquarists. Both of these groups contain a number of smaller, readily available species that can be housed in small- to medium-sized aquariums with a wide range of fish tankmates.

Genus *Serranus* (Dwarf Seabasses)

The dwarf seabasses are commonly encountered in North American aquarium stores and by underwater visitors to Caribbean reefs. They are well-suited to captivity because of their small sizes, with most members of the genus *Serranus* not exceeding 15 cm (6 in.) in maximum length. The largest species in the genus attains 36 cm (14 in.) in maximum length.

Hypoplectrus puella, Barred Hamlet (blue-phase specimen): member of a large family of fishes of special interest to aquarists and divers (Bonaire).

Biology

The dwarf seabasses are circumtropical in distribution, but are most common in the tropical Western Atlantic. The majority of these fishes associate with rocky and coral reefs; some also occur in seagrass meadows or on open bottoms comprised of a mixture of sand and rubble. Several members of the genus are more common on deep-reef slopes. The Orangeback Bass (*Serranus annularis*), for example, is abundant at depths greater than 27 m (88 ft.), while the Snow Bass (*Serranus chionaraia*) is rarely encountered in less than 45 m (146 ft.) of water. While most dwarf seabasses are limited to tropical seas, a handful of species are found in warm temperate waters.

The majority of dwarf seabasses are diurnal, opportunistic carnivores that feed most heavily on crustaceans and small fishes. The Chalk Bass (*Serranus tortugarum*) is an exception; it feeds mainly on zooplankton. All the dwarf seabasses are substrate-bound and, with the exception of their spawning ascents, rarely move more than 30 cm (12 in.) off the bottom. Some species are territorial, while others form aggregations (see individual species accounts, starting on page 520).

One of the unique aspects of dwarf seabass biology is their sexuality and the various mating systems displayed by different species. All the dwarf seabasses studied thus far are simultaneous hermaphrodites; that is, an individual has functional male and female sex organs at the same time. Sperm and eggs are released at different times and through separate openings to prevent self-fertilization, although this will occur if reproductively ready individuals are isolated from conspecifics. Many of the seabasses do not release all their eggs at the same time, but instead expel them in several batches during the spawning period (in most species, the spawning period is several hours before sunset). This is known as egg parceling.

In most cases, seabasses also alternate sexual roles. That is, each individual will release eggs and sperm during a single spawning period. This is referred to as egg trading. Those individuals that do not exhibit this alternation of sexual roles will be discriminated against by potential mates in the future. The dwarf seabasses also engage in egg advertisement: during courtship, individuals advertise the fact that they have ripe eggs by displaying their swollen abdomens to a potential partner.

Dwarf seabasses employ a variety of mating systems, including serial monogamy and permanent monogamy. Serial monogamy describes the behavior in which an individual spawns with the same mate for an extended period of time, but not for life (e.g., Chalk Bass, *Serranus tortugarum*). Permanent monogamy is the pattern in which individuals form lifelong pair bonds (e.g., Harlequin Bass, *Serranus tigrinus*). In these monogamous mating systems, being larger does not equate with greater mating success. Other seabasses engage in polygynous, or haremic, mating systems in which large individuals mate with, and are able to defend, more than one mate at a predictable location (e.g., Lantern Bass, *Serranus baldwini*).

Captive Care

Dwarf seabasses are well suited to the home aquarium. They are relatively diminutive in size; they accept most aquarium fare, including finely chopped fresh and frozen seafoods, brine shrimp, mysid shrimp, black worms, live baby guppies, frozen preparations, and even flake foods; and they are colorfast and disease-resistant.

One prerequisite for the dwarf seabass aquarium is that it have an abundance of hiding places. This will help reduce aggression between seabass individuals, as well as toward other fish tankmates. Dwarf seabasses can be kept in reef aquariums, but most species will eat small crustaceans and fishes that are small enough to fit into their mouths. In a fish-only aquarium, feed dwarf seabasses at least once a day; in a reef aquarium, feed them a minimum of every other day. Although not a common occurrence, dwarf seabasses may jump out of an open aquarium.

The dwarf seabasses vary considerably in their disposition from one species to the next. Some members of this genus will behave aggressively toward smaller, more docile species like cardinalfishes, small wrasses, dartfishes, and gobies. They are also likely to attack and chase other substrate-bound fishes with similar dietary habits, especially if the seabasses are already resident in the aquarium when these new fishes are introduced. Other dwarf seabasses are quite mild-mannered and are more likely to be the targets of aggressive behavior. Their smaller maximum sizes make them more vulnerable to piscivorous predators like lizardfishes, frogfishes, scorpionfishes, groupers, and jacks.

Because of their hardiness and small size, dwarf seabasses are great candidates for captive breeding. At least one species, the Belted Sandfish (*Serranus subligarius*), has already been bred in aquarium confines. The best way to induce spawning is to place several adult specimens in a large aquarium (minimum 135 gallons for smaller species) that contains several coral heads spaced equidistant from one another. Feed a diet that includes live foods, such as enriched adult brine shrimp.

DWARF SEABASS SPECIES

Serranus annularis (Günther, 1880)
Common Name: Orangeback Bass.
Maximum Length: 9 cm (3.5 in.).
Distribution: South Florida and Bermuda to Venezuela.
Biology: The Orangeback Bass occurs on deep sand flats, near rocky outcroppings, or over coral rubble mounds. It can be found at depths from 10 to 70 m (33 to 228 ft.), but it is usually not seen in water less than 27 m (88 ft.) deep and is most abundant at depths greater than 36 m (117 ft.). It swims just above the bottom and shelters among loggerhead sponges, rocks, and coral rubble. Not much is known about the social organization of this fish, but it is frequently observed in pairs.
Captive Care: The Orangeback Bass is a durable fish that feeds on most aquarium fare. Only one specimen should be kept per tank, unless you can acquire a pair, and even then they should only be housed in a larger aquarium (11,600 cm^2 [1,800 in.^{2}] of surface area or larger) with numerous hiding places. The two fish must be added to the tank simultaneously. This species may behave aggressively toward congeners in smaller tanks. I have seen trios kept in large tanks with a surface area greater than 12,900 cm^2 (2,000 in.^{2}). In this situation, a dominant fish would move between two subordinates, restricting their movements to opposite ends of the aquarium. The larger specimen would frequently chase the two subordinates for short periods of time, but was not observed to do any physical harm. The Orangeback Bass is also a threat to passive fish species—like certain anthias, juvenile grammas, small wrasses, fire gobies, dart gobies, and small shrimp gobies—if space and hiding places are in short supply.

Although this species prefers the lower-light levels of the deep fore reef, it can be acclimated to the brighter conditions characteristic of a shallow-water reef tank (although its color may fade in brighter conditions). It will eat smaller ornamental shrimps and may attack and nip at larger specimens. Because the Orangeback Bass lives in deeper water, it is uncommon in the aquarium trade and commands a higher price than its cousins.
Aquarium Size: 20 gal. **Temperature:** 22 to 27°C (72 to 80°F).
Aquarium Suitability Index: 5.
Remarks: The orange on this fish can vary in intensity. Although it has been suggested that these color differences may represent chromatic differences between the sexes, this has not been demonstrated.

Serranus baldwini (Evermann & Marsh, 1900)
Common Name: Lantern Bass.
Maximum Length: 7 cm (2.8 in.).
Distribution: South Florida and Bermuda to Venezuela.
Biology: The Lantern Bass occurs on coral rubble and in Turtle Grass (*Thalassia testudinum*). In Turtle Grass meadows, it is most abundant where the grass is thin, on the seaward edge of the bed. The density of Lantern Bass in this habitat can range from two to eight fish in an area of 10 m^2 (108 ft.^{2}). It also frequents the rubble mounds constructed by the Sand Tilefish (*Malacanthus plumieri*). *Serranus baldwini* is a diurnal species that feeds on caridean shrimps and small fishes. Its relatively small size means that it is vulnerable to piscivores and therefore rarely moves more than 25 cm (10 in.) off the bottom. At dusk it hides in holes or under coral rubble.

The Lantern Bass mating system is quite unusual for a serranid. Small individuals are simultaneous hermaphrodites, while large specimens function as males only. Males defend an exclusive area, containing one or more hermaphrodites, from other large Lantern Bass. Hermaphrodites are usually ignored by males (except during courtship or mating), but they will occasionally chase them from one hiding place to another. Defending a territory can be costly for a male Lantern Bass. For example, a male that was observed fighting with a conspecific was eaten by a lizardfish (*Synodus* sp.). If a male territory holder should perish, the most dominant hermaphrodite will take his place. Unlike most of the other hermaphroditic seabasses, male Lantern Bass initiate the mating process. Males are much more aggressive and more active (i.e., patrolling their territories) than hermaphroditic individuals.

The Lantern Bass begins spawning about 1½ hours before sunset. Courtship begins when a male begins to bob and jerk as he approaches a hermaphrodite. To bob, the fish erects its median fins and moves up and down while keeping its body horizontal; to jerk, the individual moves forward in a lurching and erratic fashion. If the hermaphrodite does not swim away, the male begins nudging it with his snout. A sexually receptive hermaphrodite will point; that is, it will hover with its body in a slight S-curve and its head pointed slightly upward. This is an invitation to the male to spawn. The male will move alongside the hermaphrodite, placing his chin on the posterior part of its back. Then the two fish rapidly ascend 25 to 75 cm (9.8 to 30 in.) into the water column to disperse their gametes. If a hermaphrodite ignores a courting male, the male will swim away or chase the hermaphrodite. Streaking behavior (in which a noncourting individual intercepts a spawning pair and releases its gametes) is also rare in Lantern Bass mating systems.

Serranus annularis, Orangeback Bass: somewhat uncommon but hardy.

Serranus annularis, Orangeback Bass: variant.

Serranus baldwini, Lantern Bass: hardy with a mildly aggressive disposition.

Captive Care: *Serranus baldwini* is a hardy aquarium fish that is disease-resistant and will accept most aquarium fare. It should be placed in a tank with numerous hiding places and housed with moderately aggressive tankmates (e.g., hamlets, grunts, pygmy angelfishes, the Spotted Hawkfish [*Cirrhitichthys aprinus*], hogfishes, other large wrasses, damselfishes, and/or surgeonfishes). It should not be kept with passive fishes, especially in smaller aquariums. Keeping two of these fish in a larger tank (i.e., 11,600 cm^2 [1,800 in.^{2}] of surface area or larger) is a possibility. Select smaller specimens, add them simultaneously, and observe them carefully for the first week or more in case aggressive encounters occur. If fights begin, be prepared to remove one specimen. The Lantern Bass is suitable for a shallow- or deep-water reef aquarium, although it will eat ornamental shrimps.
Aquarium Size: 20 gal. **Temperature:** 22 to 27°C (72 to 80°F).
Aquarium Suitability Index: 5.
Remarks: The color of *S. baldwini* is somewhat variable, with the body markings ranging from rusty brown to yellowish orange. The **Snow Bass (*Serranus chionaraia*) Robins & Starck, 1961** is a deep-water species (it occurs at a depth range from 45 to almost 300 m [146 to 975 ft.]) that ranges from south Florida to the northern Caribbean. This small bass should be kept with peaceful tankmates in a tank with plenty of cover. It will also adjust more readily to the captive environment if the tank is dimly lit, making it a better candidate for the deep-water reef aquarium than its shallow-water counterpart. The Snow Bass has three blue stripes on its head and white on its belly.

Serranus flaviventris (Cuvier & Valenciennes, 1829)
Common Name: Twospot Bass.
Maximum Length: 7.5 cm (2.9 in.).
Distribution: Greater Antilles to Uruguay.
Biology: The Twospot Bass is a resident of rocky and coral reefs and seagrass beds, at depths from 2 to 402 m (7 to 1,307 ft.).
Captive Care: *Serranus flaviventris* is a hardy aquarium fish, suitable for the beginning aquarist as well as the seasoned veteran. This species is disease-resistant and will accept flake, fresh, and frozen seafoods and frozen prepared foods. It may behave aggressively toward other dwarf seabasses and more passive fish species, especially in smaller aquariums. The Twospot Bass can be kept in a shallow-water or deep-water reef aquarium, although it will consume smaller ornamental shrimps. This species is not often seen in aquarium stores because of its more southern distribution and its muted coloration. There is a strong possibility that this species, like some of its close relatives, could be successfully bred in captivity.
Aquarium Size: 20 gal. **Temperature:** 23 to 27°C (74 to 80°F).
Aquarium Suitability Index: 5.
Remarks: This species is similar to the Belted Sandfish (*Serranus subligarius*) but lacks spots on the rays of the pectoral and caudal fins and has two bold spots on the caudal peduncle.

Serranus phoebe Poey, 1852
Common Name: Tattler Bass.
Maximum Length: 10 cm (3.9 in.).
Distribution: Bermuda, North Carolina, South Carolina, Bermuda, and the Yucatan Peninsula to Venezuela.
Biology: The Tattler Bass occurs on rocky reefs at depths from 27 up to 180 m (88 to 585 ft.), but in many areas it is most abundant at depths greater than 50 m (163 ft.). It has also been observed living in burrows under rocks lying on deep sand slopes.
Captive Care: The Tattler Bass tank should have plenty of hiding

Serranus flaviventris, Twospot Bass: small, easily kept Western Atlantic fish.

Serranus phoebe, Tattler Bass: attractive little Caribbean-Atlantic species.

Serranus subligarius, Belted Sandfish: will spawn readily in captivity.

places. It is not unusual for this fish to hide for several days when first introduced to the aquarium, but it will soon learn to associate the aquarist with food. While juvenile Tattler Bass can be kept in a docile community tank, adults may pick on smaller, less aggressive species. It is better suited for deep-water reef aquariums.
Aquarium Size: 20 gal. **Temperature:** 19 to 26°C (66 to 78°F).
Aquarium Suitability Index: 5.

Serranus subligarius Cope, 1870
Common Names: Belted Sandfish, Belted Sandbass, Mouse Bass.
Maximum Length: 10 cm (3.9 in.)
Distribution: Northern Gulf of Mexico from Texas to Florida and along the Atlantic coast from Florida to North Carolina.
Biology: The Belted Sandfish is most common in turbid conditions on limestone reef outcroppings, near jetties, and over mixed sand and rubble bottoms. It occurs at depths from less than 1 m (3.3 ft.) to at least 26 m (85 ft.). Specimens larger than about 5 cm (2 in.) feed mainly on amphipods, crabs, shrimps, and fishes, while those less than 5 cm (2 in.) feed mostly on copepods, amphipods, and shrimps. The Belted Sandfish will also feed on members of its own species on occasion. *Serranus subligarius* usually defends an exclusive territory, except during the breeding season when pairs and trios of these fish occur in the same areas. Belted Sandfish are simultaneous hermaphrodites that develop male reproductive organs in the first year of life, while the ovarian tissue appears in the second year. In northern Florida, the spawning season lasts from late April or early May to September, with spawning taking place in the late afternoon and early evening before sunset. Courtship begins when the individual playing the female role swims alongside or in front of a likely mate, contorts her body into an S-curve, raises all her fins, and quivers. The other fish, which will potentially function as the male, responds by ignoring, nipping at, or swimming in a jerky fashion alongside the S-curving female. In the latter case, the "male" will begin nudging the "female's" abdomen and back with his snout. Then the pair will dash up into the water column, release their gametes at the apex of their ascent, and rush back to the bottom. Courtship resumes again, but this time the individuals reverse sexual roles. During courtship, the bands on the side of the body and the dark spot at the base of the dorsal fin fades in the "female," while the markings on the "male" darken. Although individuals usually mate with conspecifics, isolated individuals in captivity have been known to engage in self-fertilization; that is, they fertilize their own eggs.
Captive Care: The Belted Sandfish is a durable aquarium fish that has spawned in captivity. All that is necessary to encourage spawning is a medium-sized aquarium, some hiding places (e.g., ceramic flowerpots or live rock) and two Belted Sandfish, which should be introduced to the tank together. Feeding them frequently may also help encourage spawning.
Aquarium Size: 20 gal. **Temperature:** 20 to 27°C (68 to 80°F).
Aquarium Suitability Index: 5.

> ### The Deep-Water Dwarf Seabass Community Aquarium
>
> The dwarf seabass aficionado may want to set up an aquarium for small serranids and the fishes that share their natural habitat. Use an aquarium of 75 gallons or larger, and place 5 cm (2 in.) of live sand on the bottom. Add enough live rock to form a low profile reef with one or two prominent spires that reach halfway up the tank. Leave at least half the aquarium bottom free of large pieces of live rock, and scatter smaller pieces of rubble over some of this area. To simulate the blue light conditions of deep water, use two actinic bulbs for each daylight bulb or up to three actinics and one daylight bulb in a four-bulb hood. Add four or more Chalk Bass (*Serranus tortugarum*) to the tank first. Over the next several months, add a juvenile Cuban Hogfish (*Bodianus pulchellus*), one or two Blackcap Basslets (*Gramma melacara*) and a small school (three or more, depending on the size of your tank) of larger Sunshine Chromis (*Chromis insolatus*). Finally, introduce a small Wrasse Bass (*Liopropoma eukrines*) and an Orangeback Bass (*Serranus annularis*). Once all the fishes have been introduced, you will have successfully re-created a deep-water bass community.

Serranus tabacarius, Tobacco Fish: coloration displayed over rubble substrate.

Serranus tabacarius, Tobacco Fish: coloration exhibited over sand.

Serranus tabacarius (Cuvier & Valenciennes, 1829)
Common Names: Tobacco Fish, Tobacco Bass.
Maximum Length: 18 cm (7.1 in.).
Distribution: South Florida and Bermuda to southern Brazil.
Biology: The Tobacco Fish occurs on sand slopes near reefs and on mixed sand, rock, and coral rubble at the edge of the reef. It also is found in Turtle Grass (*Thalassia testudinum*) beds. It occurs at depths from 3 to 70 m (10 to 228 ft.), but is most common at depths between 10 and 45 m (33 and 146 ft.). Population density can measure as many as seven individuals in an area of 1,000 m^2 (10,760 ft.^{2}). During the day, *S. tabacarius* sits on the sand or swims just above it, while at night, it shelters under rocks and rubble. This bass feeds mainly on fishes, but will also eat small crustaceans that live on the sand surface. Individual *S. tabacarius* have large, overlapping home ranges that correlate with their size (the larger the individual, the larger its territory).

A Tobacco Fish does not defend its home range from conspecifics during the nonreproductive period of the day; in fact, two to four individuals often forage together in the same area. When mating, individuals perform lateral displays (the median fins are erected when conspecifics are parallel), frontal displays (the gill covers are flared when conspecifics are facing), and chase away other conspecifics. Larger *S. tabacarius* engage in more aggressive behaviors than smaller ones.

Tobacco Fish mate from midafternoon to shortly after dusk, anywhere within a home range. Courtship begins when individuals, separated by a distance of 1 to 10 m (3.3 to 33 ft.), display to each other by hanging up to 1 m (3.3 ft.) over the bottom and performing "short arching swims" with their tails curved upward. One fish (the initiator) then approaches a prospective mate (the follower), quivering and distorting its body into an S-shaped curve. The follower either ignores the initiator, swims away, or begins bumping the vent area of the initiator with its mouth. After a variable number of bumps, the initiator turns to face the follower and the pair dashes up into the water column to release their gametes. At the apex of the ascent, the follower expels sperm and the initiator releases eggs. On rare occasions, a third individual may engage in streaking behavior. In streaking, the third fish (which in nonsimultaneous hermaphrodites would be a male) joins the pair in the spawning ascent, releasing gametes along with the other two fish. After spawning, the pair swims back to the bottom, at which time one fish may attempt to initiate spawning again. Individuals typically reverse sexual roles, with the partner that expelled eggs now taking on the male role, while the individual that released sperm now becoming the female partner. There are some advantages in being a bigger bass; larger individuals tend to spawn with more mates and spawn more often as males. A Tobacco Fish may spawn as many as 16 times in one day, with from one to nine different partners. In about half of the spawning events, an individual will act as a male; in the other half, it will function as a female.

Captive Care: The Tobacco Fish is a durable aquarium species that is suitable for aquarists at all levels of experience. Although it is not one of the most colorful members of the group, its interesting behavior and relatively peaceful disposition make it a great choice for a fish-community tank as well as a reef tank (although *S. tabacarius* will eat any ornamental shrimps or fishes that can fit into its mouth). Because this species attains a larger maximum size than many other dwarf seabasses, it will become a greater threat to more diminutive species like damselfishes, gobies, and blennies as it grows. More than one Tobacco Fish can be kept in a larger aquarium (11,600 cm^2 [1,800 in.^{2}] of surface area or

Serranus tigrinus, Harlequin Bass (juvenile): durable but a natural predator.

Serranus tigrinus, Harlequin Bass: cooperatively hunt their prey.

larger), but the individuals selected should all be small in size and introduced to the tank at the same time. Avoid larger Tobacco Fish if you are attempting to keep more than one, because they are socially dominant and may harass smaller specimens. This species may be bullied by more aggressive fishes, especially those that are bottom-dwelling, such as large hawkfishes and large sand perches.
Aquarium Size: 55 gal. **Temperature:** 22 to 27°C (72 to 80°F).
Aquarium Suitability Index: 5.

Serranus tigrinus (Bloch, 1790)
Common Name: Harlequin Bass.
Maximum Length: 10 cm (3.9 in.).
Distribution: North Florida and Bermuda to Venezuela.
Biology: This is the most common dwarf seabass on shallow reefs in the Caribbean. It occurs at depths of 2 to 36 m (7 to 117 ft.) among coral rubble on the reef flat. The diet of the Harlequin Bass is mainly caridean shrimps, but this species also feeds on fishes, mantis shrimps, and crabs. Adult Harlequin Bass form long-term pair bonds. Pairs, solitary adults, and juveniles defend a specific area from conspecifics and other small fishes that are food competitors. Adult pair members stay within 2 m (7 ft.) of each other for most of the day; if one partner is lost, a solitary adult from a nearby territory will usually take its place. Pairs of these fish hunt cooperatively. As they patrol their territory together, they often move to opposite sides of a small coral or rubble outcrop, rapidly descending on it in unison. This behavior, known as synchronous hunting, functions to drive small prey out of one fish's way and into the path of the other.

The average territory size of a pair of Harlequin Bass measures 88 m^2 (947 ft.^{2}), while the size of the area defended by solitary adults and juveniles averages 37 m^2 (398 ft.^{2}) and 11 m^2 (188 ft.^{2}), respectively. Territorial boundaries are contiguous, with squabbles regularly breaking out when neighbors encounter one another at their borders. When neighbors do meet, they perform frontal or lateral displays. In the lateral display, they fully erect their median fins and tilt their bodies so that their dorsal fins are directed toward their opponent. If aggression escalates, the fish may swim in tight head-to-tail circles, chase, or even strike one another. If one pair member is engaged in a dispute, the other often arrives on the scene to aid in defense of the territory. Harlequin Bass have also been observed attacking food competitors like hamlets (*Hypoplectrus* spp.). For example, one Harlequin Bass chased a Black Hamlet (*Hypoplectrus nigricans*) 43 times on 13 consecutive nights. These bass will also drive small parrotfishes from their nocturnal shelter sites; the Harlequin Bass, in turn, are chased by small groupers and larger damselfishes.

Harlequin Bass spawn in their territories just before sunset. The individual acting as the female initiates spawning by holding its body in an S-curve for 1 to 2 seconds, with its belly facing its suitor. If it is interested in spawning, the other pair member will approach the initiating fish. When close together, the pair will rapidly ascend into the water column 1 to 2 m (3.3 to 7 ft.). At the apex of the spawning ascent, the gametes are released. After the first spawning, the fish usually switch sexual roles and spawn one more time, after which they seek shelter for the night. On rare occasions, pairs will group spawn with neighboring, solitary individuals.
Captive Care: *Serranus tigrinus* is a hardy species well suited for small- to large-sized aquariums. It will eat any fishes, including cleaner species like neon gobies (*Gobiosoma* spp.) or crustaceans small enough to ingest. Do not keep more than one Harlequin Bass in a smaller aquarium unless you can acquire a mated pair. If

you have a larger tank, you can add two unpaired specimens simultaneously, but you will need to watch them carefully to make sure no fighting occurs. If they start chasing and biting each other, remove one specimen immediately. On the other hand, if they ignore each other or swim close together, there is good chance that they will form a pair. This species can be kept in a shallow- or deep-water reef aquarium.

Aquarium Size: 20 gal. **Temperature:** 22 to 27°C (72 to 80°F).
Aquarium Suitability Index: 5.

Serranus tortugarum Longley, 1935
Common Name: Chalk Bass.
Maximum Length: 8 cm (3.1 in.).
Distribution: South Florida and the Bahamas east to Honduras.
Biology: The beautiful little Chalk Bass is common on the leeward side of fringing reefs. It occurs on reef faces and fore-reef slopes at depths from 2 to 396 m (7 to 1,287 ft.). *Serranus tortugarum* is most abundant over rubble bottoms, but also occurs near coral outcrops in sand channels and on sandy slopes with less than 50% coral cover. In some areas, it also shelters in the rubble mounds constructed by Sand Tilefish (*Malacanthus plumieri*). The Chalk Bass lives in loose aggregations, numbering from 10 to 300 individuals, and feeds on zooplankton, including amphipods, copepods, and fish eggs. It has more numerous gill rakers than its congeners, which is an anatomical adaptation to feeding on small prey (i.e., zooplankton). It will swim up to 3 m (10 ft.) above the bottom when feeding, quickly retreating to cover when a potential predator swims past.

During the reproductive period of the day, pairs of Chalk Bass form three-dimensional territories, measuring 1 to 2 m (3.3

Serranus tortugarum, Chalk Bass: may be kept in groups and a wonderful fish for new aquarists, offering small size, dazzling colors, and a calm disposition.

to 7 ft.) on each side. Those engaged in mating can range from 3 to 5 cm (1 to 2 in.) Standard Length, but mating pairs usually consist of individuals of about the same size. Those Chalk Bass that do not find a mate move along the periphery of these territories in search of a partner. They employ two different courtship displays: the dip and the parallel swim. In the dip, an individual "pitches its body forward and down, then rights itself several times in succession." Dipping occurs during the spawning period, with females engaging in this behavior more than males. It is also employed by individuals when they leave a hiding place or when they move to sleeping sites at night. The parallel swim is a display performed when separated partners reunite. It consists of two fish swimming upward simultaneously for two or three body lengths.

During the spawning period, the individual that initiates mating is the first to release eggs. A pair can spawn as many as 17 times in a single day. In the vast majority of cases, individuals switch sex roles during subsequent spawnings. Courtship begins when one individual swims in front of the other, rises one or two body lengths into the water column, and erects its dorsal fin. The initiating fish may remain in this position for several minutes, until the lower fish suddenly dashes forward and the two fish "snap together in a quick embrace." Solitary and paired individuals often engage in delayed streaking behavior. These individuals dart to the position where a neighboring pair has just engaged in a spawning clasp, snap their bodies to one side, and then dart back to their original position. The function of this type of streaking is not known.

Captive Care: The Chalk Bass is a durable aquarium fish and a great first fish for beginning aquarists. Provide your Chalk Bass with plenty of hiding places and keep it with nonaggressive tankmates. It will spend most of its time hanging a few inches above the aquarium bottom, usually in the open. The Chalk Bass is usually not aggressive, even toward inoffensive species (e.g., cardinalfishes, small wrasses, and gobies), and even in smaller aquariums. It is best kept in small groups. Individuals will form dominance hierarchies, their rank in the pecking order being determined by their size. If you are keeping more than one *S. tortugarum* per aquarium, all individuals should be introduced simultaneously. This species is great for shallow- or deep-water reef tanks. It is a zooplankton feeder and will not bother crabs or most shrimps, with the possible exception of the delicate *Periclimenes* species.

Aquarium Size: 20 gal. **Temperature:** 22 to 27°C (72 to 80°F).
Aquarium Suitability Index: 5.
Remarks: The base color of this species can be blue, brown, or orange.

Diplectrum formosum, Sand Perch

The Durable Sand Perch

A number of species occur along the shores of North America that have yet to be fully appreciated by aquarists. One of these is the **Sand Perch (*Diplectrum formosum*)** Linnaeus, 1766. This is a smaller serranid (at least by grouper standards) that should not be confused with the sand perches of the Family Pinguipedidae. Although it has the ability to change its color pattern rapidly, it always has alternating bright blue and orange stripes running along its back and sides. The stripes tend to become more bold as it moves over the substrate. Large adults have a prolonged upper caudal lobe. *Diplectrum formosum* ranges from North Carolina to Uruguay and the Gulf of Mexico and attains a maximum length of 30 cm (11.8 in.). It typically occurs in bays and on shallow bank reefs at depths of 60 cm to at least 8 m (2 to 26 ft). The Sand Perch is often found in the open, on sand, mud, and rubble substrates, and frequently inhabits seagrass beds. Individuals usually refuge in a burrow under rocks, which they construct by lying next to the rock and undulating their bodies to displace the substrate. This voracious, diurnal predator feeds on amphipods, shrimps, and brachyuran crabs. To a lesser degree, it eats polychaete worms, mantis shrimps, brittlestars, and fishes. Like many serranids, it is a simultaneous hermaphrodite.

The Sand Perch is an ideal aquarium fish that should be housed in a sand or rubble tract biotope aquarium of at least 100 gallons at temperatures of 20 to 27°C (68 to 80°F). Place a large, flat piece of live rock on a live sand substrate at least 7.5 to 10 cm (3 to 4 in.) deep. This will provide a structure under which the Sand Perch can burrow. It will jump out of an open aquarium, so a top is necessary. Keep it with fishes that are too large for it to swallow and are capable of defending themselves (i.e., moderately aggressive).

Genus *Hypoplectrus* (Hamlets)

The hamlets have been a hot topic of debate in the ichthyological community for a number of years. There are ten described hamlet species and one undescribed form, all of which differ only in their coloration. This characteristic alone is typically not used to recognize a fish as a true species, so many ichthyologists consider the genus to be monotypic—containing only one species that displays a variety of different color morphs. A study conducted to see if hamlet morphs could be distinguished on the molecular level found that there were no significant differences between the proteins of the various forms. This lent more credence to the monotypic hypothesis. However, in a more recent study conducted by Michael Domeier, some important discoveries shed new light on the *Hypoplectrus* enigma. This study looked at the progeny that resulted from the cross-breeding of two morphs, the geographical distribution of the various color forms, and mate selection between the different hamlets.

By looking at the offspring produced by crossing two hamlet species or morphs, Domeier was able to determine whether it was a single gene or several linked genes that controlled the colors of all the morphs, or whether each color form was genetically distinct. If coloration were controlled by a single gene or linked genes, it would be a recessive/dominant characteristic. For example, in crossing two Shy Hamlets (*Hypoplectrus guttavarius*), you will get progeny that look like Shy Hamlets. But if you cross a Shy Hamlet with a Yellowbelly Hamlet (*Hypoplectrus aberrans*), the single- or linked-gene theory would predict that the offspring would resemble their parents or some other known hamlet color morph. In contrast, if each color morph were genetically distinct, a cross between two different hamlet morphs would result in progeny with characteristics of both parents (i.e., hybrids).

Domeier's study demonstrated that coloration was genetically distinct; that is, the genes controlling the coloration of each morph are different, which suggests that the morphs are actually separate species.

One way that a species may change with time is if it is geographically isolated. This occurs when a group of individuals is cut off from the rest of the population, which stops the exchange of genetic material. The two populations may now evolve independently and, over millions of years, two very distinct populations, or "species" may arise. Many hamlet species are wide-ranging in the Caribbean and tropical Western Atlantic, but this study demonstrated that there are population centers for several of the morphs. This finding suggests that these populations were isolated in the distant past, which allowed the different color forms to differentiate. For example, the population center for the Golden Hamlet (*Hypoplectrus gummigutta*) is off the coast of Nicaragua. Outside of this area, it is rarely seen. The study also showed that at least in some morphs, there were differences in the habitat they utilized. These findings lend support to the theory that the genus *Hypoplectrus* is comprised of numerous species, not one polymorphic form.

The final question was whether gene flow between the various morphs was prevented by mate selection or by reproductive isolation. When presented with a choice between a morph with the same coloration and one that was different in color, all individuals tested chose to mate with a like color morph. This demonstrated that their mating behavior serves to isolate the various morphs from one another, supporting the multi-species hypothesis. You can make up your own mind as to how many species exist in the genus *Hypoplectrus*, but I will be treating the color morphs as valid species in the species accounts beginning on page 532.

Biology

Hamlets are limited in distribution to the tropical Western Atlantic, the Gulf of Mexico, and the Caribbean, with the vast majority of species found in the latter location. They live on coral and rocky reefs and are usually found in relatively shallow water. Some species, however, occur at greater depths outside the areas where they are most common (e.g., Golden Hamlet, *Hypoplectrus gummigutta*). Although one hamlet species may be most abundant in a particular geographical location (its population center), as many as seven hamlet species have been observed on the same reef.

All hamlets are active during the day and hide in reef crevices at night. Those that live in shallow water on the reef flat may migrate to the reef slope at dusk to find a hole in which to slumber. Hamlets stalk their quarry by moving slowly just above the bottom with their heads directed toward the seafloor. When they detect a potential prey item, they stop their forward motion and hover in the water column, using their pectoral fins to stay in position. Then, using the tail and pectoral fins for thrust, they dash forward to strike at their prey. Hamlets feed off the surfaces of hard corals, gorgonians, sea fans, filamentous algae, and sandy bottoms. Although hamlet diets vary slightly, crustaceans and small fishes are their preferred prey. The *Hypoplectrus* species have also been observed stalking and eating cleaner species, including neon gobies (*Gobiosoma* spp.) and cleaner shrimps.

Hamlets will join groups of foraging herbivores, like parrot-

Hypoplectrus puella, Barred Hamlet (Curaçao): underappreciated by aquarists, hamlets are handsome, active by day, and tolerant of other species.

fishes and surgeonfishes, in order to feed on small fishes and crustaceans flushed out of the algal mat by these feeding assemblages. The hamlet will position itself toward the rear of the group, with its body pitched slightly forward and directed toward the center of the feeding activity.

Individual hamlets, or pairs of these fishes, are strongly site-attached and drive conspecifics away from their feeding areas. Field studies suggest that their territorial boundaries are not well defined and may overlap. Hamlets may hunt over a home range of 100 to 200 m^2 (1,076 to 2,152 ft.^{2}), but usually restrict their activities to a much smaller portion of their home range (around 10 m^2 [108 ft.^{2}]). Although hamlets are aggressive toward conspecifics and congeners, they rarely behave aggressively toward other fishes, including those with similar diets. However, I have seen hamlets being chased by Graysby (*Cephalopholis cruentatus*), Creolefish (*Paranthias furcifer*), and other serranids. Oddly enough, although they are similar in shape, the more aggressive damselfishes of the genus *Stegastes* usually ignore hamlets, which move around these pomacentrids' territories with almost total immunity. If two hamlets of appreciably different sizes cross paths, the larger individual will race toward the smaller specimen, which will typically flee. But if the individuals are of similar size, they will display toward one another. When they display, one individual presents its side to its rival, with its head pointed slightly downward and its median fins and pelvic fins fully extended. The body may also assume a slight S-curve and the head may be snapped to one side. This is known as the head-snap display. Individuals will also engage in dorsal fin rolls (they orient their body so that their erect dorsal fin is facing their opponent) and opercular flaring (they lift their gill covers while facing their rival). Aggressive encounters are typically short and limited to displays and chasing, but hamlets will occasionally fight fiercely.

Hypoplectrus aberrans, Yellowbelly Hamlet: most likely an unusual variant of the species, but possibly a hybrid specimen (Bonaire).

In these encounters, individuals tail-beat, ram, and bite each another, which can result in torn fins and lacerations on the head and body.

Hamlets are simultaneous hermaphrodites, and like some of the dwarf seabasses, they engage in egg parceling and egg trading. Hamlets breed all year round, with spawning commencing two hours before sunset. Some hamlets breed in their feeding territories, while others swim to specific areas, usually near the reef edge or on the reef face, where they form pairs and spawn. Courtship is initiated by the fish that will release eggs first. This fish, referred to as the initiator, rises up into the water column and begins displaying. The two most common displays performed are the head snap (described above) and the dorsal pitch. In the dorsal pitch, the initiator, while facing away from its potential partner, swims forward, pitches its head down, and brakes with its pectoral fins. This causes the tail to rise and exposes the distended abdomen to its mate. The follower, acting as the male, swims up to the initiator and places the top of its head between the anal and caudal fins of its partner. The initiator then moves around so that its head is in a similar position to the follower (i.e., between the tail and anal fins) and adopts a shallow S-posture, while the follower bows its body into a U-shape. Then the initiator begins to quiver and sculls backwards with its pectoral fins. While still maintaining physical contact, the pair roll onto their sides, with the follower positioned on top of the initiator. The initiating fish quivers some more, releasing eggs into the space between their bodies. At the same time, the follower releases the sperm. Then both fish snap out of the embrace and dart back to the substrate. The individuals then reverse sex roles and spawn again. A pair of hamlets may spawn as many as nine times, but usually only four or five times, in one evening.

Hamlet eggs are planktonic, and the larvae settle out onto the reef about 22 days after they hatch. *Hypoplectrus* larvae are unique among serranids in having shorter pelvic fin rays and a fleshier head and mouth. Once on the reef, they live a reclusive life, moving among reef crevices and macroalgae. Youngsters are often more common in deeper water than their adult counterparts. The color pattern of young hamlets is similar in most species, consisting of a gray body with two white spots and a black spot on each side of the caudal peduncle. Adult coloration begins to develop when the hamlet attains a length of about 5 cm (2 in.).

As explained earlier, hamlets almost always choose to breed with members of their own species, but if there are no conspecifics available, they will crossbreed. Thus, hybridization will be most common in areas where one species is rare and another is common. For example, of 189 pairings observed in one study, only 7 involved heterospecific pairs. In two surveys conducted on

Hypoplectrus puella, Barred Hamlets: spawning (Bonaire).

Hamlet Love Songs

Vocalizations are often a part of the courtship repertoire of terrestrial animals like mammals and birds. But there are also some fishes that produce sounds to facilitate spawning. Hamlets are one group of reef fishes that produce sounds by stimulating a muscle that is connected to the swim bladder. Dr. Phillip Lobel, a well known fish behaviorist, studied sound production in these fishes and was able to recognize two different "courtship calls." One call, which consisted of pulses of sound with a duration of 0.2 to 1.5 seconds, was produced just prior to spawning by the individual acting as the male. The dominant frequency of this sound was about 500 hertz. A second sound was produced when the pair member assuming the female role released her gametes. This sound, which lasted only about 1.5 seconds, was produced in part by the vibration of the swim bladder, caused by the abdominal muscles contracting to expel the eggs. Sound was also produced during egg expulsion by the "female's" fluttering pectoral fins. These sounds are barely audible to the human ear, but are easily recorded by a hydrophone. Hamlet courtship calls may serve to give information about a partner's readiness to spawn, may help pair members recognize each other, and may assist in coordinating gamete release.

hamlet abundance, only 1 or 2% of the hamlets observed were hybrids. A hybrid fish would find it difficult to entice another hamlet to spawn with it, because hamlets tend to mate with similarly colored individuals.

Captive Care
Hamlets are usually quite easy to maintain in the home aquarium if you practice good husbandry techniques. Young fishes tend to adjust more readily to captivity than adult specimens. Larger hamlets are more prone to acclimation difficulties when transferred from one tank to another. Every time an adult individual is moved, it will have a harder time adjusting to its new captive environment. Hamlets that don't acclimate will hide constantly and refuse to feed. In general, hamlets should be offered a varied diet, including chopped fresh seafood, live grass shrimp, frozen preparations for carnivores, and frozen mysid shrimp. After numerous months in captivity, it is not uncommon for a hamlet's color to fade, especially if it is not given a varied diet.

Hamlets should be housed in aquariums of at least 30 gallons, complete with a number of suitable hiding places. Only one hamlet should be kept per tank, unless your aquarium is at least 75 gallons or larger. If you have a medium- to large-sized aquarium, it is possible to keep two species of *Hypoplectrus* together. You will have greater success if you add all individuals to the tank simultaneously. If this is not possible, you may have to place the new fish in a clear plastic jar that has holes drilled in the side and let it float around in the tank, or install a see-through tank divider so that the fish can habituate to each other before you allow them to intermingle. Occasionally, a belligerent hamlet will behave aggressively toward congeners, regardless of tank size. These individuals will have to be kept in aquariums without other hamlets.

Although there is more risk inherent in placing two hamlets of the same species together, it can be done. You should have a tank of at least 75 gallons, and as with heterospecifics, both hamlets should be added to the tank at the same time. Spend several hours carefully observing them to see if they display any aggression toward each other. Because of their small size and the fact that they are simultaneous hermaphrodites (i.e., sexing is not necessary), hamlets are good candidates for captive breeding.

Although these fishes are rarely aggressive toward unrelated species, they are occasionally attacked by more belligerent fishes like other groupers (e.g., *Cephalopholis* spp. and Creolefish [*Paranthias furcifer*]), larger dottybacks (e.g., *Labracinus* spp., *Ogilbyina* spp.), larger hawkfishes (e.g., *Paracirrhites* spp.), larger damselfishes, and triggerfishes. Hamlets will consume shrimps, crabs, and smaller fishes. They can be kept in reef aquariums and can serve to help reduce populations of smaller mantis shrimps in a tank full of live rock. A very interesting display would include a hamlet that mimics a nonpredatory fish together with its model. For example, you could keep a small Blue Hamlet (*Hypoplectrus gemma*) in a tank that includes a small aggregation of adult Blue Chromis (*Chromis cyanea*); or keep a Shy Hamlet (*Hypoplectrus guttavarius*) with a Rock Beauty Angelfish (*Holacanthus tricolor*). Make sure in the latter pairing that the hamlet is acclimated to the aquarium before the angelfish is introduced (see page 537). All hamlets are well suited to both the shallow- and deep-water reef aquarium, if the aquarist is not eager to maintain healthy shrimp populations. Larger hamlets will also eat small fish tankmates.

HAMLET SPECIES

Hypoplectrus aberrans (Poey, 1868)
Common Name: Yellowbelly Hamlet.
Maximum Length: 12 cm (4.8 in.).
Distribution: Central America (color form 1) and the Greater Antilles and the Virgin Islands (color form 2). The population center of color form 1 is Panama.
Biology: This species occurs on the reef face and fore-reef slopes at depths from 3 to 15 m (10 to 49 ft.). The Yellowbelly Hamlet feeds mainly on shrimps, but also eats crabs, mantis shrimps, small fishes, and mysid shrimps. On rare occasions, this species has been observed to pair-up and spawn with the Barred Hamlet (*Hypoplectrus puella*) and the Black Hamlet (*Hypoplectrus nigricans*). The mostly brown color form (form 1) is thought to be a mimic of the Cocoa Damselfish (*Stegastes variabilis*).
Captive Care: The Yellowbelly Hamlet is infrequently encountered in the aquarium trade. For details on the husbandry of this fish, see the Captive Care section in the genus account, at left.
Aquarium Size: 30 gal. **Temperature:** 22 to 27°C (72 to 80°F).
Aquarium Suitability Index: 4.
Remarks: *Hypoplectrus aberrans* displays two different color forms that may be genetically distinct. Color form 1 is brown on its back down to the midline of its body, while the rest of the sides and belly are yellow. The dorsal fin of color form 1 is brown, while the rest of the fins are yellow or yellowish brown. Color form 2 is blue on the back, but most of the body is yellow and there are bright blue spots and lines on the face. The dorsal fin of this form is yellow and blue, while all the rest of the fins are yellow. If it is determined that color form 2 is a distinct species, it will be referred to as *Hypoplectrus maculiferus*. The two color forms have been observed to pair-up and spawn on rare occasions.

Hypoplectrus aberrans, Yellowbelly Hamlet: typical form.

Hypoplectrus chlorurus, Yellowtail Hamlet: juvenile form.

H. aberrans: Central American hybrid color form 1.

H. chlorurus (adult): possible mimic of the Yellowtail Damsel.

H. aberrans: Eastern Caribbean color form 2 ("*H. maculiferus*").

Hypoplectrus chlorurus: variant or possible hybrid.

Hypoplectrus gemma, Blue Hamlet: common and a good aquarium species.

Hypoplectrus gemma, Blue Hamlet: nocturnal color phase.

Hypoplectrus gummigutta, Golden Hamlet: a beauty prized by aquarists.

Hypoplectrus chlorurus (Valenciennes, 1792)
Common Name: Yellowtail Hamlet.
Maximum Length: 13 cm (5.1 in.).
Distribution: The population center of this hamlet is the islands off the coast of Venezuela (e.g., Bonaire, Curaçao), but it also occurs around the Bahamas, Virgin Islands, and Lesser Antilles. It is rare along the continental Western Caribbean.
Biology: The Yellowtail Hamlet occurs on fringing reef faces and fore-reef slopes, usually in areas with rich stony coral growth. It occurs at depths of 3 to 33 m (10 to 98 ft.). *Hypoplectrus chlorurus* feeds mainly on shrimps (including anemone shrimps [*Periclimenes* spp.]), but it also eats small fishes (including blennies), crabs, polychaete worms, and isopods. This species is thought to be a mimic of the Yellowtail Damselfish (*Microspathodon chrysurus*), but in the Dutch Antilles these species are rarely found in the same habitat. The Yellowtail Hamlet is usually found at depths from 7 to 21 m (23 to 68 ft.), while adult Yellowtail Damselfish occur in shallow areas, usually amid fire corals (*Millepora* spp.). I have seen *H. chlorurus* behave aggressively toward Barred Hamlets (*Hypoplectrus puella*), chasing smaller specimens over the reef. The Yellowtail Hamlet has been observed to spawn with the Black Hamlet (*Hypoplectrus nigricans*), in areas where it is rare; I have seen individuals that appeared to be a cross between *H. chlorurus* and *H. puella*.
Captive Care: *Hypoplectrus chlorurus* is rare in the aquarium trade. For details on the husbandry of this fish, see the Captive Care section in the genus account, page 532.
Aquarium Size: 30 gal. **Temperature:** 22 to 27°C (72 to 80°F).
Aquarium Suitability Index: 4.
Remarks: The color of this species can vary slightly from one geographical location to the next. For example, in the northern Bahamas, individuals are brown with a yellow tail; in the southern Bahamas and Jamaica, they are black with a yellow tail; off the Virgin Islands, they are dark blue with a yellow tail. Some individuals have blue lines on the face.

Hypoplectrus gemma (Goode & Bean, 1882)
Common Name: Blue Hamlet.
Maximum Length: 13 cm (5.1 in.).
Distribution: Florida and Belize.
Biology: The Blue Hamlet occurs on reef faces at depths of 3 to 12 m (10 to 39 ft.). It often occurs in areas with profuse gorgonian or stony coral growth. The Blue Hamlet is thought to be a mimic of the zooplankton-feeding Blue Chromis (*Chromis cyanea*).
Captive Care: This is one of the most common species in the aquarium trade. For details on the husbandry of this fish, see the Captive Care section in the genus account, page 532.

Aquarium Size: 30 gal. **Temperature:** 22 to 27°C (72 to 80°F).
Aquarium Suitability Index: 4.
Remarks: *Hypoplectrus gemma* is blue with black borders on the edges of the caudal fin. This is second only to the Butter Hamlet (*Hypoplectrus unicolor*) in abundance off the coast of Florida. There is an apparent color morph of this species that sometimes shows up in the aquarium trade: it is sky blue with what appear to be wavy, pigment-free lines and spots on the head and body. It has black margins on the caudal fin like *H. gemma*, but in some individuals, the tail is light yellow.

Hypoplectrus gummigutta (Poey, 1852)
Common Name: Golden Hamlet.
Maximum Length: 13 cm (5.1 in.).
Distribution: The population center of this species is on the Mosquito Bank, off the coast of Nicaragua, but it also occurs off the Bahamas, Cuba, Grand Cayman, Jamaica, the Dominican Republic, the Grenadines, and Tobago. It is rare outside of its population center.
Biology: It was once thought that the Golden Hamlet was a rare species limited to deep-reef areas (depths greater than 30 m [98 ft.]). But a recent study demonstrated that this is the most common *Hypoplectrus* species observed off the Nicaraguan coast. Here it is abundant on the reef face at depths from 1 to 8 m (3.3 to 26 ft.). This species has also been reported in water as shallow as 2 m (7 ft.) off the Grenadines. The Golden Hamlet is not known to mimic any other reef fish. It has been observed to hybridize with the Yellowbelly Hamlet (*Hypoplectrus aberrans*).
Captive Care: This highly desirable species is rare in the aquarium industry, because no collecting exists where its population center occurs. For details on the husbandry of this fish, see the Captive Care section in the genus account, page 532.
Aquarium Size: 30 gal. **Temperature:** 22 to 27°C (72 to 80°F).

Hypoplectrus gemma, Blue Hamlet (possibly *H. gemma* x *H. puella* hybrid): hamlet reproduction and crossbreeding is of great interest to marine biologists.

Hypoplectrus guttavarius, Shy Hamlet: amount of black on body varies.

Hypoplectrus guttavarius, Shy Hamlet: hybrid.

Hypoplectrus indigo, Indigo Hamlet: a Blue Chromis predator.

Aquarium Suitability Index: 4.
Remarks: *Hypoplectrus gummigutta* is bright yellow, gold, or orange overall. The occasional specimen may have gray on its back. The amount of black and blue markings on its face may vary (in some specimens, the dark pigmentation is limited to a small black area in front of each eye that is outlined with blue lines).

Hypoplectrus guttavarius (Poey, 1852)
Common Name: Shy Hamlet.
Maximum Length: 13 cm (5.1 in.).
Distribution: Florida, Bahamas, Greater Antilles, Lesser Antilles, Honduras. The population center for this species is Jamaica and Grand Cayman.
Biology: The Shy Hamlet usually occurs on reef faces, reef slopes, and dropoffs, at depths from 3 to 15 m (10 to 49 ft.). It has also been reported as deep as the continental shelf break. Off the Florida coast, it is most abundant at depths greater than 45 m (146 ft.). This species apparently mimics the Rock Beauty Angelfish (*Holacanthus tricolor*), which feeds primarily on sponges (see "Hamlet Trickery," page 537).
Captive Care: This is one of the easiest hamlets to maintain in captivity, although the differences in durability between the various species are slight. It is frequently collected for the marine aquarium trade. For more details on the husbandry of this fish, see the Captive Care section in the genus account, page 532.
Aquarium Size: 30 gal. **Temperature:** 22 to 27°C (72 to 80°F).
Aquarium Suitability Index: 4.
Remarks: The black saddle on the back and sides of the Shy Hamlet can vary in size.

Hypoplectrus indigo (Poey, 1852)
Common Name: Indigo Hamlet.
Maximum Length: 14 cm (5.5 in.).
Distribution: The population center for this species is the reefs near Hispaniola and Great Inagua. It is also common near Jamaica and the Cayman Islands and is occasionally observed off Florida and the continental Caribbean.
Biology: The Indigo Hamlet is most abundant on reef faces and fore-reef slopes at depths from 12 to 39 m (39 to 127 ft.), but it is an infrequent resident of the back-reef habitat as well. It is seen singly or in pairs, which defend a feeding territory from members of their own species. Juvenile Indigo Hamlets, like other members of the genus, feed mainly on benthic crustaceans. But adults of this species have a very specialized diet. Studies have shown that larger specimens feed extensively on the Blue Chromis (*Chromis cyanea*). They do so by stalking *C. cyanea* when these damselfishes feed above the reef. The hamlet will

Hamlet Trickery?

Hypoplectrus guttavarius, Shy Hamlet:
The Mimic

Holacanthus tricolor, Rock Beauty Angelfish:
The Model

One of the most fascinating aspects of *Hypoplectrus* biology is the mimetic relationship that apparently exists between hamlets and other fish species that do not share their taste for small crustaceans. Most of the hamlets display color patterns similar to fish species that are herbivores or predators that feed infrequently on crustaceans. Motile invertebrates, like shrimps and crabs, learn to recognize which species are a threat and will flee when these fishes approach too closely. It has been hypothesized that hamlets mimic species that are not a threat to crustaceans so that they can approach within striking distance without being perceived as dangerous. Of course, the model species (the fish that is being mimicked) must be more common than the mimic in that geographic area, or the potential prey animal would duck for cover whenever it saw either the harmless or the predatory fish.

As a human, you may look at a hamlet and its model and question whether the appearance of the two species is really that similar. But you are not perceiving them through the eyes of a shrimp or crab. The compound eye of the crustacean is good for distinguishing colors and sensing movement, but it is poor at differentiating shapes. Your human eye may find it easy to tell a Shy Hamlet (*Hypoplectrus guttavarius*) from a Rock Beauty Angelfish (*Holacanthus tricolor*) because the two species differ in form, but to a crustacean, with its poor visual acuity, the two similarly colored fishes look the same. This type of mimicry, where a predatory species mimics a nonpredatory form to gain a hunting advantage over its prey, is known as aggressive mimicry.

Although not as appealing an explanation for the color similarity between hamlets and their supposed models, it has also been suggested that it is just a coincidence that the *Hypoplectrus* species look similar to nonpredatory fishes with a similar distribution.

Aquarists may match the model with the mimic hamlet in the aquarium, but in this case the sponge-eating Rock Beauty requires an expert's care.

swim up to 1 m (3.3 ft.) over the bottom, slowly approaching schools of Blue Chromis until it is within striking range. The Indigo Hamlet's blue bars help conceal it as it moves through the water column. Adult hamlets also feed on benthic fishes on occasion. This species is eaten by larger piscivores like the Tiger Grouper (*Mycteroperca tigris*).

Captive Care: This handsome hamlet is regularly available to marine hobbyists. The piscivorous nature of *H. indigo* means it is a greater threat to small fish tankmates than most of its congeners. For more details on the husbandry of this fish, see the Captive Care section in the genus account, page 532.

Aquarium Size: 30 gal. **Temperature:** 22 to 27°C (72 to 80°F).
Aquarium Suitability Index: 4.
Remarks: The color pattern of *H. indigo* is similar to that of the Barred Hamlet (*Hypoplectrus puella*), but the bands of *H. indigo* are blue and white, rather than brown and white. The Indigo Hamlet attains maturity at a larger size than the other hamlet species.

Hypoplectrus nigricans, Black Hamlet: may also be chocolate brown or blue.

Hypoplectrus providencianus, Masked Hamlet: beautiful but seldom available.

Hypoplectrus nigricans (Poey, 1852)
Common Name: Black Hamlet.
Maximum Length: 15 cm (5.9 in.).
Distribution: This species is widely distributed in the Caribbean, but its population centers occur around Puerto Rico and the Virgin Islands.
Biology: The Black Hamlet occurs on shallow reef flats, reef faces, and reef slopes, usually at depths of less than 6 m (20 ft.). However, it has been reported to a maximum depth of 12 m (39 ft.). This hamlet feeds mainly on small fishes and shrimps, but also eats crabs, mysids, and mantis shrimps. The diet of larger specimens (greater than 9 cm [3.5 in.] Standard Length) includes more small fishes than does the diet of smaller individuals. *Hypoplectrus nigricans* is a solitary species that defends its feeding territory from conspecifics. It migrates to areas near the edge of the reef or to the reef face to spawn, with some individuals traveling up to 100 m (325 ft.) from their foraging territory to preferred spawning sites. In some areas, as many as 28 fish will occur in an area of 0.5 hectares (1.23 acres) equivalent to one Black Hamlet every 178 m^2 (1,915 ft.^{2}).
Captive Care: Although not highly sought after because of its more muted coloration, the Black Hamlet is occasionally available to hobbyists. Its piscivorous nature and larger maximum size make it a greater threat to small fish tankmates than most of its congeners. For more details on the husbandry of this fish, see the Captive Care section in the genus account, page 532.
Aquarium Size: 30 gal. **Temperature:** 22 to 27°C (72 to 80°F).
Aquarium Suitability Index: 4.
Remarks: The Black Hamlet can be chocolate brown, black, or bluish gray overall. In captivity, black specimens often fade to a pale gray.

Hypoplectrus providencianus (Acero, Gazon-Ferreira & Nieto, 1993)
Common Names: Masked Hamlet, Blacktail Hamlet.
Maximum Length: 13 cm (5.2 in.).
Distribution: Providencia Island (Colombia), Belize, Honduras, Jamaica, and Grand Cayman.
Biology: *Hypoplectrus providencianus* species occurs on the reef face and fore-reef slopes, often in areas with rich stony coral growth, at depths of 6 to 15 m (20 to 50 ft.).
Captive Care: This species is rarely encountered in the aquarium trade. For details on its husbandry, see the Captive Care section in the genus account, page 532.
Aquarium Size: 30 gal. **Temperature:** 22 to 27°C (72 to 80°F).
Aquarium Suitability Index: 4.
Remarks: The Masked Hamlet species is easily recognized by the triangular black mask that extends down from the eyes.

Hypoplectrus puella (Cuvier, 1828)
Common Name: Barred Hamlet.
Maximum Length: 13 cm (5.1 in.).
Distribution: This hamlet is found throughout the Caribbean and is the only hamlet found in the Gulf of Mexico and off Bermuda. It is one of the most abundant of the hamlet species.
Biology: Although the Barred Hamlet occurs on reef faces and fore-reef slopes, it is most abundant in back-reef areas that have low relief and dense gorgonian populations. It is also more common in turbid water than most other hamlets. This species is observed at depths from 3 to 30 m (10 to 98 ft.) and feeds primarily on shrimps (including snapping shrimps [*Alpheus* spp.] and cleaner shrimps [*Periclimenes* spp.]) and crabs, but it also eats small fishes, mysid shrimps, mantis shrimps, and isopods. Larger

Hypoplectrus puella, Barred Hamlet (juvenile): widespread in the Caribbean.

Hypoplectrus puella, Barred Hamlet (adult): variable color pattern.

Hypoplectrus puella, Barred Hamlet: adult with courtship colors.

Hypoplectrus puella, Barred Hamlet: faded adult just prior to spawning.

specimens (greater than 9 cm [3.5 in.] Standard Length) feed more heavily on fishes (e.g., wrasses, juvenile parrotfishes) than do smaller individuals. Adult individuals will slowly approach swarms of mysid shrimps and turn on their sides before swooping in to attack them. This species will pair spawn at the same site on consecutive evenings. Pair members meet at the courtship site about an hour before sunset. Initially they engage in cooperative hunting behavior, stalking small shrimps and fishes in the general area of the spawning site. If they encounter other hamlet pairs, they behave aggressively toward them and also chase heterospecifics, like *Chromis* damselfishes and parrotfishes. They engage in hunting behavior, display toward one another, chafe the substrate, and chase other fishes for about 30 to 40 minutes before spawning occurs. The initiating pair member will then attempt to lead its mate to the spawning site (usually a high coral head or the top of a patch reef). When in position, the initiator's color fades drastically, with the bars almost disappearing. The other fish then moves behind and alongside the initiator, their bodies clasp together, and gametes are released. They will change roles and spawn as many as seven times in a single night. It has been suggested that the reason the Barred Hamlet is so wide-ranging is that its larvae are more tolerant of suboptimal conditions than other hamlet species. *Hypoplectrus puella* will hybridize with Butter (*Hypoplectrus unicolor*), Yellowbelly (*H. aberrans*), Blue (*H. gemma*), and Indigo (*H. indigo*) Hamlets.

Captive Care: This species is frequently available to marine aquarists. Large individuals are a threat to fish tankmates, while all sizes are a threat to ornamental shrimps. For more husbandry details, see the Captive Care section in the genus account, page 532.

Aquarium Size: 30 gal. **Temperature:** 22 to 27°C (72 to 80°F).

Aquarium Suitability Index: 4.

Remarks: *Hypoplectrus puella* shows some variation in the col-

Hypoplectrus unicolor, Butter Hamlet: adult variant without spot on snout.

Hypoplectrus sp. 1, Tan Hamlet: well known but undescribed.

oration of the six bars on the body: they vary in darkness and in the evenness of their shading.

Hypoplectrus unicolor (Walbaum, 1792)
Common Name: Butter Hamlet.
Maximum Length: 13 cm (5.1 in.).
Distribution: Found throughout the entire Caribbean, it is the most abundant hamlet.
Biology: Like *Hypoplectrus puella*, the Butter Hamlet is most often found on areas of low relief with prolific gorgonian growth, but also occurs on fringing reef faces, fore-reef slopes, and under piers among sponges and human debris. It is found at depths ranging from 3 to 23 m (10 to 76 ft.). When this species is about to strike at its prey, the black markings in front of its eyes fade, possibly because they would make the hamlet more conspicuous. Butter Hamlets sometimes form pairs, with individuals typically staying within 20 cm to 1 m (7.9 in. to 3.3 ft.) of each other in a large territory that they defend from conspecifics. This species pair spawns at the same spawning site every night just before sunset, often selecting a site over large gorgonians. In rare cases, the Butter Hamlet has been observed to pair-up and spawn with the Barred Hamlet (*H. puella*).
Captive Care: The Butter Hamlet is occasionally available to marine aquarists. For details on the husbandry of this fish, see the Captive Care section in the genus account, page 532.
Aquarium Size: 30 gal. **Temperature:** 22 to 27°C (72 to 80°F).
Aquarium Suitability Index: 4.
Remarks: Some Butter Hamlets possess a blue-ringed black spot on each side of the snout, while others lack this chromatic char-

Hypoplectrus unicolor, Butter Hamlet: the most abundant Caribbean hamlet, best known by the black saddle on the caudal peduncle (Grand Cayman).

acteristic. Those individuals lacking the nasal spots are more common along the Florida coast and in the southern Caribbean. A characteristic feature of the Butter Hamlet is the black saddle on the caudal peduncle that extends down below the level of the lateral line. In rare individuals, this black saddle may actually form a wide band around the entire peduncle. An occasional specimen may exhibit lemon yellow on the lower part of the sides and ventrum.

Hypoplectrus sp. 1
Common Names: Tan Hamlet, Blue-lip Hamlet.
Maximum Length: 13 cm (5.1 in.).
Distribution: Florida and Panama.
Biology: This undescribed hamlet is found on reef faces and reef slopes at depths of 6 to 15 m (20 to 49 ft.). It apparently mimics the adult Dusky Damselfish (*Stegastes dorsopunicans*).
Captive Care: The Tan Hamlet is regularly encountered in the marine aquarium trade, but is not highly sought after because of its subdued coloration. For details on the husbandry of this fish, see the Captive Care section in the genus account, page 532.
Aquarium Size: 30 gal. **Temperature:** 22 to 27°C (72 to 80°F).
Aquarium Suitability Index: 4.
Remarks: This species has been referred to as the Blue-lip Hamlet in the scientific literature.

References
Barlow (1975), Bohlke & Chaplin (1968), Clark (1959), Domeier (1994), Fischer (1980a, 1980b, 1984), Fischer & Petersen (1986), Graves & Rosenblatt (1980), J. Hancock (personal communication), Lieske & Myers (1994), Lobel (1992), Petersen (1995), Pressley (1981), Randall (1967, 1968), Robins et al. (1986), Thresher (1978, 1980).

SUBFAMILY ANTHIINAE
ANTHIAS

THE TERM "GROUPER" USUALLY CALLS TO MIND A LARGE, voracious predator that is a threat to smaller fishes and a menace in any passive community aquarium. The grouper family, Serranidae, however, is diverse both in form and behavior and includes many small, elegant, and strikingly pigmented reef fishes.

Subfamily Anthiinae, especially, differs greatly from the common perception of groupers and is comprised of many modestly sized, colorful reef dwellers. Many of them form gaudy aggregations of hundreds of individuals over the reef where they capture minute food items carried by ocean currents. The anthias are also welcome additions to a more peaceful community setting and, because they do not feed on sessile invertebrates, are considered by most to be suitable for the reef aquarium. Aquarists may have difficulty, however, maintaining some anthias species and an understanding of their biology and species characteristics is important when choosing specimens for captive systems.

Classification

Anthias occur in all the tropical oceans of the world. The first species recognized in this group was described from the Mediterranean and Northeast Atlantic in 1758 and is known as *Anthias anthias*. In the past, many species from around the world were assigned to this genus. But subsequent studies concluded that the "true" *Anthias* species are restricted to the Atlantic and Mediterranean. All other forms that had previously been included in this group were shown to belong to different genera, at least eight of which are known to enter the aquarium trade. The subfamily now includes: *Anthias, Holanthias, Luzonichthys, Nemanthias, Plectranthias, Pseudanthias, Rabaulichthys,* and *Serranocirrhitus*. (All are commonly lumped under the label "anthias" in everyday usage by aquarists and divers.) The biology of these genera is briefly discussed in the species accounts, beginning on page 548.

In the Captive Care section, below, we will direct our attention to the most commonly kept anthias species—the members of the genus *Pseudanthias*. In order to better understand the behavior and care of these fishes, a brief taxonomic dissection of the genus is provided. This group can be broken down into three subgenera: *Franzia, Pseudanthias,* and *Mirolabrichthys*. These subgenera vary not only morphologically, but also in their captive behavior and hardiness (see Tables 26 and 27, pages 544 and 545).

Captive Care

One common, widely repeated misconception about anthias is that they need to be kept in groups to ensure their survival. This is incorrect. In fact, this practice can hinder your success in keeping some species. The belief that they are best kept in groups comes from the fact that most anthias species shoal in their natural habitat. However, unlike a school of freshwater Neon Tetras (*Paracheirodon innesi*) in which every individual is equal in so-

Pseudanthias evansi, Evan's Anthias (magenta and purple) with *Pseudanthias squamipinnis,* Lyretail Anthias: typical shoaling pattern on a shallow fore reef.

A mixed shoal of anthias and damselfishes feed in the current near a stand of *Acropora* coral, into which they can dart at the approach of predators.

TABLE 26

Morphological and Behavioral Differences Among *Pseudanthias* Subgenera

Subgenus	Morphological Characteristics	Behavioral Characteristics
Franzia	Heavily scaled dorsal and anal fins; lunate tail; the third dorsal spine becomes elongate in males.	Aggressive toward members of their own and other fish species; easy to keep.
Mirolabrichthys	A thickened protuberance on the upper lip in males; both sexes have deeply incised (forked) tails.	Many are not aggressive; conspecific males will fight; most are difficult to keep.
Pseudanthias	Anterior spines show different degrees of development in the various species; no protuberance on the upper lip; tail shape varies greatly.	Extremely variable; can be belligerent, passive, hardy, or extremely sensitive.

cial status (an egalitarian school), members of an anthias shoal compete for a position in the group's pecking order. For example, in a typical Lyretail Anthias (*Pseudanthias squamipinnis*) assemblage (which can consist of 1,000 or more individuals), there are mainly females and nonterritorial males (these low-ranking males literally hang toward the bottom of the group). Within the swarm of females, the territorial males that are present perform acrobatic U-swim displays and vigorously defend both an area of the reef and an associated harem of females. The size of the male's territory is a function of the female density, and can range from about 0.5 to 3 m^2 (5 to 32 ft.^{2}) in area. Within each group of females, a hierarchy exists, with larger fish dominating smaller conspecifics. If the territorial male should die, the dominant female in the harem changes sex (in as little as two weeks) and becomes the new territory holder. To maintain dominance, males and larger females display at, charge, chase, and sometimes nip their neighbors. (See illustrations on page 579.)

All of this makes maintaining a group of anthias in a home aquarium difficult, because their aggression and dominance behaviors are not left behind on the reef. Males will attempt to constrain female sex change by asserting their dominance, while females work to maintain a pecking order among themselves. The subordinate females are harassed by both male and female tankmates and do not have enough room to avoid these attacks. Consequently, the females eventually hide, stop feeding, and die. In several captive anthias colonies (each consisting of one of the following species: *P. squamipinnis*, *Pseudanthias huchtii*, and *Pseudanthias pleurotaenia*), I have observed that females get

Pseudanthias squamipinnis, Lyretail Anthias: male displaying.

Pseudanthias bicolor, Bicolor Anthias: males in mouth-to-mouth combat.

TABLE 27

Anthias Species in the Aquarium Trade Grouped by Subgenus

Subgenus *Franzia*	Subgenus *Pseudanthias*
Pseudanthias huchtii	*Pseudanthias bimaculatus*
Pseudanthias squamipinnis	*Pseudanthias cooperi*
	Pseudanthias fasciatus
Subgenus *Mirolabrichthys*	*Pseudanthias hawaiiensis*
Pseudanthias aurulentus	*Pseudanthias heemstrai*
Pseudanthias bartlettorum	*Pseudanthias hypselosoma*
Pseudanthias bicolor	*Pseudanthias luzonensis*
Pseudanthias dispar	*Pseudanthias marcia*
Pseudanthias evansi	*Pseudanthias olivaceus*
Pseudanthias ignitus	*Pseudanthias pictilis*
Pseudanthias lori	*Pseudanthias pleurotaenia*
Pseudanthias parvirostris	*Pseudanthias pulcherrimus*
Pseudanthias pascalus	*Pseudanthias randalli*
Pseudanthias smithvanizi	*Pseudanthias rubrizonatus*
Pseudanthias tuka	*Pseudanthias sheni*
	Pseudanthias sp. 1 (Bloodspot)
	Pseudanthias sp. 2 (Harlequin)
	Pseudanthias sp. 3 (Cave)
	Pseudanthias sp. 4 (Reticulated)
	Pseudanthias taeniatus
	Pseudanthias thompsoni
	Pseudanthias townsendi
	Pseudanthias ventralis

sick or die in order of their rank within the dominance hierarchy—the lowest fish becomes ill or dies first, followed by the next, and so on. Another deleterious phenomenon that often occurs in a captive anthias colony is that the male will start losing weight because of the number of calories expended chasing conspecifics.

Since aggression is density dependent, the aquarist may get lucky and reach an equilibrium point where the density of individuals is low enough and aggression becomes uncommon enough that the remaining fishes live in relative peace. Unfortunately, I do not know of a magic compatibility formula.

While many aquarists dream of recreating a large assemblage of anthias in their home aquariums, it is important to remember that—unless you have a huge tank—much greater likelihood of success will come by keeping only one anthias per tank. A single healthy and long-lived anthias is always better than a group that quickly self-destructs. One of the only drawbacks with keeping some male anthias, such as *P. squamipinnis*, in an aquarium without conspecifics is that their coloration may change and become more like that of the female.

For aquarists determined to keep more than one of the more belligerent anthias species (e.g., members of the subgenus *Franzia* and many species in the subgenus *Pseudanthias*, and Bartlett's Anthias [*Pseudanthias bartlettorum*]), there are two different strategies that can be tried. In the simplest approach, I suggest purchasing approximately one anthias per 3,800 cm^2 (600 $in.^2$) of tank surface area—and only one male per aquarium. (In more approximate terms, this means just one anthias per 40 to 50 gallons in a system housing other community fishes.) If the tank is large enough—that is, there is enough room for subordinates to elude more aggressive conspecifics—you might succeed in keeping a small number of individuals together.

The other potentially effective method, especially for those aquarists with a less spacious tank, is to crowd the aquarium with female specimens—at least six, and preferably eight or more, individuals in the group. By doing this, a dominance hierarchy will be more difficult for them to maintain. Rather than one or two subordinate fishes receiving all of the abuse, aggression will be spread around the captive population. (A similar strategy is used by freshwater aquarists keeping aggressive African cichlids.) If you decide to try this procedure, it is important to introduce all the shoal members to the tank at once. The drawback to this approach is that, in a medium-sized aquarium (e.g., 55 to 75 gallons) you will limit the number of other fish species you can have, possibly put an excessive biological load on your filter system, and increase the chances of a disease epidemic. It will be imperative to install a protein skimmer on a tank with this many hungry anthias. Another consideration when trying to establish a captive anthiine shoal is that, if there is a great difference in the sex ratio in a captive population of anthias, a dominant female may begin to change into a male. This will typically result in excessive fighting between the established and the transforming male.

It should be pointed out again that keeping anthias in groups is particularly problematic when dealing with most of the species from the subgenera *Franzia* and *Pseudanthias*. Among the less aggressive species that an experienced aquarist might consider for a shoal are members of the subgenus *Mirolabrichthys* like the Dispar Anthias (*Pseudanthias dispar*), Flame Anthias (*Pseudanthias ignitus*), Lori's Anthias (*Pseudanthias lori*), Purple Queen Anthias (*Pseudanthias pascalus*), Princess Anthias (*Pseudanthias smithvanizi*), Yellowstripe Anthias (*Pseudanthias tuka*), as well as four choices from subgenus *Psuedanthias*: the Hawaiian Longfin

Anthias and Social Mimicry

Nemanthias carberryi, Threadfin Anthias (male):
The Mimic

Pseudanthias evansi, Evan's Anthias (male):
The Model

The old adage that "there is safety in numbers" is often true—especially in the coral reef fish community. One of the greatest advantages to grouping with members of your own kind, or with species that are similar in appearance, is that it reduces the chances that you will become some piscivore's lunch. This phenomenon is referred to as the "dilution effect." Simply put, the more potential prey individuals in a group, the less likelihood there is that any one individual will be the one selected. (A large aggregation of fishes also tends to confuse some would-be predators.) But if you don't look like the rest of the group members, you are *more* likely to be the one chosen by a predator, because you stand out. Therefore, some fishes possess color patterns that allow them to blend in with other species and become part of a homogeneous-looking group—this is called social mimicry.

In the anthias, some species mimic each other, while other anthias are mimicked by unrelated species. For example, in the Maldives, the Threadfin Anthias (*Nemanthias carberryi*) and the Fusilier Damselfish (*Lepidozygus tapeinosoma*) engage in social mimicry. The Threadfin Anthias displays two different color forms: one orange and red, the other purple and yellow. The Threadfin Anthias is sympatric with both the Flame Anthias (*Pseudanthias ignitus*) and Evan's Anthias (*Pseudanthias evansi*), and in the Maldives, the Threadfin is less common than either of these two forms.

When diving in the Maldives, I have often observed small groups of purple and yellow Threadfin Anthias swimming amid shoals of the more numerous Evan's Anthias, which is also purple with a yellow dorsal region. On the other hand, the orange and red color morphs of the Threadfin Anthias were found mixing with groups of the more abundant Flame Anthias, which are similarly colored. One of these heterospecific anthias groups was joined by Fusilier Damselfish, which are similar in color and in overall shape to the anthias. This damselfish is known to mimic other species of anthias in different locations. In the Line Islands, the Fusilier Damselfish resembles the Olive Anthias (*Pseudanthias olivaceus*), while in other locations it looks like the Purple Queen Anthias (*Pseudanthias pascalus*). Likewise, in the Western Pacific, juvenile Bluehead Tilefish (*Hoplolatilus starcki*) associate and appear to mimic the Purple Queen Anthias and the male Yellowstripe Anthias (*Pseudanthias tuka*). The Midas Blenny (*Ecsenius midas*) mimics and associates with female Lyretail Anthias (*Pseudanthias squamipinnis*) and Evan's Anthias.

Any of these mimetic associations can make for an interesting display in the home aquarium, although most of the fishes involved in these relationships present special husbandry challenges. As discussed elsewhere, creating shoals of captive anthias requires careful planning and abundant swimming space to avoid serious territorial conflicts.

Anthias (*Pseudanthias hawaiiensis*), Resplendent Anthias (*Pseudanthias pulcherimmus*), Randall's Anthias (*Pseudanthias randalli*), and the Longfin Anthias (*Pseudanthias ventralis*). Some of these species will actually do better if kept in a group, although it is still advisable to keep only one male per aquarium. (Some of the more diminutive forms, like *P. dispar*, *P. hawaiiensis*, and *P. ventralis* will be more amenable to the presence of multiple males in larger systems.) Unfortunately, many of these less aggressive anthias species are also less hardy, demanding more expert care, or are infrequently encountered in the aquarium trade.

Before mixing anthias species, consider that an aggressive individual may not restrict its attacks to members of its own species. Therefore, keeping a "mixed" shoal of anthias can result in disaster for subordinate members no matter what species they happen to be.

Anthias can make an attractive piscine addition to any reef tank. However, because they feed on zooplankton (including copepods, crustacean larvae, and fish eggs) and are very active, and because large populations of these foods do not usually occur "naturally" in reef aquariums, it is important to feed them frequently—I recommend at least twice, and preferably three or four times, a day. Some may argue that this is a poor practice as it can lead to an increase in the level of dissolved organic compounds and a lowering of the redox potential, which can be deleterious to sensitive invertebrates and encourage microalgae growth. However, ample quantities of live rock, live sand, and a protein skimmer can be employed to help maintain good water quality. Anthias are best housed with more durable hard corals (e.g., Elegance [*Catalaphyllia jardinei*], and Open Brain [*Trachyphyllia geoffroyi*]), soft corals, mushroom anemones, and zoanthids. These species are less sensitive to the buildup of dissolved organic compounds than small-polyped stony corals. Although anthias will not harm invertebrates, they may fall prey to the Elephant Ear Anemone (*Amplexidiscus fenestrafer*), carpet anemones (*Stichodactyla* spp.), Corkscrew Tentacle Anemone (*Macrodactyla doreensis*), large Elegance Corals (*C. jardinei*), large crabs, and piscivorous mantis shrimps.

It is important to feed your anthias (as well as all your marine fishes) a varied diet. Some of the frozen foods with added vitamins, pigments, and amino acids will help maintain good condition and color. Salmon flesh is fed in some public aquariums to maintain the bright colors of captive anthias. Frozen *Mysis* shrimp are also voraciously accepted by many anthias species and are one of the most complete food sources an aquarist can provide. Live food (e.g., brine shrimp, baby livebearers) can be used to elicit feeding in those specimens that refuse to eat. Remember: anthias feed on organisms floating in the water column and rarely take food off the substrate. For more information on anthias nutrition, see "Keys to Successful Anthias Husbandry," page 548.

Anthias appreciate a strong current and clean, well-oxygenated water. One way to duplicate the water movements of their natural habitat is to hook up a battery of water pumps or powerheads at one end of your aquarium. These pumps should be set on a timer to run for several hours, shut off for a similar time span, run for several hours, and so on. Water movement may also help discourage aggression. For example, it has been demonstrated in the Lyretail Anthias (*P. squamipinnis*) that inter-individual distances decrease when currents are strong, and increase when they are slack. Anthias also make great "dither" fishes, especially those species that spend a lot of time swimming together in the water column. This bustle of activity helps incite more nervous species to spend time in the open.

Anthias are often skittish when initially introduced to the aquarium; a sudden change in light level or an aquarist's hand moving through the tank can lead to some spectacular aerial displays. Large Squarespot Anthias (*Pseudanthias pleurotaenia*) are particularly prone to this potentially suicidal behavior. Aggressive tankmates can also be a curse to newly acquired anthiines. I have seen dottybacks, angelfishes, hawkfishes, and larger damselfishes pester the anthias to the point of death.

When selecting individuals for your tank, choose fishes that are swimming about and avoid specimens that are hiding among the coral (this is atypical daytime behavior for an anthias unless it is being threatened by a predator or rival). Also avoid anthias in which the posterior part of the skull is clearly demarcated from the rest of the body (i.e., the head appears to be enlarged) and the back looks sunken. This condition indicates that a fish has lost weight (including dorsal musculature) and will be more difficult to maintain. Ask the retailer to feed the fish before you buy it and

Anthias, like this juvenile *Pseudanthias hypselosoma*, frequently visit the cleaning stations of the Common Cleaner Shrimp, *Lysmata amboinensis*.

Keys to Successful Anthias Husbandry

Anthias have presented aquarists with difficult husbandry challenges for years. However, with the recent inclusion of refugiums and the culturing of zooplankton in these isolated chambers, the keeping of anthias has become much easier. For example, some of the species listed in the species accounts as very difficult to keep (e.g., Yellowstripe Anthias [*Pseudanthias tuka*]) have been successfully kept in a tank with a productive refugium.

Some refugiums are placed either below or alongside the aquarium, while others are actually hung inside the tank. In the external refugium, the water and associated plankters are typically pumped into the main aquarium. The problem with this system is that some small crustaceans may be killed when they are pulled through the pump. In the internal refugium, water is slowly pumped (e.g., 10 to 15 gallons per hour) from the display tank into the refugium, while the refugium water, along with some of the small animals it contains, pours directly into the tank over an overflow. This prevents the zooplankters from being either disabled or destroyed by the pump's impeller. Zooplankton cultures, like mysid shrimp, copepods, and amphipods, are available for refugiums. These small crustaceans can be fed aquarium flake food and plant material and are typically very prolific. They provide a natural and constant food source for any anthias. Zooplankton also provide a more nutritional food source to help maintain chromatic fidelity in these fishes, which are notorious for losing their color. An advantage to having a well-stocked refugium is that you will not have to introduce food as frequently in order to ensure that your anthias get enough to eat.

Another way to succeed with anthias is to offer them frozen mysid shrimp. This is the most nutritional food source available to aquarists, and anthias usually cannot resist it. Make sure the frozen mysids you use are not a mushy mass when thawed. Rather, the shrimp should be whole and solid. If you don't have a refugium, or it is not productive, feed your anthias the mysid shrimp at least twice and preferably three or four times a day.

avoid specimens that do not eat with gusto.

For your viewing pleasure, introduce a cleaner shrimp (*Lysmata* spp.) with your anthias. Anthias seem to have a special affinity for these crustaceans and will usually race up to a newly introduced cleaner shrimp and pose to be cleaned. Action patterns used by the fish to facilitate the shrimp's inspection include lying on the substrate, extending the jaws, lifting the opercula, and erecting the fins.

ANTHIAS SPECIES

Genus *Anthias* (Anthias)

The members of the genus *Anthias* have scales on the top of the head and maxilla, and a crescent-shaped tooth patch on the vomer. They are restricted in their distribution to the Atlantic Ocean and the Mediterranean Sea. The best known member of the genus is the Anthias, or Common Anthias (*Anthias anthias*), which is a resident of rocky reefs in the Mediterranean, Portugal, and the east coast of northern Africa. Two other species have been reported from the Eastern Atlantic, while five species occur on deep-water reefs of the tropical Western Atlantic and Gulf of Mexico. At least one of these species is occasionally collected for the aquarium trade. Like many of their relatives, the members of the genus *Anthias* form shoals in current-prone areas and feed on zooplankton.

Anthias tenuis Nichols, 1920
Common Name: Threadnose Anthias.
Maximum Length: 11 cm (4.3 in.).
Distribution: North Carolina and Bermuda to the eastern Gulf of Mexico, Puerto Rico, and the southern Caribbean.
Biology: This uncommon, deep-dwelling anthiine is known from depths in excess of 77 m (250 ft.). It occurs in shoals and is occasionally preyed upon by larger groupers.
Captive Care: The Threadnose Anthias, like its deep-water counterparts, is best housed in a dimly lit tank at low water temperatures. It can be kept in small groups in large tanks, and can share the tank with other deep-water anthias. It tends to be less boisterous than the Roughtongue Bass (*Holanthias martinicensis*),

Anthias tenuis, Threadnose Anthias (female): rarely collected deep-water fish.

another deep-water species that is often collected with this anthias. If you are mixing these two species, make sure the anthias is introduced to the tank before *H. martinicensis*.
Aquarium Size: 55 gal. **Temperature:** 12.5 to 23°C (55 to 74°F).
Aquarium Suitability Index: 4.
Remarks: This species differs from other anthiines of the region in possessing a slender filament on the posterior border of the front nostril. The filament almost reaches the orbit of the eye.

Genus *Hemanthias* (Streamer Bass)

Like those in the genus *Anthias*, the members of the genus *Hemanthias* are restricted in their distribution to the Atlantic Ocean. But unlike their relatives, they have no scales on the top of the head or on the maxilla. All of the *Hemanthias* species live in deep water (usually 60+ m [195+ ft.]). They also form shoals and feed on zooplankton. Deep-water aquarium fish collectors catch one of the three species that occur in the tropical Western Atlantic.

Hemanthias vivanus (Jordan & Swain, 1884)
Common Name: Red Barbier.
Maximum Length: 25 cm (9.8 in.).
Distribution: North Carolina and Northern Gulf of Mexico, south to Brazil.
Biology: The Red Barbier occurs in large shoals on rocky reef slopes, or around rock outcroppings, at depths of 45 to 610 m (146 to 1,983 ft.). The macroinvertebrates found in the same habitat include gorgonians of the genus *Paramuricea*, basket stars, long-spined sea urchins (*Diadema* spp.), serpent stars, and sea stars. The fishes in this habitat include the Roughtongue Bass (*Holanthias martinicensis*), Short Bigeye (*Pristigenys alta*), Tattler Bass (*Serranus phoebe*), Bank Butterflyfish (*Prognathodes aya*), Wrasse Bass (*Liopropoma eukrines*), Twospot Cardinalfish (*Apogon pseudomaculatus*), Blue Goby (*Ptereleotris calliurus*), and the Sharpnose Puffer (*Canthigaster rostrata*). The Red Barbier occurs in large, fast-moving shoals. Both juveniles and females feed on zooplankton—especially copepods—near the seafloor, while large males move farther away from the bottom to capture similar prey. When the Red Barbier is approached, it will take cover in the holes and crevices of the reef. It has been observed sharing a burrow with the Wrasse Bass and the Sand Perch (*Diplectrum formosum*).
Captive Care: This species should be housed in a dimly lit tank, at water temperatures slightly lower than those often maintained in a tropical marine aquarium. They can be housed in small to large groups; they will form size-related dominance hierarchies, with large individuals chasing smaller conspecifics. The Red Barbier has recently become available in the aquarium trade as a result of the employment of mixed gas to collect deep-water fish species. This is a relatively dangerous procedure, so fish collected in this manner command a high price. Currently, most specimens are exported to Japan.
Aquarium Size: 55 gal. **Temperature:** 12.5 to 23°C (55 to 74°F).
Aquarium Suitability Index: 4.
Remarks: The head and body of the male is deep red, with small yellow spots and violet on the side. There are two golden stripes on the head that extend from the eye to the pectoral fin base, and a red caudal fin. Adults have filaments extending from the caudal fin lobes and pelvic fins, and the dorsal fin has three to five elongate spines. Both females and juveniles are much less spectacular-looking than large males. The **Longtail Bass (*Hemanthias leptus*) Ginsburg, 1952** is a member of this genus that ranges from South Carolina to the northern Gulf of Mexico and throughout the Caribbean. Adult Longtail Bass are red above and silvery below, with fine yellow mottling on the flanks and a broad yellow stripe extending from the back of the eye to the front edge of the operculum. Larger individuals have an elongate third dorsal spine and filaments extending from the pelvic fins. *Hemanthias leptus* is found over hard substrates at depths of 60 to 300 m (195 to 975 ft.). Its care requirements are similar to those of *H. vivanus*, although it is larger and needs a larger aquarium.

Genus *Holanthias* (Deep-Water Anthias)

This genus contains at least 14 deep-bodied species that are typically limited to deeper fore-reef areas (usually greater than 100 m [325 ft.]) These fishes have scales on the head and maxilla, but the vomer tooth patch has an extension (unlike *Anthias* species). Because of their bathymetric distribution, few of the deep-water

Hemanthias vivanus, Red Barbier (juvenile): uncommon Caribbean species.

Holanthias martinicensis, Roughtongue Bass (male): rarely collected.

Luzonichthys earlei, Earle's Slender Anthias: best kept in small groups.

anthias ever make it into aquarium stores or are encountered by divers. This is unfortunate, as many of these fishes are brightly colored. Consider the Hawaiian Deep-water Anthias (*Holanthias fuscipinnis*), which is bright orange with fuchsia markings on the face and fins. It is sometimes found in water as shallow as 55 m (179 ft.) off the island of Maui and is reported to be a durable aquarium fish (although it often takes several days to acclimate fully). The only species regularly collected, but not readily available in North America, is the Roughtongue Bass (*Holanthias martinicensis*). Deep-water anthias vary in their social structure. Although they feed on zooplankton, many occur singly and stay near the seafloor. Others form shoals well away from the bottom. Sexual dichromatism is also not as common in *Holanthias* species as it is in the other anthiine groups.

Holanthias martinicensis Guichenot, 1868
Common Name: Roughtongue Bass.
Maximum Length: 20 cm (7.9 in.).
Distribution: Bermuda, North Carolina, Florida, and the Greater Antilles south to northern South America.
Biology: This species is found on deep rocky reef slopes and on limestone outcroppings, at depths of 60 to 610 m (195 to 1,983 ft.). It occurs either singly or in shoals numbering to 20, but it most commonly lives in pairs or small groups of up to five. Unlike the sympatric Red Barbier, this species usually swims away from predators. In certain areas, such as off the North Carolina coast, the Roughtongue Bass is found in association with clumps of stony corals in the genera *Oculina* and *Madrepora*. See the species account for *Hemanthias vivanus*, page 549, for a list of some of the macroinvertebrates and fishes that occur in the same habitat as the Roughtongue Bass.

Captive Care: *Holanthias martinicensis* is a very durable fish that does best if kept in a dimly lit tank at cool water temperatures. Females and smaller males are not overly aggressive and can be kept with other deep-water anthias, as well as smaller zooplanktivores. Large males, however, can be pugnacious, especially toward congeners, once they have been in captivity for a while. It is prudent to house only one male per tank, unless the aquarium is of considerable size. Most of the individuals collected are sent to Japan and command a very high price.
Aquarium Size: 55 gal. **Temperature:** 12.5 to 23°C (55 to 74°F).
Aquarium Suitability Index: 4.
Remarks: This is a beautiful fish, with deep blue or bright green eyes, depending on where the fish is in relation to the light. Small individuals (under 5 cm [2 in.]) Standard Length) have a brown saddle from the dorsal fin base to the midline of the body.

Genus *Luzonichthys* (Slender Anthias)
The members of genus *Luzonichthys* are elongate with a divided dorsal fin. They are sometimes called splitfins. Six species are currently recognized, with most of these associating with coral reefs. They form large shoals, which often include other zooplankton-feeding fish like their cousins in the genus *Pseudanthias*. They tend to inhabit current-swept dropoff areas at depths of 1 to 205 m (3.3 to 666 ft.), although most species are more common at depths greater than 20 m (65 ft.). Unlike many of their relatives, male and female slender anthias do not differ in coloration. At least three species occasionally show up in aquarium stores: Earle's Slender Anthias (*Luzonichthys earlei*), the Magenta Slender Anthias (*Luzonichthys waitei*), and Whitley's Slender Anthias (*Luzonichthys whitleyi*). The other species in genus *Luzonichthys* tend to occur in much deeper water.

Luzonichthys earlei Randall, 1981

Common Names: Earle's Slender Anthias, Earle's Splitfin.
Maximum Length: 6 cm (2.4 in.).
Distribution: Hawaii to the Maldives.
Biology: Earle's Slender Anthias occurs in large groups—often with other zooplankton feeders—on steep outer-reef slopes. It has been reported at depths from less than 15 down to 205 m (49 to 666 ft.) and has been taken from the stomach of the snapper *Pristipomoides filamentosus*.
Captive Care: This species should be kept in a small group (of five or more individuals) in a large aquarium with strong water movement. Live foods like brine shrimp may be necessary to incite feeding. Belligerent fishes often pick on Earle's Slender Anthias, including some of their more aggressive anthias relatives—choose tankmates carefully. A small group of chromis damselfishes and dart gobies, like the Zebra Dart Goby (*Ptereleotris zebra*), may encourage *L. earlei* to come out from hiding and feed. This species is not aggressive toward other fishes and will not harm invertebrates. It can be kept in a shallow-water or deep-water reef aquarium, but should be fed at least twice a day.
Aquarium Size: 55 gal. **Temperature:** 22 to 26°C (72 to 78°F).
Aquarium Suitability Index: 2.

Luzonichthys waitei (Fowler, 1931)

Common Name: Magenta Slender Anthias.
Maximum Length: 7 cm (2.8 in.).
Distribution: Philippines, Indonesia, and the Great Barrier Reef.
Biology: The Magenta Slender Anthias occurs in large groups, often with other zooplankton feeders, on steep outer-reef slopes. It has been reported at depths of 1 to 55 m (3.3 to 179 ft.).
Captive Care: See the Captive Care section for *Luzonichthys earlei*, above.
Aquarium Size: 55 gal. **Temperature:** 22 to 26°C (72 to 78°F).
Aquarium Suitability Index: 2.

Luzonichthys whitleyi (Smith, 1955)

Common Name: Whitley's Slender Anthias.
Maximum Length: 7 cm (2.8 in.).
Distribution: Christmas Island, eastern Indian Ocean, and the Line, Canton, and Phoenix Islands in the Central Pacific.
Biology: Whitley's Slender Anthias occurs in large groups, often with other zooplankton feeders, on steep outer-reef slopes. It has been reported at depths of 22 to 200 m (72 to 650 ft.). In the Line Islands, this species joins groups comprised of up to five other zooplankton feeders, including Bartlett's Anthias (*Pseudanthias bartlettorum*), the Dispar Anthias (*Pseudanthias dispar*), the Fusilier Damselfish (*Lepidozygus tapeinosoma*), and the

Luzonichthys waitei, Magenta Slender Anthias: female specimen.

Luzonichthys waitei, Magenta Slender Anthias: color variant.

Luzonichthys whitleyi: specimen from Christmas Island (Pacific).

Midas Blenny (*Ecsenius midas*). All of these species share a similar color pattern at this location and may derive protection from aggregating as they feed. Whitley's Slender Anthias has also been observed joining aggregations of *L. waitei*.
Captive Care: See the Captive Care section for *Luzonichthys earlei*, page 551.
Aquarium Size: 55 gal. **Temperature:** 22 to 26°C (72 to 78°F).
Aquarium Suitability Index: 2.

Genus *Nemanthias* (Threadfin Anthias)

This genus contains one attractive species, the Threadfin Anthias (*Nemanthias carberryi*), which is limited in its distribution to the Indian Ocean. It differs from the similar *Pseudanthias* in having 11 dorsal spines rather than 10. The first and second dorsal spines are also prolonged in this species, and the upper lip of the adults is thick and pointed. Threadfin Anthias form shoals on the reef-face and fore-reef slopes—like their relatives the *Pseudanthias*—feed on zooplankton. This species is a protogynous hermaphrodite.

Nemanthias carberryi Smith, 1954
Common Name: Threadfin Anthias.
Maximum Length: 10 cm (3.9 in.).
Distribution: East Africa to the Maldive Islands.
Biology: *Nemanthias carberryi* inhabits depths of 4 to 30 m (13 to 98 ft.) on reef faces, outer-reef slopes, and dropoffs. Around the Maldive Islands, it is most common on the reef face in areas that are rich in fire, hard, and soft coral growth. Males are often found in small groups within the larger aggregations, with up to four males swimming together—tilting on their sides and displaying toward each other. Also near the Maldives, the Threadfin Anthias is often found in association with the ubiquitous Flame Anthias (*Pseudanthias ignitus*), Evan's Anthias (*Pseudanthias evansi*), and Lyretail Anthias (*Pseudanthias squamipinnis*).

Nemanthias carberryi, Threadfin Anthias (males): as with many anthias, keep singly or in groups of one male to eight or more females to diffuse aggression.

Nemanthias carberryi, Threadfin Anthias: violet form, male specimen.

Nemanthias carberryi, Threadfin Anthias: pinkish form, male specimen.

Captive Care: The Threadfin Anthias will do best if housed in a medium- to large-sized aquarium with nonaggressive tankmates and plenty of hiding places. It is best kept in a group consisting of one male and eight or more females. Strong water movement and good water quality are prerequisites for keeping this sensitive species, while live foods (e.g., brine shrimp) may be necessary to induce feeding. Introducing this fish into a tank that already contains an established shoal of less aggressive anthias may facilitate its acclimation. This species can be kept in either a shallow-water or deep-water reef aquarium.

Aquarium Size: 55 gal. **Temperature:** 22 to 27°C (72 to 80°F).
Aquarium Suitability Index: 2-3.
Remarks: The Threadfin Anthias has two color forms. One is reddish pink with yellow spots on each scale and lighter pink on the ventrum. The other is purplish violet with a violet dorsal fin and yellow on the posterior portion of the body and caudal fin. Intermediate color forms are not uncommon. The sympatric Evan's Anthias (*P. evansi*) is also violet and yellow, but it does not have prolonged first and second dorsal spines. The Evan's Anthias also has a yellow, rather than a violet, dorsal fin.

Genus *Plectranthias* (Perchlets)

The genus *Plectranthias* is divergent in both form and behavior from the other anthias. All of the perchlets have a robust body, a deeply notched dorsal fin, a square tail, lower pectoral rays that are thickened (an adaptation to resting on the substrate), a large mouth, and large scales, which are present on the head as far forward as the posterior nostrils. There are over 40 known species in this genus and only one of these occurs in the Atlantic. This species, the **Apricot Perchlet** (*Plectranthias garrupleus*) **Robins & Starck, 1961**, has been exported to Japan by deep-water fish collectors. The rest are known from tropical and subtropical areas of the Indo-Pacific. Members of this genus are small (many attain a maximum length of less than 6 cm [2.4 in.]), secretive fishes rarely seen by divers or aquarists. They look and act more like hawkfishes than anthias, spending time either sitting on or hovering just above the bottom. They feed on small fishes and crustaceans and usually inhabit deep water in areas of coral rubble. Some of the shallow-water forms also occur in areas rich in hard coral. Many of the *Plectranthias* species are attractively marked, displaying shades of brown, red, or orange. However, Pelicier's Perchlet (*Plectranthias pelicieri*), which was recently described from Mauritius, is the most visually stunning member of the genus.

Plectranthias longimanus Weber, 1913
Common Name: Longfinned Perchlet.
Maximum Length: 3.5 cm (1.4 in.).
Distribution: East Africa to Fiji, north to southern Japan, and south to Queensland.
Biology: The Longfinned Perchlet occurs on coastal reefs, on both reef faces and fore-reef slopes, at depths from to 6 to 73 m (20 to 237 ft.). It is most common below 20 m (65 ft.). This fish is reported to behave much like a hawkfish.
Aquarium Care: This species is collected for the aquarium trade on rare occasions. Because of its small size, it can be kept with a wide range of less aggressive species, although it is potential prey for many piscivores. Although it can be kept in a shallow or deep-water reef aquarium, it will spend more time in the open in the latter environment.
Aquarium Size: 30 gal. **Temperature:** 22 to 26°C (72 to 78°F).
Aquarium Suitability Index: 5.

Plectranthias longimanus, Longfinned Perchlet: hawkfish-like rarity.

Plectranthias pelicieri, Pelicier's Perchlet: specimen from Okinawa.

Remarks: *Plectranthias longimanus* is very similar to the **Midget Perchlet** (*Plectranthias nanus*) **Randall, 1980**. They are almost identical in color, but *P. nanus* has two distinct dark spots on the posterior region of the caudal peduncle, while *P. longimanus* has two white spots in the same location. The Longfinned Perchlet has 12 or 13 pectoral rays (*P. nanus* has 14 to 18) and 12 to 15 tube-bearing lateral line scales (*P. nanus* has 14 to 22). The Midget Perchlet is more common around small, oceanic islands, while *P. longimanus* more often frequents reefs around continents or large islands. The Midget Perchlet attains a maximum length of 3.5 cm (1.4 in.) and is distributed from Christmas and Cocos-Keeling Islands east to the Line and Hawaiian Islands, north to the Philippines, and south to the Pitcairn group. It occurs on coastal reefs, in reef channels, on reef faces, fore-reef slopes, and dropoffs, at depths from to 6 to 57 m (20 to 185 ft.). Although still a secretive fish, this perchlet lives in more exposed habitats than its relatives. It occurs in dense coral growth, near coral heads on sand slopes, on rubble, and on mixed rubble/sand bottoms; it has also been found in caves. Midget Perchlets from around the Hawaiian Islands are redder than those from other locations.

Plectranthias pelicieri Randall & Hoese, 1995
Common Name: Pelicier's Perchlet.
Maximum Length: 6 cm (2.4 in.).
Distribution: Mauritius and Okinawa.
Biology: Pelicier's Perchlet occurs on fore-reef slopes at depths of 50 to 70 m (163 to 228 ft.). It lives in pairs on coral rubble slopes and often refuges among plate corals (*Fungia* spp.). It is reported to swim off the bottom to capture zooplankton in a manner similar to certain hawkfishes.
Captive Care: On rare occasions, this species is collected for the

Plectranthias sp.: undescribed but similar to *P. inermis*.

Highfin Perchlets

Several species of perchlets have a high third dorsal spine with a pennantlike flap. These include **Plectranthias morgansi Smith, 1961**, from Kenya; **Plectranthias altispinnatus Katayama & Masuda, 1980**, from Japan; and the **Unarmed Perchlet (*Plectranthias inermis*) Randall, 1980**, from Indonesia, the Philippines, and New Britain. As a result of its distribution, it is possible to encounter *P. inermis* in your local aquarium store. This fish is a resident of rubble slopes, where it can be found among coral rubble, soft corals, and mushroom or disc corals (*Fungia* spp.). (It shares this habitat with several species of fairy wrasses, *Cirrhilabrus* spp.). The Unarmed Perchlet has been reported at depths of 14 to 65 m (46 to 211 ft.). The specimen pictured here is apparently an undescribed species from Okinawa that is quite similar to *P. inermis*.

aquarium trade and it always commands a high price. *Plectranthias pelicieri* can be aggressive toward smaller fishes—like gobies and dartfishes—that stay near the aquarium bottom. Although Pelicier's Perchlet can be kept in a shallow-water or deep-water reef aquarium, it will spend more time in the open in the latter environment.

Aquarium Size: 30 gal. **Temperature:** 22 to 26°C (72 to 78°F).
Aquarium Suitability Index: 5.
Remarks: This recently discovered species is the most striking member of the genus. It has 10 dorsal spines, 16 or 17 dorsal rays, 15 branched caudal rays, 13 unbranched pectoral rays, a long third dorsal spine, an emarginate caudal fin, and 3 ventrally directed to antrorse spines on the lower edge of the preopercle. It also has a very distinct color pattern. This fish is named in honor of David Pelicier, an astute fish collector in Mauritius who captured the first specimens.

Genus *Pseudanthias* (Fairy Basslets or Anthias)

The anthias most often encountered by divers and aquarists are members of the genus *Pseudanthias*. These fishes are commonly referred to as fairy basslets, or simply anthias (even though their genus name means "false anthias"). There are approximately 30 species in this group, which occur in the tropical and subtropical Indo-Pacific. Most of these fishes are sexually dichromatic and sexually dimorphic; some also exhibit more spectacular colors during courtship and spawning. Most of the *Pseudanthias* species form aggregations near the reef, which provides shelter from their enemies. Some species occur in fairly shallow water and are occasionally found in reef channels and clear or turbid lagoons, but the majority of these fishes are most prolific in the clean, clear water near dropoffs or steep reef slopes.

Although some fairy basslets encountered in the aquarium trade range into deep water (e.g., Twinspot Anthias, *Pseudanthias bimaculatus*), others are only found at great depths. For example, *Pseudanthias fucinus*, a species known only from the Hawaiian Islands and Johnston Atoll, occurs at depths of 122 to 180 m (397 to 585 ft.). The *Pseudanthias* species are always found in areas subjected to moderate or strong currents, which they depend on to transport their zooplankton prey. Most occur in shoals, with the size of these social groups varying greatly from one species to the next. For example, the Lyretail Anthias (*P. squamipinnis*) forms immense shoals in some locations, while Randall's Anthias (*Pseudanthias randalli*) is typically found in smaller groups that "hug" the substrate.

All the fairy basslets studied to date are protogynous hermaphrodites. At least one member of this genus has spawned in captivity.

Pseudanthias cooperi, Cooper's Anthias: shoaling near black coral on a deep fore reef, hovering in the currents to feed on passing zooplankton.

Pseudanthias bartlettorum (Randall and Lubbock, 1981)
Common Name: Bartlett's Anthias.
Maximum Length: 9 cm (3.5 in.).
Distribution: Belau, Caroline, Marshall, Nauru, and Line Islands.
Biology: This species is found at depths ranging from 4 to 30 m (13 to 98 ft.) on steep outer-reef slopes, dropoffs, and in reef channels. It forms groups that typically consist of several males and 30 or more females and juveniles. At shallow depths, Bartlett's Anthias often forms aggregations with Dispar Anthias (*Pseudanthias dispar*), Whitley's Slender Anthias (*Luzonichthys whitleyi*), Fusilier Damselfish (*Lepidozygus tapeinosoma*), and the Midas Blenny (*Ecsenius midas*). All of these species will develop a similar coloration (i.e., yellow dorsally, pink ventrally) when they associate with each other, a phenomenon known as social mimicry.

Pseudanthias bartlettorum, Bartlett's Anthias (male): an easily kept anthias.

Pseudanthias bartlettorum, Bartlett's Anthias (male): variant.

Pseudanthias bicolor, Bicolor Anthias (male in foreground): a durable species.

Captive Care: *Pseudanthias bartlettorum* is one of the easiest anthias to keep in an aquarium. Although it is not a large species, it needs swimming room in the upper part of the tank. Bartlett's Anthias will quickly acclimate to captivity as long as there are plenty of hiding places available and the aquarium does not already contain aggressive fish species. This anthias can be pugnacious, especially toward both other anthias and similarly shaped zooplankton feeders. Male specimens should not be kept with members of their own kind or even with other *Pseudanthias* species, unless they are housed in larger aquariums (135+ gallons). I once had a male fight with a large Blackcap Basslet (*Gramma melacara*) over rights to a shelter site. Bartlett's Anthias succeeded in driving the Blackcap Basslet out of the hole. In the process, it tore skeletal elements of the Blackcap's upper jaw loose. *Pseudanthias bartlettorum* is great for shallow-water and deep-water reef aquariums, but (like all anthias) it is important to feed it at least twice a day.

Aquarium Size: 55 gal. **Temperature:** 22 to 27°C (72 to 80°F).
Aquarium Suitability Index: 4.
Remarks: Females have a yellow back and caudal fin and a lavender body. There is a narrow violet line on the top of the head, along the anterior dorsal fin base. Males are violet with a yellow band starting just behind the eye, running along the back, and onto the upper caudal lobe. The lower caudal lobe is also bright yellow. This species is quite unique in its appearance, but there are several color forms present that may represent undescribed species, are the result of hybridization, or are simply color variations of this fish. In some areas—like the Line Islands—the Dispar Anthias (*Pseudanthias dispar*) mimics the color of Bartlett's Anthias, developing a lavender hue to the ventrum and a yellow dorsal coloration (see photograph, page 561). However, the Dispar Anthias can be distinguished by its red dorsal fin.

Pseudanthias bicolor (Randall, 1979)

Common Name: Bicolor Anthias.
Maximum Length: 13 cm (5.1 in.). Hawaiian specimens are reported to attain a larger size than those from other areas.
Distribution: Mauritius to the Hawaiian and Line Islands, south to the Loyalty Islands, and north to the Yaeyamas.
Biology: The Bicolor Anthias is found at depths between 5 and 70 m (16 to 228 ft.), on low-profile lagoon patch reefs and near crevices, caves, and ledges on steep outer-reef slopes. It is a deep-water anthias, being most abundant between 20 and 70 m (65 and 228 ft.). *Pseudanthias bicolor* is observed in small- to medium-sized aggregations as high as 3 to 4 m (10 to 13 ft.) up in the water column. In Hawaii, the Bicolor Anthias is occasionally seen associating with the Hawaiian Anthias (*Pseudanthias*

The Bloodspot Anthias: A New Species of Fish?

Several years ago, I happened upon an unusual species of anthias. It was pink overall, with a yellowish orange line running from the upper jaw, under the eye, and ending at the base of the pectoral fin. One of the most distinct characteristics of this species was a bright red spot on the back and the base of the dorsal fin.

After searching the literature, I was unable to identify this lovely fish, so I sent several photos off to Dr. John Randall, the world's leading authority on reef fish taxonomy. Since Dr. Randall was also unable to identify the fish, I was convinced that it was an undescribed species. This discovery was not made on a reef off Fiji, New Guinea, or the Red Sea—but at a fish store in Omaha, Nebraska.

Little information exists on the distribution of this fish, which I refer to as the Bloodspot Anthias (*Pseudanthias* sp. 1). Those individuals entering the aquarium trade (often called "pink anthias") are apparently coming out of the Philippines, while Richard Pyle reported seeing this fish in water about 77 m (250 ft.) deep off Belau. They apparently occur at shallower depths in the Philippines, or they would probably show up with less regularity in the aquarium trade. This species has also been reported from southern Japan and Fiji. The largest specimen I have seen was a male that was about 10 cm (3.9 in.) in total length.

The most exciting thing for aquarists is that this species is not a difficult species to keep (it has an Aquarium Suitability Index of 3). The smaller females do tend to acclimate more readily than larger males. The Bloodspot Anthias accepts a variety of commercial fish foods and makes a wonderful display animal. Care should be taken if you want to keep more than one in your tank. They can be kept in groups, but make sure the tank is large (100+ gallons) and keep only one male per aquarium. Make sure you don't add this fish to a tank that contains aggressive tankmates. It will spend more time in the open and may be more likely to retain its striking coloration in a dimly lit tank.

Bloodspot Anthias (female): "discovered" in a Nebraska aquarium shop.

Bloodspot Anthias (male): easily kept, by anthias standards.

Bloodspot Anthias (male?): one male per tank helps prevent lethal territorial battles.

thompsoni); in Indonesia, it forms mixed aggregations with an undescribed species of slender anthias (*Luzonichthys* sp.).

Captive Care: This is a durable aquarium fish, but young specimens are easier to acclimate to aquarium life than large adults. If you want to keep a group of these fish—which should consist of a single male and eight or more females—use a tank of at least 135 gallons. Adult specimens can be kept with moderately aggressive tankmates, like pygmy angelfishes, small- to medium-sized dottybacks, and surgeonfishes, as long they are introduced after the Bicolor Anthias is established in the tank. This species will not harm invertebrates, but will acclimate more readily to a dimly lit aquarium. It can be kept in a shallow-water reef tank, but needs to be gradually exposed to higher light levels. The Bicolor Anthias is prone to color loss; to avoid this, it is important to feed it a diet high in carotenoids.

Aquarium Size: 55 gal. **Temperature:** 22 to 27°C (72 to 80°F).
Aquarium Suitability Index: 3-4.

Remarks: In male Bicolor Anthias, the second and third dorsal spines are greatly elongated and have yellow tufts (cirri) at the tips, while in the female, only the third dorsal spine is prolonged. The upper half of the body is orange, the lower part is lavender. At depth, the back of this anthias looks bright yellow and the ventral surface appears blue, making it easy to identify. Two other anthias resemble this species. The Hawaiian Anthias (*Pseudanthias thompsoni*) is similar in appearance, but lacks the prolonged dorsal spines and the purple ventrum of the Bicolor Anthias. (The Hawaiian Anthias is endemic to the Hawaiian Island chain.) The females of the Striped Anthias (*Pseudanthias taeniatus*), a species endemic to the Red Sea, are also similar in appearance to the Bicolor Anthias.

Pseudanthias bimaculatus (Smith, 1955)
Common Names: Twinspot Anthias, Twospot Anthias.
Maximum Length: 14 cm (5.5 in.).
Distribution: East Africa, Maldives, and Indonesia.
Biology: This anthias occurs at depths ranging from 10 to 70 m (33 to 228 ft.) on outer-reef slopes and at the base of dropoffs, and is most common below 40 m (130 ft.). In the Java Sea, this species occurs on dead reefs in relatively turbid water. *Pseudanthias bimaculatus* individuals form small aggregations that contain several males and numerous females, and also forms mixed groups with Squarespot Anthias (*Pseudanthias pleurotaenia*) in certain areas. For example, off the north coast of Bali, *P. pleurotaenia* is common at depths of 30 m (98 ft.) but is replaced by *P. bimaculatus* at about 45 m (146 ft.). At approximately 35 to 40 m (114 to 130 ft.), the two species form mixed shoals and interbreed. In the Maldives, Twinspot Anthias aggregations usually contain about 12 individuals; they swim up to 4 m (13 ft.) into the water column.
Captive Care: The Twinspot Anthias needs plenty of swimming space, good hiding places, and clean water in order to thrive in the home aquarium. The tank should include several large shelter sites into which it can quickly retreat if it feels threatened. Due to its preference for deeper water, the Twinspot Anthias acclimates more readily in an aquarium with lower light levels. Do not add this species to a tank that contains aggressive fishes—if it is bothered by tankmates, it will fail to acclimate. *Pseudanthias bimaculatus*, especially larger specimens, can be difficult to feed. Be prepared to offer live brine shrimp and baby guppies in order to elicit a feeding response. When first introduced to the aquarium, the Twinspot Anthias will typically hide for several days to

Pseudanthias bimaculatus, Twinspot Anthias (female): excellent care needed.

Pseudanthias bimaculatus, Twinspot Anthias: specimen from Java.

Pseudanthias bimaculatus, Twinspot Anthias (male): variant.

Pseudanthias sp. 2, Harlequin Anthias (male): specimen from Belau.

Pseudanthias bimaculatus, Twinspot Anthias (male): spectacular fish, but one demanding at least two feedings per day and superior aquarium conditions.

a week before making forays out into the open. Once it acclimates, it will spend most of its time in the water column and may display aggression toward smaller planktivores—especially other anthiines. Keep only one per aquarium, unless your tank is large (180+ gallons). If you want to keep a group of Twinspots, add one male and five or more females. Be careful when selecting a specimen for your aquarium. Twinspot Anthias may suffer from maladies related to being captured in deep water. *Pseudanthias bimaculatus* will not harm invertebrates, but it is not well suited for most shallow-water reef aquariums. It does best at lower light levels and needs plenty of swimming room—often lacking in a tank packed with live rock. Like all anthias, it must be fed at least twice (preferably several times) a day.

Aquarium Size: 70 gal. **Temperature:** 22 to 26°C (72 to 78°F).
Aquarium Suitability Index: 2-3.
Remarks: Males of this species have either one or two spots on the dorsal fin. The male is pink on the head, which changes to red toward the middle of the body and extends to the tail. There are pink squiggle lines on the red, with two pink lines running toward the ventrum. Over some parts of their range, male *P. bimaculatus* are pink with red bands on the body and a red blotch on the soft portion of the posterior dorsal fin. Females are pink overall with a yellow dorsal, anal, and caudal fin, and a yellow caudal peduncle. This is a larger, heavy-bodied anthias. The Squarespot Anthias (*P. pleurotaenia*) is probably most similar in form, but is easily distinguished by its color pattern. Male Stocky Anthias (*Pseudanthias hypselosoma*) and Luzon Anthias (*Pseudanthias luzonensis*) have a spot on the dorsal fin but are otherwise dissimilar in coloration. Another spectacular deep-water anthias is the **Harlequin Anthias** (*Pseudanthias* sp. 2). The females of this species are yellowish orange, while the males are very gaudy, as you can see in the photograph on page 558. This species has only been reported from the German Channel in Belau, although it no doubt occurs elsewhere. It was observed at depths of 55 to 90 m (179 to 293 ft.) and attains a maximum length of about 12 cm (4.7 in.).

Pseudanthias cooperi, Cooper's Anthias (male): a less-demanding species.

Pseudanthias cooperi, Cooper's Anthias (male): displaying.

Pseudanthias cooperi: specimen from Christmas Island (Pacific).

Pseudanthias cooperi (Regan, 1902)
Common Names: Cooper's Anthias, Redbar Anthias, Silverstreak Anthias.
Maximum Length: 14 cm (5.5 in.).
Distribution: East Africa to the Line Islands, north to Japan, and south to the Great Barrier Reef.
Biology: This anthias occurs at depths of 16 to 60 m (52 to 195 ft.) on dropoffs and outer-reef slopes. Like many anthias, it prefers areas that are affected by strong currents. Cooper's Anthias live in small, loose aggregations and often hang over or among the branches of large black corals (*Antipathes* spp.) and Green Cup Coral trees (*Tubastraea micrantha*). In the Maldives, *P. cooperi* is occasionally found associating with the Resplendent Anthias (*Pseudanthias pulcherimmus*) near large cave and archway openings in water deeper than 35 m (114 ft.). Cooper's Anthias also forms mixed aggregations with the Lyretail Anthias (*Pseudanthias squamipinnis*) in the Maldives at depths between 22 and 32 m (72 to 104 ft.). In Micronesia, Cooper's Anthias is commonly found associating with the Squarespot Anthias (*Pseudanthias pleurotaenia*) and the Purple Queen Anthias (*Pseudanthias pascalus*). Males will display to females about 2 m (7 ft.) off the bottom. During these displays, the males adopt a silvery dorsal coloration.
Captive Care: This is a less demanding anthias that can be kept in small groups in larger aquariums (135+ gallons). Keep only one male per tank. Cooper's Anthias will not harm invertebrates. Plenty of hiding places, good water movement, and nonaggressive tankmates will facilitate acclimation. Reduced light levels and either artificial or live branching gorgonians will also make this fish "feel" more at home. *Pseudanthias cooperi* prefers light levels that are lower than in most shallow-water reef aquariums, although it has been known to acclimate to brighter conditions.
Aquarium Size: 55 gal. **Temperature:** 22 to 26°C (72 to 78°F).
Aquarium Suitability Index: 3.
Remarks: Males of this species have a well-developed short red bar on their sides and a red tail. The tail of this species is lunate, and the tips of both the upper and lower lobes are prolonged in males. Females have red-tipped caudal lobes and are pinkish orange overall, with a small, faint red bar on the sides. Around Christmas Island, in the Central Pacific, Cooper's Anthias are more brightly colored—having bright yellow on their flanks—than their counterparts from other regions. This species was once thought to be the same as the Striped Anthias (*Pseudanthias taeniatus*), but the Striped Anthias is endemic to the Red Sea and differs from *P. cooperi* in its coloration. *Pseudanthias kashiwae* is a synonym of *P. cooperi*.

Pseudanthias dispar, Dispar Anthias (male): note characteristic red dorsal.

Pseudanthias dispar, Dispar Anthias: male yawning.

Pseudanthias dispar, Dispar Anthias (male): mimic from Christmas Is. (Pacific).

Pseudanthias bartlettorum, Bartlett's Anthias: model from Christmas Island.

Pseudanthias dispar (Herre, 1955)
Common Names: Dispar Anthias, Redfin Anthias, Peach Anthias.
Maximum Length: 9.5 cm (3.7 in.).
Distribution: Western Pacific east to Samoa and the Line Islands.
Biology: The Dispar Anthias is a shallow-water species that occurs at depths of 1 to 15 m (3.3 to 49 ft.). It inhabits reef crests, reef faces, and reef slopes, usually in areas of rich hard coral growth. Male Dispar Anthias often form small aggregations at the periphery of female shoals. Here, they display at consexual rivals and attempt to entice potential female partners. In certain parts of its range, *P. dispar* forms mixed aggregations with other anthias species, like Bartlett's Anthias (*P. bartlettorum*) or the Lyretail Anthias (*Pseudanthias squamipinnis*).
Captive Care: The Dispar Anthias is a demanding species that is often difficult to feed and is prone to being picked on by more aggressive tankmates. They are best kept in groups consisting of six or more females and a single male. More than one male can be kept in the same aquarium if the tank is large enough (100+ gallons). Because this species inhabits shallow reef-face areas, it is a suitable choice for a well-illuminated, shallow-water reef tank. It should be fed at least twice (preferably several times) a day.
Aquarium Size: 55 gal. **Temperature:** 22 to 27°C (72 to 80°F).
Aquarium Suitability Index: 2-3.
Remarks: The color of this species varies to some degree, but male Dispar Anthias always have a bright red dorsal fin and lack red bands on the tail. The females are yellowish orange above, pale lavender to white below, and the dorsal fin is a paler red—especially the anterior portion. Both males and females have an orange line, bordered in lavender, running from the snout to the pectoral fin base. The pelvic fins are slightly prolonged in females,

Pseudanthias dispar, Dispar Anthias: a male displays at a consexual.

Pseudanthias evansi, Evan's Anthias (male): difficult to maintain.

Pseudanthias fasciatus, Redstripe Anthias (female): a deep-water species.

and greatly so in males. The Flame Anthias (*Pseudanthias ignitus*) is almost identical to *P. dispar*, but it has red bands on the edge of the upper and lower caudal fin. Dispar Anthias from the Line Islands mimic Bartlett's Anthias (*P. bartlettorum*). Some individuals of both species are yellow dorsally and have pink on their ventrums. However, *P. dispar* always has a red dorsal fin. In the Ryukyus, an unusual male Dispar Anthias has been photographed that was purple overall and became silver when it displayed. This individual lived among a shoal of normally colored *P. dispar* for several months, until it suddenly disappeared.

Pseudanthias evansi (Smith, 1954)
Common Names: Evan's Anthias, Yellowback Anthias, Yellowtail Anthias.
Maximum Length: 13 cm (5.1 in.).
Distribution: Indian Ocean from Kenya south to Mozambique, east to the Maldives, Mauritius, and the Cocos-Keeling Islands.
Biology: This species occurs at depths of 5 to 30 m (16 to 98 ft.) on reef faces and reef slopes. It is usually found in areas with rich hard and soft coral growth, where it lives in large shoals that may number in the hundreds. Evan's Anthias will rise several meters into the water column to pick off zooplankton carried by ocean currents. This species has been taken from the stomach of a piscivorous snapper (the Green Jobfish, *Aphareus furcata*). The Midas Blenny (*Ecsenius midas*) will associate with Evan's Anthias and may enhance its resemblance to this species by developing a yellow dorsal and lavender-blue ventral coloration. The Threadfin Anthias (*Nemanthias carberryi*) is also a social mimic of this anthias species.
Captive Care: Evan's Anthias is a difficult species to maintain and is best left to more experienced aquarists. It can be kept in a reef

P. fasciatus, Redstripe Anthias: female in background, male in foreground.

aquarium, but is difficult to keep in any aquarium for long periods of time. Zooplankton provided by a productive refugium will increase your chances of success with this species. Evan's Anthias should be housed with peaceful tankmates.
Aquarium Size: 55 gal. **Temperature:** 22 to 27°C (72 to 80°F).
Aquarium Suitability Index: 2.
Remarks: Evan's Anthias is violet overall with yellow dots on its sides. The back is yellow from the origin of the dorsal fin to the lower caudal fin base. The dorsal fin and tail are also mostly yellow. There is an orange line from the snout, through the eye, to the pectoral fin base. In *P. evansi* males, the second pelvic ray, fourth and fifth anal ray, and tenth to thirteenth dorsal rays are prolonged. The Threadfin Anthias (*N. carberryi*) is similar in overall coloration, but while it has a violet or pink dorsal fin, Evan's Anthias has a yellow dorsal fin. The Threadfin Anthias also has 11 dorsal spines rather than 10, and the first and second dorsal spines are prolonged.

Pseudanthias fasciatus (Kamohara, 1954)
Common Names: Redstripe Anthias, Striped Anthias.
Maximum Length: 21 cm (8.3 in.).
Distribution: South Africa and the Red Sea east to Indonesia, north to southern Japan (where it is common), and south to the Great Barrier Reef. This species was only recently documented from deep water in the Red Sea and southern Africa.
Biology: The Redstripe Anthias occurs at depths ranging from 20 to over 150 m (65 to 489 ft.), but is most common deeper than 30 m (98 ft.). Adults frequent dropoff caves and overhangs, often swimming upside down with their ventral surfaces oriented toward the cave or overhang ceiling. Juveniles are most common in small aggregations in 20 to 30 m (65 to 98 ft.) of water.

During the breeding period, the tips of the male's pelvic fins and caudal fin turn red, and red also appears on the head.
Captive Care: Redstripe Anthias prefer low-light conditions and should be housed in a dimly lit tank with a large cave or overhang. They should not be kept with overly aggressive tankmates, but instead should live with cardinalfishes, assessors, comets, chromis, flasher wrasses, gobies, and dart gobies. The Redstripe Anthias can be kept in small aggregations, but maintain only one male per aquarium. This species will not harm invertebrates, but is best in a deep-water reef aquarium. The Redstripe Anthias is prone to suffering from decompression problems associated with being captured at greater depths. For this reason, it is important to examine specimens carefully before making a purchase to be sure they are able to maintain their position in the water column.
Aquarium Size: 55 gal. **Temperature:** 20 to 26°C (68 to 78°F).
Aquarium Suitability Index: 3.

Pseudanthias hawaiiensis Randall, 1979
Common Name: Hawaiian Longfin Anthias.
Maximum Length: 7.7 cm (3.0 in.).
Distribution: Hawaiian and Johnston Islands.
Biology: This species is often found swimming upside down in caves or under overhangs in water 26 to 199 m deep (85 to 647 ft.), but is most common below 40 m (130 ft.). It feeds on zooplankton—including copepods, crustacean larvae, fish eggs, mollusk larvae, and polychaete larvae—but does not venture far from the bottom the way many other anthias species do.
Captive Care: Although this species often ships poorly, healthy individuals will usually fare better in a home aquarium than their counterparts, Longfin Anthias (*Pseudanthias ventralis*).

Pseudanthias fasciatus, Redstripe Anthias: male displaying courtship colors.

Pseudanthias hawaiiensis, Hawaiian Longfin Anthias: female specimen.

Pseudanthias hawaiiensis, Hawaiian Longfin Anthias (male) : a stunningly beautiful species that can be kept in pairs and may fare well in a dimly lit aquarium.

Hawaiian Longfin Anthias can be kept in male/female pairs, and are best kept in a dimly lit tank. They are very susceptible to bacterial and protozoan infections, should not be kept with aggressive tankmates, and should be moved as little as possible. This species will not harm invertebrates, but it will have difficulty acclimating to the intense lighting often present over a shallow-water reef aquarium. It can be kept in a more dimly lit deep-water reef tank, but if a specimen does contract a parasite or bacterial infection, it would be difficult to treat without removing it and stressing it further.

Aquarium Size: 30 gal. **Temperature:** 21 to 24°C (70 to 76°F).
Aquarium Suitability Index: 2-3.
Remarks: *Pseudanthias hawaiiensis* has prolonged pelvic and anal fins. Males are orangish red with a violet section toward the tail, the head is yellow with fuchsia lines behind the eyes, and the anal fin is orange in front and yellow at the rear. In females, the head, back, and anal fin are mostly yellow, and the ventral half of the body is lavender.

Pseudanthias heemstrai Schumacher, Krupp & Randall, 1989
Common Names: Heemstra's Anthias, Redhead Anthias.
Maximum Length: 13 cm (5.1 in.).
Distribution: Gulf of Aqaba, Red Sea.
Biology: This species occurs at a depth range of 13 to 67 m (42 to 218 ft.) on fore reefs and at the base of the reef slope. They occur in loose aggregations and forage from 3 to 6 m (10 to 20 ft.) above the reef (males are found higher in the water column than females). This species typically forms unisexual groups. Occasionally during the day, the sexes will mix together and/or with other species of anthias like the Striped Anthias (*Pseudanthias taeniatus*). About one hour before sunset, some male Heemstra's begin to establish territories, a minimum of 80 cm (31 in.) apart, over prominent coral outcrops. These males adopt courtship colors, which consist of the scale margins turning from pinkish red to dark red, the scale centers becoming darker, a white band forming from the back of the yellow head to the

caudal fin origin, a white, oval spot forming on the upper part of the caudal peduncle, the posterior margin of the caudal fin turning bright red, the dorsal fin becoming darker red, and the anal fin taking on a reddish tinge. The courting males hang about 1 m (3.3 ft.) over the reef, display to females by performing U-swim displays, and evict conspecific males, some females, Zebra Swallowtail Angelfish (*Genicanthus caudovittatus*), and chromis (*Chromis* spp.). After 10 to 30 minutes of this territorial behavior, the males resume their normal coloration and leave their courtship sites.

Captive Care: This is a moderately hardy species that should be kept with nonaggressive tankmates. Heemstra's Anthias can be kept alone or in groups composed of one male and eight or more females. It will accept most aquarium foods, will not harm invertebrates, and can be kept in a shallow-water or deep-water reef aquarium. However, *P. heemstrai* will acclimate more readily to the latter environment.
Aquarium Size: 55 gal. **Temperature:** 21 to 26°C (70 to 78°F).
Aquarium Suitability Index: 3.

Pseudanthias huchtii (Bleeker, 1857)
Common Names: Redcheek Anthias, Green Anthias, Threadfin Anthias.
Maximum Length: 12 cm (4.7 in.).
Distribution: Indonesia and Philippines to Vanuatu and southern Great Barrier Reef. This species is common on coastal reefs in the Philippines, Indonesia, and New Guinea.
Biology: The Redcheek Anthias occurs at depths of 0.3 to 20 m (1 to 65 ft.). It is usually found on shallow reef faces, reef slopes, or near the edge of dropoffs where there is rich hard and soft coral growth. It is also found over coral heads in lagoon habitats and around more nutrient-rich coastal reefs. This species often associates with groups of Lyretail Anthias (*Pseudanthias squamipinnis*).
Captive Care: This is a hardy and aggressive anthias species. It is best to keep solitary individuals, unless you have a large aquarium. If you want to keep a group of Redcheek Anthias, it should consist of one male and eight or more females, and be housed in a tank of at least 180 gallons. Be sure that the females you introduce are not undergoing sex changes if they are going to be housed with another male. Because of its pugnacious disposition, it is also risky to keep *P. huchtii* with most other anthias species or with peaceful zooplankton feeders (e.g., dart gobies, fairy wrasses, and flasher wrasses). An interesting aquarium display might be made up of three or four female Redcheek Anthias, five or more female Lyretail Anthias, and a male of either species. If fed frequently, the Redcheek Anthias can be expected to do well in both

Pseudanthias heemstrai, Heemstra's Anthias (male): moderately hardy.

Pseudanthias huchtii, Redcheek Anthias (female): hardy with proper feeding.

Pseudanthias huchtii, Redcheek Anthias (male): a pugnacious personality.

Pseudanthias huchtii, Redcheek Anthias (male): males vary in coloration and are often referred to in the aquarium trade as "Green Anthias."

the shallow-water and the deep-water reef aquarium.
Aquarium Size: 55 gal. **Temperature:** 22 to 27°C (72 to 80°F).
Aquarium Suitability Index: 4.
Remarks: Male *P. huchtii* have a red line on each cheek and are greenish yellow overall with red margins on the fins. Females are yellowish orange or greenish orange, with orange stripes on their cheeks.

Pseudanthias hutomoi (Allen & Burhanuddin, 1976)
Common Name: Hutomo's Anthias.
Maximum Length: 11.5 cm (4.5 in.).
Distribution: Indonesia and the Philippines.
Biology: This is a deep-water anthias found on fore-reef slopes, often in nutrient-rich coastal waters. In Bali, *P. hutomoi* is observed on sandy slopes where it hangs near small patch reefs composed of boulders, sponges, and soft corals at depths in excess of 30 to at least 63 m (98 to 205 ft.). It occurs in small female-dominated shoals in current-prone areas.

Captive Care: Hutomo's Anthias is not common in the aquarium trade, but is offered through Bali fish distributors on occasion. This species should be housed in an aquarium with reduced illumination, like a deep-water reef tank. For more details on care requirements see the Captive Care section of the subfamily account, page 543.
Aquarium Size: 55 gal. **Temperature:** 22 to 27°C (72 to 80°F).
Aquarium Suitability Index: 3.
Remarks: The original description of *P. hutomoi* was based on specimens collected in a fishing trawl. Both males and females have a thick orange bar running from the posterior edge of the eye to the pectoral fin base. Females and males have four small, light blotches along the back (these may be less conspicuous or even absent in some males). Females are pinkish orange overall, while males are lighter on the sides and ventrum and have blue trim on the margins of the pelvic and median fins. Males also have purple trim on the bar behind the eye and some have a large blue patch under the soft portion of the dorsal fin.

Pseudanthias hypselosoma Bleeker, 1878

Common Names: Stocky Anthias, Pink Anthias, Truncate Anthias.

Maximum Length: 19 cm (7.5 in.).

Distribution: Maldives to Samoa, north to Taiwan and southern Japan, and south to the Great Barrier Reef and Loyalty Island.

Biology: The Stocky Anthias occurs at depths of 6 to 50 m (20 to 163 ft.) and is most common on protected lagoon patch reefs—often in more turbid conditions. It is also encountered on outer-reef slopes. Stocky Anthias form small- to medium-sized aggregations, and males aggressively defend females within their harems. When males display, their head lightens and the tail becomes a deep red color. I have seen this species intermingling with small groups of Red-belted Anthias (*Pseudanthias rubrizonatus*) around a large shipwreck in 26 m (85 ft.) of water.

Captive Care: This is a hardy anthias that can be kept in small aggregations in larger aquariums (135+ gallons), but only one male per tank should be included. Plenty of hiding places, good water movement, and nonaggressive tankmates will make acclimation easier. This species can be kept in a shallow-water or deep-water reef aquarium.

Aquarium Size: 55 gal. **Temperature:** 22 to 27°C (72 to 80°F).

Aquarium Suitability Index: 4.

Remarks: The males of *P. hypselosoma* have a red spot on the spinous portion of the dorsal fin. In juveniles and females, the dorsal spot is lacking, but their caudal fin has red upper and lower tips and a narrow red edge. The caudal fin of males truncates (the posterior edge is rounded), although males may have thin streamers present on the upper tip. In females, the caudal fin is slightly emarginate. The Luzon Anthias (*Pseudanthias luzonensis*) is most

Pseudanthias hypselosoma, Stocky Anthias (females): a hardy choice.

Pseudanthias hypselosoma, Stocky Anthias (male): coastal reef dweller.

Pseudanthias hutomoi, Hutomo's Anthias (female): a deep-water rarity.

Pseudanthias hutomoi, Hutomo's Anthias (male): occasional Bali import.

similar in overall appearance, with males of both species having a red spot on the dorsal fin. However, the Luzon Anthias also has yellow stripes on the body and a lunate tail. Females are most easily identified by their caudal fin shape, which is slightly emarginate in *P. hypselosoma* and lunate in *P. luzonensis*. The latter species also lacks the bright red posterior caudal fin margin. *Anthias truncatus* is a synonym of *P. hypselosoma*.

Pseudanthias ignitus (Randall & Lubbock, 1981)
Common Names: Flame Anthias, Indian Flame Anthias.
Maximum Length: 8 cm (3.1 in.).
Distribution: Indian Ocean, from the Maldives and Andaman Sea.
Biology: The Flame Anthias occurs at a depth range of 10 to 35 m (33 to 114 ft.) on patch reefs in lagoons, on the reef face, and on fore-reef slopes. It is typically found in areas with rich fire, hard, and soft coral growth. This anthias is found in huge aggregations and sometimes forms mixed aggregations with the Lyretail Anthias (*Pseudanthias squamipinnis*) or the Threadfin Anthias (*Nemanthias carberryi*).
Captive Care: Flame Anthias can be difficult to keep, often refusing anything but live food. They are also prone to being picked on by more aggressive tankmates. They are best kept in groups consisting of six or more females and a single male. More than one male can be kept in the same aquarium if the tank is large enough (100+ gallons). Because this species inhabits shallow reef faces and fore-reef areas, it is a good choice for the well-illuminated shallow-water reef tank. It should be fed at least twice (preferably several times) a day. Flame Anthias tend to be slightly more durable than Dispar Anthias (*Pseudanthias dispar*), which may be a result of how they are handled in their countries of origin.
Aquarium Size: 55 gal. **Temperature:** 22 to 27°C (72 to 80°F).

Pseudanthias ignitus, Flame Anthias: crowded shoal includes a few *Pseudanthias squamipinnis*, Lyretail Anthias. Note red caudal fins of male *P. ignitus*.

Aquarium Suitability Index: 2-3.
Remarks: In female Flame Anthias, only the outer edge of the dorsal fin is red, while the caudal fin is not red at all. The males do have a red caudal fin, which is a characteristic that distinguishes it from the closely related Dispar Anthias. I have seen males in the Maldives, however, that had apparently changed sex recently and still lacked the red coloration on the tail.

Pseudanthias lori (Lubbock & Randall, 1976)
Common Names: Lori's Anthias, Tiger Queen Anthias.
Maximum Length: 12 cm (4.7 in.).
Distribution: Philippines and Christmas Island to the Tuamotu Islands, north to the Yaeyamas, south to the Loyalty Islands.
Biology: Lori's Anthias occurs at depths of 7 to 70 m (23 to 228 ft.) on the reef face, steep reef slopes, or dropoffs, usually around caves, archways, and ledges. It is most abundant in the deeper parts of its range. For example, in Micronesia it is found at depths of 20 to 70 m (65 to 228 ft.). It forms smaller aggregations and sometimes associates with the closely related Princess Anthias (*Pseudanthias smithvanizi*).
Captive Care: This species is moderately hardy and is easier to keep than most of the other members of the subgenus *Mirolabrichthys*. Lori's Anthias should be kept in an aquarium with plenty of hiding places, nonaggressive tankmates, and reduced lighting. They also do best if kept in groups comprised of one male and several females. Unless they are given plenty of space to avoid one another (135+ gallons), males will fight among themselves. Once acclimated, Lori's Anthias will eat a variety of foods, including finely chopped seafoods, frozen preparations, and flake food, but live food can be helpful in inducing finicky specimens to feed. This species will not harm invertebrates and can be kept in a shallow- or deep-water reef aquarium.
Aquarium Size: 55 gal. **Temperature:** 22 to 27°C (72 to 80°F).
Aquarium Suitability Index: 3.
Remarks: The Princess Anthias (*Pseudanthias smithvanizi*) is a similar species, but lacks the red bars on the body. *Pseudanthias imeldae* is a synonym of this species.

Pseudanthias luzonensis (Katayama & Masuda, 1983)
Common Names: Luzon Anthias, Yellowline Anthias.
Maximum Length: 12 cm (4.7 in.).
Distribution: Philippines to northern Australia and the Great Barrier Reef.
Biology: This species is found at depths of 20 to 60 m (65 to 195 ft.) on protected coastal reefs, often where there is rich coral and sponge growth. It also lives at the base of dropoffs over rubble bottoms with scattered larger coral rock. The Luzon Anthias oc-

Pseudanthias ignitus, Flame Anthias (male displaying): a challenge to keep.

Pseudanthias lori, Lori's Anthias (female): moderately hardy.

Pseudanthias lori, Lori's Anthias (male): also called Tiger Queen Anthias.

Pseudanthias luzonensis, Luzon Anthias (male): prefers dim conditions.

Pseudanthias olivaceus, Olive Anthias (female): a durable aquarium fish.

Pseudanthias olivaceus, Olive Anthias (male): note caudal filaments.

curs in small groups, in which females greatly outnumber males. The Lyretail Hawkfish (*Cyprinocirrhites polyactis*) occasionally swims among aggregations of these anthias, which it apparently mimics.

Captive Care: This anthias can be kept in small groups in larger aquariums (135+ gallons), but only one male should be housed per tank. Plenty of hiding places, good water movement, and nonaggressive tankmates will help ensure its acclimation. The Luzon Anthias is best kept in a dimly lit aquarium. This species will not harm invertebrates, but prefers lower light levels than are present in most shallow-water reef aquariums.

Aquarium Size: 55 gal. **Temperature:** 22 to 27°C (72 to 80°F).
Aquarium Suitability Index: 3.

Remarks: Males have a red spot on the spinous portion of the dorsal fin and three yellow lines on the body, just below the lateral line. Females are pink overall and lack the spot and body markings. Both males and females have a lavender-edged orange band from the eye to the pectoral base. *Pseudanthias luzonensis* is most similar to the Stocky Anthias (*Pseudanthias hypselosoma*)—males of this species have the red spot on the dorsal fin, but they lack the yellow stripes. The tail of the Stocky Anthias is also truncate, while that of the Luzon Anthias can be either emarginate or lunate.

Pseudanthias olivaceus Randall & McCosker, 1982
Common Name: Olive Anthias.
Maximum Length: 12 cm (4.7 in.).
Distribution: Southeast Oceania (including Cook Islands, Austral Islands, Line Islands, Society Islands, and Tuamotus).
Biology: This species is found on reef faces and fore-reef slopes at depths of 1 to 34 m (3.3 to 111 ft.). It occurs in small aggregations over coral heads and rock substrates. The Fusilier Damselfish (*Lepidozygus tapeinosoma*) apparently mimics, and may associate with, the Olive Anthias around the Line Islands.
Captive Care: This is a durable aquarium species that is occasionally available from the Cook and Christmas Islands. It is a fairly aggressive fish and should not be housed in small aquariums with diminutive zooplanktivores. It can be kept in groups, as long as they are placed in a large tank (135+ gallons). Add only one male per tank, however.
Aquarium Size: 55 gal. **Temperature:** 22 to 27°C (72 to 80°F).
Aquarium Suitability Index: 4.
Remarks: Olive Anthias males have a dusky spot on the pectoral fins, the pelvic fins have a dusky margin, and the males are more brightly colored overall with orange patches on the side of the body and blue margins on the tail lobes and dorsal fin. The caudal lobes of males also have filamentous extensions.

Pseudanthias parvirostris (Randall & Lubbock, 1981)

Common Names: Diadem Anthias, Shortsnout Anthias, Sunset Anthias.
Maximum Length: 9 cm (3.5 in.).
Distribution: Solomon Islands, Philippines, southern Japan, the Maldives, and the Mascarenes.
Biology: *Pseudanthias parvirostris* lives at depths of 35 to 60 m (114 to 195 ft.) over patch reefs, on sand and rubble slopes, and along dropoffs. I have observed small groups of Diadem Anthias near the mouth of a large cave at 42 m (137 ft.) in the Maldives, along with a larger aggregation of Resplendent Anthias (*Pseudanthias pulcherimmus*). At this same location, large aggregations of Diadem Anthias were encountered at about 61 m (198 ft.) amid black corals. In the Western Pacific, the Diadem Anthias has been observed aggregating with the Princess Anthias (*Pseudanthias smithvanizi*).
Captive Care: This is a moderately hardy species that rarely enters the aquarium trade. It should be housed in a tank that contains plenty of hiding places, nonaggressive tankmates, and reduced lighting. It can be kept in groups, but house only one male per aquarium. Once acclimated, the Diadem Anthias will eat a variety of foods, but live food may be required to induce finicky specimens to feed. This species can be housed in a shallow-water reef tank, but will acclimate more readily to a deep-water reef aquarium.
Aquarium Size: 55 gal. **Temperature:** 22 to 27°C (72 to 80°F).
Aquarium Suitability Index: 3.
Remarks: *Pseudanthias parvirostris* has a short snout; head length can be divided by snout length from 4.5 to 5.6 times. The tail is yellow, with violet upper and lower margins. The males of this species lack the pointed protuberance on the upper lip common to all other members of the subgenus *Mirolabrichthys*. Instead, the upper lip of *P. parvirostris* is thicker than that of the females. The populations from the Indian Ocean differ in color and may represent a distinct species.

Pseudanthias pascalus (Jordan & Tanaka, 1927)

Common Names: Purple Queen Anthias, Amethyst Anthias, Sailfin Anthias.
Maximum Length: 17 cm (6.7 in.).
Distribution: North Sulawesi, Indonesia, and Taiwan to French Polynesia, north to Japan, and south to the Great Barrier Reef and New Caledonia.
Biology: This species occurs at depths of 5 to 60 m (16 to 195 ft.), but is most abundant in the deeper parts of its range. For example, in Enewetak, *P. pascalus* is most common at depths greater than 30 m (98 ft.). It is found in areas subjected to strong

Pseudanthias parvirostris, Diadem Anthias (female): specimen from Maldives.

Pseudanthias parvirostris, Diadem Anthias (male): specimen from Japan.

Pseudanthias parvirostris, Diadem Anthias (male): specimen from Maldives.

currents, over rubble bottoms, or near large caves on coral outcrops, outer-reef slopes, or dropoffs. The Purple Queen Anthias occurs in loose groups and feeds high in the water column (2 to 3 m [7 to 10 ft.] above the bottom). Juvenile Bluehead Tilefish (*Hoplolatilus starcki*), which look similar in color to this species at depth, have been observed associating with the Purple Queen Anthias as they feed and apparently mimic them. These anthias also form aggregations with the Yellowstripe Anthias (*Pseudanthias tuka*) in some areas (e.g., Belau).

Captive Care: This is a difficult species to maintain in captivity. It often refuses to feed, wasting away as a result. The Purple Queen Anthias is best kept in groups of one male and five or more females. This aggregation should be housed in a medium- to large-sized aquarium (70+ gallons) with plenty of swimming room in the upper levels of the tank. Provide plenty of shelter sites and do not house them with aggressive species. The best way to keep *P. pascalus* is to have a plankton-laden refugium attached to the tank (see "Keys to Successful Anthias Husbandry," page 548). Adding individuals to a tank that contains docile anthias that are already established and feeding may facilitate the acclimation of this species. The Purple Queen Anthias is also prone to losing its intense coloration. It will not harm invertebrates, but should not be housed in a shallow-water reef aquarium—it will be less likely to acclimate under such intense lighting. *Pseudanthias pascalus* should be fed at least once (preferably several times) a day and may be more prone to parasitic infections due to its fragility.

Aquarium Size: 55 gal. **Temperature:** 22 to 27°C (72 to 80°F).
Aquarium Suitability Index: 2.
Remarks: This species is bright violet in color with an orange band from the tip of the snout under the eye to the pectoral fin base. In males, the posterior portion of the dorsal fin has a large red patch. The female Purple Queen Anthias has no yellow band on the back, or yellow on the caudal fin. It is closely related to the Yellowstripe Anthias (*P. tuka*). The males of these two species are very similar in appearance. The throat and abdominal area of *P. tuka* males is yellow, and they have a small patch of purple on the dorsal fin. Females of *P. tuka* have a yellow stripe down the back.

Pseudanthias pictilis (Randall & Allen, 1978)
Common Name: Painted Anthias.
Maximum Length: 15 cm (5.9 in.).
Distribution: West Pacific Ocean from New Caledonia, Lord Howe Island, and the Great Barrier Reef. Most of the specimens that enter the aquarium trade are reported to come from Tonga, which would be a range extension for this species.
Biology: *Pseudanthias pictilis* is found at depths of 10 to 40 m (33 to 130 ft.) at the edge of steep reef slopes. It is most common at depths greater than 20 m (65 ft.), and occurs in shoals in current-prone areas.
Captive Care: This is a large anthias that needs a lot of swimming space as well as several suitable hiding places. Live foods (e.g., brine shrimp) are usually required to induce an initial feeding response. The Painted Anthias should not be introduced to a tank that contains aggressive tankmates, although it can become aggressive toward other zooplankton feeders once it acclimates. More than one Painted Anthias can be kept per tank, although male individuals may pick on females. Never place more than one male in an aquarium. These anthias can be kept in a large shallow-water or deep-water reef aquarium, although they will acclimate more rapidly in a tank with reduced lighting.

Pseudanthias pascalus, Purple Queen Anthias (male): sadly, difficult to keep.

Pseudanthias pictilis, Painted Anthias (female): often found in cooler water.

Pseudanthias pictilis, Painted Anthias (male): demands a large tank and ample swimming room and will actively harass many other zooplankton feeders.

Aquarium Size: 70 gal. **Temperature:** 21 to 26°C (70 to 78°F).
Aquarium Suitability Index: 3.

Pseudanthias pleurotaenia (Bleeker, 1857)

Common Names: Squarespot Anthias, Squareblock Anthias, Squareback Anthias, Mirror Anthias.
Maximum Length: 20 cm (7.9 in.).
Distribution: Philippines south to the Great Barrier Reef and east to Samoa.
Biology: This species is found at depths of 10 to 180 m (33 to 585 ft.), but is most common at depths exceeding 30 m (98 ft.). For example, at Enewetak, this species is most abundant between 60 and 120 m (195 to 390 ft.). It occurs on steep reef slopes and walls, and is most often encountered at the upper edge of the dropoff. It is most common in areas affected by tidal currents. The Squarespot Anthias forms loose aggregations consisting of several males and numerous females. Individuals in these groups feed well above the bottom on zooplankton. At the depths that this species normally occurs, the pink blotches on the males glow like blue neon lights. These conspicuous markings, in addition to the acrobatic swimming displays of territorial males, serve as signals to rival male conspecifics and potential mates.

Captive Care: Adult *P. pleurotaenia* need a large aquarium (no smaller than a standard 55-gallon tank) with several hiding places that they can dive into when they feel threatened. Acclimation is often slow—your specimen may hide for a week or more before you catch a glimpse of it. In time, however, it will usually come out of hiding and accept live and prepared foods, including baby livebearers, frozen and live brine shrimp, frozen preparations, and even flake food. Juveniles and smaller females (under 8 cm [3.1 in.]) adjust more readily to aquarium confines. Only one specimen should be kept per aquarium, unless the tank is large (180+ gallons). Even then you should keep only one male per tank and six or more females. This species may also behave aggressively toward other zooplankton feeders. The Squarespot Anthias will not harm invertebrates, but it is not well suited for most shallow-water reef aquariums. It does best at lower light levels and needs plenty of swimming room, which is often lacking in a tank packed with live rock. Another drawback to keeping this species in a brightly lit tank is that its color often fades. The Squarespot Anthias must be fed at least twice (preferably several times) a day.

Pseudanthias pleurotaenia, Squarespot Anthias (female): feed frequently.

Pseudanthias pleurotaenia, Squarespot Anthias (male): ample space needed.

Pseudanthias sheni, Shen's Anthias (male): rarity from NW Australia.

Pseudanthias pleurotaenia, Squarespot Anthias (male): Flores variant.

Aquarium Size: 70 gal. **Temperature:** 22 to 27°C (72 to 80°F). **Aquarium Suitability Index:** 3.

Remarks: As the name implies, the male Squarespot Anthias has a large pink spot or square on each side of its body (an occasional specimen may lack this blotch). The Red-belted Anthias (*Pseudanthias rubrizonatus*) has a red smudge on each side of its body, but otherwise is very different in color. Male Cooper's Anthias (*Pseudanthias cooperi*) also have a narrow red bar on each side. The Squarespot Anthias is most closely related to the Twinspot Anthias (*Pseudanthias bimaculatus*), (with which it has been known to crossbreed off Bali) and **Shen's Anthias (*Pseudanthias sheni*) Randall & Allen, 1989**. The latter species is only known from Rowley Shoals off the northwestern coast of Australia and differs from the Squarespot both in color and in the number of gill rakers. Male Shen's Anthias lack the distinct square blotch on the side, while females of these two species are difficult to distinguish. Female Shen's Anthias are more orange (the female Squarespot is yellow), with a lavender belly. There is also an apparent color form of the Squarespot Anthias that has been reported from the reefs of Flores, Indonesia. This unusual morph, which was originally dubbed the Flores Basslet, suddenly appeared after a massive earthquake struck the area in 1993. It occurs in shoals at depths of 1 to 50 m (3.3 to 163 ft.), and inhabits reef slopes and dropoffs.

Pseudanthias pulcherimmus (Heemstra & Randall, 1986)
Common Name: Resplendent Anthias.
Maximum Length: 11 cm (4.3 in.).
Distribution: Mauritius, Chagos Archipelago, and the Maldives.
Biology: The Resplendent Anthias resides on fore-reef dropoffs

Pseudanthias pulcherimmus, Resplendent Anthias (female): delicate species.

Pseudanthias pulcherimmus, Resplendent Anthias (male): deep-water fish.

Pseudanthias randalli, Randall's Anthias (male): prefers dim conditions.

Pseudanthias randalli, Randall's Anthias (male): rare and challenging.

at depths greater than 33 m (107 ft.). It is most commonly encountered at arches, the mouths of caves, and under large overhangs. Aggregations of 20 to 30 individuals, consisting mostly of females, hang around large black coral trees. These groups often mix with Cooper's Anthias (*Pseudanthias cooperi*) and the Lyretail Anthias (*Pseudanthias squamipinnis*). Other fishes found in this habitat include the Diadem Anthias (*Pseudanthias parvirostris*), Redscale Fairy Wrasse (*Cirrhilabrus rubrisquamis*), Longnose Hawkfish (*Oxycirrhites typus*), and Indian Butterflyfish (*Chaetodon mitratus*).

Captive Care: See the Captive Care section for *Pseudanthias randalli*, below, for husbandry information.
Aquarium Size: 55 gal. **Temperature:** 22 to 27°C (72 to 80°F).
Aquarium Suitability Index: 3.
Remarks: This species is very similar to Randall's Anthias (*P. randalli*), but Resplendent males are pink with a yellow band along the back and along the lower part of the side. Randall's males are pink overall with a bright red line down the side. Female Resplendent Anthias are orange, shading to pink, with a yellow snout, dorsal fin, and caudal fin, while female Randall's Anthias are yellowish to reddish orange overall with yellow outer caudal rays.

Pseudanthias randalli (Lubbock & Allen, 1978)
Common Name: Randall's Anthias.
Maximum Length: 7 cm (2.8 in.).
Distribution: Southern Japan south to Indonesia and east to the Marshall Islands.
Biology: This species occurs at depths ranging from 15 to 120 m (49 to 390 ft.) on reef dropoffs. It is most common at depths

Pseudanthias sp. 3, Cave Anthias: undescribed anthias from Guam.

Pseudanthias rubrizonatus, Red-belted Anthias (male): durable and fiesty.

Pseudanthias rubrizonatus, Red-belted Anthias (male): variant.

exceeding 20 m (65 ft.). Randall's Anthias is found in aggregations of 10 to 20 individuals and, unlike some of its congeners, it remains close to the bottom even when feeding.

Captive Care: This is a delicate anthias that should be kept in a dimly lit aquarium with docile fish species like small cardinalfishes, assessors, flasher wrasses, small fairy wrasses, fire gobies, dart gobies, shrimp gobies, etc. If Randall's Anthias is housed with pugnacious species, it will remain hidden and refuse to feed. Although I have had a *P. randalli* eat on the same day it was placed in my aquarium, this species is often difficult to feed. Adding larger specimens to a tank that already contains an acclimated shoal of smaller Dispar Anthias (*Pseudanthias dispar*) or juvenile Bartlett's Anthias (*P. bartlettorum*) may help initiate feeding. Do not add this species to a tank that contains an adult Bartlett's Anthias, which can be very aggressive. Finicky specimens should be offered live brine shrimp and baby guppies. A male and several females can be kept in larger aquariums (100+ gallons). When selecting specimens, be sure they are not swimming with their bodies pitched forward while laboring to maintain their position in the water column—this is an indication of a gas bladder problem. Unfortunately, this gorgeous fish is relatively uncommon in the hobby. It will not harm invertebrates, but is best kept in a deep-water reef aquarium because it is less likely to acclimate to the more intense light levels in a shallow-water reef tank. Feed *P. randalli* at least twice a day.

Aquarium Size: 55 gal. **Temperature:** 22 to 27°C (72 to 80°F).
Aquarium Suitability Index: 3.

Remarks: The third dorsal spine of Randall's Anthias is prolonged. The Resplendent Anthias (*P. pulcherimmus*) is a very similar species known from East Africa and the Maldives and Chagos Islands. There is also a similar, but undescribed, species (commonly referred to as the Cave Anthias) that has been observed off Guam at depths of 25 to 45 m (81 to 146 ft.) and in the Line Islands and Johnston Atoll. It is reported to be similar in form and behavior to Randall's Anthias, but differs in coloration.

Pseudanthias rubrizonatus (Randall, 1983)
Common Names: Red-belted Anthias, Red-girdled Anthias, Red-bar Anthias, Redband Anthias, Tricolor Anthias.
Maximum Length: 10 cm (3.9 in.).
Distribution: Andaman Sea to Fiji, north to the Philippines, and south to the Great Barrier Reef.
Biology: This species is found at depths of 10 to 58 m (33 to 189 ft.) around coral heads and rocks, in open sandy areas, around shipwrecks, and on outer-reef slopes. It is most abundant in areas exposed to strong currents. Male Red-belted Anthias are quite aggressive toward each other. I have seen this species in

mixed aggregations with the Stocky Anthias (*P. hypselosoma*).
Captive Care: This is a hardy and aggressive anthias species. It is best to keep solitary individuals, unless you have an aquarium that is 180+ gallons. If you want to keep a group, it should consist of one male and eight or more females. Because of its pugnacious disposition, it is also risky to keep Red-belted Anthias with most other anthias species and peaceful zooplankton feeders. It is prone to color and weight loss if not given a varied diet and an ample quantity of food. This species thrives in both shallow-water and deep-water reef aquariums. It must be fed at least once a day.
Aquarium Size: 55 gal. **Temperature:** 22 to 27°C (72 to 80°F).
Aquarium Suitability Index: 3.
Remarks: The males of this species are yellow posteriorly and have an orange head and a broad red bar on their sides. Females are light red with yellow marks on the scales and a white ventrum. Both sexes have a violet band from below the eye to the pectoral fin base. Specimens from Western Australia, which may represent a different species, differ in coloration and lateral line scale counts. The Red-belted Anthias has a distinct color pattern, but is most similar in its chromatic attire to Cooper's Anthias (*P. cooperi*) and Marcia's Anthias (*Pseudanthias marcia*).

Pseudanthias smithvanizi (Randall & Lubbock, 1981)
Common Name: Princess Anthias.
Maximum Length: 9.5 cm (3.7 in.).
Distribution: Cocos-Keeling to the Marshall Islands, north to the Yaeyamas, and south to the Great Barrier Reef.
Biology: The Princess Anthias occurs on steep outer-reef slopes in 6 to 70 m (20 to 228 ft.) of water. It is often found in areas of profuse hard coral and sponge growth, where it forms small aggregations that usually number less than 30 and consist mainly of females and juveniles. This species usually stays within 1 m (3.3 ft.) of the bottom and is often found in association with Lori's Anthias (*P. lori*) and the Yellowstripe Anthias (*Pseudanthias tuka*).
Captive Care: The Princess Anthias is not easy to keep. It should be housed in small shoals (about eight individuals with one male per group) in a medium- to large-sized aquarium. Provide this species with plenty of hiding places and nonaggressive tankmates. The aquarium should be dimly lit, with a combination of daylight and actinic bulbs. These anthias usually do not adapt to shallow-water reef aquariums because of the intense lighting.
Aquarium Size: 55 gal. **Temperature:** 22 to 27°C (72 to 80°F).
Aquarium Suitability Index: 3.
Remarks: Males have a pink band on the upper lobe of the caudal fin; females have red tail lobes. There is a yellow spot on each scale, except those on the ventrum, and no red bars on the back. Lori's Anthias (*P. lori*) is similar, but has short red bars on the back. The Princess Anthias is also closely related to the **Golden Anthias** (*Pseudanthias aurulentus*), **Randall & McCosker, 1982**, which differs from *P. smithvanizi* in having 15 soft dorsal rays, a larger eye, and two red stripes running down the body. The Golden Anthias is restricted in its distribution to the Line Islands and is rarely seen in the North American aquarium trade.

Pseudanthias sp. 4
Common Name: Reticulated Anthias.
Maximum Length: 10 cm (3.9 in.).
Distribution: Maldive Islands.
Captive Care: I have kept several of what may be this species (collected from the Maldives), and they proved to be quite durable aquarium fish. The Reticulated Anthias fed on frozen brine

Pseudanthias smithvanizi, Princess Anthias (female): forms aggregations.

Pseudanthias smithvanizi, Princess Anthias (male): not easy to keep.

Pseudanthias sp. 4, Reticulated Anthias (male): undescribed Maldivian fish.

Pseudanthias marcia, Marcia's Anthias (males): found in waters of Oman.

shrimp immediately after I released them from the shipping bag, and also accepted frozen preparations. Two individuals housed together in a smaller tank did not display any aggression toward each other. One specimen did arrive with an abrasion on its lower jaw caused by rubbing against the plastic shipping bag.
Aquarium Size: 55 gal. **Temperature:** 22 to 27°C (72 to 80°F).
Aquarium Suitability Index: 4.
Remarks: This anthias has yellow reticulations on the posterior portion of the body and the caudal peduncle. The Reticulated Anthias is similar to **Marcia's Anthias** (*Pseudanthias marcia*) **Randall & Hoover, 1993**, which is known from the Gulf of Oman and southern Oman. In Marcia's Anthias, the tail of the female is deeply emarginate, while the male's caudal fin has rounded lower lobes and a long red or yellow filament on the upper lobe. The females are orangish red over most of the body, head, and tail—except for the abdomen and lower portion of the head, which are pale. There is also a pale lavender line that extends from the lower edge of the eye to the pectoral fin base, and the caudal fin has red tips. Males are similar in overall coloration, but they have a red bar on the upper flank and a pale area on the upper portion of the caudal peduncle. The male's caudal fin is yellow, becoming red toward the posterior margin. Marcia's Anthias is found on rugged, rocky reefs at depths of 14 to 30 m (46 to 98 ft.). It occurs in shoals and sometimes forms mixed groups with Townsend's Anthias (*Pseudanthias townsendi*).

Pseudanthias squamipinnis (Peters, 1855)
Common Names: Lyretail Anthias, Scalefin Anthias, Jewel Anthias.
Maximum Length: 12 cm (4.7 in.).
Distribution: Red Sea to the Fijian Islands, north to Japan, and south to New South Wales, Australia.

Biology: The Lyretail Anthias occurs above clear lagoon pinnacles, in channels, on reef faces, and on fore-reef slopes at depths of 2 to at least 40 m (6.5 to 130 ft.). However, it is usually found at depths of less than 20 m (65 ft.). This species forms shoals of varying sizes, from small, isolated groups that are scattered sporadically over the reef, to huge shoals, numbering in excess of 2,000 individuals, that cover immense sections of the vertical reef face. The size and composition of these groups is a function of the microhabitat where they occur and the "age" of the group (that is, how long the group has been in existence). Lyretail Anthias shoals are comprised mainly of juveniles and adult females, and in some cases no males are present. However, most Lyretail Anthias shoals include nonterritorial as well as territorial males, although they are greatly outnumbered by juveniles and females. For example, shoals studied in the Red Sea had an average of one territorial male for every eight females, while multimale groups in Japan had an average ratio of approximately one male to every five females. Lyretail Anthias feed mainly on larger zooplankton, such as hydromedusans, pteropods, large copepods, and chaetognathans. They feed to a lesser degree on floating filamentous algae and small zooplankton, such as radiolarians, tintinnids, and the nauplii of copepods. *Pseudanthias squamipinnis* groups maintain their position in the water column by swimming at a rate equal to the speed of the oncoming current. In this way, the whole shoal remains stationary, usually above a specific coral head or rock. When the direction of the current changes, the anthias change their orientation. Group members swim from less than 20 cm (7.9 in.) to over 7 m (23 ft.) over their coral head. This distance is dependent on several factors, including size (larger specimens stray farther from shelter), light or visibility (the more light penetration, the higher they swim in the water column), and

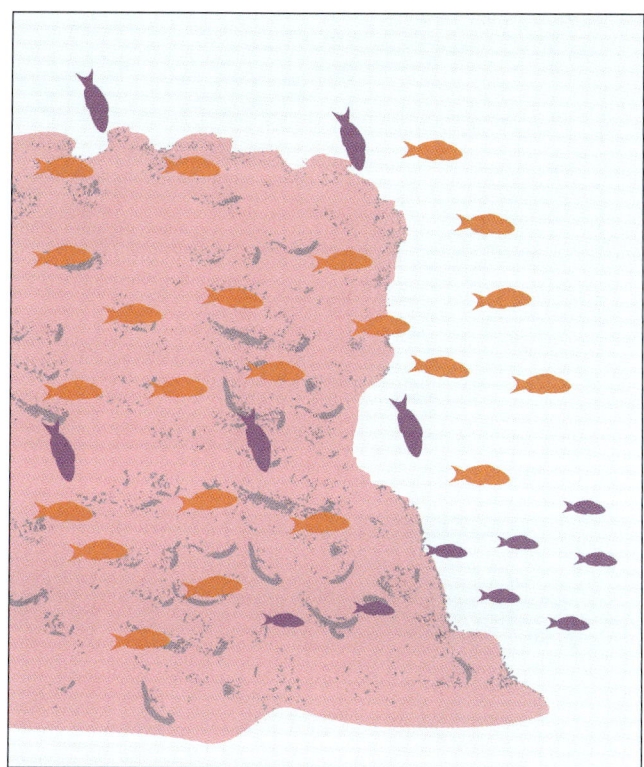

Typical distribution of a *Pseudanthias squamipinnis* shoal by gender: terminal males (larger purple), females (orange), subadult males (smaller purple).

During courtship, the *Pseudanthias squamipinnis* male (purple) performs a U-swim under the female (orange), dashing toward the bottom, then pulling up.

the size of the group (the larger the group, the more dispersed the individuals will be). *Pseudanthias squamipinnis* shoals are often joined by other zooplankton feeders, like Dispar Anthias (*P. dispar*), Redcheek Anthias (*P. huchtii*), Bicolor Chromis (*Chromis dimidiatus*), sergeants (*Abudefduf* spp.), Klein's Butterflyfish (*Chaetodon kleini*), and Twotone Wrasses (*Thalassoma amblycephalum*). Female Lyretail Anthias are mimicked by the Midas Blenny (*Ecsenius midas*), which associates and feeds among the Lyretail shoals. In the Red Sea, the Lyretail Anthias is the primary food of the Coral Hind (*Cephalopholis miniata*). In the Red Sea, this species spawns in the cooler months (November through June), when the water temperatures are about 20°C (68°F), while on the Great Barrier Reef and Japan, spawning occurs in the summer, when water temperatures are 25 to 26°C (77 to 78°F). This and other anthias species spawn every night throughout the spawning period. The Lyretail Anthias spawns at dusk. Courtship begins with territorial males engaging in zigzag swimming (they descend in the water column in a back-and-forth trajectory). Males also perform U swims: from a height of about 2 m (7 ft.) they dash toward the bottom, then pull up to the height at which they started. All the fins are erected during the U-swim, and the pectoral fins are held out, fully exposing the purple blotches on the fin. A receptive female will then approach the male and the two will swim ahead together and release their gametes. Females spawn once a night, while territorial males spawn multiple times. Nonterritorial males occasionally spawn with groups of females when the territorial males are occupied.

Captive Care: The Lyretail Anthias is a hardy and aggressive anthias species. It is best to keep solitary individuals, unless you have a large aquarium. If you want to keep a group, it should consist of one male and eight or more females and should be housed in a tank of 180+ gallons. Make sure the females you introduce are not undergoing sex change if they are to be housed with a male. During aggressive encounters, individuals will chase and nip at each other, or may even lock jaws. Because of their pugnacious disposition, it is also risky to keep male Lyretail Anthias with most other members of the genus, or with peaceful zooplankton feeders (e.g., dart gobies, fairy wrasses, or flasher wrasses). Lyretail Anthias will aggressively accept most forms of aquarium fare, but make sure a varied diet is presented to ensure good health and

Pseudanthias squamipinnis, Lyretail Anthias (female): common and hardy.

Pseudanthias squamipinnis, Lyretail Anthias (female): variant.

Pseudanthias squamipinnis, Lyretail Anthias: female changing to male.

Pseudanthias squamipinnis, Lyretail Anthias (male): variant from Maldives.

Pseudanthias squamipinnis, Lyretail Anthias (male): variant from Sulawesi.

Pseudanthias squamipinnis, Lyretail Anthias (male): one per aquarium.

color retention. They will not harm invertebrates and will do well in both shallow-water and deep-water reef aquariums. Feed this species at least twice a day.

Aquarium Size: 55 gal. **Temperature:** 22 to 27°C (72 to 80°F).
Aquarium Suitability Index: 4.
Remarks: Females are orange-gold overall, with a red line edged in purple running from the eye to the pectoral fin base. Females also lack a violet marking on the pectoral fins. Male coloration varies somewhat, but most are dark red or violet with a large pink smudge on the pectoral fins. The first signs of female sex change consist of a darkening of the head, back, posterior dorsal fin, and pelvic fins. The pectoral fins begin to develop the violet pectoral spot, which starts as thin parallel lines on the fin. These lines gradually broaden, forming the spot that is characteristic of the male. The caudal fin begins to darken after the pectoral spot begins to appear. These short-term changes are complete about 16 days after sex change begins. It will take months for the colors to attain the brilliant reddish violet of the fully transformed male. An increase in body size and elongation of the third dorsal spine and caudal fin streamers are also characteristic of sex change. Sex change can occur at a variety of sizes depending on the anthias population in question. For example, in the Red Sea, female Lyretail Anthias change sex at a length of 6.5 to 10 cm (2.6 to 3.9 in.) SL, while at Aldabra, sex change occurs at 5.3 to 6.2 cm (2.1 to 2.4 in.) SL in one population and 4.0 to 4.5 cm (1.6 to 1.8 in.) SL in another population. Female sex change typically does not take place until the individual is more than 2 years old.

Pseudanthias taeniatus Klunzinger, 1884
Common Names: Striped Anthias, Red Sea Anthias.
Maximum Length: 13 cm (5.1 in.).
Distribution: Red Sea.
Biology: The Striped Anthias occurs at depths of 10 to 50 m (33 to 163 ft.) on dropoffs, reef faces, and outer-reef slopes. Like many anthias, *P. taeniatus* prefers areas affected by strong currents. They live in loose groups and often aggregate with the Lyretail Anthias (*P. squamipinnis*); however, they stay closer to the reef. Male Striped Anthias will form small aggregations within these groups and display at each other. When they display, the red and white stripes on their bodies become more pronounced and the orange dorsal and caudal fins turn snowy white and often have a blue hue. Male *P. taeniatus* will also display at and fight with the Lyretail Anthias.
Captive Care: This is a moderately hardy anthias that can be kept in shoals in larger aquariums (135+ gallons). Keep only one male per tank and eight or more females. Provide plenty of hiding places, good water movement, and nonaggressive tankmates to

Pseudanthias squamipinnis: displaying male from Papua New Guinea.

Pseudanthias taeniatus, Striped Anthias: male at right, smaller female at left.

Pseudanthias townsendi, Townsend's Anthias: male in foreground.

ANTHIAS 581

Once A Hawkfish

Serranocirrhitus latus, Fathead Anthias

The story of the Fathead Anthias (*Serranocirrhitus latus*) begins in 1949, when a small colorful fish, collected off the island of Okinawa, was described by the Japanese ichthyologist Dr. M. Watanabe. The fish was not only a new species, it also represented an undescribed genus. It was given the name *Serranocirrhitus latus* (the generic name meaning "grouper-hawkfish") and placed in the hawkfish Family Cirrhitidae. Thirteen years later on the island continent of Australia, the renowned ichthyologist Dr. G. Whitley described an apparently unknown anthiaslike species from the Coral Sea, and named it *Dactylanthias mcmichaeli*. Whitley placed his "new" discovery in the Family Serranidae and the Subfamily Anthiinae. Although the color of Whitley's species differed somewhat from that of *S. latus*, it turned out to be the same fish. In 1978, Dr. J. Randall and Dr P. Heemstra formally moved *S. latus* from the hawkfish family to the grouper family and made it synonymous with *D. mcmichaeli*. This completed the somewhat confusing taxonomic heritage of the Fathead or Hawkfish Anthias.

In 1986, I had my first encounter with this fish that had even fish taxonomists at odds. My initial contact was not underwater, but in one of the holding tanks at Aquarium Fish Fiji, in Viti Levu, Fiji. I was taken aback by the subtle beauty of this delicate-looking fish and was thrilled to hear that Tony Nahacky, part owner of this fish-collecting operation, was regularly sending a few of these fish to the United States. The following day, on my last afternoon dive, I had the good fortune of locating Fathead Anthias in their natural environment near Beqa Island, Fiji. I was diving along a steep reef face when I spotted a trio of these beauties in a small cave at 17 m (55 ft.).

The Fathead Anthias differs from its more regularly encountered *Pseudanthias* cousins in both morphology and behavior. Meristically, it is characterized by a very deep body and elongate pectoral fins that extend back as far as the posterior part of the anal fin. The shape of the eye and mouth give it a menacing expression, although this species is the antithesis of mean. It is a relatively small fish, reaching a maximum length of 13 cm (5.1 in.).

Unlike the majority of the *Pseudanthias* species, which form sizable shoals and hang above the reef feeding on zooplankton, the Fathead Anthias can be found in most areas swimming upside down under overhangs, archways, and in caves. I have also seen these fish hovering out in the open on sheer dropoffs, usually near crevices in which they quickly retreat if threatened. They occur singly, in pairs, or in trios. In Savu Savu, Fiji, where this species is common, it is found in association with hard corals, soft corals, and gorgonians. Other authors have observed this species in small to large groups along vertical dropoff ledges and caves. It may be that these shoals occur in deeper water where this fish is more abundant. The specimens I have encountered in Fiji have been at shallow depths of 14 to 23 m (46 to 75 ft.), but it has been reported to occur on steep outer-reef slopes down to 70 m (228 ft.). Its geographical range is from the Moluccan Islands east to the Fijian Islands, north as far as the Izu Islands off Japan, and south to the Great Barrier Reef and New Caledonia.

There are a few secrets to keeping Fathead Anthias successfully. One is to provide them with plenty of hiding places. Since they seem to prefer the subdued light levels of caves and archways, a dimly lit tank may help them to overcome their initial timidity more quickly. I kept a specimen in a 10-gallon aquarium with a Highfin Banded Goby (*Stonigobiops nematodes*) and a small Bluelined Dottyback (*Pseudochromis cyanotaenia*). The anthias was introduced first and was initially shy. When I fed it, I had to introduce the food, move to the back of the room, and watch from a distance to see if it was eating. Not long after being introduced to its new home, the Fathead Anthias began eating live brine shrimp and frozen preparations. However, it took some time before the fish would venture out of hiding when I was near the aquarium.

Another factor that will aid an aquarist in keeping this delicate fish is to house it with passive tankmates like gobies, comets, reef basslets, assessors, and dragonets. Although I did keep mine with a Blueline Dottyback, I would not recommend dottybacks as good tankmates for such a shy fish. This species has been observed to lie on top of, and follow, a small Snowflake Moray (*Echidna nebulosa*) in captivity. Whether this interesting association is an artifact of being kept in captivity or something that occurs in nature is unknown, but some groupers have been known to follow and even rub up against eels on the reef. It is thought that eel locomotion may flush out or expose small fishes and invertebrates that are preyed on by the groupers. I would also be reluctant to put more than one of these fishes together in a small- to medium-sized aquarium because of potential aggression. In my observations of pairs and trios in the wild, one individual was always larger than the other(s). The larger specimen was probably the male. If you want to try to acquire a pair, purchase individuals that differ greatly in size.

***Serranocirrhitus latus*, Fathead Anthias: a beautiful but shy and often delicate fish that requires ample hiding places and placid tankmates.**

Fathead Anthias are especially sensitive to inadequate decompression. These individuals will perch between rocks constantly and will have difficulty maintaining their position in the water column. This fish is not well suited for the shallow-water reef aquarium, as the bright environment will cause it to stay hidden in a cave or crevice. It can be kept in the more dimly lit deep-water reef tank, with green star polyps, mushroom anemones, zoanthids, *Dendronephthya* soft corals, and colt coral.

You may be wondering what happened to my Fathead Anthias. I decided to move him from my 10-gallon tank to a larger reef aquarium. After acclimating the fish, I released it into its new tank and watched it disappear into a crevice in the reef. Apparently, this Fathead never adjusted to life in its new environment (possibly due to resident bullies) for it was the last time I ever saw that fish. Its cause of death was never determined.

Although it is apparently common in some parts of its range, it is by no means common on the ornamental marine fish market. If you do have access to one of these beauties, I would highly recommend it for an aquarium that contains nonaggressive fishes or for a smaller-species tank.

Pseudanthias thompsoni, Hawaiian Anthias (female): Hawaiian endemic.

Pseudanthias tuka, Yellowstripe Anthias (female): tempting but hard to keep.

Pseudanthias tuka, Yellowstripe Anthias, male: demands expert feeding.

facilitate acclimation. Striped Anthias will not harm invertebrates and can be kept in shallow-water or deep-water reef aquariums. However, this species will acclimate more readily to the latter environment.

Aquarium Size: 70 gal. **Temperature:** 21 to 26°C (70 to 78°F).
Aquarium Suitability Index: 3.
Remarks: Male Striped Anthias have a narrow white stripe on each side of the body (which becomes broader and more pronounced when the male displays) and a wide stripe extending from the chin onto the ventrum. Females have red-tipped caudal lobes and are pinkish orange overall with a broad area of pink on the lower flank and a white ventrum. **Townsend's Anthias (*Pseudanthias townsendi*) (Boulenger, 1897)** is a very similar species that is restricted in its distribution to the Gulf of Oman and the Arabian Sea. The females of the two species are almost indistinguishable, while the males are easily separated by the color of the caudal fin (*P. townsendi* has a crimson red semicircular band on the outer edge of the tail, which is bordered by luminescent blue bands). Townsend's Anthias is most often found on rocky reefs at depths in excess of 15 m (49 ft.).

Pseudanthias thompsoni (Fowler, 1923)
Common Names: Hawaiian Anthias, Thompson's Anthias.
Maximum Length: 22 cm (8.7 in.).
Distribution: Hawaiian Islands and Bonin Island, Japan.
Biology: This species is found at depths ranging from 10 to 188 m (33 to 611 ft.), but is most common below 50 m (163 ft.). It occurs on dropoffs or steep outer-reef slopes. It swims as high as 9 m (29 ft.) over the bottom and feeds on copepods and shrimp larvae. Aggregations consist of numerous females and few males. The Hawaiian Anthias often forms mixed groups with the zooplankton-feeding Oval Chromis (*Chromis ovalis*), which it somewhat resembles at the depths at which they are found. During courtship, the male erects the dorsal fin and its color changes—the dorsal fin becomes a deeper red, a red line appears along the dorsum, and a red border appears on the operculum. The Hawaiian Anthias is eaten by the Bluefin Jack (*Caranx melampygus*).
Captive Care: This is a relatively hardy aquarium fish. It can be kept in groups in larger aquariums (135+ gallons), but keep eight or more females and only one male. The Hawaiian Anthias can be aggressive toward small zooplankton-feeding fish—especially other anthias. It may prove more difficult to acclimate if kept in a tank with intense lighting, like a shallow-water reef aquarium; they are best kept in the more dimly lit deep-water reef tank.
Aquarium Size: 70 gal. **Temperature:** 21 to 26°C (70 to 78°F).
Aquarium Suitability Index: 3.
Remarks: Males of this species differ from females in having a

broader magenta streak on the head and a wide yellow band on each side, a yellower pectoral fin base with a distinct lavender V, magenta upper and lower lobes of the caudal fin, and more pronounced red submarginal lines. It is most similar to the Bicolor Anthias (*Pseudanthias bicolor*), which differs in having an orange dorsal fin, prolonged first and second dorsal fin spines (in males), and an elongate third dorsal spine (in females).

Pseudanthias tuka (Herre & Montalban, 1927)
Common Names: Yellowstripe Anthias, Purple Anthias.
Maximum Length: 12 cm (4.7 in.).
Distribution: Indonesia to the Solomon Islands, north to southern Japan, and south to the northern Great Barrier Reef.
Biology: The Yellowstripe Anthias occurs at depths of 2 to over 30 m (7 to 98 ft.) on clear coastal and outer-reef slopes and dropoffs. In parts of Micronesia, *P. tuka* aggregates with the more abundant Purple Queen Anthias (*P. pascalus*). Juvenile Bluehead Tilefish (*Hoplolatilus starcki*) have been observed swimming with these anthias; they resemble them and feed at depths where Yellowstripe Anthias occur. Normally solid blue, *H. starcki* individuals develop a yellow line on their backs to more closely resemble the female anthias. *Pseudanthias tuka* also forms mixed aggregations with the Magenta Slender Anthias (*Luzonichthys waitei*).
Captive Care: This is a delicate, hard-to-keep species. See the Captive Care section for *Pseudanthias pascalus*, page 572.
Aquarium Size: 55 gal. **Temperature:** 22 to 27°C (72 to 80°F).
Aquarium Suitability Index: 2.
Remarks: Male Yellowstripe Anthias are a brilliant purple with a dark purple spot on the posterior part of the base of the dorsal fin, and yellow on the throat, abdomen, and thorax. Females have a yellow stripe down the back and yellow bands on the upper and lower caudal lobes. In the Purple Queen Anthias, females lack a yellow stripe down the back, while males have a white lower jaw and throat region and a large red spot on the posterior part of the dorsal fin.

Pseudanthias ventralis (Randall, 1979).
Common Name: Longfin Anthias.
Maximum Length: 5.5 cm (2.2 in.).
Distribution: Marianas east to the Pitcairn group, north to southern Japan, and south to the Great Barrier Reef.
Biology: This species occurs at depths of 40 to 120 m (130 to 390 ft.), but is most abundant at depths greater than 90 m (293 ft.). For example, at Enewetak Atoll, *P. ventralis* is the most common fish species at depths from 90 to 120 m (293 to 390 ft.). This habitat is a medium to steep reef slope, with sand, rocky

Pseudanthias ventralis, Longfin Anthias (female): shy and not easy to keep.

Pseudanthias ventralis, Longfin Anthias (female): variant from Japan.

Pseudanthias ventralis, Longfin Anthias (male): variant from Japan.

rubble, small caves, shallow ledges, gorgonians, black corals, *Halimeda*, and encrusting sponges. The Longfin Anthias feeds on zooplankton, but does not venture far from the bottom the way many other anthias species do.

Captive Care: The Longfin Anthias is a stunning deep-water species that has been available with some regularity from the Cook Islands. I have had limited success in the long-term maintenance of the Cook Island form. A shy species, it is often reluctant to eat and is a regular victim of both tankmate aggression and disease. Because *P. ventralis* is a delicate deep-water fish, it is possible that it could suffer more physical damage when collected. The Longfin Anthias tends to ship better than its Hawaiian counterpart, *Pseudanthias hawaiiensis*, but may be less hardy once introduced to the aquarium. It is best to special-order Longfin Anthias and take them as soon as they arrive at the retail store. The majority of fish stores can not give them the special care they need and often place them in brightly lit tanks with aggressive tankmates. The Longfin Anthias can be induced to eat live brine shrimp and similar-sized crustaceans, as well as some frozen foods (e.g., brine shrimp and small mysid shrimp). They will also ingest small motile invertebrates off the sides of the aquarium, or off the tank bottom. A refugium, as discussed in "Keys to Successful Anthias Husbandry," page 548, will also aid in the successful care of these anthias. Male Longfin Anthias may fight if they are placed in the same aquarium and might also pick on females, especially in smaller aquariums. However, they are not as aggressive as many of their congeners. This species will not harm invertebrates, but will be less likely to acclimate to the intense lighting and high water temperatures associated with a shallow-water reef aquarium. They can be kept in the more dimly lit deep-water reef aquariums.

Aquarium Size: 30 gal. **Temperature:** 20 to 24°C (68 to 76°F).

Pseudanthias ventralis, Longfin Anthias (male): a lovely fish, but demanding of expert husbandry techniques (specimen from Cook Islands).

The Ventralis Zone

On the fore-reef slope off the island of Enewetak, Micronesia, there is a particular section of the reef referred to as the Ventralis Zone, located at a depth range of 90 to 120 m (297 to 396 ft.). The substrate consists of 50% sand and 50% rubble, with a scattering of deep-water gorgonians and encrusting sponges. As its scientific name implies, the Longfin Anthias (*Pseudanthias ventralis*) is abundant here. In fact, it was reported that 82% of all fishes seen at this depth range were Longfin Anthias. The admirer of the Longfin Anthias can recreate this environment, with some associated fish species, in a home aquarium. Use a larger tank (75+ gallons) with dim lighting and cover the substrate with live sand and coral rubble. Then make several small coral heads out of rubble or pieces of live rock for your fish to shelter in, and provide vigorous water movement. You can also add clumps of the calcareous green algae known as *Halimeda*. Purchase a group of Longfin Anthias consisting of five to seven females and one or two males. Quarantine them in several smaller tanks (two 20-gallon tanks with air-driven sponge filters, heaters, and PVC pipe for behavioral substrate) for two weeks before placing them in your main display tank. Make sure you have a ready supply of live brine shrimp to feed the Longfin Anthias, in case they refuse frozen brine or mysid shrimp, or even better, connect a refugium to the display aquarium. (Note: *P. ventralis* should only be kept by experienced aquarists.) To complete your Ventralis Zone aquarium, it would be appropriate to add any of the following less aggressive fishes that occur in the same habitat: Randall's Anthias (*Pseudanthias randalli*), Helfrich's Firefish (*Nemateleotris helfrichi*), Bluehead Tilefish (juvenile) (*Hoplolatilus starcki*), and the Green Tilefish (juvenile) (*Hoplolatilus cuniculus*).

Aquarium Suitability Index: 2.

Remarks: This species has prolonged pelvic and anal fins. The tips of the pelvic fins reach past the base of the anal fin in males, while in females they reach well past the anal origin. In *P. ventralis*, males have a violet section toward the tail, the head is yellow with fuchsia lines behind the eyes, and the anal fin is yellow. In females, the head, back, and anal fin are mostly yellow, and the ventral half of the body is lavender, with a more distinct demarcation between the lavender of the dorsum and the yellow of the ventral region than its Hawaiian counterparts. Some ichthyologists have suggested that this species represents three distinct forms, or valid species. They consider the *P. ventralis* populations from Japan and Australia to be distinct from each other and from those that inhabit the rest of the Western and South Pacific.

Rabaulichthys stigmaticus, Spotfin Anthias (male): Indian Ocean rarity.

Genus *Rabaulichthys* (Sailfin Anthias)

There are two described species in this marvelous genus. (A third undescribed form has been collected off the Marshall Islands.) The Spotfin Anthias (*Rabaulichthys stigmaticus*) is known from Mauritius and the Maldives; the Sailfin Anthias (*Rabaulichthys altipinnis*) has only been reported from New Britain, a small island near Papua New Guinea. Both species attain a maximum length of 6 cm (2.4 in.). They have one continuous dorsal fin; in males, the front portion of the fin is enlarged and looks like a sail. These fishes use this structure to communicate to rivals and potential mates. *Rabaulichthys* occur in small aggregations, usually over coral rubble bottoms in moderately deep water (30 to 50 m [98 to 163 ft.]). Although I have not seen them in the aquarium trade, the Indian Ocean species may show up on rare occasions. Their color, small size, and feeding habits suggest that they would be wonderful aquarium fish.

References

Allen & Burhanuddin (1976), Chave & Mundy (1994), Colin (1976), Diamant & Shpigel (1985), Hoover (1993), K. Imai (personal communication), Katayama & Masuda (1980), Krupp & Paulus (1991), Kuiter (1990, 1992), Kuiter & Debelius (1994), Linquist & Clavijo (1993), M. Lister (personal communication), Myers (1989), Popper & Fishelson (1973), Randall (1979, 1980, 1985), Randall & Heemstra (1978), Randall & Hoese (1995), Randall & Hutomo (1988), Randall & Lubbock (1981), Randall & McCosker (1982, 1993), Randall & Shimizu (1994), Randall et al. (1990), Senou & Imai (1998), Shapiro (1977, 1979, 1980, 1981a, 1981b, 1981c), H. Tanaka (personal communication), G. Teodora (personal communication), Thresher (1984), Thresher & Colin (1986), Yogo (1986), F. Young (personal communication).

Japanese Anthias

The rocky reefs of subtropical Japan support a unique fish assemblage comprised of representatives from warmer, tropical waters as well as those restricted to cooler climes. One group that is very well represented on reefs like those of the Izu Peninsula of central Japan is the Subfamily Anthiinae. Keisuke Imai, an accomplished photographer and friend of the author, has reported observing over 20 species of anthias on the reefs of this region. Some of these also occur on other reefs in the Indo-Pacific, while others are known only from this area. The Japanese anthias are usually found in deeper water than their warm-water counterparts. For example, the anthias community around the Izu Peninsula is most diverse at depths in excess of 60 m (195 ft.), where water temperatures range from 11 to 16°C (52 to 60°F). This anthias community includes some of the most magnificent fishes in the sea.

Two of the most beautiful Japanese anthias belong to the genus *Tasanoides*. The **Filament-fin Anthias (*Tasanoides filamentosus*)** occurs at depths in excess of 50 m (163 ft.), while the even more stunning **Yellowlined Anthias (*Tasanoides flavofasciatus*)** occurs at depths of around 60 m (195 ft.). Male and female *T. filamentosus* are similar in appearance, while the genders of *T. flavofasciatus* are chromatically disparate. The latter species occurs in harems, consisting of one male and numerous females. The young of *T. flavofasciatus* appear in the summer. In a "good" summer, shoals made up of hundreds of young Yellowlined Anthias can be observed. The **Yellowspotted Anthias (*Pseudanthias flavoguttatus*)** is a sister species of Lori's Anthias (*Pseudanthias lori*), a tropical species that is commonly observed in the aquarium trade (see page 569). *Pseudanthias flavoguttatus* occurs in small groups at depths in excess of 30 m (98 ft.). It is most common in current-prone areas and sometimes mixes with aggregations of Redstripe (*Pseudanthias fasciatus*) and Lyretail Anthias (*Pseudanthias squamipinnis*). Male Yellowspotted Anthias have a slightly longer third dorsal spine than females. The **Elongate Anthias (*Pseudanthias elongatus*)** is another Japanese endemic that often associates with whip corals at depths in excess of 30 m (98 ft.). This species mates in December, when the male exhibits nuptial coloration and performs U-swims among groups of females. The **Blotchy Deep Anthias (*Holanthias borbonius*)** is a wide-ranging deep-water species that is found at relatively shallower depths in the cooler waters around Japan (at about 60 m [195 ft.]); it is often found singly and never strays far from a crevice or cave in which to hide.

Although most of these Japanese anthias are not likely to show up in your local aquarium store, they are included for the determined rare fish collector and those aquarists who love the anthiines as much as I do.

Holanthias borbonius, Blotchy Deep Anthias: one of more than 20 anthiines that are found in Japanese waters, some of which are endemic.

Pseudanthias elongatus, Elongate Anthias (male).

Pseudanthias elongatus, Elongate Anthias: male with spawning coloration.

Pseudanthias flavoguttatus, Yellowspotted Anthias (male).

Tasanoides filamentosus, Filament-fin Anthias (male).

Tasanoldes flavofasciatus, Yellowlined Anthias (female).

Tasanoides flavofasciatus, Yellowlined Anthias (male).

Glossary

aggregation: a social group consisting of members of the same or different species that are not attracted to each other but to some other mutually attractive stimulus (e.g., food, shelter).
aggressive mimicry: a type of imitation wherein a predatory species resembles a nonpredatory form to gain a hunting advantage over its prey.
ahermatypic corals: corals that do not have zooxanthellae and do not contribute directly to the development of coral reefs.
alpheid shrimp: a member of the Family Alpheidae, with greatly enlarged pincers that are used to produce a snapping sound, hence their common name, snapping shrimp. Many engage in commensal relationships.
amphipod: a group of small crustaceans belonging to the Order Amphipoda, including the genus *Gammarus*, used as a common aquarium fish food.
anterior margin: the leading edge of the fin.
antrorse: upward or forward.
band: a thick, pigmented vertical marking that encircles the circumference of the fish's body.
bar: a thick, pigmented vertical marking that does not encircle the body.
barbel: a long, fleshy protuberance that is often located under the lower parts of the head and is equipped with sensory cells and used to locate prey.
base: the portion of the fin that is joined to the body.
Batesian mimicry: a type of imitation wherein an innocuous species resembles a noxious species to gain protection from predators.
bathymetric: pertaining to the depth of water.
bathypelagic: describing the part of the ocean water column 1,000 to 4,000 m (3,300 to 13,500 ft.) deep; not in contact with the seafloor.
benthic: pertaining to organisms that live on or just over the seafloor.
bioherm: a structure of biological origin (e.g., coral reef).
bivalve: a member of the mollusk Class Bivalvia, having a dorsally hinged, calcareous shell comprised of two valves; includes the oysters, clams, and mussels.

black coral: a member of the Order Antipatharia, gorgonian-like corals having polyps arranged around a horny axial skeleton.
blotch: a patch or spot of pigment with irregular edges.
bony fishes: members of the Class Actinopterygia, a diverse group that contains most of the modern fish species.
brackish: water that is slightly less "salty" than "normal" strength seawater.
branchial: related to the gills.
buccal: related to the mouth.
canine teeth: pointed, conical teeth located at the front or edge of the jaws.
carapace: a rigid shell or exoskeleton that encases the body.
caridean shrimp: a member of the Infraorder Caridea, which contains a number of conspicuous coral reef-dwelling families, including the snapping, cleaner, and anemone shrimps.
caudal: referring to the tail.
caudal peduncle: the narrow portion of the body of a fish located just before the caudal fin.
cephalopods: members of the Class Cephalopoda, including the squids, octopuses, cuttlefishes, and nautiloids.
chitons: members of the mollusk Class Polyplacophora, which adhere tightly to the substrate and have flattened, ovoid bodies and shells comprised of eight overlapping plates.
chromatophore: a pigment cell located in the integument of a fish.
cirrus (pl., cirri): a filamentlike projection that is sometimes present on the head, fin, nape, nostril, lateral line, etc. of some species.
commensalism: a relationship between members of different species in which one member benefits while the other is unaffected (compare to **parasitism**).
congeners: of the same genus.
consexual: of the same sex.
conspecific: of the same species.
copepods: very small crustaceans that belong to the extremely large Class Copepoda. Some are ectoparasites of fishes, while others are planktonic.

cryptic: pertaining to concealment, usually in reference to color pattern or behavior (e.g., hiding in reef crevices).

cumaceans: small, mysidlike crustaceans that belong to the Order Cumacea, many of which burrow in bottom sediments.

decapod shrimps: shrimps that belong to the largest order of crustaceans, Decapoda; characterized by having the first three pairs of thoracic appendages modified as maxillipeds.

demersal: living on the sea bottom.

dermal appendage: a flap or tassel of skin.

distal: the portion of an appendage farthest from the point of origin (compare to **proximal**).

diurnal: active during the day (compare to **nocturnal**).

dorsum: pertaining to the back or the upper part of the body.

echinoderms: members of the Phylum Echinodermata, which encompasses radially symmetrical invertebrates, some of which have sharp spines; includes sea stars, serpent stars, sea cucumbers, and sea urchins.

echinoids: members of the Class Echinoidea, including sea urchins, heart urchins, and sand urchins.

emarginate: having a notched margin, but not so deeply as to be forked.

endemic: restricted in distribution to a specific area or region.

errant: free-swimming.

euryhaline: pertaining to organisms that can withstand a wide salinity range (compare to **stenohaline**).

exoskeleton: outer shell or skeleton (e.g., carapace of a crab).

facultative: capable of living in varying conditions; e.g., facultative cleaners do not rely strictly on parasites for food (compare to **obligatory**).

falcate: sicklelike, long and curved; deeply concave.

filamentous: long and thin.

gastropod: members of the mollusk Class Gastropoda, including the limpets, top shells, snails, cowries, moon shells, whelks, bubble shells, sea hares, nudibranchs, and sea slugs.

gonochorism: the condition wherein the sexes are separate, predetermined at birth or hatching, and do not change throughout the individual's lifetime.

gorgonian: a soft coral of the Order Gorgonacea, having a horny, organic skeleton; includes sea whips and sea fans.

grapsid crab: a crustacean in the Family Grapsidae; can be found in freshwater, marine, or terrestrial environments; includes the sally lightfoot crabs (*Grapsus* spp.).

grass shrimp: a species of small, transparent shrimp often sold for freshwater aquariums and as food for other fishes; also called ghost shrimp.

group spawning: reproductive behavior in which a group of individuals simultaneously release their gametes; these groups usually consist of one female and several males.

hermatypic: corals with zooxanthellae that contribute directly to the development of coral reefs.

heterocercal: describing a caudal fin in which the upper lobe is larger than the lower lobe.

heterospecific: members of different species.

homocercal: describing a caudal fin in which the upper and lower lobes are nearly equal in size.

hypersaline: having a salinity higher (more salty) than "normal" strength seawater.

hyposaline: having a salinity lower (less salty) than "normal" strength seawater.

incisiform: describing a chisel-shaped tooth used for cutting, typically wider than it is thick.

infaunal: pertaining to organisms that live in the sediment of the seafloor.

initial phase: in a sequentially hermaphroditic species, the color exhibited before the sex change (compare to **terminal phase**).

inner margin: the rear edge of a fin.

interorbital: describing the space between the eyes.

interspecific: between members of different species.

intromittent organ: a structure employed by males of those species that practice internal fertilization to transfer sperm.

isopods: crustaceans belonging to the Order Isopoda (including the gnathid isopods, some of which are ectoparasites on coral reef fishes); most are quite small (less than 1.5 cm).

lanceolate: shaped like a spear head, being tapered at each end.

large-polyped stony corals: hard corals that are less important in reef development, having a large, fleshy polyp (or polyps); also called LPS corals.

lateral: pertaining to the side.

leptocephalus larvae: long, ribbonlike larvae, characteristic of the tarpons, bonefishes, and eels.

line: a narrow, straight-sided chromatic marking (thinner than a stripe or bar), that can radiate from the eyes, run longitudinally or vertically on the body or tail, or can be chevron-shaped on the fish's side.

lobate: resembling a lobe.

lunate: shaped like a crescent.

majid crab: a member of the crustacean Family Majidae, having a triangular-shaped carapace and long legs; these crabs are often called spider or decorator crabs because they carry sponges and/or other marine organisms on their carapaces to enhance their camouflage.

mantis shrimp: a member of the crustacean Order Stomatapoda, having well-developed compound eyes on stalks; mantis shrimps are highly predatory, employing a pair of raptorial thoracic appendages to capture their prey.
marginal: just along the fin edge.
molariform: describing molarlike or pebblelike teeth.
monogamy: a mating system in which a male and female form a mating pair for an entire reproductive season or for their entire lives.
mutualism: a relationship between members of different species in which both members benefit (compare to **commensalism** and **parasitism**).
mysid shrimp: a member of the crustacean Order Mysidacea; often called possum shrimps because of the pouch on their ventrum; most reef-dwelling mysid species are small and swarm near the ocean floor.
nape: area behind the back of the head, extending from the back of the skull to the dorsal fin origin.
nauplius (pl., nauplii): the free-swimming, planktonic, larval stage of many crustaceans.
nocturnal: active at night (compare to **diurnal**).
obligatory: obligate or required; e.g., an obligatory cleaner fish relies entirely on this feeding mode to obtain nutrients (compare to **facultative**).
occipital pit: a pit on top of the head, located between the eyes.
oceanic: pertaining to the open ocean and the organisms or structures found in this environment.
ocellus (pl., ocelli): a spot with a lighter outer margin (also known as an eyespot).
ontogenetic: referring to a change that occurs with age.
operculum: a bony gill cover.
ophiuroid: a member of the Subclass Ophiuroidea, including the basket stars, serpent stars, and brittle stars.
opisthobranchs: members of the mollusk Subclass Opisthobranchia, many of which have a reduced or no shell. Most have a pair of tentacles on the head. This group includes the nudibranchs, pyramidellid snails, and sea hares.
orbit: bony eye socket.
osculum: a large excurrent pore that allows water to exit from the internal cavity of sponges.
ostracod: a member of the crustacean Subclass Ostracoda, with a body encased in a bivalve shell; resembles a minute clam.
oviparity: the reproductive mode in which eggs are released from the body and hatch at a later time.

ovoviviparity: the reproductive mode in which the eggs hatch and develop within the female's reproductive tract (or within a specialized pouch in the males of some species), are not nourished in any way by the female, and are free-swimming when expelled from the parent (compare to **viviparity**).
palatine bones: a pair of bones on the roof of the mouth.
panaeid shrimp: a member of the Family Penaeidae, commercially important for human consumption. Many of these shrimps bury under the substrate during the day
papillae: small, fleshy protuberances.
parasitism: a relationship between members of different species in which one benefits while the other is harmed (compare to **commensalism**).
peanut worm: a member of the Phylum Sipuncula; drably colored worms that typically hide in coral crevices, bore into coralline substrate, or bury under coral rubble, mud, or sand.
pelagic: pertaining to the open sea and to the organisms that inhabit it.
pharyngeal teeth: teeth located on the bones in the pharynx, which is located between the mouth and the esophagus.
photophore: an organ that emits light.
piscivorous: fish-eating.
poisonous: an organism that contains poison (a substance causing illness or death) in its tissues that can be harmful if the organism is ingested (compare to **venomous**).
polychaetes: worms in the Class Polychaeta, many of which are marine and infaunal; are part of the Phylum Annelida (the segmented worms).
porcelain crabs: crabs in the Infraorder Brachyura, Family Porcellanidae, including the anemone crabs (genus *Neopetrolisthes*) and others commensal with invertebrates.
preorbital: the area under and in front of the eyes.
primary male or female: a male or female whose sex is genetically determined at birth or hatching and is not the result of a sex change.
protandry: sequential hermaphroditism in which individuals transform from male to female (compare to **protogyny**).
protogyny: sequential hermaphroditism in which individuals transform from female to male (compare to **protandry**).
protractile: capable of being protruded or thrust out.
protunid crabs: crabs in the Infraorder Brachyura, Family Protunidae, commonly referred to as swimming crabs; they have a broad carapace, often armed with large spines along its edges, and the last pair of legs are flattened to form paddles that are used for swimming and burying in the substrate.

proximal: nearest to the point of origin (compare to **distal**).

rostrum: an elongate or extended snout.

school: a social group consisting of individuals of the same species, with individuals being similar in size, equal in their social status, and moving in a highly coordinated fashion (compare to **shoal**).

secondary male or female: a male or female that is the result of a sex change; a secondary male would be derived from a protogynous female, while a secondary female would be derived from a protandrous male (compare to **primary male or female**).

sequential hermaphroditism: a form of hermaphroditism in which individuals can change sex, but the sexes are separate (compare to **simultaneous hermaphroditism**).

sessile: attached to the substrate; stationary.

sexual dichromatism: color differences between the sexes.

sexual dimorphism: structural or size differences between the sexes.

shoal: a social group consisting of individuals of the same species that are not always similar in size, not equal in social status, and that usually do not move in a highly coordinated fashion (compare to **school**).

simultaneous hermaphroditism: a form of hermaphroditism in which individuals have functional testes and ovaries at the same time and can release either sperm or eggs during spawning (compare to **sequential hermaphroditism**).

slipper lobster: a member of the Family Scyllaridae; dorsally flattened crustaceans with antennae that are shield-shaped. They are nocturnal.

small-polyped stony corals: reef-building stony corals having small polyps that retract completely into their calyces; also called SPS corals.

snout: the portion of the head that is just in front of the eyeball.

soft corals: members of the Order Alcyonacea, which have a skeleton formed of calcareous spicules, and include the genera *Dendronephthya, Sarcophyton, Sinularia*, and many others.

spot: a circular area of pigment.

stenohaline: pertaining to organisms that can only withstand a narrow salinity range (compare to **euryhaline**).

stony corals: members of the Order Scleractinia, which secrete a heavy, external, calcareous skeleton, and many of which are primary contributors to the building of coral reefs; these can be further divided into the small-polyped stony corals (SPS corals) and the large-polyped stony corals (LPS corals).

stripes: a straight area of pigment that can vary in width (wider than a line), and can be oriented vertically, horizontally, or obliquely on the head, body, or fins.

submarginal: just before the fin margin.

suborbital: below the eye.

substrate: the solid surface or material on or over which an organism lives.

supraorbital: above the eye.

swimming crabs: see protunid crabs.

sympatric: having a similar geographical and/or bathymetric distribution.

tanaids: small, marine crustaceans in the Order Tanaidacea, most of which live in bottom sediments or in reef interstices.

terminal: at the end of the head.

terminal phase: in sequentially hermaphroditic species, the color pattern developed after sex change (compare to **initial phase**).

thermocline: a zone in the water column where there is a sharp discontinuity in temperature and water density with increasing depth.

thoracic: lying below or just before the pectoral fin base.

tubercle: a modified, thornlike scale.

truncate: having the end squared-off.

upwelling: a process in which subsurface, nutrient-rich, and usually cooler water is carried up into the ocean's surface layers.

venomous: pertaining to an organism that has a poison, usually secreted by glandular tissue, that is injected through hollow spines or teeth (compare to **poisonous**).

ventrum: pertaining to the underside or belly.

vermiculations: fine, wavy lines.

villiform teeth: minute, slender teeth that usually are crowded into small patches so that they resemble a brush.

viviparity: a form of reproduction in which the young are nourished in the reproductive tract of the female (other than by a yolk sac) and expelled from the mother as free-swimming young. It is often used loosely to refer to any species that gives birth to live young (compare to **ovoviviparity**).

vomer: a bone located just behind the upper jaw, or the front portion of the roof of the mouth; often bears teeth.

xanthid crab: crabs in the Infraorder Brachyura, Family Xanthidae, often referred to as coral crabs because of their association with coral reefs; all have black-tipped claws and some live in association with stony corals (e.g., *Trapezia* spp.).

zooplankter: an individual animal within the zooplankton.

zooplankton: free-floating, typically minute animals (e.g., protozoans, copepods, crustacean larvae, fish larvae).

zooxanthellae: dinoflagellate photosynthetic algae living within the tissues of corals and other organisms.

Bibliography

Abrams, D.W., M.D. Abrams and M. W. Schein. 1983. Diurnal observations on the behavioral ecology of *Gymnothorax moringa* (Cuvier) and *Muraena miliaris* (Kuap) on a Caribbean coral reef. *Coral Reefs*, 1:185-192.

Ahnesjö, I. 1996. Apparent resource competition among embryos in the brood pouch of a male pipefish. *Behav. Ecol. Sociobiol.* 38:167-172.

Allen, G.R. 1997. *Marine Fishes of tropical Australia and south-east Asia.* Western Australian Museum, Perth, 292 pp.

Allen, G. R. and Burhanuddin. 1976. *Anthias hutomoi*, a new species of serranid fish from Indonesia (Perciformes, Serranidae). *Mar. Res. Indonesia*, 16:45-50.

Aronson, R.B. 1983. Foraging behavior of the West Atlantic trumpetfish, *Aulostomus maculatus*: use of large, herbivorous reef fishes as camouflage. *Bull. Mar. Sci.* 33:166-171.

Atiya, F.S. 1991. *The Red Sea in Egypt. Part 1: Fishes.* Farid Surial Atiya Publisher, 232 pp.

Baba, O. and M. Sano. 1987. Diel feeding patterns of the congiopodid fish *Hypodytes rubripinnis* in Aburatsubo Bay, Japan. *Japan. J. Ichthyol.* 34:209-213.

Barbour, T. 1942. The northwestern Atlantic species of frog fishes. *Proc. New England Zool. Club*, 19:21-40.

Barlow, G. W. 1975. On the sociobiology of some hermaphroditic serranid fishes, the hamlets, in Puerto Rico. *Mar. Biol.* 33:295-300.

Bernadsky, G. and D. Goulet. 1991. A natural predator of the lionfish, *Pterois miles. Copeia*, 1991:230-231.

Böhlke, J.E. and J.E. McCosker. 1997. Review of the moray eel genus *Scuticaria* and included species (Pisces: Anguilliformes: Muraenidae: Uropterygiinae). *Proc. Acad. Nat. Sci. Phil.* 148:171-176.

Böhlke, J.E. and J.E. Randall. 1981. Four new garden eels (Congridae, Heterocongrinae) from the Pacific and Indian Oceans. *Bull. Mar. Sci.* 31:366-382.

Böhlke, J. E. and C.C.G. Chaplin. 1993. *Fishes of the Bahamas and Adjacent Tropical Waters.* 2nd Edition. University of Texas Press, Austin, 771 pp.

Bortone, S.A., P.A. Hastings and S.B. Collard. 1977. The pelagic-sargassum ichthyfauna of the eastern Gulf of Mexico. *Northeast Gulf Sci.* 1:60-67.

Bradbury, M.G. 1980. A revision of the fish genus *Ogcocephalus* with descriptions of new species from the Western Atlantic Ocean (Ogcocephalidae; Lophiiformes). *Proc. Calif. Acad. Sci.* 42:229-285.

Breder, C.M. Jr. 1941. On the reproduction of *Opsanus beta* Goode & Bean. *Zoologica, NY*, 26:229-232.

———1949. On the relationship of social behavior to pigmentation in tropical shore fishes. *Bull. Amer. Mus. Nat. Hist.* 94:85-106.

Breder C.M. Jr. & D.E. Rosen. 1966. *Modes of Reproduction in Fishes.* T.F.H. Publ., Jersey City, 941 pp.

Burke, V.J., S. Morreale, and A.G.J. Rhodin. 1993. *Lepidochelys kempii* (Kemp's Ridley Sea Turtle) and *Caretta caretta* (Loggerhead Sea Turtle). *Herpetol. Rev.* 24:31-32.

Campson, P.J. and G.A. Paleudis. 1995. Captive breeding and culture of the lined seahorse (*Hippocampus erectus*). *Aquar. Front.* Summer: 10-13.

Casadevall, M, J. Matallanas, and B. Bartoli. 1994. Feeding habits of *Ophichthus rufus* (Anguilliformes, Ophichthidae) in the Western Mediterranean. *Cybium*, 18:431-440.

Chave, E.H. and B.C Mundy. 1994. Deep-sea benthic fish of the Hawaiian Archipelago, Cross Seamounts, and Johnston Atoll. *Pac. Sci.* 48:367-409.

Chave, E.H. and H.A. Randall. 1971. Feeding behavior of the moray eel (*Gymnothorax pictus*). *Copeia*, 1971:570-574.

Clark, E. 1959. Functional hermaphroditism and self-fertilization in a serranid fish. *Science*, 129:215-216.

Clark, E, J.F. Pohle, and D. C. Shen. 1990. Ecology and population dynamics of garden eels at Ras Mohammed, Red Sea. *Nat. Geo. Res.* 6:306-318.

Colin, P.L. 1976. Observations of deep-reef fishes in the Tongue of the Ocean, Bahamas. *Bull. Mar. Sci.* 26:603-605.

Colin, P.L., D. M. Devaney, L. Hillis-Colinvaux, T.H. Suchanek and J.T. Harrison, III. 1986. Geology and biological zonation of the reef slope, 50-360 M depth at Enewetak Atoll, Marshall Islands. *Bull. Mar. Sci.* 38:111-128.

Collette, B.B. 1974. A review of the coral toadfishes of the genus *Sanopus* with descriptions of two new species from Cozumel Island, Mexico. *Proc. Biol. Soc. Wash.* 87:185-204.

Collette, B.B. and J.L. Russo. 1981. A revision of the scaly toadfishes, genus *Batrachoides*, with descriptions of two new species from the Eastern Pacific. *Bull. Mar. Sci.* 31:197-233.

Collette, B.B. and F.H. Talbot. 1972. Activity patterns of coral reef fishes with emphasis on nocturnal-diurnal changeover. *Nat. Hist. Mus. L.A. Count. Soc. Bull.* 14: 98-109.

Cressey, R. 1981. Revision of the Indo-Pacific fishes of the genus *Synodus* (Pisces; Synodontidae). *Smithson. Contr. Zool.* No. 342, 53 pp.

Danemann, G. D. 1992. Prey storing behavior in the Panamic green moray eel (*Gymnothorax castaneus*). *Calif. Fish Game*, 78:172.

Dawson, C.E. 1977. Review of the pipefish genus *Corythoichthys* with description of three new species. *Copeia*, 1977: 295-338.

———1982. Review of the Indo-Pacific pipefish genus *Trachyrhamphus* (Syngnathidae). *Micronesica*, 18: 163-191.

Debelius, H. 1993. *Indian Ocean Tropical Fish Guide*. Aquaprint Verlags, Neu Isenburg, 319 pp.

Dee, A. 1986. Growth, reproduction and diet of *Myripristis amaenus* at Johnston Island Atoll. Abstr. Tester Paper Series. *Pac. Sci.* 40:115.

De Graaf, F. 1973. *Marine Aquarium Guide*. Pet Library, Ltd. Harrison, 284 pp.

Dennis, G.D. and T.J. Bight. 1988. Reef fish assemblages on hard banks in the northwestern Gulf of Mexico. *Bull. Mar. Sci.* 43:280-307.

Deraniyagala, P.E.P. 1930. Notes on the breeding habit of the eel *Leiuranus semicinctus*. *Spolia Zeylanica*, 16:107.

Diamant, A and M. Shpigel. 1985. Interspecific feeding associations of groupers (Teleostei: Serranidae) with octopuses and moray eels in the Gulf of Eilat (Aqaba). *Env. Biol. Fish.* 13:153-159.

Dinesen, Z.D. and W.J. Nash. 1982. The scorpionfish, *Rhinopias aphanes* Eschmeyer from Australia. *Japan. J. Ichthyol.* 29:179-184.

Domeier, M. L. 1994. Speciation in the serranid fish *Hypoplectrus*. *Bull. Mar. Sci.* 54:103-141.

Donaldson, T.J. 1990. Lek-like courtship by males, and multiple spawnings by females of *Synodus dermatogenys* (Synodontidae). *Japan. J. Ichthyol.* 37:292-301.

Doublilet, D. (1987). Scorpionfish: danger in disguise. *Natl. Geogr. Mag.* 172:634-643.

Edwards, A. and J. Roswell. 1981. Vertical zonation of coral reef fishes in the Sudanese Red Sea. *Hydrobiol.* 79:21-31.

Endean, R. 1961. A study of the distribution, habitat and behavior, venom apparatus, and venom of the stone-fish. *Austr. J. Mar. Fresh. Res.* 12:177-190.

Eschmeyer, W.N. 1997. A new species of dactylopteridae (Pisces) from the Phillipines and Australia, with a breif synopsis of the family. *Bull. Mar. Sci.* 60:727-738.

Eschmeyer, W.N., Y. Hirosaki and T. Abe. 1973. Two new species of the scorpionfish genus *Rhinopias*, with comments on related genera and species. *Proc. Calif. Acad. Sci.* 40:285-310.

Eschmeyer, W. N., K.V. Rama-Rao and L.E. Hallcher. 1979a. Fishes of the scorpionfish genus *Minous* (Scorpaenidae, Minoinae) including new species from the Indian Ocean. *Proc. Calif. Acad. Sci.* 41:453-473.

———1979b. Fishes of the scorpionfish subfamily Choridactylinae from the Western Pacific and the Indian Ocean. *Proc. Calif. Acad. Sci.* 41:475-500.

Ferraris, C.J. Jr. 1985. Redescription and spawning of the muraenid eel *Gymnothorax herrei*. *Copeia*, 1985:518-520.

Fischer, E. A. 1980a. The relationship between mating system and simultaneous hermaphroditism in the coral reef fish, *Hypoplectrus nigricans* (Serranidae). *Anim. Behav.* 28:620-633.

———1980b. Speciation in hamlets (*Hypoplectrus unicolor*) - a continuing enigma. *Copeia*, 1980:649-659.

———1984. Egg trading in the chalk bass, *Serranus tortugarum*, a simultaneous hermaphrodite. *Z. Tierpsychol.* 66:143-151.

Fischer, E.A. and C.W. Petersen. 1986. Social behavior of males and simultaneous hermaphrodites in the lantern bass. *Ethology*, 73:235-246.

Fishelson, L. 1966. *Solenostomus cyanopterus*, Bleeker (Teleostei, Solenostomidae) in Eilat (Gulf of Akaba). *Isr. J. Zool.* 15:95-103.

———1975. Ethology and reproduction of the pteroid fishes found in the Gulf of Aqaba (Red Sea), especially *Dendrochirus brachypterus* (Cuvier) (Pteroidae, Teleostei). *Publ. Staz. Zool. Napoli*, 39 (Suppl.): 635-656.

———1978. Oogenesis and spawn-formation in the pigmy lionfish *Dendrochirus brachypterus* (Pteroidae). *Mar. Biol.*, 46:341-348.

———1990. *Rhinomuraena* spp. (Pisces: Muraenidae): the first vertebrate genus with post-anally situated urogenital organs. *Mar. Biol.* 105:253-257.

———1992. Comparative gonad morphology and sexuality of the Muraenidae (Pisces, Telesotei). *Copeia*, 1992: 197-209.

———1996. Skin morphology and cytology in marine eels adapted to different lifestyles. *Anat. Rec.* 246:15-29.

Francis-Floyd, R., L. Roth, T. Ardelt, M. Andrew, P. Reed and E. Rose. 1992. Contact dermatitis in green moray eels (*Gymnothorax funebris*) exposed to fiberglass. *J. Zoo Wildlife Med.* 23:328-335.

Friese, U.E. 1973. Anglerfishes. *Mar. Aquarist*, 4:29-36.

———1974. Anglerfishes. *Koolewong*, 3:7-11.

Galzin, R. 1987. Structure of fish communities of French Polynesian coral reefs. I. Spatial scales. *Mar. Ecol. Prog. Ser.* 41:129-136.

Galzin, R. and P. Legendre. 1987. The fish communities of a coral reef transect. *Pac. Sci.* 41:158-165.

Gischler, E. and R. N. Ginsburg. 1996. Cavity dwellers (coelobites) under coral rubble in southern Belize barrier and atoll reefs. *Bull. Mar. Sci.* 58:570-589.

Giwojina, J.K. 1996a. Seahorse nutrition. Part 1. Live food for adults. *Freshwat. Mar. Aquar.* 19 (10):40-56.

———1996b. Seahorse nutrition. Part 2: frozen foods for adults. *Freshwat. Mar. Aquar.* 19 (11):72-78.

———1996c. Seahorse nutrition. Part 3: hand-feeding adults. *Freshwat. Mar. Aquar.* 19 (12):30-46.

———1997. Seahorse nutrition. Part 5: feeding juveniles and dwarf seahorses. *Freshwat. Mar. Aquar.* 20 (2): 30-48.

Gorelova, T.A. and B.I. Fedoryako. 1986. Topic and trophic relationships of fishes associated with drifting sargassum algae. *Voprosy Ikhtiologii*, 1986: 94-102.

Graves, J. E. and R. H. Rosenblatt. 1980. Genetic relationships of the color morphs of the serranid fish *Hypoplectrus unicolor*. *Evol.* 34:240-245.

Green, A.L. 1996. Spatial, temporal and ontogenetic patterns of habitat use by coral reef fishes (Family Labridae). *Mar. Ecol. Prog. Ser.* 133:1-11.

Grieg, R.A. and R.H. Gnaedinger. 1971. Occurence of thiaminase in some common aquatic animals of the United States and Canada. *Spec. Sci. Rpt. Fish.* No. 631, U.S. Nat. Mar. Fish. Serv. 7 pp.

Grobecker, D.B. 1983. The 'lie-in-wait' feeding mode of a cryptic teleost, *Synanceia verrucosa. Env. Biol. Fish.* 8:191-202.

Gronell, A.M. 1984. Courtship, spawning and social organization of the pipefish, *Corythoichthys intestinalis* (Pisces: Syngnathidae) with notes on congeneric species. *Z. Tierpsychol.* 65:1-24.

Grovhoug, J.G. and R.S. Henderson. 1976. Distribution of fishes at Canton Atoll *in* S. V. Smith and R.S. Henderson (Eds.). *An Environmental Survey of Canton Atoll lagoon.* Naval Undersea Research and Development Center, San Diego: 99-157.

Harmelin-Vivien, M.L. and C. Bouchon. 1976. Feeding behavior of some carnivorous fishes (Serranidae and Scorpaenidae) from Tulear (Madagascar). *Mar. Biol.* 37:329-340.

Hatooka, K. 1986. Sexual dimorphism found in teeth of three species of moral eels. *Japan. J. Ichthyol.* 32:379-385.

Hemdal, J. 1987. A horse of a different color. *Sea Scope*, Winter: 1-3.

———1986. The ribbon eel (*Rhinomuraena quaesita*). *Freshwat. Mar. Aquar.* 9(2):62-63.

———1992. Captive husbandry of the flashlight fish, *Anomolops katoptron* (Bleeker, 1856). *J. Aquaricul. Aquat. Sci.* 6(2):55-52.

Herold, D. and E. Clark. 1993. Monogamy, spawning and skin-shedding of the sea moth, *Eurypegasus draconis* (Pisces: Pegasidae). *Env. Biol. Fish.* 37:219-236.

Hiatt, R.W. and D.W. Stratsburg. 1960. Ecological relationships of the fish fauna on coral reefs of the Marshall Islands. *Ecol. Monogr.* 30:65-127.

Hillis-Colinvaux, L. 1986. Deepwater populations of *Halimeda* in the economy of an atoll. *Bull. Mar. Sci.* 38:155-169.

Hobson, E.S. 1968. Predatory behavior of some shore fishes in the Gulf of California. *Fish. & Wildlife Res. Rpt.* 73, 92 pp.

———1974. Feeding relationships of teleostean fishes on coral reefs in Kona, Hawaii. *Fish. Bull.* 72: 915-103.

Hoffman, S.G. and D.R. Robertson. 1983. Foraging and reproduction of two Caribbean reef toadfishes (Batrachoididae). *Bull. Mar. Sci.* 33:919-927.

Hoover, J.P. 1993. *Hawaii's Fishes; a guide for snorkelers, divers, and aquarists*. Mutual Publishing, Honolulu, 178 pp.

Hornell, J. 1921. The Madaras aquarium. *Madras Fish. Bull.* 14:57-96.

Howe, J., G. Crow, and J. Herbert. 1988. The strange-eyed scorpionfish (*Rhiopias xenops*) with comments on its Hawaiian distribution and aquariology. *Freshwat. Mar. Aquar.* 11 (9):8-11.

Hueter, J. 1998. An American seahorse. Trop. Fish Hobby. 46(9):50-56.

Hughes, G.M. and S. Umezawa. 1983. Gill structure of the yellowtail and frogfish. *Japan. J. Ichthyol.* 30:176-183.

Humann, P. 1994. *Reef fish identification. Florida, Caribbean, Bahamas.* 2nd edition. New World Publ. Jacksonville, 396 pp.

Hutchins, B. and R. Swainston. 1986. Sea *fishes of Southern Australia*. Swainston Publishing, Perth, 180 pp.

Jones, R.S. and J.A. Chase. 1975. Community structure and distribution of fishes in an enclosed high island lagoon in Guam. *Micronesica*, 11: 127-148.

Kajikawa, H. 1973. Determination of age in the marine catfish *Plotosus anguillaris* by the use of the otolith. *Sci. Rpt. Shima Marineland*, 2:5-22.

Katayama, M. and H. Masuda. 1980. Two new anthiine fishes from Sagami Bay, Japan. *Japan. J. Ichthyol.* 27:185-190.

Kaufman, L. 1976. Feeding Behavior and functional coloration of the Atlantic trumpetfish, *Aulostomus maculatus. Copeia*, 1976: 378-379.

Kizer, K.W., H.E. McKinney and P.S. Averbach. 1985. Scorpaenidae envenomation: A five-year poison center experience. *Trop. Fish Hobby.* 33 (11):54-63.

Krupp, F. and T. Paulus. 1991. Territoriality and courtship behavior in the coral reef fish *Pseudanthias heemstrai* (Pisces: Serranidae). *Revue fr. Aquariol.* 18:43-46.

Kuiter, R. H. 1990. *Pseudanthias bimaculatus* x *Pseudanthias pleurotaenia*, a hybrid anthiid fish from Indonesia. *Revue fr. Aquariol.* 17:17-18.

———1992. *Tropical Reef-Fishes of the Western Pacific: Indonesia and Adjacent Waters.* PT Gramedia Utama, Jakarta. 314 pp.

———1993. *Coastal Fishes of South-Eastern Australia.* University of Hawaii Press, Honolulu, 437 pp.

———1996. *Guide to Seafishes of Australia.* New Holland Ltd., Sydney. 433 pp.

Kuiter, R.H. and H. Debelius. 1994. *Southeast Asia Tropical Fish Guide.* IKAN-Underwasserarchiv, Frankfurt, 321 pp.

Larson, H.K. 1983. Notes of the biology of the goby *Kelloggella cardinalis* (Jordan and Seale). *Micronesica*, 19: 157-164.

Lieske, E and R. Myers. 1994. *Collins pocket guide. Coral reef fishes: Indo-Pacific and Caribbean.* HarperCollins Publ., London, 400 pp.

Linquist D.G. and I.E. Clavijo. 1993. Quantifying deep reef fishes from a submersible and notes on a live collection and diet of the red barbier, *Hemanthias vivanus. J. Elisha Mitchell Sci. Soc.* 109:135-140.

Lobel, P.S. 1992. Sounds produced by spawning fishes. *Env. Biol. Fish.* 33:351-358.

Longley, W. H. and S. F. Hildebrand. 1941. Systematic catalog of the fishes of the Tortugas, Florida with observations on color, habits, and local distribution. *Carnegie Inst. Wash. Publ.* 535:331 pp.

Machida, Y. 1994. Description of two new and one resurrected species of the bythitid genus *Dinematichthys* (Ophidiiformes). *Japan. J. Ichthyol.* 40:451-464.

Martin, F.D. and M Cooper. 1981. A comparison of fish faunas found in pure stands of two tropical Atlantic seagrasses, *Thalassia fesudinum* and *Syringodium filiforme. Northeast Gulf Sci.* 5:31-37.

Masonjones, H.D. and S.M. Lewis. 1996. Courtship behavior in the dwarf seahorse, *Hippocampus zosterae. Copeia*, 1996:634-640.

McCormik, M.I. 1995. Fish feeding on mobile benthic invertebrates: influence on spatial variability in habitat selection. *Mar. Biol.* 121:627-637.

McCosker, J.E. and J.E. Randall. 1977. Three new species of Indo-Pacific moray eels (Pisces: Muraenidae). *Proc. Calif. Acad. Sci.* 41:161-168.

McCosker, J.E. and R.H. Rosenblatt. 1987. Notes on the biology, taxonomy, and distribution of flashlight fishes (Beryciformes:Anomalopidae). *Japan. J. Ichthyol.* 34:157-163.

———1993. A revision of the snake eel genus *Myrichthys* (Anguilliformes: Ophichthidae) with the description of a new eastern Pacific species. *Proc. Calif. Acad. Sci.* 48:153-169.

Medvick, P.A. and J.M. Miller. 1979. Behavioral thermoregulation in three Hawaiian reef fishes. *Env. Biol. Fish.* 4:23-28.

Meesters, E., R. Knijn, R. Pennartz, G. Roebers and R.W. M. van Soest. 1991. Sub-rubble communities of Curacao and Bonaire coral reefs. *Coral Reefs,* 10:189-197.

Miller, T. 1987. Knotting: a previously undescribed feeding behavior in muraenid eels. *Copeia,* 1987: 1055-1057.

Morin, J.G., A. Harrington, K. Nealson, N. Krieger, T.O. Baldwin, and J.W. Hastings. 1975. Light for all reasons: versatility in the behavioral repertoire of the flashlight fish. *Science,* 190:74-76.

Moriuchi, S. and Y. Dotsu. 1973. Spawning and larva rearing of the sea catfish, *Plotosus anguillaris. Bull. Fac. Fish.*, Nagasaki Univ. 36:7-12.

Mosher, C. 1954. Observations on the behavior and the early larval development of the sargassum fish *Histrio histrio* (Linnaeus). *Zoologica,* NY, 39:141-152.

Moyer, J.T. and M.J. Zaiser. 1981. Social organization and spawning behavior of the pteroine fish *Dendrochirus zebra* at Miyake-jima, Japan. *Japan. J. Ichthyol.* 28:52-69.

———1982. Reproductive behavior of moray eels at Miyake-jima, Japan. *Japan. J. Ichthyol.* 28:466-468.

Moyer, J.T., T. Yoshikawa and Kazue Asoh. 1995. Spawning behavior and social organization of the congiopodid fish *Ablabys taenianotus* at Miyake-jima, Japan. *Japan. J. Ichthyol.* 32:265-267.

Müller, K. 1995. *Underwater Indonesia*. Periplus Editions Ltd. 326 pp.

Myers, R.F. 1989. *Micronesian reef fishes. A practical guide to the identification of the coral reef fishes of the tropical Western Pacific*. Coral Graphics, Guam, 298 pp.

Nelson, J.S. 1994. *Fishes of the world*. 3rd Edition. John Wiley and Sons Inc., New York, 600 pp.

Nemtzov, S.C., J.E. McCosker and L.M. Albert-Nemtzov. 1986/1987. First record of the snake-eel *Brachysomophis cirrocheilos* (Pisces: Ophichthidae) in the Red Sea. *Israel J. Zool.* 34:13-14.

Ohnishi, N. A. Iwata and W. Hiramatsu. 1997. *Antennatus flagellatus* (Teleostei: Antennariidae) a new species of frogfish from southern Japan. *Ichthyol. Res.* 44:213-217.

Orr, J.W. and R.A. Fritzsche. 1993. Revision of the ghost pipefishes, family Solenostomidae (Teleostei: Syngnathoidei). *Copeia,* 1993:168-182.

Palsson, W.A and T.W. Pietsch. 1989. Revision of the acanthopterygian fish family Pegasidae (Order Gasterosteiformes). *Indo-Pacific Fishes,* No. 18, 38 pp.

Parker, R.O. Jr. and S.W. Ross. 1986. Observing reef fishes from submersibles off North Carolina. *Northeast Gulf Sci.* 8:31-49.

Patton, W.K. 1994. Distribution and ecology of animals associated with branching corals (*Acropora* spp.) from the Great Barrier Reef. *Bull. Mar. Sci.* 55:193-211.

Penrith, M.L., S.S. Bastianello and M.J. Penrith. 1994. Hepatic lipidosis and fatty infiltration of organs in a captive African stonefish, *Synanceia verrucosa* Bloch and Schneider. *J. Fish Disease,* 17:171-176.

Petersen, C.W. 1995. Reproductive behavior, egg trading, and correlates of male mating success in the simultaneous hermaphrodite, *Serranus tabacarius. Env. Biol. Fish.* 43:351-361.

Pietsch T. W. and D. B. Grobecker. 1980. Parental care as an alternative reproduction mode in an antennariid anglerfish. *Copeia,* 1980:551-553.

———1987. *Frogfishes of the World*. Stanford University Press, Stanford, 420 pp.

Pinto, L. and N.N. Punchihewa. 1996. Utilization of mangroves and seagrasses by fishes in the Negombo Estuary, Sri Lanka. *Mar. Biol.* 126: 333-345.

Polunin, N.V.C. and E.B. Brothers. 1989. Low efficiency of dietary carbon and nitrogen conversion to growth in an herbivorous coral reef fish in the wild. *Fish. Biol.* 35:869-879.

Polunin, N.V.C. and D.W. Klumpp. 1989. Ecological correlates of foraging periodicity in herbivorous reef fishes of the Coral Sea. *J. Exp. Mar. Biol.* 126:1-20.

Popper, D. and L. Fishelson. 1973. Ecology and behavior of *Anthias squamipinnis* (Peters, 1855) (Anthiidae, Teleostei) in the coral habitat of Eilat (Red Sea). *J. Exp. Zool.* 184:409-424.

Potts, C. and K. Swart. 1984. Water temperature as an indicator of environmental variability on a coral reef. *Amer Soc. Limnol. Oceanogr.* 29:504-516.

Pressley, P.H. 1981. Pair formation and joint territoriality in a simultaneous hermaphrodite—the coral-reef fish *Serranus tigrinus. Z. Tierpsychol.* 56:33-45.

Preston, E.M. and J.L. Preston. 1975. Ecological structure in a west Indian gorgonian fauna. *Bull. Mar. Sci.* 25:248-258.

Randall, J.E. 1967. Food habits of reef fishes of the West Indies. *Stud. Trop. Oceanogr., Miami,* 5:665-847.

———1979. A review of the serranid fish genus *Anthias* of the Hawaiian Islands, with descriptions of two new species. *Contrib. Nat. Hist. Mus. L.A. Count.* 302:1-13.

———1980. Revision of the fish genus *Plectranthias* (Serranidae: Anthinnae) with descriptions of 13 new species. *Micronesica,* 16:101-187.

———1983a. *Caribbean Reef Fishes*. T.F.H. Publ., Neptune City, 350 pp.

———1983b. *Red Sea Reef Fishes*. Immel Publishing, London, 192 pp.

———1985. *Guide to Hawaiian reef fishes*. Harrowood Books, Newton Square, 77 pp.

———1995. *Coastal fishes of Oman*. University of Hawaii Press, Honolulu, 439 pp.

———1996. *Shore fishes of Hawaii*. Natural World Press, Vida, 216 pp.

Randall, J.E. and J.R. Chess. 1979. A new species of garden eel (Congridae: Heterocongrinae) of the genus *Gorgasia* from Hawaii. *Pac. Sci.* 33:17-23.

Randall, J.E and L.H. DiSalvo. 1997. *Rhinopias cea*, a new species of scorpionfish from Easter Island. *Bull. Mar. Sci.* 60:1035-1039.

Randall, J.E. and D. Golani. Review of the moray eels (Anguilliformes: Muraenidae) of the Red Sea. *Bull. Mar. Sci.* 56:849-880.

Randall, J.E. and D.W. Greenfield. 1996. Revisions of the Indo-Pacific holocentrid fishes of the genus *Myripristis*, with descriptions of three new species. *Indo-Pacific Fishes*, No. 25, 61 pp.

Randall, J.E. and P.C. Heemstra. 1978. Reclassification of the Japanese cirrhitid fishes *Serranocirrhitus latus* and *Isobuna japonica* to the Anthiinae. *Japan J. Ichthyol.* 25:165-172.

Randall, J.E. and D.F. Hoese. 1995. Three new species of Australian fishes of the genus *Plectranthias* (Perciformes: Serranidae: Anthinnae). *Rec. Aust. Mus.* 47:327-335.

Randall, J.E. and M. Hutomo. 1988. Redescription of the Indo-Pacific serranid fish *Pseudanthias bimaculatus* (Smith). *Copeia*, 1988:669-673.

Randall, J.E. and R. Lubbock. 1981. A revision of the serranid fishes of the subgenus *Mirolabrichthys* (Anthiinae: *Anthias*), with descriptions of five new species. *Contrib. Nat. Hist. Mus. L.A. Count.* 333:1-27.

Randall, J.E. and J.E. McCosker. 1982. Two new serranid fishes of the genus *Anthias* from the central Pacific. *J. Aquaric.* II (3):59-69.

Randall, J.E. and J.E. McCosker. 1993. Revision of the fish genus *Luzonichthys* (Perciformes: Serranidae: Anthiinae), with descriptions of two new species. *Indo-Pacific Fishes*, No. 21, 21 pp.

Randall, J. E. and H. A. Randall. 1960. Examples of mimicry and protective resemblance in tropical marine fishes. *Bull. Mar. Sci.* 10:444-480.

Randall, J.E. and T. Shimizu. 1994. *Plectranthias pelicieri*, a new anthiine fish (Perciformes: Serranidae) from Mauritius, with notes on *P. gardineri*. *Japan. J. Ichthyol.* 41:109-115.

Randall, J.E., G.R. Allen and R.C. Steene. 1990. *Fishes of the Great Barrier Reef and Coral Sea*. University of Hawaii Press, Honolulu, HI, 507 pp.

Ray, C. 1961. Spawning behavior and egg raft morphology of the ocellated fringed frogfish, *Antennarius nummifer* (Cuvier). *Copeia*, 1961:230-231.

Reynolds, W.W. and M.E. Casterlin. 1980a. Thermoregulatory behavior of a tropical marine fish: *Forcipiger longirostris* (Broussonet). *Contrib. Mar. Sci.* 23:111-113.

———1980b. Thermoregulatory behavior of juvenile *Cromileptes altivelis* (Serranidae), a tropical marine fish. *Hydrobiol.* 75:281-282.

Roberts, C. M. and R.F.G. Ormond. 1987. Habitat complexity and coral reef fish diversity and abundance on Red Sea fringing reefs. *Mar. Ecol. Prog. Ser.* 41:1-8.

Robertson, D.R. 1987. Responses of two coral reef toadfishes (Batrachoididae) to the demise of their primary prey, the sea urchin *Diadema antillarum*. *Copeia*, 1987:637-642.

Robins, C.R., G.C. Ray, J. Douglass and E. Freund. 1986. *A field guide to Atlantic coast fishes of North America*. Houghton Mifflin Co., Boston, MA, 354 pp.

Rooker, J.R. and G.D. Dennis. 1991. Diel, lunar and seasonal changes in a mangrove fish assemblage off southwestern Puerto Rico. *Bull. Mar. Sci.* 49:684-698.

Sano, M., M. Shimizu, and Y. Nose. 1984. Food habits of teleostean reef fishes in Okinawa Island, southern Japan. Univ. Mus., *Univ. Tokyo Bull.* No. 25, 128 pp.

Saurez, S.S. 1975. The reproductive biology of *Ogilbia cayorum*, a viviparous brotulid fish. *Bull. Mar. Sci.* 25:143-175.

Scarratt, A.M. 1996. Techniques for raising Lined Seahorses (*Hippocampus erectus*). *Aquar. Front.* 3:24-29.

Schallenberger, R. J. and W.D. Madden. 1973. Luring behavior in the scorpionfish, *Iracundus signifer*. *Behav.* 67:3-47.

Schleser, D.M. 1994. Captive husbandry of batfish (family Ogcocephalidae). *Aquar. Front.* Spring: 27-29.

Schroeder, R.E. 1980. Philippine shore fishes of the western Sulu Sea. National Media Production Center, Manila, 266 pp.

Schultz, E.T. 1986. *Pterois volitans* and *Pterois miles*: two valid species. *Copeia*, 1986:686-690.

Sedberry, G.R. and J. Carter. 1993. The fish community of a shallow tropical lagoon in Belize, Central America. *Estuaries*, 16:198-215.

Senou, H. and K. Imai. 1998. Life color of *Pseudanthias hutomoi* (Allen & Burhanuddin, 1976) (Perciformes, Anthiinae). *I.O.P. Diving News*, 9:5-7.

Shapiro, D.Y. 1979. Social behavior, group structure, and the control of sex reversal in hermaphrodite fish. in *Adv. Study Behav.*, eds: J.S. Rosenblatt, R.A. Hinde, C. Beer, and M.C Busnell, Academic Press, New York, Vol 10:43-102

———1980. Serial female sex change after simultaneous removal of males from a social groups of a coral reef fish. *Science*, 195:1136-1137.

———1981a. Size, maturation and the social control of sex reversal in the coral reef fish *Anthias squamipinnis*. *J. Zool., Lond.* 193:105-128.

———1981b. Sequence of coloration changes during sex reversal in the tropical marine fish *Anthias squamipinnis*. *Bull. Mar. Sci.* 31: 383-398.

Smith, M.M. and P.C. Heemstra (eds.) 1986. *Smith's sea fishes*. Springer-Verlag, New York. 1047 pp.

Sonnier, F., J. Teerling and H.D. Hoese. 1976. Observations on the offshore reef and platform fish fauna of Louisiana. *Copeia*, 1976:105-111.

Sprung, J. 1995. Magnificent Mangroves. Aquar. Fish Mag. 7(15):50-58.

St. John, J., G.P. Jones and P.F. Sale. 1989. Distribution and abundance of soft-sediment meiofauna and a predatory goby in coral reef lagoons. *Coral Reefs*, 8:51-57.

Straughan, R.P.L. 1954. The sargassum fish, *Histrio pictus*. *Aquarium*, 23:277-279.

———1970. *The Salt-Water Aquarium in the Home*. 2nd revised edition. A.S. Barnes & Co., New York, 360 pp.

Strawn, K. 1958. Life history of the pigmy seahorse (*Hippocampus zosterae* Jordan and Gilbert, at Cedar Key, Florida. *Copeia*, 1958:16-22.

Steinitz, H. 1959. Observations of *Pterois volitans* (L.) and its venom. *Copeia*, 1959:158-160.

Strawn, K. 1958. Life history of the pigmy seahorse, *Hippocampus zosterae* Jordan & Gilbert, at Cedar Key, Florida. *Copeia*, 1958: 16-22.

Sweatman, H.P. 1984. A field study of the predatory behavior and feeding rate of the piscivorous coral reef fish, the lizardfish *Synodus englemani*. *Copeia* 1984:187-194.

Thayer, G.W., D.R. Colby, abd W.F. Hettler Jr. 1987. Utilization of the red mangrove prop root habitat by fishes in south Florida. *Mar. Ecol. Prog. Ser.* 35:25-38.

Thollot, P. 1996. A list of fishes inhabiting mangroves from the south-west lagoon of North Carolina. *Micronesica*, 29:1-19.

Thomson, D.A., L.T. Findley and A.N. Kerstitch. 1979. *Reef Fishes of the Sea of Cortez*. John Wiley and Sons, New York, 302 pp.

Thresher, R. E. 1978. Polymorphism, mimicry, and the evolution of hamlets. *Bull. Mar. Sci.* 28:345-353.

———1980. *Reef fish: Behavior and Ecology on the Reef and in the Aquarium*. The Palmetto Publ. Co. St. Petersburg, 171 pp.

———1984. *Reproduction in Reef Fishes*. TFH Publ. Inc. Neptune City, 399 pp.

Thresher, R.E. and P.L. Colin. 1986. Trophic structure, diversity and abundance of fishes of the deep reef (30-300m) at Enewetak, Marshall Islands. *Bull. Mar. Sci.* 38:253-272.

Tipton, K and S. S. Bell. 1988. Foraging patterns of two syngnathid fishes: importance of harpacticoid copepods. *Mar. Ecol. Prog. Ser.* 47:31-43.

Turner, C.L.1946. Male secondary sexual characters of *Dinematichthys ilucoeteoides*. *Copeia*, 1946:92-96.

Tyler, J.C. 1971. Habitat preferences of the fishes that dwell in shrub corals on the Great Barrier Reef. Proc. *Natl. Acad. Sci.* 123:1-26.

Tyler, J.C. and J.E. Böhlke. 1972. Records of sponge-dwelling fishes, primarily of the Caribbean. *Bull. Mar. Sci.* 22:601-642.

Tyler, J.C. and B.E. Luckhurst. 1994. Unusual features of the colonies of the common western Atlantic garden eel (Heterocongrinae) with a new record for Bermuda. *Northeast Gulf Sci.* 13:89-99.

Tursch, B. 1982. Chemical protection of a fish (*Abudefduf leucogaster* Bleeker) by a soft coral (*Litophyton viridis* May). *J. Chem. Ecol.* 8:1421-1425.

Vincent, A.C.J. 1994a. Seahorses exhibit conventional sex roles in mating competition, despite male pregnancy. *Behav.* 128:135-151.

———1994b. Operational sex ratios in seahorses. *Behav.* 128:153-167.

———1995. A role for daily greeting in maintaining seahorse pair bonds. *Anim. Behav.* 49: 258-260.

Vincent, A.C.J. and L. M. Sadler. 1995. Faithful pair bonds in wild seahorses, *Hippocampus whitei*. *Anim. Behav.* 50:1557-1569.

Vivien, M.L. and M.P. Peyrot-Clausade. 1974. A comparative study of the feeding behaviour of three coral reef fishes (Holocentridae), with special reference to the polychaetes of the reef cryptofauna as prey. *Proc. 2nd Int. Coral Reef Symp*. 179-1992.

Wallace, R.K. Jr. 1977. Thermal acclimation, upper temperature tolerance, and preferred temperature of juvenile yellowtail snappers, *Ocyurus chrysurus* (Bloch) (Pisces: Lutjanidae). *Bull. Mar. Sci.* 27:292-298.

Weinstein, M.P. and K.L. Heck, Jr. 1979. Ichthyfauna of seagrass meadows along the Caribbean Coast of Panama and in the Gulf of Mexico: composition, structure and community ecology. *Mar. Biol.* 50:97-107.

Wells, J.W. 1952. The coral reefs of Arno Atoll, Marshall Islands. *Atoll Res. Bull.* No. 9. 14 pp.

Wetzel, J. and J.P. Wourms. 1995. Adaptations for the reproduction and development in the skin-brooding ghost pipefish, *Solenostomus*. *Env. Biol. Fish.* 44:363-384.

Wilder Orr, J. and R. A. Fritsche. 1993. Revision of the ghost pipefish, family Solenostomidae (Teleostei: Syngnathoidei). *Copeia*, 1993:168-182.

Wilkie, D. 1986. *Aquarium Fish*. Pelham Books, London, 214 pp.

Woo, N.Y.S. & K.C. Chung. 1995. Tolerance of *Pomacanthus imperator* to hypoosmotic salinites: changes in body composition and hepatic enzyme activites. *J. Fish. Biol.* 47:70-81.

Wourms, J.P. and O. Bayne. 1973. Development of the viviparous brotulid fish, *Dinematichthys ilucoeteoides*. *Copeia*, 1973:32-40.

Yogo, Y. 1986. Protogyny, reproductive behavior and social structure of the anthiine fish *Anthias* (*Franzia*) *squamipinnis*. Indo-Pacific Fish Biology, *Ichthyological Society of Japan*, p. 964.

Young, R.F. 1992. Habitat utilization, diet, and foraging behavior of two species of Caribbean moray eels, *Gymnothorax moringa* and *Gymnothorax vicinus*. Ph.D. Dissertation, University of Rhode Island, 211 pp.

Yukihira, H., T. Shibuno, H. Hashimoto and K. Gushima. 1994. Feeding habits of moray eels (Pisces: Muraenidae) at Kuchierabujima. *J. Fac. Appl. Biol. Sci.* 33:159-166.

Photography Credits

All photographs by Scott W. Michael unless otherwise indicated.

FRED BAVENDAM: 17, 21, 39(R), 88, 117, 158, 169, 192, 210, 217, 218, 232, 234, 244, 247, 255(C), 287, 290, 292(T), 293(T), 294(BL, BR), 299(T), 308, 310, 321, 328, 329, 330(L), 348(T), 349(T), 351(TL), 353(C), 395, 396(R), 415, 418, 420, 424(T), 425(R), 428, 433(L), 436, 440, 442(B), 448(L), 456(C), 464, 465(BL, BC), 488(B), 493, 504(B), 507, 511(C), 542, 547

PAUL HUMANN: 53, 59, 205, 206, 304(L), 306(B), 324, 326, 343(B), 350(TR), 354(T), 358, 366(L), 372, 377(C), 384, 387(L), 409, 417, 423(T), 424(BR), 425(C), 433(R), 455(TR), 470(B), 471(C,B), 472(T), 514, 527, 533(BL), 534(T,B), 536(C, B), 538(R), 541(R)

JOHN E. RANDALL: 268(L), 282(L), 291(B), 301(R), 316(TR), 323, 345, 373(R), 374(L), 377(T), 378, 379(B), 380(R), 381(B), 383(L), 386(R), 388(L), 391(L), 430(C), 434(R), 435(C), 437(R), 481(TL), 517(B), 551(C), 567(BL, BR), 570(C, B), 574(BL), 575(BR), 587

RUDIE H. KUITER: 52, 258(R), 262(B), 263(T), 317, 331(TL), 335, 336(B), 351(BL, BC), 352(C), 365(B), 366(R), 368, 376(R), 382(L), 387(R), 400(R), 405(TR, B), 508(TR), 512(C), 550(R), 554(TL), 556(B), 558(TR, BL), 574(BR), 575(TL), 577(R)

KEISUKE IMAI: 334(TL), 342(TL, BL, BR), 351(CL), 369, 443, 482(BL), 505(R), 508(TL, TC), 562(BR), 563(L), 588, 589

ROGER STEENE: 160, 163, 181, 186(L), 198, 242, 288(B), 292(C,B), 294(T,C), 299(C), 300(L), 301(L), 403(T), 408(TR), 412, 421(R), 458(L), 465(TC), 624

DENISE NIELSEN TACKETT: 166, 176, 184, 191, 195, 251(R), 256(L), 263(C), 276(R), 288(T), 303(L), 312(L), 346(C), 353(T), 403(B), 405(TL), 406(BR), 424(BL)

JOHN P. HOOVER: 249, 259(L), 266(R), 267(B), 270(C), 274(B), 291(T, C), 394, 480, 502(R), 544(R), 578(R), 581(B)

JANINE CAIRNS-MICHAEL: 316(BL), 331(TR), 333(T) 336(T), 398, 447, 454, 455(TL), 472(C), 482(TR), 484(BL), 492(R), 518

FOSTER BAM: 46, 62, 67, 86, 110, 141, 147, 171, 465(TR)

LARRY TACKETT: 263(BL), 427, 429, 435(B), 438(R), 439

TSUYOSHI KAWAMOTO: 554(TR, B), 557(R), 585(B,C)

ROBERT F. MYERS: 375(L), 379(C), 575(BL), 576(T)

JOHN GREENAMYER: 35, 407, 450(B), 468(BL)

WOODY MAYHEW: 257(L), 306(C), 307(L), 327(C)

MIKE BACON: 360, 361(TL), 470(C)

KEN MARKS: 293(BR), 361(BL, BR)

D.R. AND T.L. SCHRICHTE: 22, 177(L), 189

GERALD ALLEN: 197, 388(R)

HELMUT DEBELIUS/IKAN: 441, 462(BL)

GRAEME TEAGUE: 71, 362

MASAE UEDA: 263(BR), 340

SATOSHI UEDA: 269(T), 505(L)

NORBERT WU/MO YUNG PRODUCTIONS: 363, 371

C. CHESEK/COURTESY DEPARTMENT OF LIBRARY SCIENCE/AMERICAN MUSEUM OF NATURAL HISTORY: 32

KEVIN DEACON/WATERHOUSE: 37(L)

STEVEN FRINK/WATERHOUSE: 14

JOSEPH H. FROELICH: 361(TR)

MASAO KASAI: 558(BR)

ALISON KUITER: 193

R. LUBBOCK/IKAN: 239

HIROSHI NAGANO: 571(C)

AARON NORMAN: 320

DOUG PERRINE: 327(B)

R. ROBERTSON: 252

MARTY SNYDERMAN: 327(T)

P. WIRTZ/IKAN: 457

ILLUSTRATIONS:
All illustrations by Joshua Highter

Index

Boldface page numbers refer to main entries for species covered in detail in this volume.

Abalistes stellatus (Starry Triggerfish), 180
Ablabys, 447-448
   binotatus (Indian Ocean Waspfish), **447**
   macracanthus (Spiny Waspfish), 167, **447**; photo, 447
   taenianotus (Cockatoo Waspfish), 167, 447, **448**; photos, 445, 446, 448
Abudefduf, 579
   saxatilis (Sergeant Major), 180, 190
   septemfasciatus (Banded Sergeant), 188
   sordidus (Blackspot Sergeant), 188
   vaigiensis (Indo-Pacific Sergeant Major), 346-347
   whitleyi (Whitley's Sergeant), 190
Acanthemblemaria, 214
Acanthclininae, 103
Acanthostracion quadricornis (Scrawled Cowfish), 177, 183
Acanthuridae, 69, 144-146, 337
Acanthurinae, 144
Acanthuroidei, 69
Acanthurus
   achilles (Achilles Surgeonfish), 23, 190, 220; photo, 22
   bahianus (Ocean Surgeonfish), 177, 180
   blochii (Ringtail Surgeonfish), 180
   chirurgus (Doctorfish), 177, 180
   coeruleus (Atlantic Blue Tang), 65, 202
   guttatus (Whitespotted Surgeonfish), 190; photo, 22
   leucosternon (Powderblue Surgeonfish), 185
   lineatus (Lined Surgeonfish), 190
   mata (Elongate Surgeonfish), 180
   nigricans (Whitecheek Surgeonfish), 190
   nigrofuscus (Lavender Surgeonfish), 217
   olivaceous (Orange-shoulder Surgeonfish), 23
   pyroferus (Chocolate Surgeonfish), 185; photo, 145
   sohal (Sohal Surgeonfish), 188
   triostegus (Convict Surgeonfish), 185, 217, 219, 357, 394; photo, 394
   xanthopterus (Yellowfin Surgeonfish), 180, 183
Acentronura, 427
   tentaculata (Pipehorse), 89
Acreichthys tomentosus (Seagrass Filefish), 183
Acropora palmata, photo, 171
   zone, 171
Adioryx, 370
Aeoliscus, 440, 441-442
   punctulatus (Speckled Shrimpfish), **441**; photo, 441

   strigatus (Coral Shrimpfish), **441-442**; photos, 442
Albulidae, 68, 70-72
Albuliformes, 68, 249
Alepisauroidei, 68
Alphestes afer (Mutton Hamlet), 251
Algae, coralline / sponge zone, 203
Algal ridge habitat, 171, 189-191
Aluterus
   schoepfi (Orange Filefish), 206
   scriptus (Scrawled Filefish), 177, 206
Amblycirrhitus bimacula (Twospotted Hawkfish), 190
Amblyeleotris, 209, 214
   randalli (Randall's Shrimp Goby), 196
   steinitzi, (Steinitz's Shrimp Goby), 516
Amblyglyphidodon leucogaster (Whitebelly Damselfish), 212
Amblygobius
   bynoensis (White Goby), 180
   decussatus (Crosshatch Goby), 216
   hectori (Hector's Goby), 175
   linki (Link's Goby), 180
   nocturnus (Nocturn Goby), 180
   phalaena (Banded Goby), 180, 516
   rainfordi (Rainford's Goby), photo, 139
   sphynx (Sphinx Goby), 183
Amphichthys cryptocentrus (Cryptic Toadfish), 322
Amphiprion, 214
   clarkii (Clark's Anemonefish), photos, 29, 61
   leucokranos, 126
   melanopus (Red and Black Anemonefish), 167
   nigripes (Maldives Anemonefish), 190; photo, 125
   ocellaris (Ocellaris Anemonefish), 42; photo, 213
   percula (Percula Anemonefish), 42, 43-44
   perideraion (Pink Skunk Anemonefish), 167, 190
   polymnus (Saddleback Anemonefish), 175
   sandaracinos (Orange Skunk Anemonefish), 190
Amphiprioninae, 125-126
Anal fins, 45
Anampses
   caeruleopunctatus (Bluespotted Wrasse), 190
   chrysocephalus (Redtail Tamarin Wrasse), photo, 237
   cuvier (Cuvier's Wrasse), 190
   twistii (Twisti Wrasse), 190

Anatomy of reef fishes, 34-61; illustration, 50
Andros Barrier Reef, 170
Anemonefishes, 125-126, 214
   Clark's, photos, 29, 61
   Maldives, 190; photo, 125
   Maroon, 51, 167, 188, 219
   Ocellaris, 42; photo, 213
   Percula, 42, 43-44
   Red and Black, 167
   Saddleback, 175
   Skunk, Orange, 190
   Skunk, Pink, 167, 190
Anemones
   Magnificent Sea, photos, 125, 213
Angelfishes, 69, 120-122, 337
   African Flameback, 209
   Bandit, 194
   Bicolor, 209
   Blackspot Pygmy, 232
   Blackspot, 194, 212
   Blue, 201, 203
   Blueface, 396
   Boyle's, 212
   Cherub, 203, 209
   Clarion, photo, 197
   Cocos Pygmy, 209
   Colin's, 196, 212
   Debelius, 194, 212
   Emperor, 185, 228; photos, 37, 121
   French, 201, 203
   Golden, 232; photo, 231
   Gray, 180; photo, 204
   Halfblack, 167
   Herald's, 60
   Hotumatua's, 23; photo, 20
   Keyhole, 167, 209
   Koran, photo, 51
   Lemonpeel, 185
   Lemonpeel x Halfblack hybrid, photo, 64
   Manybar, 212
   Multicolor, 195, 209, 212
   Nahacky's, 209, 212
   Narcosis, 212
   Ornate, 194, 212
   Passer, 496
   Potter's, 209
   Queen, 202, 203; photo, 239
   Regal, 176, 196; photo, 30
   Rock Beauty, 203, 532, 536, 537; photo, 537
   Scribbled, 205
   swallowtail, 337
   swallowtail, Zebra, 565

INDEX   601

Venustus, 196; photo, 243
Vermiculated, 167
Watanabe's, 212
Yellowtail, 205
Anglerfishes
Prickly, 334
Tasseled, 334
Anguilliformes, 68
Anisochrominae, 100
Anisotremus virginicus, 180
Anomalopidae, 68, 83, 363-366
Anomalops, 364
katoptron (Twofin Flashlight Fish), **365**, 366; photos, 365
Antennariidae, 68, 79-81, 329-357
Antennarioidei, 68
Antennarius, 200
avalonis (Roughjaw Frogfish), 347
biocellatus (Twinspot Frogfish), 334, **339-340**; photos, 334, 339
biocellatus group, 339-340
coccineus (Scarlet Frogfish), 188, **341**, 343; photos, 340, 341
commerson (Giant Frogfish), 167, 216, 330, **345-347**, 352; photos, 328, 330, 336, 338, 346
dorehensis (New Guinean Frogfish), 179, **341-342**; photo, 341
drombus (Hawaiian Freckled Frogfish), **341**
hispidus (Hispid Frogfish), 167, 330, **352-353**; photo, 352
indicus (Indian Frogfish), **344**; photo, 344
maculatus (Wartskin Frogfish), 167, 179, 202, 329, **347-349**, 351-352; photos, 330, 332, 333, 347, 348
moluccensis, 347
multiocellatus (Longlure Frogfish), 201, 216, 330, **349-350**; photos, 80, 215, 336, 349, 350
nummifer (Coinbearing Frogfish), 329-330, **342-343**; photo, 334, 342
nummifer group, 340-343
ocellatus (Ocellated Frogfish), 335, **344-345**; photos, 344
ocellatus group, 343-345
pauciradiatus (Dwarfed Frogfish), **345**
pauciradiatus group, 345
phymatodes, 349
pictus (Painted Frogfish), 167, 175, 202, 332, 349, **350-352**; photos, 329, 351
pictus group, 345-352
randalli (Randall's Frogfish), **345**; photo, 345
rosaceus (Rosey Frogfish), **343**
sanguineus (Bloody Frogfish), 59, 331, 342, **343**; photos, 59, 343
scaber, 354
striatus (Striated Frogfish), 57, 167, 183, 216, 329, 330, 337, **353-354**, 451, 465, 471; photos, 42, 331, 333, 336, 353

striatus group, 352-354
tridens, 354
Antennatus, 354-355; photo, 354
flagellatus (Flagellated Frogfish), **354**
strigatus (Bandtail Frogfish), **354-355**; photo, 354
tuberosus (Tuberculated Frogfish), 334-335, 354, **355**; photo, 355
Anthias, 68, 98-100, 543-589
anthias (Anthias), 543, 548
tenuis (Threadnose Anthias), **548-549**; photo, 548
truncatus, 568
Anthias, photo, 542
Amethyst, **571-572**
Bartlett's, 551, **555-556**, 561, 562, 576; photos, 556, 561
Bicolor, **556-557**, 585; photos, 544, 556
Bloodspot, **557**; photos, 557
Blotchy Deep, **588**; photo, 588
captive care, 543-548
captive feeding, 547, 548
Cave, photo, 576
classification, 543
Common, 548
Cooper's, **560**, 574, 575, 577; photos, 555, 560
deep-water, 549-550
Diadem, **571**, 575; photos, 571
Dispar, 190, 545, 551, 555, 556, **561-562**, 568, 576, 579; photos, 561, 562
Elongate, **588**; photos, 589
Evan's, 546, 552, 553, **562-563**; photos, 543, 546, 562
Fathead, **582-583**; photos, 582, 583
Filament-fin, **588**; photo, 589
Flame, 260, 545, 546, 552, 562, **568-569**; photos, 236, 568, 569
Golden, **577**
Green, **565-566**
Harlequin, **559**; photo, 558
Hawaiian, 556-557, **584-585**; photo, 584
Hawaiian Deep-water, 212, 550
Hawaiian Longfin, 212
Hawkfish, **582-583**
Heemstra's, **564-565**; photo, 565
Hutomo's, **566**; photos, 567
Indian Flame, **568-569**
Jewel, **578-581**
Longfin, 161, 212, 223, 226-227, 546, 563, **585-587**
Longfin, Hawaiian, 545-546, **563-564**; photos, 161, 563, 564, 585, 586
Lori's, 545, **569**, 577, 588; photos, 569
Luzon, 559, 567-568, **569-570**; photo, 570
Lyretail, 16, 60, 161, 185, 190, 220, 260, 544, 546, 547, 552, 555, 560, 561, 565, 568, 575, **578-581**, 588; photos, 14, 220, 544, 568, 580, 581
Marcia's, 577, **578**; photo, 578
Mirror, **573-574**

of Japan, 588-589
Olive, 546, **570**; photos, 570
Painted, **572-573**; photos, 572, 573
Peach, **561-562**
Pink, **567-568**
Princess, 194, 545, 569, 571, **577**; photos, 577
Purple, **585**
Purple Queen, 194, 226, 545, 546, 560, **571-572**, 585; photo, 572
Randall's, 212, 546, 555, **575-576**, 587; photos, 575
Red Sea, **581**, 584
Redband, **576-577**
Redbar (*Pseudanthias cooperi*), **560**
Redbar (*Pseudanthias rubrizonatus*), 576-577
Redcheek, 167, **565-566**, 579; photos, 565, 566
Red-belted, 567, 574, **576-577**; photos, 576
Redfin, **561-562**
Red-girdled, **576-577**
Redhead, **564-565**
Redstripe, **563**, 588; photos, 562, 563
Resplendent, 546, 560, 571, **574-575**, 576; photos, 575
Reticulated, **577-578**; photo, 578
Sailfin, (*Pseudanthias*), **571-572**
Sailfin (*Rabaulichthys*), 587
Scalefin, **578-581**
Shen's, **574**; photo, 574
Shortsnout, **571**
Silverstreak, **560**
slender, 550-552
slender, Earle's, 550, **551**; photo, 550
slender, Magenta, 550, **551**, 585; photos, 551
slender, Whitley's, 550, **551-552**, 555; photo, 551
social mimicry, 546
Splitfin, Earle's, **551**
Spotfin, **587**; photo, 587
Squareback, **573-574**
Squareblock, **573-574**
Squarespot, 212, 547, 558, 559, 560, **573-574**; photos, 574
Stocky, 167, 202, 559, **567-568**, 570, 577; photos, 547, 567
Striped (*Pseudanthias fasciatus*), **563**
Striped (*Pseudanthias taeniatus*), 557, 560, 564, **581-584**; photo, 581
Sunset, **571**
Thompson's, **584-585**
Threadfin (*Nemanthias carberryi*), 546, **552-553**, 562, 563, 568; photos, 546, 552, 553
Threadfin (*Pseudanthias huchtii*), **565-566**
Threadnose, **548-549**; photo, 548
Tiger Queen, **569**
Townsend's, 578, **584**; photo, 581
Tricolor, **576-577**

Truncate, **567-568**
Twinspot, 194, 555, **558-559**, 574; photos, 558, 559
Twospot, **558-559**
Yellowback, **562-563**
Yellowline, **569-570**
Yellowlined, **588**; photos, 589
Yellowspotted, **588**; photo, 589
Yellowstripe, 545, 546, 548, 572, 577, **585**; photos, 584
Yellowtail, **562-563**
Anthiinae, 98, 543-589
Antipatharian zone, 204-205
Aphareus furcata (Green Jobfish), 562
Apistinae, 458
Apistus carinatus (Longfin Waspfish), **458**; photo, 458
Aploactinidae, 68, 95
Aplysina fistularis (Yellow Tube Sponge), photo, 201
Apogon
 altus (Bronze Cardinalfish), 179
 angustatus (Broadstriped Cardinalfish), 188
 apogonides (Goldbelly Cardinalfish), 175
 aureus (Golden Cardinalfish), 167
 aurolineatus (Bridled Cardinalfish), 179, 214
 chrysotaenia (Manyline Cardinalfish), 167
 compressus (Ochre-striped Cardinalfish), 167, 175
 cooki (Blackbanded Cardinalfish), 167
 cyanosoma (Orangestriped Cardinalfish), 175
 gilberti (Gilbert's Cardinalfish), 179
 hartzfeldii (Hartzfeld's Cardinalfish), 167
 lateralis (Inshore Cardinalfish), 206
 leptacanthus (Threadfin Cardinalfish), 175, 179
 maculatus (Flamefish), 202, 203, 320
 properupta (Northern Orangestriped Cardinalfish), 167
 pseudomaculatus (Twospot Cardinalfish), 320, 549
 quadrisquamatus (Sawcheek Cardinalfish), 214, 216
 sealei (Seale's Cardinalfish), photos, 162, 226
 semilineatus (Semilined Cardinalfish), 167
 taeniatus (Twobelt Cardinalfish), 167
Apogonidae, 69, 106-108
Apterichthus klazingai (Sharpsnout Snake Eel), **299**; photos, 299
Aquariums
 choosing suitable species, 30-31, 236
 conditions, 220-233
 duplicating deep-water habitat, 212
 duplicating mangrove swamp, 179
 duplicating oceanic desert, 210-211
 duplicating rubble zone, 208-209
 duplicating seagrass habitat, 182
 ethical responsibilities, 28-31

 light levels, 225-227
 providing natural habitats in, 17-19
 salinity, 227-229
 size of, 240
 substrates in, 229-233
 suitability ratings for, 240-242
 temperatures in, 222-224
 water movement in, 220-221
Aracaninae, 153
Archamia fucata (Orangestriped Cardinalfish), 175
Archway habitats, 195-196
 fishes in (chart), 196
Armorheads, 69, 122
 Whiskered, 122
Arno Atoll, 221
Arothron, 200
 hispidus (Whitespotted Puffer), 180, 183
 immaculatus (Immaculate Puffer), 180, 183, 188
 manilensis (Manila Puffer), 180
 mappa (Map Puffer), 199, 396; photo, 40
 meleagris (Guinea Fowl Puffer), 61, 185, 190; photo, 61
 nigropunctatus (Blackspotted Puffer), 61, 216, 190
 reticularis (Reticulate Puffer), 180
Artificial habitats, 198-202
Assessor, 102, 196
Assessors, 102, 196
Associations of fish with other organisms (chart), 214
Asterropteryx semipunctatus (Bluespotted Goby), 180, 183
Astore Atoll, 170
Astrapogon stellatus (Starry Conchfish), 177, 214
Atolls, 170
 Arno, 221
 Astore, 170
 Canton, 175-176
 Chinchirro, 170
 Enewetak, 222-223, 226
 Hogsty, 170
 Kaukura, 170
 Kwajelin, 170
 Rangiroa, 170; photo, 170
Aulopiformes, 68
Aulostomidae, 68, 85-87, 393-397
Aulostomus
 chinensis (Pacific Trumpetfish), 185, 311, 394, **396-397**; photos, 392, 394, 396
 maculatus (Atlantic Trumpetfish), 201, 393, 394, **397**; photos, 86, 393, 394, 397
 strigosus, 397
Back-reef slope habitat, 184-185; photo, 186
 fishes in (chart), 185
Balistapus undulatus (Orangelined Triggerfish), 190, 219
Balistes capriscus (Gray Triggerfish), 201, 207
Balistidae, 69, 150-152, 337

Balistoides conspicillum (Clown Triggerfish), 16, 185, 496
Bandfishes, 69, 124
Bank reefs, 168
Bannerfishes
 Humphead, 176
 Masked, 185, 190
 Schooling, 185; photo, 119
Barbels, 54
Barbfish, 421, **468-470**; photos, 469, 470
Barbier, Red, 198, **549**, 550; photo, 549
Barracudas, 69, 146
 Chevron, 146
 Great, 146; photo, 147
Barrier reefs, 168-170; photo, 168
Basses. See also Seabasses, dwarf
 Candy, 212, 232
 Chalk, 209, 211, 519, 520, 523, **526-527**; photo, 526
 Harlequin, 183, 209, 520, **525-526**; photos, 525
 Lantern, 183, 520, **521-522**; photo, 521
 Leather, 396
 Longtail, **549**
 Mouse, **523**
 Orangeback, 194, 203, 209, 519, 523, **520**; photos, 521
 Ridgeback, 194, 232
 Roughtongue, 203, 204, 212, 548-549, **550**; photo, 550
 Snow, 519, **522**
 streamer, 549
 Tattler, 198, 205, **522-523**, 549; photo, 522
 Tobacco, **524**
 Twospot, 183, **522**; photo, 522
 Wrasse, 198, 203, 212, 523, 549
Basslets
 Blackcap, 194, 212, 523, 556
 fairy, 555-587; photo, 169
 Flores, 574
 Heliotrope, 212
 reef, 98, 196
 spiny, 103
Batfishes, 69, 141-142, 337
 Gulf, **362**
 Orbiculate, 180
 Oval, 359, **362**
 Pancake, **360**; photo, 360
 Pinnate, 30, 141, 206
 Polkadot, 183, **361**, 517; photos, 361
 Red-finned, 141
 Redlip, 359; photo, 358
 Roughback, **362**; photo, 362
 Shortnose, **361-362**, 517; photos, 361
 South American, 359, **362**
 Spiny, **360**
 Spotted, **361**
Batfishes, walking, 68, 81, 209, 358-362
 biology, 358-359
 captive care, 359-360

INDEX 603

Batrachoides
    gilberti (Large-eye Toadfish), **324-325**; photo, 324
    lacinia (Twofaced Toadfish), 322; photo, 323
    manglae, 322
Batrachoididae, 68, 78-79, 321-327
Batrachoidiformes, 68
Batrachoidinae, 78
Batrachomoeus trispinosus (Threespined Toadfish), photo, 321
Bearded ghouls, 459-462. See also Devilfishes
Beaugregory, 180
Belonidae, 68, 82
Beloniformes, 68
Belonoidei, 68
Berciformes, 68
Bigeyes, 68, 104, 196, 203, 205
    Short, 198, 549
Binomial system of nomenclature, 64-65
Biological information in species accounts, 239
Black Widow, **320**
Blennies, 69, 135-136
    clinid, 69, 134, 209
    combtooth, 69, 135-136
    Convict, 69, 129-130, 309
    Diamond, 214
    Gosline's Scale Eating, 117
    Hair-tail, 37
    Midas, 546, 552, 555, 562, 579
    pike, 69, 134-135, 209
    Redspeckled, 190
    Redspotted, photo, 35
    sailfin, 209
    "scooter" (misapplied name), 237-238
    Seaweed, photo, 136
    Striped Fang, 180
    tube, 69, 134-135, 214
    weed, 69, 133-134
Blenniidae, 69, 135-136
Blennioidei, 69
Blisterhead, 290
Boarfishes, 69, 122
Bodianus
    bimaculatus (Twinspot Hogfish), photo, 211
    pulchellus (Spotfin Hogfish), 203, 205, 212, 523
    rufus (Spanish Hogfish), 297, 394, 397
Body forms of reef fishes, 36-41
    anguilliform, 36
    box-shaped, 40-41
    compressiform, 36-37
    depressiform, 39
    fusiform, 39
    globiform, 40
    sagittiform, 38-39
    taeniform, 37
Bonefishes, 68, 70-72
Bothidae, 69, 146-147, 516, 517

Bothus lunatus (Peacock Flounder), 177; photo, 39
Boxfishes
    Blue, 190
    Reticulate, photo, 40
    Yellow, 185, 216
Brachionichthyidae, 79
Brachysomophis, 288, 296, 298, 299-300
    cirrocheilos (Stargazer Snake Eel), 288, **299-300**; photos, 298, 299
    crocodilinus (Crocodile Snake Eel), 177, **300**; photos, 288, 295, 298, 300
    henshawi (Henshaw's Snake Eel), 300
    sauropsis (Reptilian Snake Eel), 300
Breams
    large-eye, 69, 113-114
    threadfin, 114
Bristletooth, Striped, 175, 185, 188, 217
Brotulas
    Black, 318, **320**; photo, 320
    Black Widow, **320**
    free-tailed, 319-320
    Large-eye, **319-320**
    livebearing, 68, 76-77, 318-320
    livebearing, biology, 318-319
    livebearing, captive care, 319
    Lycopod Goby, **320**
    Randall's, **319-320**
    Yellow, **320**; photo, 318
Brotulina fusca, 320
Bryaninops
    natans (Redeye Goby), 214
    tigris (Black Coral Goby), 214
    yongei (Whip Goby), 214
Bunaken Island Manado Tua Marine National Park, photo, 158-159
Buoyancy and swim bladder, 47
Burrfishes, 69, 156-157
    Bridled, 183
    Striped, 183
    Web, 183
Butterflyfishes, 69, 119-120, 337
    Banded, 180
    Bank, 203, 205, 212, 549
    Bennett's, 190
    Blackback, 185, 188
    Burgess', 193-195, 212
    Chevron, 185
    Doublesaddle, 185, 190
    Eightbanded, 167
    Foureye, 180, 183
    Fourspot, 190
    Golden, photo, 27
    Goldenstriped, 175
    Indian, 196, 212, 575
    Klein's, 16, 185, 346-347, 579
    Latticed, 167
    Longnose, Big, photo, 221
    Longnose, Caribbean, 194, 212
    Longnose, Yellow, 190, 222
    Margined, 205
    Merten's, 185

    Ornate, 53
    Pacific Redfin, 175, 185, 188
    Pyramid, 337; photo, 192
    Raccoon, 175, 185, 188
    Rainford's, 175
    Reef, 203
    Saddled, 185, 190
    Scythe, 212
    Speckled, 175, 185, 188, 217
    Speculum, 190
    Spotfin, 201, 202
    Teardrop, 175, 188
    Threadfin, 180, 185, 188
    Tinker's, 212
    Vagabond, 175, 188, 217
    Western, 205
    Yellowcrowned, 195
    Yellowhead, 188
Bythitidae, 68, 76-77, 318-320
Bythitoidei 68
Caesio, 185
Caesioninae, 111
Callechelys
    catostomus (Darkline Snake Eel), **301**
    luteus (Freckled Snake Eel), **301**
    marmorata (Marbled Snake Eel), 288, **300-301**; photo, 301
Callionymidae, 69, 137-138
Callionymoidei, 69
Callionymus enneactis (Mangrove Dragonet), 180
Calloplesiops altivelis (Comet), 102, 167, 270, 338; photo, 102
Callyspongia vaginalis (Branching Vase Sponge), photo, 200
Cantherhines macrocerus (Whitespotted Filefish), 394, 397
Canthidermis
    maculatus (Rough Triggerfish), 206
    sufflamen (Ocean Triggerfish), 206-207
Canthigaster, 416
    bennetti (Bennett's Toby), 211
    compressa (Fingerprint Toby), 183, 211
    coronata (Crowned Toby), 211
    cyanetron (Easter Island Toby), 196
    janthinoptera (Honeycomb Toby), 188
    leoparda (Leopard Toby), 196, 232
    pygmaea (Pygmy Toby), 232
    rostrata (Sharpnose Puffer), 177, 180, 183, 202, 205, 549
    solandri (Ocellated Toby), 185, 217; photo, 155
    tyleri (Tyler's Toby), 196
    valentini (Saddled Toby), 188, 216
Canthigastrinae, 155
Canton Atoll, 175-176
Captive bred marine fishes, 29-30
Captive care information in species accounts, 240
Caracanthidae, 68, 91-92, 443-444

Caracanthus, 214
   maculatus (Spotted Coral Croucher), **444**; photo, 443
   madagascariensis (Madagascar Coral Croucher), **444**
   typicus (Hawaiian Coral Croucher), **444**
   unipinna (Pygmy Coral Croucher), **444**; photo, 444
Carangidae, 69, 110-111
Carangiform locomotion, 39
Caranx
   crysos (Blue Runner), 201
   melampygus (Bluefin Jack), 584
   ruber (Bar Jack), 297; photo, 110
   sexfasciatus (Bigeye Trevally), photo, 39
Carapidae, 68, 77-78, 214
Carapinae, 77
Carcharhinus
   limbatus (Blacktipped Shark), 179
   signatus (Night Shark), 355
Cardinalfishes, 69, 106-108
   Aurita, 188
   Banggai, 183
   Bay, 179
   Blackbanded, 167
   Bridled, 179, 214
   Broadstriped, 188
   Bronze, 179
   Crocodile, 180
   Crown-of-Thorns, 214
   Dusky, 177
   Fivelined, 175, 183; photo, 107
   Gilbert's, 179
   Goldbelly, 175
   Golden, 167
   Hartzfeld's, 167
   Inshore, 206
   Manyline, 167
   Ochre-striped, 167, 175
   Orangestriped (*Apogon*), 175
   Orangestriped (*Archamia*), 175
   Orangestriped, Northern, 167
   Orbiculate, 180, 183
   Pajama, 175; photo, 58
   Sawcheek, 214, 216
   Sea Urchin, 214
   Seale's, photos, 162, 226
   Semilined 167
   Slender, photos, 117, 166
   Sponge, 216
   Threadfin, 175, 179
   Twobelt, 167
   Twospot, 320, 549
   Variegated, 180
Carlson, Dr. Bruce, 347
Catfishes
   Coral, **308-309**
   eel, 68, 74-75
   Eel, Striped, 130, 177, 179, 188, **308-309**; photos, 308, 309
Caudal fins, 45-46

Caudal peduncle, 46
Caulolatilus affinis (Goldeneyed Pacific Tilefish), 331
Cave habitats, 195-196
   fishes in (chart), 196
Centriscidae, 68, 91, 440-442
Centriscus, 440
   scutatus (Rigid Shrimpfish), **442**; photos, 440, 442
Centropyge
   acanthops (African Flameback Angelfish), 209
   argi (Cherub Angelfish), 203, 209
   aurantia (Golden Angelfish), 232; photo, 231
   bicolor (Bicolor Angelfish), 209
   bispinosa (Coral Beauty), 188
   colini (Colin's Angelfish), 196, 212
   debelius, (Debelius Angelfish), 194, 212
   flavissima (Lemonpeel Angelfish), 65, 185
   flavissima x *C. vroliki* hybrid, photo, 64
   heraldi (Herald's Angelfish), 60
   hotumatua (Hotumatua's Angelfish), 23; photo, 20
   joculator (Cocos Pygmy Angelfish), 209
   multicolor (Multicolor Angelfish), 195, 209, 212
   multifasciata (Manybar Angelfish), 212
   nahackyi (Nahacky's Angelfish), 209, 212
   narcosis (Narcosis Angelfish), 212
   nigriocella (Blackspot Pygmy Angelfish), 232
   potteri (Potter's Angelfish), 209
   tibicen (Keyhole Angelfish), 167, 209
   vroliki (Halfblack Angelfish), 167
Cephalopholis, 312, 532
   argus (Peacock Hind), 188, 217, 251, 269
   cruentatus (Grayshy), 530
   cyanostigma (Bluespotted Hind), 167
   formosa (Blueline Hind), 167
   microprion (Freckled Hind), 167
   miniata (Coral Hind), 16, 190, 579; photo, 99
   polleni (Harlequin Hind), 196
   sexmaculata (Sixspot Hind), photo, 194
   urodeta (V-tailed Hind), 16, 190
Cepolidae, 69, 124
Chaenopsidae, 69, 134-135
Chaenopsis, 209
Chaetoderma penicilligera (Tasseled Filefish), 57
Chaetodipterus faber (Atlantic Spadefish), 201; photo, 141
Chaetodon
   assarius (Western Butterflyfish), 205
   aureofasciatus (Goldenstriped Butterflyfish), 175
   auriga (Threadfin Butterflyfish), 180, 185, 188

   bennetti (Bennett's Butterflyfish), 190
   burgessi (Burgess' Butterflyfish), 193-195, 212
   captistratus (Foureye Butterflyfish), 180, 183
   citrinellus (Speckled Butterflyfish), 175, 185, 188, 217
   ephippium (Saddled Butterflyfish), 185, 190
   flavocoronatus (Yellowcrowned Butterflyfish), 195
   kleini (Klein's Butterflyfish), 16, 185, 346-347, 579
   lunula (Raccoon Butterflyfish), 175, 185, 188
   lunulatus (Pacific Redfin Butterflyfish), 175, 185, 188
   melannotus (Blackback Butterflyfish), 185, 188
   mertensii (Merten's Butterflyfish), 185
   mitratus (Indian Butterflyfish), 196, 212, 575
   ocellatus (Spotfin Butterflyfish), 201, 202
   octofasciatus (Eightbanded Butterflyfish), 167
   ornatissimus (Ornate Butterflyfish), 53
   quadrimaculatus (Fourspot Butterflyfish), 190
   rafflesi (Latticed Butterflyfish), 167
   rainfordi (Rainford's Butterflyfish), 175
   sedentarius (Reef Butterflyfish), 203
   semilarvatus (Golden Butterflyfish), photo, 27
   speculum (Speculum Butterflyfish), 190
   striatus (Banded Butterflyfish), 180
   tinkeri (Tinker's Butterflyfish), 212
   trifascialis (Chevron Butterflyfish), 185
   ulietensis (Doublesaddle Butterflyfish), 185, 190
   unimaculatus (Teardrop Butterflyfish), 175, 188
   vagabundus (Vagabond Butterflyfish), 175, 188, 217
   xanthocephalus (Yellowhead Butterflyfish), 188
Chactodontidae, 69, 119-120, 337
Chaetodontoplus
   duboulayi (Scribbled Angelfish), 205
   mesoleucus (Vermiculated Angelfish), 167
   personifer (Yellowtail Angelfish), 205
Channels, reef, as habitat, 184
   fishes in (chart), 185
Channomuraena
   bauchotae, 252
   vittata (Longjaw Moray Eel), 232, **252-253**; photo, 252
Chaunacidae, 79

Cheilinus
    bimaculatus (Twospot Maori Wrasse), 202
    diagrammus (Cheekline Maori Wrasse), 312
    fasciatus (Redbreasted Maori Wrasse), 217
    undulatus (Napoleon Wrasse), 15, 31, 190
Cheilio inermis (Cigar Wrasse), 167, 183
Cheilodactylidae, 69, 106
Cheilodipterus, 434
    quinquelineatus (Fivelined Cardinalfish), 175, 183; photo, 107
Cheiloprion labiatus (Biglip Damselfish), 175
Chelmon marginalis (Margined Butterflyfish), 205
Chelonodon laticeps (Laticeps Puffer), 180
Chilomycterus
    antennatus (Bridled Burrfish), 183
    antillarum (Web Burrfish), 183
    schoepfi (Striped Burrfish), 183
Chinchirro Atoll, 170
Choerodon
    cyanodus (Blue Tuskfish), 205
    fasciatus (Harlequin Tuskfish), 190
Choriaster granulatus (Sea Star), photo, 217
Choridactylinae, 458-462
Choridactylus, 458
    multibarbus (Many-barbed Stingfish), 457, **459**; photos, 458, 459
Chromatophores, 59-60
Chrominae, 126
Chromis
    acares (Midget Chromis), 190
    analis (Yellow Chromis), 194
    caudalis (Blueaxil Chromis), 194
    cyanea (Blue Chromis), 315, 394, 397, 532, 534, 536-537
    delta (Deep-reef Chromis), 194
    dimidiatus (Bicolor Chromis), 16, 579
    enchrysura (Caribbean Chromis), 198, 203, 205
    insolatus (Sunshine Chromis), 523
    lineata (Lined Chromis), 190
    ovalis (Oval Chromis), 584
    vanderbilti (Vanderbilt's Chromis), 190
    viridis (Blue Green Chromis), 16, 175, 185, 188, 444; photo, 174
    weberi (Weber's Chromis), 185
Chrysiptera
    parasema (Yellowtail Blue Damselfish), 247
    rex (King Demoiselle), 190
Chuk Lagoon, 200
Ciguatera, 249
Cirrhilabrus
    cyanopleura (Bluehead Fairy Wrasse), 209
    filamentosus (Whipfin Fairy Wrasse), 202, 209; photo, 202
    jordani (Flame Wrasse), 194, 209, 212
    lineatus (Lined Fairy Wrasse), photo, 24
    pylei (Pyle's Fairy Wrasse), 212
    rhomboidalis (Rhomboid Fairy Wrasse), 194; photo, 38
    rubripinnis (Redfin Fairy Wrasse), 209
    rubrisquamis (Redscale Fairy Wrasse), 575
    rubriventralis (Longfin Fairy Wrasse), 209
    scottorum (Scott's Fairy Wrasse), photo, 57
    solorensis (Redheaded Fairy Wrasse), 59, 167, 203; photo, 55
    temminckii (Bluestreak Fairy Wrasse), 209
Cirrhitichthys
    aprinus (Spotted Hawkfish), 216, 522
    oxycephalus (Coral Hawkfish), photo, 105
Cirrhitidae, 69, 104-106
Cirripectes variolosus (Redspeckled Blenny), 190
Class, definition, 66-67
Classification of fishes, 63-69
    chart, 68-69
Cleidopus gloriamaris (Pineapple Fish), **368**, **369**; photos, 367, 368
Clepticus parrae (Creole Wrasse), 397
Clingfishes, 69, 137
    Stippled, photo, 45
    Urchin, 211
Clinidae, 69, 134
Cociella punctata (Mangrove Crocodilefish), **510**
Cod, Butterfly, **505-508**
Coffinfishes, 79
Coloration of reef fishes, 24-25, 57-61, 57-61
    color form, 60
    color morph, 60
    color phase, 60
    pigmentation, 59-60
    theories to explain, 57-59
    variability of, 59, 60-61
Comet, 102, 103, 167, 270, 338; photo, 102
Commerson, Philibert, 347
Conchfish, Starry, 177, 214
Coney, 297, 394
Conger cinereus (Mustache Conger Eel), **291**; photos, 291
Conger eels, 68, 73-74, 287-294
    Barred, **291**; photo, 291
    biology, 287-289
    captive care, 289-290
    Mustache, **291**; photos, 291
Congrinae, 73
Congrogadinae, 100
Congroidei, 68
Conniella apterygia, 127
Copepod parasites, photo, 251
Coradion melanopus (Twoeye Coralfish), 167
Coral Beauty, 188
Coral crouchers, 68, 91-92, 214, 443-444
    biology, 443
    captive care, 443-444
    Hawaiian, **444**
    Madagascar, **444**
    Pygmy, **444**; photo, 444
    Spotted, **444**; photo, 443
Coral heads, 175-176; photo, 174
    fishes found in (chart), 175
Coral reef habitats. See Habitats
Coralfish, Twoeye, 167
Coralline algae / sponge zone, 203
Corals
    antler, photo, 177
    black, photo, 205
    black, zone, 204-205
    hard, photo, 17
    Leather, photo, 14
    pink-tipped, photo, 176
    pinnacle, photo, 177
    Plate, photo, 14
    soft, photos, 177, 219
    Staghorn, photo, 542
Coris
    africana (African Coris), 209
    aygula (Twinspot Coris), 185
    batuensis (Batu Coris), 167, 177, 312
    chlopterus (Pastel Green Coris), 177
    frerei (Formosan Coris), 209
    gaimard (Yellowtail Coris), 185, 209
Corises
    African, 209
    Batu, 167, 177, 312
    Formosan, 209
    Pastel Green, 177
    Yellowtail, 185, 209
Cornetfishes, 68, 87, 395; photo, 395
    Bluespotted, 183
    Serrate, 188
    Smooth, 185, 492; photo, 395
Coryphaena hipppurus (Dolphinfish), 355
Coryphopterus
    glaucofraenum (Bridled Goby), 290
    personatus (Masked Goby), 394
Corythoichthys, 427-428, 429-432
    amplexus (Brownbanded Pipefish), 179, **429**-430; photo, 429
    flavofasciatus (Network Pipefish), 175, 188, **430**; photo, 430
    haematopterus (Yellowstreaked Pipefish), **430**; photo, 430
    insularis (Insular Pipefish), **431**; photo, 431
    intestinalis (Messmate Pipefish), 175, 183, 428, **431**; photo, 430
    nigripectus (Blackbreasted Pipefish), **431**; photos, 431
    schultzi (Guilded Pipefish), **431-432**; photos, 432
Cowfishes
    Longhorn, 183
    Scrawled, 177, 183
Creolefish, 530, 532
Crinoids, photos, 217, 234
    feather star, photos, 169, 232, 493
Croakers, 69, 115
Crocodilefishes, 96-97, **510**
    Beaufort's, **510**; photos, 96, 510
    Mangrove, **510**
    Tentacled, **511**
Cromileptes altivelis (Panther Grouper), 43

Cryptocentrus, 214
   cinctus (Yellow Shrimp Goby), 516
Ctenocella, photo, 17
Ctenochaetus striatus (Striped Bristletooth), 175, 185, 188, 217
Ctenogobiops, 214
Ctenoid scales, 54
Cubbuyu, 205
Cyanide, use of in capturing reef fishes, 28
Cycloid scales, 54
Cymbacephalus, 510
   beauforti (Beaufort's Crocodilefish), **510**; photos, 96, 510
Cymolutes
   praetextatus (Knife Razorfish), 516
   torquatus (Finescale Razorfish), 516
Cynarina lacrymalis, photo, 162
Cyprinocirrhites polyactis (Lyretail Hawkfish), 570
Dactylanthias mcmichaeli, 582
Dactyloptena
   orientalis (Oriental Helmut Gurnard), 290, 476, **516**; photos, 516, 517
   tiltoni (Tilton's Helmut Gurnard), 515
Dactylopteridae, 68, 97, 515-517
Dactylopteroidei, 68
Dactylopterus
   volitans (Flying Gurnard), 290, **517**; photos, 514, 517
Dactylopus dactylopus (Fingered Dragonet), 167, 203, 516
Dactyloscopidae, 69, 133
Damselfishes, 69, 125-126, 247; photos, 169, 542
   Bicolor, 16
   Biglip, 175
   Black, 217
   Brighteye, 188
   Cocoa, 532
   dascyllus, 214
   Dusky, 541
   Fusilier, 126, 551, 546, 555, 570
   Jewel, 224
   Neon, 190
   Philippine, 190
   Phoenix, 188
   Speckled, 188
   Ward's, 190
   White, 175
   Whiteband, 188
   Whitebelly, 212
   Yellowtail, 534
   Yellowtail Blue, 247
Dartfishes, 69, 140-141
   Filament, 516
   Green, 516
   Spottail, 209, 516
Dascyllus, 214
   albisella (Hawaiian Dascyllus), photo, 177
   aruanus (Humbug Dascyllus), 175, 188, 219, 247; photo, 176
   melanurus (Blacktail Dascyllus), 175
   reticulatus (Reticulated Dascyllus), 185
Deep fore-reef habitat, 193-195
Deep-water fishes (chart), 212
Demoiselles
   King, 190
   Yellowtail, 190
Dendrochirus, 491, 497-501
   barberi (Green Lionfish), 491, **497**; photos, 497
   bellus (Bellus Lionfish), **508**; photo, 508
   biocellatus (Ocellated Lionfish), 494, **497-498**, 508; photos, 498
   brachypterus (Shortfin Lionfish), 167, 200, 451, 494, 496, **498-500**, 508; photos, 499
   zebra (Zebra Lionfish), 167, 216, 357, 494, 496, **500-501**, 505, 508; photos, 494, 500
Density (charts), 228, 229
Dermal appendages, 56-57
Desert, oceanic, as habitat, 210-211
Desmoholacanthus arcatus (Bandit Angelfish), 194
Devilfishes, 209, 459-462, **505-508**, 516
   Caledonian, **460**; photo, 460
   Filamented, **462**; photo, 462
   Spiny, 167, 179, 202, **460-461**, 476; photos, 460, 461, 462
Diadema, 433
Diademichthys lineatus (Urchin Clingfish), 211
Dilution effect, 546
Dinematichthys, 319-320
   iluocoeteoides (Large-eye Brotula), **319-320**
   randalli (Randall's Brotula), **319-320**
   riukiuensis (Yellow Brotula), **320**; photo, 318
Diodon
   eydouxii, 156
   holacanthus (Spiny Puffer), 177, 183, 207, 265; photo, 157
   hystrix (Porcupinefish), 185, 196, 207
Diodontidae, 69, 156-157, 337
Diodontiform swimming, 40
Diplectrum formosum (Sand Perch), 198, 527, 549; photo, 527
Diploprionini, 98
Diproctacanthus xanthurus (Wandering Cleaner Wrasse), 167
Dischistodus perspicillatus (White Damselfish), 175
Doctorfishes, 144-146, 177, 180
Dolphinfish, 355
Domeier, Michael, 528
Doratonotus megalepis (Dwarf Wrasse), 183
Dorsal fins, 42-43
Doryrhamphus, 432-435
   dactyliophorus (Banded Pipefish), **432**, 434, 435; photo, 432
   excisus (Bluestripe Pipefish), 247, **433**; photos, 433
   janssi (Janss's Pipefish), **433-434**; photo, 434
   multiannulatus (Multibar Pipefish), **434**, 435; photo, 434
   negrosensis (Negros Pipefish), **433**
   pessuliferus (Yellowbanded Pipefish), **434-435**; photo, 435
Dottybacks, 68, 100-101
   Australian, 385
   Bluelined, 190, 444, 583
   Lined, 385
   Longfin, 167, 216
   Magenta, 212
   Orchid, photo, 18
   Red, 385
   Splendid, 167, 216; photo, 242
   Spotted, 205
   Steene's, 194
   Sunrise, 355
Dragonets, 69, 137-138, 209
   Fingered, 167, 203, 516
   Mangrove, 180
   Stellate, 175
Dragonfishes
   Hawaiian, **400**
   Little, **399**
   Slender, **400**
Drums, 69, 115, 196
   Spotted, 205; photo, 115
Dunkerocampus baldwini (Redstripe Pipefish), **435**; photo, 435
Durgon, Black, 190
Ebosia bleekeri (Bleeker's Lionfish), **508**; photo, 508
Echeneidae, 69, 109-110
Echidna, 246, 253-255
   catenata (Chainlink Moray Eel), **253**; photo, 253
   delicatula (Finespeckled Moray Eel), **253-254**; photo, 253
   nebulosa (Snowflake Moray Eel), 185, 188, 248, 250, 251, **254**; photos, 254, 583
   polyzona (Banded Moray Eel), 188, 254, **255**, 259, 263; photos, 246, 255
Echinophryne crassispina (Prickly Anglerfish), 334
Echiophis intertinctus (Spotted Spoonnose Eel), **307**; photo, 307
Ecsenius midas (Midas Blenny), 546, 552, 555, 562, 579
Eels. See also Conger eels; Garden eels; Moray eels; Ribbon eels; Snake eels
   cusk, 68, 78
   Spoonnose, Spotted, **307**; photo, 307
   Vulture, photo, 296
   wolf, 100
   worm, 68, 74, 295-296

Elizabeth Reef, 166
Elopiformes, 68
Emblemaria, 209
Enchelycore, 256-258
    bayeri (Bayer's Moray Eel), **256**; photo, 256
    bikiniensis (Bikini Atoll Moray Eel), **256**
    carychoa (Chestnut Moray Eel), **256-257**; photo, 256
    nigricans (Viper Moray Eel), **257**; photo, 257
    pardalis (Dragon Moray Eel), 256, **257-258**; photos, 257, 258; photo, 52
Enchelynassa, 256, **258-259**
    canina (Longfang Moray Eel), 188, **258-259**; photo, 259
Enewetak Atoll, 222-223, 226
Ephippidae, 69, 141-142, 337
Epibulus insidiator (Slingjaw Wrasse), 190
Epinephelinae, 98, 519
Epinephelini, 98
Epinephelus
    adscensionis (Rock Hind), 297, 394
    cruentatus (Graysby), 397
    cyanopodus (Speckled Grouper), 179
    dermatolepis (Leather Bass), 396
    fulva (Coney), 297, 394
    lanceolatus (Giant Grouper), 30
    maculatus (Highfin Grouper), 179
    merra (Honeycomb Grouper), 188
    morio (Red Grouper), 183, 251
    nigritus (Warsaw Grouper), 201
    striatus (Nassau Grouper), 183, 251; photo, 62
Equetus, 196
    lanceolatus (Spotted Drum), 205; photo, 115
    umbrosus (Cubbuyu), 205
Esca, 43, 329-330
Eurypegasus
    draconis (Dragon Sea Moth), 210, **399**, 516; photos, 398, 399
    papilio (Hawaiian Dragonfish), **400**
Evermannichthys, 215
Eviota pellucida (Neon Pygmy Goby), 167
Evistias acutirostris (Whiskered Armorhead), 122, 194
Exyrias puntang (Puntang Goby), 180, 206
Family, definition, 66
Filefishes, 69, 152-153, 337
    Fringed, 177, 180, 183
    Longnosed, 153; photo, 152
    Orange, 206
    Orangehead, 496
    Planehead, 202, 206
    Pygmy, 183
    Saddled, 185
    Scrawled, 177, 206
    Seagrass, 183
    Slender, 180, 183
    Tasseled, 57
    Whitespotted, 394, 397

Fins, 41-46
    anal, 45
    caudal, 45-46
    dorsal, 42-43
    median, 41
    paired, 41-42
    pectoral, 43-44
    pelvic, 44-45
Firefishes, 140
    Deep-water, **502**
    Helfrich's, 212, 587; photo, 140
    Plaintail, **504-505**
    Ragged-finned, **501-502**
    Red, **505-508**
Fishes
    anatomy, 34-61; illustration, 50
    body form and locomotion, 36-41
    classification, 63-69; chart, 68-69
    coloration, 57-61
    definition, 63-64
    distribution in habitats, 216-220
    families, 70-157
    gills, 51-52
    history, 33-34
    lateral line organ, 49
    mouth, 52-54
    scales, 54-57; illustration, 54
    skin, 54-57
    swim bladder, 47-49
    teeth, 52-54
    that associate with other organisms (chart), 214
Fishes of the World, by Joseph S. Nelson, 64
Fistularia, 492
    commersonii (Smooth Cornetfish), 185, 492; photo, 395
    corneta, 395
    petimba (Serrate Cornetfish), 188
    tabacaria (Bluespotted Cornetfish), 183
Fistulariidae, 68, 87, 395
Flagtails, 69, 123
    Hawaiian, photo, 189
Flamefish, 202, 203, 320
Flammeo, 370
    scythrops, 374
Flashlight fishes, 68, 83, 363-366
    Atlantic, **365-366**; photo, 366
    biology, 364
    captive care, 364
    Great, **365**
    Onefin, **366**; photos, 363, 366
    Red Sea, 364, **366**
    Small, **366**
    Twofin, **365**; photos, 365
Flatheads, 68, 96-97, 509-513
    biology, 509-510
    Broadhead, **512**; photo, 512
    captive care, 510
    Fringelip, **513**, 516
    Longsnout, **513**, 516; photo, 513
    Sand, **512**
    Spiny, **511**; photo, 511

    Sulawesi, **512-513**; photo, 512
    Tentacled, **511**; photos, 511
    Welander's, **512**; photos, 509, 512
Florida Reef Tract, 176
Flounders
    lefteye, 69, 146-147, 516, 517
    Peacock, 177; photo, 39
    samarid, 69, 148
    Threespot, 148
Flower Garden Reefs, 168
Flutemouths. See Cornetfishes
Foa brachygramma (Bay Cardinalfish), 179
Forcipiger
    flavissimus (Yellow Longnose Butterflyfish), 190, 222
    longirostris (Big Longnose Butterflyfish), photo, 221
Fore reef habitats. See Reef face habitat; Reef slope habitat
Fowleria
    aurita (Aurita Cardinalfish), 188
    variegata (Variegated Cardinalfish), 180
Franzia, 543, 544, 545
Fredricksted Pier, 201
Fringing reefs, 163-166; photos, 163, 187
    fishes in (chart), 167
Frogfishes, 68, 79-81, 329-357
    Bandtail, **354-355**; photo, 354
    biology, 329-335
    Bloody, 59, 331, 342, **343**; photos, 59, 343
    Brackishwater, **339-340**
    captive care, 335-339
    captive compatibility, 336-337
    captive diseases, 338-339
    captive feeding, 337-338
    Clown, **347-349**
    Coinbearing, 329-330, 331, 332, **342-343**; photos, 334, 342
    Commerson's, **345-347**
    Cryptic, 334
    Dwarfed, **345**
    egg rafts, 333
    eggs, photos, 334
    Flagellated, **354**
    Freckled, **341**
    Freckled, Hawaiian, **341**
    Giant, 167, 216, 330, 331, 332, 334, 335, 336, **345-347**, 352; photos, 328, 330, 336, 338, 346
    habitat, 334-335
    Hispid, 167, 330, 332, 338, **352-353**; photos, 352
    Indian, **344**; photo, 344
    Longlure, 201, 216, 330, 331, **349-350**; photos, 80, 215,, 336, 349, 350
    Marblemouthed, 334, **357**; photo, 357
    New Guinean, 179, **341-342**; photo, 341
    Ocellated, 335, **344-345**; photos, 344
    Painted, 167, 175, 202, 332, 334, 336, 349, **350-352**; photos, 329, 351
    Pygmy, **355**

Randall's, **345**; photo, 345
reproduction, 332-334
Rosey, **343**
Roughjaw, 347
Sanguine, **343**
Sargassum, 207, 335, 337, 353, **355-356**; photos, 240, 335, 356
Scarlet, 188, **341**, 343; photos, 340, 341
Shaggy, **352-353**
social behavior, 335
Striated, 57, 167, 183, 216, 329, 330, 331, 334, 337, **353-354**, 451, 465, 471; photos, 42, 331, 333, 336, 353
Striped, **353-354**
tankmates, suitable and unsuitable, 337
Threespot, 330, 333-334, **357**; photo, 357
Tuberculated, 334-335, 354, **355**; photo, 355
Twinspot, 334, **339-340**; photos, 334, 339
Wartskin, 167, 179, 202, 329, 332, 334, 336, **347-349**, 352; photos, 330, 332, 333, 347, 348
Warty, **347-349**
Whitefingered, **342-343**
Fusiliers, 185
Galeocerdo cuvier (Tiger Shark), 359
Garden eels, 68, 73-74, 287-294
Atlantic, 288, **293**
biology, 287-289
Black, **293-294**
captive care, 289-290
Cobra, **294**
Freckled, **293**
Hawaiian, 288, **292**
Leopard, **294**; photos, 210, 294
Manytoothed, **293-294**; photo, 294
Orangebarred, **292**
Red Sea, 288-289, **292**
Speckled, **292**; photo, 292
Splendid, **292**; photo, 292
Spotted, 289, **293**; photos, 290, 293
Striped, **294**; photos, 287, 294
suitable tankmates for, 290
Taylor's, **294**
Whitespotted, **291-292**, 294; photo, 292
Yellow, **293**
Gas bubble disease, 417-418
Gasterosteiformes, 68
GBR. See Great Barrier Reef
Genicanthus, 337
bellus (Ornate Angelfish), 194, 212
caudovittatus (Zebra Swallowtail Angelfish), 565
melanospilos (Blackspot Angelfish), 194, 212
watanabei (Watanabe's Angelfish), 212
Genus
definition, 66
name, 64-65
Gerreidae, 69, 112

Gerres, 180, 188, 517
Ghost pipefishes, 68, 88-89, 401-408
biology, 401-404
captive care, 404
Filamented, **407-408**; photos, 408
Hairy, **407**; Hairy, photo, 407
Longtailed, **404**; photos, 403, 404, 405
Ornate, 167, 403, **406**; photos, 41, 401, 402, 403, 406
Robust, 167, 403, **405**; photos, 88, 405
Velvety, **408**; photos, 408
Gills, 51-52
Glugea heraldi, 416-417
Gnathanodon speciosus (Golden Jack), 180
Gnatholepis thompsoni (Goldspot Goby), 209
Goatfishes, 69, 116-117, 247
Blackspot, 180
Blackstriped, 167, 177, 180, 233
Dash-and-Dot, 162, 183, 188, 232
Indian, 180, 516, 233
Manybar, 167, 175, 177, 183, 185, 209, 217, 232, 312
Red Sea, 217
Redspot, 233
Sidespot, 185, 516
Spotted, 177, 183, 206, 209, 517
Twobar, 190, 233
Whitelined, 167, 177, 209, 233
Whitesaddle, 183
Yellow, 394, 517
Yellowbanded, 180
Yellowlined, 232
Yellowsaddle, 233, 283, 312
Gobies, 69, 138-140
Banded, 180, 516
Black Coral, 214
Blue, 290, 517, 549
Bluespotted, 180, 183
Bridled, 290
Candycane, 196
Catalina, 222; photo, 222
Cave, Bluestriped, 196
Citron, 161, 188
clown, 214
"clown," 213
Crested, 180
Crosshatch, 216
Dash, 209
Decorated, 180
Fire, photo, 208
Flagfin Prawn, 180
Fuzzy, 214
"fuzzy nut," 213
Girdled, 196
Goldspot, 209
Hector's, 175
Highfin Banded, 583
hover, 180
Hovering, 290, 517
Link's, 180
Lycopod, **320**
Masked, 394

Neon Pygmy, 167
Nocturn, 180
Orangespotted, 290, 517
Orangespotted Sleeper, 516
Ornate, 180
Puntang, 180, 206
Purple Fire, 209
Rainford's, photo, 139
Redeye, 214
ribbon, Bluebarred, photo, 37
Rivulate, 188
Rusty, 196
sand, 290
Seminole, 290
Shadow, 56
Shortstripe, 215-216
shrimp, 209, 214
shrimp, Graceful, 43-44
shrimp, Ornate, 183
shrimp, Randall's, 196
shrimp, Steinitz's, 516
shrimp, Yellow, 516
Sphinx, 183
Spinecheek, 180
Sponge, 216
Teardrop Sleeper, 180, 230
Whip, 214
White, 180
Yellow Eel, **320**
Yellow Prow, 216
Yellowhead Sleeper, 161, 188; photo, 230
Zebra Dart, 551
Gobiesocidae, 69, 137
Gobiesocoidei, 69
Gobiesox punctulatus (Stippled Clingfish), photo, 45
Gobiidae, 69, 138-140
Gobiodon, 214
citrinus (Citron Goby), 161, 188
rivulatus (Rivulate Goby), 188
Gobioidei, 69
Gobionellus saepepallens (Dash Goby), 209
Gobiosoma, 525, 528
chancei (Shortstripe Goby), 215-216
xanthiprora (Yellow Prow Goby), 216
Gomphosus
caeruleus (Indian Ocean Bird Wrasse), 217
varius (Bird Wrasse), 175, 185, 188
Gonochorist, 248
Goosefishes, 79
Gorgasia, 291-292
hawaiiensis (Hawaiian Garden Eel), 288, **292**
maculatus (Whitespotted Garden Eel), **291-292**; photo, 292
preclara (Splendid Garden Eel), **292**; photo, 292
sillneri (Red Sea Garden Eel), 288-289, **292**
sp. (Speckled Garden Eel), **292**; photo, 292

Gorgonian zone, 203-204; photo, 204
Gorgonians, photo, 17
Gracila albomarginata (Whitemargined Grouper), 190
Gramma, 101
  linki (Dusky Gramma), 212
  loreto (Royal Gramma), 101; photo, 101
  melacara (Blackcap Basslet), 194, 212, 523, 556
Grammas, 68, 101
  Dusky, 212
  Royal, 101; photo, 101
Grammatidae, 68, 101
Grammistes sexlineatus (Sixline Soapfish), 175
Grammistini, 98
Graysbys, 397, 530
Great Barrier Reef, 169-170, 222; photo, 160
Gregory, Bluntsnout, 190
Grinners
  Blotched, **313-314**
  Slender, **313-314**
Groupers, 68, 98-100, 247, 337
  Giant, 30
  Highfin, 179
  Honeycomb, 188
  Lyretail, 190, 251-252, 283; photo, 238
  Nassau, 183, 251; photo, 62
  Panther, 43
  Red, 183, 251
  Roving Coral, photo, 227
  Saddleback Coral, 185
  Speckled, 179
  Tiger, 397, 537; photo, 393
  Warsaw, 201
  Whitemargin Lyretail, 251
  Whitemargined, 190
Grunters, 69, 123
Grunts, 69, 112-113, 337
  Bluelined, 180, 183
  French, 180
Gunnelichthys pleurotaenia (Blacklined Wormfish), 183
Gurnards
  Flying, 290, **517**; photos, 514, 517
  helmut, 68, 97, **515-517**
  helmut, Atlantic, **517**
  helmut, biology, 515
  helmut, captive care, 515-516
  helmut, Oriental, 290, 476, **516**; photos, 516, 517
  helmut, Tilton's, 515
Gymnomuraena, 246
  zebra (Zebra Moray Eel), 232, 249, 252, 254, **259-260**, 284; photos, 72, 259
Gymnothorax, 200, **260-277**
  albimarginatus (Whitemargin Moray Eel), 249; photo, 249
  breedeni (Tinsnip Moray Eel), 190, 249, **260**; photo, 260
  brunneus (Brown Moray Eel), **260-261**, 277; photo, 260

buroensis (Latticetail Moray Eel), 190, **261**, 277; photo, 261
castaneus (Panamic Green Moray Eel), 247, **267**
chilospilus (Whitelip Moray Eel), **261-262**; photos, 261, 262
cribroris (Australian Moray Eel), **262**; photo, 262
dovii (Finespotted Moray Eel), 267
enigmaticus (Tiger Moray Eel), 188, 255, **262-263**; photos, 263
eurostus (Stout Moray Eel), **263-264**; photos, 263, 264
favagineus (Honeycomb Moray Eel), 248, 250, 262, **264-265**; photos, 264
fimbriatus (Fimbriated Moray Eel), 167, 175, **265-266**, 284; photos, 246, 251, 265
flavimarginatus (Yellowmargin Moray Eel), **266**, 486; photos, 266
flavopicta, 272
funebris (Green Moray Eel), **267**, 273; photos, 267
gracilicaudus (Slendertail Moray Eel), **267-268**; photo, 267
herrei (Herre's Moray Eel), 248-249, **268**; photo, 268
insigteena (Blackspotted Moray Eel), **265**; photo, 244
javanicus (Giant Moray Eel), 196, 245, 247-248, 264-265, **268-269**; photos, 248, 268
kidako (Kidako Moray Eel), **269**; photo, 269
kolpos (Blacktail Moray Eel), **275**
margaritophorous, 188
melanospilos, 265
melatremus (Golden Moray Eel), **270**; photos, 269
meleagris (Whitemouth Moray Eel), 175, **270-271**, 272; photos, 36, 270
miliaris (Goldentail Moray Eel), 270, **271-272**; photos, 271, 272
monochrous (Monochrome Moray Eel), 175
mordax (California Moray Eel), 245
moringa (Spotted Moray Eel), 201, 245, 246, 247, 251, 252, 267, **272-273**, 276-277; photos, 251, 272
nigromarginatus (Blackmargin Moray Eel), **275**
nudivomer (Yellowmouth Moray Eel), 56, 252, **273**; photo, 273
obesus (Speckled Moray Eel), 248
permistus (Blackblotched Moray Eel), 265
polyuranodon, 245
prasinus (Yellow Moray Eel), 248
richardsonii (Richardson's Moray Eel), 248, 251, **273-274**; photo, 274
rueppelliae (Yellowhead Moray Eel), 175, 249, 255, 263, **274-275**; photos, 250, 274

saxicola (Ocellated Moray Eel), **275**; photo, 275
steindachneri (Steindachner's Moray Eel), **275-276**; photo, 275
undulatus (Undulated Moray Eel), 179, 188, 249, **276**; photos, 276
vicinus (Purplemouth Moray Eel), 188, 246, 247, 272, **276-277**; photo, 277
zonipectus (Barredfin Moray Eel), 167, 196, 261, **277**; photos, 277
Habitats, 159-233
  artifical, 198-202
  back-reef slope, 184-185
  black coral zone, 204-205
  cave, overhang, and archway, 195-196
  channels, 184
  coralline algae / sponge zone, 203
  definition, 171
  distribution of fishes in, 216-220
  gorgonian zone, 203-204
  macroalgae / sponge beds, 202-203
  mangrove, 178-181; photo, 178
  marine lakes, 205-206
  oceanic desert, 210-211
  oil platforms, 201-202
  pier pilings, 200-201
  reef face, 191-193
  reef flat, 186-189
  reef slope, 193-195
  rocky reef, 196-198
  rubble zone, 207-209
  sand bottom, 210-211
  Sargassum rafts, 206-207
  seagrass, 181-183; photo, 181
  shipwrecks, 199-200
  sponge gardens, 205
  sponges, 214-216
  suitability for different fishes, 161-162
  variability of, 160-161
Haeckel, Ernst, 233
Haemulidae, 69, 112-113, 337
Haemulinae, 112
Haemulon
  flavolineatum (French Grunt), 180
  sciurus (Bluelined Grunt), 180, 183
Halfbeaks, 68, 82
Halicampus, **435-436**; photo, 427
  brocki (Brock's Pipefish), **435-436**; photo, 435
  macrorhynchus (Ornate Pipefish), **436**; photo, 436
Halichoeres
  argus (Peacock Wrasse), 188
  binotopsis (Saowisata Wrasse), 180
  biocellatus (Twospot Wrasse), 180
  bivittatus (Slippery Dick), 177, 180, 272, 276, 517
  centriquadrus (Checkered Wrasse), 185, 188
  leucurus (Purplestriped Wrasse), 167
  maculipinna (Clown Wrasse), 290
  melanurus (Tailspot Wrasse), 312

pictus (Rainbow Wrasse), 290
prosopeion (Twotone Wrasse), 167
radiatus (Pudding Wife), 517
richmondi (Chainlink Wrasse), 167
scapularis (Zigzag Wrasse), 167, 188
schwartzi (Schwartz's Wrasse), 183
trimaculatus (Threespot Wrasse), 162, 177, 180, 183
Halieutichthys aculeatus (Pancake Batfish), **360**; photo, 360
Hamlets, 528-541
    Barred, 532, 534, **538-541**; photos, 518, 529, 531, 539
    biology, 528-532
    Black, 525, 532, 534, **538**; photo, 538
    Blacktail, **538**
    Blue, 532, **534-535**, 539; photos, 534, 535
    Butter, 179, 535, 539, **541**; photos, 540, 541
    captive care, 532
    courtship calls, 531
    feeding behavior, 528-530
    Golden, 528, **535-536**; photo, 534
    Indigo, **536-537**, 539; photo, 536
    Masked, **538**; photo, 538
    mimetic relationships, 537
    Mutton, 251
    reproduction, 531-532
    Shy, 528, 532, **536**, 537; photos, 536, 537
    Tan, **541**; photo, 541
    Yellowbelly, 528, **532**, 535, 539; photos, 530, 533
    Yellowtail, **534**; photos, 533
Handfishes, 79
Hawk Channel, 176
Hawkfishes, 69, 104-106, 337
    Arc-eye, 185
    Coral, photo, 105
    Flame, 190, 213, 214
    Freckled, 16; photos, 16, 48
    Longnose, 194, 212, 213, 214, 575
    Lyretail, 570
    Spotted, 216, 522
    Twospotted, 190
    Whitespot, 185, 190
Hearing and swim bladder, 48
Heemstra, Dr. P., 582
Helcogramma striata (Striped Triplefin), photo, 132
Helmet gurnards. See Gurnards, helmet
Hemanthias, 549
    leptus (Longtail Bass), **549**
    vivanus (Red Barbier), 198, **549**; photo, 549
Hemigymnus melapterus (Blackedge Thicklip Wrasse), 180
Hemipteronotus niger (Green Razorfish), 290
Hemiramphidae, 68, 82

Hemitaurichthys, 337
    polylepis (Pyramid Butterflyfish), photo, 192
Heniochus
    diphreutes (Schooling Bannerfish), 185; photo, 119
    monoceros (Masked Bannerfish), 185, 190
    varius (Humphead Bannerfish), 176
Hermaphrodites
    sequential, 248
    simultaneous, 248, 519
Heron Island, 222
    reef flat, 189
Heteractis magnifica (Magnificent Sea Anemone), photos, 125, 213
Heteroconger, 293-294
    cobra (Cobra Garden Eel), **294**
    hassi (Spotted Garden Eel), 289, **293**; photos, 290, 293
    lentiginosus (Freckled Garden Eel), **293**
    longissimus (Atlantic Garden Eel), 288, **293**; photo, 293
    luteolus (Yellow Garden Eel), **293**; photo, 293
    maculatus (Whitespotted Garden Eel), 294
    perissodon (Manytoothed Garden Eel), **293-294**; photo, 294
    polyzona (Striped Garden Eel), **294**; photos, 287, 294
    taylori (Leopard Garden Eel), **294**; photos, 210, 294
Heterocongridae, 68, 73-74, 287-294
Heterocongrinae, 73
Heterodontus quoyi (Galapagos Hornshark), 359
Hinds
    Blueline, 167
    Bluespotted, 167
    Coral, 16, 190, 579; photo, 99
    Freckled, 167
    Harlequin, 196
    Peacock, 188, 217, 251, 269
    Rock, 297, 394
    Sixspot, photo, 194
    V-tailed, 16, 190
Hippocampinae, 89, 409, 410-426
Hippocampus, 200, 409, 420-426
    bargabanti (Pygmy Seahorse), **420**; photos, 412, 420
    erectus (Lined Seahorse), 179, 183, 206, 418, **421**, 422, 424, 438; photos, 411, 414, 419, 421
    histrix (Thorny Seahorse), 167, 179, **421-422**; photos, 418, 421, 422
    hudsonius, 421
    ingens (Pacific Seahorse), **422-423**; photos, 409, 423
    jayakarai, **422**, photo, 422
    kuda (Common Seahorse), 422, **423-424**; photos, 415, 423, 424
    punctulatus, 421

    reidi (Longsnout Seahorse), 183, 201, 421, **424**; photos, 90, 413, 417, 424, 425
    trimaculatus (Longnose Seahorse), **424**; photo, 424
    zosterae (Dwarf Seahorse), 183, 412, 413, 414, 418, **425-426**, 438; photo, 426
Histiophryne cryptacanthus (Cryptic Frogfish), 334
Histrio histrio (Sargassum Frogfish), 207, 335, 337, 353, **355-356**; photos, 240, 335, 356
Hogfishes, 180
    Spanish, 297, 394, 395, 397
    Spotfin, 203, 205, 212, 523
    Twinspot, photo, 211
Hogsty Atoll, 170
Holacanthus
    bermudensis (Blue Angelfish), 201, 203
    ciliaris (Queen Angelfish), 202, 203; photo, 239
    clarionensis (Clarion Angelfish), photo, 197
    passer (Passer Angelfish), 496
    tricolor (Rock Beauty Angelfish), 203, 532, 536, 537; photo, 537
Holanthias, 543, 549-550
    borbonius (Blotchy Deep Anthias), **588**; photo, 588
    fuscipinnis (Hawaiian Deep-water Anthias), 212, 550
    martinicensis (Roughtongue Bass), 203, 204, 212, 548-549, **550**; photo, 550
Holocentridae, 68, 84-85, 196
Holocentrinae, 84, 337, 370-383
Holocentroidei, 68
Holocentrus, 370, 372-373
    ascensionis (Squirrelfish), 198, **372-373**; photo, 372
    rufus (Longspine Squirrelfish), 175, **373**; photos, 370, 371, 373
Hologymnosus annulatus (Ring Wrasse), 190
Hoplolatilus, 209
    chlupatyi (Flashing Tilefish), 194, 212; photo, 109
    cuniculus (Green Tilefish), 212, 587
    marcosi (Skunk Tilefish), 194, 212
    starcki (Bluehead Tilefish), 212, 546, 572, 585, 587
Hornshark, Galapagos, 359
Hybrids, 65
Hypodytes rubripinnis, 447
Hypoplectrus, 519, 528-541
    aberrans (Yellowbelly Hamlet), 528, **532**, 535, 539; photos, 530, 533
    chlorurus (Yellowtail Hamlet), **534**; photos, 533
    gemma (Blue Hamlet), 532, **534-535**, 539; photos, 534, 535
    gummigutta (Golden Hamlet), 528, **535-536**; photo, 534

guttavarius (Shy Hamlet), 528, 532, **536**, 537; photos, 536, 537
indigo (Indigo Hamlet), **536-537**, 539; photo, 536
maculiferus, 532
nigricans (Black Hamlet), 525, 532, 534, **538**; photo, 538
providencianus (Masked Hamlet), **538**; photo, 538
puella (Barred Hamlet), 532, 534, **538-541**; photos, 518, 529, 531, 539
sp. 1 (Tan Hamlet), **541**; photo, 541
unicolor (Butter Hamlet), 179, 535, 539, **541**; photos, 540, 541
Ichthyapus vulturis (Vulture Eel), photo, 296
Illicium, 43, 329
Inimicus, 209, 454, 455, 458, 459-462, 516
caledonicus (Caledonian Devilfish), **460**; photo, 460
didactylus (Spiny Devilfish), 167, 179, 202, **460-461**, 476; photos, 460, 461, 462
filamentosus (Filamented Devilfish), **462**; photo, 462
Iracundus signifier (Decoy Scorpionfish), 43, 454, **463**, 467, 494; photos, 463
Istiblennius
chrysospilos (Redspotted Blenny), photo, 35
edentulus (Rippled Rockskipper), 180
Istigobius, 290
decoratus (Decorated Goby), 180
ornatus (Ornate Goby), 180
Jacks, 69, 110-111
Bar, 297; photo, 110
Bluefin, 584
Golden, 180
Yellowtail, 51-52
Jawfishes, 68, 103
Ringeye, 167
Spotfin, 517
Yellowhead, 517
Jobfish, Green, 562
Kaukura Atoll, 170
Keys to species accounts, 237-243
Knolls, 176
Knotting behavior in moray eels, 246-247; illustration, 247
Kryptophanaron alfredi (Atlantic Flashlight Fish), 365-366; photo, 366
Kuhlia sandvicensis (Hawaiian Flagtail), photo, 189
Kuhliidae, 69, 123
Kühlmann, Dietrich, 160-161
Kuiter, Rudie, 466, 508
Kwajelin Atoll, 170
Kyphosidae, 69, 122-123
Labracinus, 532
cyclophthalmus (Red Dottyback), 385
lineatus (Lined Dottyback), 385
Labridae, 69, 126-128
Labriform locomotion, 39

Labrisomidae, 69, 133-134
Labroidei, 69
Labroides, 247, 416
dimidiatus (Bluestreak Cleaner Wrasse), 219; photo, 25
unilineatus (Oneline Tubelip Wrasse), 167
Lachnolaimus maximus (Hogfish), 180
Lactophrys trigonus (Buffalo Trunkfish), 183
Lactoria cornuta (Longhorn Cowfish), 183
Lagoons, 174-175
bottoms, 176-178
Chuk (Truk), 200
inner, 174-175
Lakes, marine, as habitats, 205-206
Lanternfishes, 75. See also Flashlight fishes
Lateral line organ and detection of water movement, 49
Laticauda colubrina (Banded Sea Snake), 301-302, 302-303
Leaf Fish, 487-488
Leiuranus semicinctus (Saddled Snake Eel), 179, 288, 297, **301-302**; photo, 301
Leks, 312
Length, description of, in species accounts, 239
Lepidozyginae, 126
Lepidozygus tapeinosoma (Fusilier Damselfish), 126, 546, 551, 555, 570
Lethrinidae, 69, 113-114
Lethrininae, 114
Liberty shipwreck, 199-200
Light levels, 225-227
Linnaeus, Carolus, 64
Linnean system of nomenclature, 64-65
Lionfishes, 247, 491-508
African, **502**
and octopus mimics, 492
Antennata, **501-502**
Bellus, **508**; photo, 508
biology, 491-494
Blackfin, **508**; photo, 508
Bleeker's, **508**; photo, 508
captive care, 494-496
captive feeding, 495-496
Clearfin, 54, 493, 495, 501, **502-503**, 505, 508; photos, 503
Common, **505-508**
Deep-water, **502**; photos, 502
disorders, 496
Dwarf (*Dendrochirus brachypterus*), **498-500**
Dwarf (*Dendrochirus zebra*), **500-501**
Dwarf, Fuzzy, **498-500**
Fu Manchu, **497-498**
Green, 491, **497**; photos, 497
Hawaiian (*Dendrochirus*), **497**
Hawaiian (*Pterois*), 491, **503**; photos, 495, 503
Japanese, 491, 503, **505**, 508; photos, 505
Miles's, 503, **506-507**
Mombasa, 54

Ocellated, 494, **497-498**, 508; photos, 498
of Japan, 508
Radiata, **502**
reproduction, 494
Russell's, 491, 493, 495, 503, **504-505**; photos, 492, 504
Shortfin, 167, 200, 451, 494, 496, **498-500**, 508; photos, 499
Soldier, **504-505**
Spotfin, 167, 331, 343, 495, 496, **501-502**, 502-503, 508; photos, 43, 490, 501
Spotless, **504-505**
stings, 491-492
tankmates, 496
Twinspot, **497-498**
Volitans, 199, 492, 493, 495, 496, 501, 503, **505-508**; photos, 25, 493, 506, 507, 508
Volitans Group, 503-508
Volitans, Red, **504-505**
Zebra, 167, 216, 357, 494, 496, 499, **500-501**, 505, 508; photos, 494, 500
Liopropoma, 196
carmabi (Candy Bass), 212, 232
eukrines (Wrasse Bass), 198, 203, 212, 523, 549
mowbrayi (Ridgeback Bass), 194, 232
Liopropomini, 98
Lipogramma, 101
klayi (Heliotrope Basslet), 212
Live sand, 230-231
Lizardfishes, 68, 75-76, 311-317
biology, 311-312
Blackblotch, 177, **315**, 476, 516; photos, 315
captive care, 312-313
Clearfin, **314**
Graceful, 177, 188, 311, **313-314**; photo, 313
Inshore, 183, 517
leks, 312
Nebulous, **313-314**
Painted, **317**
Red, **316**; photos, 316, 457
Redmarbled (*Synodus rubromaculatus*), **315-316**, 516; photo, 316
Reef, **317**
Rockspear, **316**
Sand, 312, **314**, 516; photo, 314
Snakefish, **317**; photos, 313, 317
Tailblotch, **315**
Twospot, **314**; photo, 314
Variegated, 185, 188, 311, 314, **317**; photos, 310, 311, 312, 316
Lobet, Dr. Phillip, 531
Longfins, 68, 102-103
Bluegill, 188
Redfinned, 188
Lophiidae, 79
Lophiiformes, 68

Lophiocharon, 356-357
    lithinostomus (Marblemouthed Frogfish), 334, **357**; photo, 357
    trisignatus (Threespot Frogfish), 330, 333-334, **357**; photo, 357
Lophogobius cyprinoides (Crested Goby), 180
Lorenz, Konrad, 24-25, 58
Lotilia graciliosa (Graceful Shrimp Goby), 43-44
Lutjanidae, 69, 111, 337
Lutjanus, 297
    apodus (Schoolmaster), 252, 395; photo, 111
    biguttatus (Twospotted Snapper), photo, 17
    jocu (Dog Snapper), 251, 298
    kasmira (Bluestriped Snapper), 185
    monostigma (Onespot Snapper), photo, 198
    viridis (Blue and Gold Snapper), 247
Luzonichthys, 543, 550-552
    earlei (Earle's Slender Anthias), 550, **551**; photo, 550
    waitei (Magenta Slender Anthias), 550, **551**, 552, 585; photos, 551
    whitleyi (Whitley's Slender Anthias), 550, **551**-552, 555; photo, 551
Lysmata amboinensis (Common Cleaner Shrimp), photos, 247, 547
Lythrypnus dalli (Catalina Goby), 222; photo, 223
Macroalgae / sponge beds, 202-203; photo, 202
Macropharyngodon bipartitus (Vermiculate Leopard Wrasse), photo, 241
Mahidolia mystacina (Flagfin Prawn Goby), 180
Malacanthidae, 69, 108
Malacanthinae, 108
Malacanthus, 209
    plumieri (Sand Tilefish), 474, 517, 521, 526
Malacoctenus, 209
    boehlkei (Diamond Blenny), 214
Mandarinfishes, 138
    Green, 56, 167
Mangrove habitats, 178-181; photo, 178
    fishes in (chart), 179-180
    in aquariums, 179
Mangrove, Red, cultivation in aquariums, 179
Map of coral reefs of the world, 172-173
McCosker, John E., 65
Megalopidae, 68, 70
Megalops atlanticus, photo, 71
Meiacanthus
    anema, 135
    grammistes (Striped Fang Blenny), 180
Melanism, 61
Melichthys
    niger (Black Durgon), 190
    vidua (Pinktail Triggerfish), 16, 185

Melithaea, photo, 21
Mene rhombeus, photo, 32
Microcanthidae, 69, 124
Microcanthus strigatus (Stripey), 124
Microdesmidae, 69, 140-141
Microdesminae, 140
Micrognathus andersonii (Anderson's Shortnose Pipefish), 183
Microgobius carri (Seminole Goby), 290
Microhabitats, 211-213
Microspathodon chrysurus (Yellowtail Damselfish), 534
Middleton Reef, 166
Mimicry, 492, 546
Minoinae, 462-463
Minous trachycephalus (Blue-eyed Stingfish), **463**; photo, 462
Mirolabrichthys, 543, 544, 545
Mojarras, 69, 112, 180, 188, 517
Molas, 150-151
Molidae, 150-151
Monacanthidae, 69, 152-153
Monacanthus
    ciliatus (Fringed Filefish), 177, 180, 183
    hispidus (Planehead Filefish), 202, 206
    setifer (Pygmy Filefish), 183
    tuckeri (Slender Filefish), 180, 183
Monocanthidae, 68, 83-84, 337, 367-369
Monocentris japonicus (Pinecone Fish), **369**; photo, 369
Monodactylidae, 69, 118
Monodactylus, 337
    argenteus (Mono), 180
    sebae, 118
Monogamy, 520
Monos, 69, 118, 179, 180, 337
Monotaxinae, 114
Monte Bolca, 33
Moorea Island, French Polynesia, photo, 170
Moorish Idol, 54, 69, 143-144, 185; photo, 42
Moray eels, 68, 72-73 245-286
    Argus, **278-279**
    Australian, **262**; photo, 262
    Banded, 188, 254, **255**, 259, 263; photos, 246, 255
    Barred, **255**
    Barredfin, 167, 196, **261**, 277; photos, 277
    Bayer's, **256**; photo, 256
    Bikini Atoll, **256**
    biology, 245-249
    Blackblotched, 265
    Blackear, **279-280**; photo, 279
    Blackmargin, **275**
    Blackspotted, **265**; photo, 244
    Blacktail, **275**
    Blotchnecked, 188
    bluntnosed, **283-284**
    Broadbanded, **252-253**
    Brown, **260-261**, 277; photo, 260
    Brown, Little, **278**; photo, 278

    California, 245
    captive care, 249-252
    captive feeding, 250
    captive troubleshooting, 252
    Chain, **253**
    Chainlink, **253**; photo, 253
    Chestnut, **256-257**; photo, 256
    Clouded, **254**
    Comet, **270-271**
    compatibility with other captive species, 250-252
    dangerous, 249
    Dinosaur, **273**
    Dirty Yellow, **270**
    Dragon, 256, **257-258**; photos, 52, 257, 258
    Dragon, Hawaiian, **257-258**
    Dragon, West African, **279**
    Enigmatic, **262-263**
    Estuarine, **285**
    feeding habits and behavior, 245-247
    Fimbriated, 167, 175, **265-266**, 284; photos, 246, 251, 265
    Finespeckled, **253-254**; photos, 253
    Finespotted, 267
    Geometric, **283**
    Giant, 196, 245, 247-248, 264-265, **268-269**; photos, 248, 268
    Golden (*Gymnothorax melatremus*), **270**; photo, 269
    Golden (*Gymnothorax miliaris*), 270, **271-272**
    Golden Brazilian, 272
    Goldentail, **271-272**; photos, 271, 272
    Gray, 247, 248, **283**; photo, 283, 505
    Grayface, **284**
    Green, **267**, 273; photos, 267
    Guineafowl, **270-271**
    Hertre's, **268**; photo, 268
    Honeycomb, 248, 250, **264-265**; photos, 264
    Hourglass, **278-279**; photo, 278
    interspecies associations, 247
    Javanese, **268-269**
    Jewel, 278, **279**; photos, 279
    Kidako, **269**; photo, 269
    knotting behavior, 246-247; illustration, 247
    Latticetail, 190, **261**, 277; photo, 261
    Leopard, **283-284**
    Lipspot, **261-262**
    Longfang, 188, **258-259**; photo, 259
    Longjaw, 232, **252-253**; photo, 252
    Longtail, 179, **285**; photo, 285
    Masked, **260**
    Mexican, 279
    Monochrome, 175
    Ocellated, **275**; photo, 275
    Painted, **283-284**
    Panamic Green, 247, **267**
    pebbletooth, 253-255
    Pencil, **270**

Peppered, 188, **283-284**; photo, 283
Purplemouth, 183, 246, 247, 272, **276-277**; photo, 277
reproduction, 248-249
Reticulate, **280**
Reverse Comet, 271
Richardson's, 248, 251, **273-274**; photo, 274
Ringed, **255**
Salt and Pepper, **263-264**
sexuality and sexual dimorphism, 248
sharp-toothed, 260-277
shortfinned, 282-283
Sievepatterned, **262**
Slendertail, **267-268**; photo, 267
snake, 285-286
snake, Barred, **285-286**; photo, 285
snake, Horned, **285**-286
snake, Largehead, 269, **286**; photo, 286
snake, Manyspotted, **282-283**
snake, Okinawan, **282**; photo, 282
snake, Tiger, **282-283**; photo, 282
snake, Unicolor, 285
Snowflake, 185, 188, 248, 250, 251, **254**, 583; photos, 254
social organization, 247-248
Speckled, 248
Spotted, 201, 245, 246, 247, 251, 252, 267, **272-273**, 276-277; photos, 251, 272
Starry, **254**
Steindachner's, **275-276**; photo, 275
Stout, **263-264**; photos, 263, 264
Tessellated, **264-265**
Tiger, 188, 255, **262-263**; photos, 263
Tinsnip, 190, 249, **260**; photo, 260
undescribed, 278; photos, 278
Undulated, 179, 188, 249, **276**; photos, 276
Viper, **257**; photos, 257
White-eye, 167, 188, 261, 265, 277, **284**; photos, 247, 284
Whitelip, **261-262**; photos, 261, 262
Whitemargin, 249; photo, 249
Whitemouth, 175, **270-271**; photos, 36, 270
Wrinkled, 278; photo, 278
Yellow, 248
Yellowhead, 175, 249, 255, 263, **274-275**; photos, 250, 274
"Yellowhead" (misapplied name), 266, 276
Yellowmargin, 266, 486; photos, 266
Yellowmouth, 56, 252, **273**; photo, 273
Zebra, 232, 249, 252, 254, **259-260**, 284; photos, 72, 259
Morphs, color, 60
Morwongs, 69, 106
Mouths of reef fishes, 52-54
Mugilidae, 69, 116
Mullets, 69, 116
Mullidae, 69, 116-117

Mulloides flavolineatus (Yellowlined Goatfish), 232
Mulloidichthys martinicus (Yellow Goatfish), 394, 517
Muraena, 278-280
 argus (Argus Moray Eel), **278-279**
 clepsydra (Hourglass Moray Eel), **278-279**; photo, 278
 lentiginosa (Jewel Moray Eel), 278, **279**; photos, 279
 melanotis (Blackear Moray Eel), **279-280**; photo, 279
 retifera (Reticulate Moray Eel), **280**
Muraenidae, 68, 72-73
Muraenoidei, 68
Mustelus californica (Smoothhound Shark), 275
Mycteroperca tigris (Tiger Grouper), 397, 537; photo, 393
Myctophidae, 75
Myrichthys, 302-304
 acuminatus, 302
 bleekeri, 303
 breviceps (Sharptail Snake Eel), 209, 272, 276, 297, **302**, 394; photos, 297, 302
 colubrinus (Banded Snake Eel), **302-303**; photos, 302, 303
 elaps, 303
 maculosus (Pacific Spotted Snake Eel), 177, 188, 296, **303-304**; photos, 296, 303
 magnificus (Magnificent Snake Eel), **304**
 ocellatus (Goldspotted Snake Eel), 302, **304**; photo, 304
 pantostigmius (Clipperton Snake Eel), **304**
 tigrinus (Tiger Snake Eel), **304**
Myripristinae, 337, 384-391
Myripristis, 196, 200, 385, 386-391
 adusta (Bronze Soldierfish), **386**, 390; photo, 386
 amaena (Brick Soldierfish), 185, **386-387**; photo, 386
 berndti (Bigscale Soldierfish), 188, 386, **387**, 390; photo, 387
 botche (Finspot Soldierfish), 194, **387**; photo, 387
 chryseres (Yellowfin Soldierfish), **387-388**; photo, 388
 hexagona (Doubletooth Soldierfish), **388**; photo, 388
 jacobus (Blackbar Soldierfish), **388**; photos, 385, 389
 kuntee (Pearly Soldierfish), **388-389**; photo, 389
 melanosticta, 387
 murdjan (Red Soldierfish), 175, 185, 386, 387, **389-390**; photo, 389
 pralina (Scarlet Soldierfish), 175, **389**
 violacea (Violet Soldierfish), 175, **390**; photo, 390
 vittata (Whitetip Soldierfish), **390-391**; photos, 85, 194, 384, 390

 xanthacara (Yellowtip Soldierfish), **391**; photo, 391
Myrispristinae, 84
Myrophinae, 74
Nagreda, Bronson, 359
Nahacky, Tony, 582
Names
 common, in species accounts, 237-239
 scientific, 64-65, 237
Nasinae, 144
Naso
 hexacanthus (Sleek Unicornfish), 23
 lituratus (Orangespine Unicornfish), 23, 46, 190, 217-219
 vlamingii (Vlamingi's Unicornfish), 185
Needlefishes, 68, 82
Needling, 49
Negaprion brevirostris (Lemon Shark), 179
Nelson, Joseph S., 63-64, 66
 Fishes of the World, 64
Nemanthias, 543, 552-553
 carberryi (Threadfin Anthias), 546, **552-553**, 562, 563, 568; photos, 546, 552, 553
Nemateleotris decora (Purple Fire Goby), 209
 helfrichi (Helfrich's Firefish), 212, 587; photo, 140
 magnifica (Fire Goby), photo, 208
Nemipteridae, 69, 114
Neocirrhites armatus (Flame Hawkfish), 190, 213, 214
Neoniphon, 370, 373-375
 argenteus (Clearfin Squirrelfish), **373-374**; photo, 373
 aurolineatus (Goldlined Squirrelfish), 374, 378; photo, 374
 marianus (Longjaw Squirrelfish), **374-375**; photo, 374
 opercularis (Blackfin Squirrelfish), **375**; photo, 375
 sammara (Bloodspot Squirrelfish), 185, 188, **375**, 373; photo, 375
Neopomacentrus, 434
 azysron (Yellowtail Demoiselle), 190
Nes longus (Orangespotted Goby), 290, 517
Niphonini, 98
Novaculichthys
 macrolepidotus (Seagrass Wrasse), 183
 taeniourus (Rockmover Wrasse), 357
Nystactes hallis, 293
Oceanic desert habitat, 210-211
Octopuses, Mimic, 492; photo, 492
Ocyurus chrysurus (Yellowtail Snapper), 183, 201
Ogcocephalidae 68, 81, 358-362
Ogcocephalioidei, 68
Ogcocephalus, 209, 361-362
 cubifrons (Polkadot Batfish), 183, **361**, 362, 517; photos, 361
 darwini (Redlip Batfish), 359; photo, 358
 declivirostris (Gulf Batfish), **362**

nasutus (Shortnose Batfish), **361-362**, 517; photos, 361
notatus (Oval Batfish), 359, **362**
pantostictus (Spotted Batfish), **361**
parvus (Roughneck Batfish), **362**; photo, 362
vespertilio (South American Batfish), 359, **362**
Ogilbyina, 532
   novaehollandiae (Australian Dottyback), 385
Oil platforms as fish habitats, 201-202
Onigocea spinosa (Spiny Flathead), **511**; photo, 511
Ophichthidae 68, 74, 295-307
Ophichthinae, 74
Ophichthus, 296, 298, 304-307
   bonaparti (Bonapart's Snake Eel), 300, **304**; photos, 304, 305
   cephalozona (Blacksaddle Snake Eel), 179, **305**; photo, 305
   melanochir (Blackfinned Snake Eel), **305-306**, 451; photos, 306
   ophis (Spotted Snake Eel), 209, **306-307**; photos, 306
   polyophthalmus (Manyeyed Snake Eel), **307**; photo, 307
   rufus, 296
Ophidiidae, 68, 78
Ophidiiformes, 68
Ophoidioidei, 68
Opistognathidae, 68, 103
Opistognathus, 167, 517
   aurifrons (Yellowhead Jawfish), 517
Oplopomus oplopomus (Spinecheek Goby), 180
Opportunistic feeders and snake eels, 297
Opsanus, 325-326
   beta (Gulf Toadfish), 183, 324, **325-326**; photos, 325
   pardus (Leopard Toadfish), **326**; photo, 324
   tau (Oyster Toadfish), **326**; photo, 326
Order, definition, 66
Osprey Reef, 168
Osraciidae, 69
Ostraciform swimming, 40-41
Ostraciidae, 153-154, 337
Ostraciinae, 153
Ostracion
   cubicus (Yellow Boxfish), 185, 216
   meleagris (Blue Boxfish), 190
   solorensis (Reticulate Boxfish), photo, 40
Outer slope habitat, 193-195
Overhang habitats, 195-196
   fishes in (chart), 196
Oxycirrhites typus (Longnose Hawkfish), 194, 212, 213, 214, 575
Oxycomanthus bennetti (Feather Star Crinoid), photo, 232
Oxymetopon cyanoctenosum (Bluebarred Ribbon Goby), photo, 37

Oxymonacanthus longirostris (Longnosed Filefish), 153; photo, 152
Paper Fish, **487-488**
Papilloculiceps longiceps (Tentacled Flathead), **511**; photos, 511
Parablennius marmoreus (Seaweed Blenny), photo, 136
Paracentropogon, 202, 449-450; photos, 450
   longispinus (Longspine Waspfish), 167, **449-450**; photos, 449, 450
   sp. (Sailfin Waspfish), **450**
Paracentropyge
   boylei (Boyle's Angelfish), 212
   venusta (Venustus Angelfish), 196; photo, 243
Paracheilinus (Pink Flasher Wrasse), 167
   angulatus (Lyretail Flasher Wrasse), photo, 127
   carpenteri (Carpenter's Flasher Wrasse), 194
   filamentosus (Filamented Flasher Wrasse), 167, 190, 203, 209
   lineopunctatus (Dot-and-Dash Flasher Wrasse), 209
   mccoskeri (McCosker's Flasher Wrasse), 209; photo, 45
Paracheirodon innesi (Neon Tetra), 543-544
Paracirrhites, 337, 532
   arcatus (Arc-eye Hawkfish), 185
   forsteri (Freckled Hawkfish), 16; photos, 16, 48
   hemistictus (Whitespot Hawkfish), 185, 190
Paragobiodon, 214
Paraluteres prionurus (Saddled Filefish), 185
Paranthias furcifer (Creolefish), 530, 532
Parapercis
   cylindrica (Cylindrical Sand Perch), 180, 188, 209, 312
   hexophthalma (Speckled Sand Perch), 209
   millepunctata (Blackdotted Sand Perch), 209
   nebulosus (Nebulosus Sand Perch), 209
   schauinslandi (Schauinsland's Sand Perch), 290
   signata (Blackflag Sand Perch), 209
   snyderi (U-marked Sand Perch), 290
Parapriacanthus, photo, 234
   ransonneti (Slender Sweeper), photos, 117, 166
Parapterois heterura (Blackfin Lionfish), **508**; photo, 508
Parascorpaena, 456, 467-468
   mcadamsi (Ocellated Scorpionfish), **467-468**; photo, 468
   mossambica (Mozambique Scorpionfish), **467-468**; photos, 467, 468
Pardachirus
   marmoratus (Moses Sole), 210
   pavoninus (Peacock Sole), 148; photo, 149
Pariah, 215

Parioglossus, 180
Parma polylepis (Banded Scaleyfin), 190
Parrotfishes, 69, 128-129
   Bucktooth, 183
   Bullethead, 183
   Queen, photo, 394
   Stoplight, photos, 46, 129
Parupeneus
   barberinus (Dash-and-Dot Goatfish), 162, 183, 188, 232
   bifasciatus (Twobar Goatfish), 190, 233
   ciliatus (Whitelined Goatfish), 167, 177, 209, 233
   clyclostomus (Yellowsaddle Goatfish), 233, 283, 312
   forsskali (Red Sea Goatfish), 217
   heptacanthus (Redspot Goatfish), 233
   indicus (Indian Goatfish), 180, 516, 233
   maculatus (Spotted Goatfish), 517
   multifasciatus (Manybar Goatfish), 167, 175, 177, 183, 185, 209, 217, 232, 312
   pleurostigma (Sidespot Goatfish), 185, 516
   porphyreus (Whitesaddle Goatfish), 183
   spilurus (Blackspot Goatfish), 180
Passes (channels) as habitats, 184
   fishes in (chart), 185
Patch reefs, 175-176
   fishes found in (chart), 175
Pearlfishes, 68, 77-78, 214
Pectoral fins, 43-44
Pegasidae, 68, 87-88, 398-400
Pegasus
   lancifer, 400
   volitans (Slender Sea Moth), **400**; photos, 400
Pelvic fins, 44-45
Pempheridae, 69, 117-118
Pempheris oualensis (Copper Sweepers), 188
Pentacerotidae, 69, 122
Pentapodus, 290
   emeryii (Double Whiptail), 205
Perches, sand, 69, 131, 198, 527, 549; photo, 527
   Blackdotted, 209
   Blackflag, 209
   Cylindrical, 180, 188, 209, 312
   Nebulosus, 209
   Schauinsland's, 290
   Speckled, 209
   U-marked, 290
Perchlets, 553-555
   Apricot, **553**
   highfin, 554
   Longfinned, **553-554**; photo, 554
   Midget, **554**
   Pelicier's, 553, **554-555**; photo, 554
   Unarmed, **554**
Perciformes, 68
Percoidei, 68

Pervagor melaocephalus (Orangehead Filefish), 496
Phaeoptyx
  conklini (Dusky Cardinalfish), 177
  xenus (Sponge Cardinalfish), 216
Pholidichthyidae, 69, 129-130
Pholidichthys leucotaenia (Convict Blenny), 129-130, 309
Photoblepharon, 364
  palperbratus (Onefin Flashlight Fish), **366**; photos, 363, 366
  steinitzi (Red Sea Flashlight Fish), 364, **366**
Phycodurus eques (Leafy Seadragon), 409
Phyllopteryx taeniolatus (Weedy Seadragon), 409
Physoclistous swim bladder, 47
Physostomous swim bladder, 47
Pier pilings as fish habitats, 200-201; photos, 200, 201
Pineapple fishes, 68, 83-84, 367-369
  biology, 367
  captive care, 368
  Japanese, **369**
  Pineapple Fish, **368**; photos, 367, 368
Pinecone Fish, **369**; photos, 369
Pinecone fishes, 68, 83-84
Pinguipedidae, 69, 131
Pipefishes, 68, 89-91, 403, 409, 427-439
    See also Ghost pipefishes
  Alligator, **437**; photos, 428, 437
  Anderson's Shortnose, 183
  Banded, **432**; photo, 432
  biology, 427-428
  Blackbreasted, **431**; photos, 431
  Bluestripe, 247, **433**; photos, 433
  Brock's, **435-436**; photo, 435
  Brownbanded, 179, **429-430**; photo, 429
  captive care, 428-429
  captive reproduction, 429
  commensal, 437
  coral, Soft, 214, 437
  Double-ended, **437**
  dragon, 429-432
  Dragon, **431**
  Florida, 183
  Guilded, **431-432**; photos, 432
  Gulf, 426, **438**; photo, 438
  hovering, 432-435
  Insular, **431**; photo, 431
  Janss's, **433-434**; photo, 434
  Longsnout, **439**; photo, 439
  Messmate, 175, 183, 428, **431**; photo, 430
  Multibar, **434**; photo, 434
  Negros, **433**
  Network, 175, 188, **430**; photo, 430
  Ornate, **436**; photo, 436
  Redstripe, **435**; photo, 435
  reproduction, 428
  Ringed, **432**
  Sargassum, 207; photo, 206
  seagrass, 438
  Short-tailed, **438-439**; photos, 438, 439
  Stick, **438-439**
  Tasseled, **435-436**
  White, 214, **437**; photo, 437
  Yellowbanded, **434-435**; photo, 435
  Yellowstreaked, **430**; photo, 430
Pipehorse, 89
Plagiotremus goslinei (Gosline's Scale Eating Blenny), 117
Platax
  orbicularis (Orbiculate Batfish), 180
  pinnatus (Pinnate Batfish), 30, 141, 206
Platycephalidae, 68, 96-97, 509-513
Platycephaloidei, 68
Plectorhinchus
  albovittatus (Twostriped Sweetlips), 180
  gibbosus (Brown Sweetlips), 180
  lineatus (Lined Sweetlips), 180
  polytaenia (Yellow-ribbon Sweetlips), photos, 113, 195
Plectorhynchinae, 112
Plectranthias, 543, 553-555; photo, 554
  altispinnatus, **554**
  garrupleus (Apricot Anthias), **553**
  inermis (Unarmed Perchlet), **554**
  longimanus (Longfinned Perchlet), **553-554**; photo, 554
  morgansi, **554**
  nanus (Midget Perchlet), **554**
  pelicieri (Pelicier's Perchlet), 553, **554-555**; photo, 554
Plectroglyphidodon
  imparipennis (Brighteye Damselfish), 188
  lacrymatus (Jewel Damselfish), 224
  leucozonus (Whiteband Damselfish), 188
  phoenixensis (Phoenix Damselfish), 188
Plectropomus, 396
  laevis (Coral Saddleback Grouper), 185
  pessuliferus (Roving Coral Grouper), photo, 227
Plectrypops, 385
  lima (Roughscale Soldierfish), 175, 196, **391**; photo, 391
  retrospinis (Cardinal Soldierfish), **391**
Plesiopidae, 68, 102-103
Plesiopinae, 102
Plesiops
  caeruleolineatus (Redfinned Longfin), 188
  corallicola (Bluegill Longfin), 188
Pleuronectiformes, 69
Pleuronectoidei, 69
Pleurosicya elongata (Sponge Goby), 216
Plotosidae, 68, 74-75, 308-309
Plotosus
  lineatus (Striped Eel Catfish), 130, 177, 179, 188, **308-309**; photos, 308, 309
Poeciloconger fasciatus (Barred Conger Eel), **291**; photo, 291
Pomacanthidae, 69, 120-122, 337
Pomacanthus
  arcuatus (Gray Angelfish), 180; photo, 204
  imperator (Emperor Angelfish), 185, 228; photos, 37, 121
  paru (French Angelfish), 201, 203
  semicirculatus (Koran Angelfish), photo, 51
  xanthometopon (Blueface Angelfish), 396
Pomacentridae, 69, 125-126
Pomacentrinae, 126
Pomacentrus
  bankanensis (Speckled Damselfish), 188
  coelestis (Neon Damselfish), 190
  philippinus (Philippine Damselfish), 190
  wardi (Ward's Damselfish), 190
Porcupinefishes, 69, 156-157, 185, 196, 207, 265, 337
Porichthyinae, 79
Porkfish, 180
Premnas biaculeatus (Maroon Anemonefish), 51, 167, 188, 211, 214, 219
Priacanthidae, 68, 104, 196
Priacanthus arenatus (Bigeye), 203, 205
Priolepis
  cincta (Girdled Goby), 196
  hipoliti (Rusty Goby), 196
Prionotus
  ophryas (Bandtail Sea Robin), 517
  scitulus (Leopard Sea Robin), 179
  tribulus (Bighead Sea Robin), 179
Prionurinae, 144
Pristigenys alta (Short Bigeye), 198, 549
Pristipomoides filamentosus, 551
Prognathodes
  aculeatus (Caribbean Longnose Butterflyfish), 194, 212
  aya (Bank Butterflyfish), 203, 205, 212, 549
  falcifer (Scythe Butterflyfish), 212
Pseudamia amblyuroptera (Crocodile Cardinalfish), 180
Pseudanthias, 199, 543, 544, 545, 555-587; photos, 219, 232, 234
  aurulentus (Golden Anthias), **577**, 545
  bartlettorum (Bartlett's Anthias), 551, 545, 545, **555-556**, 561, 562, 576; photos, 561, 556
  bicolor (Bicolor Anthias), 545, **556-557**, 585; photos, 544, 556
  bimaculatus (Twinspot Anthias), 194, 545, 555, **558-559**, 574; photos, 558, 559
  cooperi (Cooper's Anthias), 545, **560**, 574, 575, 577; photos, 555, 560
  dispar (Dispar Anthias), 190, 551, 545, 546, 555, 556, **561-562**, 568, 576, 579; photos, 561, 562
  elongatus (Elongate Anthias), **588**; photos, 589
  evansi (Evan's Anthias), 545, 546, 552, 553, **562-563**; photos, 543, 546, 562
  fasciatus (Redstripe Anthias), 545, **563**, 588; photos, 562, 563

flavoguttatus (Yellowspotted Anthias), **588**; photo, 589
fucinus, 555
hawaiiensis (Hawaiian Longfin Anthias), 212, 545, 546, **563-564**, 586; photos, 563, 564
heemstrai (Heemstra's Anthias), 545, **564-565**; photo, 565
huchtii (Redcheek Anthias), 167, 544-545, **565-566**, 579; photos, 565, 566
hutomoi (Hutomo's Anthias), **566**; photos, 567
hypselosoma (Stocky Anthias), 167, 202, 545, 559, **567-568**, 570, 577; photos, 547, 567
ignitus (Flame Anthias), 260, 545, 546, 552, 562, **568-569**; photos, 236, 568, 569
imeldae, 569
kashiwae, 560
lori (Lori's Anthias), 545, **569**, 577, 588; photos, 569
luzonensis (Luzon Anthias), 545, 559, 567-568, **569-570**; photo, 570
marcia (Marcia's Anthias), 545, 577, **578**; photo, 578
olivaceus (Olive Anthias), 545, 546, **570**; photos, 570
parvirostris (Diadem Anthias), 545, **571**, 575; photos, 571
pascalus (Purple Queen Anthias), 194, 226, 545, 546, 560, **571-572**, 585; photo, 572
pictilis (Painted Anthias), 545, **572-573**; photos, 572, 573
pleurotaenia (Squarespot Anthias), 212, 544-545, 547, 558, 559, 560, **573-574**; photos, 574
pulcherimmus (Resplendent Anthias), 545, 546, 560, 571, **574-575**, 576; photos, 575
randalli (Randall's Anthias), 212, 545, 546, 555, **575-576**, 587; photos, 575
rubrizonatus (Red-belted Anthias), 545, 567, 574, **576-577**; photos, 576
sheni (Shen's Anthias), 545, **574**; photo, 574
simthvanizi (Princess Anthias), 194, 545, 569, 571, 577; photos, 577
sp. 1 (Bloodspot Anthias), 545, **557**; photos, 557
sp. 2 (Harlequin Anthias), 545, **559**; photo, 558
sp. 3 (Cave Anthias), 545; photo, 576
sp. 4 (Reticulated Anthias), 545, **577-578**; photo, 578
squamipinnis (Lyretail Anthias), 16, 60, 161, 185, 190, 220, 260, 544-545, 546, 547, 552, 555, 560, 561, 565, 568, 575, **578-581**, 588; photos, 14, 220, 544, 568, 580, 581

subgenera, 543, 544, 545
taeniatus (Striped Anthias), 545, 557, 560, 564, **581-584**; photo, 581
thompsoni (Hawaiian Anthias), 545, 556-557, **584-585**; photo, 584
townsendi (Townsend's Anthias), 545, 578, **584**; photo, 581
tuka (Yellowstripe Anthias), 545, 546, 548, 572, 577, **585**; photos, 584
ventralis (Longfin Anthias), 161, 212, 223, 226-227 545, 546, 563, **585-587**; photos, 161, 585, 586
Pseudechidna brummeri (White Ribbon Eel), 188, 248, 273, **280**; photo, 280
Pseudobalistes fuscus (Blueline Triggerfish), photo, 150
Pseudocheilinops ataenia (Pink-streaked Wrasse), photo, 207
Pseudocheilinus
  evanidus (Secretive Wrasse), 209
  tetrataenia (Fourline Wrasse), 216
Pseudochromidae, 68, 100-101
Pseudochrominae, 100
Pseudochromis
  cyanotaenia (Bluelined Dottyback), 190, 444, 583
  flavivertex (Sunrise Dottyback), 355
  fridmani (Orchid Dottyback), photo, 18
  polynemus (Longfin Dottyback), 167, 216
  porphyreus (Magenta Dottyback), 212
  quinquedentatus (Spotted Dottyback), 205
  splendens (Splendid Dottyback), 167, 216; photo, 242
  steenei (Steene's Dottyback), 194
Pseudocoris yamashiro (Yamashiro's Wrasse), 209
Pseudogramma polyacantha (Secretive Soapfish), 188
Pseudoplesiopinae, 100
Pseudupeneus maculatus (Spotted Goatfish), 177, 183, 206, 209; photo, 55
Pterapogon kauderni (Bangaii Cardinalfish), 107, 183
Ptereleotrinae, 140
Ptereleotris
  calliurus (Blue Goby), 290, 517, 549
  hanae (Filament Dartfish), 516
  helenae (Hovering Goby), 290, 517
  heteroptera (Spottail Dartfish), 209, 516
  microlepis (Green Dartfish), 516
  monoptera, 140
  zebra (Zebra Dart Goby), 551
Pteroidichthys amboinensis (Ambon Scorpionfish), 211, 451, **466**; photos, 56, 466
Pteroinae, 93, 491-508
Pterois, 491, 501-508
  antennata (Spotfin Lionfish), 167, 331, 343, 495, **501-502**, 502-503, 508; photos, 43, 490, 501

  lunulata (Japanese Lionfish), 491, **505**, 508; photos, 505
  miles, **506-507**
  mombasae (Deep-water Lionfish), 54, **502**; photos, 502
  radiata (Clearfin Lionfish), 54, 493, 495, 501, **502-503**, 505, 508; photos, 503
  russelli (Russell's Lionfish), 491, 493, 495, **504-505**; photos, 492, 504
  sphex (Hawaiian Lionfish), 491, , 497, **503**; photos, 495, 503
  volitans (Volitans Lionfish), 199, 491, 492, 493, 495, 501, **505-508**; photos, 25, 493, 506, 507, 508
Pudding Wife, 517
Puffers, 69, 154-156, 337
  Bandtail, 177, 180, 183
  Blackspotted, 61, 190, 216; photo, 61
  Greeley's, 177
  Guinea Fowl, 61, 185, 190
  Immaculate, 180, 183, 188
  Laticeps, 180
  Manila, 180
  Map, 199, 396; photo, 40
  Reticulate, 180
  Sharpnose, 177, 180, 183, 202, 205, 549
  Southern, 177, 183
  Spiny, 177, 183, 207; photo, 157
  Whitespotted, 180, 183
Pygoplites diacanthus (Regal Angelfish), 176, 196; photo, 30
Pyle, Richard, 557
Rabaulichthys, 543, 587
  altipinnis (Sailfin Anthias), 587
  stigmaticus (Spotfin Anthias), 587; photo, 587
Rabbitfishes, 69, 142-143
  Forktail, 183
  Foxface, 190, 396
  Golden, 180
  Lined, 180
  Scribbled, 183
  Seagrass, 183
  Vermiculate, 180
Rafinesque, M., 409
Randall, Dr. John E., 65, 557, 582; photo, 67
Range description in species accounts, 239
Rangiroa Atoll, 170; photo, 170
Rays, 42
Razorfishes, 91, **441-442**
  Black, 210, 290
  Finescale, 516
  Fivefinger, 290
  Green (*Hemipteronotus niger*), 290
  Green (*Xyrichtys splendens*), 312, 517
  Knife, 516
  Melanopus, 290
  Pavo, 288, 516; photo, 289
  Pearly, 290, 517
  Rosy, 290, 517
  Yellowblotch, 516

INDEX 617

Reef crest habitat, 171, 189-191
   fishes in (chart), 190
Reef face habitat, 191-193
   fishes in (chart), 190
Reef fishes. See Fishes
Reef flat habitat, 171, 186-189; photo, 186
   fishes in (chart), 188
   outer, photo, 187
Reef front. See Reef face habitat
Reef habitats. See Habitats
Reef slope habitat, 193-195; photos, 193, 211
   fishes in (chart), 194
Reefs
   aerial view, illustration, 203
   Andros Barrier, 170
   atoll, 170
   bank, 168
   barrier, 168-170; photo, 168
   cross-section, illustration, 164-165
   ecosystems, 19
   Elizabeth, 166
   Florida Reef Tract, 176
   Flower Garden, 168
   fringing, 163-166, 167; photos, 163, 187
   Grand Bahama Bank, 168
   Great Barrier, 169-170, 222; photo, 160
   Middleton, 166
   Osprey, 168
   patch, 175-176
   platform, 166-168
   rocky, 196-198
   Swain, 169
   Ten Mile Banks, 168
   types, 162-170
Refugiums for feeding anthias, 548
Remarks section in species accounts, 243
Remoras, 69, 109-110
Reproduction in reef fishes, 27
Rhabdamia gracilis (Slender Cardinalfish), photos, 117, 166
Rhinecanthus aculeatus (Picasso Triggerfish), 175
Rhinecanthus verrucosa (Blackbelly Triggerfish), 183
Rhinomuraena
   amboinensis, 282
   quaesita (Ribbon Eel), 167, 248, 252, 273, **280-282**; photos, 281
Rhinopias, 455, 464-466
   aphanes (Lacey Scorpionfish), 455, **464**, 493; photos, 464, 465
   argoliba (Japanese Scorpionfish), 464, **465**
   cea (Easter Island Scorpionfish), 464, **465**
   eschmeyeri (Eschmeyer's Scorpionfish), 457, **464-465**; photo, 465
   frondosa (Weedy Scorpionfish), 454, **464**; photos, 465
   xenops (Strange-eyed Scorpionfish), 464, **465**; photo, 466

Rhizophora mangle (Red Mangrove), cultivation, 179
Rhycherus filamentosus (Tasseled Anglerfish), 334
Ribbon eels, 167, 248, 252, 273, **280-282**; photos, 281
   Black, **280-282**
   Blue, **280-282**
   White, 188, 248, 273, **280**; photo, 280
   "White" (misapplied name), 285
   Yellow, **280-282**
Richardsonichthys, photos, 445, 451
   leucogaster (Whiteface Waspfish), 447, **451**; photos, 451
Ridge, algal, habitat, 171, 189-191
Risor, 215
   ruber, 215
Rockcod, Pygmy, 473
Rockskipper
   Jeweled, 188, 416
   Rippled, 180
Rockspear, 316
Rocky reef habitats, 196-198; photo, 197
Roundheads, 68, 102-103
Rubble bottoms, fishes in (chart), 177
Rubble zone as habitat, 207-209; photos, 207, 208
Rubble zone, fishes in (chart), 209
Runner, Blue, 201
Rypticus
   maculatus (Whitespotted Soapfish), 201
   saponaceus (Greater Soapfish), 297
Salarias fasciatus (Jeweled Rock Skipper), 188, 416
Salinity and how to calculate, 227-229
Samaridae, 69, 148
Samariscus triocellatus (Threespot Flounder), 148
Sand bottom habitat, 210-211; photo, 230
   fishes in (chart), 177
Sand Diver (*Synodus*), **314-315**; photos, 76, 315
Sand divers, 69, 130, 290, 516
   Goldbar (*Trichonotus*), 479
Sand, live, 230-231
Sand perches. See Perches, sand
Sandbass, Belted, **523**
Sandfish, Belted, 520, 522, **523**; photo, 523
Sanopus, 209, 326-327
   astrifer (Whitespotted Toadfish), **326**; photo, 327
   barbatus (Barbeled Toadfish), 322-323, **327**
   johnsoni (Johnson's Toadfish), **327**; photo, 327
   reticulatus (Reticulate Toadfish), 322
   splendidus (Splendid Toadfish), 322, **327**; photo, 327
Sarcophyton, photo, 14
Sargassum rafts as habitats, 206-207
Sargassumfish, **355-356**
Sargocentron, 370, 376-383

   caudimaculatum (Tailspot Squirrelfish), **376**; photo, 376
   cornutum (Threespot Squirrelfish), **376**; photo, 376
   coruscum (Reef Squirrelfish), 372, **376-377**; photos, 377
   diadema (Crown Squirrelfish), 188, **377**; photo, 377
   ensiferum (Yellowstriped Squirrelfish), **378**; photo, 378
   ittodai (Samurai Squirrelfish), 377, **378**; photo, 378
   melanospilos (Blackspot Squirrelfish), 377, **378-379**; photo, 379
   microstoma (Fineline Squirrelfish), 372, 378, **379**; photo, 379
   praslin (Darkstriped Squirrelfish), **380**; photo, 380
   punctatissimum (Speckled Squirrelfish), **379-380**; photo, 379
   rubrum (Redcoat Squirrelfish), **380**; photo, 380
   spiniferum (Giant Squirrelfish), 185, 376, **380-381**, 383; photos, 184, 381
   tiere (Blueline Squirrelfish), **381-382**; photo, 381
   tieroides (Pink Squirrelfish), **382**; photo, 382
   vexillarius (Dusky Squirrelfish), **382**; photo, 382
   violaceum (Violet Squirrelfish), **383**; photo, 383
   xantherythrum (Hawaiian Squirrelfish), 377, **383**; photo, 383
Saurida
   gracilis (Graceful Lizardfish), 177, 188, 311, **313-314**; photo, 313
   nebulosa (Nebulous Lizardfish), **313-314**
Scaleless fishes, 55-56
Scales of reef fishes, 54-55; illustration, 55
Scaleyfin, Banded, 190
Scaridae, 69, 128-129
Scarus
   sordidus (Bullethead Parrotfish), 183
   vetula (Queen Parrotfish), photo, 394
Scatophagidae, 69, 142
Scatophagus argus (Spotted Scat), 180
Scats, 69, 142, 180
Schleser, Dr. David, 359
Schooling, advantages, 546
Schoolmaster, 252, 395; photo, 111
Sciaenidae, 69, 115
Scolopsis
   bilineatus (Twolined Spinecheek), 180
   trilineatus (Threelined Spinecheek), 188
   xenochrous (Pearlstreaked Spinecheek), 290
Scombroidei, 69
Scorpaena, 468-472
   bergi (Goosehead Scorpionfish), **470**
   brasiliensis (Barbfish), 421, **468-470**; photos, 469, 470

calcarata (Smoothhead Scorpionfish), **471**
grandicornis (Plumed Scorpionfish), 183, **470**; photo, 470
inermis (Mushroom Scorpionfish), 216, **470-471**; photo, 471
mystes, 471
plumieri (Spotted Scorpionfish), 183, **471-472**; photos, 53, 455, 471, 472
Scorpaenidae, 68, 93-94, 337, 453-489
Scorpaeniformes, 68
Scorpaeninae, 463-467
Scorpaenodes, 472-475
　caribbaeus (Reef Scorpionfish), 177, **472**, 474, 475; photo, 472
　guamensis (Guam Scorpionfish), 188, **473**, 474; photos, 473
　guamensis scabra, 65
　parvipinnis (Lowfin Scorpionfish), **474**; photos, 474
　scaber (Pygmy Rockcod), 473
　tredecimspinosus (Deepreef Scorpionfish), **474-475**; photo, 474
　varipinnis (Blotchfin Scorpionfish), **475**; photos, 475
Scorpaenoidei, 68
Scorpaenopsis, 455, 475-484
　barbatus (Bearded Scorpionfish), **480**; photo, 480
　brevifrons (Shortsnout Scorpionfish), **475-476**; photo, 476
　cacopsis (Titan Scorpionfish), **480-481**; photo, 481
　cirrhosa (Bearded Scorpionfish), **482**; photo, 482
　diabola (Devil Scorpionfish), 209, 455, 456, 476, **477**; photos, 455, 477
　fowleri (Dwarf Scorpionfish), **476**; photos, 476
　gibbosa (Humpback Scorpionfish), 454, 455, 456, 476, **477-479**; photo, 478
　macrochir (Flasher Scorpionfish), 477, **479**; photos, 209, 478
　neglecta (Bandtail Scorpionfish), **479**; photo, 479
　oxycephala (Tasseled Scorpionfish), 60, 167, 216, 454, 456, 476, **481-482**; photos, 26, 456, 481, 482
　papuensis (Papuan Scorpionfish), 167, **482-483**; photos, 44, 94, 452, 482, 483
　sp. (Spinycrown Scorpionfish), **484**; photos, 454, 479, 484
　venosa (Raggy Scorpionfish), 167, 202, 481, **483-484**; photo, 483
Scorpionfishes, 68, 93-94, 337, 453-489
　Ambon, 211, 451, **466**; photos, 56, 466
　antipredator behavior, 454-455
　Bandtail, **479**; photo, 479
　Barchin, 467, **486**; photos, 486
　Bearded (*Scorpaenopsis barbatus*), **480**; photo, 480

　Bearded (*Scorpaenopsis cirrhosa*), **482**; photo, 482
　Bigmouth, **475-476**
　biology, 453-456
　Blotchfin, **475**; photos, 475
　captive care, 456
　captive feeding, 457
　Coral, **474**
　Decoy, 43, 454, 457, **463**, 467, 494; photos, 463
　Deepreef, **474-475**; photo, 474
　Devil, 209, 455, 456, **477**; photos, 455, 477
　disorders, 457-458
　Dwarf, **476**; photos, 476
　Easter Island, 464, **465**
　Eschmeyer's, 457, **464-465**; photo, 465
　False, **477**
　feeding behavior, 454
　Flasher, 209, 477, **479**; photos, 478
　Goosehead, **470**
　Grass, **470**
　Guam, 188, **473**, 474; photos, 473
　habitat, 453-454
　Humpback, 455, 456, **477-479**; photo, 478
　humpbacked group, 476-479
　Japanese, 464, **465**
　Lacey, **464**, 493; photos, 464, 465
　Leaf, 344, 454, 455, 457, **487-488**; photos, 487, 488
　Lowfin, **474**; photos, 474
　Mauritius, **486**
　Merlet's, **464**
　Mozambique, **467-468**; photos, 467, 468
　Mushroom, 216, 331, **470-471**; photo, 471
　Ocellated, **467-468**; photo, 468
　Orange, **468-470**
　Papuan, 167, **482-483**; photos, 44, 94, 452, 482, 483
　Plumed, 183, **470**; photo, 470
　Raggy, 167, 202, 481, **483-484**; photo, 483
　Reef, 177, **472**; photo, 472
　reproduction, 455
　shedding of cuticle, 455-456
　Shortfin, **474**
　Shortsnout, **475-476**; photo, 476
　Smallscale, **481-482**
　Smoothhead, **471**
　Speckled, 214, 453, **485**; photo, 485
　Spinycrown, **484**; photos, 454, 479, 484
　Spotfin (*Scorpaenodes*), **474-475**
　Spotfin (*Sebastapistes*), **485**; photo, 485
　Spotted, 183, **471-472**; photos, 53, 455, 471, 472
　stings, 453
　Strange-eyed, 464, **465**; photo, 466
　tankmates, 457
　tasseled group, 480-484

　Tasseled, 60, 167, 216, 456, 476, **481-482**; photos, 26, 456, 481, 482
　Titan, **480-481**; photo, 481
　Weedy, 454, **464**; photos, 465
　Yellowspotted, **485-486**; photo, 485
Scropaeninae, 93
Scuticaria, 282-283
　okinawae (Okinawan Snake Moray Eel), **282**; photo, 282
　tigrina (Tiger Snake Moray Eel), **282-283**; photo, 282
Sea chubs, 69, 122-123
Sea dragons, 89
Sea fans, photo, 117
　gorgonian, photo, 21
Sea Goblin, **460-461**
Sea moths, 68, 87-88, 398-400
　biology, 398
　captive care, 399
　Dragon, 210, 398, **399**, 516; photos, 398, 399
　Hawaiian Dragonfish, **400**
　Sculptured, 400
　Slender, **400**; photos, 400
　Volitans, **400**
Sea robins, 68, 95-96
　Bandtail, 517
　Bighead, 179
　Leopard, 179
Sea snake, Banded, 301-302, 302-303
Sea Star, photo, 217
Seabasses, dwarf, 519-527. See also Basses
　biology, 519-520
　captive care, 520
　community aquarium, 523
　reproduction, 519-520
Seadragons
　Leafy, 409
　Weedy, 409
Seagrass, collection and cultivation, 182
Seagrass habitat, 181-183
　aquariums, 182
　fishes in (chart), 183
Seahorses, 68, 89-91, 409, 410-426
　aquarium conditions, 412-415
　biology, 410-412
　Black, **423-424**
　captive care, 412-420
　captive feeding, 415-416
　captive reproduction, 419-420
　Common, 422, **423-424**; photos, 415, 423, 424
　diseases, 416-418
　Dwarf, 183, 412, 413, 414, 418, **425-426**, 438; photo, 426
　Giant Brazilian, **424**
　Lined, 179, 183, 206, 418, **421**, 422, 424, 438; photos, 411, 414, 419, 421
　Longnose, **424**; photo, 424
　Longsnout, 183, 201, 421, **424**; photos, 90, 413, 417, 424, 425
　Pacific, **422-423**; photos, 409, 423

Pygmy, **420**; photos, 412, 420
reproduction, 410-412
selecting, 418-419
Spiny, **421-422**
Spotted, **423-424**
tankmates, 416
Thorny, 167, 179, **421-422**; photos, 418, 421, 422
threatened survival, 413
Yellow, **423-424**
Sebastapistes, 456, **485-486**
  ballieui (Spotfin Scorpionfish), **485**; photo, 485
  coniorta (Speckled Scorpionfish), 214, 453, **485**; photo, 485
  cyanostigma (Yellowspotted Scorpionfish), **485-486**; photo, 485
  mauritiana (Mauritius Scorpionfish), **486**
  strongia (Barchin Scorpionfish), 467, **486**; photos, 486
Sebastes, 453
Sergeants
  Banded, 188
  Blackspot, 188
  Indo-Pacific, 346-347
  Major, 180, 190
  Whitley's, 190
Seriola quinqueradiata (Yellowtail Jack), 51-52
Serranidae, 68, 98-100, 337, 519, 543
Serraninae, 98, 519-541
Serranocirrhitus, 543
  latus (Fathead Anthias), **582-583**; photos, 582, 583
Serranus, 519-527
  annularis (Orangeback Bass), 194, 203, 209, 519, **520**, 523; photos, 521
  baldwini (Lantern Bass), 183, 520, **521-522**; photo, 521
  chionaraia (Snow Bass), 519, **522**
  flaviventris (Twospot Bass), 183, **522**; photo, 522
  phoebe (Tattler Bass), 198, 205, **522-523**, 549; photo, 522
  subligarius (Belted Sandfish), 520, 522, **523**; photo, 523
  tabacarius (Tobacco Fish), 209, 211, 290, 517, **524**; photos, 524
  tigrinus (Harlequin Bass), 183, 209, 520, **525-526**; photos, 525
  tortugarum (Chalk Bass), 209, 211, 519, 520, 523, **526-527**; photo, 526
Shallow fore reef, 191-193
Sharks
  Blacktipped, 179
  Lemon, 179
  Night, 355
Sharks, Smoothhound, 275
  Tiger, 359
Sharksuckers, 69, 109-110
Shipwrecks as fish habitats, 199-200; photo, 198

Shrimps
  Common Cleaner, photos, 247, 547
  grass, photo, 312
Shrimpfishes, 68, 91, 440-442
  biology, 440-441
  captive care, 440-441
  Coral, **441-442**; photos, 442
  Grooved, **442**
  Razorfish, **441-442**
  Rigid, **442**; photos, 440, 442
  Speckled, **441**; photo, 441
  Spotted, **441**
  Striped, **441-442**
Siderea, 246, 283-284
  grisea (Gray Moray Eel), 247, 248, **283**, 505; photo, 283
  picta (Peppered Moray Eel), 188, **283-284**; photo, 283
  prosopeion, 284
  thyrsoidea (White-eye Moray Eel), 167, 188, 261, 265, 277, **284**; photos, 247, 284
Siganidae, 69, 142-143
Siganus
  argenteus (Forktail Rabbitfish), 183
  canaliculatus (Seagrass Rabbitfish), 183
  guttatus (Golden Rabbitfish), 180
  lineatus (Lined Rabbitfish), 180
  spinus (Scribbled Rabbitfish), 183
  vermiculatus (Vermiculate Rabbitfish), 180
  vulpinus (Foxface Rabbitfish), 190, 396
Siluriformes, 68
Siokunichthys
  breviceps (Soft Coral Pipefish), 214, 437
  nigrolineatus (White Pipefish), 214, **437**; photo, 437
Siphamia
  fuscolineata (Crown-of-Thorns Cardinalfish), 214
  versicolor (Sea Urchin Cardinalfish), 214
Skin of reef fishes, 55-57
Slime secreted by fishes, 56
Slippery Dick, 177, 180, 272, 276, 517
Snake eels, 68, 74, 295-307
  and opportunistic feeders, 297
  Banded, **302-303**; photos, 302, 303
  biology, 295-297
  Blackfinned, **305-306**, 451; photos, 306
  Blacksaddle, 179, **305**; photo, 305
  Bonapart's, 300, **304**; photos, 304, 305
  Brownsaddled, **304**
  captive care, 297-298
  Clipperton, **304**
  Crocodile, 177, 288, **300**; photos, 288, 295, 298, 300
  Darkline, **301**
  Freckled, **301**
  Goldspotted, 302, **304**; photo, 304
  Harlequin, **302-303**
  Henshaw's, 300
  Magnificent, **304**

Manyeyed, **307**; photo, 307
Marbled, 288, **300-301**; photo, 301
Onebanded, **305**
Reptilian, 300
Saddled, 179, 288, 297, **301-302**; photo, 301
Sharpsnout, **299**; photos, 299
Sharptail, 209, 272, 276, 297, **302**, 394; photos, 297, 302
Spotted, 209, **306-307**; photos, 306
Spotted, Pacific, 177, 188, 296, **303-304**; photos, 296, 303
Stargazer, 288, **299-300**; photos, 298, 299
Tiger, **304**
Snakefish, 177, **317**; photos, 313, 317
Snappers, 69, 111, 297, 337
  Blue and Gold, 247
  Bluestriped, 185
  Dog, 251, 298
  emperor, 69, 113-114
  Onespot, photo, 198
  Twospotted, photo, 17
  Yellowtail, 183, 201
Soapfishes, 98, 247
  Greater, 297
  Secretive, 188
  Sixline, 175
  Whitespotted, 201
Social behavior of reef fishes, 28
Soldierfishes, 68, 84-85, 196, 337, 384-391
  Bigscale, 185, **386**, 387; photo, 387
  biology, 384-385
  Black, **386-387**
  Blackbar, **388**; photo, 385, 389
  Brick, 185, **386-387**; photo, 386
  Bronze, **386**; photo, 386
  captive care, 385-386
  Cardinal, **391**
  Crimson, **389-390**
  Doubletooth, **388**; photo, 388
  Finspot, 194, **387**; photo, 387
  Orangefin, **390**
  Pearly, **388-389**; photo, 389
  Red, 175, 185, 386, 387, **389-390**; photo, 389
  Roughscale, 175, 196, **391**; photo, 391
  Scarlet, 175, **389**
  Violet, 175, **390**; photo, 390
  Whitetip, **390-391**; photos, 85, 194, 384, 390
  Yellowfin, **387-388**; photo, 388
  Yellowtip, **391**; photo, 391
Soleichthys heterorhinos (Banded Sole), 476
Soleidae, 69, 148-149, 516
Solenostomidae, 68, 88-89, 401-408
Solenostomus
  armatus (Longtailed Ghost Pipefish), **404**; photos, 403, 404, 405
  cyanopterus (Robust Ghost Pipefish), 167, 403, **405**; photos, 88, 405

paradoxus (Ornate Ghost Pipefish), 167, 403, **406**, 407; photos, 41, 401, 402, 403, 406
  sp. 1 (Hairy Ghost Pipefish), **407**; photo, 407
  sp. 2 (Filamented Ghost Pipefish), **407-408**; photos, 408
  sp. 3 (Velvety Ghost Pipefish), **408**; photos, 408
Soles, 69, 148-149, 516
  Banded, 476
  Moses, 210
  Peacock, 148; photo, 149
Sorsogona welanderi (Welander's Flathead), **512**; photos, 509, 512
Sound production and swim bladder, 48
Spadefishes, 69, 141-142
  Atlantic, 201; photo, 141
Sparisoma
  radians (Bucktooth Parrotfish), 183
  viride (Stoplight Parrotfish), photos, 46, 129
Specialization in reef fishes, 23
Species accounts, keys to, 237-243
Species
  definition, 66
  names, 65
Specific gravity (chart), 228
Sphaeramia
  nematoptera (Pajama Cardinalfish), 175; photo, 58
  orbicularis (Orbiculate Cardinalfish), 180, 183
Sphoeroides
  greeleyi (Greeley's Puffer), 177
  nephelus (Southern Puffer), 177, 183
  spengleri (Bandtail Puffer), 177, 180, 183
Sphyraena
  barracuda (Great Barracuda), 146; photo, 147
  putnamiae (Chevron Barracuda), 146
Sphyraenidae, 69, 146
Spikefishes, 150
Spinecheeks, 69, 114
  Pearlstreaked, 290
  Threelined, 188
  Twolined, 180
Spines, 42
Sponge dwellers, 214-216
Sponge gardens, 205
Sponges
  as habitats, 214-216
  barrel, photos, 21, 217, 493
  Branching Vase, photo, 200
  tube, photos, 201, 215
Squirrelfishes, 68, 84-85, 196, 337, 370-383
  biology, 370
  Blackfin, **375**; photo, 375
  Blackspot, 377, **378-379**; photo, 379
  Blooddrop, **375**
  Bloodspot, 185, 188, 373, **375**; photo, 375

Blueline, **381-382**; photo, 381
captive care, 372
Clearfin, **373-374**; photo, 373
Crown, 188, **377**, 378; photo, 377
Darkstriped, **380**; photo, 380
Duckbilled, **380-381**
Dusky, **382**; photo, 382
Fineline, 372, 378, **379**; photo, 379
Giant, 185, 376, **380-381**; photos, 184, 381
Goldlined, **374**, 378; photo, 374
Hawaiian, 377, **383**; photo, 383
Longjaw (*Neoniphon marianus*), **374-375**; photo, 374
Longjawed (*Sargocentron spiniferum*), **380-381**
Longspine, 175, **373**; photos, 370, 371, 373
Peppered, **379-380**
Pink, **382**; photo, 382
Redcoat, **380**; photo, 380
Reef, 372, **376-377**; photos, 377
Samurai, 377, **378**; photo, 378
Speckled, **379-380**; photo, 379
Squirrelfish, **372-373**; photo, 372
Tahitian, **381-382**
Tailspot, **376**; photo, 376
Threespot, **376**; photo, 376
Violet, **383**; photo, 383
Yellowstriped, **378**; photo, 378
Stargazers, 69, 131-132
  sand, 69, 133
Stegastes, 530
  dorsopunicans (Dusky Damselfish), 541
  leucostictus (Beaugregory), 180
  lividus (Bluntsnout Gregory), 190
  nigricans (Black Damselfish), 217
  variabilis (Cocoa Damselfish), 532
Steinetz, H., 491-492
Stethojulis
  interrupta (Cutribbon Wrasse), 188
  strigiventer (Threeribbon Wrasse), 183
Stingers
  Caledonian, **460**
  demon, 459-462
  Filament-finned, **462**
Stingfishes, 459, 462-463
  Blue-eyed, **463**; photo, 462
  Many-barbed, **459**; photos, 458, 459
Stingray, Yellow, 177, 183
Stonefishes, 93, 488-489
  Common, **489**
  Dwarf, **489**
  Estuarine, **488-489**
  Horrid, 179, **488-489**; photos, 456, 488
  Reef, 453, 454, 455, 456, 457, **489**; photos, 456, 489
"Stonefishes," 477
Stongobiops, 214
  nematodes (Highfin Banded Goby), 583
Stridulation, 48
Stripies, 69, 124

Strophidon sathete (Longtail Moray Eel), 179, 268, **285**; photo, 285
Stygnobrotula latebricola (Black Brotula), 318, **320**; photo, 320
Subcarangiform swimming, 37
Substrates, 229-233
Surgeonfishes, 69, 144-146, 337
  Achilles, 23, 190, 220; photo, 22
  Chocolate, 185; photo, 145
  Convict, 185, 217, 219, 357, 394; photo, 394
  Elongate, 180
  Lavender, 217
  Lined, 190
  Ocean, 177, 180
  Orange-shoulder, 23
  Powderblue, 185
  Ringtail, 180
  Sohal, 188
  Whitecheek, 190
  Whitespotted, 190; photo, 22
  Yellowfin, 180, 183
Swain Reefs, 169
Swamps, mangrove, 178-181; photo, 178
Sweepers, 69, 117-118; photo, 234
  Copper, 188
  Slender, photos, 117, 166
Sweetlips, 69, 112-113, 337
  Brown, 180
  Lined, 180
  Twostriped, 180
  Yellow-ribbon, photos, 111, 195
Swim bladders, 47-49
  and buoyancy, 47
  and decompression, 48-49
  and hearing, 48
  and sound production, 48
Synanceia
  horrida (Horrid Stonefish), 179, **488-489**; photos, 456, 488
  nana (Dwarf Stonefish), **489**
  verrucosa (Reef Stonefish), 453, 454, **489**; photos, 456, 489
Synanceinae, 93, 488-489
Synchiropus, 209
  picturatus, 138
  splendidus (Green Mandarinfish), 56, 138, 167
  stellatus (Stellate Dragonet), 175
Syngnathidae, 68, 89-91, 409-439
Syngnathinae, 89
Syngnathoidei, 68
Syngnathoides biaculeatus (Alligator Pipefish), **437**; photos, 428, 437
Syngnathus, 427
  floridae (Florida Pipefish), 183
  pelagicus (Sargassum Pipefish), 207; photo, 206
  scovelli (Gulf Pipefish), 426, **438**; photo, 438
Synodontidae, 68, 75-76, 311-317
Synodontinae, 75

Synodus, 314-317; photo, 312
    binotatus (Twospot Lizardfish), **314**; photo, 314
    dermatogenys (Sand Lizardfish), 312, **314**, 516; photo, 314
    englemani, 317
    foetens (Inshore Lizardfish), 183, 517
    intermedius (Sand Diver), **314-315**; photos, 76, 315
    jaculum (Blackblotch Lizardfish), 177, **315**, 476, 516; photos, 315
    rubromaculatus (Redmarbled Lizardfish), **315-316**, 516; photo, 316
    synodus (Red Lizardfish), **316**; photos, 316, 457
    ulae (Ulae), **316-317**; photo, 316
    variegatus (Variegated Lizardfish), 185, 188, 311, **314**, **317**; photos, 310, 311, 312, 316
Taenianotus triacanthus (Leaf Scorpionfish), 344, 454, 455, **487-488**; photos, 487, 488
Tangs, 144-146
    Atlantic Blue, 65, 202
    Brown, 185
    Gem, 64
    Sailfin, 190
    Sailfin, Indian Ocean, 188, 219
    Yellow, 23, 64, 65, 190; photos, 22, 65
Tarpons, 68, 70; photo, 71
Tasanoides
    filamentosus (Filament-fin Anthias), **588**; photo, 589
    flavofasciatus (Yellowlined Anthias), **588**; photos, 589
Taxonomy of reef fishes, 63-69
Teeth of reef fishes, 52-54
Teeth-bearing bones, illustration, 54
Temperature
    effect on fishes, 221-224
    ranges given in species accounts, 240
    variations (chart), 225
    variations in reef habitats, 221-222
Ten Mile Banks, 168
Teraponidae, 69, 123
Tetra, Neon, 543-544
Tetraodontidae, 69, 154-156, 337
Tetraodontifom locomotion, 40
Tetraodontiformes, 69
Tetraodontinae, 154
Tetraodontoidei, 69
Tetraroge barbata (Mangrove Waspfish), 179
Tetrarogidae, 68, 92-93, 445-451
Tetrasomus gibbosus (Humpback Turretfish), 183
Thalassoma
    amblycephalum (Twotone Wrasse), 16, 579
    bifasciatum (Bluehead Wrasse), 216, 290
    hardwicke (Hardwick's Wrasse), 175, 188
    hebraicum (Goldbar Wrasse), 188
    klunzingeri (Klunzinger's Wrasse), 188

    lunare (Moon Wrasse), 219
    purpureum (Surge Wrasse), 190
Thalassophryne amazonica, 79
Thalassophryninae, 79
Thysanophrys, 512-513
    arenicola (Broadhead Flathead), **512**; photo, 512
    celebica (Sulawesi Flathead), **512-513**; photo, 512
    chiltonae (Longsnout Flathead), **513**, 516; photo, 513
    otaitensis (Fringelip Flathead), **513**, 516
Tigerfishes, 69, 123
Tilefishes, 69, 108
    Blanquillo, 209
    Bluehead, 212, 546, 572, 585, 587
    Flashing, 194, 212; photo, 109
    Green, 212, 587
    Pacific Goldeneyed, 331
    sand, 108, 209, 474, 517, 521, 526
    Skunk, 194, 212
Toadfishes, 68, 78-79, 321-327
    Atlantic, **326**
    Barbeled, 322-323, **327**; photo, 327
    biology, 321-323
    captive care, 323-324
    common, 325-326
    coral, 326-327
    Cryptic, 322
    Gulf, 183, 324, **325-326**; photos, 325
    Johnson's, **327**; photo, 327
    Large-eye, **324-325**; photo, 324
    Leopard, **326**; photo, 324
    Orange, **325-326**
    Oyster, **326**; photo, 326
    reef, 209
    reproduction, 323
    Reticulate, 322
    scaly, 324-325
    Splendid, 322, **327**; photo, 327
    Threespined, photo, 321
    Twofaced, 322; photo, 323
    Whitespotted, **326**; photo, 327
Tobacco Fish, 209, 211, 290, 517, **524**; photos, 524
Tobies, 69, 154-156
    Bennett's, 211
    Crowned, 211
    Easter Island, 196
    Fingerprint, 183, 211
    Honeycomb, 188
    Leopard, 196, 232
    Ocellated, 185, 217; photo, 155
    Pygmy, 232
    Saddled, 188, 216
    Tyler's, 196
Trachichthyoidei, 68
Trachinocephalus myops (Snakefish), 177, **317**; photos, 313, 317
Trachoinoidei, 69

Trachyrhamphus, 438-439
    bicoarctatus (Short-tailed Pipefish), **438-439**; photos, 438, 439
    longirostris (Longsnout Pipefish), **439**; photo, 439
Trevally, Bigeye, photo, 39
Triacanthidae, 150
Trichonotidae, 69, 130
Trichonotus, 290, 516
    halstead, 479
Triggerfishes, 69, 150-152, 337
    Blackbelly, 183
    Blueline, photo, 150
    Bluethroat, 194
    Clown, 16, 185, 496
    Gray (*Balistes capriscus*), 201, 207
    Ocean (*Canthidermis sufflamen*), 206-207
    Orangelined, 190, 219
    Picasso, 175
    Pinktail, 16, 185
    Rough, 206
    Sargassum, 207
    Starry, 180
Triglidae, 68, 95-96
Trimma, 196
    tevegae (Bluestriped Cave Goby), 196
Triodontidae, 150
Triplefins, 69, 132, photo, 132
Triplespines, 150
Tripterygiidae, 69, 132
Truk Lagoon, 200
Trumpetfishes, 68, 85-87, 393-397
    Atlantic, 201, **397**, 393, 394, 395; photos, 86, 393, 394, 397
    biology, 393-395
    captive care, 395-396
    hunting techniques, 393-394
    Pacific, 185, 311, 394, 395, **396-397**; photos, 392, 394, 396
Trunkfishes, 69, 153-154, 337
    Buffalo, 183
Turbinaria mesenterina (Plate Coral), photo, 14
Turkeyfishes, 493, **505-508**
    Hawaiian, **503**
    Largetail, **504-505**
    Military, **504-505**
    Mombasa, **502**
Turretfish, Humpback, 183
Tuskfishes
    Blue, 205
    Harlequin, 190
Ulae, **316-317**; photo, 316
Unicornfishes, 144
    Orangespine, 23, 46, 190, 217-219
    Sleek, 23
    Vlamingi's, 185
Upeneus
    tragula (Blackstriped Goatfish), 167, 177, 180, 233
    vittatus (Yellowbanded Goatfish), 180

Uranoscopidae, 69, 131-132
Urolophus jamaicensis (Yellow Stingray), 177, 183
Uropterygius, 285-286
   concolor (Unicolor Snake Moray Eel), 285
   fasciolatus (Barred Snake Moray Eel), **285-286**; photo, 285
   goslinei, 286
   macrocephalus (Largehead Snake Moray Eel), 269, **286**; photo, 286
   polyspilus (Manyspotted Snake Moray Eel), **282-283**
Valenciennea
   longipinnis (Teardrop Sleeper Goby), 180, 230
   puellaris (Orangespotted Sleeper Goby), 516
   strigata (Yellowhead Sleeper Goby), 161, 188; photo, 230
Vanderhorstia ornatissima (Ornate Shrimp Goby), 183
Vanderloos, Rob, 464
Variola albimarginata (Whitemargin Lyretail Grouper), 251
Variola louti (Lyretail Grouper), 190, 252, 283; photo, 238
Velvetfishes, 68, 95
   orbicular. See Coral crouchers
Ventralis Zone, 587
Vincent, Dr. Amanda, 413
Voet, Jeff, 457
Vordermann, 363
Waspfishes, 68
   68, 92-93, 445-451
   Bearded, **458**
   biology, 445
   captive care, 447
   Cockatoo, 167, 447, **448**; photos, 445, 446, 448
   Indian Ocean, 447
   Longfin, **458**; photo, 458
   Longspine, 167, **449-450**; photos, 449, 450
   Mangrove, 179
   Sailfin, **450**; photos, 450
   Spiny, 167, **447**; photo, 447
   Whiteface, 447, **451**; photos, 451
Watanabe, Dr, M., 582
Water movement
   detection of, and lateral line organ, 49
   effect on fishes, 220-221
Wetmorella
   albofasciata (Whitebarred Pygmy Wrasse), 196
   nigropinnata (Blackspot Pygmy Wrasse), 196
Whiptails
   blue, 290
   Double, 205

Whitley, Dr. G., 582
Wormfishes, 69, 140-141
   Blacklined, 183
Wrasses, 69, 126-128
   Bird, 175, 185, 188
   Bird, Indian Ocean, 217
   Blackedge Thicklip, 180
   Bluehead, 216, 290
   Bluespotted, 190
   Chainlink 167
   Checkered, 185, 188
   Cheekline Maori, 312
   Cigar, 167, 183
   cleaner, 247
   cleaner, Bluestreak, 219; photo, 25
   cleaner, Wandering, 167
   Clown, 290
   Creole, 397
   Cutribbon, 188
   Cuvier's, 190
   Dwarf, 183
   fairy, Bluehead, 209
   fairy, Bluestreak, 209
   fairy, Lined, photo, 24
   fairy, Longfin, 209
   fairy, Pyle's, 212
   fairy, Redfin, 209
   fairy, Redheaded, 59, 167, 203; photo, 55
   fairy, Redscale, 575
   fairy, Rhomboid, 194, photo, 38
   fairy, Scott's, photo, 57
   fairy, Whipfin, 202, 209; photo, 202
   Flame, 194, 209, 212
   flasher, Carpenter's, 194
   flasher, Dot-and-Dash, 209
   flasher, Filamented, 167, 203, 209
   flasher, Lyretail, photo, 127
   flasher, McCosker's, 209; photo, 45
   flasher, Pink, 167, 194
   Fourline, 216
   Goldbar, 188
   Hardwick's, 175, 188
   Klunzinger's, 188
   Moon, 219
   Napoleon, 15, 31, 190
   Oneline Tubelip, 167
   Peacock, 188
   Pink-streaked, photo, 207
   Purplestriped, 167
   pygmy, Blackspot, 196
   pygmy, Whitebarred, 196
   Rainbow, 290
   razor, 210
   Redbreasted Maori, 217
   Redtail Tamarin, photo, 237
   Ring, 190
   Rockmover, 357
   Saowisata, 180
   Schwartz's, 183

   Seagrass, 183
   Secretive, 209
   Slingjaw, 190
   Surge, 190
   Tailspot, 312
   Threeribbon, 183
   Threespot, 162, 177, 180, 183
   Twinspot, 185
   Twisti, 190
   Twospot, 180
   Twospot Maori, 202
   Twotone, 16, 167, 579
   Vermiculate Leopard, photo, 241
   Yamashiro's, 209
   Zigzag, 167, 188
Xanthichthys
   auromarginatus (Bluethroat Triggerfish), 194
   ringens (Sargassum Triggerfish), 207
Xanthism, 61
Xestospongia testudinaria (Barrel Sponge), photo, 21
Xiphasia setifer (Hair-tail Blenny), 37
Xyrichtys, 210
   aneitensis (Yellowblotch Razorfish), 516
   martinicensis (Rosy Razorfish), 290, 517
   melanopus (Melanopus Razorfish), 290
   niger (Black Razorfish), 210, 290
   novacula (Pearly Razorfish), 290, 517
   pavo (Pavo Razorfish), 288, 516; photo, 289
   pendactylus (Fivefinger Razorfish), 290
   splendens (Green Razorfish), 312, 517
Yongeichthys nebulosus (Shadow Goby), 56
Zanclidae, 69, 143-144
Zanclus cornutus (Moorish Idol), 54, 143-144, 185; photo, 42
Zebrasoma
   desjardinii (Indian Ocean Sailfin Tang), 188, 219
   flavescens (Yellow Tang), 23, 64, 65, 190; photos, 22, 65
   gemmatum (Gem Tang), 64
   scopas (Brown Tang), 185
   veliferum (Sailfin Tang), 190
Zones, coral reef. See also Habitats
   Acropora palmata, 171
   aerial view, illustration, 203
   antipatharian, 204-205
   black coral, 204-205
   coralline algae / sponge, 203
   cross section, illustration, 164-165
   gorgonian, 203-204
   reef flat, 171
   rubble, 207-209

About the Author

Author Scott W. Michael in Bonaire.

SCOTT W. MICHAEL is an internationally recognized writer, underwater photographer, and marine biology researcher specializing in reef fishes. He is a regular contributor to *Aquarium Fish Magazine* and *SeaScope* and is the author of *Reef Sharks & Rays of the World* (Sea Challengers) and *Aquarium Sharks & Rays* (Microcosm).

Having studied marine biology at the undergraduate and graduate levels at the University of Nebraska, he has been involved in research projects on sharks, rays, frogfishes, and the behavior of reef fishes. He has also served as scientific consultant for National Geographic Explorer, the Discovery Channel, and French educational television.

His research and photographic endeavors have led him from Cocos Island in the Eastern Pacific to various points in the Indo-Pacific, including the Maldive Islands, Sulawesi, the Fiji Islands, Papua New Guinea, Australia's Great Barrier Reef, as well as the Red Sea, the Gulf of Mexico, and many reefs in the Caribbean.

A marine aquarist since boyhood, he has kept tropical fishes for more than 25 years, with many years of extensive involvement, including a period of retail store ownership, in the aquarium trade. He lives with his wife, underwater photographer Janine Cairns-Michael, their Golden Retriever, and an Ornate Wobbegong (*Orectolobus ornatus*) in Lincoln, Nebraska.

Author's Camera Equipment
Nexus F4 camera housing; Nikon F4 camera; Nikkor 60 and 105 mm macro lenses; Ikelite substrobe 50 and substrobe Ai; TLC and Oceanic strobe arms; Nikon V with 20 mm lense; SB 103 Speedlight.

Future Editions
The author and publisher are committed to making all future editions of this series as complete, accurate, and up-to-date as possible. Readers with suggestions, information, or photographs for possible publication are encouraged to contact one of the following in writing:

Reef Impressions
Attn: Scott W. Michael
4310 Garfield Street
Lincoln, NE 68506

Microcosm Ltd.
P.O. Box 580
Shelburne, VT 05482
e-mail: jml@microcosm-books.com